A FRENCH SONG COM

A FRENCH SONG COMPANION

GRAHAM JOHNSON

RICHARD STOKES

OXFORD

UNIVERSITY PRESS

OXFORD
UNIVERSITY PRESS

Great Clarendon Street, Oxford OX2 6DP

Oxford University Press is a department of the University of Oxford.
It furthers the University's objective of excellence in research, scholarship,
and education by publishing worldwide in

Oxford New York

Auckland Cape Town Dar es Salaam Hong Kong Karachi
Kuala Lumpur Madrid Melbourne Mexico City Nairobi
New Delhi Shanghai Taipei Toronto

With offices in

Argentina Austria Brazil Chile Czech Republic France Greece
Guatemala Hungary Italy Japan Poland Portugal Singapore
South Korea Switzerland Thailand Turkey Ukraine Vietnam

Oxford is a registered trade mark of Oxford University Press
in the UK and in certain other countries

Published in the United States
by Oxford University Press Inc., New York

First published 2000

First published in Paperback 2002

British Library Cataloguing in Publication Data
Data available

Library of Congress Cataloging in Publication Data
Johnson, Graham, 1950–
A French Song Companion/Graham Johnson; Richard Stokes.
p. cm.
Includes indexes
1. Songs, French—Texts.   2. Songs, French—History and criticism.
I. Stokes, Richard.   II. Title.
ML54.6.J76 F74   2000   782.42168′0268—dc21   99–057524

ISBN 978–0–19–924966–4 (Pbk)

13

Typeset by Hope Services (Abingdon) Ltd.
Printed in Great Britain
on acid-free paper by
CPI Group UK Ltd,
Croydon, CR0 4YY

To the memory of Francis Poulenc and Pierre Bernac
—the Schubert and Vogl of French song—
in their shared centenary year

ACKNOWLEDGEMENTS

There are many people to thank in the preparation of this book. Without the inspiring example and friendship of the late Pierre Bernac it would not have been written at all. Bernac's *The interpretation of French song* is a pioneering work, and the English-speaking public has long regarded it as a mélodie bible. *A French song companion* is certainly a more extensive source of commentary and translation, but it makes no attempt, as Bernac did, to talk the student through song interpretation in detail. His book remains a classic, as do monographs concerning the teaching of great singers like Jane Bathori, Claire Croiza, Charles Panzéra and others. These books are listed in more detail in the afterword, beginning on p. 500.

Some years ago the music library of the Swiss tenor Hugues Cuenod was generously posted to me in small consignments, wrapped up in brown paper. Without those parcels, many songs mentioned in these pages would not have come into my ken. Huguie (b. 1902) remains an inspiring friend, and an astonishingly sprightly survivor from a golden age. The baritone François Le Roux has always been particularly generous in sharing his knowledge of a repertoire he knows so well. My recent collaboration with the tenor Jean-Paul Fouchécourt has also yielded new information. My friendship, over many years, with Rosine Seringe, Poulenc's niece, and her remarkable husband Jean, has also been a source of joy and instruction. It has been my privilege to regard Rosine, my hostess during countless concert trips to Paris, as my "mère d'outre-Manche".

There have always been great friends of French mélodie in England: Betty Bannerman, a Croiza disciple, was a splendid teacher—I only met her once as she lived in the north of England; but I became a close friend of the late Winifred Radford; she was a great influence on me, and devoted much of her life, as both singer and teacher, to the mélodie. It was thanks to her that the remarkable Sidney Buckland, whose help I also acknowledge here, became a Poulenc scholar and translator of the first rank. I am indebted to Eric Sams, as ever, and to Felix Apprahamian, doyen of French music in England, for many years of friendship and advice. I would also like to thank the following friends and colleagues: Eugene Asti; Dalton Baldwin (who has worked at the centre of the mélodie for forty years); Robin Bowman of the Guildhall School of Music and Drama; Albert Fuller; Gérard Hayman; Rosemary Hyler of the University of California, Irvine; M. Vuichoud of the Librairie Vers et Prose in Paris, Roger Nichols, Ned Rorem, Christopher Sayward (United Music Publishers) and Robert White. I remember with affection many conversations with the late Alice Tully, pupil of Jean Périer (the first Pélleas), connoisseur of French song, and a beacon of cultural life in New York City. I am grateful to Thomas Dewey and Brandon Velarde who painstakingly catalogued my French song collection. I would also like to acknowledge the superb hospitality of my friend Jill Balcon under whose roof I struggled with 'Debussy' and 'Duparc'.

And finally a word of gratitude to the British singers whose musical insights have helped me to know this repertoire as a working musician, and from the inside. My love affair with the mélodie began twenty-five years ago with Felicity Lott when we were both students at the Royal Academy of Music. Since then I treasure memories of countless hours of mélodie-making with such fine artists as Martyn Hill, Richard Jackson, Anthony Rolfe Johnson, Ann Murray, Patricia Rozario, Jennifer Smith, Stephen Varcoe and Sarah Walker.

Graham Johnson

London
December 1999

I would like to express my warmest thanks to Anne Holmes of Hertford College, Oxford, for her careful checking of the manuscript and many valuable suggestions.

Richard Stokes

London
December 1999

The authors would also like to thank the following for permission to reproduce published material:

Éditions Gallimard—Robert Desnos: 'Couplets de la rue Saint-Martin' from *État de veille*, 'Le dernier poème' from *Domaine public*. Paul Éluard: 'À Pablo Picasso, I', 'Je croyais le repos possible', 'Être', 'Rideau', 'Intimes, II, IV, V', 'Balances, III from *Les yeux fertiles*; 'Nous avons fait la nuit' from *Facile*; 'Vue donne vie' from *Les yeux ouverts*; 'Georges Braque', 'Paul Klee', 'Joan Miró' from *Capitale de la douleur*; 'Cheval', 'Vache', 'Oiseau', 'Chien', 'Chat', 'Poule', 'Porc' from *Les animaux et leurs hommes, les hommes et leurs animaux*; 'Entoure ce citron de blanc d'oeuf informe' from *Poésie ininterrompue*; 'Juan Gris', 'Irrémédiable vie' from *Voir*. Max Jacob: 'Voyage', 'Sous les ormeaux . . .' from *Ballades*. Jules Supervielle: 'J'étais toute petite', 'En attendant je serai . . .', 'Pour les enfants sans feu ni lieu' from *Bolivar*. Louise de Vilmorin: 'La dame d'André', 'Dans l'herbe', 'Il vole', 'Mon cadavre est doux comme un gant', 'Violon', 'Fleurs' from *Fiançailles pour rire*; 'Portrait', 'Métamorphoses' from *Le sable du sablier*. Jean Cocteau: 'Attelage' from *Poésie 1916–1923*. Léon-Paul Fargue: 'Rêves' from *Pour la musique*; 'Chanson du rat', 'Chanson du chat', 'Art du poète', 'La grenouille américaine', 'Spleen' from *Ludions*.

Éditions Bernard Grasset—Jean Giraudoux: 'Jeanne', 'Adèle', 'Cécile', 'Irène', 'Rosemonde' from *Suzanne et le Pacifique*; Rosemonde Gérard: 'Villanelle des petits canards', 'Les cigales' from *Les pipeaux*.

Mercure de France—Francis Jammes: 13 poems from *Clairières dans le ciel*. Tristan Klingsor: 'Chanson du chat' from *Le valet de coeur*; 3 poems from *Shéhérazade*.

Les Nouvelles Éditions Debresse—Maurice Fombeure: 'Chanson du clair-tamis', 'Les gars qui vont à la fête', 'C'est le joli printemps', 'Le mendiant', 'Chanson de la fille frivole', 'Le retour du sergent' from *Chansons de la grande hune*, 'Le menuisier du roi'.

Librairie Ernest Flammarion—'Cloche d'aube', 'La ronde', 'Notre chaumière en Yveline', 'Songe d'une nuit d'été', 'L'adieu en barque'.

Éditions Robert Laffont Fixot Seghers—Louis Aragon: 'C', 'Fêtes galantes' from *Les yeux d'Elsa*; Paul Éluard: 'Marc Chagall' from *Le dur désir de durer*.

Gründ—Robert Desnos: 'Le gardénia' and 'L'alligator' from *Chantefables et Chantefleurs*.

All possible efforts have been made to reach copyright owners. The publishers would be glad to hear from any person who can assist in tracing poems that are in copyright but not acknowledged.

CONTENTS

AVANT-PROPOS

France gentille et verdoyante,
Qui fait les femmes et le vin
Comme on chercherait en vain
Sur toute Europe environnante,

Si je te chante à ma façon,
Chacun se détourne et me moque,
Mais un jour arrive l'époque
Où l'oreille entend la chanson.

(Jean Cocteau)

The linking of 'Wine, women, and song' is something we associate with Vienna, a town where music has always been front-page news. Not so Paris, or London. Cocteau bemoaned the fact that France, the envy of neighbouring countries for its women and wine, was indifferent to 'chanson'. The definition of that word in Jean-Jacques Rousseau's *Dictionnaire de la musique* (1768) shows that words and music had long been understood to belong together: 'A short lyric poem, to which one adds an air to be sung on intimate occasions at table, with friends, mistress, or even alone, to relieve temporarily the ennui if one is rich, and to help one to bear more easily misery and toil, if one is poor.' The time would come, Cocteau said with his legendary self-confidence, when the ear of the public would be attuned to his song. But which public did he mean? Certainly, his work was of great importance to twentieth-century musicians (the lines above were set to music by Marcel Delannoy), but one can hardly imagine a Cocteau song (with music by Auric or Sauguet, for example) comforting the daily grind of the poor in their late twentieth-century 'intimate moments'. There is something curiously lacking in intimacy about a ghetto-blaster, and something surrealistically unlikely about the idea of the Spice Girls mouthing Cocteau.

How much simpler it was when serious and popular music did not inhabit different worlds. The majority of the descendants of Rousseau's nobleman and pauper are now happy consumers of the superficial sonic commodities that form part of a multi-million dollar 'industry'. Is it merely elitist arrogance to claim that their musical inheritance is rather more complex and rewarding than they suspect? It is in any case a sad fact that, compared with many other pleasures of life, song of any serious kind remains neglected and misunderstood. This book is devoted to the exploration of as fabulous a treasure trove as was ever part of a country's heritage, a musical cache even less appreciated and vaunted than the German lied. A visit to a bookshop will, with luck, unearth one or two treatises on French song, but when measured against the many tomes devoted to French wine, and in praise of French women, these are slim pickings. A different Johnson (the industrious Hugh) has written guides aplenty to the wines; the media (and the hormones of a majority of males) need no further encouragement to respond to the fairer sex. Unaided by the powerful forces which encourage inebriation and procreation, poor old song has had a raw deal. This book aims to redress the balance, at least in the direction of France. Its readers will be those who are predisposed to the idea that great poetry and classical music are not only separately delectable, but even more delightful when conjoined.

Of these enthusiasts, many will be surprised, even intimidated, by the range of the subject; they will dip into the book when necessary, rather than read it from cover to cover. Fortunately, it has been designed for exactly this purpose: the English-speaking music-lover needs accurate, accessible translations of the poems as a starting point to understanding the repertoire. The alphabetic format (by composer) and more than one comprehensive index enable these texts to be found, without having to read the prose evaluations of the repertoire. The latter may prove useful to those with a more practical interest in French song. Young singers and accompanists begin their careers as much in the dark as the amateur listener and they will hopefully find this part of the book helpful. Every young performer needs help to build a repertoire, and live music-making is as crucial to the survival of the art song as are recital discs from established professionals. Even famous singers are always looking for something new to record, and have been known to welcome a good translation of a tricky text. It is our hope that this book will encourage artists of all ages and stages to explore this field (much of it *terra incognita*), and that the public will follow suit in a happy spiral of supply and demand. A composer's reputation can be miraculously restored to life when requests for photocopies (authorized, of course) from a few adventurous performers lead to the reissue of his works. There are hopeful signs in French publishing, that after a number of decades in the doldrums, song is coming back into fashion, and if this book, and its readers, helps speed that process, the principal aim of its authors will have been achieved.

It might have been thought that interest in song had never died (many songsters of modern times are millionaires and even life peers), but, going back to Cocteau, and conflicting definitions of chanson, it rather depends on what kind of song we are talking about. The authors neither decry the great composers of popular music, nor care to court controversy by printing here a list of who (we think) they are, but the decibel-laden wallpaper which decorates almost every house, car, and shopping mall in modern times seems both dangerous and dull. In these booze and muzak surroundings, the originally romantic phrase 'wine, women, and song' might be reduced to 'plonk, bonk, and honky-tonk'. This sense of musical let-down is nothing new. In a letter to his wife, Gabriel Fauré bemoaned the fact that his music would take a long time to be justly valued; he wrote of 'the mediocrities the public likes to indulge in, and with which it is indulged'. *Plus ça change.* But we can, whenever we choose, remove ourselves from musical banality and go on a Baudelairian voyage where 'luxe, calme et volupté' hold sway. Here a different music prevails, a little old-fashioned perhaps, but none the worse for that. Thanks to poets from five centuries, and musicians from three, it contains the whole world within its boundaries. This music is spun gold rather than heavy metal, bright diamond rather than hard rock. The explosion of cultural activity which brought this art form into being in the nineteenth century continues to resound with a depth of resonance (for those who care to listen) which makes the monosyllabic pop seem aptly named in comparison.

The so-called 'art song', an unfortunately prissy term for something so vital and versatile, is the most urbane and civilized of pastimes. Its most famous manifestations are the German lied and the French mélodie, although there are also important repertoires for English and American song, Spanish canción, and the songs of Russia, eastern Europe, and Scandinavia. It is with the mélodie that French vocal music reaches its apogee. It is something to delight the ear—just as wine delights the palate, and beauty the eye; but because it engages both head and heart, it also brings a deep and lasting satisfaction. Like a long-term romance between two people, a mélodie is judged by the success and maturity of the relationship which sustains it. When we approach the lyric and the music which has been grafted onto it, we may marvel at the separate skills of both poet and composer, but it is the reaction between the two which will make the sparks fly, a fusion which has produced countless moments of incandescent magic. The music can be enjoyed and savoured on the most uncomplicated of levels—as a pretty tune, as a vehicle for a lovely voice, and so on. But if we wish to know why a composer produced *this* music for *that* verbal phrase, we have to work a little harder (it *is* worth it) to understand how a song can seem to burst into flame, and rocket into immortality. The best place to start is with the poems: while listening to the music, the recently converted enthusiast is encouraged to follow the translations printed in this book. The balance between composer and poet is of crucial importance, as is the balance between singer and pianist, once the work has left the drawing board, and entered the concert hall. Because each poem is different, each musical work (obeying the direction of the text) cannot help but be different also—a one-off time-capsule containing layer after layer of background, where the double parentage of composer and poet creates a fascinating web of cultural genealogy.

Every song of this kind has come into being as a result of compromise between the differing interests of words and music. This liaison between poet and musician is seldom conducted face to face (indeed, it is a collaboration that often happens across the centuries) and, although much less stormy than that between opera composer and librettist, it has its ups and downs. A song (except where the composer has written his own words) is the love-child of two artists, where the onus is on the composer to treat the defenceless text with courtesy and honour. That this has so often been accomplished with a selfless devotion and gallantry (despite the sometimes cavalier attitudes described by Richard Stokes on p. xvi) is an indication of the manners of another age—perhaps that is why, as we stand on the threshold of the twenty-first century, we encounter fewer composers of the mélodie, and its various cousins from other nationalities.

Classical song, then, despite its deferential manners which hardly push its cause, can hold its own with the greatest wines and the most beautiful people—indeed the famous Viennese phrase might be revised to something like 'a finer class of wine, human beings, and art song'. In this music-making, women are not just number two on a shopping list of male student fantasies, but indispensable to the art. Women composers form an important part of this book, and women accompanists are establishing themselves more and more in the heart of the profession. (At least one woman pianist, Jacqueline Bonneau, ranks as one of the greatest of all mélodie accompanists on record.) And then, without the female singing voice there would be no such thing as the song repertoire; the sounds of soprano, mezzo, and deeper-hued contralto are built into the cultural life of every nation, and no male artist can ever replace or compete with these. Discrimination of any kind cannot survive long in a sphere which has no patience with the narrow mind. As Auden once wrote: 'You alone, imaginary song | Are unable to say an existence is wrong | And pour out your forgiveness like a wine.' (In the context of this book, that healing beverage is more likely to be Poulenc than plonk.)

But if broad-minded is not the same as *laissez-faire*, and if one imagines that artists regularly permit themselves unbridled artistic licence, other qualities necessary in the performance of French song must be mentioned: the voluntary self-effacement, the giving up of freedom, the holding back out of love rather than fear, the musical phrases where it is just as important *not* to do something, as to add a layer of self-conscious interpretation. And then, the opposite challenge to the singer who may be dutiful and obedient by nature: not to allow fidelity to the text to make of this music something pinched which lacks daring, colour and spontaneity. Again, it is a question of balance. To sing and play French song is a Sisyphean task: the struggle for control, and the battle to let go; the search for the deepest expressivity in songs of the most economical means, and the determination to hold onto the simplest emotion in the midst of musical extravagance. And just when the artist thinks he or she has accomplished something definitive, it is time to go back to the bottom of the slope, and begin again. Shouldering that stone of tones up the hill takes time, and, thank heavens, youth in its confident tyranny cannot easily displace experience. The latest vocal sensations of either sex may make a splash at the opera house, but they can sink without trace in the recital hall, particularly if they have to do battle with the subtleties of mélodie and lied. The seasoned interpreter, whose hard-won mastery in song interpretation is evident in every considered phrase, is not automatically thrown away in favour of the stunning newcomer. In terms of balance (the *sine qua non* of people and music as well as wine), age brings with it a sense of equilibrium, as well as greater depth and taste, in every sense of that word. In the sophisticated company of older vintages, I have learned and savoured much. Having said that on behalf of my middle-aged contemporaries, the younger sparklers cannot be easily discounted, much less dismissed. The old and seasoned congratulate themselves on a superior and more mature viewpoint; the young, as much in love with the medium as their elders, come to challenge and refresh, to rephrase and redefine, and this too is the way of the world. In time, they too will be the venerated doyens and doyennes. Indeed, we look to this new generation of interpreters for the survival of the mélodie into the twenty-first century.

The only sad fact about writing a book of this kind is that the field is too vast for a study which is containable in a single volume, and still affordable for the music lover. I admit to basing the para-meters of this study on my own experience of playing French song over the last twenty-five years, and above all on my own song collection which is representative of the medium, without being exhaustively comprehensive in the manner of the Bibliothèque Nationale. My selection of com-posers and songs is far from all-encompassing and foolproof—how could it be? Chance has played too important a role in my acquisitions from catalogues, and countless dusty-fingered expeditions to the second-hand music shops of France. I might be tempted to reassure myself by thinking that if, after years of sifting through countless piles of music, I have not encountered a name, it is unlike-ly to be a significant one, but I make no such claim. This, after all, is still the most appropriate of all disciplines in which to find unsung heroes.

Much music that I have mentioned is out of print, but the reader should not despair. An enquiry to United Music Publishers or a reputable music shop will often reveal the publisher, and French publishing houses now have much better archive departments, where photocopies may be ordered. There is also a continuing programme of reprints, where material that has been unavailable for years suddenly reappears in the music shops. In any case, song enthusiasts are often avid collectors, and searching for new treasures is part of the joy of it. In this field where possession of the printed music is nine-tenths of a concert, all performers have the greatest incentive to hunt for their next musical meal. In most cases, the most significant ingredient of success is the sheer luck of being at the right music shop at the right time, or being close to a phone when a second-hand music catalogue arrives. The important thing, surely, is to know that a song exists in print, somewhere and somehow; then the fun of 'cherchez la mélodie' begins.

For the musical evaluations in this book, I alone can take responsibility. That I have more sympathy towards certain kinds of French music than to others—preferring, in this particular field, the pithy and unpretentious to the self-consciously sublime—is inarguable. (In this regard I would quote Debussy in my defence: 'One may regret that French music had during too long a period of time been following roads that, in a perfidious way, led us astray from that clarity of expression, from that preciseness and that concentration of form which are particular and significant qualities of the French genius.') I have perhaps been too hard on the creations of great composers which have not (in my opinion, at least) hit their mark, and too indulgent with songs by manifestly less significant figures which seem successful within narrower, and less ambitious, parameters. If I prefer one song to another, the judgements of this book are neither final nor binding, for I am as open to persuasion as any member of a recital audience. I will be delighted to discover that the music in question is better than I believed, rather than worse. Only one fine performance by a convinced champion is needed to begin a song's (or composer's) rehabilitation and rescue from oblivion. It is surely the responsibility of all performers to expand the repertoire through rediscovery and advocacy. The music thus unearthed and lovingly brought back to life will not only be a source of unrivalled joy and pleasure for performers and their listeners, it will improve French song's chances of survival in the modern world.

The vast majority of songs discussed in *A French song companion* were chosen from a musician's working collection, rather than as a result of library research and this has been as good a means as any of containing the articles and translations within the covers of a single volume. Gaps and oversights are inevitable, however, quite apart from composers who have been regretfully, but deliberately, excluded to make way for someone else, or for extra song translation. If I continually encounter works, new to me, which jostle for inclusion in this book, it follows that readers will also know composers whose omission will cause hackles to rise. We have done our best, but in this field of the perfectionist, nothing is good enough. Besides, we all have musical causes close to our heart, and it is fun to fight for neglected music which is threatened with oblivion by a clumsy and uncaring world. Perhaps the most serious omission in this book are the younger composers who are writing mélodies at the moment—those who are composing songs in a new musical climate of freedom and permission where it no longer seems necessary to follow the chilly dictates of Darmstadt, or wherever the Mecca of new music now claims to be. So the mélodie lingers on, somehow. Of course, it no longer flourishes as it did in bygone times, but there is life in it yet. A later edition of a work of this kind should attempt to take such recent developments into account, but at the moment it is too difficult a task to undertake from across a misty Channel. In the meantime, the more that is known about the glories of the mélodie's past (and it is the aim of this book to vaunt them), the more likely it is that it will have an audience. And this, above all, will determine the future of French song.

Graham Johnson

TRANSLATOR'S PREFACE

Sir Michael Tippett, in his conclusion to *A History of Song* (Hutchinson, 1960), writes that 'the moment the composer begins to create the musical verses of his song, he destroys our appreciation of the poem as poetry'. Very often, however, the composer will affect our appreciation of the poem even *before* he sets pen to manuscript paper; for song composers down the ages—even the most literary—have sometimes treated their texts in cavalier fashion. They do so in a variety of ways. Some change the title of a poem, others provide a title when none previously existed; some omit stanzas, others add stanzas, while others place them in a different order or even conflate two different poems; some add words (Ravel's famous Madagascan 'Aoua!' springs to mind), others delete words. And almost all, at some point in their songwriting career, repeat verses as a refrain.

Occasionally, it is clear why a composer should decide to change a poet's original title of a poem, as when Fauré asked Albert Samain, in a letter of 13 April 1896, to supply a new title (*Pleurs d'or*) for *Larmes*, to avoid confusing the new song with the earlier Richepin setting of the same name. But often we can only speculate on the reasons. Bizet's *Guitare*, for example, and Fauré's *Rêve d'amour* were presumably considered by the composers to be punchier titles than Victor Hugo's *Autre guitare* and *Nouvelle chanson sur un vieil air*. And perhaps Hahn called his song *Offrande* to distinguish his setting of Verlaine's *Green* from the earlier versions of the same poem by Debussy (1888) and Fauré (1891). There are countless other examples of such adaptations, which cause confusion to song and literary scholar alike.

A poem which originally formed part of a collection of verse would often be given no title by the poet. For a work of art, however, to have no title can be commercially unviable, as Rothenstein explains to Soames in Max Beerbohm's hilarious satire 'Enoch Soames' from *Seven Men*:

Rothenstein objected that absence of title might be bad for the sale of a book [Soames had another book coming out and intended giving it no title]. 'If', he urged, 'I went into a bookseller's and said simply "Have you got?" or "Have you a copy of?" how would they know what I wanted?'

And so composers often supplied their own titles. Verlaine's poem from *Sagesse* about his imprisonment after the Rimbaud episode (beginning 'Le ciel est, par-dessus le toit | Si bleu, si calme!') is re-titled *Prison* by Fauré, and *D'une prison* by Hahn. On other occasions composers simply named the song after the first line, especially if it had a ring about it and was syntactically complete. Debussy, for example, was happy with the evocative first line of Verlaine's *Il pleure dans mon cœur* from *Romances sans paroles*, but baulked at giving a song the cumbersome title of 'Tournez, tournez, bons chevaux de bois', preferring instead the simpler *Chevaux de bois*. As for song cycles, a composer could either follow the poet, like Fauré in LA BONNE CHANSON, or opt for a title laden with autobiographical significance, like CINQ MÉLODIES 'DE VENISE', to imply that composition began in Venice. Or he could choose a phrase that linked the songs with a poet's *art poétique*, as Hahn did with his CHANSONS GRISES, whose title clearly refers to the famous line from Verlaine's *Art poétique*: 'Rien de plus cher que la chanson grise'; or simply provide a euphonious title of his own, as Berlioz did in *LES NUITS D'ÉTÉ*.

Having established the title of his song, a composer must then decide what part of the poem to set. Even when that poem is short, he will often omit a verse, as Fauré did when setting Baudelaire's *Chant d'automne*, whose second verse was clearly unmanageable for his purposes. But when the poem is long, the composer has to proceed ruthlessly. Gounod reduced Lamartine's *Le vallon* from 16 to 5 verses, *Le soir* from 13 to 6, *Au rossignol* from 19 to 9; Niedermeyer cut *Le lac* from 16 to 6 strophes; while minimalist Satie used only one of the 13 quatrains of *L'isolement* for his *Élégie*. Sometimes a composer not only truncates the original poem, but changes the order of the verses, as Lalo did in *Souvenir*, his own title for a setting of a Victor Hugo poem from *Les contemplations*. Examples of even more drastic abridgements include *LE PROMENOIR DES DEUX AMANTS*, where Debussy uses only 9 of Tristan l'Hermite's 24 verses to create three separate songs; and *Belaud, mon petit chat gris* by Jean Françaix, who picked from here, there, and everywhere to salvage a mere 25 of du Bellay's 202 lines. Chabrier took the liberty of virtually rewriting two of Rosemonde Gérard's animal poems, *Villanelle des petits canards* and *Les cigales*; while Massenet actually conflated verses from two different poems to create the final song of his Armand Silvestre cycle *POÈME D'AVRIL*.

Even the most literary of all composers of mélodies, Claude Debussy, would occasionally tamper with his texts, and the compiler of poems for a book such as this, which aims to supply singers, accompanists, and listeners with the *sung* text, must be on his guard—even Pléiade editions of Baudelaire and Verlaine *et al.*, however authoritative, will not always be the correct sung version. The differences can be minimal, as in *Green*, where Debussy introduces a barely noticeable orthographical variant, by adding a final 'e' to 'encor'. Elsewhere, though, the divergences are more substantial, as the following examples from Debussy's songs show. The composer's version is preceded in each case by the poet's original:

'Ô le chant de la pluie' > 'Ô le bruit de la pluie' (*Il pleure dans mon cœur*)
'Bien dans le ventre et mal dans la tête' > 'Rien dans le ventre et mal dans la tête' (*Chevaux de bois*)
'De ses lueurs' > 'De ses pâleurs' (*Le jet d'eau*)
'Dont un langoureux rossignol' > 'Dont un amoureux rossignol' (*Fantoches*).

It is possible, of course, that the composer was working from earlier editions of the poems which included these words.

The grounds for changing individual words of a poem are as fascinating as they are various. In his recent definitive book on Fauré, *Gabriel Fauré: les voix du clair-obscur* (Flammarion, 1990), Jean-Michel Nectoux even suggests that Fauré (whose altered versions appear second in the following list) scoured a text in order to remove such obstacles to a smooth vocal line as

1. sibilants: 'Sur moi la nuit immense | S'étend comme un linceul' > 'Sur moi la nuit immense | Plane comme un linceul' (*La chanson du pêcheur*);

2. palatalized consonants: 'J'entends déjà tomber avec des chocs funèbres' > 'J'entends déjà tomber avec un choc funèbre' (*Chant d'automne*);

3. 'è' sounds: 'Et qu'il parfume encor les fleurs de l'oranger' > 'Et qu'il parfume encor la fleur de l'oranger' (*Les roses d'Ispahan*).

Establishing bona fide texts for this volume has not been easy, and there are a few poets whose works I have been unable to find in French, English, or American libraries. Amongst these are the poems of those hybrid creatures, the occasional poet-composers, whose verses were presumably set from manuscript: Berlioz, Debussy, Gounod, d'Indy, Koechlin, Lekeu, Messiaen, Ravel, Saint-Saëns, Sauguet, and Sévérac. Some composer-modifications will inevitably have been missed, and I have not always included exclamations (such as Bizet's at the start of *Guitare*) or repetitions of refrains. Orthography has not always been standardized, so that poems from the fifteenth century by Villon and Charles d'Orléans, the sixteenth by Marot, Passerat, du Bellay, and Ronsard, the seventeenth by de Viau, Corneille, La Fontaine, and Tristan l'Hermite, and the eighteenth by Voltaire, Florian, and de Parny often retain their contemporary flavour.

I have resisted the temptation to explain, either in footnotes or in the process of translation, the background to a song, when it forms part of a play, story, or novel, but singers and accompanists, when preparing the songs for performance, might like to consult these works: Victor Hugo's *Marie Tudor* (Gounod's *Sérénade*), Alexandre Arnoux's *Le chevalier errant* (Ibert's QUATRE CHANSONS DE DON QUICHOTTE), Jean Anouilh's *Léocadia* (Poulenc's *Les chemins de l'amour*), Jules Supervielle's *Bolivar* (Milhaud's TROIS CHANSONS DE NÉGRESSE), Pierre Corneille's *Psyché* (Émile Paladilhe's *Psyché*), Jean Giraudoux's *Suzanne et le Pacifique* (Arthur Honegger's PETIT COURS DE MORALE), Jean-Pierre Claris de Florian's *Estelle, pastorale* and *Célestine* (Benjamin Godard's *Chanson d'Estelle*, Johann Paul Martini's *Plaisir d'amour*), and Henry Wadsworth Longfellow's *The Spanish student* (Charles Gounod's *Viens, les gazons sont verts*).

Fearful of dumbing down, I have kept footnotes to a minimum, and placed them at the bottom of each page for ease of reference. When Graham Johnson's essays have already explained a word or phrase from a poem, I have avoided further comment. I hope that I have neither condescended the reader, nor assumed too much knowledge. It seemed sensible, for example, in Poulenc's LE TRAVAIL DU PEINTRE (Éluard), to gloss Juan Gris and Jacques Villon, but not Picasso, Chagall, Braque, Klee and Miró. I have similarly refrained from commenting on the familiar *Commedia dell' Arte* figures from Verlaine's *Fêtes galantes*, except for Scaramouche (Debussy's *Fantoches*), whose black attire is relevant to the poem. I have glossed foreign words, taken from the French poems and used in my translations, when there seemed to be no adequate English equivalent: 'alguazils' from Hugo's *Guitare* (Bizet); 'hidalgo' from Musset's *Les filles de Cadix* (Delibes); 'khanjar' from Gautier's *La fuite* (Duparc); 'spahi' from Hugo's *La captive* (Berlioz); 'Selene' from Jean de la Ville de Mirmont's *Diane, Séléné* (Fauré); 'cadis' and 'calumets' from Klingsor's *Schéhérazade* (Ravel); and 'Alcade', 'Almirante' and 'mirador' from Chalupt's *Le bachelier de Salamanque* (Roussel). I have also supplied the briefest notes on place-names (mythical, ancient and modern), and on characters from myth, history, politics and the Arts, when such information contributes to an understanding of the poem.

As far as possible I have observed in translation the French line-order, and have attempted to render the sense and tone of the poem without any slavish adherence to the original rhymes and metre.

Richard Stokes

THE HISTORY OF THE MÉLODIE:
A POCKET INTRODUCTION

(Composers in bold lettering have an alphabetical entry article in this book.)

Mélodie, the younger and more serious sibling of chanson (a word which, strictly speaking, should be used to describe only songs of a lighter, more popular nature), has long been one of France's best-kept secrets. The name, funnily enough, comes about thanks to an Irishman. In 1808, Thomas Moore, the friend of Byron, and estimable poet, issued the first of his *Irish melodies*, a collection of lyrical and patriotic poems including *The last rose of summer*. It so happened that **Hector Berlioz** fell in love with an Irish actress, Harriet Smithson, at about this time, and, driven to embrace the culture of his beloved, set a number of poems from this collection (in French translation of course). These employed voice and piano in equal partnership, and made quite a stir. 'Have you heard Berlioz's *mélodies*?' people asked, meaning the *Irish melodies* of course. But the label stuck for all piano-accompanied songs in this mould. It was a useful means to describe a new form of song which was different from the much simpler established forms: the romance, a strophic song with simple melody and anodyne accompaniment; the bergerette, a nymphs and shepherds survivor from the eighteenth century; the *scène*, a melodramatic tableau to be delivered with operatic pathos, and so on. The role of the piano in much of this earlier music was kept to a minimum. We can still find many rather pretty examples of eighteenth-century song arranged by J. B. Weckerlin (1821–1910)—these pieces had a vogue at one time. New interest in women composers has unveiled the name of **Pauline Duchambge** who was one of the first to realise that a lyric from a great poet adds to the significance of a song. It was none other than **Wolfgang Amadeus Mozart** who had served notice on the old regime of Grétry, Monsigny, and Philidor—theatre composers all, and thus outside the range of this study—by showing in two small but important songs, impeccable parodies of French musical taste, that romance and bergerette could blossom into something musically significant. And of course there were other imports, less distinguished than Mozart, but further evidence of the important role that foreigners have played in nourishing the roots of French music. **Johann Paul Martini**, a German who worked in France, wrote at least one immortal song, *Plaisir d'amour*; the hugely successful opera composer **Giacomo Meyerbeer** wrote songs in French alongside his lieder; **Franz Liszt** set Victor Hugo, sometimes achieving astonishing results like *Oh! quand je dors*, and no less a composer than **Richard Wagner** had a go at writing songs in French, even if one suspects that he did so for commercial rather than aesthetic reasons.

The German lied, with Schubert posthumously at its helm, exercised an enormous influence. Of course, serious settings of important German poetry had been made long before Schubert's ascendancy, and this made it natural for German-speakers who visited France, and could also speak French, to be utterly at home in writing songs which seemed deeper than the home-grown article. The influence of certain singers on French musical life was also inestimable: examples are the tenor

Adolphe Nourrit (who was one of the first to include Schubert and Schumann in his repertoire) and **Pauline Viardot,** whose worldly sophistication and celebrated salon shaped many a budding song composer, including the young Fauré. When native composers, and their audiences, were still hankering after the old-fashioned romance (**Loïsa Puget** was a composer who did very well financially by sticking faithfully to the past), there were a number of transitional figures who paved the way for important change. The Swiss-born composer **Louis Niedermeyer** set the poetry of Lamartine in such an innovative way that his music seemed worthy of the important texts; **Hippolyte Monpou** brought a daring and energy to a form that too easily suffered from the ladylike vapours; **Henri Reber** brought a fastidious craftsmanship that derived from his knowledge of the German classics; **Victor Massé** attempted to endow the mélodie with the theatrical flair which he more easily expressed in his operettas; **Félicien David** introduced a taste for oriental evocation to the musical public, a love-affair with this type of stylization which was to last for nearly a century—an exotic feature which distinguishes the mélodie from other song cultures.

After the walk-on appearances of all these preparatory figures, the stage is now set for the emergence of **Charles Gounod,** the first mélodie composer of genius, apart that is from Berlioz whose pioneering work stands alone, inimitable and still controversial. Inspired by Niedermeyer, Gounod also set Lamartine; he owed much to Schumann, and he learned much from Monpou, Reber, and others, but his melodic gift and graceful polish were all his own. In later life, he wore a cloak of religiosity, but in his earlier career his output was characterized by worldly elegance and a sovereign ability in the theatre. Gounod's songs, reflect these urbane talents, and two other composers follow in this tradition. They both wrote some fine songs, and both composed at least one opera of significance: **Édouard Lalo** and **Léo Delibes.** Lalo in particular had an individual voice as a song composer. More famous in the world of opera was **Georges Bizet** whose early death deprived the mélodie of great things; the melodic freshness and spontaneity of the best of his songs are worthy of his great opera *Carmen.* At this time, three other composers of great renown, one German and two Italian, wrote songs in French which stand outside the tradition of the recently emerging mélodie. **Gaetano Donizetti** wrote a great many songs and duos in French, only a few of which are available in modern editions. The works in the style of the romance seem unexceptional, if always elegantly tuneful, but Donizetti's influence on composers such as Delibes and Liszt in the realm of the more theatrical and operatically inspired *scène* was considerable. **Jacques Offenbach,** famous for his operettas, set the fables of La Fontaine (Offenbach's successor in this and other ways was **Charles Lecocq**), and **Gioachino Rossini** produced comic songs, written in the later years of his life, which are both delightful and perplexing. This music still belongs to the dazzling and opulent world of Napoleon III and his fairy-tale empire of sand-castles—it was fortunate for French music that the tide of events was soon to sweep these away.

With the emergence of **César Franck**, we find an adept, if not prolific, song composer, and also a great teacher. Franck probably had more influence on the song form in France than any other single man. The debacle of the Franco-Prussian War, the collapse of the Second Empire, and the sorry episode of the Commune inaugurated a new era of seriousness. French musicians had had enough of bowing to the imported works of Meyerbeer and Offenbach; there was a newly awakened taste among young composers for writing symphonic and chamber music. The word 'profound' was no longer risible, and Franck turned to the great German masters Bach and

Beethoven, not to mention Wagner, and made them part of his teaching. From now on, a decided-ly Franckian strain is to be found in French music. Allegiance to this school of lofty aspirations (and its successor, the Schola Cantorum) marks out certain composers as different from their rather more light-hearted contemporaries. Much great music was written under this banner, but the turgid and self-conscious side of Franckism at its least inspired loses sight of the clarity and balance which is usually characteristic of French art. One of Franck's first pupils was **Alexis de Castillon,** a name now forgotten; he died early, and is one of the great might-have-beens in French music. (Two other pupils of the 'Pater Seraphicus' from a later generation, **Guillaume Lekeu** and **Albéric Magnard,** were both composers of intense and highly strung music; they died before their time, so a question mark also hovers over what they might have achieved.) The first Franck pupil to write song master-pieces was **Henri Duparc,** whose sixteen surviving mélodies have been enough to win him his place among the great. It is thanks to his setting of Baudelaire's *L'invitation au voyage* that we are able to speak of French song's 'luxe, calme et volupté'. The spirit of Wagner had now begun to influence French music in no uncertain terms, and had a powerful effect on this group of musicians in par-ticular. Duparc showed how to absorb many of the lessons of the Bayreuth master without losing the essential French qualities of order, understatement, and a sense of human proportion. The other giant among the first (and never excelled) wave of composers to be influenced by Franck was **Ernest Chausson,** who wrote mélodies of charm, depth, and inimitable melancholy. Not all of Franck's pupils were as talented as this, of course, but they usually had strong personalities: the fascinating **Augusta Holmès** was someone to be reckoned with in French social and musical life at the time, and **Vincent d'Indy** seems now less celebrated as a composer than as a propagandist of Franckian ideals, and as founder of the Schola Cantorum, the school which was later to be set up in competi-tion to the Conservatoire.

Not all composers needed Franck to turn them to grander aspirations. A symphonist of early sig-nificance, and a composer of many bold and original songs, was **Camille Saint-Saëns,** who is some-thing of a wild card: during his long life, he was to play the role of both pioneer and reactionary. Some of his finest songs were to the poetry of Victor Hugo, the first of the great French writers to influence and inspire almost every single one of his composer contemporaries. Saint-Saëns was also a teacher, and his greatest pupil—only ten years younger—was **Gabriel Fauré,** one of the giants of the medium, whose first songs date from the 1860s, and his last from the 1920s. In a bird's-eye view of this kind, it is difficult to know when to introduce Fauré's name into the narrative, so important was his work in each phase of his organic development from salon composer to twentieth-century master. In the beginning he set Victor Hugo, then Armand Silvestre, Paul Verlaine, Albert Samain, Van Lerberghe—his song catalogue is a miniature history of changing literary tastes over a career lasting sixty years. In musical history there are always great composers who do not belong to any school or lineage, but whose individuality places them alone and *sans pareil*. In this category, between Saint-Saëns and Fauré, in chronological terms, comes **Emmanuel Chabrier.** His songs are not many, but they are entirely typical of an inimitable artist and human being who adored Wagner's music, but remained a great Frenchman absolutely individual in terms of his style, humour, and melodic exuberance.

The Conservatoire continued to spawn musicians whose ambitions were not to change and enlighten the world through music (there was always an element of this missionary zeal, to a lesser or greater degree, among the followers of Franck), but rather to write successfully in all forms, and, particularly, to succeed in the world of opera. There are a band of composers, many of them winners of the Prix de Rome (prestigious, but hardly a litmus test of greatness), who wrote good songs, some of them of great charm, and whose work should not be entirely forgotten: **Théodore Dubois, Émile Pessard, Émile Paladilhe, Benjamin Godard** (famous for his *Jocelyn*, but a prolific song composer), and the Goncourt-like brothers **Paul** and **Lucien Hillemacher.** Much more famous than any of these, but essentially of their number, as far as composing songs was concerned, was **Jules Massenet,** whose many mélodies have not held the concert platform as one might have expected from a still popular opera composer. The songs of **André Messager** seem no match for his stage works, and **Ernest Reyer** is an example of a composer whose mélodies were once performed in deference to the fame of his operas. The songs of neither composer now see the light of day, but they are part of the history of the mélodie. Occasionally we are surprised that a musician who was well known in another sphere was a fine song composer—as is the case with the great organist **Charles Widor.** Thirty years after Liszt composed his mélodies, we also encounter a second wave of foreigners who were drawn to write French songs from time to time: **Paolo Tosti, Ruggero Leoncavallo,** and **Maude Valérie White.** Some of the French operatic arias of **Pietro Mascagni** were published as mélodies. The American **Amy Beach,** although younger than these composers, also chose to write French songs in a style which pre-dates Debussy, and which seems much influenced by the example of her fellow woman composer, the prolific and popular **Cécile Chaminade.**

The advent of **Claude Debussy** marks the beginning of modernity in this study of song, although the musical revolution which he brought about was achieved in various stages of his career. In the first of these we can easily detect the style of Massenet, but this quickly gave way to an individuality and a daring which were to propel French music into the twentieth century. Like Fauré, and contemporary with him more or less, Debussy is one of the central figures of this book. As with all the great composers of this medium, it is his choice of poetry which marks him out: in the beginning Verlaine and Mallarmé (he was to revisit both, particularly Verlaine, who stands at the centre of his *œuvre*), then Baudelaire and, in the manner of Wagner, his own poetry. As he began to style himself 'Claude de France', a national figure for the new century, he turned to the earlier French poets Charles d'Orléans and Villon.

Of course the majority of the old guard, and a large number of their pupils and acolytes, did not see Debussy's path as the true way forward. There were many composers whose huge romantic operas, sometimes influenced by Italian verismo models, and successful enough at the time, now seem dinosaurs. In an age remarkable for its musical vulgarity and professional dishonesty, these artists missed the boat, as far as the future was concerned; vain composers burnished their Nero (or whatever other historical character they chose for their sumptuous operatic spectacles), while the Prix de Rome was fiddled. Of course it is with hindsight that we can see that the larger works of **Herman Bemberg, Alfred Bruneau, Alexandre George, Xavier Leroux, Georges Hüe,** and **Alfred Bachelet** were part of a doomed species—*Pelléas et Mélisande* saw to that—but some of their songs, very much of their epoch, should be considered for revival. It is one of the glories of the mélodie that to revive a song costs rather less than to unearth a forgotten opera. **Gustave Charpentier** wrote at least one fine opera, *Louise*, but his Verlaine settings are interesting—though of course they cannot rival those of Debussy.

Those composers with a Franckian aesthetical background were better placed to greet the Debussian onslaught with a certain amount of sympathy. Debussy flirted with composers like Chausson and **Charles Bordes** (one of the earliest composers to set Verlaine, and one of the founders of the Schola Cantorum) and derived much more inspiration from them than from the reactionaries at the Conservatoire. They had, after all, an admiration for Wagner in common, although later on their paths diverged. **Pierre de Bréville** allowed himself to be influenced by Debussy, as did the forgotten **Sylvio Lazzari**, but composers like **Gabriel Pierné** (a pupil of both Franck and Massenet) took a more independent line, like **Maurice Emmanuel.** The cost of being an imitator (and not quite a genius) is a certain musical anonymity, and the same applies to the loners who aspire to an individuality they do not possess. In a class on his own as an influence on Debussy (and countless other younger composers) was **Erik Satie,** both a loner and a genius. We first encounter his name in the 1890s when Debussy took him under his wing, but Satie was uncontainable in this way. He shook free of his erstwhile mentor, and went on to become one of the most important prophets and gurus of twentieth-century music. Another 'loner' in the Satie mould was **Charles Koechlin,** only slightly younger than Debussy but, because he was long-lived, seeming to belong to a more modern age. Koechlin is only recently coming into his own with the public as a composer of real individuality.

For English-speakers in the 1880s and Naughty Nineties, French music had meant the operettas of Offenbach and his successors; these were Edward, Prince of Wales's 'wine, women, and song' years. The tidal wave of impressionism which emanated from France provided Paris with a new artistic profile as distinct as the Eiffel Tower. For younger Francophiles, French music was now epitomized by Debussy and his exquisite bag of tricks. It was Debussyism which went out into the world at large and enchanted foreigners with its mystery, incipient decadence, and the delicious unwholesomeness of the whole-tone scale which had been mocked by Rossini fifty years before. Veiled eroticism, a theme ideally suited to the Debussy style, is heard in the music of foreign composers such as **Isaac Albéniz,** and the songs of the Poles **Jósef Szulc** and **Poldowski** who owe a great deal to Debussy's settings of Verlaine (though the Catulle Mendès songs of **Ignacy Paderewski** are more individual of musical language). The music of the Americans **Charles Griffes, Charles Loeffler,** and **John Alden Carpenter,** the Dutchman **Alphons Diepenbrock,** and, in the handful of his French settings, the Englishman **Frederick Delius** are impossible to imagine without the example of Debussy and Ravel—the second of these a composer some thirteen years younger, and a genius in his own right but whose name will always be linked with Debussy's in the public imagination.

In the wake of Debussy's innovations, composers of the next generation had some difficulty in establishing their own sound and style. Some like **Gabriel Dupont** chose to live in the past and to write songs of elegance which looked back to his teachers Massenet and Widor. **Jane Vieu** also refused to look forwards in her songwriting, but published her own songs for a faithful clientele. Some chose to take the best from both worlds—**Gabriel Grovlez** for example was a pupil of Fauré, and a teacher at the Schola Cantorum; **Henri Büsser** was a friend of Debussy, as well as composition professor at the Conservatoire. Others had too strong a musical personality for this fence-sitting, and evolved their own voice—few more successfully than **Albert Roussel,** whose harmonic language and style have an integrity and piquant individuality which are reflected in his fine songs. Roussel's harmonic vocabulary derived from study at the Schola, but is not typical of that establishment; for this, one need look no further than the deeply felt but rather monochrome work of **Guy Ropartz.** Like Roussel, in respect of carving his own niche, was **Déodat de Sévérac,** who was much influenced by Debussy but, inspired by his native south of France, succeeded in finding an individual voice of considerable charm. Less fortunate, and even less known than Séverac's output, is the highly crafted music of **Max d'Ollone.** Far better-known as a song composer, **Reynaldo Hahn,** had a precocious salon success as a teenager in the late 1880s, and managed somehow to remain insulated from the modern Debussian world. His music, which owes much to Massenet, wove many a spell for those who, like him, regarded Fauré's *LA BONNE CHANSON* as the last word in modern music. So powerful and haunting are some of these nostalgic evocations of the *belle époque* that Hahn now counts unexpectedly as a much more significant composer than many of his more musically ambitious contemporaries: post-Debussyists such as **Louis Aubert** and **Florent Schmitt,** for example, or **Louis Vierne,** famous as a composer for organ, but actually rather a keen songwriter, particularly in his later years.

There were a few composers who took a great deal from Debussy but nevertheless were able to turn it into something completely their own. Chief among these was **Maurice Ravel,** born in the same year as Hahn, but destined for a starring role in twentieth-century music and aesthetics. Ravel is usually not considered as innovative a figure as Debussy, but the older composer was not ashamed to adopt the 'impressionistic' pianism of Ravel's *Jeux d'eau*, and the Spanish manner of his *Habanera*. There is no equivalent in Debussy's songs to the experimental manner of Ravel's *HISTOIRES NATURELLES*. The two composers are so different in terms of personality that similarities of musical language and manner are soon discounted in the face of Ravel's songs which are undeniably unique and mesmerizing. Of the other composers of Debussian hue, one of the most important and talented was **André Caplet,** whose songs are a treasure trove of sensibility and colour. **Joseph Canteloube** showed even greater interest than Ravel in arranging folksongs; in recent years, his Auvergne settings have become more famous than he could have dreamed. Born in the same year as Canteloube, Ravel's pupil **Maurice Delage** experimented with music for voice and chamber ensemble. Like **Jean Cras,** another composer born in 1879, Delage was an inveterate traveller as far afield as India. Both composers had something in common with Roussel in this respect, and also with his refined and delicate sound-world. But Roussel was ten years older; both Delage and Cras were left behind in terms of the musical developments after the First World War when the prevailing taste for a combination of accessible neo-classicism and popular culture made their music seem over-refined, the product of a pre-war hothouse. And it was also difficult to perform.

Each generation of mélodie history brought its share of foreign visitors, in this case the Spaniard **Manuel de Falla,** the American **Charles Ives** (who was influenced by Godard and Massenet in his French songs, rather than Debussy), the Romanian **Georges Enescu,** the Italians **Alfred Casella** and **Gian Francesco Malipiero,** and the American-Jewish composer of Swiss birth **Ernst Bloch.** A curiosity is the young Portuguese composer **Luis de Freitas Branco,** whose precocious settings of Baudelaire were made before he had studied in France. The Belgian violinist Eugène Ysaÿe and his brother Théodore were both song composers; but the most influential composer of foreign extraction was undoubtedly to be **Igor Stravinsky.** He only wrote two French songs, but at one time or another he held almost every twentieth-century French composer in his thrall, not only avant-gardistes like **Edgard Varèse,** but members of Les Six as well. Of all the composers mentioned above, it was only Ives who had not lived or worked in Paris for a time.

We now arrive at those composers who were young and active at the beginning of the new century. In musical terms, by a trick of cultural chronology, this does not refer to 1900, but rather to 1918. It was the First World War which changed everything in French cultural life. In 1918, Debussy was dying, and with him the old order. Even then, there were astonishing survivors: the irrepressible Saint-Saëns was still alive and active, as was the sure-footed Fauré; Ravel was composing less than at the turn of the century, but the quality of his work was still astounding—only in 1933 was he to fall ill with the neurological disease which would eventually kill him; Duparc was alive and ill, a relic of long-distant glories condemned to a living hell of musical silence; Roussel was at the height of his powers; Hahn was approaching middle age and taking refuge in the world of operetta and light music, his productive years as a writer of songs largely behind him. One of the saddest events of the year was the death of the prodigiously gifted **Lili Boulanger** aged only 24. Her elder sister **Nadia Boulanger,** also a composer, was to become the most famous of composition teachers anywhere in the world. Against this background, the *Zeitgeist* had to have ready a surprise for the times, and this was provided by a conveniently packaged group of composers whom the critic and song composer **Henri Collet** labelled Les Six—a type of French equivalent to that mighty handful—the Russian Five. The Russian composers really had been a school united by aesthetic and aspiration, but despite the efforts of Jean Cocteau, these six French composers, though on amicable terms, were all too different to remain an active co-operative for long. **Louis Durey** was eleven years older than the youngest, Poulenc. He was a remote and politically aware composer who quickly disappeared from the collective scene to follow his own path; his substantial body of work awaits rediscovery. **Germaine Tailleferre** wrote some charming songs but was not, in the end, an important figure in mélodie history. **Georges Auric** had the reputation of an intellectual, a critic, and a writer of film music, roles which rather swamped his reputation as a serious composer, perhaps unfairly. More significant were the remaining three names: **Arthur Honegger,** a Swiss with a serious streak, who did not feel really at one with the Parisian 'jeunesse dorée', but whose substantial body of songs now seem very much part of the mainstream French tradition; **Darius Milhaud,** an astonishingly prolific composer, blessed with the emotional warmth of a Jewish background and the sunlight of his native Aix, whose songs are an important, but somewhat uneven, part of his vast musical legacy; and finally **Francis Poulenc,** a figure almost as literate as Debussy, as loveable as Chabrier, and as important a song composer as any in this book. Poulenc is an unlikely successor to the great masters perhaps, but he is nothing less than that. His name is as much linked to the poetry of Apollinaire and Éluard as Debussy's was to Verlaine and Baudelaire.

Of course, not everybody fitted into cliques as neat (if artificial) as that of Les Six, but some of them tried to imitate the success (at least in terms of marketing reputations) of that chic conglomerate. The École d'Arcueil (so called because it was grouped around an affiliation to Satie, and named after the Parisian suburb in which he lived) included the composers **Henri Sauguet** and **Maxime Jacob,** both extremely prolific song composers. Sauguet has survived better in the public imagination, but both men deserve to be reassessed. This is equally true of **Jacques Leguerney** who, rather than attaching himself to a group of composers, became affiliated with a group of poets—the sixteenth-century band known as La Pléiade, with Ronsard chief among their number. Leguerney

xxvi THE HISTORY OF THE MÉLODIE

forged for himself a style which, though it owes something to Poulenc, seems more individual as the years go by. In reality, this was a time of 'every man for himself'. Eclecticism was the order of the day and Poulenc claimed to have made his style from an amalgam of Palestrina, Mozart, Verdi, Mussorgsky, Chabrier, Debussy, and so on, not to mention Stravinsky, Prokofiev, and the French music hall; it was a time which allowed musicians to walk out of step with fashion and nevertheless survive if they had something to say in the medium. This is a very big 'if', however. The great organists **Charles Tournemire** and **Marcel Dupré**, individualists both, wrote songs, very different from each other, which still rank as musical rarities. And there are names like **Maurice Jaubert,** and **Pierre Octave Ferroud,** both fine mélodistes, who had the misfortune to die young before they had a chance to establish themselves in the increasingly competitive welter of composers who pestered performers and publishers with their works. In fact, Ferroud was founder member of another set of composers, this time known as Le Groupe de Triton, which contained another very capable song composer—**Jean Rivier**. Someone who belonged to no group at all was the singular **Georges Migot,** who forged a musical language of his own inspired by the modal music of the Renaissance; he composed a large number of songs, few of them ever performed outside France. Composers like **Louis Beydts** and **Pierre Vellones** were popular in their own time, but paid for the fluidity and accessibility of their music with a neglect which has continued to this day. Others like **Jacques Ibert** have survived better thanks to their fine instrumental writing, and their unpretentious ability to turn their talents in every direction, including providing music for the commercial world of cinema. **Marcel Delannoy** was another good example of a composer with a flair for writing for the theatre, and the woman composer **Claude Arrieu** of one with a deft gift for writing concise and charming mélodies in the Poulenc mode. **Manuel Rosenthal,** who had been a close friend of Ravel, was a first-class conductor, but he has left a significant body of songs, the best of them enchantingly humorous. This is also true of **Jean Wiener,** one-time cabaret pianist at Le Boeuf sur le Toit, whose songs are an early example of the jazz style applied to the mélodie. This style of modernity is also to be found in the songs of **Jacques de Menasce** and **Henri Barraud.** Even more of a crossover artist was **Joseph Kosma,** darling of the intellectual Left, and chanson composer, but also attracted to the discipline, and fine literature, typical of the mélodie. This was also an age when famous singers wrote their own material—a throwback to the age of Pauline Viardot, and a prophesy of the Beatles. **Charles Trenet** was not only one of the singing idols of his time, he was a modern-day Aristide Bruant unafraid to enlist great poets in the cause of popular song.

The foreign composers who set French texts now came from amazingly diverse backgrounds, and were attracted to various aspects of the art form. Those whose own language was French included the Belgian composers **Joseph Jongen** and **Jean Absil,** only two names on this country's long roster of unexplored achievement in this field. Equally impressive is the work of many Swiss composers, represented in this book by **Pierre Maurice, Frank Martin, Jean Binet,** and the conductor **Ernest Ansermet.** Some of the gentle songs of the Catalan **Frederic Mompou** are in French—a testimony to many years of residency in Paris. **Joaquín Rodrigo** also wrote songs which acknowledge Spain's enduring debt to the art of Debussy. The French songs of English Francophiles ranged from the ultra-chromatic wanderings of **Bernard van Dieren** and **Kaikhosru Sorabji** to the insouciant trifles of **Lord Berners,** and the more substantial, exquisitely well-mannered songs of **Lennox Berkeley** (the fruit of his study with Nadia Boulanger). Boulanger was a force to be reckoned with, and stands second only to Franck as a teaching influence in this medium. (The songs of **Jean Françaix** and those of **Marcelle de Manziarly** show ample evidence of the fastidious craftsmanship which she famously instilled into her pupils.) Another Boulanger protégé was the divinely gifted Romanian pianist **Dinu Lipatti,** whose songs show literary sensibility, and also surprisingly well-developed skills as a composer. Never utterly at home in the French language, and rather hostile to the Boulanger school, **Benjamin Britten** nevertheless wrote important works to French texts when still a teenager. His orchestral cycle *Les illuminations* is as exquisite an evocation of French *volupté* seen through Anglo-Saxon eyes as will ever be written. Britten's Polish contemporary **Witold Lutoslawski** was drawn to French culture and literature like few other twentieth-century composers born outside France. He selected French texts for the majority of his vocal music where Polish passion is coloured and moderated by a Francophile musical sensibility. Most other non-French composers were content to bow in the direction of France without becoming 'thoroughly assimilated' as the Voltaire-inspired musical *Candide* would have it. **Leonard Bernstein,** not the most retiring of composers, confined his setting of French song to an amusing cookery cycle with recipes. Britten's American contemporary **Samuel Barber** wrote a much smaller cycle for voice and piano; as he was not himself a Frenchman, his choice of Rilke's verse (a German writing in French) displays a certain apposite tact. Certainly Britten, with all the recklessness of genius, rushed into Rimbaud where French-born angels feared to tread. Less controversial French folksong arrangements were also made by Britten, and in this line, the British composers **Alan Rawsthorne** and **Antony Hopkins** also wrote interesting material where the French language adds a note of cross-Channel sensuality to English music.

Bernstein's cycle is not the only time we hear of a French song composer in the kitchen. Poulenc once gave an interview to an American magazine in which he stated that not all great composers had been innovators: 'it is not necessary that one *innove,*' he is reported to have said. Poulenc then went on to decry 'dirty' modern music, made with what he mysteriously termed 'teen pote'. The mystified reporter of the *Atlantic Monthly* described what happened next: 'he went into a recess of the apartment and emerged with a small saucepan on which he hammered with a spoon. "Teen pote" he said.' It was easier for Poulenc to make fun of *musique concrète* than to stop the tidal wave of new music that began to dominate the scene in the years after the Second World War. Some of his younger contemporaries, like **Jacques Chailley,** integrated their discoveries of new music into a type of writing for the voice which Poulenc could still understand. But as early as the 1930s, he had first encountered a powerful new school of composition that had sown the seeds for the downfall of mélodie. This was La Jeune France, a group which was founded by **Olivier Messiaen,** together with **André Jolivet** and **Daniel-Lesur.** The latter two composers, after an avant-garde start, developed in a more conventional way—they have both written songs that come well within the standard definition of song with piano: a collaboration of composer and poet. With the vocal works of Messiaen, however, the mélodie in the form we know it ceases to exist. His music for voice and piano (to his own texts) is overwhelmingly powerful, but no longer the urbane collaboration of word and tone that had been the guiding aesthetic which hundreds of composers had taken for granted. Messiaen, a law unto himself, made no attempt to destroy the works of others; his only concern was to construct his own astonishing musical world. Nevertheless, notice was served on the mélodie, not only from within France itself, but by the developments in the German musical world which had stemmed from the atonality of Schoenberg and the serial techniques of Webern. Figures like Stockhausen in Germany reigned supreme in the 1960s, as did **Pierre Boulez** in France. Of course vocal works continued to be written in the new dispensation, many of them with French texts. Very sensual and appealing examples of pieces for voice and ensemble (for the piano as an accompanying instrument was now somewhat *démodé*) are by the German **Hans Werner Henze,** and the English serialist **Elizabeth Lutyens.** But the old relationship between composer and singer as exemplified by the Bernac–Poulenc duo (or the Pears–Britten duo in English song) was a thing of the past.

Of course people continued to write songs, and this book contains the names of living composers who look back on their writing of mélodies with a sort of nostalgia: **Henri Dutilleux** (who wrote some fine songs, but is not regarded as a mélodie composer by the French public); the Americans **Paul Bowles** who lived in Morocco, and **Ned Rorem** who wrote songs in French when he lived in France, but who has since remained faithful to song in his mother tongue. The youngest composer in this book is **Jean-Michel Damase** (b. 1928), and the only slightly older American **Lee Hoiby** wrote a Rimbaud cycle fairly recently for a young American singer, the late Will Parker, who was a French song specialist.

The following paragraphs, the last section of this book to be written, contains names, latecomers and strays, who do not have separate articles devoted to them in *A French song companion*. These composers might be treated at greater length in a later edition of this book (the lifelong habit of acquiring printed music is impervious to publishing deadlines) but there are a few composers here whose link with the mélodie, however worthy of mention, is merely tangential.

A French song companion is reasonably comprehensive in covering the mélodie composers of the belle époque. Various names, however, have slipped through the net, including the opera composer *Ambroise Thomas* (1811–1896) whose work-list boasts numerous mélodies, all unknown to me. The interesting salon songs of *Louis Diémer* (1843–1919) are a recent acquisition; they seem more than worthy to stand next to contemporary composers like Pessard and the Hillemacher brothers. *Paul Dukas* (1865–1935) is a celebrated composer and great teacher (he is frequently mentioned as such in this book) but his only mélodie seems to be a single Ronsard setting published in a supplement to *La Revue musicale* in 1924. *Rhené-Baton* (1879–1940) was a fine conductor who composed songs which have surprisingly recently re-emerged on a recording devoted to them. *Paul Le Flem* (1881–1984) was an influential figure in French music; his songs are not central to his work, but they should be worth looking at. *Claude Delvincourt* (1888–1954), a prolific composer and one-time director of the Paris Conservatoire wrote a number of mélodies (ONCHET, Chalupt settings written for Bernac, for example); and the composer-critic *Roland-Manuel* (1891–1966) contributed a Ronsard setting to the same supplement as Dukas. The pointed and witty cycle PONCTUATION FRANÇAISE (C. Oulmont, 1946) by *Alexandre Tansman* (1897–1986), a French composer of Polish origin, encourages further exploration of his vocal works. Three composers born in 1906 are also of note: *Yves Baudrier* (1906–1988), the founder of 'Jeune France', whose *Poèmes* cycles to the texts of Tristan Corbière and Jean Cassou are important, sadly unknown outside France; the unlucky *Jean Cartan* (1906–1932) pupil of Dukas and protégé of Roussel who set Klingsor, Mallarmé, and Villon; *Pierre Capdevielle* (1906–1969) whose *Je n'ai oublié, voisine de la ville* is one of the loveliest, and shyest, of all Baudelaire settings. *Léo Preger* (1907–1965) is known to me, alas, only through his prayer-like *Étude* for the Louise de Vilmorin Chopin-inspired anthology Mouvements de coeur. Another highly talented Dukas pupil was the formidable **Elsa Barraine** (1910–1999). The composer of the symphonic poem *Song-koï* is regarded by some as the most gifted French woman composer since Lili Boulanger. Once again song composition was not at the top of the list of her priorities, but I would like to come across her work in this field. As far as I know **Jehan Alain** (1911–1940) a fallen war hero and an enormous talent, wrote only two songs (settings of Jammes and Kipling). I have recently encountered settings from Apollinaire's LE BESTIAIRE (LE CORTÈGE D'ORPHÉE) by **Claude Ballif**, b. 1924. He has also apparently set poems by Michaux, Mallarmé, and Tzara. Some years ago the pianist Billy Eidi showed me some fine Cocteau settings in manuscript by the young composer **Guy Sacre**, and I was interested to see that these are now published by Durand. Much more recently, after I had accompanied a recital in Tours, **Monique Gabus** (b. 1924) sent me her published songs: QUATRE MÉLODIES DE GIDE, and settings of Ronsard, Vilmorin, Rimbaud and Rilke.

Of non-French composers working in this language, I would like to know more about the vocal works of the distinguished Hungarian composer **Laslo Lajtha** (1892–1963). Three German composers, all of them working outside the traditions of their fatherland have had a passing relationship with French song. Among the vast vocal output of **Hanns Eisler** (1898–1962) is to be found a sombre *Rimbaud-Gedicht*, various agit prop chansons, and settings of Pascal in English translation. **Kurt Weill** (1900–1950) wrote at least three French chansons: *Youkali* (Roger Fernay) *Complainte de la Seine* and *Je ne t'aime pas.* The poet of these last two is Maurice Magre, librettist and friend of Déodat de Séverac—a curious linking of different worlds. A recent recording in Decca's *Entartete Musik* series revealed that **Berthold Goldschmitt** (b. 1903) was the composer of a substantial orchestrally-accompanied cycle to words by Robert Desnos, Paul Éluard, and Clément Marot, entitled LES PETITS ADIEUX. Also interesting are the Louise Labé settings of **Aribert Reimann** (b. 1936) although pianists should be warned of their difficulty.

In comparison with other lands, America now seems to have the most vibrant and living of song cultures, and it has also long been famous for its appreciation and cultivation of the mélodie. **Virgil Thomson** (1896–1989), **Daniel Pinkham** (b. 1923), **Jacob Druckman** (1928–1996), and **John Corigliano** (b. 1938) are among many names that have a French connection. There are also some fine Canadian composers of song, such as **Pierre Mercure** (1927–1966) whose cycle DISSIDENCE (Gabriel Charpentier, 1955) is worthy of attention, **Keith Bissell** (1912–1992) who made some interesting settings of Ronsard and his contemporaries, and **Malcolm Forsyth** (b. 1936) who made fine arrangements of Métis folksongs from Saskatchewan. In this geographical area alone, I am sure that a separate monograph could be written, and the same is true of the history of the mélodie in Belgium and Switzerland.

Graham Johnson

HOW TO USE THIS BOOK

Within the body of *A French song companion*, composers are listed alphabetically, each with an essay of differing length devoted to his or her work. Translations of a selection of songs follow some, but not all, of these articles. Song titles in bold italics (as in **Les berceaux** in the essay on Fauré) indicate that the text and translation of the song may be found at the end of that article. The titles of translated song cycles are shown in bold italic capital letters as in (*LA BONNE CHANSON*) to differentiate them from the titles of single songs. For reasons of limited space, many of the songs mentioned and discussed in the articles have not been translated. The titles of these appear, when single songs, in non-bold italics. Song cycles mentioned, and not translated, are in non-bold italic capitals.

When a composer has set a poem which is better known in another setting, articles are cross-referenced. Because it has normally not been possible to print a poem with its translation more than once, even if that poem has been set many times by various composers, the translation will often be found with the help of a reference to another composer and number. Thus the text of Josef Szulc's Verlaine's setting *Clair de lune* can be found under FAURÉ 25, and the article on Szulc tells you so. It is a simple matter to turn to Fauré in the book's alphabetical sequence, and find song 25. Single songs and song-cycles are given a normal arabic numbering, and single songs within cycles are treated as subsections of the larger work. For example, the eleventh work to be translated in the Ravel section is the five-song *HISTOIRES NATURELLES* [RAVEL 11 i–v] and all the individual songs within it are separately indexed—thus the second song in that cycle (*Le grillon*) is listed as RAVEL 11 ii.

If the reader can only remember the title of a song, rather than its composer, *Index 3: Titles of translated poems* (right at the back of the book) should be consulted where all translated songs are listed alphabetically by title. *Index 2: Composers in translation* is also arranged alphabetically. This provides a convenient list of Richard Stokes's translations in the same order as they are to be found in the book. This helps pinpoint a particular song where only the composer's name can be recalled, but memory of the title or its spelling is hazy (or if the song is difficult to find in a long sequence of printed texts). Whether a cycle or a single song, the title is always followed by a number, if translated. For example, in *Index 3: Titles of translated poems*, the title of the cycle *LE BESTIAIRE* is followed by POULENC 1 i–vi. If one looks up POULENC in *Index 2: Composers in translation* the numbers 1 i–vi and the title of his first cycle *LE BESTIAIRE* are the first things printed under his name. The cycle appears again in the *Index 1: Selected Poets*, this time under the entry for its poet, Apollinaire, where the reference i–vi is printed next to Poulenc's name.

Index 1: Selected poets is one of the most useful features in the book, particularly for programme planners interested in grouping recitals around poets' names for a change, rather than composers'. But as in much of the information in *A French song companion*, further research and exploration is needed to make the most of this. Selected French poets are listed alphabetically (from ACKERMANN to ZIMMER) and the composers who have set their texts appear under their names. Once again, translations are given numbered references, but this index also leads the reader to composer articles, and thus song titles, which are not translated in this book. The index entry for VERLAINE, for example, lists Poldowski among that poet's many composers, although the article on Poldowski lists only the titles of her songs. It is up to the resourceful reader to follow these leads.

A FRENCH SONG
COMPANION

ABSIL, Jean (1893–1974)

This Belgian composer, unjustly neglected outside his own country, wrote a large number of songs. The earlier work includes *Cimetière* (Moréas, 1927) and a cycle with words by Absil's compatriot Maeterlinck, *QUATRE POÈMES* (1933) for either piano or string quartet accompaniment. These songs show the polytonal influence of Absil's mentor Darius Milhaud, as well as his interest in the second Viennese school. There is also a very effective setting of Hugo's *Autre guitare* [BIZET 2]. From this period the *CINQ CHANSONS DE PAUL FORT* for two equal voices are a useful and piquant contribution to the duet repertoire. The late 1930s and 1940s brought a new lyricism to Absil's work. Especially fine are the *TROIS POÈMES DE TRISTAN KLINGSOR* (1940), a small Absil bestiary: the collection opens with **Chanson du chat** (one of the best cat songs ever written) and continues with *Ma mère l'oye* and *Où le coq a-t-il la plume?* (Absil was later to make choral settings of a selection of Apollinaire's *Bestiaire* poems.) Also to be recommended are a set of *ENFANTINES* (Madeleine Ley, 1942) where the nursery poems range in subject from spiders to mechanical dolls, and the transparently lucid miniature cycle *RÊVES* (René Lyr, 1952). Absil set the Belgian poet Maurice Carême (*HEURE DE GRÂCE* Op. 98) in 1958, anticipating by a few years Poulenc's discovery of that poet for the cycle *LA COURTE PAILLE* [POULENC 22 i–vii]. The last cycle, *CACHE-CACHE* (1963), also includes a Carême setting.

1 *Chanson du chat*
(Tristan Klingsor)

Chat, chat, chat,
Chat noir, chat blanc, chat gris,
   Charmant chat couché,
   Chat, chat, chat,
N'entends-tu pas les souris
Danser à trois les entrechats
   Sur le plancher?

Le bourgeois ronfle dans son lit
De son bonnet de coton coiffé
Et la lune regarde à la vitre:
Dansez souris, dansez jolies,
   Dansez vite,
En remuant vos fines queues de fées.

Dansez sans musique tout à votre aise
   À pas menus et drus
Au clair de la lune qui vient de se lever,
Courez: les sergents de ville dans la rue
   Font les cent pas sur le pavé
   Et tous les chats du vieux Paris
   Dorment sur leur chaise,
Chats blancs, chats noirs, ou chats gris.

Song of the cat

Cat, cat, cat,
Black cat, white cat, grey cat,
   Graceful recumbent cat.
   Cat, cat, cat,
Don't you hear the mice
Dancing entrechats in threes
   On the floor?

The bourgeois are snoring in their beds,
A cotton nightcap on their heads
And the moon peers through the window-pane:
Dance, dance, you pretty mice,
   Dance swiftly,
Swishing your delicate fairy-like tails.

Dance without music just as you will,
   With your pattering little steps
In the light of the moon just risen,
Run: the policemen in the street
   All are on their beat
   And all the cats of old Paris
   Are sleeping in their chairs.
White cats, black cats, or grey cats.

ALBÉNIZ, Isaac (1860–1909)

The songs of this composer are interesting mainly in the light of his unique achievements in the field of Spanish piano music. He was the most wandering of bohemians, and an itinerant life is reflected in his work-list which includes a number of songs in Spanish, Italian, French, and, rather more surprisingly, English. The poor man found himself having to set a great deal of the poetry of his patron, the English banker Francis Money-Coutts. At least Albéniz's handful of French songs seem to have been the result of a more spontaneous affinity with the texts, and an admiration for Debussy, as well as Chausson, Fauré, and Bordes. The best known of these is probably *Chanson de Barberine* (Musset, 1897), although *Il en est de l'amour* (Costa de Beauregard) is included in the Salabert anthology *Mélodies et chansons du XXᵉ siècle*. There are also the songs *Crépuscule* and *Tristesse* which make up the *DEUX MORCEAUX DE PROSE DE LOTI* (1897). In terms of atmosphere the *QUATRE MÉLODIES* of 1909 seem most influenced by the French aesthetic. The poems are by Money-Coutts (*In sickness and health, Paradise regained, The retreat,* and *Amor summa injuria*) but this is a rare instance when French translations (by Calvocoressi) sound more acceptable than the original language. The titles are *Quand je te vois souffrir, Paradis retrouvé, Le refuge,* and *Amour, souffrance suprême.* As accomplished as these songs are, we hear only occasional hints in Albéniz's vocal writing of the bold originality of the *Iberia* suite for piano, a work which was to have an unexpected influence on the piano-writing of Messiaen. The seldom-performed songs of Chopin, another composer known chiefly for his pianistic output, seem similarly uncharacteristic.

ANSERMET, Ernest (1883–1969)

It is not unknown for conductors to aspire to the composition of large works—after all who can better understand the workings of an orchestra? Weingartner and Klemperer composed symphonies, and many composers such as Mahler, Strauss, and Boulez achieved their first recognition as conductors. It is more rare to find a conductor whose songs with piano fit the medium so well that they show no signs of misplaced orchestral thinking. The Swiss conductor Ansermet composed a piece named *Feuilles d'automne* for orchestra, but his seven *CHANSONS* to the texts of the Swiss poet Ramuz (librettist of Stravinky's *L'histoire du soldat*) are models of clarity and delicacy, chansons as opposed to mélodies. Their sound-world is a combination of French impressionism and folksong. The *Chanson de dragon* has something of the neo-classical Stravinsky about it, as does the last of the set, *Les filles du village.* They show Ansermet to have had a melodic gift and a perfect sense of scale. If ever there was a famous conductor whose ear and sensibility showed him capable of the refinement of mélodie composition, it was Ansermet. With the same wit and a lightness of touch we find in these songs, Ansermet conducted the first performances of *El sombrero de tres picos* of Falla, Satie's *Parade,* as well as *L'histoire du soldat, Renard,* and *Pulcinella* by Stravinsky.

ARRIEU, Claude (1903–1990)

Had she been ten years older, Claude Arrieu might have qualified for membership of Les Six (the critic Henri Collet's grouping together of Auric, Durey, Honegger, Milhaud, Poulenc, and Tailleferre). Her music lacks the pre-war frivolity of those composers, but it shares with them a neo-classical grace and economy of means, and a feeling for lyricism that goes back to Chabrier. Like Oliver Messiaen, she was a pupil of Paul Dukas at the Conservatoire, and she spent much of her career working for French radio. Some of Arrieu's work seems indebted to Poulenc: the set (without collective title, words by Roumanez) consisting of *La vache*, *Le crapaud*, *La sauterelle*, *Froid, très froid*, and *Chanson*, each song over in a trice, is inspired by the pithiness of Poulenc's LE BESTIAIRE; and three of her fastidious POÈMES DE LOUISE DE VILMORIN (1946) are dedicated to the soprano Geneviève Touraine, that remarkable friend and exponent of contemporary composers, who had created Poulenc's FIANÇAILLES POUR RIRE. Another of Poulenc's poets, Maurice Fombeure, was an Arrieu favourite (*Bonjour village, Prière pour dormir heureux*). English singers may also like to try her *Les filles de Mayfair* (Claude-André Puget). Arrieu's CHANSONS BAS (Mallarmé, 1933) show a different side of this poet from that exploited by Debussy and Ravel; it is interesting that these poems had also been set by Milhaud in 1917, and Arrieu's work does not suffer in comparison.

AUBERT, Louis (1877–1968)

This namesake of the eighteenth-century violinist and composer is all but forgotten on the recital platform today. A child prodigy and pupil of Fauré (he sang the treble solo in the first performance of the Requiem), Aubert composed an enchanting opera after Perrault (*La forêt bleue*, 1904–13) which is still valued by aficionados of the epoch. Unrepentantly influenced by his teacher, Aubert owes more to the sensuality of Caplet and Ravel (he was the dedicatee of *Valses nobles et sentimentales*) than to the Stravinsky-influenced Parisian musical world after the First World War. He thus became quickly unfashionable, and, unlike his contemporary Reynaldo Hahn, has not yet discovered a new public. Among Aubert's many successful songs are the SIX POÈMES ARABES (Franz Toussaint, 1907) which are evocative of the east in the manner of Ravel's SHÉHÉRAZADE; the incantation 'Messaouda! Souviens-toi!', which concludes *Le destin*, the final song of the set, is reminiscent of the same composer's CHANSONS MADÉCASSES. The TROIS CHANTS HÉBRAÏQUES (Klingsor, 1925) are at least as interesting as Ravel's harmonizations and settings of Jewish texts, and were also inspired by the singer Madeleine Grey. Durand published a recueil of DOUZE CHANTS which contains songs mainly from the turn of the century, including RIMES TENDRES (1898), three settings of Armand Silvestre, one of Fauré's favourite poets. There is also a beautiful duet setting (entitled *Nocturne*) of Verlaine's *La lune blanche* [FAURÉ 30 iii, HAHN 1 v] and a black-humoured chanson written for the celebrated diseuse Marie Dubas entitled *La mauvaise prière*. Aubert also made an orchestration of Fauré's *Soir* [FAURÉ 32].

AURIC, Georges (1899–1983)

The teenage Auric arrived in Paris from Montpellier with a letter of recommendation addressed by Déodat de Séverac to Florent Schmitt. Much was expected of him. Cocteau had considered him the most important of his young composer friends—the group known as Les Six (also including Durey, Honegger, Milhaud, Poulenc, and Tailleferre). He was early considered the wise man of the group, and Poulenc consulted Auric on which settings of his LE BESTIAIRE to discard; it was also Auric who pointed out to Poulenc that he had taken a wrong direction with his POÈMES DE RONSARD. He had a brilliant mind and was widely read; both he and his wife Nora were at the centre of the cultural life of Paris for an astonishingly long period, as is shown by his autobiography *Quand j'étais là* (1979). This ubiquity as a permanent member of *le tout Paris*, and his gifts as a conversationalist, writer, and administrator (he was a distinguished critic, as well as director of the Paris Opéra 1962–8), disguised a lack of depth as a composer, although he could always claim that he had never aspired to profundity. He was perhaps at his best in the early years of Les Six when a deliberate simplicity and use of popular song was at the core of the communal style. This was a youthful affectation for some of the group, but for Auric this ability to evoke popular music with the added spice of modern harmony was at the heart of his talent as clown and wry commentator. His urbanity concealed a barbed tongue and a keen musical wit. As Claude Rostand put it, the malice of Auric was situated somewhere between Couperin and Dada. He could also write music with commercial potential, and he will perhaps be best remembered, to his chagrin, for the waltz song from the film *Moulin Rouge*, as well as the music for *Bonjour tristesse* and *Aimez-vous Brahms?*—films based on Françoise Sagan's novels. His scores for Cocteau's films, as well as Clair's make him an important figure in the development of film music as a serious art.

Auric's wide knowledge of contemporary literature ensured a fascinating and discerning choice of poetry for his mélodies. He favoured publishing short groups of songs to single poets throughout his life. This pattern is established in his first cycle, composed when he was only 15, TROIS INTERLUDES (Chalupt, 1914). This contains the charming if slight *Le pouf, Le gloxinia*, and *Le tilbury*. These songs are of similar length and density to a much later set like TROIS POÈMES DE MAX JACOB of 1946. Already an old hand in 1918, he wrote HUITS POÈMES DE JEAN COCTEAU, a set which contains such titles as *Hommage à Satie, Marie Laurencin*, and *Portrait d'Henri Rousseau*—the last of which ends with a wry quotation from *La Marseillaise*. This work was an important and influential one in the history of French song in that it turned its back on romantic lyricism in favour of the carefree spirit of the Parisian music-hall. During the same period he composed two miniature cycles to the words of Cocteau's brilliant young protégé Raymond Radiguet—LES JOUES EN FEU and ALPHABET (both 1920). In the second of these two works the letter 'M' stands for *Mallarmé*, a charming musical evocation of the poet's style. Whatever the intrinsic musical worth of these songs (the quality is uneven) they document and evoke, perhaps better than any other, Parisian cultural life during the 1920s.

By the early 1930s Poulenc rather than Auric was already setting the pace in terms of the new mélodie. Auric's song **Printemps** with a text by Ronsard was composed for Édouard Bourdet's play *Margot* (1935), where the role of Marguerite of Navarre was taken by Yvonne Printemps; it is a useful and worthy companion piece to another Ronsard setting, *À sa guitare* [POULENC 23], written for the same production. *TROIS POÈMES DE LOUISE VILMORIN* (1940) and *TROIS POÈMES DE LÉON-PAUL FARGUE* (1951) further show Auric's identification with Poulenc's literary world as well as that of Auric's one-time mentor Érik Satie. His most ambitious song cycle is *QUATRE CHANTS DE LA FRANCE MALHEUREUSE* (1943) where the words of Aragon, Supervielle, and Éluard comment on the plight of occupied and humiliated France. Perhaps this was an attempt to equal an almost instantly famous song written in the same year: Poulenc's *C* [POULENC 13 i], where the text was also by Aragon. But Poulenc's less complex, and more lyrical, music gets to the heart, and the pity, of the matter in a way denied to Auric. The *SIX POÈMES DE PAUL ÉLUARD* (1947–8) are also worthy of investigation, though, here again, the exalted tone of the love poetry and the way the cycle ends in the key in which it began foster a suspicion that it is merely an imitation of Poulenc's Éluard masterpiece *TEL JOUR TELLE NUIT* [POULENC 5 i–ix].

Although primarily sympathetic to modern poetry, Auric also included settings of Marceline Desbordes-Valmore and Théodore de Banville in his catalogue of eighty or so mélodies. The *CINQ POÈMES DE GÉRARD DE NERVAL* (1925, Heugel) show Auric's understanding of an important nineteenth-century poet otherwise undervalued by musicians. This was the tragic poet whose reworkings of Goethe were used by Berlioz in parts of his *Damnation de Faust*, but whose lyrics have largely been ignored by mélodie composers. The dedication of the cycle to Louis Aragon, a fellow Nerval enthusiast, shows how the composer's tastes were formed by contact with the most gifted literary men of his time. Auric's slightly quirky style, sometimes whimsical, sometimes abrasive, but never sentimental, suits the words, which sound at least as modern as the music. The harmonic language suggests amused detachment, and perhaps even the poet's mental instability (here only evident as engaging eccentricity). In the gently unhinged world evoked by this cycle, Auric does not suffer in comparison with his greater contemporaries.

1 *Printemps*

(Pierre de Ronsard)

Quand ce beau printemps je vois,
    J'aperçois
  Rajeunir la terre et l'onde,
  Et me semble que le jour,
    Et l'Amour,
  Comme enfants naissent au monde.

Le jour qui plus beau se fait,
    Nous refait
  Plus belle et verte la terre,
  Et Amour armé de traits
    Et d'attraits,
  Dans nos cœurs nous fait la guerre.

Spring

When I see this lovely Spring,
    I behold
  The land and sea grow young again,
  And it seems to me as if the day
    And Love
  Are born into the world like children.

The day which grows more beautiful
    Makes for us
  The land more lovely and green,
  And Cupid, armed with arrows
    And charms,
  Wages war in our hearts.

Il répand de toutes parts
           Feux et dards,
Et dompte sous sa puissance
Hommes, bêtes et oiseaux,
           Et les eaux
Lui jurent obéissance.

He scatters on all sides
           Fire and darts,
And with his power he tames
Men, beasts and birds,
           And the waters
Vow to obey him.

CINQ POÈMES DE GÉRARD DE NERVAL

FIVE POEMS OF GÉRARD DE NERVAL

2 i *Fantaisie*

Fantasy

Il est un air pour qui je donnerais
Tout Rossini, tout Mozart, tout Wèbre,
Un air très vieux, languissant et funèbre,
Qui pour moi seul a des charmes secrets!

Et, chaque fois que je viens à l'entendre,
De deux cents ans mon âme rajeunit...
C'est sous Louis treize; et je crois voir s'étendre
Un coteau vert, que le couchant jaunit,

Puis un château de brique à coins de pierre,
Aux vitraux teints de rougeâtres couleurs,
Ceint de grands parcs, avec une rivière
Baignant ses pieds, qui coule entre des fleurs;

Puis une dame, à sa haute fenêtre,
Blonde aux yeux noirs, en ses habits anciens,
Que, dans une autre existence peut-être,
J'ai déjà vue... et dont je me souviens!

There is a tune for which I'd give
All Rossini, all Mozart, and all Weber,
An ancient, languorous, funereal tune,
Which for me alone has hidden charms!

Now every time I hear that air,
My soul grows younger by two hundred years...
Louis XIII reigns; before me I seem to see
A green slope yellowed by the setting sun,

Then a chateau of brick with quoins of stone,
With stained glass windows of reddish hue,
Girded by great parks, with a river
That laps its walls and flows amidst flowers;

Then a lady, at her high window,
Fair-haired, dark-eyed, in old-fashioned dress,
Whom, in another life, perhaps,
I've already seen... and now remember!

2 ii *Chanson gothique*

Gothic song

Belle épousée
J'aime tes pleurs!
C'est la rosée
Qui sied aux fleurs.

Les belles choses
N'ont qu'un printemps,
Semons de roses
Les pas du Temps!

Beautiful bride,
I love your tears!
They are the dew
That befits the flowers.

Things of beauty
Live but one spring,
Let us sow with roses
The tracks of Time!

Soit brune ou blonde
Faut-il choisir?
Le Dieu du monde,
C'est le Plaisir.

Brunette or blonde,
Must one choose?
The God of this world
Is Pleasure.

2 iii *Les Cydalises**

Où sont nos amoureuses?
Elles sont au tombeau:
Elles sont plus heureuses,
Dans un séjour plus beau!

Elles sont près des anges,
Dans le fond du ciel bleu,
Et chantent les louanges
De la mère de Dieu!

Ô blanche fiancée!
Ô jeune vierge en fleur!
Amante délaissée,
Que flétrit la douleur!

L'éternité profonde
Souriait dans vos yeux...
Flambeaux éteints du monde,
Rallumez-vous aux cieux!

The Cydalises

Where are the women we loved?
They are in their tomb:
They are happier
In a more beautiful abode!

They are alongside angels
At the heart of blue heaven,
And sing the praises
Of the mother of God!

O white betrothed!
O blossoming young virgin!
Forsaken beloved,
Whom grief has withered!

Profound eternity
Once smiled in your eyes...
Extinguished torches of this world,
Rekindle yourselves in heaven!

2 iv *Avril*

Déjà les beaux jours,—la poussière,
Un ciel d'azur et de lumière,
Les murs enflammés, les longs soirs;—
Et rien de vert:—à peine encore
Un reflet rougeâtre décore
Les grands arbres aux rameaux noirs!

Ce beau temps me pèse et m'ennuie.
—Ce n'est qu'après des jours de pluie
Que doit surgir, en un tableau,
Le printemps verdissant et rose,
Comme une nymphe fraîche éclose,
Qui, souriante, sort de l'eau.

April

Fair days already—dust,
A blue sky filled with light,
Walls on fire, drawn-out evenings;
And nothing green: scarcely yet
A reddish reflection to adorn
The tall trees with their black boughs!

These fine days oppress and weary me.
—It is only after days of rain
That an image of spring can suddenly rise,
Verdant and pink,
Like a freshly born nymph
Who steps from the water, smiling.

---

* The name given to actresses and dancers of the 18th century, who wore Regency dresses; see Camille Rogier's famous painting La Cydalise 'en costume Régence, en robe de taffetas feuille morte'.

2 v *Une allée du Luxembourg*   *An avenue in the Luxembourg*

Elle a passé, la jeune fille
Vive et preste comme un oiseau:
À la main une fleur qui brille,
À la bouche un refrain nouveau.

C'est peut-être la seule au monde
Dont le cœur au mien répondrait,
Qui venant dans ma nuit profonde
D'un seul regard l'éclairerait!

Mais non,—ma jeunesse est finie...
Adieu, doux rayon qui m'as lui,—
Parfum, jeune fille, harmonie...
Le bonheur passait,—il a fui!

The young girl has flitted by
Quick and nimble as a bird:
In her hand a dazzling flower,
On her lips a new song,

The only girl on earth perhaps
Whose heart would answer mine,
Who entering my deep night
Would brighten it with a single glance!

But no—my youth is over...
Farewell, sweet ray that shone on me,—
Perfume, young girl, harmony...
Happiness passed by—and fled!

BACHELET, Alfred (1864–1944)

As a composer of French verismo operas, Bachelet is hardly remembered today for such stage-works as *Quand la cloche sonnera* and *Un jardin sur l'Oronte*. An expert orchestrator, his speciality was the use of local colour and pastiche, and in this way he was something of a successor to Saint-Saëns. As a mélodie composer, Bachelet is known only for his opulently romantic song *Chère nuit* (Adenis), chosen by Sergius Kagen to open the widely used anthology entitled *40 French songs* (International Music Company). This is typical of a certain type of mélodie of the time which is virtually an operatic aria with piano accompaniment.

BARBER, Samuel (1910–1981)

Although this famous American composer (and accomplished singer) never studied in France (Barber's foreign links were almost exclusively with Italy), it seems he was at home with the French language from an early age. Among his unpublished compositions are *La nuit* (Meurath, 1925), and *Au clair de la lune* (1926). In 1950–1 he composed *MÉLODIES PASSAGÈRES* (Rilke) for the baritone Pierre Bernac accompanied by Francis Poulenc. The cycle is dedicated to this duo. There are five songs in the set (available in two keys) including a meltingly liquid *Un cygne* (surely inspired by Ravel's swan in *HISTOIRES NATURELLES*), and a Debussian exercise for middle pedal in *Le clocher chante*. This cycle has a dignified elegance but it is seldom programmed, probably because it makes rather a muted impression on the platform. Rilke settings in French are sadly rare, and this short cycle might have gained stature with the addition of a few more songs. It is possible that Barber felt rather awkward writing in French, not because he was unfamiliar with the language, but because he felt it the duty of English-speaking composers to write in their own language. (Barber's younger compatriot Ned Rorem was more of a Francophile, but nevertheless felt this to be the case.) If this was so, Barber's choice of the Rilke texts has a delicate logic: Rilke worked as Rodin's secretary in Paris, and French was his second language.

MÉLODIES PASSAGÈRES

(Rainer Maria Rilke)

I i *Puisque tout passe*

Puisque tout passe,
faisons la mélodie passagère;
celle qui nous désaltère
aura de nous raison.

Chantons ce qui nous quitte
avec amour et art;
soyons plus vite
que le rapide départ.

I ii *Un cygne*

Un cygne avance sur l'eau
tout entouré de lui-même,
comme un glissant tableau;
ainsi à certains instants
un être que l'on aime
est tout un espace mouvant.

Il se rapproche, doublé,
comme ce cygne qui nage,
sur notre âme troublé...
qui à cet être ajoute
la tremblante image
de bonheur et de doute.

I iii *Tombeau dans un parc*

Dors au fond de l'allée,
tendre enfant, sous la dalle,
on fera le chant de l'été
autour de ton intervalle.

Si une blanche colombe
passait au vol là-haut,
je n'offrirais à ton tombeau
que son ombre qui tombe.

FLEETING MELODIES

Since all things flit by

Since all things flit by,
let's create a fleeting melody;
the one that slakes our thirst
shall be the one to win us.

Let us sing what leaves us
with love and art;
let us be swifter
than a swift departure.

A swan

A swan moves over the water
ringed all around by itself,
like a painting that glides;
thus, at certain moments,
a being that one loves
is a whole moving space.

It draws near, bent double,
like the drifting swan,
over our troubled soul...
adding to that being
the trembling image
of happiness and doubt.

Tomb in a park

Sleep at the end of the row,
dear child, beneath the stone;
around your space we shall sing
the song of summer.

Should a white dove
pass overhead,
as sole offering for your tomb,
I'll present its falling shadow.

I iv *Le clocher chante*

Mieux qu'une tour profane,
je me chauffe pour mûrir mon carillon.
Qu'il soit doux, qu'il soit bon
aux Valaisannes.

Chaque dimanche, ton par ton,
je leur jette ma manne;
qu'il soit bon, mon carillon,
aux Valaisannes.

Qu'il soit doux, qu'il soit bon;
samedi soir dans les channes
tombe en gouttes mon carillon
aux Valaisans des Valaisannes.

The bell-tower sings

Better warmed than a secular tower
am I to ripen my carillon.
May it be sweet, may it be good
for the girls of the Valais.

Every Sunday, tone by tone,
I cast to them my manna;
may it be good, my carillon,
for the girls of the Valais.

May it be sweet, may it be good;
into their beers on Saturday nights
my carillon falls, drop by drop,
for the boys of the girls of the Valais.

I v *Départ*

Mon amie, il faut que je parte.
Voulez-vous voir
l'endroit sur la carte?
C'est un point noir.
En moi, si la chose
bien me réussit, ce sera
un point rose
dans un vert pays.

Departure

My love, I must leave.
Would you care to see
the place on the map?
It's marked in black.
In me, if things
work out, it will be
a pink mark
in a green land.

BARRAUD, Henri (b. 1900–1997)

This Bordelais composer of operas, instrumental music, and vocal music of all kinds was influential, as the director of Radiodiffusion Française, in encouraging new music in all its forms. As an opera composer he was perhaps most successful with *Lavinia* (1959). As a composer of mélodies he set Reverdy and Mme de Sévigné among others, but his most charming collection is HUIT CHANTEFABLES POUR LES ENFANTS SAGES (Desnos, 1947). These small animal poems (some of which are also wonderfully set by Jean Wiener and Lutoslawski) triumphantly update Apollinaire's LE BESTIAIRE while doing homage to the older poet's original concept. In *L'alligator*, Barraud's sly quotation from Gershwin's *Porgy and Bess* shows the alligator's passion for the man he loves . . . to eat. Barraud's spare but witty style, more reminiscent perhaps of Milhaud and Honegger than of Poulenc, is perfectly attuned to these jewelled texts. Other cycles include the CHANSONS DE GRAMADOCH (Victor Hugo, 1944) with its jolly opening *Le sorcier et le pirate*, and QUATRE POÈMES DE LANZA DEL VASTO (1942).

BEACH, Amy Marcy (1867–1944)

The songs of Mrs H. H. A. Beach are a treasure trove of early American art song, and are now being progressively rediscovered and reassessed. Like her European contemporaries Cécile Chaminade and Maude Valérie White, Amy Beach displayed qualities of professionalism and craftsmanship in her songwriting (not to mention melodic resourcefulness) which might have received greater attention had she been a male composer. Her prolific output includes settings of French from the outset. *Jeune fille et jeune fleur* (Chateaubriand) is among her first songs and dates from 1887, and the three songs of Op. 19 (1893) are settings of Hugo and F. Bovet. Two further French songs from 1902–3 to texts by the ubiquitous Armand Silvestre have been reprinted by Southern Music Company; these are *Canzonetta* and *Je demande à l'oiseau*.

BEMBERG, Herman (1861–1931)

This Franco-Argentine composer, a pupil of Massenet, achieved considerable renown with his stage-works, and some of his sentimental but effective songs. He was most famous for his Arthurian opera *Élaine* which was well received at both Covent Garden and the Metropolitan, New York. Bemberg's songs were hugely popular with the singers of the day, for he had a real feel for melody. The most celebrated were *Chant hindou* (Ocampo), which appeared in various arrangements with optional *obbligato* instruments, and *Il neige* (with a text by the composer). Bemberg also composed a version of *La fée aux chansons* which is better known in Fauré's setting, and Sully Prudhomme's *Soupir* [DUPARC 2]. It was a brave man who could set this poem in 1909 when the Duparc song was already immortal, but there seems to have been a foolhardy streak in Bemberg's nature which was ready to take risks. As a result of this lack of discretion, his career was overshadowed by sexual scandal, and suffered a decline at the turn of the century.

BERKELEY, Sir Lennox (1903–1989)

The most Francophile of all English composers, Berkeley felt most at home with the refined Gallic sensibility of, say, Fauré and Mallarmé; not for him the France of berets, bicycles, and garlic. He admired Chabrier and Poulenc without being in the least like them, for his France was neither that of Offenbach and the naughty Second Empire, nor the boulevards and pavements of nocturnal Paris rich in amorous adventure. In his music (and not only his songs in French) his creative spirit was governed by the rational: exquisite taste, understatement, discipline were all second nature to him, partly because of his own temperament (he was a Catholic convert) and partly the result of the influence of his redoubtable teacher Nadia Boulanger. Through her he came to value and emulate the transparent clarity, logic, and economy of means we find in the neo-classical Stravinsky. There are fifteen songs in French (published in a collected edition by Chester), among which we can find some of Berkeley's most characteristic work. He has a marked taste for the poetry of the sixteenth century or earlier (Joachim du Bellay, Charles d'Orléans, Louise Labé, Jean Passerat) but he also wrote cycles with poems by his contemporaries—Jean Cocteau (*TOMBEAUX*—five songs, 1926) and Charles Vildrac (*TROIS POÈMES DE VILDRAC*, 1929), a poet he shares with Darius Milhaud. His best-known French songs are **D'un vanneur de blé aux vents** to a text by du Bellay (C. Day Lewis, poet and singer, pronounced this 'one of the most musical pieces of song-writing of our period' (1925)) and the enchanting *Ode du premier jour de mai* (Passerat, 1940) [GOUNOD 8] with a gentle lilt typical of Berkeley's music at its most ingratiating. The death of Poulenc inspired Berkeley to an Apollinaire setting (*Automne*, 1963), for which, as in Ned Rorem's similarly memorial homage *For Poulenc* (O'Hara), the composer deliberately took on a tinge of his old friend's style.

1 *D'un vanneur de blé aux vents*
   (Joachim du Bellay)

À vous, troppe légère,
   Qui d'aele passagère
     Par le monde volez,
Et, d'un sifflant murmure
   L'ombrageuse verdure
     Doulcement esbranlez,

J'offre ces violettes,
   Ces lis, et ces fleurettes,
     Et ces roses icy,
Ces vermeillettes roses,
   Tout freschement écloses,
     Et ces oeilletz aussi.

De vostre doulce halaine
   Éventez ceste plaine,
     Éventez ce séjour:
Ce pendant que j'ahanne
   À mon blé, que je vanne
     À la chaleur du jour.

From a winnower of corn to the winds

To you, troop so fleet,
   Who with winged wandering feet
     Through the world do fly,
And with soft murmuring
   Gently shake
     The shady foliage,

I offer these violets,
   These lilies and these flowerets
     And these roses here,
These bright red roses,
   All freshly blooming,
     And these carnations too.

With your sweet breath
   Fan this plain,
     Fan this dwelling-place:
While I toil away
   At my corn, which I winnow
     In the heat of the day.

BERLIOZ, Hector (1803–1869)

Berlioz's greatness as a symphonist and composer of operas is no longer in doubt, but the songs remain controversial. The tenor Hugues Cuenod, for example, was not fond of them, and his disdain for what he called their lack of elegance was not untypical of his generation, whose mind had been made up long before the Berlioz revival, which was launched in the 1960s by the conductor Colin Davis, among others. Pierre Bernac writes of the songs that 'they often have a quality of romantic grandiloquence, which is certainly opposed to the essential characteristics and finest merits of the French mélodie'. On the other hand the mezzo-soprano Sarah Walker from a much younger generation feels more closely attuned to Berlioz than to almost any other composer. This is largely due to his highly developed sense of drama, prized by all artists who have had anything to do with the Berlioz operas. But perhaps it has also something to do with the composer's own dislike of high sopranos—the majority of his finest vocal music for female voice is written for the middle range, and he had a love of the mezzo timbre.

Whatever the vicissitudes of taste and fashion, it is true that these songs lie outside the normal definitions of French mélodie; they are more closely related to the strophic romance which preceded them, and bear little relation to the songs of Gounod which follow them. It is significant that Ravel thought of Gounod, not Berlioz, as the father of the mélodie. Berlioz was nevertheless the founding father of romanticism, and one of the few French composers to be taken seriously by forward-thinking German artists in a century where cultural influence came mostly from the opposite direction. Indeed Ravel's verdict acknowledges, perhaps unintentionally, the important influence of the German lied on French music. Gounod could not have been the song composer he was without the example of Schubert, whose songs were performed in Paris by the tenor Adolphe Nourrit in the late 1830s. The first Berlioz songs on the other hand were composed in Schubert's lifetime, well before that composer was imported to France, and Berlioz's first important cycle IRLANDE (Gounet, after Thomas Moore) was complete by 1829, only a year after Schubert's death. This set stands alone in the French song repertoire, magnificently free of foreign musical influence (apart from the shade of Gluck in the background), largely ignored, but challenging and fascinating. One can feel in these songs the composer's obsession with Harriet Smithson, the Shakespearian actress and Thomas Moore's compatriot; Berlioz has adopted the Irish cause with the passion and partiality of a man who wishes to identify with the background of his beloved at all costs. Most of these long songs are dedicated to Thomas Moore himself, and are strophic in the rather laboured manner of the French romance. This, and a glance at the height of the demanding tenor tessitura, makes singers pass over them when planning recitals. This is a pity, for *Le coucher du soleil*, *L'origine de la harpe*, *La belle voyageuse*, and *Adieu Bessy* contain much that is rewarding. It is interesting that the composer's identification with these texts should have sprung from a haphazard personal connection with Smithson; the quality of the literature itself, or Berlioz's own connection with poets, seems to have played a less than crucial part in his selection of poems. He was, for example, a close friend of Vigny and acquainted with Heine, neither of whom he set to music. Nevertheless these IRLANDE songs fascinate; what Bernac dubs grandiloquence here often seems passionate, brave, and quixotically modern.

These qualities are even more pronounced in the last song of the set entitled *Élégie* which is dedicated 'to the shade of the unfortunate Robert Emmet' who was executed by the British in 1803 for his part in an uprising. There is nothing like this vehement outburst in all French song; as the elegy is written in prose, Berlioz abandons convention and gives free rein to his emotions. All of his frustration and pain over the Smithson romance is poured into the music, where for once the percussive nature of the piano seems suited to the drama (the song, unlike most of the others, was never orchestrated). In this music, gauche and inspired by turns, we can hear the very birth-pains of romanticism: the awkward writing, where major and minor tonalities clash in wilful juxtaposition, seems consistent with the painful and ecstatic emergence of a new way of responding to literature. Musical architecture yields to emotion, and words dictate the shape of the music in seemingly arbitrary fashion; this disguises the fact that the work is written in a fairly conventional ABA form. The title of Thomas Moore's collection—*Irish melodies*—also bequeathed to French song its new name: 'Have you heard Berlioz's mélodies?' music-lovers asked each other, and the word stuck as a label for the countless masterpieces of piano-accompanied song to come in future generations.

Of course, some of the Berlioz songs are quiet and contemplative, inspired by the lilting 6/8 rhythm of the bergerette. Nevertheless this velvet-gloved gentleness cannot really disguise that the composer is thinking in epic terms with almost everything he does. One is often aware of a gigantic musical personality not quite at home with a miniaturist medium, and somehow uncomfortably constrained by the limits of the single human voice, and the inadequacies of the pianoforte in terms of colour and power. (He was not a pianist, after all.) It is not surprising for example that the solo voice in the piano-accompanied version of the haunting *La mort d'Ophélie* (1842) is replaced by a female chorus in the version with orchestra, however persuasive were the composer's first ideas. (In the same way Wolf replaces the solo voice with a chorus in his orchestral version of the Mörike song *Der Feuerreiter*.) One feels Berlioz ever aspiring to the grander and more universal, especially in the case of a work like *La mort d'Ophélie* which is inspired by his beloved Shakespeare, a universal poet if ever there was one. In these heady regions of the spirit, the orchestra is his strongest ally and one suspects that the piano version has been something of a substitute for the 'real thing'. Nevertheless much of the vocal music was conceived for piano in the first place, and can be performed unashamedly on the recital platform. In this respect Berlioz is similar to Gustav Mahler, whose original piano versions for works like LIEDER EINES FAHRENDEN GESELLEN and the songs from *Des Knaben Wunderhorn* have a definite authenticity of their own. A recent edition of these Mahler songs has reinstated the original piano parts which are rather different from the piano reductions of the orchestral scores.

François Lesure has recently done a similar service for LES NUITS D'ÉTÉ in an edition published in the Patrimoine series (Éditions Musicales de Marais). The old Costallat scores (in two keys), which performers have used for generations, are a reduction of the orchestral score. The new edition goes back to the composer's original version for piano accompaniment and reveals many new interesting details; for example in *Le spectre de la rose* the familiar long prelude (always a great challenge to the pianist, and strangely unconvincing without orchestral colours) is replaced by a single bar of introduction. This set of songs, however it is accompanied, is a marvellous compendium of Berlioz's art. It is the fruit of the composer's friendship with the poet and fellow-critic Théophile Gautier, and was written in 1840–1, the period of Robert Schumann's greatest lieder, and yet utterly unlike them. The *Villanelle* with its almost Mozartian elegance and wit has the lightest touch of any of the songs and is a perfect appetizer. *Le spectre de la rose* is justly famous (above all in Régine Crespin's remarkable recording with Ansermet) for the languid beauty of its long unfolding lines; the ecstatic phrase 'Et j'arrive du paradis' leaps high into the air in such a way, and with such an orchestral shimmer to support it, that the spirit of Nijinsky is somehow conjured before our eyes (although he danced the ballet of this name to Weber's *Invitation to the waltz*, for which Berlioz provided only the orchestration). The dark majesty of *Sur les lagunes* is broodingly impressive; it was a poem set later (and less remarkably) by Gounod, Fauré, and Duparc. Then there is the plaintive and statuesque *Absence*, a poem which Bizet also set (though in truncated form) under the same title. This and *Au cimetière* (often taken far too slowly) could only have been written by Berlioz. His debt to the static grandeurs of Gluck is as apparent in the former song as is his restless harmonic originality in the latter. It is interesting to compare this *Au cimetière* with the Duparc setting entitled *Lamento* from many years later: Berlioz cedes nothing to the younger man, innovator though Duparc was, in terms of a bold and original response to the words. And nothing could better illustrate the difference between Berlioz's songs and the mainstream mélodie than to compare *L'île inconnue,* the last of LES NUITS D'ÉTÉ, with Gounod's setting of the same poem, *Où voulez-vous aller?* The Gounod is all charm with a delightful melody, light of touch and ideal for the salon. The Berlioz is painted on a much larger canvas, a seascape with the intrepid composer at the helm. There is a reckless quality here as the imaginary barque ploughs through the water with sails flapping in the breeze. But this delight in travel is combined with a dark pathos, not to be found in the Gounod, which perfectly captures the poem's undertones of deception, cynicism, and betrayal.

I suspect that singers will remain happy with the old Costallat version of LES NUITS D'ÉTÉ, if only because they are familiar with the orchestral score. A work which can have a double life on both the concert and recital platform is considered good value for money in terms of a performer's learning time. It is, however, a far from ideal recital piece, no matter how well it works in the concert hall with a good conductor and a world-class soloist. It is extremely taxing for almost any singer (perhaps more so in the piano version, for the orchestra provides a different kind of support) and it is very seldom that all the songs in the set suit the same performer, tessitura-wise. One understands conductors who opt for a performance shared between two or more soloists; indeed, this seems to have been the composer's intention. The piano-accompanied version was conceived for mezzo-soprano or tenor, but the orchestral version (if performed in the composer's chosen keys) calls for all four voice types: soprano (*Villanelle, Absence,* and *L'île inconnue*); mezzo-soprano (*Le spectre de la rose*); tenor (*Au cimitière*); baritone (*Sur les lagunes*). Ever impractical in the grand manner, Berlioz even employs different instrumentation for each song.

A glance through the complete Berlioz songs (there is a Kalmus reprint of the old Breitkopf & Härtel edition) yields a number of unusual treasures. The early song *Le pêcheur* is an extraordinarily turbulent adaptation of Goethe's *Der Fischer* (although no tenor recitalist I know would countenance the high C sharp). In *Chant du bonheur* (1833), to the composer's own text, the tessitura is once again very high, and there is a remarkable extended piano postlude which shudders in sweet anticipation of the lover's kiss. *Premiers transports* (Deschamps) has a chorus as well as an obbligato cello. The collection known as FEUILLES D'ALBUM Op. 19 (a title later adopted by Bizet) is as good an introduction to the variety of these mélodies as any, with songs dating from various periods of the composer's life. *Les champs* (Béranger) is an old-fashioned romance rescued by Berlioz from a first version made as early as 1834; *La belle Isabeau* (Dumas) from 1843 is an opera scène with optional chorus and the recurring feature of thunderclaps suggested by the elaborate piano writing; *Le chasseur danois* (Leuven) of 1844 for bass voice is a varied strophic song influenced by the fashion for hunting music that followed Weber's success with *Der Freischütz*; the last of the set is *Zaïde* (Beauvoir, 1845), which is a bolero in the Moorish manner. Here Berlioz, habitually the innovator, owes something to the oriental works of Félicien David, but he carries the idea to a higher plane of energy; after this we find countless examples of Spanish-inspired music throughout the pages of

French song. There is an optional castanet part in *Zaïde*, but where can one find a castanet player? It is a tempting challenge for a singer who fancies that she can click away as she sings, matching the composer's quirky exuberance. The separate song **La captive** (1832), a Hugo evocation, also displays Berlioz luxuriating in an exotic world of sybaritic delights. His ability as a pasticheur with a penchant for armchair travel is displayed in these oriental evocations, both of which exist in orchestral versions.

The collection FLEUR DES LANDES Op. 13 once again gathers together songs from different periods. These works contain influences as various and disparate as the naivety of Breton folk music, and a meeting in 1853 with Johannes Brahms, whom Berlioz immediately recognized as a musical innovator. *Le matin* is a strophic song with harmonies recherché enough to challenge the younger composer; *Petit oiseau* (both songs have indifferent texts by the Abbé de Bouclon) is more deliberately archaic; *Le jeune pâtre breton* (Brizeux, 1833) has a horn obbligato; one remembers that Schubert's *Auf dem Strom* had been published in 1829. The composer suggests that the horn should be 'in a room, somewhat away from the piano'. Ensemble may be rather difficult between the players, but Berlioz never let mere practical considerations dampen the quality of his febrile imagination. *Le chant des bretons* (Brizeux, 1835) is for four-part men's chorus. Short works such as these are sadly seldom heard on the concert platform, simply because it is not cost-effective to hire a large number of artists for something that is over in minutes. Less expensive to mount is the delectable duet *Le trébuchet* (Bertin and Deschamps, 1849 or earlier) which, with its inventive use of hiatus and silence, is surprisingly modern (like so much of Berlioz's music), and seems to have been composed without taking the rest of the musical world into account. This composer is only ever capable of being himself.

Even more than the usual run of his unbiddable compatriots, Berlioz was a rugged pioneer and complete individualist. His songs bear little resemblance to anyone else's, a quality which frightens many performers and listeners who feel happier with music that has a natural place in a hierarchy or lineage. These songs stand outside the traditions that are to be found almost everywhere else in this book. The same could be said of Érik Satie's very different mélodies which, despite their eccentricity, are similarly indispensable to the canon.

1 *Élégie*
(Thomas Gounet)

*Elegy**

Quand celui qui t'adore n'aura laissé derrière lui que le nom de sa faute et de ses douleurs, oh! dis, pleureras-tu s'ils noircissent la mémoire d'une vie qui fut livrée pour toi? Oui, pleure! Et quel que soit l'arrêt de mes ennemis, tes larmes l'effaceront. Car le Ciel est témoin que, coupable envers eux, je ne fus que trop fidèle pour toi.

When he who adores you has left behind him naught but the name of his transgression and grief, ah say! will you weep if they darken the memory of a life devoted to you? Yes, weep! And whatever my enemies decree, your tears shall efface it. For Heaven can bear witness, that though guilty to them, I have been only too faithful to you.

* On the death of Robert Emmet, an Irish nationalist executed by the British in 1803 for his part in an uprising.

Tu fus l'idole de mes rêves d'amour, chaque pensée de ma raison t'appartenait. Dans mon humble et dernière prière ton nom sera mêlé avec le mien. Oh! bénis soient les amis, oui, bénis soient les amants qui vivront pour voir les jours de ta gloire! Mais, après cette joie, la plus chère faveur que puisse accorder le Ciel, c'est l'orgueil de mourir pour toi.

You were the idol of my dreams of love; you were the object of all my thoughts. In my final humble prayer your name shall be mingled with mine! Ah! may friends be blessed, yes, may lovers be blessed, who shall live to see your days of glory! But after this joy, the dearest blessing that Heaven can grant is the pride of dying for you!

2 *La mort d'Ophélie*

(Ernest Legouvé, after Shakespeare*)

The death of Ophelia

Auprès d'un torrent Ophélie
Cueillait, tout en suivant le bord,
Dans sa douce et tendre folie,
Des pervenches, des boutons d'or,
Des iris aux couleurs d'opale,
Et de ces fleurs d'un rose pâle
Qu'on appelle des doigts de mort.

Beside a brook, Ophelia
Gathered along the water's bank,
In her sweet and gentle madness,
Periwinkles, crow-flowers,
Opal-tinted irises
And those pale purples
Called dead men's fingers.

Puis, élevant sur ses mains blanches,
Les riants trésors du matin,
Elle les suspendait aux branches,
Aux branches d'un saule voisin.
Mais trop faible le rameau plie,
Se brise, et la pauvre Ophélie
Tombe, sa guirlande à la main.

Then, raising up in her white hands,
The morning's laughing trophies,
She hung them on the branches,
The branches of a nearby willow.
But the bough, too fragile, bends,
Breaks, and poor Ophelia
Falls, the garland in her hand.

Quelques instants sa robe enflée
La tint encor sur le courant,
Et, comme une voile gonflée,
Elle flottait toujours chantant,
Chantant quelque vieille ballade,
Chantant ainsi qu'une naïade,
Née au milieu de ce torrent.

Her dress, spread wide,
Bore her on the water awhile,
And like an outstretched sail
She floated, still singing,
Singing some ancient lay,
Singing like a water-sprite
Born amidst the waves.

Mais cette étrange mélodie
Passa, rapide comme un son.
Par les flots la robe alourdie
Bientôt dans l'abîme profond
Entraîna la pauvre insensée,
Laissant à peine commencée
Sa mélodieuse chanson.

But this strange melody died,
Fleeting as a snatch of sound.
Her garment, heavy with water,
Soon into the depths
Dragged the poor distracted girl,
Leaving her melodious lay
Hardly yet begun.

* *Hamlet*, Act IV, scene VII.

LES NUITS D'ÉTÉ

(Théophile Gautier)

3 i *Villanelle*

Quand viendra la saison nouvelle,
Quand auront disparu les froids,
Tous les deux nous irons, ma belle,
Pour cueillir le muguet au bois;
Sous nos pieds égrenant les perles
Que l'on voit au matin trembler,
Nous irons écouter les merles
                    Siffler!

Le printemps est venu, ma belle;
C'est le mois des amants béni,
Et l'oiseau, satinant son aile,
Dit ses vers au rebord du nid.
Oh! viens donc sur ce banc de mousse,
Pour parler de nos beaux amours,
Et dis-moi de ta voix si douce:
                    Toujours!

Loin, bien loin, égarant nos courses,
Faisons fuir le lapin caché,
Et le daim au miroir des sources
Admirant son grand bois penché;
Puis, chez nous, tout heureux, tout aises,
En panier enlaçant nos doigts,
Revenons rapportant des fraises
                    Des bois!

3 ii *Le spectre de la rose*

Soulève ta paupière close
Qu'effleure un songe virginal;
Je suis le spectre d'une rose
Que tu portais hier au bal.
Tu me pris encore emperlée
Des pleurs d'argent de l'arrosoir,
Et parmi la fête étoilée
Tu me promenas tout le soir.

Ô toi qui de ma mort fus cause,
Sans que tu puisses le chasser,
Toutes les nuits mon spectre rose
À ton chevet viendra danser.

SUMMER NIGHTS

Villanelle

When the new season comes,
When the cold has gone,
We two will go, my sweet,
To gather lilies-of-the-valley in the woods;
Scattering as we tread the pearls of dew
We see quivering each morn,
We'll go and hear the blackbirds
                    Sing!

Spring has come, my sweet;
It is the season lovers bless,
And the birds, preening their wings,
Sing songs from the edge of their nests.
Ah! Come, then, to this mossy bank
To talk of our beautiful love,
And tell me in your gentle voice:
                    Forever!

Far, far away we'll stray from our path,
Startling the rabbit from his hiding-place
And the deer reflected in the spring,
Admiring his great lowered antlers;
Then home we'll go, serene and at ease,
And entwining our fingers basket-like,
We'll bring back home wild
                    Strawberries!

The spectre of the rose

Open your eyelids,
Brushed by a virginal dream;
I am the spectre of a rose
That yesterday you wore at the dance.
You plucked me still sprinkled
With silver tears of dew,
And amid the glittering feast
You wore me all evening long.

O you who brought about my death,
You shall be powerless to banish me:
The rosy spectre which every night
Will come to dance at your bedside.

Mais ne crains rien, je ne réclame Ni messe ni *De profundis*; Ce léger parfum est mon âme, Et j'arrive du paradis.	But be not afraid—I demand Neither Mass nor De Profundis; This faint perfume is my soul, And I come from Paradise.
Mon destin fut digne d'envie: Et pour avoir un sort si beau, Plus d'un aurait donné sa vie, Car sur ton sein j'ai mon tombeau,* Et sur l'albâtre où je repose Un poëte avec un baiser Écrivit: Ci-gît une rose Que tous les rois vont jalouser.	My destiny was worthy of envy; And for such a beautiful fate, Many would have given their lives— For my tomb is on your breast, And on the alabaster where I lie, A poet with a kiss Has written: Here lies a rose Which every king will envy.

3 iii *Sur les lagunes* — *On the lagoons*

Ma belle amie est morte: Je pleurerai toujours; Sous la tombe elle emporte Mon âme et mes amours. Dans le ciel, sans m'attendre, Elle s'en retourna; L'ange qui l'emmena Ne voulut pas me prendre. Que mon sort est amer! Ah! sans amour, s'en aller sur la mer!	My dearest love is dead: I shall weep for evermore; To the tomb she takes with her My soul and all my love. Without waiting for me She has returned to Heaven; The angel who took her away Did not wish to take me. How bitter is my fate! Alas! to set sail loveless across the sea!
La blanche créature Est couchée au cercueil. Comme dans la nature Tout me paraît en deuil! La colombe oubliée Pleure et songe à l'absent; Mon âme pleure et sent Qu'elle est dépareillée. Que mon sort est amer! Ah! sans amour, s'en aller sur la mer!	The pure white being Lies in her coffin. How everything in nature Seems to mourn! The forsaken dove Weeps, dreaming of its absent mate; My soul weeps and feels Itself adrift. How bitter is my fate! Alas! to set sail loveless across the sea!
Sur moi la nuit immense S'étend comme un linceul; Je chante ma romance Que le ciel entend seul. Ah! comme elle était belle, Et comme je l'aimais! Je n'aimerai jamais Une femme autant qu'elle. Que mon sort est amer! Ah! sans amour, s'en aller sur la mer!	The immense night above me Is spread like a shroud; I sing my song Which heaven alone can hear. Ah! how beautiful she was, And how I loved her! I shall never love a woman As I loved her. How bitter is my fate! Alas! to set sail loveless across the sea!

* The new Patrimoine edition by François Lesure has 'Car j'ai ta gorge pour mon tombeau'.

3 iv *Absence*

Reviens, reviens, ma bien-aimée;
Comme une fleur loin du soleil,
La fleur de ma vie est fermée
Loin de ton sourire vermeil!

Entre nos cœurs quelle distance!
Tant d'espace entre nos baisers!
Ô sort amer! ô dure absence!
Ô grands désirs inapaisés!

Reviens, reviens, ma bien-aimée!
Comme une fleur loin du soleil,
La fleur de ma vie est fermée
Loin de ton sourire vermeil!

D'ici là-bas, que de campagnes,
Que de villes et de hameaux,
Que de vallons et de montagnes,
À lasser le pied des chevaux!

Reviens, reviens, ma bien-aimée!
Comme une fleur loin du soleil,
La fleur de ma vie est fermée
Loin de ton sourire vermeil!

Absence

Return, return, my sweetest love!
Like a flower far from the sun,
The flower of my life is closed
Far from your crimson smile!

Such a distance between our hearts!
So great a gulf between our kisses!
O bitter fate! O harsh absence!
O great unassuaged desires!

Return, return, my sweetest love!
Like a flower far from the sun,
The flower of my life is closed
Far from your crimson smile!

So many intervening plains,
So many towns and hamlets,
So many valleys and mountains
To weary the horses' hooves!

Return, return, my sweetest love!
Like a flower far from the sun,
The flower of my life is closed
Far from your crimson smile!

3 v *Au cimetière*

Connaissez-vous la blanche tombe
Où flotte avec un son plaintif
         L'ombre d'un if?
Sur l'if, une pâle colombe,
Triste et seule, au soleil couchant,
         Chante son chant;

Un air maladivement tendre,
À la fois charmant et fatal,
         Qui vous fait mal
Et qu'on voudrait toujours entendre,
Un air, comme en soupire aux cieux
         L'ange amoureux.

On dirait que l'âme éveillée
Pleure sous terre à l'unisson
         De la chanson,
Et du malheur d'être oubliée
Se plaint dans un roucoulement
         Bien doucement.

At the cemetery

Do you know the white tomb,
Where the shadow of a yew
         Waves plaintively?
On that yew a pale dove,
Sad and solitary at sundown
         Sings its song;

A melody of morbid sweetness,
Delightful and deathly at once,
         Which wounds you
And which you'd like to hear forever,
A melody, such as in the heavens,
         A lovesick angel sighs.

As if the awakened soul
Weeps beneath the earth together
         With the song,
And at the sorrow of being forgotten
Murmurs its complaint
         Most meltingly.

Sur les ailes de la musique	On the wings of music
On sent lentement revenir	You sense the slow return
Un souvenir;	Of a memory;
Une ombre, une forme angélique	A shadow, an angelic form
Passe dans un rayon tremblant,	Passes in a shimmering beam,
En voile blanc.	Veiled in white.

Les belles-de-nuit, demi-closes,
Jettent leur parfum faible et doux
    Autour de vous,
Et le fantôme aux molles poses
Murmure, en vous tendant les bras:
    Tu reviendras?

The Marvels of Peru, half-closed,
Shed their fragrance sweet and faint
    About you,
And the phantom with its languid gestures
Murmurs, reaching out to you:
    Will you return?

Oh! jamais plus, près de la tombe
Je n'irai, quand descend le soir
    Au manteau noir,
Écouter la pâle colombe
Chanter sur la pointe de l'if
    Son chant plaintif!

Ah! nevermore shall I approach that tomb,
When evening descends
    In its black cloak,
To listen to the pale dove
From the top of a yew
    Sing its plaintive song!

3 vi *L'île inconnue*   *The unknown isle*

Dites, la jeune belle,
Où voulez-vous aller?
La voile ouvre son aile,
La brise va souffler!

Tell me, pretty young maid,
Where is it you would go?
The sail is billowing,
The breeze about to blow!

L'aviron est d'ivoire,
Le pavillon de moire,
Le gouvernail d'or fin;
J'ai pour lest une orange,
Pour voile une aile d'ange,
Pour mousse un séraphin.

The oar is of ivory,
The pennant of watered silk,
The rudder of finest gold;
For ballast I've an orange,
For sail an angel's wing,
For cabin-boy a seraph.

Dites, la jeune belle,
Où voulez-vous aller?
La voile ouvre son aile,
La brise va souffler!

Tell me, pretty young maid,
Where is it you would go?
The sail is billowing,
The breeze about to blow!

Est-ce dans la Baltique,
Dans la mer Pacifique,
Dans l'île de Java?
Ou bien est-ce en Norvège,
Cueillir la fleur de neige
Ou la fleur d'Angsoka?*

Perhaps the Baltic,
Or the Pacific
Or the Isle of Java?
Or else to Norway,
To pluck the snow flower
Or the flower of Angsoka?

* Engklokke (literally 'meadow bell') is the *Campanula patula*, a small harebell found in Norwegian meadows.

Dites, la jeune belle,
Où voulez-vous aller?

Menez-moi, dit la belle,
À la rive fidèle
Où l'on aime toujours.
—Cette rive, ma chère,
On ne la connaît guère
Au pays des amours.

Où voulez-vous aller?
La brise va souffler.

Tell me, pretty young maid,
Where is it you would go?

Take me, said the pretty maid,
To the shore of faithfulness
Where love endures forever.
—That shore, my sweet,
Is scarce known
In the realm of love.

Where is it you would go?
The breeze is about to blow!

4 *La belle Isabeau*

(Alexandre Dumas, père)

Dans la montagne noire,
Au pied du vieux château,
J'ai ouï conter l'histoire
De la jeune Isabeau.
Elle était de votre âge,
Cheveux noirs et l'œil bleu.

Enfants, voici l'orage!
À genoux! priez Dieu!

La belle jeune fille
Aimait un chevalier.
Son père sous la grille
La tint comme geôlier.
Le chevalier volage
L'avait vue au saint lieu.
Un soir, dans sa cellule
Isabeau vit soudain,
Sans crainte et sans scrupule,
Entrer le paladin.
L'ouragan faisait rage,
Le ciel était en feu.

Enfants, voici l'orage!
À genoux! priez Dieu!

De frayeur Isabelle
Se sentit le cœur plein:
'Où donc est, disait-elle
Le sire chapelain?'
Il est, suivant l'usage,
À prier au saint lieu.

Fair Isabeau

On the black mountain,
At the foot of the old castle,
I heard them tell the tale
Of young Isabeau.
She was your age,
With black hair and blue eyes.

Children, the storm is brewing!
Fall to your knees! Pray to God!

The fair young maiden
Loved a knight.
Her father, like a jailer,
Kept her behind bars.
The fickle knight
Had seen her in church.
One evening, Isabeau
Suddenly saw the paladin
Enter her prison cell
Without fear or qualms.
The hurricane raged,
The sky was ablaze.

Children, the storm is brewing!
Fall to your knees! Pray to God!

Isabelle's heart
Filled with fear:
'But where', she said,
'Can the chaplain be?'
He is, as he is wont to be,
At his prayers in church.

'Venez! avant l'aurore
Nous serons de retour.'
Hélas! son père encore
L'attend depuis ce jour.

Enfants, voici l'orage!
À genoux! priez Dieu!

'Come with me! Before dawn
We shall be back!'
Her father, alas, from that day on,
Awaits her still.

Children, the storm is brewing!
Fall to your knees! Pray to God!

5 *Zaïde*

(Roger de Beauvoir)

'—Ma ville, ma belle ville,
C'est Grenade au frais jardin;
C'est le palais d'Aladin,
Qui vaut Cordoue et Séville!
Tous ses balcons sont ouverts,
Tous ses bassins diaphanes;
Toute la cour des sultanes
S'y tient près des myrtes vertes!'

Ainsi près de Zoraïde,
À sa voix donnant l'essor,
Chantait la jeune Zaïde,
Le pied dans ses mules d'or.

'—Ma ville, ma belle ville,
C'est Grenade au frais jardin;
C'est le palais d'Aladin,
Qui vaut Cordoue et Séville!'

La reine lui dit: 'Ma fille,
D'où viens-tu donc?—Je n'en sais rien.
—N'as-tu donc pas de famille?
—Votre amour est tout mon bien!
Ô ma reine, j'ai pour père
Ce soleil plein de douceurs.
La sierra, c'est ma mère,
Et les étoiles, mes sœurs!'

'—Ma ville, ma belle ville,
C'est Grenade au frais jardin;
C'est le palais d'Aladin,
Qui vaut Cordoue et Séville!'

Cependant, sur la colline,
Zaïde à la nuit pleurait:
'Hélas! Je suis orpheline;
De moi qui se chargerait?'

Zaïde

'My city, my beautiful city—
That's Granada with its cool gardens,
That's the palace of Aladdin,
Worth all of Cordoba and Seville!
All its balconies are open wide,
All its fountains crystal clear,
The entire court of the Sultans
Is there beneath green myrtle trees!'

Thus by Zoraïde's side,
With passion in her voice,
Young Zaïde sang,
Golden sandals on her feet.

'My city, my beautiful city—
That's Granada with its cool gardens,
That's the palace of Aladdin,
Worth all of Cordoba and Seville!'

The queen said to her: 'My child,
Where are you from?' 'I do not know.'
'Have you no family, then?'
'Your love is all I have!
O my queen, for father
I have this gentle sun;
The Sierra is my mother
And my sisters the stars!'

'My city, my beautiful city—
That's Granada with its cool gardens,
That's the palace of Aladdin,
Worth all of Cordoba and Seville!'

But on the hillside
Zaïde cried into the night:
'Alas, I am an orphan,
Who will take care of me?'

Un cavalier vit la belle,
La prit sur sa selle d'or.
Grenade, hélas! est loin d'elle,
Mais Zaïde y rêve encor!

'—Ma ville, ma belle ville,
C'est Grenade au frais jardin;
C'est le palais d'Aladin,
Qui vaut Cordoue et Séville!'

A knight saw the beautiful girl,
Lifted her onto his golden saddle.
Alas, she is far from Granada now,
But Zaïde still dreams of it!

'My city, my beautiful city—
That's Granada with its cool gardens,
That's the palace of Aladdin,
Worth all of Cordoba and Seville!'

6 *La captive*
(Victor Hugo)

The captive girl

Si je n'étais captive,
J'aimerais ce pays,
Et cette mer plaintive,
Et ces champs de maïs,
Et ces astres sans nombre,
Si le long du mur sombre
N'étincelait dans l'ombre
Le sabre des spahis.

If I were not a captive,
I should love this country,
And this plaintive sea,
And these fields of maize,
And these stars without number,
If in the wall's dark shadow
There did not glint
The spahis'* scimitar.

Je ne suis point tartare
Pour qu'un eunuque noir
M'accorde ma guitare,
Me tienne mon miroir.
Bien loin de ces Sodomes,
Au pays dont nous sommes,
Avec les jeunes hommes
On peut parler le soir.

I was not born a Tartar
For a black eunuch
To tune my guitar
And hold up for me my mirror.
Far away from this land of Sodom,
In our native country, we are permitted
When evening falls,
To talk with the young men.

Pourtant j'aime une rive
Où jamais des hivers
Le souffle froid n'arrive
Par les vitraux ouverts.
L'été, la pluie est chaude,
L'insecte vert qui rôde
Luit, vivante émeraude,
Sous les brins d'herbe verts.

And yet I love a land
Where winter's chill breath
Never crosses
Wide-open windows.
In summer the rain is warm,
And the hovering insects
Gleam bright emerald
Beneath green blades of grass.

J'aime en un lit de mousses
Dire un air espagnol,
Quand mes compagnes douces,
Du pied rasant le sol,
Légion vagabonde
Où le sourire abonde,
Font tournoyer leur ronde
Sous un rond parasol.

I love on a bed of moss
To sing a Spanish air,
While my sweet companions,
Feet grazing the ground,
Nomadic throng
With generous smiles,
Dance and whirl
Beneath an open parasol.

* Spahi—A Turkish or Algerian horseman, serving in the army.

Mais surtout, quand la brise	But most of all when a breeze
Me touche en voltigeant,	Lightly brushes my cheek,
La nuit j'aime être assise,	I love to sit at night,
Être assise en songeant,	Sit and dream,
L'œil sur la mer profonde,	Gazing on the deep sea,
Tandis que pâle et blonde,	While the pale moon
La lune ouvre dans l'onde	Opens across the water
Son éventail d'argent.	Its silver fan.

BERNERS, Lord (Sir Gerald Hugh Tyrwhitt-Wilson) (1883–1950)

The music of Berners has some of the hallmarks of the wealthy amateur dilettante, but even composers as distinguished as Stravinsky found him interesting and diverting. (Berners's piano piece *Le poisson d'or* is dedicated to Stravinsky; it is prefaced by a French poem also written by Berners.) He had a genuine gift for light music, and although it would be an exaggeration to call him the English Satie, his good taste and understanding were veiled by irony, mockery, and wilful eccentricity in a way that suggests the master of Arcueil. None of the Berners ballets is as important as Satie's *Parade*, but the songs present a similar combination of melodic charm to divert the music-lover, and a use of dissonance to *épater les bourgeois*, as well as shock Berners's fellow aristocrats. He tended to mock the music (such as Strauss's *Der Rosenkavalier*) which one suspects he secretly loved. Berners was at home in the French language, and his Mérimée opera *Le carrosse du Saint Sacrement* was given in Paris in 1924. The three songs in French all date from four years earlier: the texts of all these TROIS CHANSONS are by the critic and musicologist G. Jean-Aubry who had a strong connection with the firm of Chester, Berners's publisher. Both *Romance* and *L'étoile filante* are quirky little philosophical reflections, over in a trice. *La fiancée du timbalier* (no relation of Saint-Saëns's Hugo setting) with its spiky fanfares and military precision seems a relative of Stravinsky's *Histoire du soldat*, and of the Cocteau settings of Poulenc and other members of Les Six.

BERNSTEIN, Leonard (1918–1990)

There is a single cycle in French from this multi-talented American musician. *LA BONNE CUISINE* was written in 1947 for his recital partner, the celebrated Jenni Tourel. These are zany settings of recipes from Émile Dumont's *La bonne cuisine française* and the titles of the songs speak for themselves: *Plum pudding* (no French equivalent given), *Queues de bœuf*, *Tavouk guenksis*, and *Civet à toute vitesse*. The English performing version is by the composer himself.

BEYDTS, Louis (1895–1953)

The name of this deft and elegant composer of songs is almost forgotten, but there was a time when certain singers championed his music over Poulenc's. Ninon Vallin was affronted when that composer asked her to sing a song entitled *Mon cadavre est doux comme un gant* (My corpse is as soft as a glove) [POULENC 6 iv]. Her retort was that she much preferred the music of Beydts, and his choice of texts. On the whole he avoided 'difficult' poetry, including the surrealists—the very poets who give such strength and purpose to Poulenc's song output. An exception to this is an atmospheric setting (reminiscent of Poulenc's *La Grenouillère* [POULENC 8]) of Apollinaire's *Le pont Mirabeau*, as well as *Le présent* (Louise Lalanne/Marie Laurencin). Beydts also set *Si tu aimes* of Cocteau and Henri de Régnier's *Crépuscule*. This composer had more than a little in common with his contemporary Poulenc in that he had a genuine feel for the voice (particularly that of the soprano), and an awareness of just how evocative the art of a chansonnière in a smoke-filled *boîte* could be when transplanted to the serious mélodie. On occasion he can topple into the sort of sentimentality which dates his music in a way avoided by Poulenc, and he often lacks a sharply defined sense of melody, preferring to spin long parlando lines, infinitely French in their ingratiating indolence. On the other hand, Beydts has a real feeling for poets who have not been given their full due by other mélodie composers: chief among these is Marceline Desbordes-Valmore whom he celebrates in the set LA GUIRLANDE DE MARCELINE (1943–4) which includes the pulsatingly feminine *Un billet de femme* (written for Ninon Vallin), the lovely lullaby *Pour l'enfant*, and *Amour partout* with its text reminiscent of a popular song.

Beydts wrote nearly a hundred mélodies: some of these, never less than gratefully written, would repay revival from enterprising singers. Apart from the Desbordes-Valmore cycle mentioned above, the best are settings of Beydts's favourite poet, Paul Fort. The SIX BALLADES FRANÇAISES (1926) bring Caplet's relationship with Fort's poetry to mind, and *Ronde autour du monde* (1934) was once considered a rallying cry for the peaceful coexistence of nations. CHANSONS POUR LES OISEAUX (1948) also have Fort texts. The third of these, *L'oiseau bleu*, is a catalogue of exotic names which recalls the ornithological Messiaen (and which was prophetic of that composer's preoccupation with birdsong), as does the final *Le petit serin en cage*, which shows Beydts's musical humour in a sad tale of a canary eaten by a cat (*Le bengali* by Manuel Rosenthal also succumbs to a sad fate). Among earlier cycles the CINQ HUMORESQUES of Tristan Klingsor (1927) and QUATRE ODELETTES (Henri de Régnier, 1928) are worthy of mention. *La lyre et les amours* (Tristan l'Hermite) was recorded by Pierre Bernac, and one should not forget three haunting little songs to poems by Louis Codet—*La flûte verte* (with flute obbligato), *Nocturne* (which was one of Cuenod's favourite encores), and *La petite noix*. There is another song with flute obbligato titled *En Arles* (Toulet) which is a homage to the famous farandole from Bizet's *L'arlésienne*. It is also notable that Beydts orchestrated Debussy's LE PROMENOIR DES DEUX AMANTS, *Mandoline*, and *Colloque sentimental*. The piano versions of Beydts's own songs are to be preferred to the orchestrations, which have touches of modernity (the vibraphone!) which have not worn well, and suggest the film music of the 1930s—this is if the recording of *La lyre et les amours* is anything to go by.

BINET, Jean (1893–1960)

This Swiss composer studied in Geneva at the Jaques-Dalcroze Institute and his music is a delicate blend of the influences of French impressionism and Dalcrozian theory. He went to America in 1919 where he studied with Bloch, and helped found the Dalcroze Rhythmic School in New York, as well as the Cleveland Conservatory. He returned to Switzerland to occupy an honoured place in that nation's musical life; many of his orchestral works were first performed by Ansermet. His songs deserve to be better known. Among the most attractive are the TROIS MÉLODIES on poems of Apollinaire (1933). The opening of *Annie*, the first song in that set, pays charming tribute to Binet's connection with the United States: 'Sur la côte de Texas | Entre Mobile et Galveston il y a | Un grand jardin tout plein de roses.' The other songs are *Clotilde* (also set by Honegger, among others) and *Aubade*. Although these graceful mélodies were written for voice and orchestra, the piano reductions work admirably well. Binet also set poems by Paul Fort (*Le bonheur*), Stravinsky's collaborator Ramuz (QUATRE CHANSONS, 1927) and there is a fine collection of songs (SIX MÉLODIES) to the poems of Clément Marot (1928). Of later songs, the SIX CHANSONS (Jean Cuttat, 1949) exist in both piano-accompanied and orchestral versions.

BIZET, Georges (1838–1875)

Unaccountably, the Bizet songs have received rather a bad press from a number of scholars who point out that in his desire to achieve success as an opera composer Bizet treated the writing of mélodies as hackwork. If music of this quality is hackwork, it is a pity that there is not more of it to be found in French song. The same genius which delights and moves us in *Carmen* can be heard at work here. It is true that the songs have something operatic about them, but this is seldom shown by grandiose vocal demands and orchestrally inspired accompaniments—indeed the voice is always used with the greatest skill within the smaller frame of song (there was singing on both sides of the Bizet family), and the piano parts are lively and idiomatic for the instrument. Bizet simply places most of his mélodies in something of a dramatic context, for this is how his mind works as a composer for the stage.

The parallel example of Britten comes to mind, whose genius for theatre is felt everywhere in his songs: for example, the flashback in *The choirmaster's burial* (Hardy) is superbly managed because the composer had already used the same device on a much grander scale in the opera *Billy Budd*. In *La coccinelle* (a Hugo text set less interestingly by Saint-Saëns) Bizet is not content to recount the story of a young man losing his nerve as a lover, he gives us an enchanting off-stage orchestra playing a waltz. In his imagination the whole incident takes place at a ball in a large country house, and Bizet is his own *régisseur* in providing a backcloth for the scene. In this 'staging' of a lyric, where the poet's ideas are supplemented and given new dimensions, Bizet is in good company, for this is also one of Schubert's great gifts. Another Hugo setting, *Guitare* (also set by Liszt, Lalo, and many others less free with the poet's verses), is intoxicatingly effective precisely because Bizet has surrounded the poem with a frame of his own. He adds 'Tra, la, las' to the short lyric, a device which lengthens the song and enables us to meet the singer and come to terms with her as a character. Settings of this lyric by other composers, however charming and allusive, are anonymous by comparison, for in this superb Spanish stylization (composed nine years before *Carmen*) it is *one* dancer who comes to the fore as a star turn, with her reckless melismas, and a triumphantly steely change to the major key when she sings of love. 'Don't meddle with me because I mean business' is the subtext, and we hear this behind, and in addition to, the lyric. It is a song which brings the house down, and which, despite the textual *lèse-majesté*, reveals the meaning behind Hugo's words.

Guitare is the fourth of six *FEUILLES D'ALBUM* (1866) which is not only a compendium of mostly fine poetry (Ronsard, Hugo, Millevoye, Lamartine), but an anthology of the composer's style. (Bizet seems to have taken the title of his set of songs from Berlioz's Op. 19.) The differing tessitura of the songs (*Guitare* for a soprano, and *Rose d'amour* for a contralto, for example) thwarts any inclination to treat it as a cycle. The first two songs are to Musset texts. *À une fleur* looks back to the flowing 6/8 songs of Berlioz and is poised between melody and speech, an arioso of great difficulty, not in any sense on account of its tessitura, but because the lengthy poem has to be held together by a flawless vocal legato, and enlivened with an uncommonly subtle rubato. Bizet, again imagining his singer as a character, has caught the musing sense of uncertainty, as in a game of 'he loves me, he loves me not'. *Adieux à Suzon* (the same poet's *Bonjour, Suzon* is better known [DELIBES 2]) is an essay in the manner of Schubert's *Willkommen und Abschied* (Goethe) where a daunting and vocally exhausting horse-ride of thundering triplets is contrasted with moments of reflection and doubt. This song calls for the stamina of an intrepid tenor. Utterly different is the gentle *Sonnet* (Ronsard) which is as lovely a piece of time-travel as one could wish; long before pastiche was the last refuge of bad film music composers, Bizet evokes the sixteenth century with haunting archaisms which match the grave beauty of the text to perfection. *Rose d'amour* is perhaps the weakest of the set; it is a neo-classical hymn which Gounod, in one of his lofty moments, might have tackled successfully, but which Bizet finds devoid of dramatic interest. *Le grillon* (Lamartine) is an astonishing tour de force, very different from the Jules Renard setting of the same name by Ravel. The coloratura acrobatics demanded of the poor singer are just not cricket—they suggest something approaching a bat out of hell. For those who can sing Donizetti's Lucia this will pose few problems, but the average lyric soprano is warned. The piano part is very piquant and uses right-hand staccato chords to depict the insect's chirp. There was a volume of Schubert songs in Bizet's library, and the motif of four semiquavers preceded by an acciaccatura which pervades *Le grillon* was certainly lifted from Schubert's *Der Einsame*, a song about the cricket on the hearth, and published in France under the title *Les grillons*. Bizet's song was conceived for the great Swedish soprano Christine Nilsson who wanted a display piece to show off her coloratura; she received just such a vehicle without the composer having to compromise himself in the process.

There are two Choudens volumes (or *recueils*) of Bizet songs. The first, and more easily obtainable, is available in two keys, and has twenty items. This volume is packed with interest, although certain mélodies stand out effortlessly. The delightfully fresh *Chanson d'avril* (Bouilhet, 1866) opens the collection with its wonderful tune. How Fauré must have loved this song with its purling semiquaver accompaniment, open-hearted yet delicate; his own *Nell* was born of this lineage. The piano rustles with just the right amount of frisson to suggest the stirrings of spring. In contrast it swoons and sulks and dances in sultry fashion in ***Adieux de l'hôtesse arabe*** (Hugo, 1866), perhaps Bizet's most celebrated song, and also perhaps the greatest of all the oriental evocations in French music, Ravel's orchestrally accompanied SHÉHÉRAZADE excepted. I was led to this song (and persuaded Felicity Lott to learn it) when reading in Poulenc's *Journal de mes mélodies* of his admiration for Bizet's Arab hostess. Of this piece he remarks that the composer 'knew how to vary a strophic song in detail. That is often what is missing in Gounod.' The scenario is over the top, and in lesser hands the text could have been set along the same lines as the appropriately named Armando Ocampo's oriental poems for Bemberg. But this is Hugo after all, and although Bizet ruthlessly cut four of the great man's strophes, and adapted some of the remainder, the result is a haunting masterpiece. The sinuous lilt of much of Carmen's music here has its beginning; the gait of the piano writing suggests hips swaying to the sound of tinkling bell or cymbal accompanied by the hypnotic throbbing of the tabor. The direction on the last page which instructs the singer to use a voice 'broken by sobs' now seems ill-advised. As in *Guitare*, Bizet uses melisma much more extensively than most composers of mélodie; the final page, with its demandingly long phrases weaving languid tendrils on the trellis of the stave, needs a very good singer indeed.

The other delights of the first *recueil* are less exotic by far: the courtly ***Vieille chanson*** (Millevoye, 1865?), with its suggestions of the charms and gallantries of the *ancien régime*; ***Ma vie a son secret*** (Arvers, 1868), with its beautifully serene melody where Bizet affectionately parodies an older com-poser's style (note the seraphic piano interludes) with a Gounod and a wink; the *Pastorale* (Regnard, 1868) which, though the bergerette of this type is associated with the fake shepherds and shep-herdesses of Versailles, evokes the earthier landscapes of Provence (there are the beginnings here of the *L'arlésienne* music which Bizet would write four years later); the lilting 6/8 of the *Berceuse* of 1868 (one of the very few settings since the time of Pauline Duchambge of that fine poet Marceline Desbordes-Valmore) derives unashamedly from the famous Hugo *Sérénade* of Gounod; the enchanting barcarole *Douce mer* (1866) for a high tenor, where Lamartine's poem is reduced from eighteen to three verses. It is also influenced by Gounod, and by Berlioz too, but the water glows mysteriously under Bizet's own inimitable stage lighting. We have already discussed *La coccinelle* above, but mention should also be made of the outrageous ***Tarentelle*** (1872), a delicious trifle where Pailleron's poem is quite overwhelmed by 'Tra la las', and we do not even notice. I would hesitate to ask most singers to battle with these runs, arpeggios, and chromatic scales, but Ann Murray has exactly the right cheeky insouciance to see it off the stage.

The second *recueil* is a disappointment by comparison; it was published as a type of posthumous homage to the composer. Bleeding chunks of unfinished and unpublished works were shamelessly adapted to make a new volume of songs; the texts were on the whole added to music that had already been composed for other purposes. It is no surprise, therefore, that this *recueil* contains much indifferent poetry. Here we find no Hugo, Ronsard, or Lamartine. ***Ouvre ton cœur*** (Delâtre) is one of the items with an original text. It is relatively often performed as a song (it is an infectious bolero with touching changes between major and minor) but it actually comes from the ode-symphony *Vasco de Gama* (1859–60). This is seldom if ever performed, and the recitalist can be for-given for appropriating this material. *Chanson de la rose* (Barbier, date unknown) is a charming trifle, in the same dancing mood as *Tarentelle*, but without the hair raising technical difficulties. The gen-tly tripping accompaniment shows Bizet's rather surprising interest in the music of Scarlatti and the *clavecinistes.* Hidden shyly towards the back of the volume is **Pastel** (Gille, date unknown). It evokes exactly the gentle charms that its title implies, and is a useful song for recitals built on a theme of art and artists. It pictures the past in the same way as Schumann's duet *Familien-Gemälde.* And speaking of duets, we should not forget *La fuite* (Gautier, 1872) for soprano and tenor, an Arabic extravagance also set by Duparc. *Rêvons* (Barbier) and other published duets by Bizet are publishing sharp practice—reworkings of mélodies from the second *recueil* (not even the best of them) with shamelessly adapted texts.

1 *La coccinelle*
(Victor Hugo)

Elle me dit: 'Quelque chose
Me tourmente.' Et j'aperçus
Son cou de neige, et, dessus,
Un petit insecte rose.

J'aurais dû—mais, sage ou fou,
À seize ans on est farouche,—
Voir le baiser sur sa bouche
Plus que l'insecte à son cou.

On eût dit un coquillage;
Dos rose et taché de noir.
Les fauvettes pour nous voir
Se penchaient dans le feuillage.

Sa bouche fraîche était là:
Hélas! je me penchai sur la belle,
Et je pris la coccinelle;
Mais le baiser s'envola.

'Fils, apprends comme on me nomme',
Dit l'insecte du ciel bleu,
'Les bêtes sont au bon Dieu;*
Mais la bêtise est à l'homme.'

The ladybird

She said to me: 'Something's
Bothering me.' And I saw
Her snow-white neck, and on it
A small rose-coloured insect.

I should have—but right or wrong,
At sixteen one is shy—
I should have seen the kiss on her lips
More than the insect on her neck.

Like a shell it shone;
Red back speckled with black.
The warblers, to catch a glimpse of us,
Craned their necks in the branches.

Her fresh mouth was there:
I leaned over the lovely girl, alas,
And picked up the ladybird,
But... the kiss flew away!

'Son, learn my name,'
Said the insect from the blue sky,
'Creatures belong to our good Lord,
But only men behave like cretins.'

2 *Guitare*
(Victor Hugo)

Comment, disaient-ils,
Avec nos nacelles,
Fuir les alguazils?
—Ramez, disaient-elles.

Guitar

How, said the men,
In our small craft
Can we flee the alguazils?†
—Row, said the women.

* A 'bête à bon Dieu' is colloquial French for a ladybird.
† Spanish officers whose task is to arrest offenders and see execution done.

Comment, disaient-ils, Oublier querelles, Misère et périls? —Dormez, disaient-elles.	How, said the men, Can we forget feuds, Poverty and peril? —Sleep, said the women.
Comment, disaient-ils, Enchanter les belles Sans philtres subtils? —Aimez, disaient-elles.	How, said the men, Can we bewitch the fair Without rare potions? —Love, said the women.

3 *Sonnet*
(Pierre de Ronsard)

Sonnet

Vous méprisez nature: êtes-vous si cruelle
De ne vouloir aimer? voyez les passereaux
Qui démènent l'amour, voyez les colombeaux,
Regardez le ramier, voyez la tourterelle.
Voyez deçà, delà d'une frétillante aile
Voleter par les bois les amoureux oiseaux,
Voyez la jeune vigne embrasser les ormeaux,
Et toute chose rire en la saison nouvelle.
Ici la bergerette en tournant son fuseau
Dégoise ses amours, et là le pastoureau
Répond à sa chanson; ici toute chose aime,
Tout parle de l'amour, tout s'en veut enflammer.
Seulement votre cœur froid d'une glace extrême
Demeure opiniâtre et ne veut point aimer.

You disdain nature: can you be so cruel
And not wish to love? See the sparrows
Who dance with love, see the little doves,
See the ring-doves, see the turtle-doves.
See how, with quivering wings, the amorous birds
Flit to and fro among the woods.
See the young vine embrace the young elm,
And all things laugh in the new season.
Here the shepherd-lass, plying her spindle,
Pours out her love, and there the shepherd-lad
Replies to her song; here all things love,
All speak of love, all wish to blaze with love.
Your heart alone, with excessive frost,
Remains stubborn and will not love.

4 *Chanson d'avril*
(Louis Bouilhet)

April song

Lève-toi! lève-toi! le printemps vient de naître.
Là-bas, sur les vallons, flotte un réseau vermeil,
Tout frissonne au jardin, tout chante, et ta fenêtre,

Comme un regard joyeux, est pleine de soleil.

Du côté des lilas aux touffes violettes,
Mouches et papillons bruissent à la fois;
Et le muguet sauvage, ébranlant ses clochettes,
A réveillé l'amour endormi dans les bois.

Puisqu'avril a semé ses marguerites blanches,
Laisse ta mante lourde et ton manchon frileux;
Déjà l'oiseau t'appelle, et tes sœurs les pervenches
Te souriront dans l'herbe en voyant tes yeux bleus.

Arise! Arise! Spring has just been born.
Rosy gossamer floats over those distant valleys,
The whole garden quivers and sings, and your
    window,
Like a happy glance, is full of sun.

Beside the purple-clustered lilac,
Flies and butterflies hum together;
And the wild lilies-of-the-valley, shaking their bells,
Have awakened love asleep in the woods.

Since April has sown its white daisies,
Leave off your heavy cloak and wintry muff;
Birds call you, and your sister periwinkles
Will smile in the grass at your blue eyes.

Viens, partons! Au matin, la source est plus limpide;
N'attendons pas du jour les brûlantes chaleurs;
Je veux mouiller mes pieds dans la rosée humide,
Et te parler d'amour sous les poiriers en fleurs!

Come, let us go! Morning springs are clearer!
Let us not wait for the heat of the day,
I would moisten my feet in the damp dew,
And talk to you of love beneath the flowering pears!

5 *Adieux de l'hôtesse arabe*
(Victor Hugo)

Farewell of the Arabian hostess

Puisque rien ne t'arrête en cet heureux pays,
Ni l'ombre du palmier, ni le jaune maïs,
    Ni le repos, ni l'abondance,
Ni de voir à ta voix battre le jeune sein
De nos sœurs, dont, les soirs, le tournoyant essaim
    Couronne un coteau de sa danse,

Since nothing can keep you in this happy land,
Neither shade-giving palm nor yellow corn,
    Nor repose nor abundance,
Nor the sight of our sisters' young breasts trembling
At your voice as, in a wheeling throng at evening,
    They garland a hillside with their dance,

Adieu, beau voyageur! Hélas adieu! Oh! que n'es-tu
    de ceux
Qui donnent pour limite à leurs pieds paresseux
    Leur toit de branches ou de toiles!
Qui, rêveurs, sans en faire, écoutent les récits,
Et souhaitent, le soir, devant leur porte assis,
    De s'en aller dans les étoiles!

Farewell, fair traveller! Ah! Why are you not like
    those
Whose indolent feet venture no further
    Than their roofs of branch or canvas!
Who, musing, listen passively to tales
And dream at evening, sitting before their door,
    Of wandering among the stars!

Si tu l'avais voulu, peut-être une de nous,
Ô jeune homme, eût aimé te servir à genoux

    Dans nos huttes toujours ouvertes;
Elle eût fait, en berçant ton sommeil de ses chants,

Had you so wished, perhaps one of us,
O young man, would willingly have served you,
    kneeling,
    In our ever-open huts;
Lulling you asleep with songs, she would have
    made,

Pour chasser de ton front les moucherons méchants,
    Un éventail de feuilles vertes.

To chase the tiresome midges from your brow,
    A fan of green leaves.

Si tu ne reviens pas, songe un peu quelquefois
Aux filles du désert, sœurs à la douce voix,
    Qui dansent pieds nus sur la dune;
Ô beau jeune homme blanc, bel oiseau passager,
Souviens-toi, car peut-être, ô rapide étranger,
    Ton souvenir reste à plus d'une!

If you do not return, dream at times
Of the daughters of the desert, sweet-voiced sisters,
    Who dance barefoot on the dunes;
O handsome young white man, fair bird of passage,
Remember—for perhaps, O fleeting stranger,
    More than one maiden will remember you!

Hélas! Adieu! bel étranger! Souviens-toi!

Alas! Farewell, fair stranger! Remember!

6 *Vieille chanson*
(Charles Hubert Millevoye)

Dans les bois l'amoureux Myrtil
Avait pris Fauvette légère:
'Aimable oiseau, lui disait-il,
Je te destine à ma bergère.
Pour prix du don que j'aurai fait,
Que de baisers!... Si ma Lucette
M'en donne deux pour un bouquet,
J'en aurai dix pour la Fauvette.'

La Fauvette dans le vallon
A laissé son ami fidèle,
Et tant fait que de sa prison
Elle s'échappe à tire-d'aile.
'Ah! dit le berger désolé,
Adieu les baisers de Lucette!
Tout mon bonheur s'est envolé
Sur les ailes de la Fauvette.'

Myrtil retourne au bois voisin,
Pleurant la perte qu'il a faite;
Soit par hasard, soit à dessein,
Dans le bois se trouvait Lucette:
Sensible à ce gage de foi,
Elle sortit de sa retraite,
En lui disant: 'Console-toi, Myrtil,
Tu n'as perdu que la Fauvette.'

Old song

Amorous Myrtil in the woods
Once caught a merry warbler;
'Lovely bird', he said,
'I'll give you to my shepherdess.
As a reward for this gift,
The kisses she'll give me! If Lucette
Gives me two for a posy,
For a warbler there'll be ten!'

The warbler had left in the dale
Its faithful friend,
And so escaped the prison
As swiftly as it could.
'Ah', said the anguished shepherd,
'Farewell, then, to Lucette's kisses!
My whole happiness has flown away
On the warbler's wings!'

Myrtil returns to the nearby woods,
Weeping the loss he'd suffered.
Whether by chance or by design,
Lucette was also there;
And, touched by this pledge of faith,
She slipped from her retreat
And said: 'Ah, Myrtil, be of good cheer—
It's only the warbler you've lost!'

7 *Ma vie a son secret*
(Félix Arvers)

Ma vie a son secret, mon âme a son mystère.
Un amour éternel en un moment conçu:
Le mal est sans remède, aussi j'ai dû le taire,
Et celle qui l'a fait n'en a jamais rien su.

Ainsi j'aurai passé près d'elle inaperçu,
Toujours à ses côtes, et toujours solitaire.
Et j'aurais jusqu'au bout fait mon temps sur la terre,
N'osant rien demander et n'ayant rien reçu.

Pour elle, que le ciel a faite douce et tendre,

Elle suit son chemin, distraite et sans entendre
Le murmure d'amour élevé sur ses pas.

My life has its secret

My life has its secret, my soul its mystery.
An eternal love conceived in a moment:
Since the ill has no cure, I have had to conceal it,
And she, the cause, has never known it.

Thus I shall have passed unnoticed near her,
Ever at her side and ever alone.
And I shall have spent my life on earth,
Daring to ask for—and receiving—nothing!

And she, whom heaven has made so sweet and
        tender,
She goes dreaming on her way, nor hearing
Love's murmur stirring in her wake.

À l'austère devoir, pieusement fidèle,
Elle dira, lisant ces vers tout remplis d'elle:

'Quelle est donc cette femme?' et ne comprendra
    pas.

Devoutly faithful to her austere duty,
She will say, reading these lines imbued with her
    being:
'Who, then, is this woman?' and will not
    understand!

8 *Tarentelle*
(Édouard Pailleron)

Tarantella

Le papillon s'est envolé,
La fleur se balance avec grâce.
Ma belle, où voyez-vous la trace,
La trace de l'amant ailé?
Ah! Le papillon s'est envolé!

The butterfly has flown away,
The flower sways gracefully.
Where, my sweet, do you see
The trace of your winged lover?
Ah! The butterfly has flown away!

Le flot est rapide et changeant,
Toujours sillonnant l'eau profonde.
La barque passe, et toujours l'onde
Efface le sillon d'argent.

The waves are swift and changing,
Always furrowing the deep waters.
The boat passes by, and still the waves
Efface the silver wake.

Le papillon, c'est votre amour.
La fleur et l'onde, c'est votre âme
Que rien n'émeut, que rien n'entame,
Où rien ne reste plus d'un jour.
Le papillon c'est votre amour.

The butterfly is your love,
The flower and wave are your heart,
Which nothing can move nor penetrate,
Where nothing remains for more than a day.
The butterfly is your love.

Ma belle, où voyez-vous la trace,
La trace de l'amant ailé?
La fleur se balance avec grâce...
Le papillon s'est envolé!

Where, my sweet, do you see
The trace of your winged lover?
The flower sways gracefully...
The butterfly has flown away!

9 *Ouvre ton cœur*
(Louis Delâtre)

Open your heart

La marguerite a fermé sa corolle,
L'ombre a fermé les yeux du jour.
Belle, me tiendras-tu parole?
Ouvre ton cœur à mon amour.

The daisy has closed its petals,
Darkness has closed the eyes of day.
Will you, fair one, be true to your word?
Open your heart to my love.

Ouvre ton cœur, ô jeune ange, à ma flamme,
Qu'un rêve charme ton sommeil.
Je veux reprendre mon âme,
Comme une fleur s'ouvre au soleil!

Open your heart to my ardour, young angel,
May a dream beguile your sleep—
I wish to recover my soul,
As a flower unfolds to the sun!

10 *Pastel*
(Philippe Gille)

Pastel

C'est un portrait de jeune fille,
On l'a fait au siècle passé,
Les ans l'ont à peine effacé!
Ce regard où son âme brille
Est innocent et curieux,
Me dit ces mots mystérieux:
Ne cherche pas ce qu'on peut lire
Dans mes yeux bleus couleur du temps,
Et n'y vois rien que le sourire
Qui t'attendait depuis cent ans.

It is a young girl's portrait,
Painted in the past century,
The years have scarcely faded it!
This gaze where her soul shines
Is innocent and enquiring,
And speaks mysteriously to me:
'Seek to read no message
In my blue, time-coloured eyes,
And see nothing there but the smile
That has waited a century for you.'

À quoi cette enfant pensait-elle,
Quand le peintre la regardait?
Son cœur avait-il un secret?
Sur sa bouche on voit un sourire,
Est-ce ironie, est-ce bonheur?
Que dit-il sous cet air railleur?
Il dit, je crois: à quoi bon lire
Dans les feuillets noircis du temps?
Vois-y seulement le sourire,
Qui t'attendait depuis cent ans!

What were this child's thoughts,
When the painter gazed at her?
Did her heart harbour a secret?
The smile you see on her lips,
Is it irony or happiness?
What does it say beneath its mocking mien?
It says, I think: 'why ever read
The blackened pages of time?
Look only at the smile
That has waited a century for you!'

BLOCH, Ernst (1880–1959)

Born in Switzerland, but an American citizen from the 1920s, Bloch (once a fashionable composer) is primarily remembered today for his chamber and orchestral music on Jewish themes. He studied in Frankfurt and Munich, but he also spent part of his studentship in Brussels and Paris. The four HISTORIETTES AU CRÉPUSCULE (Mauclair, 1904) are not typical of the style of Bloch's later music (that of the epic Piano Quintet of 1921–3, for example) but they are attractive songs, well suited to the texts, and not over-written for the piano. *Complainte* has a folksong feel about it, and *Ronde* is a latter-day *danse macabre*, lively and appealingly grotesque, with an appearance from the devil. The four POÈMES D'AUTOMNE (Béatrix Rodès, 1906, also orchestrated) are in a grander, more dramatic manner which now seems rather inflated. The poetry strikes a melancholy pose which brings out a response from Bloch typical of his highly emotive musical manner; but the Mauclair songs benefit from more interesting texts, and are more useful recital items.

BORDES, Charles (1863–1909)

The lifelong passion of this wonderfully energetic musician was early music, and he did more than anyone else of his generation to further the cause of plainchant, and the polyphony of Josquin, Palestrina, and so on, not to mention the operas of Rameau. He established traditions of choral singing of the highest order, and his work with his own Chanteurs de Saint-Gervais achieved remarkable standards for the time. With d'Indy he was a founder of the Schola Cantorum, first as a society for sacred music, and later as a school. He is still admired in Spain for his work on the music of the Basques, and much of his own instrumental music is based on the folksongs of that region of northern Spain. His folksong arrangements (ONZE CHANSONS DU LANGUEDOC, 1906) place him next to Déodat de Séverac as a champion of that region of southern France; indeed Bordes was among the first to encourage the younger Séverac to become a composer.

With this serious attitude to musical research it may perhaps seem surprising that Bordes was also a pioneering mélodie composer with a great deal of flair (he was among the first to set the lyrics of Paul Verlaine). There is little sign of scholastic academicism in his songs, which are inventive, atmospheric, and long overdue for reassessment. There are two volumes of song, both posthumously edited by Pierre de Bréville. In the Rouart Lerolle volume there are no less than nine settings of Verlaine, including *Spleen* (also set by Fauré and Debussy [DEBUSSY 6 vi]), *La bonne chanson* ('J'allais par des chemins perfides') [FAURÉ 30 iv], *Épithalame* ('Donc, ce sera par un clair jour d'été') (from *LA BONNE CHANSON* [FAURÉ 30 vii]), and *Le son du cor s'afflige vers les bois* [DEBUSSY 9 ii]. Particularly beautiful is a setting of a Verlaine poem unessayed by the major masters: ***Sur un vieil air*** ('Le piano que baise une main frêle') weaves the melody of *Plasir d'amour* [MARTINI 1] into a texture of murmuring piano writing which seems halfway between Fauré and Debussy (cf. the Lipatti setting). The range of Bordes's circle was wide, for the songs are dedicated to Chausson and Chabrier, Albéniz and Ropartz.

Mention should also be made of Bordes's QUATRE POÈMES DE FRANCIS JAMMES, written for the different voices and vocal ranges of the 'Quatuor vocal de la Schola Cantorum'; he was attracted to the same poetry from which Lili Boulanger drew her CLAIRIÈRES DANS LE CIEL. There is also a lovely duet entitled *L'hiver* with a text by Maurice Bouchor, and *Madrigal à la musique*, a choral setting of that poet's translation of Shakespeare's *Orpheus with his lute*. A second *recueil* was published by Hamelle which includes the jolliest of all Verlaine settings, ***Dansons la gigue!***, which quotes the Northumberland traditional song *The keel row* to dizzying effect for the pianist. Debussy was to pay Bordes the compliment of lifting this tune as the basis for *Gigues*, the first of his *Images* for orchestra. The 1886 setting of Verlaine's *Ô triste, triste était mon âme* has the look of plainchant on the stave. Equally fascinating and strange are four songs from Verlaine's *Paysages tristes* from the same year which pre-date both Fauré's and Debussy's Verlainian efforts; the set opens with a majestic *Soleils couchants* and is followed by a setting of *Chanson d'automne* [HAHN 1 i, from the CHANSONS GRISES]. *Amour évanoui* (Maurice Bouchor) is a setting of the poem which, under the title of *Le temps des lilas*, found fame as part of Chausson's orchestral song cycle *POÈME DE L'AMOUR ET LA MER* [CHAUSSON 12]. This song's long postlude is typical of Schumann's undoubted influence on the piano writing of Bordes.

1 *Sur un vieil air*

(Paul Verlaine)

Le piano que baise une main frêle
Luit dans le soir rose et gris vaguement,
Tandis qu'avec un très léger bruit d'aile
Un air bien vieux, bien faible et bien charmant
Rôde discret, épeuré quasiment,
Par le boudoir longtemps parfumé d'Elle.

Qu'est-ce que c'est que ce berceau soudain
Qui lentement dorlote mon pauvre être?
Que voudrais-tu de moi, doux chant badin?
Qu'as-tu voulu, fin refrain incertain
Qui vas tantôt mourir vers la fenêtre
Ouverte un peu sur le petit jardin?

On an old air

The piano kissed by a delicate hand
Gleams dimly in the pink grey evening,
While with the lightest brush of a wing
A melody, truly old, truly faint, truly charming,
Floats quietly, as if frightened,
About the room where long her scent had lingered.

What is this sudden lullaby
That slowly caresses my poor being?
What would you want of me, sweet playful song?
What did you want, vague and subtle air
That soon will die away by the window,
Opened a little onto the tiny garden?

2 *Dansons la gigue!*

(Paul Verlaine)

　Dansons la gigue!

J'aimais surtout ses jolis yeux,
Plus clairs que l'étoile des cieux,
J'aimais ses yeux malicieux.

　Dansons la gigue!

Elle avait des façons vraiment
De désoler un pauvre amant,
Que c'en était vraiment charmant!

　Dansons la gigue!

Mais je trouve encore meilleur
Le baiser de sa bouche en fleur
Depuis qu'elle est morte à mon cœur.

　Dansons la gigue!

Je me souviens, je me souviens
Des heures et des entretiens,
Et c'est le meilleur de mes biens.

　Dansons la gigue!

Let's dance the jig!

　Let's dance the jig!

Most I loved her pretty eyes,
Brighter than the heavens' stars,
I loved her impish eyes.

　Let's dance the jig!

She truly had ways of afflicting
A poor lover's heart—
It was quite charming the way she did!

　Let's dance the jig!

But even more I love
The kiss of her mouth in bloom,
Now that she's dead to my heart.

　Let's dance the jig!

I remember, I remember
The times we spent together talking,
The best of all my memories.

　Let's dance the jig!

BOULANGER, Lili (1893–1918)

This composer, who, despite her early death, left 'an exquisite body of work' (Henri Barraud), remains something of an enigma for the performer and listener. Of formidable intelligence and individuality, she studied with her sister Nadia and Paul Vidal, and broadened her horizons through her sojourns in Italy (she was the first woman to win the coveted Prix de Rome). She was, however, a chronic invalid (she suffered from Crohn's disease) and, apart from her work in Rome for the families of the war-wounded, her life was a cosseted one in a way which suggests the young Elizabeth Barrett. After listening to Boulanger's music at length, one is amazed by the technical accomplishment and depth of feeling, particularly in the epic choral work *Du fond de l'abîme*.

The size of Boulanger's musical personality is reflected in the vitality, and one may even say vehemence, of her work. This larger than life quality is accompanied by a pre-occupation with death; her first song, written in 1907, is *Lettre de mort*. Her later songs also scorn the traditional understatement of the mélodie. The music of the long cycle CLAIRIÈRES DANS LE CIEL (Jammes, 1913–14) aspires to the sublime in a manner which sometimes approaches the self-conscious. There had of course always been an 'elevated' and deeply Catholic French style which goes back to César Franck, and which extends to Messiaen. We encounter it in some of the Caplet songs, in many composers of the Franck school (Bréville, Chausson, Lekeu, and so on), and we certainly find it in CLAIRIÈRES DANS LE CIEL, which is cyclical in form in the Franckian manner. There are also musical references to Wagner's *Tristan* which add to the work's sumptuous effect.

How different this is from the music of the man whom Boulanger calls 'Maître Fauré' in the dedication to this work, and whose middle name, not without justification, was 'Urbain'. And there is no doubt that she meant to make anything other than an urbane impression. There is much of the hothouse in the manner of her music, not least in the cycle where the perfumed atmosphere created by the Debussian harmonic language effectively suggests the mystery and eroticism of the narrator's relationship to the un-named 'Elle'. The poetry of Jammes, a Catholic convert, is partly responsible for the heady mix of sensuality and *pudeur* which pervades the work. Boulanger was not the only composer attracted to the poetry of Jammes, but if we are tempted to wonder whether her response to these texts was born of her own feelings and longings, the final impression is somehow impersonal, and that we do not hear the composer's own viewpoint behind the astonishingly accomplished music. The poems call for a male singer and are written in the first person, but the composer observes at a distance. Many will admire this as being part of the mélodie's long-established manner of detachment and veiled eroticism (cf. Debussy's CHANSONS DE BILITIS) but these songs, not surprisingly, do not seem part of this male-dominated tradition either. Rather do they suggest someone passionately religious and religiously passionate, and at a stage in her life where one state of mind was interchangeable with the other. It should be mentioned that twelve of the thirteen poems set here by Boulanger formed part of an even longer song cycle, TRISTESSES, composed by Darius Milhaud in 1956 (*Au pied de mon lit*, the text of Boulanger's fifth song, was not included in the Milhaud cycle). Still competitive with her sister, Boulanger is determined to establish herself with serious music on a grand scale, and in this she succeeds. (It is no surprise that eight of the thirteen songs were orchestrated.) However the human being who seems never to have had a carefree (or work-free) day in her childhood, and who was groomed for greatness from the cradle, is somehow obscured by the composer, brilliant beyond her years. In this case, the disparity between human experience and professional aspiration is moving, for one suspects that Lili's need for independence from her formidably possessive family was at least as great as her struggle against male musical prejudices in this era of suffragettes. If she had been spared to live a long and fulfilled life, she would have astonished us with even finer music. She seems to me to be a composer who was still in the process of growing into her redoubtable gifts. This makes her early death, ten days before Debussy's, a real tragedy for French music.

Even if there was something saint-like about Lili's short life, she was deified, not always to the advantage of her cause. Generations of the pupils of Mademoiselle (as her sister Nadia was respectfully addressed) were expected to accept without question her classification of Lili as on a par with Bach and Mozart. This special pleading, born of an understandable family devotion, obscured Lili's real accomplishments as much as it vaunted them. The burnishing of the legend included Nadia making a revision of the Jammes cycle for republication in 1970. Whether this was necessary or not, a performance of CLAIRIÈRES DANS LE CIEL is a rewarding undertaking for both singer and pianist. It is a lengthy work, however, with thematic cross-references between the songs (as in Fauré's LA BONNE CHANSON) and difficult to perform in excerpts. Easier to programme in a mixed recital are the QUATRE CHANTS, a Schirmer collection which comprises separate songs from 1910 to 1916, including the Debussian *Attente* (1910), and *Reflets* (1911), as well as two settings of Maurice Maeterlinck. *Dans l'immense tristesse* (1916) displays a remarkable empathy with the poet Bertha Galéron de Calonne who was a Helen Keller of her time, unable to see, hear, or speak. Boulanger's setting with its lugubrious movement in bare fifths reflects this isolation: it seems hermetically sealed as if attempting to depict an enormous void where music resonates in empty space. There is also a small cantata for four voices, RENOUVEAU (Silvestre, 1911–13), which can be performed with either piano or orchestral accompaniment.

CLAIRIÈRES DANS LE CIEL	*CLEARINGS IN THE SKY*
(Francis Jammes)	

1 i *Elle était descendue au bas de la prairie*	*She had gone down to the end of the meadow*
Elle était descendue au bas de la prairie,	She had gone down to the end of the meadow,
et, comme la prairie était toute fleurie	and, since the meadow was all decked
de plantes dont la tige aime à pousser dans l'eau,	with flowers whose stems thrive in water,
ces plantes inondées je les avais cueillies.	I picked those water-flowers.
Bientôt, s'étant mouillée, elle gagna le haut	She, now drenched, soon reached the top
de cette prairie-là qui était toute fleurie.	of that flowering meadow.
Elle riait et s'ébrouait avec la grâce	She was laughing and splashing with the awkward
dégingandée qu'ont les jeunes filles trop grandes.	grace of girls who are too tall.
Elle avait le regard qu'ont les fleurs de lavande.	Her eyes looked like lavender flowers.

I ii *Elle est gravement gaie*

Elle est gravement gaie. Par moments son regard
se levait comme pour surprendre ma pensée.
Elle était douce alors comme quand il est tard
le velours jaune et bleu d'une allée de pensées.

She is gravely cheerful

She is gravely cheerful. At times she looked
up as if to catch what I was thinking.
She was gentle then, like at dusk
the blue-yellow velvet of pansies along a path.

I iii *Parfois, je suis triste*

Parfois, je suis triste. Et, soudain, je pense à elle.
Alors, je suis joyeux. Mais je redeviens triste
de ce que je ne sais pas combien elle m'aime.
Elle est la jeune fille à l'âme toute claire,
et qui, dedans son cœur, garde avec jalousie
l'unique passion que l'on donne à un seul.
Elle est partie avant que s'ouvrent les tilleuls,
et, comme ils ont fleuri depuis qu'elle est partie,
je me suis étonné de voir, ô mes amis,
des branches de tilleuls qui n'avaient pas de fleurs.

Sometimes I am sad

Sometimes I am sad. And suddenly, I think of her.
Then, I am overjoyed. But I grow sad again,
not knowing how much she loves me.
She is the girl with the utterly limpid soul,
who, in her heart, jealously guards
that unique passion, reserved for one man alone.
She left before the lime trees bloomed,
and since they bloomed after she left,
I have been astonished to see, O my friends,
some lime tree branches devoid of flowers.

I iv *Un poète disait*

Un poète disait que, lorsqu'il était jeune,
il fleurissait des vers comme un rosier des roses.
Lorsque je pense à elle, il me semble que jase
une fontaine intarissable dans mon cœur.
Comme sur le lys Dieu pose un parfum d'église,
comme il met du corail aux joues de la cerise,
je veux poser sur elle, avec dévotion,
la couleur d'un parfum qui n'aura pas de nom.

A poet once said

A poet once said that, when he was young,
he blossomed with verse like a rose-tree with roses.
When I think of her, an inexhaustible fountain
seems to babble in my heart.
As God gave the lily a church's scent
and set coral on the cheeks of the cherry,
I wish devoutly to give her
the hue of a scent that shall have no name.

I v *Au pied de mon lit*

Au pied de mon lit, une Vierge négresse
fut mise par ma mère. Et j'aime cette Vierge
d'une religion un peu italienne.
Virgo Lauretana, debout dans un fond d'or,
qui me faites penser à mille fruits de mer
que l'on vend sur des quais où pas un souffle d'air
n'émeut les pavillons qui lourdement s'endorment,
Virgo Lauretana, vous savez qu'en ces heures
où je ne me sens pas digne d'être aimé d'elle,
c'est vous dont le parfum me rafraîchit le cœur.

At the foot of my bed

At the foot of my bed, my mother placed
a black Virgin. And I love this Virgin
with a somewhat Italianate piety.
Virgo Lauretana, standing on a gold ground,
you who remind me of a thousand fruits de mer
sold on quaysides where no breath of air
stirs the flags falling listlessly asleep,
Virgo Lauretana, you know that at such moments
when I feel myself unworthy of her love,
it is your scent that revives my heart.

I vi *Si tout ceci n'est qu'un pauvre rêve*

Si tout ceci n'est qu'un pauvre rêve, et s'il faut
que j'ajoute, dans ma vie, une fois encore,
la désillusion aux désillusions;
et, si je dois encore, par ma sombre folie,
chercher dans la douceur du vent et de la pluie
les seules vaines voix qui m'aient en passion:
je ne sais si je guérirai, ô mon amie…

If all this is but a poor dream

If all this is but a poor dream, and if I must,
once more in my life, add
disillusion to disillusion;
and, if I must once more, in my dark distraction,
seek in the sweetness of the wind and rain
the only voices—unreal ones—that adore me:
I do not know, my friend, if I shall recover…

I vii *Nous nous aimerons*

Nous nous aimerons tant que nous tairons nos mots,
en nous tendant la main, quand nous nous reverrons.
Vous serez ombragée par d'anciens rameaux
sur le banc que je sais où nous nous assoierons.
Donc nous nous assoierons sur ce banc, tous deux
        seuls…
D'un long moment, ô mon amie, vous n'oserez…
Que vous me serez douce et que je tremblerai…

We shall love each other

We shall love each other so, that we shall be silent
as we hold out hands when next we meet.
You will be shaded by old branches
on the bench where I know we shall both sit down.
And so we shall sit down on this bench, we two
        alone…
For a long while, my friend, you will not dare…
How gentle you will be with me and how I shall
        tremble…

I viii *Vous m'avez regardé avec toute votre âme*

Vous m'avez regardé avec toute votre âme.
Vous m'avez regardé longtemps comme un ciel bleu.
J'ai mis votre regard à l'ombre de mes yeux…
Que ce regard était passionné et calme…

You gazed at me with all your soul

You gazed at me with all your soul.
You gazed at me long like a blue sky.
I set your gaze in the shade of my eyes…
How this gaze was passionate and calm…

I ix *Les lilas qui avaient fleuri*

Les lilas qui avaient fleuri l'année dernière
vont fleurir de nouveau dans les tristes parterres.
Déjà le pêcher grêle a jonché le ciel bleu
de ses roses, comme un enfant la Fête-Dieu.
Mon cœur devrait mourir au milieu de ces choses,
car c'était au milieu des vergers blancs et roses
que j'avais espéré je ne sais quoi de vous.
Mon âme rêve sourdement sur vos genoux.
Ne la repoussez point. Ne la relevez pas,
de peur qu'en s'éloignant de vous elle ne voie
combien vous êtes faible et troublée dans ses bras.

The lilacs which had flowered

The lilacs which had flowered last year
will soon flower once more in dismal beds.
The slender peach has already strewn the blue sky
with its pinks, like a child at Corpus Christi.
My heart should have died amid these things,
for it was amid the orchard's whites and pinks
that I had hoped from you I know not what.
My soul dreams secretly on your lap.
Do not reject it. Do not raise it up,
for fear that, drawing away from you, it might see
how frail you are and troubled in its embrace.

I x *Deux ancolies se balançaient sur la colline*

Deux ancolies se balançaient sur la colline.
Et l'ancolie disait à sa sœur l'ancolie:
Je tremble devant toi et demeure confuse.
Et l'autre répondait: si dans la roche qu'use
l'eau, goutte à goutte, si je me mire, je vois
que je tremble, et je suis confuse comme toi.

Le vent de plus en plus les berçait toutes deux,
les emplissait d'amour et mêlait leurs cœurs bleus.

Two columbines swayed on the hill

Two columbines swayed on the hill.
And one columbine said to its sister columbine:
I tremble before you and feel abashed.
And the other replied: if in the rock, worn away
drop by drop by water, I mirror myself, I see
that I am trembling, and feel abashed like you.

The wind rocked them both more and more,
filled them with love and mingled their blue hearts.

I xi *Par ce que j'ai souffert*

Par ce que j'ai souffert, ma mésange bénie,
je sais ce qu'a souffert l'autre: car j'étais deux...
Je sais vos longs réveils au milieu de la nuit
et l'angoisse de moi qui vous gonfle le sein.

On dirait par moments qu'une tête chérie,
confiante et pure, ô vous qui êtes la sœur des lins

en fleurs et qui parfois fixez le ciel comme eux,
on dirait qu'une tête inclinée dans la nuit
pèse de tout son poids, à jamais, sur ma vie.

Through what I suffered

Through what I suffered, my sweetest,
I know what another suffered: for I was two...
I know of your long vigils at the dead of night
and your anguish for me that makes your breast
    heave.
It is at times as though a cherished face,
trusting and pure,—O you the sister of flowering
    flax,
who at times will also stare at the sky—
as though a face, bowing to the night
were bearing down, for evermore, with all its weight
    on my life.

I xii *Je garde une médaille d'elle*

Je garde une médaille d'elle où sont gravés
une date et les mots: prier, croire, espérer.
Mais moi, je vois surtout que la médaille est sombre:

son argent a noirci sur son col de colombe.

I keep a medallion of her

I keep a medallion of her, engraved
with a date and the words: pray, believe, hope.
But above all I see the medallion lacks lustre:

the silver has darkened on her dove-like neck.

I xiii *Demain fera un an*

Demain fera un an qu'à Audaux je cueillais

les fleurs dont j'ai parlé, de la prairie mouillée.
C'est aujourd'hui le plus beau jour des jours de
    Pâques.
Je me suis enfoncé dans l'azur des campagnes,
à travers bois, à travers prés, à travers champs.

Tomorrow will mark a year

Tomorrow will mark a year since at Audaux I
    picked
the flowers I spoke of from the drenched meadow.
Today is the most lovely Easter day.

I plunged deep into the blue countryside,
across woods, across meadows, across fields.

Comment, mon cœur, n'es-tu pas mort depuis un an? | How is it, O heart, you did not die a year ago?

Mon cœur, je t'ai donné encore ce calvaire | O heart, once more I have caused you this anguish
de revoir ce village où j'avais tant souffert, | of seeing again this village where I suffered so,
ces roses qui saignaient devant le presbytère, | these roses that bled before the vicarage,
ces lilas qui me tuent dans les tristes parterres. | these lilacs that kill me in their dismal beds.
Je me suis souvenu de ma détresse ancienne, | I have recalled my former distress
et je ne sais comment je ne suis pas tombé | and do not know why I did not fall
sur l'ocre du sentier, le front dans la poussière. | headlong in the dust on the ochre path.
Plus rien. Je n'ai plus rien, plus rien qui me soutienne. | Nothing more. I have nothing more, nothing to sustain me.
Pourquoi fait-il si beau et pourquoi suis-je né? | Why is the day so lovely and why was I born?
J'aurais voulu poser sur vos calmes genoux | I would have wished to place on your tranquil lap
la fatigue qui rompt mon âme qui se couche | the fatigue which breaks my soul and lies
ainsi qu'une pauvresse au fossé de la route. | like a poor woman by the roadside ditch.
Dormir. Pouvoir dormir. Dormir à tout jamais | To sleep. To be able to sleep. To sleep for evermore
sous les averses bleues, sous les tonnerres frais. | beneath the blue showers and the fresh thunder.
Ne plus sentir. Ne plus savoir votre existence. | No longer to feel. No longer to know you exist.
Ne plus voir cet azur engloutir ces coteaux | No longer to see this blue sky engulf these hills
dans ce vertige bleu qui mêle l'air à l'eau, | in this reeling blue which mingles air and water,
ni ce vide où je cherche en vain votre présence. | nor this void where I search for you in vain.
Il me semble sentir pleurer au fond de moi, | I seem to feel a weeping within me,
d'un lourd sanglot muet, quelqu'un qui n'est pas là. | a heavy silent sobbing, someone who is not there.
J'écris. Et la campagne est sonore de joie. | I write. And the countryside is loud with joy.

... Elle était descendue au bas de la prairie, | ... She had gone down to the end of the meadow,
et comme la prairie était toute fleurie... | and since the meadow was all decked with flowers . . .

BOULANGER, Nadia (1887–1979)

The family background was extraordinary: a father 72 years old when she was born, a mother forty years younger who claimed to be a Russian princess, and who was ambitious for, and severe with, her daughter, never giving her a word of praise. And then a sister, Lili, with whose well-being she was charged by her father at the age of 6. Nadia, pupil of Fauré, had a distinguished career at the Conservatoire but failed four times to win the Prix de Rome. She became Lili's composition teacher, and one can only imagine the guilt-inducing mixture of pride and envy Nadia felt when her sister won the prize at her second attempt. The stage was set for Nadia's retreat from her own hopes and ambitions as a composer, and a life devoted to conducting and teaching, but not until at least four years after Lili's premature death. In 1906 she made her debut as a composer with a performance of her song *Versailles* (Samain) at the Grand Palais; Hamelle published this, and at least twelve more of her early songs, including *Soleil couchant* (Verlaine), a gravely eloquent *Élégie* (also Samain, one of the older Fauré's favourite poets), a Heine setting *Was will die einsame Träne?*, and a spare *Cantique* (Maeterlinck) reminiscent of late Fauré.

As early as 1903 she had become the protégée of the distinguished pianist Raoul Pugno (1852–1914) and their relationship and collaboration was the subject of some speculation. Boulanger composed a concerto-like *Fantaisie* for him which he played, and she conducted. Pugno was also a composer, and in 1909 the pair collaborated on a large song cycle (an enterprise curiously reminiscent of Robert and Clara Schumann's LIEBESFRÜHLING cycle, Op. 37) entitled LES HEURES CLAIRES (Verhaeren). This music is rather similar in style (as in title) to Lili Boulanger's CLAIRIÈRES DANS LE CIEL which was composed a few years later.

Boulanger's last works to be published (1922) were a set of five songs to poems by Camille Mauclair (*Chanson, Le couteau, Doute, Au bord de la route,* and *L'échange*). These works are much more economical of utterance than her earlier songs. The influence of neo-classical Stravinsky can be detected, and the composer's Russian ancestry (surely a hidden link between the two lifelong friends) gives rise to a darkly introspective mood in the fourth song. They well deserve an airing, and on the strength of these works alone one can understand the remark made by Fauré as a very old man, when Nadia visited him in the rue de Vigne: 'I'm not sure you did the right thing in giving up composition.' After saying this, Fauré moved to the piano and played by heart an exercise she had written for a class when she was a teenager. We are used to acknowledging Nadia Boulanger's greatness as a teacher of composition, and the devotion of her students was legendary; but that her talents as a composer inspired this type of compliment from Fauré himself allows us to glimpse the extent, and cost, of her renunciation.

BOULEZ, Pierre (b. 1925)

Even more than Messiaen, the music of Boulez seems out of place in a study of French song as the concert enthusiast would understand it. Unlike Messiaen (who wrote his own texts) Boulez has written a number of important and masterful works where poetry by important French literary figures is of the essence. In his music, poetry suggests the musical forms without dominating them in typical mélodie fashion; nevertheless it plays a crucial part in the composer's imaginative process, something which Boulez has in common with the conventional masters of French song. From early in his career he was attracted to the poetry of René Char: Boulez provided the music for this poet's radio play *Le soleil des eaux* (1948), and he also looked to Char for the texts of one of the most celebrated of all twentieth-century avant-garde song cycles—LE MARTEAU SANS MAÎTRE (1952–4, rev. 1957). The other important poet in Boulez's output is Mallarmé; indeed such was his devotion to this poet that he may claim to have inherited him directly from Ravel, and to have become Mallarmé's most ardent champion in the second half of the century. It is a paradox that this poet, himself an ardent Wagnerian, should have become the darling of the French *avant-garde*. There are three works with the title *Improvisations sur Mallarmé* (*I, II,* and *III,* 1957–9), as well as *Tombeau* (1959) and *Don* (1960–2). All of these works were written for soprano and various instrumental combinations, and were incorporated into PLI SELON PLI. The poet may seem to be treated in cavalier fashion by the traditional standards of word-setting, but a closer study reveals that Boulez reveres these texts; his main interest in this demanding style is to reflect the poet's revolutionary syntax in musical form.

BOWLES, Paul (1910–1999)

This American composer renowned equally for his music and his fiction (his wife was the writer Jane Bowles) had a strong link with French North Africa, where he lived on and off for many years. His interest in ethnomusicology led him to spend a decade in Tangier (from 1959). His first French songs date from 1935: *Danger de mort* (G. Linze), *Memnon* (Cocteau), and *SCÈNES D'ANABASE III* (Perse). Later songs in French include *Ainsi parfois nos seuils* and *Voici la feuille* (the latter a typically Bowlesian quirky waltz) to his own texts.

BRÉVILLE, Pierre de (1861–1949)

Bréville is a surprisingly prolific composer, with some 105 songs to his credit, only 23 of which were unpublished. The most important songs are to be found in two *recueils* which were issued by Rouart Lerolle in 1913 and 1914. Bréville was a pupil of Franck, though there are signs that Fauré and Debussy had places in his pantheon. This duality is typical of the generation of musicians who were able to benefit from the musical influences of both the Schola Cantorum and the Conservatoire. It is hardly surprising that Bréville's music often brings that of Ernest Chausson to mind, a composer who had studied with both Franck and Massenet. Bréville's main weakness is a lack of true feeling for the sensuality of the voice which he sometimes treats as just another orchestral instrument; thus it is no surprise to find that he has written a set entitled *QUATRE SONATINES VOCALES*. He actually set Baudelaire's *Harmonie du soir* (1879) before Debussy [DEBUSSY 7 ii] and his setting of Moréas's *La forêt charmée* precedes the setting of the same poem (under the title of *Dans la forêt du charme et de l'enchantement*) by Chausson [CHAUSSON 11]. On the other hand, his 1922 setting of the Mallarmé poem *Sainte* post-dates the song by Ravel [RAVEL 3], as does the late and unpublished (1944) setting of Klingsor's *La flûte enchantée* [RAVEL 8 ii].

His earlier mélodies (e.g. Hugo's *Extase*) seem rather heavily Wagnerian, but the later songs (settings of Henri de Régnier 1911–16) show a fastidious choice of text and an increasingly individual and transparent musical style. Of these *Venise marine* is a favourite. Also from this period is the song *Une jeune fille parle* (Moréas) which was sung by Claire Croiza and recorded with the composer as accompanist. This exceptional singer championed Bréville's work and took the title role in his opera *Éros vainqueur*; a number of the songs are dedicated to her including some of the *DOUZE RONDELS DE CHARLES D'ORLÉANS* (1928), a book of six each for high and medium voice. These are almost minimalist in comparison to the sumptuous accompaniments of the earlier work, but are effective stylizations without adopting the guise of pastiche that we find in some of Reynaldo Hahn's *DOUZE RONDELS* to different texts of the same poet (although both composers made settings of *Gardez le trait de la fenestre*). On the other hand they also lack the charm of Hahn, for it is surely the earnest quality of many of Bréville's songs, and their rather stiff prosody, that have exiled them from the repertoire. As a critic Bréville was cut and dried in his dismissal of Bizet and his distaste for Berlioz, opinions which typified his generation's reactions against earlier masters of the mélodie.

A few other works should be mentioned: Bréville was attracted (like Chausson) to the poetry of Maurice Bouchor and *Élégie*, *Chanson d'amour*, and *Chanson triste* are all to be found in the first *recueil*; *Le furet du bois joli* (Bénédict, 1896) is a pastiche in *galant* style, and one of Bréville's best-known songs; *Childe Harold* (1899) is a Byron portrait by Heine (Bréville admired German music and literature); *Aimons-nous* (Banville) is a useful duet—both Saint-Saëns and the young Debussy set it as a solo song); there are two late Rimbaud settings, *Les corbeaux* (*c.*1942) and *Le dormeur du val* (*c.*1943), which remain unpublished. This is a pity as songs by this poet are exceedingly rare from French composers, and seem more forthcoming from foreigners (see Britten, Henze, Hoiby, Lipatti).

BRITTEN, Benjamin (1913–1976)

Unlike his friend Lennox Berkeley, Benjamin Britten was no Francophile. One thinks of a line in *Billy Budd* set with just a little too much relish not to have something of the composer himself in it: 'Don't like the French, don't like their lingo.' He had originally wanted to study with Alban Berg in Vienna, not Nadia Boulanger in Paris (the disdain seems to have been mutual, exacerbated by their differing regard for Stravinsky, and a disastrous dinner before a Queen's Hall concert in the 1930s when the nervous young composer, invited to sit at Boulanger's side, inadvertently spilled ice cream on her black velvet dress). A study of song recently published in France, which includes an admiring chapter on Britten, makes the point succinctly: 'he was never more natural or lively than when setting a foreign language, despite a prosody and accentuation which are not exactly those of the French language.'

Britten went on a jaunt to Paris in January 1937, when an innocent expedition to the *Folies bergères* turned into, to the composer's horror, a distressing (but uneventful) visit to what turned out to be a brothel. The seedy side of French life did not appeal. He was nevertheless drawn at an early age to the evocative perfume of French literature. In February 1928, at the age of 15, he composed *Dans les bois*, an orchestral piece. This seems to have been inspired by a Gérard de Nerval poem of the same title, for in June of the same year he wrote a song to that text. Soon afterwards he composed the QUATRE CHANSONS FRANÇAISES for soprano and orchestra, his biggest work to date, and dedicated it to his parents for their 27th wedding anniversary. This work reflects the young composer's composition lessons with Frank Bridge. The four songs are *Nuits de juin* (Hugo), *Sagesse* ('Le ciel est par-dessus le toit', set as *Prison* by Fauré [FAURÉ 31] and by Hahn as *D'une prison*), *L'enfance* (Hugo), and *Chanson d'automne*, the opening song of CHANSONS GRISES by an equally precocious Reynaldo Hahn [HAHN 1 i]. The music shows Bridge's influence, but also a real ability to recreate the delicate colour and evocative mood of the French manner somehow assimilated as a result of listening to concerts and radio broadcasts. These songs are the first of his many stylizations, and an astonishing achievement in one so young. When the work came to be published by Faber in 1982 (there is a piano score of the work), the composer Colin Matthews, charged with editing the work, had almost nothing to change in the orchestration. But he did alter the prosody of the vocal line where the composer had wrongly accented the words.

A lack of familiarity with the exactitudes of French prosody is also a problem in Britten's most celebrated work in French, the song cycle *LES ILLUMINATIONS* (Arthur Rimbaud, 1939). This fact was ruefully confirmed in conversations I had with Pierre Bernac. The Achilles heel of Britain's musical young Apollo has never seemed to bother English singers; but it is a work which seems not to have been taken up by French-speaking musicians, although its first performer and dedicatee was the Swiss soprano Sophie Wyss (A French tenor of the younger generation recently informed me it was easy enough to make the necessary small adaptations to the prosody). Rimbaud occupies almost a sacred place in French literature, and it is significant that on the whole French composers have left him unset. For the rest of the world, Britten's understanding of Rimbaud's various moods (the poet's work was no doubt introduced to him by W. H. Auden or Edward Sackville-West) seems beyond criticism; he does indeed possess 'la clef de cette parade sauvage'. The cycle has a flair and elegance, a sumptuous sensuality notwithstanding an economy of means, which encapsulates English-speaking longing for the 'luxe, calme et volupté' of a culture more sensual than our own. Apart from the 'calme' of Baudelaire's phrase, the work has more than a touch of the sinister and disturbing, reflecting the poet's complex and highly strung nature, and no less the composer's. Maggie Teyte performed this cycle with piano, but the piece requires the colours of the string orchestra to work its magic. The violas' evocation of trumpets in the opening *Fanfare* announces the composer's unerring touch from the beginning. *LES ILLUMINATIONS* is also almost embarrassingly (and unashamedly) tonal for its time. Indeed the awestruck Aaron Copland told Britten that Nadia Boulanger would never have let him stay so long in the key of B flat major without modulating (in the song *Antique*—'Gracieux fils de Pan').

Britten also made a volume of French folksong settings (1943–6). These include, among others, the delightful *Voici le printemps*, a melting setting of *La belle est au jardin d'amour*, and a potent and hypnotic *Il est quelqu'un sur terre*, a French *Gretchen am Spinnrade* with an obsessively grinding spinning wheel. The rollicking *Quand j'étais chez mon père* seems to have been conceived alongside *Peter Grimes*; there is a vivid resemblance between the folksong and the dance music (also marked 'alla Ländler') for off-stage band, as Mrs Sedley makes her meddling accusations in the opera's last act.

The opera *Albert Herring* is modelled on a Maupassant story, but Britten returned to the world of French literature only once in his song writing, and then only obliquely. The words of his cantata *Phaedra* for mezzo-soprano and small orchestra (1975) are drawn from Racine's *Phèdre*, but the composer, whose life was drawing to a close, decided to set the work in English to the free translation of the American poet Robert Lowell.

LES ILLUMINATIONS
(Arthur Rimbaud)

ILLUMINATIONS

1 i *Fanfare*

J'ai seul la clef de cette parade sauvage.

Fanfare

I alone hold the key to this savage parade.

I ii *Villes*

Ce sont des villes! C'est un peuple pour qui se sont montés ces Alleghanys* et ces Libans de rêve! Ce sont des villes! Des chalets de cristal et de bois se meuvent sur des rails et des poulies invisibles. Les vieux cratères ceints de colosses et de palmiers de cuivre rugissent mélodieusement dans les feux. Ce sont des villes! Des cortèges de Mabs en robes rousses, opalines, montent des ravines. Là-haut, les pieds dans la cascade et les ronces, les cerfs tettent Diane. Les Bacchantes des banlieues sanglotent et la lune brûle et hurle. Vénus entre dans les cavernes des forgerons et des ermites. Ce sont des... Des groupes de beffrois chantent les idées des peuples. Des châteaux bâtis en os sort la musique inconnue. Ce sont des villes! Ce sont des villes! Le paradis des orages s'effondre. Les sauvages dansent sans cesse la fête de la nuit. Ce sont des villes!

Quels bons bras, quelle belle heure me rendront cette région d'où viennent mes sommeils et mes moindres mouvements?

Towns

These are towns! This is a people for whom these imagined Alleghanies and Lebanons have been raised! Towns! Chalets of crystal and wood move on invisible rails and pulleys. Old craters, encircled by colossi and palms of copper, roar melodiously in the fires. These are towns! Cortèges of Queen Mabs, in russet and opaline robes, climb up from the ravines. Up there, their hoofs in the waterfalls and brambles, the deer suckle at Diana's breast. Bacchantes of the suburbs sob, and the moon burns and howls. Venus enters the caves of blacksmiths and hermits. These are... Groups of belfries ring out peoples' ideas. From castles built of bone unknown music issues. These are towns! These are towns! The paradise of storms subsides. Savages dance unceasingly the festival of night. These are towns!

What kindly arms, what lovely hour will restore to me those regions from which my slumbers and my slightest movements come?

I iii *Phrase*

J'ai tendu des cordes de clocher à clocher; des guirlandes de fenêtre à fenêtre; des chaînes d'or d'étoile à étoile, et je danse.

Phrase

I have hung ropes from steeple to steeple; garlands from window to window; golden chains from star to star, and I dance.

I iv *Antique*

Gracieux fils de Pan! Autour de ton front couronné de fleurettes et de baies tes yeux, des boules précieuses, remuent. Tachées de lies brunes, tes joues se creusent. Tes crocs luisent. Ta poitrine ressemble à une cithare, des tintements circulent dans tes bras blonds. Ton cœur bat dans ce ventre où dort le double sexe. Promène-toi, la nuit, en mouvant doucement cette cuisse, cette seconde cuisse et cette jambe de gauche.

Antique

Graceful son of Pan! Around your brow, crowned with little flowers and berries, your eyes—precious globes—move. Stained with brown sediment, your cheeks are hollowed out. Your tusks gleam. Your breast resembles a cithara, tintinnabulations course through your white arms. Your heart pulses in that belly where Hermaphrodite sleeps. Walk forth, at night, gently moving this thigh, that second thigh, and that left leg.

---

* Part of the Appalachian mountains; from the West, the Alleghany plateau slopes to the Central Plain.

I v *Royauté*

Un beau matin, chez un peuple fort doux, un homme et une femme superbes criaient sur la place publique: 'Mes amis, je veux qu'elle soit reine!' 'Je veux être reine!' Elle riait et tremblait. Il parlait aux amis de révélation, d'épreuve terminée. Ils se pâmaient l'un contre l'autre.

En effet, ils furent rois toute une matinée, où les tentures carminées se relevèrent sur les maisons, et tout l'après-midi, où ils s'avancèrent du côté des jardins de palmes.

Royalty

One beautiful morning, among a most gentle people, a man and a woman of proud presence cried out in the public square: 'Friends, I want her to be queen.' 'I want to be queen!' She laughed and trembled. To his friends he spoke of a revelation, of a trial concluded. They swooned against each other.

And during one whole morning, whilst the crimsoned hangings festooned the houses, and during the whole afternoon, as they headed for the palm gardens, they were indeed monarchs.

I vi *Marine*

Les chars d'argent et de cuivre—
Les proues d'acier et d'argent—
Battent l'écume,—
Soulèvent les souches des ronces.
Les courants de la lande,
Et les ornières immenses du reflux,
Filent circulairement vers l'est,
Vers les piliers de la forêt,
Vers les fûts de la jetée,
Dont l'angle est heurté par des tourbillons de
    lumière.

Marine

Chariots of silver and copper—
Prows of steel and silver—
Thrash the foam—
Rip up the bramble roots.
The streams of the wasteland,
And the huge ruts of the ebb-tide
Flow away in a circle toward the east,
Toward the pillars of the forest,
Toward the piles of the jetty,
Whose quoins are battered by whirlpools of light.

I vii *Interlude*

J'ai seul la clef de cette parade sauvage.

Interlude

I alone hold the key to this savage parade.

I viii *Being beauteous*

Devant une neige un Être de Beauté de haute taille. Des sifflements de mort et des cercles de musique sourde font monter, s'élargir et trembler comme un spectre ce corps adoré; des blessures écarlates et noires éclatent dans les chairs superbes. Les couleurs propres de la vie se foncent, dansent, et se dégagent autour de la Vision, sur le chantier. Et les frissons s'élèvent et grondent, et la saveur forcenée de ces effets se chargeant avec les sifflements mortels et les rauques musiques que le monde, loin derrière nous, lance sur notre mère de beauté,—elle recule, elle se dresse. Oh! nos os sont revêtus d'un nouveau corps amoureux.

Being beauteous

Against a background of snow, a tall Being of Beauty. Death's wheezing and circles of muffled music cause this adored body to rise, to swell, to quiver like a spectre; scarlet and black wounds break out on the glorious flesh. The true colours of life deepen, dance and detach themselves around the Vision in the making. And tremors rise and rumble, and the frenzied flavour of these effects, being burdened with the dying gasps and raucous music that the world, far behind us, hurls at our mother of beauty, recoils and rears up. Oh! our bones are dressed in a new and loving body.

Ô la face cendrée, l'écusson de crin, les bras de cristal! le canon sur lequel je dois m'abattre à travers la mêlée des arbres et de l'air léger!

Ah! The ashen face, the horsehair escutcheon, the crystal arms! the cannon at which I must charge across the tangle of trees and soft air!

1 ix *Parade*

Des drôles très solides. Plusieurs ont exploité vos mondes. Sans besoins, et peu pressés de mettre en œuvre leurs brillantes facultés et leur expérience de vos consciences. Quels hommes mûrs! Des yeux hébétés à la façon de la nuit d'été, rouges et noirs, tricolores, d'acier piqué d'étoiles d'or; des faciès déformés, plombés, blêmis, incendiés; des enrouements folâtres! La démarche cruelle des oripeaux!—Il y a quelques jeunes!

Ô le plus violent Paradis de la grimace enragée! Chinois, Hottentots, bohémiens, niais, hyènes, Molochs, vieilles démences, démons sinistres, ils mêlent les tours populaires, maternels, avec les poses et les tendresses bestiales. Ils interpréteraient des pièces nouvelles et des chansons 'bonnes filles'. Maîtres jongleurs, ils transforment le lieu et les personnes et usent de la comédie magnétique.

J'ai seul la clef de cette parade sauvage.

Sideshow

These are very real rogues. Several have exploited your worlds. Having no needs, and in no hurry to put into action their brilliant gifts and their experience of your consciences. What mature men! Vacant eyes like a summer night, red and black, tricoloured, steel studded with stars of gold; features deformed, leaden, livid, inflamed; wanton hoarsenesses! The cruel swagger of tawdry finery!—There are youths among them!

Most violent paradise of maddened grimaces! Chinese, Hottentots, gypsies, simpletons, hyenas, Molochs, old insanities, sinister demons, they mingle popular and maternal tricks with bestial poses and caresses. They would perform new plays and respectable songs. Master jugglers, they transform place and person and make use of magnetic comedy.

I alone hold the key to this savage parade!

1 x *Départ*

Assez vu. La vision s'est rencontrée à tous les airs.

Assez eu. Rumeurs des villes, le soir, et au soleil, et toujours.
Assez connu. Les arrêts de la vie.—O Rumeurs et Visions!
Départ dans l'affection et le bruit neufs!

Departure

Enough seen. The vision was encountered under all skies.

Enough had. Murmurs of the towns at night, and in the sun, and always.
Enough known. The decrees of life.—O Sounds and Visions!
Departure into new affection and new clamour!

BRUNEAU, Alfred (1857–1934)

A friend of Zola and a perspicacious writer on music, this prolific composer of operas in the verismo style contributed an impressive number of songs to the repertoire. These include settings of such poets as Ronsard, Gautier, and Silvestre and are seldom if ever performed today. He is best (if at all) remembered for his settings of Catulle Mendès evoking the folksong manner in *couplets* (strophes) such as *Le sabot de frêne* or *L'heureux vagabond*. Also by Mendès are the texts for songs in the pastiche mode, as in the *DIX LIEDS DE FRANCE* (1892) and *SIX CHANSONS À DANSER* (1895), the best of which is probably *La sarabande* in which Cardinal Mazarin makes an appearance, and the poet prophesies that revolutionary mobs will one day dance in the streets. Bruneau's music often has an unashamed socialist slant, or it can be sentimental in the manner of the age (such as his Christmas song, Lavedans's *Le nouveau-né*). When writing in his folksong style he can also, as Koechlin put it, evoke large horizons and a feeling of the open air. Later songs from the large *œuvre* include *Cœur au cré-puscule*, *Brumes*, and *Marine* written variously for such distinguished singers as Croiza and Bathori. These all come from a cycle entitled *CHANTS DE LA VIE* (Saint-Georges de Bouhélier, Gregh, Bataille— 1913).

BÜSSER, Henri (1872–1973)

This long-lived friend of Gounod and Debussy, conductor (with Messager) of the first performances of *Pelléas et Mélisande*, and professor of composition at the Conservatoire was a song composer of modest ambition. Chiefly interesting are his large number of settings of Charles Cros, including *L'abandonée* (1903), which uses the same poem as that of the *Chanson perpétuelle* [CHAUSSON 13]. It is instructive to see how both composers cut the poem mercilessly, Chausson in the interests of brevity, Büsser as a prudish bowdlerizer at the appearance of the sexy bits. Perhaps this is because the work was written for the famous Scottish soprano Mary Garden. The three *DUETTOS* (1900) for female voices are much more light-hearted, and a useful addition to the repertoire; the poet of these, Gabriel Vicaire, also provided the text of *Robin et Marion*, a duet for soprano and tenor.

CANTELOUBE, Joseph (1879–1957)

At the Schola Cantorum, and under d'Indy's watchful eye, Canteloube made a number of Verlaine settings, the most successful of which was *Colloque sentimental* (1903) [DEBUSSY 13 iii] with string quartet accompaniment. He also indulged his taste for orchestrated vocal music from early in his career: *Églogue d'automne* (Roger Frêne), *Au printemps* (originally written for Maggie Teyte, although she did not sing the first performance), and *TRIPTYQUE* (three songs with poems by Frêne) were written between 1909 and 1919; all had orchestral accompaniment on a rather grand scale. The most original vocal work of these years was *L'ARADA* (La terre), a cycle of six mélodies in folksong vein with elaborate piano accompaniments which traverse the whole range of the keyboard. The poems were written in the *langue d'oc* of Antonin Perbosc, and translated into French by the composer himself.

In 1895 Canteloube had embarked on the serious business of folksong collection. This work was crowned by the publication (between 1939 and 1944) of his *Anthologie des chants populaires français*, a collection of some 1,300 songs in four volumes. There are also a number of volumes dedicated to the music of other French regions like Champagne, Touraine, and the Basque country. Canteloube was certainly one of the most important of the French folksong collectors, but it is his fate that he should now be known only for his arrangements of the CHANTS D'AUVERGNE. These appeared in five volumes between 1923 and 1930 (the last *recueil* is generally thought to be weaker than the first four) and have found much favour with velvet-voiced sopranos in search of something tuneful on the borders of popular song. Audiences with a taste for easy listening have always clamoured for more of this music, and these arrangements have even given rise to a film and a ballet. The CHANTS D'AU-VERGNE have always had their ardent admirers, particularly among the singers (Madeleine Grey, Victoria de los Angeles, Kiri Te Kanawa) for whom they have made a perfect vehicle. They have even been compared to Falla's work in the realm of folksong, and it is true that the composer strictly respected the original melodies, reserving his lavish flights of fancy for the accompaniments. On the other hand, the hardy simplicity of this music can often seem lost in the lush orchestrations which threaten to overpower the tunes which gave rise to them. It might be thought that the solution is to perform the works with piano, but that too is unsatisfactory. The vocal score reductions are fussy and difficult, and one misses the highly coloured orchestrations which are as much a part of the music's charm as they are problematic. Singers and pianists should unearth the more piano-friend-ly AIRS TENDRES DES 17e ET 18e SIÈCLES, the NOËLS POPULAIRES FRANÇAIS, or the neglected cycle L'ARADA which was at least conceived for the instrument. The composer has paid for his great, though limited, popularity; his serious and deeply felt opera *Le mas*, for example, is not thought to merit a hearing.

CAPLET, André (1878–1925)

Pierre Bernac used to say that *Forêt* from the Caplet cycle LE VIEUX COFFRET was his favourite song in all the French repertoire. This is high praise indeed, but it reflected a personal connection between singer and composer. Caplet was among the first to champion the young Bernac's singing, and would have established a recital duo with him if early death had not intervened, the long-term result of war-wounds and gas poisoning in the First World War. Caplet was apparently an extraordinary accompanist with a magical command of tonal colour, and this is what one would have expected from such an ardent Debussian (he orchestrated part of *Le martyre de Saint-Sébastien*, and conducted its first performance). Of the composers who followed that master, and attempted to emulate his special world of rarefied and sensual mystery, Caplet is the most important because the most individual.

Caplet confined himself to songs and choral and chamber music in his mature years. Despite being a fine opera conductor (he was at the Boston Opera from 1910 to 1914) he never seems to have had theatrical ambitions, for this was a man of almost legendary modesty and probity. If his music has a fault, it is because it is unfailingly fastidious. This is a source of great joy to his admirers who see in him the quintessential French song composer; his work has about it the aura of the recher-ché, as if fans of Caplet ('who?' asks the average listener) have been initiated to an especially cultivated understanding of the mélodie. But there is a sameness to some of the music, particularly the arpeggio-derived accompaniments in hushed cascades of exquisiteness; and even more than Fauré, Caplet refused to make concessions to public taste, refraining from promoting his own work. Even the best of composers needs a little of that push. He lacked Debussy's ruthlessness and will to succeed, but his best songs are the equal of Debussy's in terms of refinement and acute sensitivity, if not in terms of earthiness and visceral response to the poet's texts. Apart from an early *Green* (1902) [FAURÉ 29 iii, DEBUSSY 6 v] and an exquisite setting of Hugo's *Une flûte invisible* which had attracted a number of composers, including Saint-Saëns, Caplet avoided texts composed by his great predecessors, preferring to look for poets of his own, such as Jean-Aubry, Rémy de Gourmont, and Paul Fort.

Almost all of Caplet's songs are worthy of study. The first vocal set of his maturity is TROIS POÈMES (1908) to the texts of Jean-Aubry. Of the three songs *Ce sable fin et fuyant, Angoisse*, and *Préludes*, the last two are orchestrated. The harmonic complexity of *Angoisse* suggests that Caplet was already acquainted with the work of Arnold Schoenberg (and touches of that master's dark wit and whimsy in his *Pierrot lunaire* mode can also be detected in the later La Fontaine settings). The 1914 setting of Charles d'Orléans's *En regardant ces belles fleurs* (later set by Jean Françaix) and the spare single page of *Quand reverrai-je, hélas!* (1916, du Bellay) are especially beautiful. The latter song was written under enemy fire at the battle front. This and the song *Détresse!* (Charasson, 1918), which was written in memory of a soldier lost in action, are testament to Caplet's old-fashioned determination to serve his country. They surely belong in any anthology of First World War songs, alongside Debussy's *Noël des enfants qui n'ont plus de maisons* and Poulenc's *Bleuet*, not to mention English songs by Gurney and Butterworth.

It is astonishing that some of Caplet's greatest and most concentrated works were written in these years of upheaval. *Nuit d'automne* (Régnier) and *Solitude* (Ochsé) both date from 1915; both are dark and melancholy in different ways and show the composer's anguish in those sad times. The Gourmont cycle LE VIEUX COFFRET dates from 1917. The first three songs in the set—*Songe, Berceuse, In una selva oscura*—are all masterful, but it is the fourth mélodie *Forêt* which is, above all, a must for those wishing to single out one Caplet song from the others. The poem encourages the composer to draw on a wide range of instrumental colour in the piano; the fluidity of the vocal line lends an appropriately rustling magic to the music of the forest. This is supple and full of languor, and generates at the same time a real sense of excitement, even ecstasy.

The year 1919 saw the composition of two works of extraordinary confidence, as if in a way Caplet had been liberated by Debussy's death the year before. The CINQ BALLADES FRANÇAISES DE PAUL FORT are heard increasingly in the concert hall, and justifiably so. The beautiful and succinct poems encourage a pithy musical response, no less luxuriant in terms of pianism, but almost more concentrated than LE VIEUX COFFRET. **Cloche d'aube** is perhaps more of a piano piece with vocal obbligato than a song (complete with the composer's familiar pianistic mannerisms) but the music is wholeheartedly in the service of the poem. **La ronde,** written in a straightforward 6/8 of merry childlike quavers, is less perfumed than the other songs in the set, but rather welcome for reasons of contrast. It seems to breathe an air of post-war relief and a confidence in a new order of friendship between nations. **Notre chaumière en Yveline** is the least individual of the set; the title refers to the *département* outside Paris which includes Versailles and Saint-Germain-en-Laye. **Songe d'une nuit d'été** is an ecstatic nocturne, and **L'adieu en barque** an extraordinarily ornate barcarole, where we can detect the composer's debt to the Debussy of *L'île joyeuse*. Most refreshing of all are the TROIS

FABLES DE JEAN DE LA FONTAINE, also from 1919. Here Caplet writes something that Debussy never did—a cycle of humorous songs. Let loose in a farmyard realm rather neglected since Offenbach and Chabrier (apart from Ravel's *HISTOIRES NATURELLES* of course), Caplet triumphs with sparer textures than usual, and the most delightfully graphic and piquant wit. When he has a story to tell, as opposed to the evoking of atmosphere, the composer marshals his hidden theatrical talents to wonderful effect. This set is perhaps his finest memorial in that it could not have been written by anyone else of his generation. In our own time, both Elly Ameling and François Le Roux have championed this cycle in their recitals.

Mention must be made of a few other songs; for those who are happy to see the intersection of sacred music with the mélodie, the three song-prayers published under the titles of *LES PRIÈRES* (1914–17) and *Prière normande* (Hébertot) are beautifully done, the latter a hymn to the Virgin of touching simplicity by Caplet's standards. Also remarkable are the late *DEUX POÈMES DE CHARLES BAUDELAIRE* (1922), where the composer turns to one of Debussy's seminal poets: *La cloche fêlée* and *La mort des pauvres* are among the last of the important mélodies written to this poet's words—it is strange that twentieth-century composers of songs with piano have scarcely engaged with these texts, despite the fact that Baudelaire's literary reputation has grown steadily with the century. Sopranos and tenors should be warned that these songs are rather low for them; like most of Caplet's vocal output they seem best suited to the high baritone voice, and these particular songs suggest that the young Bernac had already become Caplet's chosen singer. Suitable for high voice is the delectable *Sonnet de Pierre de Ronsard* ('Doux fut le trait') which was written, along with songs by a number of other composers including Ravel, Poulenc, and Roussel, for the 400th anniversary of that poet's birth in 1924. There are also two fine mélodies with flute: in the first of these, the early *Viens!—une flûte invisible* (Hugo, 1900), the instrument is an obbligato addition to the piano part. (This lyric was also set by Saint-Saëns for the same forces.) At the other end of Caplet's career is the exotic *Écoute, mon amour* (Tagore, 1924) which is for middle voice and flute, this time without piano.

1 *Forêt*

(Rémy de Gourmont)

Ô Forêt, toi qui vis passer bien des amants
Le long de tes sentiers, sous tes profonds feuillages,
Confidente des jeux, des cris, et des serments,

Témoin à qui les âmes avouaient leurs orages.

Ô Forêt, souviens-toi de ceux qui sont venus
Un jour d'été fouler tes mousses et tes herbes,

Car ils ont trouvé là des baisers ingénus
Couleur de feuilles, couleur d'écorces, couleur de rêves.

Forest

O forest, who have seen many lovers pass
Along your paths, beneath your dense foliage,
Have been a confidante of games and cries and vows,
Have witnessed souls disclose to you their storms;

O forest, remember those who came
One summer day to tread down your moss and grasses,
For there they found ingenuous kisses
The colour of leaves and bark and dreams.

Ô Forêt, tu fus bonne, en laissant le désir
Fleurir, ardente fleur, au sein de ta verdure.

L'ombre devint plus fraîche: un frisson de plaisir
Enchanta les deux cœurs et toute la nature.

Ô Forêt, souviens-toi de ceux qui sont venus
Un jour d'été fouler tes herbes solitaires
Et contempler, distraits, tes arbres ingénus
Et le pâle océan de tes vertes fougères.

O forest, you were kind to allow desire
To blossom, a passionate flower, enfolded by your verdure.

Shadows grew cooler: a thrill of pleasure
Enchanted two hearts and the whole of nature.

O forest, remember those who came
One summer day to tread down your lonely grasses
And to stare abstractedly at your simple trees
And the pale ocean of your green ferns.

CINQ BALLADES FRANÇAISES DE PAUL FORT

FIVE FRENCH BALLADS OF PAUL FORT

2 i Cloche d'aube

Ce petit air de cloche, errant dans le matin, a rajeuni mon cœur à la pointe du jour.

Ce petit air de cloche, au cœur frais du matin, léger, proche et lointain, a changé mon destin.

Quoi! vais-je après cette heure survivre à mon bonheur, ô petit air de cloche qui rajeunis mon cœur?

Si lointain, monotone et perdu, si perdu, petit air, petit air au cœur frais de la nue,

tu t'en vas, reviens, sonnes: errant comme l'amour, tu trembles sur mon cœur à la pointe du jour.

Quoi! la vie pourrait être monotone et champêtre et douce et comme est, proche, ce petit air de cloche?

douce et simple et lointaine aussi, comme est lointain ce petit air qui tremble au cœur frais du matin?

The bell of dawn

This little bell tune, drifting at morn, has rejuvenated my heart at daybreak.

This little bell tune in the fresh heart of morning, light, near and distant, has changed my destiny.

What! shall I, after this hour, survive my happiness, O little bell tune that rejuvenates my heart?

So distant, unvaried and lost, so lost, little tune, little tune, in the fresh heart of the sky,

you depart, return, ring out, drifting like love, you tremble on my heart at daybreak.

What! could life be unvaried and rustic and sweet, and near as this little bell tune?

sweet and simple and distant too, as distant as this little tune that trembles in the fresh heart of morning?

2 ii La ronde

Si toutes les filles du monde voulaient s'donner la main, tout autour de la mer elles pourraient faire une ronde.

The ring

If all the girls in the world were of a mind to join hands, all around the sea they could form a ring.

Si tous les gars du monde voulaient bien êtr' marins, ils f'raient avec leurs barques un joli pont sur l'onde.

Alors on pourrait faire une ronde autour du monde, si tous les gens du monde voulaient s'donner la main.

If all the boys in the world were of a mind to be sailors, they'd form with their ships a pretty bridge on the seas.

So... we could form a ring around the world, if all the people in the world were of a mind to join hands.

2 iii *Notre chaumière en Yveline*

Chaumière, vos parures sont marguerites, roses:
à vos pieds ces blancheurs, et sur vous ces couleurs.
Chaumière, la nature est bonne à quelque chose:
elle abrite nos cœurs dans un bouquet de fleurs.
Chaumière, cela dure autant que le bonheur.

Our cottage in Yveline

Cottage, your walls are daisies, roses:
such whiteness at your feet, and such colours.
Cottage, nature sometimes serves us well:
it shelters our hearts in a bouquet of flowers.
Cottage, this lasts as long as happiness.

2 iv *Songe d'une nuit d'été*

La rose libre des montagnes a sauté de joie cette nuit, et toutes les roses des campagnes, dans tous les jardins, ont dit:

'Sautons, d'un genou léger, mes sœurs, par-dessus les grilles. L'arrosoir du jardinier vaut-il un brouillard qui brille?'

J'ai vu, dans la nuit d'été, sur toutes les routes de la terre, courir les roses des parterres vers une rose en liberté!

A summer night's dream

The free rose of the mountain leapt for joy tonight, and all the roses of the plain, and in every garden, cried:

'Let us leap, with a light spring, over the gates, my sisters. Is the gardener's watering-can a match for gleaming mist?'

I saw, in the summer night, along all the roads on earth, roses running from their beds towards a rose now free!

2 v *L'adieu en barque*

C'est l'heure où le château s'endort, l'heure où les rames sont si belles, où l'hirondelle entraîne l'or du soir jusqu'au plus bleu du ciel,

où je cache le paysage à mes yeux tout remplis d'amour. Je m'en vais, pleurs de mon visage.—Quittons ces rames pour toujours!

Farewell from a boat

This is the hour when the castle falls asleep, when oars are so lovely, when the swallow bears the gold of evening to the bluest sky,

when I conceal the countryside from my eyes that brim with love. I take my leave with tear-stained face. Let us leave these oars forever!

TROIS FABLES DE JEAN DE LA FONTAINE

3 i *Le corbeau et le renard*

Maître corbeau, sur un arbre perché,
　　Tenait en son bec un fromage.
Maître renard, par l'odeur alléché,
　　Lui tint à peu près ce langage:
　　'Et bonjour, Monsieur du Corbeau.
Que vous êtes joli! que vous me semblez beau!
　　Sans mentir, si votre ramage
　　Se rapporte à votre plumage,
Vous êtes le phénix des hôtes de ces bois.'
À ces mots, le corbeau ne se sent pas de joie;
　　Et pour montrer sa belle voix,
Il ouvre un large bec, laisse tomber sa proie.
Le renard s'en saisit, et dit: 'Mon bon monsieur,
　　Apprenez que tout flatteur
　　Vit aux dépens de celui qui l'écoute.
Cette leçon vaut bien un fromage sans doute.'
　　Le corbeau honteux et confus,
Jura, mais un peu tard, qu'on ne l'y prendrait plus.

3 ii *La cigale et la fourmi*

La cigale, ayant chanté
　　　Tout l'été,
Se trouva fort dépourvue
Quand la bise fut venue.
Pas un seul petit morceau
De mouche ou de vermisseau.
Elle alla crier famine
Chez la fourmi sa voisine,
La priant de lui prêter
Quelque grain pour subsister
Jusqu'à la saison nouvelle.
'Je vous paierai, lui dit-elle,
Avant l'oût, foi d'animal,
Intérêt et principal.'
La fourmi n'est pas prêteuse;
C'est là son moindre défaut.
'Que faisiez-vous au temps chaud?
Dit-elle à cette emprunteuse.
—Nuit et jour à tout venant
Je chantais, ne vous déplaise.
—Vous chantiez? j'en suis fort aise.
Eh bien! dansez maintenant.'

THREE FABLES OF JEAN DE LA FONTAINE

The crow and the fox

Master Crow, perched on a tree,
　　Was holding in his beak a cheese.
Master Fox, lured by the scent,
　　Spoke words more or less like these:
　　'Good day, my dear Sir Crow,
How elegant you are! How handsome you look!
　　In truth, if your song
　　Be as fine as your plumage,
You are the phoenix of these woods.'
At this, the crow grew wild with glee;
　　And to display his fine minstrelsy,
He opens wide his beak and drops his booty.
The fox snaps it up, saying: 'My dear sir,
　　Learn that every flatterer
　　Depends on an audience to live at ease.
This lesson is doubtless cheap at a cheese.'
　　The crow, shamefaced and in troubled state,
Vowed to be tricked no more—a little late.

The grasshopper and the ant

The grasshopper, having sung
　　　All summer long,
Found herself most destitute,
When the North Wind came.
Not a morsel to her name
Of either fly or worm.
She blurted out her tale of want
To her neighbour Mistress Ant,
And begged her for a loan
Of grain to last her
Till the coming spring.
'I shall pay you', were her words,
'On insect oath, before the fall,
Interest and principal.'
Mistress Ant is not a lender—
That's the last thing to reproach her with!
'Tell me how you spent the summer,'
Was what she asked this borrower.
'Night and day, to every comer,
I sang, so please you ma'am.'
'You sang? I'm overjoyed.
Now off you go and dance!'

3 iii *Le loup et l'agneau*

La raison du plus fort est toujours la meilleure,
  Nous l'allons montrer tout à l'heure.
   Un agneau se désaltérait
   Dans le courant d'une onde pure.
Un loup survient à jeun qui cherchait aventure,
  Et que la faim en ces lieux attirait.
'Qui te rend si hardi de troubler mon breuvage?
   Dit cet animal plein de rage:
   Tu seras châtié de ta témérité.
—Sire, répond l'agneau, que Votre Majesté
   Ne se mette pas en colère;
   Mais plutôt qu'elle considère
   Que je me vas désaltérant
    Dans le courant,
   Plus de vingt pas au-dessous d'elle,
Et que par conséquent en aucune façon
   Je ne puis troubler sa boisson.
—Tu la troubles, reprit cette bête cruelle,
Et je sais que de moi tu médis l'an passé.
—Comment l'aurais-je fait, si je n'étais pas né?
  Reprit l'agneau, je tette encor ma mère.
   —Si ce n'est toi, c'est donc ton frère.
  —Je n'en ai point.—C'est donc quelqu'un des
   tiens:
   Car vous ne m'épargnez guère,
   Vous, vos bergers et vos chiens.
  On me l'a dit: il faut que je me venge.'
   Là-dessus au fond des forêts
   Le loup l'emporte, et puis le mange
   Sans autre forme de procès.

The wolf and the lamb

The mightiest are always right,
  Which we shall now set out to prove.
   A lamb was slaking its thirst
   In the waters of a limpid stream.
A famished wolf arrived to try his luck,
  Drawn by hunger to this place.
'Who made you so bold to foul my drink?'
   Said this animal full of rage:
   'You shall be punished for such cheek.'
'Sir,' said the lamb, 'so please your Grace,
   Do not fly into a rage;
   Consider, rather, first,
   The stream where I assuage my thirst
    Is twenty yards downstream,
   Below your place,
It can in no way therefore be the case
   That I am fouling your drink.'
'You foul it all the same,' the cruel beast went on,
'And last year I know that you slandered me.'
'How can that be, if I wasn't yet born?'
  Replied the lamb, 'My mother still suckles me.'
   'If it isn't you, it's your brother then.'
  'I have no brother.' 'Then some relation:

   For you are always plaguing me,
   You, your dogs and shepherds too.
  They tell me I should wreak revenge.'
   Whereupon the wolf dragged him through
   The forest's depths and ate him up
   Without further ado.

4 *Viens!—une flûte invisible*

(Victor Hugo)

Viens!—une flûte invisible
Soupire dans les vergers.—
La chanson la plus paisible
Est la chanson des bergers.

Le vent ride, sous l'yeuse,
Le sombre miroir des eaux.—
La chanson la plus joyeuse
Est la chanson des oiseaux.

Come!—An unseen flute

Come!—An unseen flute
Sighs in the orchards.
The most peaceful song
Is the song that shepherds sing.

The wind beneath the ilex
Ruffles the waters' dark mirror.
The most joyous song
Is the song that birds sing.

Que nul soin ne te tourmente.	Let no worry torment you.
Aimons-nous! aimons toujours!—	Let us love! Let us always love!
La chanson la plus charmante	The most sweet song
Est la chanson des amours.	Is the song that lovers sing.

CARPENTER, John Alden (1876–1951)

This American composer, sometime pupil of Elgar, flirted with the popular elements of the music of his homeland, at the same time as being deeply influenced by the music of Debussy and Ravel. Diaghilev commissioned from him the ballet *Skyscrapers* in 1923, and Carpenter wrote a *Sea drift*, something no English composer after Delius would have dared to do. Carpenter was well known for his settings of Tagore (*Gitanjali*) and Langston Hughes in which he draws on American influences. His French songs (which almost all date from 1910) are written in the style of an enthusiast smitten with impressionism, and determined to be more French than the French. These include Verlaine's *Chanson d'automne* [HAHN 1 i], *Le ciel* [FAURÉ 31], *Dansons la gigue!* [BORDES 2 and also set by Poldowski], *En sourdine* [FAURÉ 29 ii], and *Il pleure dans mon cœur* [DEBUSSY 6 ii].

CASELLA, Alfredo (1883–1947)

Casella spent nineteen years of his early creative life in Paris where he studied with Fauré, and befriended Ravel and Enescu. It was thus natural that before returning to Italy he should have set a number of French texts. There is the sombre *Soleils couchants* (Verlaine, also set by Bordes and Nadia Boulanger) with ever-changing harmonies gliding snake-like beneath the vocal line. This was performed (by Ann Murray, accompanied by the author), as part of a group of Verlaine settings by non-French composers, at a concert at the Théâtre des Champs-Elysées on 8 January 1996 to celebrate the 100th anniversary of the poet's death. There is also a setting from 1903 of Baudelaire's *La cloche fêlée*, a text later to be set by Caplet. The biggest work to a French text dates from 1915. It is *L'ADIEU À LA VIE*, four dense songs about death on the transcendental prose poems of Rabindranath Tagore, rather fashionable at the time, and translated by André Gide, no less. The set is dedicated to Claire Croiza. The piano writing of this truly hybrid work, often on three staves, is formidably difficult. It has the look of an orchestral score, and it is no surprise that the composer rearranged it eleven years later for instrumental ensemble. More approachable are a charming *Sonnet* (Ronsard) and the excitingly fleet *En ramant* (Richepin). The atmospheric accompaniment to *Soir païen* (Samain), with its ceaselessly murmuring semiquavers and sextuplets, is typical of this composer's keyboard writing. Poulenc claimed to have been influenced by Casella's pianistic virtuosity in conceiving the opening of his *Concerto pour deux pianos*.

CASTILLON, Alexis de (1838–1873)

This composer, completely forgotten by the audiences of today, was one of the great 'might-have-beens' in French music. We are familiar enough with the sad story of musicians whose careers were cut short by the First World War; Castillon, from an earlier epoch, distinguished himself in military service during the Franco-Prussian War, but his health was permanently ruined. A late developer and a pupil of Franck from the age of 30, all his music dates from the last years of his short life. Saint-Saëns played his Piano Concerto and Duparc believed in his talent, and claimed to have been deeply influenced by his songs. It was Duparc who introduced Castillon to Franck. Castillon's achievement lies in his synthesis of the style of Schumann (who was a great influence on the French composers of this generation) and a genuinely French musical brilliance and clarity, particularly in the field of chamber music. Noske criticizes Castillon's prosody, and the only surviving songs (SIX POÉSIES D'ARMAND SILVESTRE, 1868–73) are a mixed bag of gaucherie and real achievement. Nevertheless some commentators claim that these are seminal works, and Koechlin thought them important enough to orchestrate. Each of the songs is written for a different voice: the first four are for mezzo-soprano, contralto, or baritone, and the last two are for tenor. This is the sort of vocal variety, perhaps required by the publishers, which we find in Bizet's contemporary collection FEUILLES D'ALBUM. From a musical viewpoint, however, Castillon seems to have been aiming at writing a cycle unified by the themes of transience, unrequited love, and death. In Le bûcher there is a fluidity and a Germanic passion in the piano writing which strikes a note heard neither in Gounod nor in the songs of Franck. The long romantic cantilena at the heart of Le semeur is framed by passages of dance-like music in minuet style, more typically French. In both Sonnet mélancolique and La mer we understand what Duparc meant when he claimed to be in Castillon's debt. In the latter song with its ominously rolling accompaniment lies the germ of wild grandeur that was to lead to Duparc's La vague et la cloche. In Renouveau there is an extended eloquent postlude (andante molto espressivo) and we once again think of Duparc and the closing page of his La vie antérieure. Vendange begins in deceptively light-hearted manner—Bizet might have written the first page. In a manner daring for the time, Castillon weaves and contrasts this first idea with figurations of different mood and speed which are prompted by a passionate response to the name 'Rosa'. It might have been 'Clara', for here is a composer who has not been influenced merely by the melodies and poetic moods of Schumann, but by his actual piano writing, and his way of thinking about texts. It would indeed have been interesting to have seen how Castillon might have continued to contribute to a renovation of the mélodie thirty years after Gounod's first songs. As fate would have it, that role fell to his admirer Duparc.

CHABRIER, Emmanuel (1841–1894)

There is no one like him, this adorable man, and nothing in French song, indeed in all music, which is quite like his music. It must be said that those who are at all sympathetic to the French muse, and who do not love Chabrier as a composer, have not yet taken the trouble to get to know him. True, Cosima Wagner hated his visit to 'Wahnfried': wearing his inimitable cotton bonnet, Chabrier damaged Wagner's piano in an exuberant performance of *España*. The visit was not altogether a success on either side. However fond he was of the music performed at Bayreuth, he declined the heavy German sticky bun offered him at tea, and stuffed it into a drawer containing the dead master's scrupulously preserved shirts. This was also the man (at times, as if engineering a surprising modulation, he liked to appear a country bumpkin straight from the Auvergne) who warned the Princesse de Polignac in a loud voice at dinner of the urinary consequences of eating asparagus. The same individual was the friend of the most cultivated and talented men of the age, and who was welcomed everywhere with joy. Verlaine wrote a poem in his honour; although none of the Chabrier songs has a Verlaine text, there were the beginnings of operatic collaboration. And then there were his beloved painters where the admiration was entirely mutual. No French song composer has been painted by as many great masters: there are two portraits by Manet, and appearances in the works of Degas (*L'orchestre*) and Fantin-Latour (*L'atelier de Manet* and *Autour du piano*). His personal collection of art ranged from Manet's *Un bar aux Folies-Bergère* (hung above his piano) to Renoir's *Femme nue* and Cézanne's *Les moissonneurs*, at a time when few art-lovers had the eye to appreciate the greatness of that painter. Even if he failed to collaborate with the greatest poets in his mélodies, his work was touched by the visual arts to a new and unprecedented degree.

A man of contrasts, then. Amidst all the sunlit energy and overflowing exuberance of his music we hear an undertone of melancholy, and everywhere, whether the music is fast or slow, a tenderness to make you smile at the same time as it breaks your heart. No one has put it better than the musicologist and poet Jean-Aubry: 'He had all the French virtues: good humour, vivid sensibility, the sense of charm without affectation, and an inclination to tenderness that is interrupted by wit . . . There is thus nothing that he fails to elevate, even when at first vulgarity appeared in prospect. He is often on the borderline of vulgarity. But he never crosses it. If he approaches the vulgar it is only in order to raise it.' The man with everything had everything but luck in his career. Many of his works (which later numbered Debussy, Ravel, and Poulenc among their greatest admirers—a fondness for Chabrier has a way of uniting opposing factions) were ignored in his lifetime. Too late to be an Offenbach, and too early to be a Poulenc, the *Zeitgeist* had something to do with his failures, for Chabrier's sophistication was ahead of its time: people were used to composers of serious operas and songs, or to writers of operettas and popular ditties. Chabrier's genius lay between the two camps, and received the acclaim of neither, for he wanted to have his cake (no German sticky bun, this) and invite us to eat it with relish. Why could a composer not be both uproariously funny and sad, and *why not* play on the transition between the two moods with an element of surprise, as one world of feeling dissolves deliciously into its opposite? In this mood of 'Lachen und Weinen', where much of his work appears simultaneously merry and sad, Chabrier was Schubertian; he was no less cherished by a circle of friends than the Viennese composer had been loved and supported by his. As it happened, Chabrier was also Schubert's match in physical stature and embonpoint.

Another perennial problem for opera composers, and one also suffered by Schubert, was deeply flawed librettos. Chabrier had it in him to write a work for the stage which would have been to Paris what *Le nozze di Figaro* is to Vienna, and *Il barbiere di Siviglia* to Milan. But it was not to be. If *Le roi malgré lui* had had a decently worked-out plot, it would stand next to the divine *L'étoile* in the standard repertoire, and if the same perhaps may not be said for *Gwendoline* (the nearest Chabrier came to German stickiness), it is nevertheless true that there are passages of enormous beauty in that work. These are undermined by the ridiculous scenario of Catulle Mendès: in this opera, for example, a Danish chieftain is persuaded to sit at a Saxon maid's spinning wheel and sing a sort of *Harald am Spinnrade* to the dismay of his fellow warriors who burst into the room. Of course Chabrier had certain successes in his lifetime, but few realized the full and unique nature of his musical qualities until it was too late for him to benefit personally. Now there exists for him throughout the world much affection and gratitude. Although Chabriéristes are still a relatively select band, a gathering where mutual enthusiasms for this composer are discovered and amplified over a bottle of wine is always a heart-warming one. That Francis Poulenc, self-confessedly lazy, took the trouble to write a book in homage to Chabrier illustrates his debt of gratitude to a portly ghost who showed him how to cajole, tease, and seduce the French mélodie into the twentieth century.

Chabrier did not actually think of himself as a real song composer, and his own mélodies tend to send up the perfumed effusions of the salon, its singers, and the oh-so-refined sensibilities of its composers. He wrote to his publishers that his aim was to write quite different songs from those of Fauré and Augusta Holmès destined for a rarefied public. (Such a cavalier pairing of names suggests that Chabrier was not really *au courant* with the mélodie's recent developments.) His choices of text would have done honour to a home-spun Schubertiad in that he tended to set the poetry of chums rather than great poetry for its own sake. Even then, it is strange that, as a friend of Verlaine, Mallarmé, and Villiers de l'Isle-Adam, he never chose any of their texts to set to music, preferring the works of less exalted wordsmiths such as Catulle Mendès, and the husband and wife team Edmond Rostand and Rosemonde Gérard, who both contributed whimsical farmyard evocations to the Chabrier canon. The most 'important' text Chabrier was to undertake (though not the best suited to his purposes) was Baudelaire's *L'invitation au voyage* [DUPARC 7]; this setting (1870) has an optional bassoon obbligato and is published complete for the first time in the new song volume devoted to his work in the Le Pupitre series, edited by Roger Delage. With this *recueil* the Chabrier enthusiast is richer by nine new songs from the very earliest years, of unequal inspiration but nevertheless valuable. Among these we find an abbreviated setting of Musset's *Adieux à Suzon*, a poem which Bizet included at greater length in his FEUILLES D'ALBUM, as well as the tantalizingly titled *Ah! petit démon!* (Châtillon), a song in popular style which has some of the marks of the mature master. From 1866 there is a rival setting of the famous *Le pas d'armes du Roi Jean* [SAINT-SAËNS 1] and from 1872 *Ivresses!. . .* (Labarre), an extended *valse chantée*, and a forerunner of *Je te veux* by Satie. Also reprinted in this volume are two later Hugo settings, a serenade entitled simply *Ruy Blas*, and an extended song for baritone *Sommation irrespectueuse* (1880). The Rollinat setting *Tes yeux bleus* (1883), long a favourite of those lucky enough to have the music, is published in the second of M. Delage's important volumes. This shows just how much Chabrier must have loved Wagner's WESENDONCK LIEDER. The early song *Lied* (Banville) is not to be confused with the later Mendès setting, but its delicious vocal line and piquant accompaniment mark it out as one of the most characteristic of the earlier songs.

The established song canon, published by Enoch in a single volume, and available in two keys, is full of treasures. There are only ten songs here, eight of which are in the regular repertoire. The stray outsiders are *Credo d'amour* (Silvestre) which is slightly bombastic with its musical echoes (meant humorously?) of church music in the old style, that of Bach in particular. Because of its text, it is unsuitable for women singers. Chabrier loved the big voices (Wagnerian singers like Ernest Van Dyck were his ideal); a hefty tenor with a humorous sense of self-deprecation could bring these strophes to life without blasting us out of our seats, but where is such a wonder to be found? *España*, based loosely on the virtuosic rhapsody for solo piano (it is very much easier for the pianist here than in its original version) and with words by Adenis, has a certain camp appeal, like Pauline Viardot's arrangement of the Chopin mazurkas. If used in this version, it is best left as a *postres*, an outrageous dessert to an otherwise serious musical repast.

And so we come to the core of the œuvre. ***Chanson pour Jeanne*** (Mendès, 1886) is simply a miracle of beauty, and it is said to have been Ravel's favourite song. It is strophic in the old-fashioned manner of the romance (as are all Chabrier's mélodies) but here the music for each of the verses is subtly varied. At one point the voice chants on a repeated note as if caught in a web of nostalgic memories, and around it the piano embroiders a sensual filigree as only Chabrier knows how. This is inimitable and heart-stopping. The next six songs belong together, having been published as SIX MÉLODIES in 1890. It is these that one finds most often on the concert platform today. The waddling little ducks of Gérard (***Villanelle des petits canards***) have made thousands smile, and the portentous turkeys of Rostand (***Ballade des gros dindons***) mock bourgeois self-importance as effectively today as in the composer's time. Chabrier alludes to Don Giovanni's serenade in the piano interjections as if to underline how inappropriate it is to couple Mozartian delicacy with these awkward creatures. ***Pastorale des cochons roses*** (also Rostand) with its delightfully teasing melisma on 'roses' is both longer than its farmyard companions, and tougher for singer and pianist; it is heard less in recital, lacking the pithiness of the other lighter songs, but this litter has a certain porcine glitter. ***L'île heureuse*** (Mikhaël) is an out and out masterpiece. Poulenc grew up with hearing it performed by Ninon Vallin and Reynaldo Hahn, and a later generation encountered it first on Bernac's recording with Poulenc. The song is an exercise in rubato for the pianist, not only the rubato of dallying and *laissez-faire*, but the impulsive sense of freedom as waves and winds disregard the bar-line and carry the barque ever onwards to its magical island destination of sexual fulfilment. This song seems a most unlikely marriage of influences: the grand sweep of Wagner's *Tristan und Isolde* and the delicacy of Watteau's *L'embarquement pour Cythère*. As such it is typical Chabrier. ***Les cigales*** (Gérard) has an unforgettable tune and a strummed accompaniment which evokes the relentless sound of the cicadas in the southern heat. There is scarcely anything more delicious in Chabrier than the leaping sixth, quasi portamento, on 'que les' followed by those three detached syllables of 'vi-o-lons!' These abrupt changes of vocal register, leaping from a growl in the bass to a swoon in the treble, are one of the fingerprints of the composer's style. The piano interlude which follows this, the basses rumbling, the right hand reaching for splayed chords in an ecstasy of enthusiasm, is also the purest Chabrier. It is this, surely, which inspired Poulenc to the madcap energy of his *Aussi bien que les cigales* (from CALLIGRAMMES). That work is to do with trench warfare (unknown to Chabrier's generation), but equally over the top is Chabrier's ***Toutes les fleurs*** which begins by mocking the sentimental extravagances of the drawing-room ballad, and stays to enchant us; the air is heavy with perfume and languor, the composer tongue-in-cheek. Chabrier laughs at himself when he exaggerates like this, and there is a delicious complicity between composer and audience who both understand how ridiculous it all is. The music gushes and swoons, and at first it seems to be overblown and blowsy. But Jean-Aubry might have been thinking of this song when he writes what amounts to a prose poem in explaining how Chabrier plans his surprises: 'the line waves along and one expects the heart-rending eloquence of love-music for homely company. But a nervous movement insinuates itself, a nervous tremor slips in, and the melodic line is inflected into true tenderness.' The last song is *Lied* (Mendès, 1890), which Poulenc describes as the cheekiest in the entire repertoire. It concerns the strawberry-gathering Berthe and her assignation with an old roué of an elf. It is one of the few songs in my experience which never fails to make the audience laugh out loud at the end of the piquant postlude. Berthe's suitor is both gallant and ridiculous with his 'moustache très fine', and she accepts his offer with enormous good sense, knowing that one must seize the moment—*Carpe diem* in song. The poet divides his text into three numbered sections to show the different phases of the seduction. Thanks to Berthe's pragmatism, *Lied* smells of fresh grass and a roll in the hay rather than tasting of strawberries.

In the Enoch volume there are also three operatic airs. The rules barring this material from song recitals should here be relaxed, so seldom do we have the chance to hear this music, and so delicately beautiful are the *Romance de l'étoile* (from *L'étoile*) and the haunting *Chanson de l'alouette* from *Le roi malgré lui*. And then there is the spellbinding *Ode à la musique* (Rostand, 1890), a choral work which should really have an orchestra, but which should always be performed with piano when enough female singers can be found to make it practicable. 'Musique adorable' is how that work begins, and these words sum up this composer's output nicely. Any chance to perform Chabrier is a chance to be in the company of a beloved friend. Poulenc regarded Chabrier as an indulgent musical father with pockets full of tasty titbits whose music is an inexhaustible treasure house. As he wrote at the end of his heartfelt little monograph on the composer—'Cher Chabrier, comme on vous aime!'

Those familiar with the hilarious and delicious Donizetti parody *Duo de la chartreuse verte* from *L'étoile* will be delighted to find three Chabrier comic duos that one may be forgiven for performing with piano (the orchestrations of the last two are, in any case, lost). The first of these is *Duo de l'ouvreuse de l'Opéra-Comique et de l'employé du Bon Marché* which was written as a send-up of theatrical politics of the time. The other two works need a chorus as well as the two duettists: *Cocodette et Cocorico* and *Monsieur et Madame Orchestre*.

1 *Chanson pour Jeanne*
(Catulle Mendès)

Puisque les roses sont jolies
Et puisque Jeanne l'est aussi,
Tout fleurit dans ce monde-ci;
Et c'est la pire des folies
Que de mettre ailleurs son souci,
Puisque les roses sont jolies
Et puisque Jeanne l'est aussi.

Song for Jeanne

Since roses are pretty,
And Jeanne is too,
All this world's in flower,
And it's the height of folly
To be concerned about other things,
Since roses are pretty,
And Jeanne is too!

Puisque vous gazouillez, mésanges,
Et que Jeanne gazouille aussi,
Tout chante dans ce monde-ci;
Et les harpes saintes des anges
Ne feront jamais mon souci,
Puisque vous gazouillez, mésanges,
Et que Jeanne gazouille aussi.

Puisque la belle fleur est morte,
Morte l'oiselle, et Jeanne aussi,
Rien ne vit dans ce monde-ci;
Et j'attends qu'un souffle m'emporte
Dans la tombe, mon seul souci,
Puisque la belle fleur est morte,
Morte l'oiselle, et Jeanne aussi.

Since, blue-tits, you warble,
And since Jeanne warbles too,
All this world's a-singing,
And the angels' holy harps
Will never be a concern of mine,
Since, blue-tits, you warble,
And Jeanne warbles too!

Since the lovely flower is dead,
Dead the bird and Jeanne dead too...
All this world's bereft of life!
And I wait for a breeze to bear me away
To the tomb, my only concern...
Since the lovely flower is dead,
Dead the bird and Jeanne dead too.

2 *Villanelle des petits canards*

(Rosemonde Gérard)

Villanelle of the little ducks

Ils vont, les petits canards,
Tout au bord de la rivière,
Comme de bons campagnards!

Barboteurs et frétillards,
Heureux de troubler l'eau claire,
Ils vont, les petits canards.

Ils semblent un peu jobards,
Mais ils sont à leur affaire,
Comme de bons campagnards!

Dans l'eau pleine de têtards,
Où tremble une herbe légère,
Ils vont, les petits canards.

Marchant par groupes épars,
D'une allure régulière
Comme de bons campagnards;

Dans le beau vert d'épinards
De l'humide cressonnière,
Ils vont, les petits canards,

Et quoiqu'un peu goguenards,
Ils sont d'humcur débonnaire,
Comme de bons compagnards!

There they go, the little ducks,
All along the river bank,
Like good country-folk!

Paddling and waggling,
Happy to muddy the clear water,
They go on their way, the little ducks,

A little gullible, perhaps,
But they go about their business,
Like good country-folk!

Into the tadpole-teeming water,
Where a delicate weed is trembling,
They make their way, the little ducks,

Walking in scattered groups
With a regular gait,
Like good country-folk;

In the beautiful spinach green
Of the moist watercress,
They make their way, the little ducks,

And though a little mocking,
They're by nature benevolent,
Like good country-folk!

Faisant, en cercles bavards,
Un vrai bruit de pétaudière,
Ils vont, les petits canards,

Dodus, lustrés et gaillards,
Ils sont gais à leur manière,
Comme de bons campagnards!

Amoureux et nasillards,
Chacun avec sa commère,
Ils vont, les petits canards,
Comme de bons campagnards!

Chattering in circles,
Making a terrible racket,
They go on their way, the little ducks,

Plump and glossy and cheery,
With a gaiety all their own,
Like good country-folk!

Amorous and snuffling,
Each one with his lady,
They go on their way, the little ducks,
Like good country-folk!

3 *Ballade des gros dindons*

(Edmond Rostand)

Ballad of the plump turkey-cocks

Les gros dindons, à travers champs,
D'un pas solennel et tranquille,
Par les matins, par les couchants,
Bêtement marchent à la file,
Devant la pastoure qui file,
En fredonnant de vieux fredons
Vont en procession docile
    Les gros dindons.

Ils vous ont l'air de gros marchands
Remplis d'une morgue imbécile,
De baillis, rogues et méchants,
Vous regardant d'un œil hostile:
Leur rouge pendeloque oscille;
Ils semblent, parmi les chardons
Gravement tenir un concile,
    Les gros dindons.

N'ayant jamais trouvé touchants
Les sons que le rossignol file,
Ils suivent, lourds et trébuchants,
L'un d'eux, digne comme un édile;
Et lorsqu'au lointain campanile
L'angélus fait ses lents 'din! dons!'
Ils regagnent leur domicile,
    Les gros dindons.

Prud'hommes gras, leurs seuls penchants
Sont vers le pratique et l'utile,
Pour eux, l'amour et les doux chants
Sont un passe-temps trop futile;

The plump turkey-cocks plod across fields
With solemn and placid steps,
Every morning, every evening,
Brainlessly in single file,
Before the shepherd lass who spins,
While humming her old tunes—
They form a docile procession,
    Those plump turkey-cocks.

They look like plump merchants,
Full of foolish arrogance,
Or haughty, spiteful magistrates
Fixing you with hostile eyes:
Their red pendants oscillate;
They seem among the thistles
To be gravely holding council,
    Those plump turkey-cocks.

Having never been moved
By the nightingale's song,
They lumber and stumble after one
Of their number, as stately as councillors;
And when from the distant belfry
The angelus chimes its slow ding! dong!
They return to their abode,
    Those plump turkey-cocks!

Pompous and portly and partial only
To the practical and the useful,
They consider love and its sweet songs
Too trifling a diversion;

Bourgeois de la gent volatile,
Arrondissant de noirs bedons,
Ils se fichent de toute idylle,
    Les gros dindons!

Bourgeois of the feathered kind
With black and swelling bellies,
They care not a jot for any romance,
    Those plump turkey-cocks!

4 *Pastorale des cochons roses*
(Edmond Rostand)

Pastorale of the pink pigs

Le jour s'annonce à l'Orient
De pourpre se coloriant;
Le doigt du matin souriant
    Ouvre les roses;
Et sous la garde d'un gamin
Qui tient une gaule à la main,
On voit passer sur le chemin
    Les cochons roses.

Day is dawning in the East
With light of crimson hue;
Smiling morning's finger
    Opens up the roses;
And herded by a boy,
A long stick in his hand,
You can see along the way
    The pink pigs pass by.

Le rose rare au ton charmant
Qu'à l'horizon, en ce moment,
Là-bas, au fond du firmament,
    On voit s'étendre,
Ne réjouit pas tant les yeux,
N'est pas si frais et si joyeux
Que celui des cochons soyeux
    D'un rose tendre.

The rare pink of charming tint,
That on the distant horizon,
Deep in the sky
    You can now see spreading,
Does not so gladden the eye,
Is not so fresh and joyous
As the silky pigs
    With their gentle tinge of pink.

Le zéphyr, ce doux maraudeur,
Porte plus d'un parfum rôdeur,
Et, dans la matinale odeur
    Des églantines,
Les petits cochons transportés
Ont d'exquises vivacités
Et d'insouciantes gaîtés
    Presque enfantines.

The West Wind, that sweet marauder,
Brings more than one meandering scent,
And in the morning fragrance
    Of the wild roses
The blissful little pigs
Are exquisitely pugnacious
And carelessly vivacious,
    Almost childlike.

Heureux, poussant de petits cris,
Ils vont par les sentiers fleuris,
Et ce sont des jeux et des ris
    Remplis de grâces;
Ils vont, et tous ces corps charnus
Sont si roses qu'ils semblent nus,
Comme ceux d'amours ingénus
    Aux formes grasses.

Happy, emitting little cries,
They pass along the flowery paths,
Playing and laughing
    With such grace;
And these fleshy bodies, as they progress,
Are so pink as to seem nude,
Like innocent putti
    With their folds of fat.

Des points noirs dans ce rose clair
Semblant des truffes dans leur chair
Leur donnent vaguement un air
    De galantine,

The black specks in this pale pink,
Like truffles in their flesh,
Make them seem a little
    Like galantine,

Et leur petit trottinement
À cette graisse, incessamment,
Communique un tremblotement
   De gélatine.

Le long du ruisseau floflottant
Ils suivent, tout en ronflotant,
La blouse au large dos flottant
   De toile bleue;
Ils trottent, les petits cochons,
Les gorets gras et folichons
Remuant les tire-bouchons
   Que fait leur queue.

Puis, quand les champs sans papillons
Exhaleront de leurs sillons
Les plaintes douces des grillons
   Toujours pareilles,
Les cochons, rentrant au bercail,
Défileront sous le portail,
Agitant le double éventail
   De leurs oreilles.

Et, quand, là-bas, à l'Occident,
Croulera le soleil ardent,
À l'heure où le soir descendant
   Ferme les roses,
Paisiblement couchés en rond,
Près de l'auge couleur marron,
Bien repus, ils s'endormiront,
   Les cochons roses.

And as they trot along,
Their fat keeps
Wobbling
   Like gelatine.

Along the gurgling gutter
They snortingly pursue
The broad cloth smock
   Of fluttering blue;
They trot, the little pigs,
Those fat and playful porkers,
Waggling the flails
   Of their cork-screw tails.

Then when the fields with no butterflies
Emit from their furrows
The crickets'
   Repetitive complaint,
The pigs return to the sty,
And pass through the door,
Waving the dual fan
   Of their ears.

And, when yonder in the West,
The burning sun begins to wane,
At the hour when evening falls
   And closes the roses,
Peacefully at rest in the round,
Next to the chestnut-coloured trough,
Satiated they fall asleep,
   The pink pigs.

5 *L'île heureuse*
   (Ephraïm Mikhaël)

The happy isle

Dans le golfe aux jardins ombreux,
Des couples blonds d'amants heureux
Ont fleuri les mâts langoureux
   De ta galère,
Et, caressé de doux été,
Notre beau navire enchanté
Vers des pays de volupté
   Fend l'onde claire!

Vois, nous sommes les souverains
Des lumineux déserts marins,
Sur les flots ravis et sereins
   Berçons nos rêves!

By the shady gardens of the gulf,
Blond pairs of happy lovers
Have garlanded the languorous masts
   Of your galley,
And, caressed by gentle summer,
Our beautiful enchanted ship,
Bound for the land of delight,
   Cleaves the limpid waves!

Behold, we are the sovereigns
Of the ocean's luminous wastes;
On waves, delightful and serene,
   Let us rock our dreams!

Tes pâles mains ont le pouvoir
D'embaumer au loin l'air du soir,
Et dans tes yeux je crois revoir
　　Le ciel des grèves!

Mais là-bas, là-bas, au soleil,
Surgit le cher pays vermeil
D'où s'élève un chant de réveil
　　Et d'allégresse;
C'est l'île heureuse aux cieux légers
Où, parmi les lys étrangers,
Je dormirai dans les vergers,
　　Sous ta caresse.

Your pale hands have the power
To scent from afar the evening air,
And in your eyes I seem to glimpse again
　　The skyline of the shore!

But there, over there in the sun,
Looms the dear vermilion land,
Where a song of wakening rises
　　And of joy;
It is the happy isle of gentle skies,
Where among exotic lilies
I shall sleep in the orchards
　　And your embrace!

6 *Les cigales*

(Rosemonde Gérard)

Le soleil est droit sur la sente,
L'ombre bleuit sous les figuiers;
Ces cris au loin multipliés,
C'est midi, c'est midi qui chante.

Sous l'astre qui conduit le chœur,
Les chanteuses dissimulées
Jettent leurs rauques ululées
De quel infatigable cœur.

Les cigales, ces bestioles,
Ont plus d'âme que les violes;
Les cigales, les cigalons,
Chantent mieux que les violons!

S'en donnent-elles, les cigales,
Sur les tas de poussière gris,
Sous les oliviers rabougris
Étoilés de fleurettes pâles.

Et grises de chanter ainsi,
Elles font leur musique folle;
Et toujours leur chanson s'envole
Des touffes du gazon roussi!

Les cigales, ces bestioles,
Ont plus d'âme que les violes:
Les cigales, les cigalons,
Chantent mieux que les violons!

Aux rustres épars dans le chaume,
Le grand astre torrentiel,
À larges flots, du haut du ciel,
Verse le sommeil et son baume.

The cicadas

The sun's overhead above the path,
The shadow turns blue beneath the figs,
These distant chirpings multiply,
It is noon, it is noon that sings!

Beneath the sun that conducts the choir,
The hidden songsters
Utter their raucous cries
From what unflagging hearts!

The cicadas, these tiny beasts,
Have more soul than viols,
Cicadas, tiny cicadas,
Sing better than violins!

They revel in it, the cicadas,
On the heaps of grey dust,
Beneath the stunted olive-trees,
Studded with pale little flowers.

And drunk with such singing,
They make their mad music;
And their song soars unceasingly
From the tufts of russet grass!

The cicadas, these tiny beasts,
Have more soul than viols,
Cicadas, tiny cicadas,
Sing better than violins!

On the rustics across the stubble,
The great torrential sun,
From high in heaven
Pours its sleep and balm.

Tout est mort, rien ne bruit plus
Qu'elles, toujours, les forcenées,
Entre les notes égrénées
De quelque lointain angélus!

Les cigales, ces bestioles,
Ont plus d'âme que les violes:
Les cigales, les cigalons,
Chantent mieux que les violons!

All is dead, no sound but theirs,
Frenzied and insistent,
Among the far-flung notes
From some distant angelus!

The cicadas, these tiny beasts,
Have more soul than viols,
Cicadas, tiny cicadas,
Sing better than violins!

7 *Toutes les fleurs*

(Edmond Rostand)

Toutes les fleurs, certes, je les adore!
Les pâles lys aux saluts langoureux,
Les lys fluets dont le satin se dore,
Dans leur calice, d'ors poudreux!
Et les bleuets bleus
Dont l'azur décore
Les blés onduleux,
Et les liserons qu'entr'ouvre l'aurore
De ses doigts frileux...
Mais surtout, surtout, je suis amoureux,
Cependant que de folles gloses
S'emplissent les jardins heureux,
Des lilas lilas
Et des roses roses!

Toutes les fleurs, certes, je les adore!
Les cyclamens aux fragiles bouquets,
Les mimosas dont le buisson se dore,
Et les chers jasmins si coquets,
Et les doux genêts
Dont la brise odore,
Et les fins muguets,
Les muguets d'argent,
Si frais quand l'aurore
Mouille les bosquets.
Mais surtout, surtout, je suis amoureux,
Cependant que de folles gloses
S'emplissent les jardins heureux,
Des lilas lilas
Et des roses roses!

Toutes les fleurs, certes, je les adore!
Toutes les fleurs dont fleurit ta beauté,
Les clairs soucis dont la lumière dore
Tes cheveux aux blondeurs de thé,

All the flowers

All the flowers—of course I adore them!
Pale lilies with languid bows,
Slender lilies with gold-tinged satin
In calyxes of powdered gold!
Blue corn-flowers,
Whose blueness beautifies
The waving corn,
And convulvulus half-opened
By cold-fingered dawn...
But most of all I'm in love,
Though wild rumour
Fills the happy gardens,
With the lilac lilac
And rose-coloured rose!

All the flowers—of course I adore them!
Cyclamen in fragile clusters,
Mimosa that gilds the thickets,
And dear coquettish jasmine
And sweet broom
That scents the breeze,
Pretty, silver
Lilies-of-the-valley,
So fresh when dawn
Bedews the groves.
But most of all I'm in love,
Though wild rumour
Fills the happy gardens,
With the lilac lilac
And rose-coloured rose!

All the flowers—of course I adore them!
All the flowers with which your beauty blooms.
The bright marigold whose golden light
Bathes your hair the colour of tea,

L'iris velouté
Qui te prête encore
Sa gracilité,
Et l'œillet qui met ta joue et l'aurore
En rivalité!
Mais surtout, surtout, je suis amoureux,
Dans tes chères lèvres décloses
Et dans les cernes de tes yeux,
Des lilas lilas
Et des roses roses!

The velvety iris
Which lends you
Her slender form,
And the pinks that cause your cheeks
To vie with the dawn!
But most of all I'm in love—
In your dear lips in bloom
And your round eyes—
With the lilac lilac
And rose-coloured rose!

8 *Lied*

(Catulle Mendès)

I

Nez au vent; cœur plein d'aise,
Berthe emplit, fraise à fraise,
Dans le bois printanier,
    Son frais panier.

Les déesses de marbre
La regardent sous l'arbre
D'un air plein de douceur,
    Comme une sœur,

Et dans de folles rixes
Passe l'essaim des Nixes
Et des Elfes badins
    Et des Ondins.

II

Un Elfe dit à Berthe:
'Là-bas, sous l'ombre verte,
Il est dans les sentiers
    De beaux fraisiers!'

Un Elfe a la moustache
Très fine et l'air bravache
D'un reître ou d'un varlet,
    Quand il lui plaît.

'Conduisez-moi, dit Berthe,
Là-bas, sous l'ombre verte,
Où sont dans les sentiers
    Les beaux fraisiers.'

Song

I

Facing the wind and happy at heart,
Berthe fills, strawberry by strawberry,
In the springtime wood,
    Her freshly prepared basket.

Marble goddesses
Watch her beneath trees
With a look full of sweetness,
    Like a sister's,

And amid mad skirmishing
The swarms of nixies,
Of playful elves
    And water-sprites pass by.

II

One elf says to Berthe:
'Over there in the green shade,
Along the paths,
    Delicious strawberry bushes grow.'

Elves have most natty
Moustaches and the swaggering air
Of a knight or page,
    When the mood so takes them...

'Escort me,' says Berthe,
'Over there, in the green shade,
To where along the paths
    Delicious strawberry bushes grow!'

<table>
<tr><td>

III

Leste comme une chèvre,
Berthe courait. 'Ta lèvre
Est un fraisier charmant,'
   Reprit l'amant.

'Le baiser, fraise rose,
Donne à la bouche éclose,
Qui le laisse saisir,
   Un doux plaisir.

—S'il est ainsi, dit Berthe,
Laissons sous l'ombre verte
En paix dans les sentiers
   Les beaux fraisiers!'

</td><td>

III

Sprightly as a goat,
Berthe ran: 'Your lips
Are a charming strawberry bush,'
   Replied the lover.

'A kiss is like a rosy strawberry
Which gives the open mouth
That is allowed to savour it
   Sweet pleasure!'

'If that is so,' says Berthe,
'Let us leave them in peace,
In the green shade, along the paths,
   The delicious strawberry bushes!'

</td></tr>
</table>

CHAILLEY, Jacques (1910–1999)

This astonishingly versatile musician occupied some of the most important posts in French musical life, and was a major force in the field of musical education. A renowned ethnomusicologist, he took a special interest in the music of ancient Greece. A latter-day Charles Bordes, he also devoted himself to the revival of medieval music, and founded various groups for its performance. As a composer, he was most active before 1960, and if Chailley's intellectual and academic reputation would seem to suggest dry and challenging music, this could not be further from the truth. He was master of comedy, as well as capable of writing serious songs which show a high level of technical accomplishment, with particularly interesting piano writing. The harmonic language sometimes suggests the smoky lyricism of Poulenc in the slower songs, but it can also be tinged with touches of Messiaen. The faster songs recall the elegant acerbity of Albert Roussel. One of the earliest cycles is TROIS POÉSIES DE FRANÇOIS VIL-LON (1934) which, hardly surprisingly, owe something of its musical atmosphere to Debussy's settings of the same poet. Chailley does not seem, on this reckoning, to have a musical voice of his own that is easy to recognize.

However, the SEPT CHANSONS LÉGÈRES, begun in 1949 and completed only in the 1980s are fit to stand next to Poulenc's *La courte paille* as light-hearted settings of the Belgian poet Maurice Carême: *Mon oncle*, *La gamme* (where all the notes of the sol-fa are hidden within other words), *Apollinaire* (which explores the familiar theme of Don Pedro's dromedary [POULENC 1 i]), and *Le crocodile* are all small comic gems. By the same poet, but altogether more serious is the cycle À MA FEMME (1949), which celebrates marital love in four intense songs which are Chailley's answer to Messiaen's POÈMES POUR MI. Also by Carême are DEUX POÈMES SUR LA MORT where the vocal line is supplemented by speech and the musical inspiration stems from Beethoven's superscription to his F minor String Quartet Op. 95—'Muß es sein?—es muß sein!' A more conventionally religious side of the composer is shown by LE PÈLERIN D'ASSISE (Léon Chancerel, 1932), originally conceived for contralto and a quartet of Ondes Martenot; the first song *Chanson de la route* can be sung as a duet in liturgical manner. Also worthy of mention are TROIS MADRIGAUX GALANTS (Voltaire), an elegant group of time-travelling miniatures painted with pointed wit. If it were necessary to choose only one of Chailley's lighter songs, it would probably have to be the enchanting *Le menuisier du roi* (Fombeure), a setting of the same whimsical poet whom we encounter in Poulenc's CHANSONS VILLAGEOISES.

1 *Le menuisier du roi*   *The King's carpenter*
   (Maurice Fombeure)

—Je stipule,   I insist,
dit le roi,   said the King,
que les grelots de ma mule   that the bells of my mule
seront des grelots de bois.   be wooden bells.

—Je stipule,   I insist,
dit la reine,   said the Queen,
que les grelots de ma mule   that the bells of my mule
seront des grelots de frêne.   be ash-tree bells.

—Je stipule,   I insist,
dit le dauphin,   said the Dauphin,
que les grelots de ma mule   that the bells of my mule
seront en cœur de sapin.   be fir-cone bells.

—Je stipule,   I insist,
dit l'infante   said the elegant
élégante,   Infanta
que les grelots de ma mule   that the bells of my mule
seront faits de palissandre.   be rosewood bells.

—Je stipule,   I insist,
dit le fou,   said the fool,
que les grelots de ma mule   that the bells of my mule
seront des grelots de houx.   be holly-tree bells.

Mais, quand on appela le menuisier,   But when the carpenter was called,
Il n'avait que du merisier.   Wild cherry was all there was.

CHAMINADE, Cécile (1857–1944)

For a long while the music of Chaminade was a byword for the faded trifles of the salon, inoffensive music to tinkle in the background of ladies' tea-parties. Chaminade's music may be inoffensive, but it is none the worse for desiring to please and entertain. It is the work of a gifted professional, and the sheer number of her songs, some 125, show a resolute determination to compose despite the pressures on women which made the sustaining of a significant composing career difficult, if not impossible. Incidentally, she was a virtuoso pianist and wrote an even greater number of works for piano, usually characteristic pieces in the manner of *Lullaby of the little wounded soldier*. Her largest work was a 'dramatic' symphony with chorus entitled *Les amazones*.

There are four *recueils* of mélodies which were published by Enoch between 1897 and 1910. A glance through the title pages of these collections confirms a continuing fondness for Fauré's poet (and Massenet's) Armand Silvestre. There is a setting of *Fleur jetée* [FAURÉ 22] where the vocal line is impassioned, but the accompaniment tame compared to Fauré's throbbing sextuplets. More successful is Silvestre's *Amoroso* in the same volume. *L'angélus*, a useful, if sentimental, duet for mezzo soprano and baritone is yet another Silvestre setting. Another favourite poet was Rosemonde Gérard (Mme Edmond Rostand), the poet of some of the celebrated farmyard songs by Chabrier. Chaminade is included in a sumptuous *Album-Rostand*, a collection of settings of the Rostands, man and wife, in which six songs by Chabrier appear, and no less than five of Chaminade's, which is indicative of her high standing in the salon world of the time. These have been well chosen and represent some of her best work: *Ma première lettre*, a sparely accompanied parlando piece in the manner of Hahn; *Tu me dirais*, a mélodie which employs more cantabile, but once again the accompaniment is discreet; *Vieux portrait*, a delicious little pastiche evoking the elegant world of marquis and marquise—here it is the Massenet of *Manon* who comes to mind; *Malgré nous*, more impassioned with a real sweep to the music (although these arpeggios seem to run to a formula); and ***L'anneau d'argent***, world famous and much recorded—John McCormack had a smash hit with this *Little Silver Ring*.

The second *recueil* has some of Chaminade's most popular songs including *Colette* (P. Barbier), *Si j'étais jardinier* (Roger Milès), the jolly *Ronde d'amour* (Fuster), and an amusing donkey's serenade to a text of Charles Foleÿ entitled *Mandoline* which ends 'Elle a dit que je chantais faux, Et je brisais ma mandoline.' Mady Mesplé sang this song to perfection, deliberately going out of tune on 'faux' of course. This is a note of comedy that we do not often find in Chaminade's music. The third *recueil* includes many settings of Charles Fuster as well as *Au pays bleu* and *Le rendez-vous* to poems of Charles Cros. There is something of a revival of interest in Chaminade's piano music, and these songs deserve to be re-heard at least as much as, if not more than, many of the equally neglected Massenet songs.

1 *L'anneau d'argent*

(Rosemonde Gérard)

Le cher anneau d'argent que vous m'avez donné
Garde en son cercle étroit nos promesses encloses;
De tant de souvenirs réceleur obstiné,
Lui seul m'a consolée en mes heures moroses.

Tel un ruban qu'on mit autour de fleurs écloses
Tient encor le bouquet alors qu'il est fané,
Tel l'humble anneau d'argent que vous m'avez donné
Garde en son cercle étroit nos promesses encloses.

The silver ring

The dear silver ring that once you gave me
Keeps our vows enclosed in its narrow band;
Steadfast confidante of so many memories,
It alone has consoled me in my hours of gloom.

Just as a ribbon around blossoming flowers,
When faded still holds them entwined,
So the humble silver ring that once you gave me
Keeps our vows enclosed in its narrow band.

Aussi, lorsque viendra l'oubli de toutes choses,	Thus, when oblivion shall finally come,
Dans le cercueil de blanc satin capitonné,	In the coffin draped in white satin,
Lorsque je dormirai, très pâle sur des roses,	Where, so pale on roses, I shall sleep,
Je veux qu'il brille encor à mon doigt décharné,	On my bony finger I would like it still to shine,
Le cher anneau d'argent que vous m'avez donné.	The dear silver ring that once you gave me.

CHARPENTIER, Gustave (1860–1956)

Surprisingly, the man who wrote the opera *Louise*, (the *première* of which took place only two years before that of *Pelléas et Mélisande*), was an avid composer of mélodies. He responded enthusiastically to some of the greatest poetry of the age, in particular Baudelaire and Verlaine; this suggests a knowledge of Debussy's work, and a desire to paint the poems in quite another manner—on a bigger canvas, and more dramatically. His theatrical instincts, when it comes to putting music to a text, are similar to those of Bizet, perhaps, without that composer's innate sense of proportion and pianistic flair.

Many of Charpentier's songs with piano are to be found in a Heugel volume entitled POÈMES CHANTÉS (all pre-1900) where each of the songs is prefaced by a paragraph of scene-setting by Camille Mauclair (himself represented in the volume with three songs), introductions which do not make the music any more meaningful. The collection begins with settings by a handful of minor poets, but is chiefly notable for Verlaine's *Chanson d'automne* [HAHN 1 i], as well as his *La veillée rouge* and *La ronde des Compagnons*. The last two poems seem not to have been set by other composers of Verlaine, and thus have a certain novelty value, although the fact that they were conceived for tenor, orchestra, and chorus renders these IMPRESSIONS FAUSSES (1894) performable only under special circumstances. Of Baudelaire there is *La cloche fêlée* (also set by Caplet among others) and *La musique* which shows the composer's accomplishment in handling the sweep of the poem. Published separately under the title of LES FLEURS DU MAL (1895) are settings of Baudelaire's *Le jet d'eau* [DEBUSSY 7 iii], *La mort des amants* [DEBUSSY 7 v], and *L'invitation au voyage* [DUPARC 7], where Charpentier seems to throw down the gauntlet to his fellow composers. In this case, however, there is no contest. The mélodie *Les yeux de Berthe* from the same set is more interesting, both in itself and because there is no rival setting by another composer.

A number of the songs mentioned above were orchestrated, and one feels that this is how the composer had first envisaged them. Indeed, it is hardly surprising, considering the scale of his operas, that Charpentier had a penchant for setting poems with orchestral accompaniment with the addition of a chorus. Apart from the Verlaine settings mentioned above, these include the rumbustious *Les chevaux de bois* (Verlaine, 1893) [DEBUSSY 6 iv] and *Parfum exotique* (Baudelaire, 1895), the conclusion of which is a distant choral setting of lines from the same poet's 'L'invitation au voyage'. *La chanson du chemin* (Mauclair, 1893) is a *scène* for tenor and baritone; the funeral march brings Mahler's drummer-boy songs from DES KNABEN WUNDERHORN to mind. *Sérénade à Watteau* is an extended setting (for orchestra or piano accompaniment) of *Clair de lune* [FAURÉ 25, DEBUSSY 8 iii] which finishes typically (an impractical luxury) with 'voix lointaines'. Given in the Jardins du Luxembourg in 1896 in a memorial concert to the poet who had died earlier in the year, it is a rather superficial rendition of a text, where the intimacy of Fauré and Debussy are more appropriate.

CHAUSSON, Ernest (1855–1899)

His teachers were an unlikely pairing—Massenet and César Franck. He was certainly among the most gifted pupils of either, and was acknowledged as such. His place in musical history lies somewhere between Duparc and Debussy, and he can be seen as an important link between their two very different worlds. But Chausson's music does not always radiate confidence in his own star, for it is pervaded by a note of profound melancholy and diffidence. It is this quality of a personality *en sourdine*, a muted and serious response to life itself, which, together with his early death in a ridiculously unnecessary bicycling accident, has prevented his automatic entry into the pantheon of music's greatest heroes. Duparc, a composer with only a small proportion of Chausson's total output, and who proved himself great with so much less music, seems his superior in the Elysian fields of mélodie.

Chausson, unlike most of his contemporaries, and rather similar to a good number of English composers of the Victorian age, was a gentleman of means. He collected the pictures of Renoir and Degas, and was painted by Carrière. He could live without wondering where his next mouthful was coming from, and he was able to travel a good deal. He helped (with exquisite tact) such artists as Debussy and Albéniz when they were in financial difficulties, and was able to maintain a salon of his own which included the great musicians, poets, and performers of the day. But this was not a liberating influence on his own art, for it made him all too aware that the label of 'rich dilettante' awaits the wealthy when they attempt to be more than *mycène* or admiring connoisseur. Fastidious by nature, he was ruthlessly self-critical and pessimistic, and we sense this hanging like a mourning veil over his songs, even if they are in fact masterpieces, or very near it. Never mind, we say, for how beautiful many of them are! Hauntingly evocative, perfumed with a magic which seems both exotic and very French, the composer of *Le colibri* seldom fails to strike his own personal and heartfelt note. These songs lack only the capacity to make us rejoice (even the great Fauré was not afraid from time to time to *entertain* his public); the high-minded idealism of their composer sometimes makes these works appear to have been cultivated (alongside the humming bird's favourite 'açoka rouge') in a *serre chaude*, a hothouse within a monastery garden.

The trappings of Wagnerism are sometimes responsible for this (Chausson regularly visited Bayreuth) but in his case, the mood of *Tristan*-derived longing is refined into something infinitely more French: despite his admiration for the German master, his music is always his own, and this is one of its glories. Any drawbacks arise not from lack of talent or originality, but rather from Chausson's own sense of self-criticism which saps the energy from the music. His concern for the verdict of posterity, as well as of his colleagues, makes him cautious, causes him to dither. So haunted is he by the challenge of proving Chausson to be a composer in earnest, that he forgets the less formal importance of being Ernest, and the joy of it too. Of course, a highly developed sense of duty meant that the composer, religious and high-minded by nature, seldom wrote a frivolous or inappropriate note, for on the whole, some of the early songs excepted, his music is never simply pretty. It has, rather, the beauty of a shy and serious girl who seldom smiles. Chausson's lack of compromise, and an almost painful purity, endears him to listeners who somehow hear his goodness in the music, and his desire to do only his very best for an art which he regards as sacred. It is typical of the man that his only real opera *Le roi Arthus* (1886–95) is about chivalry and ideals, and the chasing of impossible dreams.

The first of Chausson's songs (they date from the late 1870s) are settings of Musset, Silvestre, and Baudelaire; these await publication in modern times. There are two *recueils* of mélodies in everyday use, the earlier published by Hamelle, and the later by Salabert. The Hamelle volume contains his most famous songs, though not always the most interesting; they were written under the supervision of Massenet. *Nanny* (Leconte de Lisle) with its wilting chromaticism, the sentimental but appealing *Le charme* (Silvestre) which seems touched by Fauré's influence, and the popular and palpitating *Les papillons* of Gautier (with its exasperatingly tricky piano part) are charming trifles from 1879–80 that are tuneful and delicate without plumbing the depths. Similarly easy on the ear is *Sérénade italienne* (Bourget) with water-borne arpeggios (which fall under the fingers a trifle too easily to avoid certain pianistic clichés) and a vocal line which any self-respecting tenor would covet. In quite another class are the volume's two uncontested masterpieces: *Hébé* (Louise Ackermann) where Chausson equals Fauré's achievement in *Lydia* (perhaps in deliberate homage) and evokes the world of antiquity with the most simple of accompaniments, and the most classically chaste of vocal lines; and *Le colibri*, as sensuous a setting of Leconte de Lisle as the best of Duparc, and with a sense of the mystery of far-away places that would do justice to Baudelaire's dreams, or Gauguin's South Seas adventures. The 5/4 time signature seems to set the seal on something exotic and out of step with the rest of the world. From a harmonic point of view this song would have been impossible without César Franck's influence on Chausson, but it also radiates a breadth of utterance, calm and ecstatic at the same time, which had been, until now, the special province of Fauré.

So far all the songs we have discussed belong to Op. 2 and were completed by 1882. There are a number of other delights in this *recueil* which date from 1887, including a luminous setting of Verlaine's 'La lune blanche' [FAURÉ 30 iii] with the title *Apaisement*, and *La cigale* of Leconte de Lisle (unusually extrovert and fast in the context of Chausson's normally contemplative songs). Towards the back of the volume sleeps a forgotten jewel, a song also composed in 1887, and later orchestrated. This is the evocative and elaborate setting of Gautier's *La caravane* which is quite the equal of any orientalism by a French song composer; it makes Saint-Saëns's *MÉLODIES PERSANES* seem positively Parisian by comparison. It is a pity that the piano doubles the vocal line as much as it does, and we sense that the composer was thinking of the orchestra all along when he wrote it. Nevertheless it has an astonishing sweep and sway (it undulates across the stave like a camel on the Sahara sands). This would ideally suit a baritone with a high A; it is too low for most tenors, yet the work usually has to be transposed downwards to put it within the range of lower voices. The Hamelle volume ends with two duets from 1883: *La nuit* (Banville) is a gentle nocturne in the Massenet style, later orchestrated; *Réveil* is perhaps more interesting, for not only is it an exceedingly rare setting of Honoré de Balzac (from the novel *Modeste Mignon*), but the progressive sense of awakening is beautifully planned, and by the end achieves something which we have already experienced in *Le colibri*, a sense of exaltation kept under tactful control.

The Salabert volume contains the songs which have yet to find their regular place on the platform; they are more difficult to perform than the Op. 2, especially for the pianist, and they do not have the heart-on-sleeve quality that gives an audience a quick fix of sentiment. But the real Chausson is here, for better or worse, with the lights and half-lights that glow within his music, and the exquisite diffidence that both defines and limits it. In Op. 8 we find gathered together four settings of Maurice Bouchor from different times (the songs were composed between 1882 and 1888, but the collection was not deemed fit for publication until 1897). Of these *Nocturne* and *Amour d'antan* are perhaps the best; the layout of *Printemps triste* seems too orchestral by contrast. *Nos souvenirs* has an extraordinary accompaniment; languid arpeggios stretching widely between treble and bass in almost eccentric manner; the older Reynaldo Hahn was capable of experiments of this type. The heart of this *recueil* is given over to the five Maeterlinck settings, SERRES CHAUDES (Op. 24, 1893–1896). Chausson was working on these while Debussy was still incubating *Pelléas*, and they were given their first performance by Thérèse Roger, the singer to whom Debussy was engaged during the period of his friendship with Chausson. The first *Serre chaude* is the liveliest; the accompaniment palpitates with semiquaver oscillations between the hands, a familiar pattern since the early *Les papillons*, but here the effect is distant and muted. The music is ravishing and subtle, but also oppressive. The languid spell of these mysterious hot-houses with their other-worldly sadness must have remained with Debussy when he created the music for the story which unfolds in the same poet's equally strange and claustrophobic kingdom of Allemonde. This song, actually the last to be written, closes with a quotation from the fifth of the set, an attempt to impose a cyclical shape on a work which is already closely knit by musical and poetic mood. The opening words of the second song, *Serre d'ennui*, encapsulate the cycle's overall colour—"Ô cet ennui bleu dans le cœur". This is moderate tempo, as is the grander, and highly chromatic, *Lassitude*. In contrast, *Fauves las* throbs in gently agitated triplets. But the emotional high-point of the cycle is the concluding *Oraison*, an impassioned prayer for redemption. Here the musical language, influenced by Franck and Wagner, recalls the majesty of those great spiritual outpourings of anguish in Wolf's contemporary SPANISCHES LIEDERBUCH—*Nun bin ich dein* and *Mühvoll komm ich und beladen*.

More approachable, because shorter and more transparent, are the TROIS LIEDER of Camille Mauclair, Op. 27. They also date from 1896 and they have the same sigh of exquisite lassitude built into the music. The first of these, **Les heures,** with its repeated octave As in the accompaniment, is as masterful a musical description of the lassitude associated with the slow passing of time as has ever been written; hypnotic in a different way is the gentle 6/4 undulation of *Ballade* (the swell of the undercurrent reminiscent of Fauré's water music for *Les berceaux*) which slowly builds into a song of real stature. The third song, *Les couronnes*, is simpler and more spare in texture, but no less haunting; it might have been written for Debussy's Mélisande. The CHANSONS DE SHAKESPEARE (Op. 28) date from various years in the 1890s. Maurice Bouchor was a great Shakespeare aficionado, but neither his translations, nor the composer's music, quite capture the pithy and unsentimental nature of 'Come away death' (*Chanson d'amour*) or 'Take, oh take those lips away' (*Chanson de clown*). The *Chanson d'Ophélie* ('They bore him on his bier') on the other hand is suitably distracted and fey, like the third of Richard Strauss's Ophelia songs to the same Shakespeare text (though the songs are translations in different languages of course). Chausson also composed incidental music for Shakespeare's *The tempest* for a marionette production in 1888, and the songs for Ariel (originally accompanied by small instrumental ensemble) are sometimes heard with piano.

In the DEUX POÈMES Op. 34 (Verlaine, 1898) the composer follows the poet where few musicians have cared to journey. For most musicians, Verlaine is above all the poet of the *Fêtes galantes* and *La bonne chanson*, but in the collection entitled *Sagesse* he enters metaphysical realms: the pagan mystery of the terracotta faun and the bourgeois world of an aspiring fiancé are set aside in favour of introspection and seraphic contemplation. (We find this side of the poet's nature also explored in the little-known Verlaine settings of Tournemire and Vierne.) In **La chanson bien douce** Chausson is utterly at home with this mood, and this song which appears to be about the vocal music of Chausson itself, seems to identify with 'L'âme qui souffre sans colère'. The tone of *Le chevalier Malheur* (published only in 1925 as a supplement to *La revue musicale*) is even more unfamiliar to the lovers of Verlaine in music; here it is as if the poet had been set by Duparc, and this is the only Verlaine setting that has the quality of an epic ballad.

Two further fine songs are to be found in the posthumously published Op. 36. **Cantique à l'épouse** (Jounet) is a heartfelt tribute to a wife from a happily married man (this is not found often in song, and only Schumann does it better) which unfolds as a paean of praise, muted by the intimacy of the boudoir. The harmonic world of the composer has developed from the early days (we can even detect the influence of Chopin in the unfolding chains of harmony), but what can seem unnecessarily complicated in some works by Chausson, here strikes the ear as rich and subtle. The same might be said for **Dans la forêt du charme et de l'enchantement** (Moréas, 1898), where the musical path of Chausson intersects with that of Debussy's *Pelléas et Mélisande*, although the hint of depression in the music, like a sad spell hanging over a magic castle, is uniquely Chaussonian. Debussy borrowed this colour from Chausson as well as others, in fashioning the music for the blighted lovers in his opera.

In POÈME DE L'AMOUR ET DE LA MER (Bouchor, 1882–90) Chausson added an important song cycle (it is actually more like a symphony with voice) to the orchestrally accompanied repertoire. The work is a triptych of movements: *La fleur des eaux* with three songs; an *Interlude*; and the final section, *La mort de l'amour* with another three mélodies. The last of these is the haunting **Le temps des lilas,** the tune of which is derived from the orchestral *Interlude*. It has long been customary to excerpt this from the work as a whole, and to include it in recitals. Here is the signature of the composer's moral and introspective art: a ravishing melody, sensual use of harmony that suggests languor innocent of sexual overtones, and a *deuil* that sees in every half-filled glass one that will soon be empty. So much in Chausson speaks to us of paradise lost. **Chanson perpétuelle** (Cros, 1898) was conceived for soprano (or mezzo) and orchestra but it is generally recognized that the version for piano and string quartet accompaniment is more powerful. This brings to mind the chamber music combination, if not the instrumental virtuosity, of one of Chausson's incontestable masterpieces, the *Concert* for violin, piano, and string quartet. The ebb and flow of the music is gently hypnotic, subdued in exquisite half-tones until the final climax. It has something of the same bereft flavour as Duparc's *Au pays où se fait la guerre*, and is related to such other great monologues of female desperation as Schoenberg's *Erwartung* and Poulenc's *La dame de Monte Carlo*. Like so many of the Chausson songs, this is a lament for love flown and past happiness, a familiar theme in his work, and curious in a happily married man. It is as if he feared disaster or mishap amidst such wealth, health, and uxurious contentment. And to the sorrow of all those who love and admire his music, the unkind fates arranged the tragedy which deprived us of more of it.

1 *Nanny*

(Charles-Marie-René Leconte de Lisle)

Bois chers aux ramiers, pleurez, doux feuillages,
Et toi, source vive, et vous, frais sentiers;
 Pleurez, ô bruyères sauvages,
 Buissons de houx et d'églantiers!

Printemps, roi fleuri de la verte année,
Ô jeune Dieu, pleure! Été mûrissant,
 Coupe ta tresse couronnée;
 Et pleure, Automne rougissant!

L'angoisse d'aimer brise un cœur fidèle.
Terre et ciel, pleurez! Oh! que je l'aimais!
 Cher pays, ne parle plus d'elle:
 Nanny ne reviendra jamais!

Nanny

Woods dear to doves, weep; gentle leaves, weep;
And you flowing spring, and you cool paths;
 Weep, O wild heather,
 Holly and sweet-briar!

Spring, flower-laden monarch of the green year,
O young god, weep! Ripening summer,
 Cut your crowned tresses;
 And reddening autumn, weep!

Love's anguish breaks a faithful heart.
Earth and heaven, weep! Oh! how I loved her!
 Beloved countryside, speak of her no more:
 Nanny will never return!

2 *Le charme*

(Armand Silvestre)

Quand ton sourire me surprit,
Je sentis frémir tout mon être;
Mais ce qui domptait mon esprit,
Je ne pus d'abord le connaître.

Quand ton regard tomba sur moi,
Je sentis mon âme se fondre;
Mais ce que serait cet émoi,
Je ne pus d'abord en répondre.

Ce qui me vainquit à jamais,
Ce fut un plus douloureux charme,
Et je n'ai su que je t'aimais
Qu'en voyant ta première larme!

The charm

When your smile caught me unawares,
I felt my whole being quiver,
But what held me in thrall
I could at first not tell.

When your gaze rested on me,
I felt my soul dissolve,
But what this emotion might be
I could at first not know.

What vanquished me forever
Was a more sorrowful charm,
And I only knew I loved you
When I saw your first tear!

3 *Les papillons*

(Théophile Gautier)

Les papillons couleur de neige
Volent par essaims sur la mer;
Beaux papillons blancs, quand pourrai-je
Prendre le bleu chemin de l'air?

Savez-vous, ô belle des belles,
Ma bayadère aux yeux de jais,
S'ils me voulaient prêter leurs ailes,
Dites, savez-vous où j'irais?

Sans prendre un seul baiser aux roses
À travers vallons et forêts,
J'irais à vos lèvres mi-closes,
Fleur de mon âme, et j'y mourrais.

Butterflies

Snow-coloured butterflies
Swarm over the sea;
Beautiful white butterflies, when might I
Take to the azure path of the air?

Do you know, O beauty of beauties,
My jet-eyed bayadere—
Were they to lend me their wings,
Do you know where I would go?

Without kissing a single rose,
Across valleys and forests
I'd fly to your half-closed lips,
Flower of my soul, and there would die.

4 *Sérénade italienne*

(Paul Bourget)

Partons en barque sur la mer
Pour passer la nuit aux étoiles;
Vois, il souffle juste assez d'air
Pour enfler la toile des voiles.

Le vieux pêcheur italien
Et ses deux fils qui nous conduisent
Écoutent, mais n'entendent rien
Aux mots que nos bouches se disent.

Sur la mer calme et sombre, vois:
Nous pouvons échanger nos âmes,
Et nul ne comprendra nos voix
Que la nuit, le ciel et les lames.

Italian serenade

Let us put to sea in a boat
And spend the night beneath the stars.
See, there is just enough breeze
To swell the canvas of the sails.

The old Italian fisherman
And his two sons who steer us
Listen, but understand
No words our lips exchange.

On the calm, dark waters—see,
Our souls may both commune,
And none will grasp what our voices say,
Save the night, the waves, and the sky.

5 *Hébé: chanson grecque dans le mode phrygien*

(Louise Ackermann)

Les yeux baissés, rougissante et candide,
Vers leur banquet quand Hébé s'avançait,
Les Dieux charmés tendaient leur coupe vide,
Et de nectar l'enfant la remplissait.

Hebe: a Greek song in Phrygian mode

When Hebe, guileless and with lowered gaze,
Blushingly drew near their feast,
The delighted Gods proffered empty beakers
Which the child replenished with nectar.

Nous tous aussi, quand passe la Jeunesse,
Nous lui tendons notre coupe à l'envi.
Quel est le vin qu'y verse la déesse?
Nous l'ignorons; il enivre et ravit.

Ayant souri dans sa grâce immortelle,
Hébé s'éloigne; on la rappelle en vain.
Longtemps encor, sur la route éternelle,
Notre œil en pleurs suit l'échanson divin.

And we too, when Youth fades,
Vie in proffering her our beakers.
What is the wine she dispenses?
We do not know; it elates and enraptures.

Having smiled with her immortal grace,
Hebe goes on her way—you call her back in vain.
For a long time still on the eternal path,
We follow the gods' cup-bearer with weeping eyes.

6 *Le colibri*

(Charles-Marie-René Leconte de Lisle)

Le vert colibri, le roi des collines,
Voyant la rosée et le soleil clair
Luire dans son nid tissé d'herbes fines,
Comme un frais rayon s'échappe dans l'air.

Il se hâte et vole aux sources voisines
Où les bambous font le bruit de la mer,
Où l'açoka rouge, aux odeurs divines,
S'ouvre et porte au cœur un humide éclair.

Vers la fleur dorée il descend, se pose,
Et boit tant d'amour dans la coupe rose,
Qu'il meurt, ne sachant s'il l'a pu tarir.

Sur ta lèvre pure, ô ma bien-aimée,
Telle aussi mon âme eût voulu mourir
Du premier baiser qui l'a parfumée!

The humming-bird

The green humming-bird, the king of the hills,
On seeing the dew and gleaming sun
Shine in his nest of fine woven grass,
Darts into the air like a shaft of light.

He hurries and flies to the nearby springs
Where the bamboos sound like the sea,
Where the red hibiscus with its heavenly scent
Unveils the glint of dew at its heart.

He descends, and settles on the golden flower,
Drinks so much love from the rosy cup
That he dies, not knowing if he'd drunk it dry.

On your pure lips, O my beloved,
My own soul too would sooner have died
From that first kiss which scented it!

7 *La caravane*

(Théophile Gautier)

La caravane humaine au Sahara du monde,
Par ce chemin des ans qui n'a plus de retour,
S'en va traînant le pied, brûlée aux feux du jour,
Et buvant sur ses bras la sueur qui l'inonde.

Le grand lion rugit et la tempête gronde;
À l'horizon fuyard, ni minaret, ni tour;
La seule ombre qu'on ait, c'est l'ombre du vautour,
Qui traverse le ciel cherchant sa proie immonde.

The caravan

The human caravan in the Sahara of the world,
Along this road of years that has no return,
Trudges on, burned by the heat of day,
And drinking from its arms the coursing sweat.

The great lion roars and the storm rumbles;
No minaret, no tower on the dwindling horizon;
The only shade is the vulture's shadow,
Sweeping the sky for its obscene prey.

L'on avance toujours, et voici que l'on voit
Quelque chose de vert que l'on se montre au doigt:
C'est un bois de cyprès, semé de blanches pierres.

Dieu, pour vous reposer, dans le désert du temps,
Comme des oasis, a mis les cimetières;
Couchez-vous et dormez, voyageurs haletants.

On it moves, and something green now
Is glimpsed, which each points out to the other:
A cypress grove scattered with white stones.

God, to offer you rest, in the desert of time
Has placed, like oases, cemeteries;
Breathless travellers, lie down and sleep.

8 *Les heures*
(Camille Mauclair)

Les pâles heures, sous la lune,
En chantant, jusqu'à mourir,
Avec un triste sourire,
Vont une à une,
Sur un lac baigné de lune,
Où, avec un sombre sourire,
Elles tendent, une à une,
Les mains qui mènent à mourir.

Et certains, blêmes sous la lune,
Aux yeux d'iris sans sourire,
Sachant que l'heure est de mourir,
Donnent leurs mains une à une,
Et tous s'en vont dans l'ombre et dans la lune
Pour s'alanguir et puis mourir
Avec les heures, une à une,
Les heures au pâle sourire.

The hours

The pallid hours beneath the moon,
Singing unto death,
With a sad smile
Move one by one,
On a lake bathed in moonlight,
Where, with a sombre smile,
They hold out, one by one,
Their hands which lead to death.

And some, deathly pale in the moonlight,
With unsmiling eyes,
Knowing that the hour of death is nigh,
Give their hands one by one,
And all depart in the moonlit dark,
To languish and then to die
With the hours, one by one,
The hours with the pallid smile.

9 *La chanson bien douce*
(Paul Verlaine)

Écoutez la chanson bien douce
Qui ne pleure que pour vous plaire.
Elle est discrète, elle est légère:
Un frisson d'eau sur de la mousse!

La voix vous fut connue (et chère?),
Mais à présent elle est voilée
Comme une veuve désolée,
Pourtant comme elle encore fière,

The very gentle song

Listen to the very gentle song
That weeps but to delight you.
It is discreet, it is delicate:
A shiver of water on moss!

The voice was known to you (and dear?),
But is at present veiled
Like a disconsolate widow,
And yet like her still proud;

Et dans les longs plis de son voile
Qui palpite aux brises d'automne,
Cache et montre au cœur qui s'étonne
La vérité comme une étoile.

And in the long folds of her veil
Which flutters in the autumn breeze,
It hides and shows the astonished heart
The truth, emblazoned like a star.

Elle dit, la voix reconnue,
Que la bonté c'est notre vie,
Que de la haine et de l'envie
Rien ne reste, la mort venue.

It says, the voice you recognize,
That kindness is our very life,
And that of hate and envy
Nothing remains, once death has come.

Accueillez la voix qui persiste
Dans son naïf épithalame.
Allez, rien n'est meilleur à l'âme
Que de faire une âme moins triste!

Welcome the voice that continues
Its simple bridal song.
Come! Nothing so becomes the soul
As making souls less sorrowful!

Elle est *en peine* et *de passage*,
L'âme qui souffre sans colère,
Et comme sa morale est claire!...
Écoutez la chanson bien sage.

It is *transient* and *in travail*,
The soul that suffers without wrath,
And how manifest its moral is!...
Listen to the very wise song.

10 *Cantique à l'épouse*

(Albert Jounet)

Song in praise of a wife

Épouse au front lumineux,
Voici que le soir descend
Et qu'il jette dans tes yeux
Des rayons couleur de sang.

Wife with the luminous brow,
Evening now descends
And casts into your eyes
Blood-red rays of light.

Le crépuscule féerique
T'environne d'un feu rose.
Viens me chanter un cantique
Beau comme une sombre rose;

The magical dusk
Surrounds you in a pink glow,
Come sing to me a song,
Beautiful as a dark rose.

Ou plutôt ne chante pas,
Viens te coucher sur mon cœur;
Laisse-moi baiser tes bras
Pâles comme l'aube en fleur.

Or rather do not sing,
Come lie on my heart,
Let me kiss your arms
Pale as the blossoming dawn.

La nuit de tes yeux m'attire,
Nuit frémissante, mystique,
Douce comme ton sourire,
Heureux et mélancolique.

The night of your eyes entices me,
Thrilling, mystical night,
Sweet as your happy
And melancholy smile.

Et soudain la profondeur
Du passé religieux,
Le mystère et la grandeur
De notre amour sérieux

And suddenly the depth
Of the devout past,
The mystery and grandeur
Of our true love

S'ouvre au fond de nos pensées
Comme une vallée immense
Où des forêts délaissées
Rêvent dans un grand silence.

Unfolds in our innermost thoughts,
Like an immense valley
Where deserted forests
Dream in a great silence.

11 Dans la forêt du charme et de l'enchantement

(Jean Moréas)

In the forest of charm and enchantment

Sous vos sombres chevelures, petites fées,
Vous chantâtes sur mon chemin bien doucement,
Sous vos sombres chevelures, petites fées,
Dans la forêt du charme et de l'enchantement.

Beneath your dark tresses, little fairies,
You sang most sweetly in my path,
Beneath your dark tresses, little fairies,
In the forest of charm and enchantment.

Dans la forêt du charme et des merveilleux rites,
Gnomes compatissants, pendant que je dormais,
De votre main, honnêtes gnomes vous m'offrîtes
Un sceptre d'or, hélas! pendant que je dormais.

In the forest of charm and magical rites,
While I slept, O tender gnomes,
From your hands, good gnomes, you offered me
A golden sceptre, alas, while I slept.

J'ai su depuis ce temps que c'est mirage et leurre
Les sceptres d'or et les chansons dans la forêt;
Pourtant, comme un enfant crédule, je les pleure,
Et je voudrais dormir encor dans la forêt.

I have since known them to be mirage and delusion,
Those golden sceptres and songs in the forest;
But like a credulous child I weep for them
And should like still to sleep in the forest.

Qu'importe si je sais que c'est mirage et leurre!

Though I know them to be mirage and delusion!

12 Le temps des lilas

(Maurice Bouchor)

Lilac time

Le temps des lilas et le temps des roses
Ne reviendra plus à ce printemps-ci;
Le temps des lilas et le temps des roses
Est passé, le temps des œillets aussi.

The time for lilac and the time for roses
Will return no more this spring;
The time for lilac and the time for roses
Is past, the time for carnations too.

Le vent a changé, les cieux sont moroses,
Et nous n'irons plus courir, et cueillir
Les lilas en fleur et les belles roses;
Le printemps est triste et ne peut fleurir.

The wind has changed, the skies are sullen,
And no longer shall we roam to gather
The flowering lilac and beautiful rose;
The spring is sad and cannot bloom.

Oh! joyeux et doux printemps de l'année,
Qui vins, l'an passé, nous ensoleiller,
Notre fleur d'amour est si bien fanée,
Las! que ton baiser ne peut l'éveiller!

Oh sweet and joyous springtime
That came last year to bathe us in sun,
Our flower of love is so far faded,
That your kiss, alas, cannot rouse it!

Et toi, que fais-tu? pas de fleurs écloses,
Point de gai soleil ni d'ombrages frais;
Le temps des lilas et le temps des roses
Avec notre amour est mort à jamais.

And what do you do? No blossoming flowers,
No bright sun, and no cool shade;
The time for lilac and the time for roses
With our love has perished for evermore.

13 *Chanson perpétuelle*
(Charles Cros)

Song without end

Bois frissonnants, ciel étoilé,
Mon bien-aimé s'en est allé,
Emportant mon cœur désolé!

Quivering woods, starlit sky,
My beloved has gone away,
Carrying off my desolate heart!

Vents, que vos plaintives rumeurs,
Que vos chants, rossignols charmeurs,
Aillent lui dire que je meurs!

Winds, let your plaintive sounds,
Bewitching nightingales, let your songs
Tell him I am dying!

Le premier soir qu'il vint ici
Mon âme fut à sa merci.
De fierté je n'eus plus souci.

The first evening he came here,
My soul was at his mercy.
I cared no more for pride.

Mes regards étaient pleins d'aveux.
Il me prit dans ses bras nerveux
Et me baisa près des cheveux.

My eyes were full of love,
He took me in his strong arms
And kissed me about the brow.

J'en eus un grand frémissement;
Et puis, je ne sais plus comment
Il est devenu mon amant.

I was seized by a great trembling;
And then, I no longer know how
He became my lover.

Je lui disais: 'Tu m'aimeras
Aussi longtemps que tu pourras!'
Je ne dormais bien qu'en ses bras.

I said to him: 'Love me
As long as you can!'
Only in his arms could I sleep soundly.

Mais lui, sentant son cœur éteint,
S'en est allé l'autre matin,
Sans moi, dans un pays lointain.

But he, feeling his heart grown cold,
Went away one morning
Without me, to a distant land.

Puisque je n'ai plus mon ami,
Je mourrai dans l'étang, parmi
Les fleurs, sous le flot endormi.

Since I no longer have my lover,
I shall die in the pool among
The flowers beneath the still water.

Sur le bord arrivée, au vent
Je dirai son nom, en rêvant
Que là je l'attendis souvent.

Halting on the edge, to the winds
I'll speak his name, dreaming
That there I often awaited him.

Et comme en un linceul doré,
Dans mes cheveux défaits, au gré
Du vent je m'abandonnerai.

And as if in a golden shroud,
With my flowing hair about me, to the will
Of the wind I'll abandon myself.

Les bonheurs passés verseront
Leur douce lueur sur mon front;
Et les joncs verts m'enlaceront.

Past joys will shed
Their gentle light on my brow,
And the green rushes will entwine me.

Et mon sein croira, frémissant
Sous l'enlacement caressant,
Subir l'étreinte de l'absent.

And my breast shall believe, trembling
Beneath enfolding arms,
It feels the absent one's embrace.

COLLET, Henri (1885–1951)

Collet is best known in English-speaking countries as the critic who, in 1920, compared a group of young French composers to the Russian group known as The Five by dubbing them Les Six (Auric, Durey, Honegger, Milhaud, Poulenc, and Tailleferre). In fact Collet was more than just the author of this chic witticism: he was a serious and accomplished composer who specialized in Spanish music. He was a teacher of Spanish as well as a musicologist. One thinks of another critic of the time, G. Jean-Aubry, who was also an esteemed poet, and it is all too easy to bemoan the passing of an age where critics themselves were prepared to put their own heads and reputations as artists on the executioner's block. Collet was a friend of Albéniz, Granados, Turina, and Mompou. Amongst many other works (including an opera, operettas, and ballets), he composed some sixty mélodies.

Collet's teachers included Séverac, Pedrell, and Falla, so it is little wonder that the majority of his output should have been related to the Spanish repertoire (folksong arrangements from Castille and Burgos are highly effective), even if all of these works have French translations. His most important French cycle is CINQ POÈMES DE FRANCIS JAMMES (1920). These songs show the influence of Fauré and Roussel but are sufficiently individual and technically assured for us to regret that Collet's name should now be so utterly unknown. Falla admitted to Collet that the third of these songs—*Ce sont de grandes lignes paisibles*—gave him the melodic idea for the first bars of his *Nuits dans les jardins d'Espagne*. There could surely be no higher compliment to Collet's success in adopting a foreign culture as his own.

CRAS, Jean (1879–1932)

This is almost an unknown name, particularly in English-speaking countries, but Cras was a composer of rare accomplishment. He was a protégé of Duparc (long after that composer had ceased to write songs) and like Roussel he was a professional sailor. Unlike Roussel, however, he remained in the navy until his premature death, and achieved the rank of rear-admiral. His most important orchestral work is *Journal de bord* (1927), judged by some to be a masterpiece, which, as the name implies, draws on his seafaring experience. Like Rimsky-Korsakov and Roussel, and also perhaps because a life on the ocean wave was their common destiny, Cras was attracted to the East for the subject matter of his songs. There is, however, a certain derivative tone in some of the music which looks back to the exoticism of Ravel's SHÉHÉRAZADE. In the cycle LA FLÛTE DE PAN, Cras appears not only to have adopted its title from Debussy, but also to have borrowed the idea of a cycle for voice and chamber ensemble from Ravel's Mallarmé or MADÉCASSE cycles. On the other hand these orientalisms seem more authentic than many of the time (the Arabian-inspired songs of Louis Aubert for example). The four songs of LA FLÛTE DE PAN (Lucien Jacques, 1928) are *Invention de la flûte, Don de la flûte* (where this is a quotation from Mussorgsky's *Boris*), *Le signal de la flûte* and *Le retour de la flûte*. These are scored for soprano, pan pipes (with only seven notes), violin, viola, and cello.

Another of the main cycles is CINQ ROBAIYAT (translations of Omar Khayyám by Franz Toussaint, 1924), which is arguably his most compelling vocal work in terms of the orchestral demands of the piano writing. It seems a culmination of the composer's oriental experiments. In FONTAINES (Lucien Jacques, 1923) the vocal line is equally assured, the piano writing equally demanding and effective. The SEPT MÉLODIES dedicated to 'mon maître bien aimé Henri Duparc' are much earlier songs (1900–5). This set includes two Verlaine settings, *L'espoir luit* and *Le son du cor* [DEBUSSY 9 ii], and concludes with *Correspondances* ('La nature est un temple'), a complex Baudelaire song written at a time when this poet was regarded as passé by some of the younger generation. This shows the influence of Duparc of course, doyen of Baudelaire composers. ÉLÉGIES (Samain, 1910) is a set of four songs with piano or orchestral accompaniment. Also of note is L'OFFRANDE LYRIQUE (1920), six settings of Tagore translated by André Gide, poems which enjoyed a considerable vogue with composers of the time. In the midst of music of this rich complexity, one should not forget that Cras could also write simple and direct music: TROIS NOËLS (1928) is a set of Christmas dialogues between several voices, and TROIS CHANSONS BRETONNES are simple strophic songs from the composer's native Brittany, all the more touching because they were written in the last year of his life.

Cras's songs are an example of music from the 1920s which resolutely refused to travel with the prevailing neo-classical (and some would say simplistic) ethic of Les Six. Without the musical reputation or influence of a name like Caplet's behind it, the music has suffered from seeming too serious (and somewhat old-fashioned) for the prevailing new-music tastes of the time. The failure of these songs to establish themselves in the mainstream repertoire has led to them remaining more or less unknown to this day outside France.

DAMASE, Jean-Michel (b. 1928)

At least five song sets by this Bordelais composer and pianist are worthy of note. The TROIS CHANSONS DE CHARLES D'ORLÉANS (1951) is a fine cycle for baritone, very much in the Poulenc style, and useful for recitalists building a mixed group of settings of that poet. The debt to Poulenc's gentle accompaniments in flowing quavers is also evident in NO EXIT (Paul Gilson), a cycle of French songs with English titles (*Absent-minded, O nightingale, Remembrance, San Francisco night*, and so on). The last of these poems was also set by Dutilleux. The little cycle JEUX DE L'AMOUR is in three sections—in effect, one continuous piece: the first two of these are reminiscent of Poulenc's late manner, the third more like the spiky, clockwork moto perpetuo style of Jean Françaix. DEUX POÈMES (Henry Jacqueton) is a later set and written for baritone; the second of these songs is an admirable scherzo entitled *Masques*. In rather a different style, more like the populist settings of Kosma, are the very much more recent CHANSONS DE MARS ET DE MAI, with poems by Jacques Prévert.

DANIEL-LESUR (b. 1908)

This composer (he was originally simply Daniel Lesur before coining his two names into one) was a fellow member with Jolivet, Messiaen, and others of La Jeune France, a group formed in 1936, which promulgated a 'return to the human', and a resistance to the neo-classicism fashionable at the time. An admiration for such composers as Tournemire and a respect for folksong ensured that Daniel-Lesur's work was more diatonic and conventional than his avant-garde colleagues. Nevertheless his friendship with Messiaen is evident in his songs; indeed the TROIS POÈMES DE CÉCILE SAUVAGE (1939) are settings of poetry by that composer's mother. They are dedicated to Geneviève Touraine, just as the rather more complex cycle CLAIR COMME LE JOUR (Claude Roy, 1945) is dedicated to Gérard Souzay. This pair of singers, sister and brother, were important supporters of new music, who encouraged the songwriting of Jacques Leguerney, among others, at the same time.

Perhaps the most characteristic of Daniel-Lesur's songs is the collection entitled BERCEUSE À TENIR ÉVEILLÉ (René de Obaldia, 1947), a set which is reminiscent of Britten's CHARM OF LULLABIES in its assembly of songs of sleep in various moods and speeds. Here the similarity ends, however, for this is a work where both the musical and poetic styles suggest Messiaen on a much smaller (and easier) scale. In Berceuse à réveiller les morts for example, the octave doublings between voice and piano in strident fanfare as well as the text ('Violente chair autour de mes os | Trompettes du sang | Montagnes d'oiseaux') could only have been set as a homage to that composer's Quatuor pour la fin du temps. Thank-you letters from Lesur's two children Béatrice and Christian were set to music by Jacques Menasce (q.v.).

DAVID, Félicien (1810–1876)

If the credit for setting the first romantic poets goes to Monpou, Félicien David was the first to introduce the oriental note into French song, a rich seam of inspiration which was to be mined by countless others. Surprisingly enough David's interest was not awoken by Hugo's Les orientales, but by personal experience: he visited Egypt in 1832 and stayed in Cairo for two years. He took a small travelling piano with him, and it was there that he began to compose songs influenced by his surroundings. He is best known for his 'ode-symphonie' Le désert (1844) and for his operas La perle de Brésil and Lalla-Roukh, but his songs (written between 1836 and 1866) found much favour, particularly such mélodies as Le bédouin (Cognat), Sultan Mahmoud (Gautier), and one of the best of David's songs—prophetic of Fauré's cantabile style—Tristesse de l'odalisque (Gautier). A collection of fifty mélodies was published by Gérard in 1866 and this included the majority of the cycle LES PERLES D'ORIENT which was composed in 1846. The first songs in the set, Reviens, reviens! as well as La chanson du pêcheur (both Gautier), had been set by Berlioz in LES NUITS D'ÉTÉ [BERLIOZ 3 iv, 3 iii], but David seems to have learned nothing from the older composer's daring and deeply felt response. In addition to the eastern influence David also looked towards Vienna: some of the songs, such as the once popular Les hirondelles (Banville wrote a new poem to fit the tune) and Plaintes amoureuses, show a Schubertian affinity. *Gronde, océan!*, written for bass voice, and with a stormy accompaniment, owes something to Schubert's *Der Atlas*.

Another important poet for this composer was Lamartine. David's setting of that poet's *Le jour des morts* is a noble plaint for baritone and orchestra which Fritz Noske counts as 'among the most remarkable French songs of the Romantic era'. Although Niedermeyer's *Le lac* is normally credited with having brought Lamartine to Gounod's attention, there is no doubt that *Le jour des morts* also played its part in encouraging the younger composer to turn to the spacious strophes of that poet. Gounod set *Le soir* and *Le vallon* in the grand and lofty manner of David at his most ambitious. Despite real achievements, David was not truly an innovator; his songwriting is too often staid and owes too much to the strophic romance and the salon. One feels that, had he been born twenty years later, his undoubted talent for putting words to music might have blossomed to a greater degree.

DEBUSSY, Claude (1862–1918)

Asked what place this composer should be accorded in French song, one would be tempted to adapt Jerome Kern on Irving Berlin, and say that Debussy *is* French song. If there is one composer who seems to encapsulate both the most delicate and passionate aspects of the mélodie, whose command of literature ranges from the lyrics of the salon to the greatest of French poetry, both new and old, and whose musical mastery is equal to the demands of the greatest texts, it is this mysterious man, as enigmatic in many ways as his greatest dramatic creations, Pelléas and Mélisande. It is the style of *his* music, not Fauré's, which musical humorists like Anna Russell have parodied, and which has come to encapsulate what foreigners take to be the decadent *fin-de-siècle* charms of French song. Of course it is outrageously easy to play a few whole-tone chords under a preciously intoned vocal line (Fauré's style is almost impossible to mock in such a way). But this immediate popular identification with a musical characteristic, however degraded and simplified, and the fact that Debussy's music almost always sounds like Debussy, is a measure of how effortlessly he stands at the top of the list as French song incarnate—turn of the century musical France personified.

In some ways the new direction he forced on French music obscured Fauré's true importance as far as the ordinary public was concerned, but one soon realizes how futile such comparisons between two great composers are. Fauré had links, through his teacher Saint-Saëns, with a musical world which was a tone's throw from composers like Berlioz and Gounod, and he was in every sense their successor; one can hear the laying-on of hands at the keyboard as one reads through Fauré's first *recueil*. Debussy on the other hand is a rank outsider, a revolutionary who was not expected to take a seat in the cabinet, much less become prime minister. His direct antecedents were less distinguished than Fauré's, and he stole from them unashamedly while he established his ascendancy. His songwriting starts off in a strangely suburban manner where his style owes much to Massenet (*Voici le printemps* would have been impossible without the model of Massenet's *Si tu veux, Mignonne*) and salon composers like the Hillemacher brothers, at least one of whose works he possibly passed off as his own during his visit to Russia as a teenager. But this was soon to change. The inspiration he derived from Russian composers, and the exceptional range of his general culture, helped provide new ingredients for a musical Molotov cocktail which exploded onto the Parisian musical scene, and little by little, as one work followed another in a war of attrition, established a new order—at least until that was toppled, in turn, by a real Russian revolution—Stravinsky, aided by Cocteau and Les Six. The influence of Érik Satie was crucially important, and largely unacknowledged. That the new aesthetic which Debussy proposed and imposed should still be considered paradigmatic of French art song as it is perceived by the rest of the world is a mark of that most typical of twentieth-century artistic figures, the guerrilla fighter, like Picasso for example, who quickly and imperceptibly becomes a classic.

The composer's background was unusual in that he seems to have been a cuckoo in a rather banal nest, a not particularly musical, lower-middle-class household where his father was a jack-of-all-trades (he had been imprisoned briefly for his activities during the Commune of 1871), and his mother a seamstress. Despite his extraordinary culture, there is a ruthless and self-possessed side to Debussy's nature which is a sign of the boy from the wrong side of the tracks who has glimpsed poverty and decided firmly against it. He was determined to get on at all costs, and to play the establishment at their own game; here is the paradox of the dreamer, the quintessential poet-musician being the same person as the opportunist who would be accused of using people, especially women, for his own ends.

One of the most important influences on his early life was his piano teacher Mme Mauté, the mother-in-law of Verlaine. Thus right from the beginning his destiny seems linked to poetry. One can only wonder whether the child received a whiff of the scandal which had erupted when the poet left his wife for Arthur Rimbaud, and embarked on his crazy period of vagabondage. Such a story might have made the youngster imagine the poet-beyond-the-pale as an utterly exotic bohemian, living the free and louche life which was despised by the bourgeois, and which others could only dream about. There is something about Debussy which is a street Arab and at one with the outsider. A special affinity with this particular poet seems borne out in the way in which he approached the ARIETTES OUBLIÉES some years later, and kept Verlaine at the heart of his career as a writer of songs. In any case, Mme Mauté paved the way for the young Claude to be admitted to the Conservatoire by the age of 10, where he studied with Marmontel, the first of a long list of teachers which included César Franck for a short and unsuccessful spell. Once he was placed in these official channels, there was no doubting that his talent would be recognized. He had first hoped to be a solo pianist, and by the age of 12 was able to do battle with Chopin's F minor Concerto. By the age of 16 and 17 he had not developed quite as he had hoped; he probably lacked the tunnel vision required of the young virtuoso bent on perfecting his technique.

Instead, like many pianists out of work before and after him, he played for singing lessons, and at the classes of Mme Moreau-Sainti he fell in love with the human voice, and with one singer in particular. *Nuit d'étoiles* (1880) is not the first Debussy song (earlier mélodies have disappeared or remain fragments) but it was the composer's first published composition, and it is dedicated to Mme Moreau-Sainti. Even here, amidst the salon commonplaces and the fascination with the dreamy world of Massenet, there are early signs of Debussian individuality and wilfulness. It was not long, however, before he was directing his attentions to one of the teacher's pupils. Here we have the classic case of a teenage boy embarking on an affair with an older woman who was haughty, bored with her husband, and flattered to be the object of adoration by a talented young musician. Among the first songs to be composed for this coloratura soprano, Marie-Blanche Vasnier, were *Caprice* and *Rêverie*; like *Nuit d'étoiles* they are both settings of Théodore de Banville, a poet who remained important in the composer's life for some time.

Just before this affair, and by a strange quirk of musical history, Debussy was hired to be a part of the musical entourage (a piano trio of young musicians) of Nadezhda von Meck, the 'beloved friend' and patroness of Tchaikovsky. In 1880–1 he stayed in her villas in Florence and Switzerland, and got to know the songs of Borodin and something of Rimsky-Korsakov's music. He allegedly also visited Vienna during this period, where he heard *Tristan und Isolde* for the first time, but he later allowed a veil of mystery to descend over this period. All through his life Debussy was an avid visitor to cultural events of every kind, and there is no doubt he absorbed much on these early travels that helped him to grow beyond the salon style of his early work. In the summer of 1881 he visited Moscow itself, where he seems to have been over-fond of one of the Meck daughters, and not fond enough of Tchaikovsky's music for Mme von Meck's liking. Nevertheless he brought back with him a knowledge of Mussorgsky's *Boris Godunov,* and with it, the seeds of *Pelléas et Mélisande.*

Even after he had won the Prix de Rome in 1884, the affair with Mme Vasnier continued unabated, and the spate of songs is evidence of this. More than half of his total output of mélodies (some forty-seven items) were composed between 1879 and 1887. Astonishingly for the output of a great composer, much of the material has not been easily available for performers until very recently. While the early Fauré songs are almost all to be found with ease, Debussy's first efforts, probably because of his lack of enthusiasm for them later in his life, long remained alluring titles in a work-list. The composer published extremely selectively. Thus *Fleur des blés* (Girod), the giddy and swirling *Mandoline* (Verlaine), **Beau soir,** and *Romance* (both Bourget) were published, but a host of other songs languished in manuscript in the Bibliothèque nationale and elsewhere. As recently as 1969 four of these were collected under the title of QUATRE CHANSONS DE JEUNESSE (not the composer's title of course, and not to be thought of as a cycle). We were thus first introduced to the real world of the Vasnier songs, high in tessitura, charmingly effective, and written as display pieces for a woman approaching middle age who still liked to play the coquette. There is Verlaine's **Pantomime** with its floating stratospheric peroration; a most elegant *Clair de lune* (also Verlaine) which was superseded by the later setting of 1891 [DEBUSSY 8 iii] but which has its own merits as a gracious minuet; Banville's **Pierrot,** based on a racy allusion to the folksong 'Au clair de la lune', and incorporating a mention of a famous stage Pierrot, the actor Jean Gaspard Deburau, later the subject of a play by Sacha Guitry and a film by Marcel Carné (*Les enfants du paradis*) with Jean-Louis Barrault; the set ends with **Apparition** (1884), an astonishingly sophisticated song, over-sweet in the Massenet manner in parts, but which suddenly sprouts Debussian wings in the final pages. The choice of poet is also unusually sophisticated for the period—Stéphane Mallarmé. Of the other poets set in this period mention should be made of Armand Renaud whose *Flots, palmes, sables* comes from the same set of poems which inspired Saint-Saëns to his MÉLODIES PERSANES, and Leconte de Lisle whose *Chansons écossaises* were plundered for two texts set also by Paladilhe: *Jane,* and *La fille aux cheveux de lin,* the latter first a song, and later a piano piece.

In 1980 Salabert issued a new Debussy volume entitled *Chansons.* This is nothing less than a shortened version of the Vasnier songbook, a volume of songs gathered together by the composer for his beloved Blanche before his departure for Rome, much in the manner that Schubert made a collection of songs for Therese Grob in 1816, and Schumann for Clara Wieck in 1840. Here we find the bizarrely necrophiliac *Coquetterie posthume* (Gautier) and *Chanson espagnole* (1883), a very tricky duet setting for two high voices of a truncated version of Musset's *Les filles de Cadix* (originally *Les filles de Madrid*) [DELIBES 1]. (In the same mock-Spanish mode the composer also set *Séguidille* by Gautier which Falla was later to put to music magnificently [FALLA 1 iii].) All the rest of the songs in the volume are settings of Paul Bourget, whose collection *Les aveux* must have been a favourite of Blanche Vasnier. Here we find *Romance* (not the famous one of 1886), *Musique, Regrets*, and early versions of two songs which were subsequently published and have been performed more often: *Paysage sentimental* and *Voici le printemps*. The most ambitious song in the *recueil* is *Romance d'Ariel* (1884), which should be sung only by a singer at home in the stratosphere. Apart from Edition Peters's efforts to impose Germanic order on this chaotic output by publishing a collection of Bourget songs, and one of 'Lieder nach verschiedenen Dichtern', further Vasnier-inspired songs were published by Jobert in 1984 under the title SEPT POÈMES DE BANVILLE. The titles of these are *Rêverie, Souhait, Le lilas, Sérénade, Il dort encore, Les roses*, and *Fête galante*, the last of course having no relation to the Verlaine settings of the same name. Once again the tessitura bears witness to a devoted admirer of a particular singer's art, working to find various means to fit a voice and personality. Nevertheless we have the impression that the composer is gradually finding his aesthetic thanks to the medium of song; indeed song is the workshop of the Debussian imagination, the means, thanks to the older woman ('Mrs Robinson' circa 1882), of his serving an apprenticeship and becoming a mélodie graduate.

It is possible of course that Marie-Blanche Vasnier had one of those nasty, squeaky voices that are sometimes to be found amongst the coloratura hopefuls of France, and Debussy was simply too besotted to register her limitations. In any case she must have been a very good musician, and a hard-working one to undertake this music, and there can be no doubt about her allure as a woman. On more than one occasion Debussy (who had won the Prix de Rome in 1884) left the Villa Medici in Rome to pay her fleeting, illicit visits in Paris. This relationship seems to have ended soon after the composer's return to France in 1887. His new lover was a girl named Gabrielle Dupont with whom he lived on and off for the next nine years. He had the grace to send Marie-Blanche a copy of the Verlaine ARIETTES (his next published compositions) and *Mandoline* [FAURÉ 29 i], published in 1890, was dedicated to her. Apart from that, only the song *Fantoches* (1882), incorporated into the FÊTES GALANTES set of 1892, and originally part of the Vasnier songbook, has been integrated into the main body of Debussy's songs as an echo of this formative relationship. During the entire affair, the composer had been helped financially by the singer's husband and had been welcomed into the home as one of the family. This brings to mind a parallel with Hugo Wolf's contemporary relationship with Melanie Köchert and her wealthy husband, the cuckolded Viennese court-jeweller.

Probably the best of these early songs are the Verlaine settings. They encourage the composer to a concentrated utterance which helps contain the inflation of the salon style with its sweetly sentimental platitudes. The stage is now set for a cycle of Verlaine masterpieces, the songs first published singly as ARIETTES in 1888, and then in 1903 as the ARIETTES OUBLIÉES, dedicated to Mary Garden, the Scottish soprano who first sang Mélisande. The Dover edition has caused some confusion to singers and pianists by reprinting the first version, which is different from the final edition in a number of significant details. Although the beginnings of the cycle belong to the Vasnier period, there is no doubt that this work marks the beginning of Debussy the great song composer—each mélodie has something utterly new about it. From the very opening of *C'est l'extase langoureuse* we are ushered into a world of sensuality and yielding languor. The music is exactly notated, but the vocal line has a freedom which suggests the naturalness of speech. The supporting piano writing, gently cradling the voice, is full of colour both sumptuous and delicate. The monotonous English drizzle of *Il pleure dans mon cœur* (the poem was written in Camden Town) is evoked by a type of writing for piano that no other French song composer could have achieved—quasi-orchestral in its colouristic demands, but absolutely translucent in its effect. *L'ombre des arbres* weaves a spell of silence and stillness; only Ravel, years later, in his *Le martin-pêcheur* could match its regal calm. In *Chevaux de bois* the steam-pistoned calliope of the funfair is brilliantly evoked in a masterful scherzo which keeps the momentum going until the composer chooses to relax into a wonderful postlude pervaded with a twilight atmosphere that we will come to recognize as sheerly Debussian—in the last of the *PROSES LYRIQUES* we will find another such magical page. *Green* uses a motif of octaves in the piano, a fall of a fifth and then a rising fourth, to bind together an exuberant paean to abundant and overwhelming love. This response to the poem is that of an accomplished and successful wooer of women. Only Reynaldo Hahn in his setting of the poem (entitled *Offrande*) proffers a sadder and more passive alternative, possibly truer to the poem's biographical background. The final song is *Spleen* which captures to perfection the sickly hothouse atmosphere of the *décadence*. It is a strangely downbeat, not to say brave, way to end a cycle, despite the fact that the tessitura climbs dramatically on the final page—a high B flat that suggests that Mme Vasnier's voice came into the composer's mind at this moment. We are left with an almost palpable portrait of the poet: sensual, vulnerable, excitable, prone to mad gaiety and depression, and tormented by the fact that his love for Rimbaud was not fully returned.

This personal core, a human relationship between composer, poet, and listener, is the only thing lacking in the next set of songs, the monumental *CINQ POÈMES DE CHARLES BAUDELAIRE* (1887–9). Only Wolf (and at exactly the same time) could claim to switch styles so suddenly in the interests of being true to a poet. The differences between Wolf's Mörike and Goethe songbooks are mirrored in Debussy's completely different attitudes to Verlaine and Baudelaire. In setting Goethe, Wolf knew that he had to capture in music some of the cosmic utterances of a giant of literature. Debussy aimed at the same thing with Baudelaire. Thus the songs have a sweep and a scale unequalled in his work, the music a fascinating demonstration of this composer's debt to Wagner, and to the music of *Parsifal* in particular (we have already heard the notes of the *Parsifal* bells used as the basis for *Chevaux de bois*). Admiration for the way that Debussy gives himself heart and soul to the poet is tempered only by the fact that there are limits to the amount of sublimity that human throat and ivory keys can convey, a fact that Duparc understood to perfection in his Baudelaire settings by writing to the edge of those limits, but not beyond. We would not be without the gigantic construction of *Le balcon* (something that might have been dreamed up by a musical Piranesi, and unique in French song) but interpreters find it almost unrealizable: wonderful to work on, almost impossible to perform. No matter how hard one tries, the music, when it changes from notes on paper to notes sung and played, falls short of the composer's vision. When there is a more intimate human dimension (as in the divinely beautiful *Le jet d'eau*), we forget for a moment that Baudelaire is a lord of literature and are drawn into a spellbinding evocation. When the scale is less vast, when there is a retreat from orchestral dimensions and a move toward intimate utterance, we can better perceive the profundities. In this respect *Recueillement* is perhaps the most successful of the songs, thoroughly true to Baudelaire, and Debussy at his peerless best; it was later orchestrated by Caplet. Interestingly, it was this poem which Duparc attempted to set after his illness set in; but he destroyed his music as not being worthy of the poem.

Debussy needed to work on a canvas of Baudelairian size to prove to himself that he could do it. Perhaps he needed to exorcize the ghosts of Bayreuth, clearing certain aspects of Wagner out of his system, and conserving what was important for the future: he now had the seeds of operatic ideas growing within him. Despite the reverence we feel for Wolf's expansive GOETHE LIEDER, we find it easier to adore his ITALIENISCHES LIEDERBUCH miniatures. In similar fashion the public is astonished by the Baudelaire orations, but falls in love with Debussy's more compact songs. In 1891–2 the composer returned to Verlaine for a triptych (from now on a favourite form for his cycles) entitled FÊTES GALANTES. On either side of the old Vasnier song *Fantoches* (now revised) he placed two new songs on poems he had set before: *En sourdine* and *Clair de lune.* The mesmeric theme of the nightingale which opens the accompaniment of *En sourdine*—repeated high G sharps in languid syncopation—announces a magician who is already master of Verlaine's world. It is as if Debussy is composing this music as a riposte to Fauré, reminding the public that he had discovered this poet many years before the older composer's CINQ MÉLODIES 'DE VENISE'. If Debussy had composed no other songs but these, he would still be celebrated by singers: these are jewels around the slender neck of Mélodie as she plays at being a Versailles courtier, painted the while in delicate brushstrokes by Watteau. If moonlight could ever be transferred into the black and white of paper and ink, it is in this *recueil.* The Verlaine winning streak reappears, this time more robustly drawn, in another set of songs from 1891 (entitled simply TROIS MÉLODIES). The outer two songs, *La mer est plus belle* and *L'échelonnement des haies,* are both ebullient pieces of music with swirling arpeggios and vocal lines which break free of the hothouse. The poems date from Verlaine's visits to England. The central panel of the set is *Le son du cor s'afflige,* which has a sense of mystery and grandeur (typified by the sombre sound of the horn) that recalls *Recueillement,* although on a smaller scale and prophesies the atmosphere of *Pelléas et Mélisande.*

If Debussy knew the Mussorgsky songs, and it seems that he did, he would have noticed that for some of them the poet was the composer himself. Wagner was no less his own librettist, and perhaps Debussy knew how a song composer like Cornelius wrote Lieder to his own poems. Debussy, the most literary of composers, whose letters are full of artful quotations recalling not only lines from his own songs, but citations from a wide range of literature, now decided to write a cycle to his own words. As a preparation for *Pelléas et Mélisande* Debussy might have wished to write a Maeterlinck song cycle, but Chausson had already done this in SERRES CHAUDES. His new work seems influenced by Maeterlinck nevertheless, and by the perfumed morbidity of the *fin de siècle.* The leafy foliage of the art nouveau cover of the first edition (which might have illustrated the Wagnerian hothouse of *Im Treibhaus* from the WESENDONCK LIEDER) seems to announce a work of exquisite mannerisms from an age of decadence. Although this is partly true, these PROSES LYRIQUES (1892–3) contain some of his most potent music for voice and piano. Each of the four songs, though substantial in comparison with the slender Verlaine settings, has a perfection of form which does not outstay its musical welcome. And if one were pressed to name a Debussy cycle which encapsulated all aspects of his pianistic style, it would be this: the dreamy vistas of *De rêve*; the enchanting dancing water music of *De grève*; the sumptuous breadth of *De fleurs* (the climactic section of which contains some of his most passionate and vocally taxing music); and the bell music of *De soir* which seems to prophesy one of the *Sea interludes* from *Peter Grimes*, and which has a mesmerizing final section which recalls the close of *Chevaux de bois*. Perfection then? Not quite, for the poems read uncomfortably like parodies of Wagner, Baudelaire, Laforgue, and Mallarmé. Mention of a hot-house in *De fleurs* invokes memories of Maeterlinck, and Chausson's SERRES CHAUDES. The English-speaking singer is able to hide behind the perfume of the French language in singing these effusions, and the audience is seduced by the music. But Debussy as a poet has been led down the garden path of an amateur's vanity, and as a result there is something artificial about the PROSES LYRIQUES. Nothing daunted, Debussy also began a second volume of PROSES LYRIQUES in 1898–1902, entitled NUITS BLANCHES (Sleepless nights). Two of the five songs have now been rediscovered, but neither of them is yet available in print.

The PROSES LYRIQUES were sung by Thérèse Roger, a soprano to whom Debussy was engaged. It was at this time in his life that he was friendly with Ernest Chausson and his family, who mightily approved of Thérèse's influence on him. The break-up of the relationship and the return to Gaby Dupont ruptured the Chausson connection. Personal chaos did not prevent progress and growing success. For some time Debussy had been thinking of writing an opera to Maeterlinck's *Pelléas et Mélisande*, a project which was encouraged by the composer's new friend, Érik Satie. The first version of the opera was ready by early 1895. In 1894 *L'après-midi d'un faune* had been performed and this had consolidated his reputation in avant-garde circles as the coming man. There were no more songs however until 1897 when he wrote CHANSONS DE BILITIS, three settings of Pierre Louÿs's evocations of ancient Greek eroticism—veiled, understated, and under-age. The great Nabokov, creator of *Lolita*, might easily have named Humbert Humbert's nymphette Bilitis, as depicted by this poet and composer. We are used to time-travel in French music, and Reynaldo Hahn set a whole cycle of Leconte de Lisle's *Études latines* where nymphs in chitons and shepherd boys strike musical poses which recall the paintings of Puvis de Chavannes and the stagy photography of Sicilian youths by Baron Corvo. The BILITIS songs however transcend any sense of pastiche, for they achieve a type of Delphic spirituality: *La flûte de Pan* begins with a delicate little instrumental scale and ends with the croaking of Aristophanes' frogs; *La chevelure*, despite its luxuriant sensuality, takes on a sense of Attic detachment, a sheerly musical purity which counterbalances the words and renders them enchanting rather than smutty; *Le tombeau des Naïades* is as mysterious as ancient myth and legend, full of unanswered questions. And we are aware that Debussy is now composing songs, highly successful ones, that in terms of form and content are unlike any that had ever been written. So complete is the composer's identification with the antique world conjured by Louÿs that it seems a pity that Debussy chose to write only three *Bilitis* songs; the existence of a later *Bilitis* work for reciter and chamber ensemble of two flutes, two harps, and celesta (1901) only makes us regret this more. The slender song cycle, later orchestrated by Maurice Delage, is a poignant homage to the beauties of youth unsullied by guilt and the strictures of Christian morality. There is a famous photograph of Debussy, *chez* Louÿs, with Zohra ben Brahim, a young Algerian girl of whom the poet was enamoured and who inspired the *Bilitis* poems.

This seems obvious enough in the light of hindsight, but the poet took steps to disguise their slightly scandalous provenance. When originally published in 1894, Louÿs claimed that these texts were his translations from the ancient Greek of Bilitis, a poetess of the sixth century BC. The first edition features a biography of this so-called student of Sappho. A distinguished Hellenist was taken in by this elaborate hoax; he even claimed to have already known the poems in their original form! Thus Louÿs takes his place besides James Macpherson (the Celtic bard 'Ossian') whose distinguished falsifications inspired another great composer—Franz Schubert—to some of his most atmospheric and mysterious music.

The CHANSONS DE BILITIS are a high point of the Debussy song-style, as it has come to be popularly understood. It is these which Anna Russell parodied, and it is these, rather than the later songs, which occasion gasps of pleasure from the French song enthusiast who wishes to swoon in a nebulous haze of high art *à la française*. Debussy moved on as a song composer, however, no longer content to weave the same old spells. There was much to change him too, above all problems in his strange and unsettled private life. In 1897 Gabrielle Dupont had attempted suicide, as did Debussy's wife Lily (née Rosalie Texier) in 1904. The first incident was less commented on as Debussy was still something of a bohemian, but by 1904 he was the famous composer of *Pelléas et Mélisande*, as well as of an impressive amount of orchestral and piano music. He had almost become part of the establishment. But the abandoning of his wife Lily and his affair with Emma Bardac, formerly a mistress of Fauré, and a married woman with a child, scandalized the Parisian musical world to such an extent that many of his colleagues refused to have anything more to do with him.

Debussy never recovered from his bitter disappointment in being deserted by his erstwhile friends. His songs became less easily accessible, like the man himself, and, with the new century, a new austerity is to be heard in the works for voice and piano. The first of these are the TROIS CHANSONS DE FRANCE (1904), two madrigal-like settings (both rondels) of the royal medieval poet Charles d'Orléans, a writer who became ineffably dear to Debussy as a role-model of French artistic genius and hard-working probity. These two stand on either side of *La grotte*, a song to a text of Tristan l'Hermite which, in a few bars, conjures the limpid sound-world of Debussy's opera. This is indeed literary and musical perfection where not a single note could be changed. The composer thought so highly of it that the same song later reappears as the first of the cycle LE PROMENOIR DES DEUX AMANTS. And then there was a return to Verlaine for a final visit, a second set of FÊTES GALANTES in 1904. In these songs, inscribed to the woman who was to be the composer's second wife, Debussy seems to bid farewell to his promiscuous life. There is a shadow over this music (and the carefully chosen texts) which seems to speak of past mistakes and the price that we pay for loving unwisely. *Les ingénus*, with music as delicate as the strands of a distant memory, meditates on past pleasures and speaks of 'our crazed young eyes', and there is something diabolical about *Le faune* and the sound of tambourines predicting an ill sequel to these hedonistic pleasures. In this we hear what Auden meant when he wrote: 'Every farthing of the cost, | All the dreaded cards foretell.' Alfred Cortot accompanied Maggie Teyte in a recording of this song with the bottom strings of the piano somehow damped in order to simulate the sinister sound of the tambourine. The last song, *Colloque sentimental*, would have many Debussy-lovers' votes as his greatest mélodie, and in some ways it is, particularly in terms of the meeting of great poetry with music which matches it in quality. This is, without question, a masterpiece—cold, forbidding, and utterly truthful about the unfairness of human relationships, despite the song's extraordinary air of haunted unreality. This dialogue of ghosts, one of whom is still pathetically dependent on the love of the other, requires masterful singing and playing. In it we can detect the chill of the autumn frost that was beginning to set in with the composer's life and work. The song of the nightingale which we have heard in *En sourdine* from the earlier set of FÊTES GALANTES makes a moving reappearance here as if to haunt the lovers with the failure of their relationship, and as if to emphasize that Debussy has come full-circle in his role as Verlaine's composer. But if we return to the much earlier ARIETTES OUBLIÉES we find a similar musical language for despair and heartbreak, betrayal and insecurity. This stems from the unifying effect of the poet's voice and its power over a composer sensitive, perhaps more than any other, to the inner music of words. It is not too much to believe that, in Verlaine, the composer had found something of an alter ego.

The cycle LE PROMENOIR DES DEUX AMANTS was completed in 1910, by the addition of two new songs to *La grotte*, which had already made an appearance in the TROIS CHANSONS DE FRANCE discussed above. These are among the composer's most intimate mélodies, songs of the half-light where vulnerable exchanges of affection are made far from the prying gaze of onlookers. It is as if the courtiers of the FÊTES GALANTES have grown up at last, and in ageing, have discovered a deeper note to human relationships. Even the middle song, **Crois mon conseil, chère Climène,** which could seem at first glance to be merely flirtatious, reveals the wistful shadow of experience; the older narrator, looking at beauty from the outside, realizes that it is a thing wasted on the young. **Je tremble en voyant ton visage** has such a spiritual quality to it that it could effortlessly stand next to a late Fauré song like *Je me poserai sur ton cœur*, the difference in musical style unimportant in comparison to a remarkably similar vision of devotion and surrender of self.

A similar sense of almost medieval abnegation is to be found in the first two songs from the TROIS BALLADES DE FRANÇOIS VILLON (1910). The composer was already ill with cancer and the anguish of the first song of this set reflects hard times. His wife had been disinherited by her rich banker uncle, and Debussy now had to travel far and wide as a conductor and pianist in order to provide for his wife and daughter Chouchou (born 1905). Debussy has already progressed far beyond an adolescent need to furnish his lover with pretty display songs; the Villon set is his only cycle written specifically for the male voice. Both the **Ballade de Villon a s'amye** and the following **Ballade que Villon feit a la requeste de sa mère pour prier Nostre-Dame** bring the art of pastiche or stylization to new and unexpected heights. Most songs in this genre are meant to charm us, but here we have a composer able to rethink himself and his music into the more rigorous aspects of a distant century. In the refrain of the second song ('En ceste foy je vueil vivre et mourir') Koechlin claimed to be able to smell the very wax, candles, and incense of medieval Catholicism. We are used to window-dressing in songs of this type, but here we get a great deal more than a costume drama: we find a lofty severity worthy of the architecture, painting, and, of course, literature of the long-vanished age. There could be no better illustration of the way in which this composer synthesized his knowledge and impressions from every sphere of art and experience, and somehow turned them into music, an illustration of what Baudelaire called *correspondances*. It is little wonder that Debussy later called himself 'Claude de France', for his works sought to reflect the entire sweep of French culture threatened by an unfriendly modern world. The last of the Villon set is **Ballade des femmes de Paris,** the only comic song of Debussy's maturity (although it has an edge which is deadly serious). It seems to mock all the Parisian gossips who had done their best to undermine the happiness of the composer's new life with wife and child. The repeated notes between the hands, devilish for the accompanist to execute cleanly, illustrate in masterful manner the jabber of wagging tongues. The 'Napolitaines' section, a momentary swaggering of southern hips, is an example of genuine musical wit.

It is now clear that Debussy belongs to that handful of great song composers—Schubert, Wolf, Britten, Poulenc—who were able to find a different musical voice for each of their different poets. The difference between the style for Verlaine and that for Baudelaire was obvious almost from the start. The composer's own poetry in PROSES LYRIQUES invokes somehow a combination of the two. Charles d'Orléans is different again from Villon, and Tristan l'Hermite from either—although all the songs by these poets embark on time-travel. Pierre Louÿs too has his musical vocabulary; even if at first we imagine that we could confuse the CHANSONS DE BILITIS with the FÊTES GALANTES, we reckon without Debussy's subtle ways of differentiating between the sacred groves of Hellas and the gardens of Versailles. As final proof of his fastidious feel for the singularity of a great poet's world we have the TROIS POÈMES DE STÉPHANE MALLARMÉ (1913), Debussy's last cycle. We know from *L'après-midi d'un faune* that he had long had an instinctive sympathy with this poetry, and the result is a set of songs of crystalline clarity and purity which experiment in sonority and weight of sound in the same way that Mallarmé measures the length of a syllable and the effect of assonance. In this fastidious control of texture and poetic form we sense two genuinely twentieth-century minds at work. In Debussy we have someone who would not only understand the songs of his young contemporaries (like his disciple Caplet), but who, on this evidence, would have seen the point of Boulez's PLI SELON PLI for example, where the poet is also Mallarmé. This link with the future is just as clear in Ravel's settings of the same poet written for voice and chamber ensemble at about the same time. By a strange coincidence, *Soupir* and *Placet futile* were also part of this set [RAVEL 14 i, 14 ii] although *Éventail* was Debussy's choice alone. Mallarmé seems to have been a poet who encouraged his musicians to time-travel forwards rather than backwards.

The final song that Debussy wrote was very much of its time. The horrors of the First World War seem to have encouraged composers to write against Boche atrocities more than the Second, and anger seems to have swamped good taste, as in the rather embarrassing patriotic works of Saint-Saëns, Magnard, and Séverac. In *Noël des enfants qui n'ont plus de maisons* (1915) at least we have a good piece of music, as if written for the child Yniold in *Pelléas*, even if the text is a grotesque follow-up to the reserved jewelled utterances of Mallarmé. (The song was later orchestrated by Inghelbrecht.) The desperation of the composer is apparent. The whole of civilization as he has known it is breaking down. Throughout his life he has fought to undermine bourgeois values, and to follow the dictates of his pleasure. In his own quiet way he conducted a guerrilla war against the rigid rule-books of the academic pedants, sensual gratification being his only guiding star. In asserting his independence as a human being, even in sexual terms, he was establishing the right of an artist to follow his fancy. After him, music would never be the same again. After all, which twentieth-century composer refuses to acknowledge Debussy, in some respects at least, as his precursor? But in this final heartfelt little rondo, we find him caught up in the horrors of the time, the breakdown of law and order on a gigantic and unmanageable scale. It was then that the bourgeois comforts in his home in the avenue du Bois de Boulogne were the only consolations for the onslaught of both war and ravaging disease. The remaining three years of his life were without songs. We can only imagine what greater contributions to twentieth-century music Debussy might have made if he had lived to do battle for ascendancy in the field of the mélodie, not only with Fauré (who outlived him by six years) but with Les Six. Poulenc's LE BESTIAIRE dates from the year of Debussy's death, and how enthralling it is to imagine a collaboration between Claude de France and the poet Guillaume Apollinaire.

1 Nuit d'étoiles

(Théodore de Banville)

Nuit d'étoiles,
Sous tes voiles,
Sous ta brise et tes parfums,
Triste lyre
Qui soupire,
Je rêve aux amours défunts.

La sereine mélancolie
Vient éclore au fond de mon cœur,
Et j'entends l'âme de ma mie
Tressaillir dans le bois rêveur.

Nuit d'étoiles,
Sous tes voiles,
Sous ta brise et tes parfums,
Triste lyre
Qui soupire,
Je rêve aux amours défunts.

Je revois à notre fontaine
Tes regards bleus comme les cieux;
Cette rose, c'est ton haleine,
Et ces étoiles sont tes yeux.

Nuit d'étoiles,
Sous tes voiles,
Sous ta brise et tes parfums,
Triste lyre
Qui soupire,
Je rêve aux amours défunts.

Night of stars

Night of stars,
Beneath your veils,
Beneath your breeze and fragrance,
Sad lyre
That sighs,
I dream of bygone loves.

Serene melancholy
Now blooms deep in my heart,
And I hear the soul of my love
Quiver in the dreaming woods.

Night of stars,
Beneath your veils,
Beneath your breeze and fragrance,
Sad lyre
That sighs,
I dream of bygone loves.

Once more at our fountain I see
Your eyes as blue as the sky;
This rose is your breath
And these stars are your eyes.

Night of stars,
Beneath your veils,
Beneath your breeze and fragrance,
Sad lyre
That sighs,
I dream of bygone loves.

2 *Beau soir*
(Paul Bourget)

Lorsque au soleil couchant les rivières sont roses,
Et qu'un tiède frisson court sur les champs de blé,
Un conseil d'être heureux semble sortir des choses
    Et monter vers le cœur troublé;

Un conseil de goûter le charme d'être au monde
Cependant qu'on est jeune et que le soir est beau,
Car nous nous en allons, comme s'en va cette onde:
    Elle à la mer—nous au tombeau!

Beautiful evening

When at sunset the rivers are pink
And a warm breeze ripples the fields of wheat,
All things seem to advise content—
    And rise toward the troubled heart;

Advise us to savour the gift of life,
While we are young and the evening fair,
For our life slips by, as that river does:
    It to the sea—we to the tomb.

3 *Pantomime*
(Paul Verlaine)

Pierrot, qui n'a rien d'un Clitandre,
Vide un flacon sans plus attendre,
Et, pratique, entame un pâté.

Cassandre, au fond de l'avenue,
Verse une larme méconnue
Sur son neveu déshérité.

Ce faquin d'Arlequin combine
L'enlèvement de Colombine
Et pirouette quatre fois.

Colombine rêve, surprise
De sentir un cœur dans la brise
Et d'entendre en son cœur des voix.

Pantomime

Pierrot, who is no Clitandre,
Gulps down a bottle without delay
And, being practical, starts on a pie.

Cassandre, at the end of the avenue,
Sheds an unnoticed tear
For his disinherited nephew.

That rogue of a Harlequin schemes
How to abduct Colombine
And pirouettes four times.

Colombine dreams, amazed
To sense a heart in the breeze
And hear voices in her heart.

4 *Pierrot*
(Théodore de Banville)

Le bon Pierrot, que la foule contemple,
Ayant fini les noces d'Arlequin,
Suit en songeant le boulevard du Temple.
Une fillette au souple casaquin
En vain l'agace de son œil coquin;
Et cependant mystérieuse et lisse
Faisant de lui sa plus chère délice,
La blanche Lune aux cornes de taureaux
Jette un regard de son œil en coulisse
À son ami Jean Gaspard Deburau.

Pierrot

Good old Pierrot, watched by the crowd,
Having done with Harlequin's wedding,
Drifts dreamily along the boulevard du Temple.
A girl in a flowing blouse
Vainly leads him on with her teasing eyes;
And meanwhile, mysterious and sleek,
Cherishing him above all else,
The white moon with horns like a bull
Ogles her friend
Jean Gaspard Deburau.

5 *Apparition*
(Stéphane Mallarmé)

La lune s'attristait. Des séraphins en pleurs
Rêvant, l'archet aux doigts, dans le calme des fleurs
Vaporeuses, tiraient de mourantes violes
De blancs sanglots glissant sur l'azur des corolles.
—C'était le jour béni de ton premier baiser.
Ma songerie aimant à me martyriser
S'enivrait savamment du parfum de tristesse
Que même sans regret et sans déboire laisse
La cueillaison d'un Rêve au cœur qui l'a cueilli.
J'errais donc, l'œil rivé sur le pavé vieilli

Quand avec du soleil aux cheveux, dans la rue
Et dans le soir, tu m'es en riant apparue

Et j'ai cru voir la fée au chapeau de clarté

Qui jadis sur mes beaux sommeils d'enfant gâté

Passait, laissant toujours de ses mains mal fermées
Neiger de blancs bouquets d'étoiles parfumées.

Apparition

The moon grew sad. Weeping seraphim,
Dreaming, bows in hand, in the calm of hazy
Flowers, drew from dying viols
White sobs that glided over the corollas' blue.
—It was the blessed day of your first kiss.
My dreaming, glad to torment me,
Grew skilfully drunk on the perfumed sadness
That—without regret or bitter after-taste—
The harvest of a Dream leaves in the reaper's heart.
And so I wandered, my eyes fixed on the old paving
    stones,
When with sun-flecked hair, in the street
And in the evening, you appeared laughing before
    me
And I thought I glimpsed the fairy with her cap of
    light
Who long ago crossed my lovely spoilt child's
    slumbers,
Always allowing from her half-closed hands
White bouquets of scented flowers to snow.

ARIETTES OUBLIÉES
(Paul Verlaine)

FORGOTTEN AIRS

6 i *C'est l'extase langoureuse*

C'est l'extase langoureuse,
C'est la fatigue amoureuse,
C'est tous les frissons des bois
Parmi l'étreinte des brises,
C'est, vers les ramures grises,
Le chœur des petites voix.

Ô le frêle et frais murmure!
Cela gazouille et susurre,
Cela ressemble au cri doux
Que l'herbe agitée expire...
Tu dirais, sous l'eau qui vire,
Le roulis sourd des cailloux.

It is languorous rapture

It is languorous rapture,
It is amorous fatigue,
It is all the tremors of the forest
In the breezes' embrace,
It is, around the grey branches,
The choir of tiny voices.

O the delicate, fresh murmuring!
The warbling and whispering,
It is like the soft cry
The ruffled grass gives out...
You might take it for the muffled sound
Of pebbles in the swirling stream.

Cette âme qui se lamente
En cette plainte dormante
C'est la nôtre, n'est-ce pas?
La mienne, dis, et la tienne,
Dont s'exhale l'humble antienne
Par ce tiède soir, tout bas?

This soul which grieves
In this subdued lament,
It is ours, is it not?
Mine, and yours too,
Breathing out our humble hymn
On this warm evening, soft and low?

6 ii *Il pleure dans mon cœur*

Tears fall in my heart

Il pleure dans mon cœur
Comme il pleut sur la ville;
Quelle est cette langueur
Qui pénètre mon cœur?

Ô bruit doux de la pluie
Par terre et sur les toits!
Pour un cœur qui s'ennuie
Ô le bruit de la pluie!

Il pleure sans raison
Dans ce cœur qui s'écœure.
Quoi! nulle trahison?...
Ce deuil est sans raison.

C'est bien la pire peine
De ne savoir pourquoi
Sans amour et sans haine,
Mon cœur a tant de peine.

Tears fall in my heart
As rain falls on the town;
What is this torpor
Pervading my heart?

Ah, the soft sound of rain
On the ground and roofs!
For a listless heart,
Ah, the sound of the rain!

Tears fall without reason
In this disheartened heart.
What! Was there no treason?...
This grief is without reason.

And the worst pain of all
Must be not to know why
Without love and without hate
My heart feels such pain.

6 iii *L'ombre des arbres*

The shadow of trees

L'ombre des arbres dans la rivière embrumée
    Meurt comme de la fumée
Tandis qu'en l'air, parmi les ramures réelles,
    Se plaignent les tourterelles.

Combien, ô voyageur, ce paysage blême
    Te mira blême toi-même,
Et que tristes pleuraient dans les hautes feuillées
    Tes espérances noyées!

The shadow of trees in the misty stream
    Dies like smoke,
While up above, in the real branches,
    The turtle-doves lament.

How this faded landscape, O traveller,
    Watched you yourself fade,
And how sadly in the lofty leaves
    Your drowned hopes were weeping!

6 iv *Chevaux de bois*

Tournez, tournez, bons chevaux de bois,
Tournez cent tours, tournez mille tours,
Tournez souvent et tournez toujours,
Tournez, tournez au son des hautbois.

L'enfant tout rouge et la mère blanche,
Le gars en noir et la fille en rose,
L'une à la chose et l'autre à la pose,
Chacun se paie un sou de dimanche.

Tournez, tournez, chevaux de leur cœur,
Tandis qu'autour de tous vos tournois
Clignote l'œil du filou sournois,
Tournez au son du piston vainqueur!

C'est étonnant comme ça vous soûle
D'aller ainsi dans ce cirque bête:
Rien dans le ventre et mal dans la tête,
Du mal en masse et du bien en foule.

Tournez, dadas, sans qu'il soit besoin
D'user jamais de nuls éperons
Pour commander à vos galops ronds:
Tournez, tournez, sans espoir de foin.

Et dépêchez, chevaux de leur âme,
Déjà voici que sonne à la soupe
La nuit qui tombe et chasse la troupe
De gais buveurs que leur soif affame.

Tournez, tournez! Le ciel en velours
D'astres en or se vêt lentement.
L'église tinte un glas tristement.
Tournez au son joyeux des tambours!

Merry-go-round

Turn, turn, you fine wooden horses,
Turn a hundred, turn a thousand times,
Turn often and turn for evermore
Turn and turn to the oboes' sound.

The red-faced child and the pale mother,
The lad in black and the girl in pink,
One down-to-earth, the other showing off,
Each buying a treat with his Sunday sou.

Turn, turn, horses of their hearts,
While the furtive pickpocket's eye is flashing
As you whirl about and whirl around,
Turn to the sound of the conquering cornet!

Astonishing how drunk it makes you,
Riding like this in this foolish fair:
With an empty stomach and an aching head,
Discomfort in plenty and masses of fun!

Gee-gees, turn, you'll never need
The help of any spur
To make your horses gallop round:
Turn, turn, without hope of hay.

And hurry on, horses of their souls:
Nightfall already calls them to supper
And disperses the crowd of happy revellers,
Ravenous with thirst.

Turn, turn! The velvet sky
Is slowly decked with golden stars.
The church bell tolls a mournful knell—
Turn to the joyful sound of drums!

6 v *Green*

Voici des fruits, des fleurs, des feuilles et des
    branches
Et puis voici mon cœur qui ne bat que pour vous.
Ne le déchirez pas avec vos deux mains blanches
Et qu'à vos yeux si beaux l'humble présent soit doux.

J'arrive tout couvert encore de rosée
Que le vent du matin vient glacer à mon front.
Souffrez que ma fatigue à vos pieds reposée
Rêve des chers instants qui la délasseront.

Green

Here are flowers, branches, fruit, and fronds,

And here too is my heart that beats just for you.
Do not tear it with your two white hands
And may the humble gift please your lovely eyes.

I come all covered still with the dew
Frozen to my brow by the morning breeze.
Let my fatigue, finding rest at your feet,
Dream of dear moments that will soothe it.

Sur votre jeune sein laissez rouler ma tête
Toute sonore encore de vos derniers baisers;
Laissez-la s'apaiser de la bonne tempête,
Et que je dorme un peu puisque vous reposez.

On your young breast let me cradle my head
Still ringing with your recent kisses;
After love's sweet tumult grant it peace,
And let me sleep a while, since you rest.

6 vi *Spleen*

Les roses étaient toutes rouges
Et les lierres étaient tout noirs.

Chère, pour peu que tu te bouges,
Renaissent tous mes désespoirs.

Le ciel était trop bleu, trop tendre,
La mer trop verte et l'air trop doux.

Je crains toujours,—ce qu'est d'attendre!—
Quelque fuite atroce de vous.

Du houx à la feuille vernie
Et du luisant buis je suis las,

Et de la campagne infinie
Et de tout, fors de vous, hélas!

Spleen

All the roses were red
And the ivy was all black.

Dear, at your slightest move,
All my despair revives.

The sky was too blue, too tender,
The sea too green, the air too mild.

I always fear—oh to wait and wonder!—
One of your agonizing departures.

I am weary of the glossy holly,
Of the gleaming box-tree too,

And the boundless countryside
And everything, alas, but you!

CINQ POÈMES DE CHARLES BAUDELAIRE

FIVE POEMS OF CHARLES BAUDELAIRE

7 i *Le balcon*

Mère des souvenirs, maîtresse des maîtresses,
Ô toi, tous mes plaisirs! ô toi, tous mes devoirs!
Tu te rappelleras la beauté des caresses,
La douceur du foyer et le charme des soirs,
Mère des souvenirs, maîtresse des maîtresses!

Les soirs illuminés par l'ardeur du charbon,
Et les soirs au balcon, voilés de vapeurs roses.

Que ton sein m'était doux! que ton cœur m'était
    bon!
Nous avons dit souvent d'impérissables choses
Les soirs illuminés par l'ardeur du charbon.

The balcony

Mother of memories, mistress of mistresses,
O you, all my pleasures, O you, all my duties!
You will recall the beauty of caresses,
The hearth's sweetness and the evenings' charm,
Mother of memories, mistress of mistresses!

Evenings lit with the glow of coals,
And evenings on the balcony, veiled in pink
    vapours.
How soft your breast was, how warm your heart!

We have often said imperishable things,
On evenings lit with the glow of coals.

Que les soleils sont beaux par les chaudes soirées!
Que l'espace est profond! que le cœur est puissant!
En me penchant vers toi, reine des adorées,
Je croyais respirer le parfum de ton sang.
Que les soleils sont beaux par les chaudes soirées!

La nuit s'épaississait ainsi qu'une cloison,
Et mes yeux dans le noir devinient tes prunelles,
Et je buvais ton souffle, ô douceur! ô poison!
Et tes pieds s'endormaient dans mes mains
    fraternelles.
La nuit s'épaississait ainsi qu'une cloison.

Je sais l'art d'évoquer les minutes heureuses,
Et revis mon passé blotti dans tes genoux.
Car à quoi bon chercher tes beautés langoureuses
Ailleurs qu'en ton cher corps et qu'en ton cœur si
    doux?
Je sais l'art d'évoquer les minutes heureuses!

Ces serments, ces parfums, ces baisers infinis,
Renaîtront-ils d'un gouffre interdit à nos sondes,

Comme montent au ciel les soleils rajeunis
Après s'être lavés au fond des mers profondes?
—Ô serments! ô parfums! ô baisers infinis!

How beautiful the suns on warm evenings!
How space is deep, how strong the heart!
Leaning toward you, queen of my loves,
I seemed to breathe the scent of your blood.
How beautiful the suns on warm evenings!

Night thickened like a wall,
And my eyes in the dark divined your own,
And I drank in your breath, O sweetness, O poison!
And your feet were cradled in my fraternal hands.

Night thickened like a wall.

I am skilled in the art of recalling rapture,
And relive my past, my head in your lap.
For where else should I seek your languid beauty
But in your dear body and most loving heart?

I am skilled in the art of recalling rapture!

These vows, these scents, these infinite kisses,
Will they rise from a pit we are forbidden to
    fathom,
As the reborn suns ascend the sky,
Having washed themselves in the depths of the sea?
O vows! O scents! O infinite kisses!

7 ii *Harmonie du soir*

Voici venir les temps où vibrant sur sa tige
Chaque fleur s'évapore ainsi qu'un encensoir;
Les sons et les parfums tournent dans l'air du soir;
Valse mélancolique et langoureux vertige!

Chaque fleur s'évapore ainsi qu'un encensoir;
Le violon frémit comme un cœur qu'on afflige;
Valse mélancolique et langoureux vertige!
Le ciel est triste et beau comme un grand reposoir.

Le violon frémit comme un cœur qu'on afflige,
Un cœur tendre, qui hait le néant vaste et noir!
Le ciel est triste et beau comme un grand reposoir;
Le soleil s'est noyé dans son sang qui se fige.

Un cœur tendre, qui hait le néant vaste et noir,
Du passé lumineux recueille tout vestige!
Le soleil s'est noyé dans son sang qui se fige.....
Ton souvenir en moi luit comme un ostensoir!

Evening harmony

Now comes the time when, quivering on its stem,
Each flower sheds perfume like a censer;
Sounds and scents turn in the evening air;
Melancholy waltz and reeling languor!

Each flower sheds perfume like a censer;
The violin throbs like a wounded heart;
Melancholy waltz and reeling languor!
The sky is sad and beautiful like a great altar.

The violin throbs like a wounded heart,
A fond heart that loathes the vast black void!
The sky is sad and beautiful like a great altar;
The sun has drowned in its congealing blood.

A fond heart that loathes the vast black void
And garners in all the luminous past!
The sun has drowned in its congealing blood.....
Your memory within me shines like a monstrance!

7 iii *Le jet d'eau*

Tes beaux yeux sont las, pauvre amante!
Reste longtemps, sans les rouvrir,
Dans cette pose nonchalante
Où t'a surprise le plaisir.
Dans la cour le jet d'eau qui jase
Et ne se tait ni nuit ni jour,
Entretient doucement l'extase
Où ce soir m'a plongé l'amour.

    La gerbe d'eau qui berce
       Ses mille fleurs,
    Que la lune traverse
       De ses pâleurs,
    Tombe comme une averse
       De larges pleurs.

Ainsi ton âme qu'incendie
L'éclair brûlant des voluptés
S'élance, rapide et hardie,
Vers les vastes cieux enchantés.
Puis, elle s'épanche, mourante,
En un flot de triste langueur,
Qui par une invisible pente
Descend jusqu'au fond de mon cœur.

    La gerbe d'eau qui berce
       Ses mille fleurs,
    Que la lune traverse
       De ses pâleurs,
    Tombe comme une averse
       De larges pleurs.

Ô toi, que la nuit rend si belle,
Qu'il m'est doux, penché vers tes seins,
D'écouter la plainte éternelle
Qui sanglote dans les bassins!
Lune, eau sonore, nuit bénie,
Arbres qui frissonnez autour,
Votre pure mélancolie
Est le miroir de mon amour.

    La gerbe d'eau qui berce
       Ses mille fleurs,
    Que la lune traverse
       De ses pâleurs,
    Tombe comme une averse
       De larges pleurs.

The fountain

Your beautiful eyes are fatigued, poor lover!
Rest awhile, without opening them anew,
In this careless pose,
Where pleasure surprised you.
The babbling fountain in the courtyard,
Never silent night or day,
Sweetly prolongs the ecstasy
Where love this evening plunged me.

    The sheaf of water
       Swaying its thousand flowers,
    Through which the moon gleams
       With its pallid light,
    Falls like a shower
       Of great tears.

And so your soul, lit
By the searing flash of ecstasy,
Leaps swift and bold
To vast enchanted skies.
And then, dying, spills over
In a wave of sad listlessness,
Down some invisible incline
Into the depths of my heart.

    The sheaf of water
       Swaying its thousand flowers,
    Through which the moon gleams
       With its pallid light,
    Falls like a shower
       Of great tears.

O you, whom night renders so beautiful,
How sweet, as I lean toward your breasts,
To listen to the eternal lament
Sobbing in the fountain's basin!
O moon, lapping water, blessed night,
Trees that quiver all around,
Your sheer melancholy
Is the mirror of my love.

    The sheaf of water
       Swaying its thousand flowers,
    Through which the moon gleams
       With its pallid light,
    Falls like a shower
       Of great tears.

7 iv *Recueillement*

Sois sage, ô ma Douleur, et tiens-toi plus tranquille.
Tu réclamais le Soir; il descend; le voici:
Une atmosphère obscure enveloppe la ville,
Aux uns portant la paix, aux autres le souci.

Pendant que des mortels la multitude vile,
Sous le fouet du Plaisir, ce bourreau sans merci,
Va cueillir des remords dans la fête servile,
Ma Douleur, donne-moi la main; viens par ici,

Loin d'eux. Vois se pencher les défuntes Années,
Sur les balcons du ciel, en robes surannées;

Surgir du fond des eaux le Regret souriant;

Le Soleil moribond s'endormir sous une arche,
Et, comme un long linceul traînant à l'Orient,
Entends, ma chère, entends la douce Nuit qui
          marche.

Meditation

Be good, O my Sorrow, and keep more calm.
You longed for Evening; it is falling; now:
A dusky atmosphere enfolds the town,
Bringing peace to some, to others care.

While the vile multitude of mortals,
Lashed by Pleasure, that pitiless tormentor,
Goes gathering remorse in abject revels,
Give me your hand, my Sorrow; come this way,

Far from them. See the departed Years leaning,
In outmoded dress, from the heavens'
          balustrades;
See smiling Regret well up from the water's depths;

The dying sun fall asleep beneath an arch,
And like a long shroud trailing in the East,
Listen, my love, listen to the tread of gentle Night.

7 v *La mort des amants*

Nous aurons des lits pleins d'odeurs légères,
Des divans profonds comme des tombeaux,
Et d'étranges fleurs sur des étagères,
Écloses pour nous sous des cieux plus beaux.

Usant à l'envi leurs chaleurs dernières,
Nos deux cœurs seront deux vastes flambeaux,
Qui réfléchiront leurs doubles lumières
Dans nos deux esprits, ces miroirs jumeaux.

Un soir fait de rose et de bleu mystique,
Nous échangerons un éclair unique,
Comme un long sanglot, tout chargé d'adieux;

Et plus tard un Ange, entr'ouvrant les portes,
Viendra ranimer, fidèle et joyeux,
Les miroirs ternis et les flammes mortes.

The death of lovers

We shall have beds drenched in light scents,
Divans as deep as tombs,
And displays of exotic flowers
That bloomed for us beneath fairer skies.

Outdoing even their most recent passions
Our two hearts will be two mighty torches,
Reflecting their twin lights
In our two twin-mirrored souls.

On an evening of pink and mystic blue,
We shall exchange a single radiant glance,
Like a long sob laden with farewells;

And later an Angel, pushing the portals ajar,
Will come, faithful and joyous, to revive
The tarnished mirrors and lifeless flames.

FÊTES GALANTES I
(Paul Verlaine)

FÊTES GALANTES I

8 i *En sourdine*

Calmes dans le demi-jour
Que les branches hautes font,
Pénétrons bien notre amour
De ce silence profond.

Fondons nos âmes, nos cœurs
Et nos sens extasiés,
Parmi les vagues langueurs
Des pins et des arbousiers.

Ferme tes yeux à demi,
Croise tes bras sur ton sein,
Et de ton cœur endormi
Chasse à jamais tout dessein.

Laissons-nous persuader
Au souffle berceur et doux
Qui vient à tes pieds rider
Les ondes de gazon roux.

Et quand, solennel, le soir
Des chênes noirs tombera,
Voix de notre désespoir,
Le rossignol chantera.

8 ii *Fantoches*

Scaramouche* et Pulcinella
Qu'un mauvais dessein rassembla
Gesticulent, noirs sous la lune.

Cependant l'excellent docteur†
Bolonais cueille avec lenteur
Des simples parmi l'herbe brune.

Lors sa fille, piquant minois,
Sous la charmille, en tapinois,
Se glisse, demi-nue, en quête

De son beau pirate espagnol,
Dont un amoureux rossignol
Clame la détresse à tue-tête.

Muted

Calm in the twilight
Cast by lofty boughs,
Let us steep our love
In this deep quiet.

Let us blend our souls, our hearts
And our enraptured senses
With the hazy languor
Of arbutus and pine.

Half-close your eyes,
Fold your arms across your breast,
And from your heart now lulled to rest
Forever banish all desire.

Let us both succumb
To the gentle and lulling breeze
That comes to ruffle at your feet
The waves of russet grass.

And when, solemnly, evening
Falls from the black oaks,
Voice of our despair,
The nightingale shall sing.

Marionettes

Scaramouche and Pulcinella,
Drawn together by some evil scheme,
Gesticulate, black beneath the moon.

Meanwhile the excellent doctor
From Bologna is leisurely picking
Medicinal herbs in the brown grass.

Then his daughter, pertly pretty,
Beneath the arbour, stealthily,
Glides, half-naked, in quest

Of her handsome Spanish pirate,
Whose grief a lovelorn nightingale
Proclaims as loudly as he can.

---

* A figure from Italian *Commedia dell' Arte* who was dressed in black from head to toe.

† Gracian Baloardo, another *Commedia dell' Arte* character.

8 iii *Clair de lune*

Votre âme est un paysage choisi
Que vont charmant masques et bergamasques
Jouant du luth et dansant et quasi
Tristes sous leurs déguisements fantasques.

Tout en chantant sur le mode mineur
L'amour vainqueur et la vie opportune,
Ils n'ont pas l'air de croire à leur bonheur
Et leur chanson se mêle au clair de lune,

Au calme clair de lune triste et beau,
Qui fait rêver les oiseaux dans les arbres
Et sangloter d'extase les jets d'eau,
Les grands jets d'eau sveltes parmi les marbres.

Moonlight

Your soul is a chosen landscape
Bewitched by masquers and bergamaskers,
Playing the lute and dancing and almost
Sad beneath their fanciful disguises.

Singing as they go in a minor key
Of conquering love and life's favours,
They do not seem to believe in their fortune
And their song mingles with the light of the moon,

The calm light of the moon, sad and fair,
That sets the birds dreaming in the trees
And the fountains sobbing in their rapture,
Tall and svelte amid marble statues.

TROIS MÉLODIES
(Paul Verlaine)

THREE MÉLODIES

9 i *La mer est plus belle*

La mer est plus belle
Que les cathédrales,
Nourrice fidèle,
Berceuse de râles,
La mer sur qui prie
La Vierge Marie!

Elle a tous les dons
Terribles et doux.
J'entends ses pardons
Gronder ses courroux...
Cette immensité
N'a rien d'entêté.

Oh! si patiente,
Même quand méchante!
Un souffle ami hante
La vague, et nous chante:
'Vous sans espérance,
Mourez sans souffrance!'

The sea is lovelier

The sea is lovelier
Than the cathedrals,
A faithful wet-nurse,
Lulling those in the grip of death,
The sea over which
The Virgin Mary prays!

It has all the qualities,
Awesome and sweet.
I hear its forgiveness
Scolding its wrath...
This immensity
Is without wilfulness.

Oh, so forbearing,
Even when wicked!
A friendly breath haunts
The wave, and sings to us:
'You without hope,
May you die without pain!'

Et puis, sous les cieux
Qui s'y rient plus clairs,
Elle a des airs bleus,
Roses, gris et verts...
Plus belle que tous,
Meilleure que nous!

And then beneath the skies,
Reflected there more brightly,
It seems blue,
Pink, grey, and green...
Lovelier than all,
Better than we!

9 ii *Le son du cor s'afflige*

The sound of the horn

Le son du cor s'afflige vers les bois
D'une douleur on veut croire orpheline
Qui vient mourir au bas de la colline
Parmi la bise errant en courts abois.

The sound of the horn wails towards the woods
With an almost orphan sorrow
Which fades away at the foot of the hill
Amid the gusts of the fierce North wind.

L'âme du loup pleure dans cette voix
Qui monte avec le soleil qui décline
D'une agonie on veut croire câline
Et qui ravit et qui navre à la fois.

The soul of the wolf weeps in that voice
Which rises with the setting sun
With an almost soothing agony,
Which delights and distresses all at once.

Pour faire mieux cette plainte assoupie,
La neige tombe à longs traits de charpie
À travers le couchant sanguinolent,

To muffle better this lament,
The snow falls in long shreds of lint
Across the blood-flecked setting sun,

Et l'air a l'air d'être un soupir d'automne,
Tant il fait doux par ce soir monotone
Où se dorlote un paysage lent.

And the air has the air of an autumn sigh,
So mild is this monotonous night
On which a languid landscape takes its ease.

9 iii *L'échelonnement des haies*

The hedgerows stretch out

L'échelonnement des haies
Moutonne à l'infini, mer
Claire dans le brouillard clair
Qui sent bon les jeunes baies.

The hedgerows stretch out
Frothing afar, sea-like
And clear in the clear mist,
Fragrant with young berries.

Des arbres et des moulins
Sont légers sur le vert tendre
Où vient s'ébattre et s'étendre
L'agilité des poulains.

Trees and windmills rise
Insubstantial on the delicate green,
Where agile colts
Come to stretch and frolic.

Dans ce vague d'un Dimanche
Voici se jouer aussi
De grandes brebis aussi
Douces que leur laine blanche.

On this lazy Sunday,
Some large ewes,
Soft as their white wool,
Join them in their play.

Tout à l'heure déferlait
L'onde, roulée en volutes,
De cloches comme des flûtes
Dans le ciel comme du lait.

Just now there broke
A curling wave
Of flute-like bells
In the milk-white sky.

<table>
<tr><td>

PROSES LYRIQUES

(Claude Debussy)

</td><td>

LYRICAL PROSE

</td></tr>
</table>

10 i *De rêve* / *Of dreams*

La nuit a des douceurs de femmes!	The night has a woman's softness!
Et les vieux arbres, sous la lune d'or, songent	And the old trees beneath the golden moon dream
À celle qui vient de passer la tête emperlée,	Of her who has just gone by, her head bespangled,
Maintenant navrée!	Now broken-hearted!
À jamais navrée!	Forever broken-hearted!
Ils n'ont pas su lui faire signe...	They were not able to beckon her...
Toutes! Elles ont passé:	All! All have gone by:
Les Frêles,	The Frail,
Les Folles,	The Foolish,
Semant leur rire au gazon grêle,	Scattering their laughter on the thin grass,
Aux brises frôleuses	Casting to the glancing breezes
La caresse charmeuse	The bewitching caress
Des hanches fleurissantes.	Of their burgeoning hips.
Hélas! de tout ceci, plus rien qu'un blanc frisson.	Alas! of all this nothing is left but a pale tremor.
Les vieux arbres sous la lune d'or pleurent	The old trees beneath the golden moon tearfully shed
Leurs belles feuilles d'or!	Their lovely golden leaves!
Nul ne leur dédiera plus la fiérte des casques d'or	No one will plight them again the pride of golden helmets
Maintenant ternis!	Now tarnished!
À jamais ternis!	Forever tarnished!
Les chevaliers sont morts sur le chemin du Grâal!	The Knights have died in their quest for the Grail!
La nuit a des douceurs de femmes!	The night has a woman's softness!
Des mains semblent frôler les âmes,	Hands seem to brush the souls,
Mains si folles, si frêles,	Hands so foolish, so frail,
Au temps où les épées chantaient pour Elles!...	In the days when swords sang for them!...
D'étranges soupirs s'élèvent sous les arbres.	Strange sighs rise from beneath the trees.
Mon âme! c'est du rêve ancien qui t'étreint!	My soul, you are gripped by some former dream!

10 ii *De grève* / *Of the shore*

Sur la mer les crépuscules tombent,	Dusk falls over the sea,
Soie blanche effilée!	Like frayed white silk!
Les vagues comme de petites folles,	The waves like wild little things
Jasent, petites filles sortant de l'école,	Chatter, little girls coming out of school,
Parmi les froufrous de leur robe,	Amid their rustling frocks
Soie verte irisée!	Of iridescent green silk!

Les nuages, graves voyageurs,
Se concertent sur le prochain orage,
Et, c'est un fond vraiment trop grave
À cette anglaise aquarelle.
Les vagues, les petites vagues,
Ne savent plus où se mettre,
Car voici la méchante averse,
Froufrous de jupes envolées,
Soie verte affolée!

Mais la lune, compatissante à tous,
Vient apaiser ce gris conflit,
Et caresse lentement ses petites amies,
Qui s'offrent, comme lèvres aimantes
À ce tiède et blanc baiser.
Puis, plus rien!
Plus que les cloches attardées
Des flottantes églises!
Angélus des vagues,
Soie blanche apaisée!

The clouds, grave travellers,
Consult over the coming storm,
A background truly too solemn
For this English watercolour.
The waves, the little waves,
No longer know which way to turn,
For here comes the malicious downpour,
The rustling of flying skirts,
The panic of green silk!

But the moon, with pity for all,
Comes to calm this grey conflict,
And slowly caresses his lady friends,
Who offer themselves like loving lips
To this warm, white kiss.
Then, nothing more!
Only the belated bells
Of floating churches!
Angelus of the waves,
Smoothed white silk!

10 iii *De fleurs*

Dans l'ennui si désolément vert
De la serre de douleur,
Les Fleurs enlacent mon cœur
De leurs tiges méchantes.
Ah! quand reviendront autour de ma tête
Les chères mains si tendrement désenlaceuses?

Les grands Iris violets
Violèrent méchamment tes yeux,
En semblant les refléter,
Eux, qui furent l'eau du songe
Où plongèrent mes rêves si doucement
Enclos en leur couleur;
Et les lys, blancs jets d'eau de pistils embaumés,
Ont perdu leur grâce blanche
Et ne sont plus que pauvres malades sans soleil!

Soleil! ami des fleurs mauvaises,
Tueur de rêves! Tueur d'illusions,
Ce pain béni des âmes misérables!
Venez! Venez! Les mains salvatrices!
Brisez les vitres de mensonge,
Brisez les vitres de maléfice,
Mon âme meurt de trop de soleil!

Of flowers

In the tedium so desolately green
Of sorrow's hothouse,
The Flowers entwine my heart
With their wicked stems.
Ah! when shall they return about my head,
Those dear hands, so tenderly disentwining?

The tall violet Irises
Wickedly violated your eyes,
While seeming to reflect them,
They, who were the dream-water
Into which my dreams plunged, so softly
Enclosed in their colour;
And the lilies, white pistil-scented fountains,
Have lost their white grace
And are but poor, sickly, sunless things!

Sun! friend of evil flowers,
Destroyer of dreams, destroyer of illusions,
This blessed wafer of wretched souls!
Come! Come! Redeeming hands!
Shatter the panes of mendacity,
Shatter the panes of evil,
My soul is dying of too much sun!

Mirages! Plus ne refleurira la joie de mes yeux,
Et mes mains sont lasses de prier,
Mes yeux sont las de pleurer!
Éternellement ce bruit fou
Des pétales noirs de l'ennui,
Tombant goutte à goutte sur ma tête
Dans le vert de la serre de douleur!

Mirages! The joy of my eyes will never reflower,
And my hands are weary of praying,
My eyes are weary of weeping!
Eternally this insane sound
Of tedium's black petals
Falling drop by drop on my head
In the green of sorrow's hothouse!

10 iv *De soir*

Of evening

Dimanche sur les villes,
Dimanche dans les cœurs!
Dimanche chez les petites filles
Chantant d'une voix informée
Des rondes obstinées
Où de bonnes Tours*
N'en ont plus que pour quelques jours!

Sunday over the cities,
Sunday in people's hearts!
Sunday for the little girls
Singing with childish voices
Persistent rounds
In which good Towers
Have only a few days left!

Dimanche, les gares sont folles!
Tout le monde appareille
Pour des banlieues d'aventure
En se disant adieu
Avec des gestes éperdus!

On Sunday, the stations are frantic!
Everyone sets out
For suburb adventures,
Saying farewell
With frenzied gestures!

Dimanche les trains vont vite,
Dévorés par d'insatiables tunnels;
Et les bons signaux des routes
Échangent d'un œil unique
Des impressions toutes mécaniques.

On Sunday, trains go fast,
Devoured by insatiable tunnels;
And the good signals
Exchange with their single eye
Wholly mechanical impressions.

Dimanche, dans le bleu de mes rêves
Où mes pensées tristes
De feux d'artifices manqués
Ne veulent plus quitter
Le deuil de vieux Dimanches trépassés.

Sunday, in the blue of my dreams,
When my thoughts,
Saddened by fizzled fireworks,
Will no longer cease
Mourning for old Sundays dead and gone.

Et la nuit à pas de velours
Vient endormir le beau ciel fatigué,
Et c'est Dimanche dans les avenues d'étoiles;
La Vierge or sur argent
Laisse tomber les fleurs de sommeil!

And night with velvet tread
Comes to lull the lovely tired sky to sleep,
And it is Sunday on the avenues of stars;
The gold-on-silver Virgin
Lets fall the flowers of sleep!

Vite, les petits anges,
Dépassez les hirondelles
Afin de vous coucher
Forts d'absolution!
Prenez pitié des villes,
Prenez pitié des cœurs,
Vous, la Vierge or sur argent!

Quick! you tiny angels,
Outstrip the swallows,
That you may go to rest
Fortified by absolution!
Take pity on the cities,
Take pity on the hearts,
You gold-on-silver Virgin!

* An old folksong ('La tour, prends garde'), popular among French children.

CHANSONS DE BILITIS
(Pierre Louÿs)

II i *La flûte de Pan*

Pour le jour des Hyacinthies, il m'a donné une syrinx faite de roseaux bien taillés, unis avec la blanche cire qui est douce à mes lèvres comme le miel.

Il m'apprend à jouer, assise sur ses genoux; mais je suis un peu tremblante. Il en joue après moi, si doucement que je l'entends à peine.

Nous n'avons rien à nous dire, tant nous sommes près l'un de l'autre; mais nos chansons veulent se répondre, et tour à tour nos bouches s'unissent sur la flûte.

Il est tard; voici le chant des grenouilles vertes qui commence avec la nuit. Ma mère ne croira jamais que je suis restée si longtemps à chercher ma ceinture perdue.

II ii *La chevelure*

Il m'a dit: 'Cette nuit, j'ai rêvé. J'avais ta chevelure autour de mon cou. J'avais tes cheveux comme un collier noir autour de ma nuque et sur ma poitrine.

'Je les caressais, et c'étaient les miens; et nous étions liés pour toujours ainsi, par la même chevelure la bouche sur la bouche, ainsi que deux lauriers n'ont souvent qu'une racine.

'Et peu à peu, il m'a semblé, tant nos membres étaient confondus, que je devenais toi-même ou que tu entrais en moi comme mon songe.'

Quand il eut achevé, il mit doucement ses mains sur mes épaules, et il me regarda d'un regard si tendre, que je baissai les yeux avec un frisson.

THE SONGS OF BILITIS*

The flute of Pan

For Hyacinthus day he gave me a syrinx made of carefully cut reeds, bonded with white wax which tastes sweet to my lips like honey.

He teaches me to play, as I sit on his lap; but I am a little fearful. He plays it after me, so gently that I scarcely hear him.

We have nothing to say, so close are we one to another, but our songs try to answer each other, and our mouths join in turn on the flute.

It is late; here is the song of the green frogs that begins with the night. My mother will never believe I stayed out so long to look for my lost sash.

The tresses of hair

He said to me: 'Last night I dreamed. I had your tresses around my neck. I had your hair like a black necklace all round my nape and over my breast.

I caressed it and it was mine; and we were united thus forever by the same tresses, mouth on mouth, just as two laurels often share one root.

And gradually it seemed to me, so intertwined were our limbs, that I was becoming you, or you were entering into me like a dream.'

When he had finished, he gently set his hands on my shoulders and gazed at me so tenderly that I lowered my eyes with a shiver.

* The fictitious daughter of a Greek and Phoenician, Bilitis spent her childhood in Pamphylia, surrounded by forests, springs, and valleys.

11 iii *Le tombeau des Naïades*

Le long du bois couvert de givre, je marchais; mes cheveux devant ma bouche se fleurissaient de petits glaçons, et mes sandales étaient lourdes de neige fangeuse et tassée.

Il me dit: 'Que cherches-tu?'—'Je suis la trace du satyre. Ses petits pas fourchus alternent comme des trous dans un manteau blanc.' Il me dit: 'Les satyres sont morts.

'Les satyres et les nymphes aussi. Depuis trente ans il n'a pas fait un hiver aussi terrible. La trace que tu vois est celle d'un bouc. Mais restons ici, où est leur tombeau.'

Et avec le fer de sa houe il cassa la glace de la source où jadis riaient les naïades. Il prenait de grands morceaux froids, et les soulevant vers le ciel pâle, il regardait au travers.

The tomb of the Naiads

Along the frost-bound wood I walked; my hair, across my mouth, blossomed with tiny icicles, and my sandals were heavy with muddy, packed snow.

He said to me: 'What do you seek?' 'I follow the satyr's track. His little cloven hoof-marks alternate like holes in a white cloak.' He said to me: 'The satyrs are dead.

The satyrs and the nymphs too. For thirty years there has not been so harsh a winter. The tracks you see are those of a goat. But let us stay here, where their tomb is.'

And with the iron head of his hoe he broke the ice of the spring, where the naiads used to laugh. He picked up some huge cold fragments, and, raising them to the pale sky, gazed through them.

TROIS CHANSONS DE FRANCE

THREE SONGS OF FRANCE

12 i *Rondel: le temps a laissié son manteau*
(Charles d'Orléans)

Rondel: the season has shed its cloak

Le temps a laissié son manteau
De vent, de froidure et de pluye,
Et s'est vestu de broderye,
De soleil raiant, cler et beau.

Il n'y a beste ne oiseau
Qui en son jargon ne chante ou crye:
Le temps a laissié son manteau.

Rivière, fontaine et ruisseau
Portent, en livrée jolye,
Goultes d'argent d'orfaverie.
Chascun s'abille de nouveau,
Le temps a laissié son manteau.

The season has shed its cloak
Of wind and cold and rain
And donned embroidered garments
Of radiant sunshine, clear and fair.

There is no beast nor bird
That in its own tongue does not sing or cry:
The season has shed its cloak.

River, fountain, and brook
Wear, as pretty livery,
Drops of silver jewellery.
Each thing clads itself anew,
The season has shed its cloak.

12 ii *La grotte*

(Tristan l'Hermite)

Auprès de cette grotte sombre
Où l'on respire un air si doux,
L'onde lutte avec les cailloux,
Et la lumière avecque l'ombre.

Ces flots, lassés de l'exercice
Qu'ils ont fait dessus ce gravier,
Se reposent dans ce vivier
Où mourut autrefois Narcisse...

L'ombre de cette fleur vermeille
Et celle de ces joncs pendants
Paraissent estre là-dedans
Les songes de l'eau qui sommeille.

The grotto

Close to this dark grotto,
Where the air is so soft,
The water contends with pebbles,
And light contends with shade.

These waves, tired of moving
Across this gravel,
Are reposing in this pond
Where long ago Narcissus died...

The shadow of this crimson flower
And of those bending reeds
Seem in the depths to be
The dreams of the sleeping water.

12 iii *Rondel: pour ce que Plaisance est morte*

(Charles d'Orléans)

Pour ce que Plaisance est morte
Ce may, suis vestu de noir;
C'est grand pitié de véoir
Mon cœur qui s'en desconforte.

Je m'abille de la sorte
Que doy, pour faire devoir;
Pour ce que Plaisance est morte,
Ce may, suis vestu de noir.

Le temps ces nouvelles porte
Qui ne veut déduit avoir;
Mais par force du plouvoir
Fais des champs clore la porte,
Pour ce que Plaisance est morte.

Rondel: Because Plaisance is dead

Because Plaisance is dead
This May, I am attired in black;
It is so pitiful to see
My heart distressed.

I dress in the manner
That is becoming;
Because Plaisance is dead
This May, I am attired in black.

The elements proclaim the news
And will brook no diversion;
Instead, by means of rain,
They make the meadows close their door,
Because Plaisance is dead.

FÊTES GALANTES II

(Paul Verlaine)

FÊTES GALANTES II

13 i *Les ingénus*

Les hauts talons luttaient avec les longues jupes,
En sorte que, selon le terrain et le vent,
Parfois luisaient des bas de jambes, trop souvent
Interceptés!—et nous aimions ce jeu de dupes.

Parfois aussi le dard d'un insecte jaloux
Inquiétait le col des belles sous les branches,
Et c'étaient des éclairs soudains de nuques blanches,
Et ce régal comblait nos jeunes yeux de fous.

Le soir tombait, un soir équivoque d'automne:
Les belles, se pendant rêveuses à nos bras,
Dirent alors des mots si spécieux, tout bas,
Que notre âme, depuis ce temps, tremble et s'étonne.

Ingénus

High heels struggled with long skirts,
So that, depending on contour and wind,
Glimpses of leg would sometimes gleam, too often
Snatched from view!—and we loved this foolish
play.

Sometimes too a jealous insect's sting
Bothered pretty necks beneath the branches,
And there were sudden flashes of white napes—
And this feast overwhelmed our crazed young eyes.

Evening fell, an equivocal autumn evening:
The pretty girls, leaning dreamily on our arms,
Then murmured such fair-seeming words,
That, ever since, our startled souls have trembled.

13 ii *Le faune*

Un vieux faune de terre cuite
Rit au centre des boulingrins,
Présageant sans doute une suite
Mauvaise à ces instants sereins

Qui m'ont conduit et t'ont conduite,
—Mélancoliques pèlerins,—
Jusqu'à cette heure dont la fuite
Tournoie au son des tambourins.

The faun

An ancient terracotta faun
Laughs in the middle of the lawns,
Predicting no doubt an unhappy
Sequel to these moments of calm

That have led both you and me,
—Melancholy pilgrims—
To this hour that flits away,
Twirling to the tambourines.

13 iii *Colloque sentimental*

Dans le vieux parc solitaire et glacé,
Deux formes ont tout à l'heure passé.

Leurs yeux sont morts et leurs lèvres sont molles,
Et l'on entend à peine leurs paroles.

Dans le vieux parc solitaire et glacé,
Deux spectres ont évoqué le passé.

Lovers' dialogue

In the ancient park, deserted and frozen,
Two shapes have just passed by.

Their eyes are dead and their lips are lifeless,
And their words can hardly be heard.

In the ancient park, deserted and frozen,
Two spectres were recalling the past.

—Te souvient-il de notre extase ancienne?   —Do you remember our past rapture?
—Pourquoi voulez-vous donc qu'il m'en souvienne?   —Why would you have me remember?

—Ton cœur bat-il toujours à mon seul nom?   —Does your heart still surge at my very name?
Toujours vois-tu mon âme en rêve?—Non.   Do you still see my soul when you dream?—No.

—Ah! Les beaux jours de bonheur indicible   —Ah, the beautiful days of inexpressible bliss
Où nous joignions nos bouches!—C'est possible.   When our lips met!—It may have been so.

—Qu'il était bleu, le ciel, et grand, l'espoir!   —How blue the sky, how hopes ran high!
—L'espoir a fui, vaincu, vers le ciel noir.   —Hope has fled, vanquished, to the black sky.

Tels ils marchaient dans les avoines folles,   So they walked on through the wild grasses,
Et la nuit seule entendit leurs paroles.   And the night alone heard their words.

LE PROMENOIR DES DEUX AMANTS

THE TWO LOVERS' PROMENADE

(Tristan l'Hermite)

14 i *Auprès de cette grotte sombre*

Close to this dark grotto

Auprès de cette grotte sombre   Close to this dark grotto,
Où l'on respire un air si doux,   Where the air is so soft,
L'onde lutte avec les cailloux,   The water contends with pebbles,
Et la lumière avecque l'ombre.   And light contends with shade.

Ces flots, lassés de l'exercice   These waves, tired of moving
Qu'ils ont fait dessus ce gravier,   Across this gravel,
Se reposent dans ce vivier   Are reposing in this pond
Où mourut autrefois Narcisse...   Where long ago Narcissus died...

L'ombre de cette fleur vermeille   The shadow of this crimson flower
Et celle de ces joncs pendants   And of those bending reeds
Paraissent estre là-dedans   Seem in the depths to be
Les songes de l'eau qui sommeille.   The dreams of the sleeping water.

14 ii *Crois mon conseil, chère Climène*

Trust my counsel, dear Climène

Crois mon conseil, chère Climène;   Trust my counsel, dear Climène;
Pour laisser arriver le soir,   While waiting for evening to fall,
Je te prie, allons nous asseoir   I beg you, let us sit
Sur le bord de cette fontaine.   At this fountain's edge.

N'ouïs-tu pas soupirer Zéphire,
De merveille et d'amour atteint,
Voyant des roses sur ton teint,
Qui ne sont pas de son empire?

Sa bouche d'odeur toute pleine,
A soufflé sur notre chemin,
Mêlant un esprit de jasmin
À l'ambre de ta douce haleine.

Can you not hear Zephyrus sigh,
Stricken with wonder and love
At the sight of roses on your cheeks,
Over which he has no power?

His mouth, so full of fragrance,
Has breathed across our path,
Mingling jasmine essence
With the amber of your sweet breath.

14 iii *Je tremble en voyant ton visage*

Je tremble en voyant ton visage
Flotter avecque mes désirs,
Tant j'ai de peur que mes soupirs
Ne lui fassent faire naufrage.

De crainte de cette aventure
Ne commets pas si librement
À cet infidèle élément
Tous les trésors de la Nature.

Veux-tu, par un doux privilège,
Me mettre au-dessus des humains?
Fais-moi boire au creux de tes mains,
Si l'eau n'en dissout point la neige.

I tremble when I see your face

I tremble when I see your face
Floating with my desires,
So frightened am I that my sighs
Might cause your face to drown.

For fear of this misfortune,
Do not endow too freely
That untrustworthy element
With all of Nature's treasures.

Will you, as a sweet privilege,
Raise me above human kind?
Let me drink from your cupped hands,
If the water melt not their snow.

TROIS BALLADES DE FRANÇOIS VILLON

THREE BALLADS OF FRANÇOIS VILLON

15 i *Ballade de Villon a s'amye*

Faulse beauté, qui tant me couste cher,
Rude en effet, hypocrite doulceur,
Amour dure, plus que fer, à mascher;
Nommer te puis de ma deffaçon sœur.
Charme felon, la mort d'ung povre cueur,
Orgueil mussé, qui gens met au mourir,
Yeulx sans pitié! ne veult droict de rigueur,
Sans empirer, ung povre secourir?

Mieulx m'eust valu avoir esté crier
Ailleurs secours, c'est esté mon bonheur:
Rien ne m'eust sceu de ce fait arracher;
Trotter m'en fault en fuyte à deshonneur.

Ballad of Villon to his love

False beauty, for whom I pay so great a price,
Harsh, in truth, behind a mask of sadness,
A love that's tougher to chew than steel,
I name you sister of my undoing.
Criminal charm, death of my poor heart,
Hidden pride that sends folk to their destruction,
Eyes devoid of pity—will not Justice
Help a poor man without crushing him?

It had been better to have begged
For help elsewhere, it might have made me happy.
Nothing could snatch me from this fate.
Now I must retreat in shame.

Haro, haro, le grand et le mineur!
Et qu'est cecy? mourray sans coup ferir,
Ou pitié peult, selon ceste teneur,
Sans empirer, ung povre secourir?

Ung temps viendra, qui fera desseicher,
Jaulnir, flestrir, vostre espanie fleur:
J'en risse lors, se tant peusse marcher,
Mais las! nenny: Ce seroit donc foleur,
Vieil je seray; vous laide et sans couleur.
Or, beuvez fort, tant que ru peult courir.
Ne donnez pas à tous ceste douleur,
Sans empirer, ung povre secourir.

Prince amoureux, des amans le greigneur,
Vostre mal gré ne vouldroye encourir;
Mais tout franc cueur doit, par Nostre Seigneur,
Sans empirer, ung povre secourir.

Help me, help me, one and all!
But what? Am I to die and not strike a blow?
Or will Pity, softened by these sad words,
Help a poor man without crushing him?

A time will come that will dry up,
Fade, and wither your full-blown flower;
Then I shall laugh, if I can still walk.
But alas! Nay—that would be folly:
I shall be old; you ugly and wan.
So drink deep, while the river still runs.
Give this pain to no one else—
Help a poor man without crushing him.

Prince of lovers, greatest of them all,
I had sooner not incur your wrath,
But every honest heart should, by Our Lord,
Help a poor man without crushing him.

15 ii *Ballade que Villon feit a la requeste de sa mère pour prier Nostre-Dame*

Ballad made at his mother's request for a prayer to Our Lady

Dame du ciel, régente terrienne,
Emperière des infernaulx paluz,
Recevez-moy, vostre humble chrestienne,
Que comprinse soye entre vos esleuz,
Ce non obstant qu'oncques riens ne valuz.
Les biens de vous, ma dame et ma maistresse,
Sont trop plus grans que ne suys pecheresse,
Sans lesquelz bien ame ne peult merir
N'avoir les cieulx, je n'en suis menteresse.
En ceste foy je vueil vivre et mourir.

À vostre Filz dictes que je suys sienne;
De luy soyent mes pechez aboluz:
Pardonnez-moy comme à l'Égyptienne,*

Ou comme il feit au clerc Théophilus,†
Lequel par vous fut quitte et aboluz,
Combien qu'il eust au diable faict promesse.
Preservez-moy que je n'accomplisse ce!
Vierge portant sans rompure encourir
Le sacrement qu'on celebre à la messe.
En ceste foy je vueil vivre et mourir.

Lady of Heaven, Regent of earth,
Empress of the infernal swamps,
Take me, your humble Christian,
To be numbered among your elect,
Though my worth has been as nothing.
Your mercy, my Lady and my Mistress,
Is much greater than my sinfulness,
Without it no soul can merit
Nor enter Heaven, I do not lie.
In this faith I wish to live and die.

Say to your Son that I am his,
By him may my sins be pardoned.
May he forgive me as he forgave the Egyptian
    woman,
Or the clerk Theophilus,
Who was acquitted and absolved by you,
Though he had made a pact with Satan.
Preserve me from doing such a thing,
Virgin, who bore without incurring blemish
The sacrament we celebrate at mass.
In this faith I wish to live and die.

---

  * Saint Mary was an Egyptian courtesan from Alexandria who implored the Virgin Mary to intercede for her.
  † Theophilus, a sixth century clerk from Asia Minor, sold his soul to the Devil. He then begged the Virgin Mary to retrieve his contract from the Devil, which she did.

Femme je suis povrette et ancienne,
Qui riens ne sçay; oncques lettre ne leuz;
Au moustier voy dont suis paroissienne,
Paradis painct où sont harpes et luz,
Et ung enfer où damnez sont boulluz:
L'ung me faict paour, l'aultre joye et liesse.

La joye avoir fais-moy haulte Déesse,
A qui pecheurs doivent tous recourir,
Comblez de foy, sans faincte ne paresse.
En ceste foy je vueil vivre et mourir.

I am a poor old woman,
Ignorant and unlettered.
In my parish church I see
A painted paradise with harps and lutes,
And a hell where the damned are boiled:
One fills me with fright, the other with joy and
    bliss.
Let me have that joy, high Goddess,
To whom all sinners in the end must come,
Full of faith, without hypocrisy or sloth.
In this faith I wish to live and die.

15 iii *Ballade des femmes de Paris*

Ballad of the women of Paris

Quoy qu'on tient belles langagières
Florentines, Veniciennes,
Assez pour estre messaigières,
Et mesmement les anciennes;
Mais, soient Lombardes, Romaines,
Genevoises, à mes périls,
Piemontoises, Savoysiennes,
Il n'est bon bec que de Paris.

De beau parler tiennent chayères,
Ce dit-on Napolitaines,
Et que sont bonnes cacquetières
Allemandes et Bruciennes;
Soient Grecques, Egyptiennes,
De Hongrie ou d'aultre païs,
Espaignolles ou Castellannes,
Il n'est bon bec que de Paris.

Brettes, Suysses, n'y sçavent guères,
Ne Gasconnes et Tholouzaines;
Du Petit Pont deux harangères
Les concluront, et les Lorraines,
Anglesches ou Callaisiennes,
(Ay-je beaucoup de lieux compris?)
Picardes, de Valenciennes...
Il n'est bon bec que de Paris.

Prince, aux dames parisiennes,
De bien parler donnez le prix;
Quoy qu'on die d'Italiennes,
Il n'est bon bec que de Paris.

Though they be reckoned good talkers,
Florentine and Venetian women,
Good enough to be go-betweens,
Even the ancient women too;
And be they Lombards or Romans
Or Genovese, I say to my peril,
Or Piedmontese or Savoyards—
There's no tongue like a Parisian one.

Chairs in the art of fine chatter, they say,
Are held by the women of Naples,
While those from Germany and Prussia
Are very good at prattle.
Yet be they Greek, Egyptian,
From Hungary or other lands,
Spanish or Catalonian—
There's no tongue like a Parisian one.

Bretons and Swiss are mere beginners,
Like Gascons and Toulousians;
Two jabberers on the Petit Pont
Would silence them, and Lorrainers, too,
And women from England and from Calais
(I've named a lot of places, eh?),
From Picardy and Valencienne...
There's no tongue like a Parisian one.

Prince, to the ladies of Paris
Present the prize for fine chatter;
Whatever is said of Italians,
There's no tongue like a Parisian one.

16 *Éventail*   *Fan*

(Stéphane Mallarmé), from *TROIS POÈMES DE STÉPHANE MALLARMÉ*

Ô rêveuse, pour que je plonge
Au pur délice sans chemin,
Sache, par un subtil mensonge,
Garder mon aile dans ta main.

Une fraîcheur de crépuscule
Te vient à chaque battement
Dont le coup prisonnier recule
L'horizon délicatement.

Vertige! voici que frissonne
L'espace comme un grand baiser
Qui, fou de naître pour personne,
Ne peut jaillir ni s'apaiser.

Sens-tu le paradis farouche
Ainsi qu'un rire enseveli
Se couler du coin de ta bouche
Au fond de l'unanime pli!

Le sceptre des rivages roses
Stagnants sur les soirs d'or, ce l'est,
Ce blanc vol fermé que tu poses
Contre le feu d'un bracelet.

O dreamer, that I may plunge
Into pure pathless delight,
Contrive, by a subtle deception,
To hold my wing in your hand.

A twilight freshness
Reaches you at each flutter,
Whose captive stroke distances
The horizon delicately.

Vertigo! See how space
Shivers like an immense kiss
Which, mad at being born for no one,
Can neither burst forth nor abate.

Can you feel the wild paradise
Just like buried laughter
Flow from the corner of your mouth
Deep into the unanimous fold!

The sceptre of rose-coloured shores
Stagnating over golden evenings—such is
This white furled flight which you set
Against a bracelet's fire.

17 *Noël des enfants qui n'ont plus de maisons*   *A carol for homeless children*

(Claude Debussy)

Nous n'avons plus de maisons!
Les ennemis ont tout pris,
   tout pris, tout pris,
   jusqu'à notre petit lit!
Ils ont brûlé l'école et notre maître aussi.
Ils ont brûlé l'église et monsieur Jésus-Christ
Et le vieux pauvre qui n'a pas pu s'en aller!

Nous n'avons plus de maisons.
Les ennemis ont tout pris,
   tout pris, tout pris,
   jusqu'à notre petit lit!
Bien sûr! papa est à la guerre,
Pauvre maman est morte!

We've no houses any more!
The enemy have taken everything,
   everything, everything
   even our little beds!
They've burned the school and our teacher too.
They've burned the church and Mister Jesus
And the poor old man who couldn't escape!

We've no houses any more!
The enemy have taken everything,
   everything, everything
   even our little beds!
Of course! Daddy's at the war,
Poor mother died!

Avant d'avoir vu tout ça.	Before seeing all this.
Qu'est-ce que l'on va faire?	What are we to do?
Noël! petit Noël! n'allez pas chez eux,	Noël, little Noël, don't visit them,
n'allez plus jamais chez eux,	don't visit them ever again.
Punissez-les!	Punish them!
Vengez les enfants de France!	Avenge the children of France!
Les petits Belges, les petits Serbes,	The little Belgians, the little Serbs,
et les petits Polonais aussi!	and also the little Poles!
Si nous en oublions, pardonnez-nous.	If we've forgotten any, forgive us.
Noël! Noël! surtout, pas de joujoux,	Noël, Noël, and above all, no toys,
Tâchez de nous redonner le pain quotidien.	Try to give us back our daily bread.
Nous n'avons plus de maisons!	We've no houses any more!
Les ennemis ont tout pris,	The enemy have taken everything,
tout pris, tout pris,	everything, everything
jusqu'à notre petit lit!	even our little beds!
Ils ont brûlé l'école et notre maître aussi.	They've burned the school and our teacher too.
Ils ont brûlé l'église et monsieur Jésus-Christ	They've burned the church and Mister Jesus
Et le vieux pauvre qui n'a pas pu s'en aller!	And the poor old man who couldn't escape!
Noël! écoutez-nous, nous n'avons plus de petits	Noël! Hear us, we no longer have our little clogs:
sabots:	
Mais donnez la victoire aux enfants de France!	But give victory to the children of France!

DELAGE, Maurice (1879–1961)

This follower and student of Ravel and friend of Stravinsky contributed a number of small cycles with instrumental accompaniment to the repertoire. Chief among these is the *QUATRE POÈMES HINDOUS* (1912) which is something of a travel diary. Delage composed the pieces in India, thus *Madras*, *Lahore*, *Bénarès* (Benares), and *Jeypur* (Jaipur) stand above the poems' titles. They form a vocal riposte to the orchestral *Évocations* of Albert Roussel (1910–11), the second and third of which had also been inspired by visits to Jaipur and Benares. Delage's songs are exceptionally atmospheric, and the evocation of real Indian music is astonishing, particularly in the second, which shows Delage's taste for the exotic side of Heine (something already explored in *Intermezzo*, the first of *TROIS MÉLODIES*—1908–10). In this version of *Ein Fichtenbaum steht einsam* (set also by Liszt and Grieg) the singer has two pages of sinuous wordless melisma which would only need the addition of quarter-tones here and there to seem utterly authentic in Indian classical music terms. It is above all in the Ravelian instrumentation of this music (flutes, oboe, clarinet, bassoon, harp, piano, and string quartet) that Delage distinguishes himself; a performance of this cycle with piano alone would be a nonsense. The dedications of the first song to Ravel and the fourth to Stravinsky somehow place the work in its historical context.

From 1923 date *SEPT HAÏ-KAÏ*, delicate little Japanese-inspired fragments; once again it is the use of the ensemble which is astonishing, particularly in the fifth of the set, *Lune d'automne*. *TROIS CHANTS*

DE LA JUNGLE date from 1934. The first two songs are settings from Rudyard Kipling's *Jungle book* in French translation. The touching *Maktah (Berceuse phoque*, also set by Koechlin) and the dramatic *Chil le vautour* are among the most unusual English contributions (via their poetry) to the mélodie repertoire. For the utterly zany third song, *Themmangú* (*Chant et danse du tigre*), Delage has invented his own fantasy text along the lines of 'Doe re kan-ne me le pou-pa-di Kan ma-ni va-ren na-di dorrekan' and so on. This derives from the composer's own transcriptions of the sounds he heard sung to an age-old raga; nevertheless, the solemn nonsense of Poulenc's *Rhapsodie nègre* comes to mind. The isolated Coctean setting *Sobre las olas* is another tangential link with Les Six.

The *DEUX FABLES DE JEAN DE LA FONTAINE* from 1931 (*Le corbeau et le renard* and *La cigale et la four-mi* [CAPLET 3 i, 3 ii]), are pleasantly discursive without really rivalling Caplet's settings, and the *TROIS POÈMES DÉSENCHANTÉS*, the composer's last set of songs, have a gently nostalgic, valedictory quality.

QUATRE POÈMES HINDOUS

I i *Madras: Une belle*
(Bhartrihari)

Une belle à la taille svelte
se promène sous les arbres de la forêt,
en se reposant de temps en temps.
Ayant relevé de la main
les trois voiles d'or
qui lui couvre les seins,
elle renvoie à la lune
les rayons dont elle était baignée.

I ii *Lahore: Un sapin isolé*
(Heinrich Heine)

Un sapin isolé se dresse sur une montagne
Aride du Nord. Il sommeille.
La glace et la neige l'environne
D'un manteau blanc.

Il rêve d'un palmier qui là-bas
Dans l'Orient lointain se désole,
Solitaire et taciturne,
Sur la pente de son rocher brûlant.

FOUR HINDU POEMS

Madras: A beautiful woman

A beautiful woman, with a slim waist,
walks beneath the forest trees,
halting to rest from time to time.
Lifting with her hand
the three golden veils
that cover her breasts,
she reflects back to the moon
the rays in which she was bathed.

Lahore: A lonely fir-tree

A lonely fir-tree stands on a mountain's
Barren northern heights. And drowses.
Ice and snow envelop it
In a white blanket.

It dreams of a palm-tree which grieves
Far away in the distant East,
Solitary and silent
On a blazing rocky wall.

I iii *Bénarès: Naissance de Bouddha*   *Benares: The birth of Buddha*
    (Anon.)

En ce temps-là fut annoncé
la venue de Bouddha sur la terre.
Il se fit dans le ciel un grand bruit de nuages.
Les Dieux, agitant leurs éventails et leurs vêtements,
répandirent d'innombrables fleurs merveilleuses.
Des parfums mystérieux et doux se croisèrent
comme des lianes dans le souffle tiède de cette nuit
    de printemps.
La perle divine de la pleine lune
s'arrêta sur le palais de marbre,
gardé par vingt mille éléphants,
pareils à des collines grises de la couleur de
    nuages.

It was then that the coming of Buddha
was announced on earth.
The sky filled with a great clamour of clouds.
The Gods, flourishing their fans and robes,
scattered innumerable marvellous flowers.
Mysterious and sweet scents intermingled
like creepers in the warm breath of that spring
    night.
The sacred pearl of the full moon
hung above the marble palace,
guarded by twenty thousand elephants,
like grey hills the colour of clouds.

I iv *Jeypur: Si vous pensez à elle*   *Jaipur: If you think of her*
    (Bhartrihari)

Si vous pensez à elle,
vous éprouvez un douloureux tourment.
Si vous la voyez,
votre esprit se trouble.
Si vous la touchez,
Vous perdez la raison.
Comment peut-on l'appeler bien-aimée?

If you think of her,
you feel an aching torment.
If you see her,
you grow distracted.
If you touch her,
you lose your reason.
How can you call her beloved?

DELANNOY, Marcel (1898–1962)

The music of Delannoy sometimes sees the light of day, but seldom outside France where, at one time, he enjoyed a high reputation. He published many songs which display a lively and sometimes acerbic style. An interest in the manner of folksong is combined with an eclectic use of such illustrative devices as blues and Renaissance pastiche. This versatility made Delannoy a good composer for the theatre, and a number of his songs were connected with plays and films. In this mode, the DEUX AIRS POUR CROMWELL DE VICTOR HUGO are great fun—particularly the racy *Chanson de Rochester*. More serious are the DEUX BALLADES (1934)—the first, *La mer et la mort*, a grandiose Paul Fort setting which mixes singing with speech, the second, *Ballade des vingt mineurs* (André de la Tourrasse), a song which is both exciting and moving, about a tragic mining disaster. This is composed in a popular style that brings Brecht and Eisler to mind. In the style of Poulenc's CHANSONS GAILLARDES (and almost contemporary with them) are QUATRE REGRETS DE JOACHIM DU BELLAY (1928). The piano writing in the last song of this set shows the composer to be a master of the instrument. Perhaps the set of songs of which Delannoy would have been most proud were CINQ QUATRAINS DE FRANCIS JAMMES (1935) where the brevity of the poetry, and its intensity, brings out the best in him—particularly in a song like *Columbine* which was also set by Lili Boulanger. The quotation by Cocteau which opens the *Avant-propos* to this book is set to music in *M'entendez-vous ainsi?*, the third of *TROIS MÉLODIES* (1929), a cycle which also includes settings of Georges Gabory and Anna de Noailles.

DELIBES, Léo (1836–1891)

The creator of *Coppélia* and *Sylvia* (in ballet terms he was France's Tchaikovsky) and of the opera *Lakmé* was a talented writer for voice and piano. Fritz Noske points out that his work derives from the chansonnette, lighter and more entertaining than the romance, and less susceptible to the German influence of the lied. Indeed, Delibes composed quite a number of these semi-popular ditties in his apprentice years. A stranger to the Delibes songs might look to the Bizet mélodies for some indication of his style, for he shared with this contemporary a natural feeling for the theatre, and an ability to spin local colour for Spanish and oriental character pieces. The most famous of these is *Chanson espagnole*—the bolero known as **Les filles de Cadix** (Musset). This was one of *TROIS MÉLODIES* published in 1863; the other two songs in the collection are also delightful: a Victor Hugo setting entitled *Églogue* (the poem 'Viens!—une flûte invisible' was later set by Saint-Saëns and others [CAPLET 4]), and another Musset lyric, **Bonjour, Suzon.** Both charm us with their unpretentious gaiety and delicacy, as well as their economy of means. It seems true that the Bizet songs have greater depth than Delibes's, but at his best this composer is irresistible. Well worth investigation is *Avril* (Rémy Belleau, also set by Leguerney, and first conceived as a song for women's chorus in 1866), which ranks with Bizet's *Sonnet* (Ronsard) as one of the earliest and best evocations of sixteenth-century madrigal style. (It is hardly surprising that Delibes was later able to write such wonderful pastiche dances for Hugo's *Le roi s'amuse*.) A debt to Gounod is apparent in the tuneful *Chanson de l'oiseleur* (Lockroy), which captures the tone of the *fabliau* in that composer's charming *Médecin malgré lui* from 1858. The poet Armand Silvestre makes an early and frequent appearance in this work-list. Worth hearing is his *Myrto*, which Delibes fashions as a dance song from antiquity, its dotted rhythms prophetic of *Danseuse* from Fauré's *MIRAGES* cycle. Exciting in its way, but less convincing, is the extended scena (or scène) *Départ* (Augier), for this composer is better suited to less hectic and less passionate effusions, indeed we most delight in him (in his songwriting at least) when his canvas is of modest dimensions.

So much for the first *recueil* of mélodies. Apart from a vocal arrangement of the waltz from *Coppélia* and a few recycled operatic fragments, there are six songs worthy of note in the second *recueil* (which comprises works written between 1872 and 1890), although one cannot avoid the impression of a composer who had peaked early and whose style was old hat before he had reached his fifties. Here we find a familiar mixture of scène, occasional piece, and pastiche as exemplified by the dramatic *Chanson hongroise* (Coppée), *Épithalame* (Grenier) on a nautical theme (and probably written for a friend's wedding), and *Crysanthème* (Fuchs), which is a chinoiserie to an imaginary lute accompaniment, and deliberately reticent in emotion. The restrained grief of Roussel's *Réponse d'une épouse sage* comes to mind. There are two duets which are useful additions to the repertoire: *Les trois oiseaux* (Coppée, 1868) for two sopranos, and the more unusual *Marchand d'oublies* (Parmentier), a jolly little ditty for tenor and baritone.

Apart from these songs, Delibes was well known as a composer of incidental music for the theatre. *Sérénade à Ninon* (written in 1879 for Musset's *À quoi rêvent les jeune filles*) reminds us of *Bonjour, Suzon* with its catchy tune. For the eponymous heroine of the play by the same poet, Delibes composed *Chanson de Barberine* in 1882 (also set by Albéniz). The *Sérénade de Ruy-Blas* (written for the Hugo play in 1879) is expertly done; it suggests the Spanish style without outstaying its welcome. Chabrier's setting, by comparison, seems to make too much of the poem for its passing importance in the play. Continuing his collaboration with Hugo, Delibes wrote *Vieille chanson*, a mandolin-accompanied serenade, for *Le roi s'amuse* in 1882. In all this we hear a charm and tact, above all a professionalism, which we rediscover in the music of Reynaldo Hahn who was having his first successes in the salon as Delibes's life was coming to its close. One feels that the two composers, charmers both, had a similarly eighteenth-century idea of the role of music in refined society: the unashamed giving of pleasure.

1 *Les filles de Cadix*

(Alfred de Musset)

Nous venions de voir le taureau,
  Trois garçons, trois fillettes,
Sur la pelouse il faisait beau
Et nous dansions un boléro
  Au son des castagnettes.
    'Dites-moi, voisin,
    Si j'ai bonne mine,
    Et si ma basquine
    Va bien, ce matin.
Vous me trouvez la taille fine?...
    Ah! ah!
Les filles de Cadix aiment assez cela.'

Et nous dansions un boléro,
  Un soir c'était dimanche.
Vers nous s'en vint un hidalgo
Cousu d'or, la plume au chapeau,
  Et le poing sur la hanche:
    'Si tu veux de moi,
    Brune au doux sourire,
    Tu n'as qu'à le dire,
    Cet or est à toi.
—Passez votre chemin, beau sire.
    Ah! ah!
Les filles de Cadix n'entendent pas cela.'

The girls of Cadiz

We'd just left the bullfight,
  Three boys, three girls,
The sun shone on the grass
And we danced a bolero
  To the sound of castanets.
    'Tell me, neighbour,
    Am I looking good,
    And does my skirt
    Suit me, this morning?
Have I a slender waist?...
    Ah! ah!
The girls of Cadiz are rather fond of that.'

And we were dancing a bolero,
  One sunday evening.
A hidalgo* came towards us,
Glittering in gold, feather in cap,
  And hand on hip:
    'If you want me,
    Dark beauty with the sweet smile,
    You've only to say so,
    And these riches are yours.'
Go on your way, fine sir.
    Ah! ah!
The girls of Cadiz don't take to that.

* One of the lower nobility; a gentleman by birth.

2 *Bonjour, Suzon*

(Alfred de Musset)

Bonjour, Suzon	***Bonjour, Suzon!***
Bonjour, Suzon, ma fleur des bois!	Bonjour, Suzon, my woodland flower!
Es-tu toujours la plus jolie?	Are you still the prettiest?
Je reviens, tel que tu me vois,	I return, just as you see me,
D'un grand voyage en Italie.	From travels throughout Italy.
Du paradis j'ai fait le tour;	I have made a tour of paradise,
J'ai fait des vers, j'ai fait l'amour.	I have made verses, I have made love.
Mais que t'importe?	But what is that to you?
Je passe devant ta maison;	I pass before your house,
Ouvre ta porte.	Open your door.
Bonjour, Suzon!	Bonjour, Suzon!
Je t'ai vue au temps des lilas.	I saw you last at lilac-time.
Ton cœur joyeux venait d'éclore.	Your heart was full of new-found joy.
Et tu disais: 'Je ne veux pas,	And you said: 'I do not wish,
Je ne veux pas qu'on m'aime encore.'	I do not wish to be loved just yet.'
Qu'as-tu fait depuis mon départ?	What have you done since I left?
Qui part trop tôt revient trop tard.	Who leaves too soon, returns too late;
Mais que m'importe?	But what is that to me?
Je passe devant ta maison;	I pass before your house,
Ouvre ta porte.	Open your door.
Bonjour, Suzon!	Bonjour, Suzon!

DELIUS, Frederick (1862–1934)

An English composer, but a true cosmopolitan, he was more attracted to the literature and culture of Scandinavia than France, as far as his songwriting was concerned. But Delius liked the country well enough to live there (in Grez-sur-Loing, outside Paris) from 1897 until his death. There are five French songs, all with Verlaine texts. *Il pleure dans mon cœur* [DEBUSSY 6 ii] captures the aimless depression of the poem to admirable effect. *Le ciel est par-dessus le toit* [FAURÉ 31] is perhaps less suited to this composer's meandering, quasi-improvised style; it fails to reflect the poem's concision and tension. These songs were composed in 1895 and were later orchestrated. *La lune blanche* [FAURÉ 30 iii, HAHN I v] was composed sixteen years later, and achieves a moonlit peacefulness and stillness despite its seemingly random chromaticism. The superimposition of fourths and fifths is one of this composer's harmonic signatures. Like *Il pleure dans mon cœur*, the languid *Chanson d'automne* [HAHN I i] effectively expresses the *deuil*, if not the linguistic economy, of the poet, and surely owes something to Debussy. The last Delius song dates from 1919 and is a setting of *Avant que tu ne t'en ailles* from LA BONNE CHANSON [FAURÉ 30 vi] with typically Delian modulations, and chords of the added sixth and seventh at its conclusion.

DIEPENBROCK, Alphons (1862–1921)

Heavily influenced by Debussy, the Dutch composer Diepenbrock rushed in where angels fear to tread. Most composers have avoided duplicating the settings of the masters, but almost every one of Diepenbrock's French songs is a familiar title, in the canon of Duparc, Fauré, and Debussy. It may be coincidence that his setting of Verlaine's *Écoutez la chanson bien douce* [CHAUSSON 9] dates from the same year as Chausson's. Equally it is hard to accuse him of copying the mood of Debussy's 1882 setting of *Clair de lune* when that song was only published in 1926. Nevertheless Diepenbrock's music (1898) is remarkably similar, and suggests the possibility of a privileged glimpse of the manuscript. Other familiar titles are *Recueillement* [DEBUSSY 7 iv], *Puisque l'aube grandit* [FAURÉ 30 ii] from *LA BONNE CHANSON* (actually nothing like Fauré's song), a rather original (and difficult to sing) *Mandoline* [FAURÉ 29 i], and a more derivative *En sourdine* [DEBUSSY 8 i]. In *Berceuse*, Diepenbrock sets a poem from Van Lerberghe's *LA CHANSON D'ÈVE* (God's warning to Eve about the serpent) which Fauré was wise enough to leave out of his cycle. The setting of *L'invitation au voyage* [DUPARC 7] puts a new gloss on a very familiar text and is not without merit; likewise the Baudelaire setting *Les chats* and *Incantation* to a text by André Gide. These songs, which sometimes lose themselves (and thus prospective interpreters) in ineffective complexities, are the work of an imaginative sensibility. His response to German literature was equally strong and, in the case of his Novalis settings, arguably more original than his excursions into French mélodie. An exception to this is *La chanson de l'hypertropique*, one of the few good Laforgue songs in the canon—it describes the staccato cries of a child with a heart condition. Diepenbrock had met Yvette Guilbert in Paris in 1891, and this song was meant to be performed in a café-chanson style almost certainly inspired by the great diseuse.

DIEREN, Bernhard van (1887–1936)

This English composer and critic of Dutch birth wrote a number of songs in French, as well as the *DEUX POÈMES* (Baudelaire, Villon, 1917) for speaker and string quartet. The songs with piano are often without bar-lines, and are of bewildering chromatic complexity, but they are the work of a man of considerable culture and imagination. The following are worthy of investigation provided the interpreters are willing to work hard in the initial process of deciphering the works: *Chanson* (Boileau, 1925), *Spleen* (Verlaine, 1927 [DEBUSSY 6 vi]), and *Rondel* ('Le temps a laissié son manteau'—Charles d'Orléans, 1928 [DEBUSSY 12 i]).

DONIZETTI, Gaetano (1797–1848)

The piano-accompanied vocal works of Donizetti are more numerous than the readily available modern editions seem to suggest. In fact this composer wrote more than 300 songs. A number of these were included in the eleven collections published in his lifetime under titles such as *NUITS D'ÉTÉ*

À PAUSILIPPE and *INSPIRATIONS VIENNOISES*. Some 160 songs were published separately, the majority of these undated. Songs composed to French poems were often translated into Italian, and vice versa. Much work remains to be done by musicologists, merely in unravelling the background to these texts. We await a scholarly edition of the works, and the recovery of music in a wide and interesting range of musical styles reflecting Donizetti's astonishing career—his employment and ascendancy in Naples, Paris, and Vienna. Until then the composer has to suffer the indignity of being lumped together with his Italian contemporaries and their shortcomings. It was Thackeray in *Vanity Fair* who referred to 'the milk-and-water *lagrime*, *sospiri* and *felicità* of the eternal Donizettian music with which we are favoured now-a-days'.

It is curious that an Italian composer born in the same year as Schubert owed his musical instruction to a German (Donizetti's mentor and teacher in Bergamo was Simon Mayr) at the same time as Schubert's talent was fostered by Antonio Salieri in Vienna. The young Italian's training included the writing of string quartets, and it is perhaps due to Mayr's influence that Donizetti's song output is more extensive and ambitious than any other nineteenth-century composer from Italy. A number of his greatest operas (*Poliuto*, *La fille du régiment*, *Don Pasquale*) were created for the Parisian public; it is little wonder, therefore, that Donizetti seems to have been as happy setting French texts as Italian. In some of his *recueils* (for example the *MATINÉE MUSICALE* from 1841 dedicated to Queen Victoria) the composer handles both languages with equal ease. In this volume one finds, among the songs in Italian, such titles as the bolero *Le retour au désert*, the oriental evocation *La nouvelle Ourika*, and the rather sentimental effusions *Ton Dieu est mon Dieu*, and *Billets doux*. The two most substantial French songs are from an earlier collection which was published simultaneously in France and Italy in 1839 under the title *UN HIVER À PARIS OU RÊVERIES NAPOLITAINES*. Poems by the famous French tenor Adolphe Nourrit enabled Donizetti to deploy his histrionic gifts: *La dernière nuit d'un novice*, a scène describing the final night of agony and temptation of a young monk as he struggles to choose the world of the spirit over that of the flesh, and *La folle de Sainte-Hélène* about a woman driven mad by her devotion to Napoleon. Her fervent patriotism gives way to reality as the Dies Irae sounds in the bass of the piano, signifying the emperor's death in exile.

Only the first of these scènes is included in the second volume of the modern selection of Donizetti's works published by Ricordi—*COMPOSIZIONI DA CAMERA*; in the same collection one also finds a highly sentimental ballad concerning a beggar woman and her child dying of starvation, *La mère et l'enfant*. Ricordi also publishes *6 ARIE* (edited by Pestalozza), a collection of late songs (1844) the most substantial of which is *Depuis qu'une autre a su te plaire*, an effective aria which shows Donizetti's French style at its most fluent. Much of this composer's music seems to rub shoulders with the songwriting of Meyerbeer, another internationally successful opera composer based in Paris; it serves as a reminder that for such luminaries the whole of Europe was a single market (in today's terms they would have a production of *Gatti* playing in every European capital). Celebrity has not always benefited the quality of such composers' musical output. Nevertheless, the jury is still out in the case of Donizetti's songs, and the list of French song titles in the composer's astonishingly long work-list contains a number of tantalizing titles: *Le dernier chant du troubadour*, *Le gondolier de l'Adriatique*, *Le miroir magique*, *Le pauvre exilé*, and, most fascinatingly, *Le violon de Crémone* with words by E. T. A. Hoffmann (here translated into French). The composer's penchant in his operas for historical tales containing an element of the fantastical and macabre is found also in his songs, thus the *duo historique* entitled *Héloïse et Abélard* and one of the most bizarre of all Donizetti's songs, *La Hart, chant diabolique pour basse*. This is based on the legend of Enguerrand de Montfaucon and his pact with the devil which led to the hangman's noose. This gives Donizetti an opportunity to use the piano in an adventurous and melodramatic way that brings to mind the music of Liszt and Alkan. Until the full range of Donizetti's song output is available in modern editions, it is impossible accurately to evaluate his influence on French music. But given that he is a composer of genius on the operatic stage, it seems likely that his music for voice and piano, once so readily available to the French public, will have played some part in the early musical experiences of such composers as Gounod, Saint-Saëns, Delibes, Bizet, and so on.

DUBOIS, Théodore (1837–1924)

A composer who attempted to resist the tide of modernity, in fact an atrocious old reactionary to some ('un personnage de zinc', according to Hélène Jourdan-Morhange). It is for his church music and his treatises on harmony that Dubois is most remembered, and that, as director of the Paris Conservatoire, he was antagonistic to the young Ravel, then a student. His mélodies have faded almost completely from the page and this is a pity because some of them have charm, and all are well written for the voice. He set Banville (*La chanson de ma mie* and the ingratiating *Iseult*), Sully Prudhomme (*Rosées* and *Le galop* [DUPARC 5]), Maurice Bouchor (one of Chausson's favourite writers—*Matin*), and Marc Monnier, poet of Fauré's *Barcarolle* and of a most effective Neapolitan *Tarentelle* from Dubois. A curiosity is a setting entitled *Madrigal*, because its poet Henri Murger (much better known as a novelist) wrote *Scènes de la vie de bohème* which was the basis of Puccini's opera.

DUCHAMBGE, Pauline (1778–1858)

To her belongs the distinction of being France's first notable woman song composer. She left a convent in order to marry the Baron Duchambge, but in 1798 she lost her parents and fortune, and was also divorced. After this she studied in earnest with Dussek, Cherubini, and Auber. She was a lifelong friend of the poetess Marceline Desbordes-Valmore (1786–1859) who provided a number of texts for her songs such as *L'adieu tout bas, La fiancée du marin, La valse et l'automne, La sincère*. Through Valmore, Duchambge met such literary luminaries as Chateaubriand, Lamartine, and Vigny, all of whom provided texts for her romances. The celebrated woman poet Amable Tastu also collaborated with Duchambge, notably in a setting of the poem *À mon ange gardien*, a poem which was famous at the time. There are about 400 romances published between 1816 and 1840. Among the many works of this genre written in France during this period, it is rare to see such important literary names above the music. The songs themselves are simple strophic creations, sometimes with short piano introductions which may mirror their subjects (as in the bell-like effect which opens

Tastu's *Les cloches de couvent*) but which often remain unadorned (apart from the pretty illustrative vignettes on the title-pages) in the simple musical style of the time. The most adventurous setting by Duchambge is probably *Cancione amorosa* (again Tastu) where, in the interests of a southern evocation, the composer throws discretion to the winds, and provides an accompaniment of much greater character than usual. But she was above all capable of touching simplicity: *La blanchisseuse de fin* (Rességuier) in its plaintive depiction of a laundry maid puts us in mind of the sweat-shop poverty in Paris: this character could have been the grandmother of Puccini's Mimi in *La bohème*.

DUPARC, Henri (1848–1933)

He is a prince among song composers, admitted into the royal enclosure without having to show a long list of credentials. He can claim immortality simply by having written *L'invitation au voyage*, and twelve or so other songs. In return, the fates exacted a strange and terrible revenge: he stopped composing in 1885, and the last forty-eight years of his life, one for each prelude and fugue of his beloved Bach, were spent in stultifying musical silence, as he took refuge in his religious faith. Where he had composed songs, he now composed prayers. Instead of being able to set poems by his younger friends, such as Paul Claudel and Francis Jammes, he accompanied them to Lourdes in the hope of a cure from his strange neurasthenic condition. This was of a physical origin certainly (for Duparc was no malingerer), but there were perplexing additional problems of crippling hyperaesthesia (and later blindness) which suggest a psychological dimension to his extraordinary case-history.

When Duparc first met his teacher and mentor César Franck, the mélodie was in the hands of Gounod and Bizet; the young Fauré had written the first of his elegant salon songs, and the fledgling form was well on its way to independence from the old strophic romance which had ruled France for generations. Partly inspired by the examples of Schubert and Schumann, Gounod was writing beautiful vocal lines with interesting accompaniments to fine poems, Lamartine's and Hugo's chief among them. These songs need no apology, for some of them are masterpieces and remain effortlessly in the repertoire. The mélodie, a form which we see struggling to emerge in the pioneering efforts of Berlioz, was at last established and developing. But it was not yet what we now know it to be. If we look in early Gounod for the prophetic early signs of a style that would lead to a sombre and majestic song like Fauré's *Automne* or *Larmes*, we look in vain. Someone was yet to bring to the mélodie a deeper strain of high-minded seriousness, free of the sanctimonious, an inner drama born of deep feeling rather than of theatrical flair (the latter was already to be found without difficulty in the songs of Bizet). In the composition classes of César Franck, notice was served on the frothy and lightweight musical values of the Second Empire, as surely as the reign of Napoleon III was doomed by Franco-Prussian conflict. The inspiration for a new artistic direction came from Germany, the political enemy whose musical history encompassed the self-discipline of Bach, the visionary qualities of Beethoven, and the alluring emotional scope of Wagner. Schubert and Schumann, so important to Gounod's songwriting, were now joined, if not replaced, by heavyweight influences both older and more modern. It was inevitable that a group of composers should seek to reflect the high seriousness of which French culture has always been capable (even if this strain is not best loved by English Francophiles) and such a circle of young men was to be found around Franck. But it was not enough to admire the Germans, and it was not enough to imitate them. Someone had to synthesize these influences and translate them into perfect French. This was the role of Henri Duparc in the history of the mélodie.

The range of Duparc's culture was astonishingly wide. He was equally a fan of Dante, Tolstoy, and Ibsen, as well as of oriental painting, theatre, and dance. The depth of his reading and his openness to other cultures prevented him from becoming blinded by Wagner, or obsessed with his music; he seems to have seen it as one of the many great and new things which could rejuvenate French art. Indeed he was one step ahead of the master of Bayreuth in terms of modernity: he imagined Brünnhilde surrounded by a simple circle of light, rather than by stage fire, and unsuccessfully tried to persuade Wagner to abandon realism in favour of symbolic staging of this kind. Here was a man ahead of his time in terms of aesthetics, who understood Japanese art, and how to take the essence of an idea and throw away its all-too-obvious physical manifestations. This ability to reduce and refine is at the heart of great song-composing; the mélodie is a form where the intensity of operatic emotions and thoughts must be rendered digestible within the smaller framework of voice and piano. Duparc borrowed the Wagnerian cauldron, and over the refining fire of an inherently different culture, he magically reduced fattening stew with dumplings to a delicate but full-flavoured consommé; the stock and some of the ingredients may be of German origin, but we are served something clearly French.

The volume of Duparc songs published by Salabert pays no attention to their chronology, which gives us the idea that he started off with the first song in the collection, a masterpiece entitled *L'invitation au voyage*. In fact the first song is **Chanson triste** (Jean Lahor—pseudonym of Henri Cazalis, 1868) which is no less a work of genius. It has a light touch despite its heartfelt words, and is as transparent as a running silvery stream, a superb musical evocation of the beloved's own 'clarté', and of the clarity of the French spirit at its best. Any pianist who has tried to accompany this song knows how hard it is to keep these flowing semiquavers at exactly the right tempo: too slow, and the singer fails to soar through the taxing long vocal lines; too fast, and the gentle melancholy suggested by the title is lost. There is a superb ground-plan traversing an adventurous range of keys, and there are many tiny details to treasure: the wilting inner voice in the accompaniment of the right hand, as discreet as a concealed sigh; the tiny rallentandos, scrupulously marked, which regulate the sentimentality in homeopathic doses; the floated high note of '*mon* amour' which is a test of style and technique for the singer; or, for example, the way the phrase 'une ballade | Qui semblera parler de nous' breaks the heart with its rise towards hope, and its exquisite fall to the home key as it makes a shy confession that, yes, we ourselves are the subjects of this wistful ballad. A *coup d'essai* is here a *coup de maître*.

The next song dates from the same period, and is also a marvel—a setting of Sully Prudhomme's **Soupir**. This is perhaps the most Chaussonian of Duparc's songs, with an accompaniment of subtly woven arpeggios drifting lazily across the stave, each movement of the hand bringing a tiny change of chromatic inflection. It is in the same key of D minor as Chausson's *Le temps des lilas* and reminds us of that composer's static melancholy which makes time stand still, as well as the sumptuousness of his cadences at 'toujours l'attendre, toujours l'aimer'. But it is Chausson who has learned much from Duparc of course, and the mood of this music goes back to their teacher Franck.

The songs that immediately follow this in Duparc's output seem slightly less original, and he thought so too; accordingly the **Romance de Mignon** (Wilder after Goethe), one of the five songs Duparc published as Op. 2 in 1869, was dropped from the *recueil* of mélodies published in 1894. Perhaps by then Duparc had got to know Wolf's *Kennst du das Land*, and found his own song wanting. It is not without power as a piece of music (the Wagner of *Lohengrin* comes to mind) but the composer was possibly impatient with its strophic repetitiveness. Both **Sérénade** (Marc) and **Le galop** (Sully Prudhomme) from Op. 2 suffered a similar fate; the former is an agreeable trifle, leaning towards Gounod's manner (the accompaniment could almost be played by the left hand alone), and the latter is useful for its exciting *Erlkönig*-like impetus in a recital of slow songs. But Duparc was famously merciless in his self-criticism, and they were exiled from grace. We catch a glimpse of the aspiring opera composer in **Au pays où se fait la guerre** (Gautier), a ballad of a lady in a tower, complete with elements of pastiche suggestive of medieval minstrelsy. This was eventually included in the 1911 *Nouvelle édition complète* of the songs, the only surviving fragment of *Roussalka*, an opera after Pushkin destroyed by its creator.

Duparc was one of the first musicians to champion the poetry of Verlaine and Baudelaire. He turned to the latter for the text of **L'invitation au voyage** (*c.*1870), which is many people's idea of the quintessential French song. Grandeur is not quite a new thing in the mélodie (Gounod's Lamartine's settings are imposing, with a lofty spiritual quality) but, as we travel with Baudelaire and Duparc across the landscapes of the Dutch East Indies into a realm of the imagination bordering the twentieth century, we discover a different grandeur from Gounod's. Despite the devotion to Christian ideals typical of the Franck circle as a whole, this music has pagan resonances of 'luxe, calme et volupté'. In this land the marble statuary of Lamartine's verse yields to poetry of flesh and blood, and vast horizons encompass sexual intimacy. But here is no unbridled orgy, for there are undreamed of refinements among these pagans: purity as well as decadence, rigour as well as sensuality, concision at the same time as expansiveness. In all French song only Duparc has the musical language to find the key to such a text, and turn it in the lock. As Debussy discovered in the CINQ POÈMES DE BAUDELAIRE, a more heated temperament and a more complicated harmonic language do not necessarily penetrate the poet's mystery more effectively. (Indeed it is one of Duparc's strong points that he modulates less frequently than is the usual Franckian habit, and that his bass lines are free of chromatic turbulence for its own sake.) Those mysterious oscillations in the piano which initiate this invitation are not an orchestral tremolando, but rather strictly controlled semiquavers. From the beginning, an aura of classicism underlines the gravity of the poet, and complements and controls the abandon of the vocal line which hovers provocatively, and then silkily soars or sinks into cadences of delight. (Who can forget, who has once heard it, the sun-drenched majesty of 'Dans une chaude lumière'? Philip Hope-Wallace once wrote of this passage as 'The crown of all lyrical effusions, specially at that marvellous deep plunge from the left hand in the piano part.') The duality of loosening the rein with one hand and tightening it with the other was a natural part of Duparc's musical personality, and when the songs were orchestrated something of it was lost. Like Wolf's lieder, the Duparc mélodies have the so-called limitations of the piano turned to advantage as part of their very nature.

La vague et la cloche (1871) shows Duparc to be less of a prophet, more a man of his time. Part of the problem is to do with the poem by François Coppée which encourages the composer to something of a cop-out. It is an epic ballad for an epic voice, superbly well crafted, and in a good performance highly effective. But histrionics of this kind are a throwback to the old-fashioned scène, and not in the mainstream mélodie tradition. We can hear that its appeal to opera singers of the period was that it allowed them to show off: part of its *raison d'être* is to give a big voice a chance to sing loud enough to show the accompanist who is boss. It is interesting to hear this side of Duparc, however, because, unlike the retiring Chausson, he shows himself to be a musical swashbuckler with a larger than life personality. He avoids such obvious rhetoric in *Élégie* (Thomas Moore, translated—according to Rémy Stricker—by Duparc's wife, 1874) and the song is a far cry from Berlioz's outburst of the same name which is also to do with the sad story of the Irish nationalist Robert Emmet. Here, and in the contemporary *Extase* (Lahor, 1874), the influence of Wagner (particularly of the WESENDONCK LIEDER, and the song *Träume*) looms large. The *Élégie*, with its ostinato of a falling minor second, is of suitably noble cast, and *Extase* is astonishingly erotic without being vulgar; a tasteless performance can cheapen it certainly, but Duparc is not to blame. He fully understands that Isolde's *Liebestod* and Mathilde Wesendonck's dreams have spiritual dimensions beyond the obvious sexual overtones. In this song, once again thanks to Duparc's rounded musical understanding, we do not hear one at the expense of the other.

Le manoir de Rosemonde (1879) has a text by Robert de Bonnières which is almost symbolist. Barbara Meister avers that this title refers to two historical Rosamonds. The first of these is celebrated by Swinburne in his epic poem *Rosamund, the queen of the Lombards*, a tale of love and murder; the second, a mistress of King Henry II, apparently could only be reached by finding one's way through a labyrinth. This problem of accessibility may be linked to the image of the unattainable 'bleu manoir' of the poem. The picture of a snarling and dangerous dog (otherwise known as love) inspires the composer to thundering triplets in the right hand that dominate the song almost throughout in dotted rhythms, as if there had been a marriage between Schubert's *Erlkönig* and the same composer's *Die Post*. As in that song, Duparc has a middle section which is less hearty and more introspective. It is skilfully written and evokes the sinister world of Edgar Allan Poe. On a recital menu it is useful as something of a palate-cleansing sorbet between the composer's more sumptuous creations. The *Sérénade florentine* (Lahor, 1880–1) surprises by its late date, for it has a desire to please which seems more typical of the composer's earlier years. Here it is quite possible that some of the *trouvailles* of Chausson had influenced Duparc, the continually syncopated accompaniment for instance. The younger composer had written a *Sérénade italienne* at this very time, and Duparc would also have been aware of Fauré's *Sérénade toscane*. The division of Italy by these composers into various regions seems a gentlemanly sharing of territory.

In 1882 Duparc composed a song which many consider their favourite among his works, whether or not it be his greatest masterpiece, a laurel which should by rights go to one of the Baudelaire settings. This is *Phidylé* (Leconte de Lisle), an evocation of Greek antiquity, and a poem scrupulously avoided by Reynaldo Hahn when he came to set a whole collection of the poet's *Études latines*. This was wise, for no one else could compete with Duparc in the region where Delphi borders the Bois de Boulogne. It is impossible not to believe that those somnolent crotchet chords at the opening did not influence Vaughan Williams in his *Silent noon*; and Brahms in his *Feldeinsamkeit* evoked with no greater opulence the calm heat of the sun suspended in mid-heaven. After a page of natural description when time seems to stand still, the lover turns his gaze to the sleeping nymph. His pulse quickens, and the music blossoms into flowing quavers, tenderness mixed with erotic tension. With the phrase 'Repose, ô Phidylé' thousands have fallen in love with French song, putty in Duparc's hands. 'How exquisite,' they may sigh, but it has more than that, a secret ingredient, a *gravitas*, which makes Duparc a far greater song composer than, say, Reynaldo Hahn. The music has an exotic sensuality certainly, and a poise beyond most composers, but it also overflows with as true and deep a feeling as one would find in the greatest of German lieder. We are having our ambrosia, and drinking it: the best of both worlds. In masterly fashion the grasses are made to murmur, and the bees hum and the music moves towards its climax where the lover allows his longing to be voiced on an almost Wagnerian scale. But not before another 'Repose, ô Phidylé', this time a third higher, and if the listener has not yet fallen under the spell of the song, he is now as truly ravished as the song's eponymous heroine expects to be. The grand vocal climax which now unfolds is no less than one would expect from this red-blooded composer, but in practical terms it has always meant that almost any singer manages one section better than the other: those able to ride the swirling accompaniment urging the voice upwards are often less suited to the hushed mood of the opening. The postlude is a glory. Although it has the feeling of an orchestral reduction, it gives the pianist the chance to sing wordlessly of those passions, both heavenly and earthy, only hinted at by the poet. After the Tristanesque coming together of voice and piano at the final 'l'attente', the music gradually dies away, stretching and swooning, enveloped in a gentle post-coital sadness, as fine a depiction of the aftermath of love as has ever been written.

If neither **Lamento** (Gautier) nor **Testament** (Silvestre) is in this exalted class, they are both nevertheless fine songs of *c*.1883–5. The mournful chromaticism and consecutive fifths of *Lamento* must have sounded the last word in modernity at the time (the composer was proud enough of this to have dedicated it to Fauré), but this now sounds one of the least individual of his songs. For once, Duparc does not seem to have taken in the emotional scale of the text (compare *Au cimetière*, the masterful setting from LES NUITS D'ÉTÉ [BERLIOZ 3 v]) and in cutting the poem (thus making the song finish all too soon) he has diminished its effectiveness. On the other hand *Testament*, a long song, sounds somewhat overblown for its text; some of the obfuscating mannerisms of Chausson when writing in the grand manner are detectable in the piano. Like *Élégie*, the work is bound together by a tiny falling figure in the accompaniment, a drooping phrase which tolls bell-like throughout, suggestive of obsession and tragedy. The quotation of the spear motif from *Parsifal* (four ascending notes, first in the right hand, and then in the left) in the song's postlude reminds us that 1883 was the year of Wagner's death; perhaps Duparc wished to pay homage to that master in this way. Despite its undeniable intensity, *Testament*, in common with *La vague et la cloche*, aspires to an epic grandeur which the poet does not help the composer sustain.

With **La vie antérieure** (1884) we return to a perfect complicity between composer and poem. In this masterpiece the composer proves once again that he has a relationship with the works of Baudelaire achieved by no other musician. Here we find epic grandeur totally without bombast, and a sense of perfect truth in the response to the poet's images. Thus the solemn dotted octaves in the accompaniment's right hand balanced on bare fifths in the bass are the 'grands piliers, droits et majestueux' rendered into visible music. It is one of Duparc's tricks (as in *Phidylé*) to balance episodes of mighty stillness with tremors of more excited feeling which gradually move towards an outburst of emotion. Thus the sea music of 'Les houles, en roulant des images des cieux' is progressively ruffled and works up to a storm. This accelerando, culminating in a virtuoso flourish down the keyboard, and then up again, is one of the famous pianistic challenges of this repertoire. The accompanist may feel that he has gone through a hoop, but the composer then takes us through a door into another realm. Turbulent demisemiquavers are stilled in favour of rapt quaver chords in the first, slower, tempo. 'It is there that I have lived,' proclaims the singer in full voice, and Duparc conveys the ache of memory, the flash of vision (perhaps drug-inspired in the case of the poet) which precedes a journey deeper into the subconscious. These images of 'des vagues, des splendeurs, des esclaves nus' are deeply exotic, but Duparc tells the singer that these wonders must be recounted in half-voice, and without nuance. In the midst of decadence we discover the innocence of a child, a purity which captures the range of the poet's fantasy better than any other. What is this dark secret of which Baudelaire speaks at the end of the poem? The remarkable postlude ponders this wordlessly; it has infinite melancholy and seems to speak of universal truths, so near our understanding that we can almost grasp them but, as in a dream, they remain far beyond our reach, and fade to pianissimo.

Mention should also be made of a work which Duparc allowed to remain in print, but which was never published as part of his mélodie collections. This was *La fuite* (1871), a duet on a quasi-Arabic theme with a text by Gautier, and also set by Bizet. The work, written in a definitely operatic manner, is rather exciting, but it is difficult both to play and to sing, and has not stayed in the repertoire. It nevertheless merits examination in light of Duparc's tiny output. (We can only mourn a destroyed setting of Baudelaire's *Recueillement* [cf. DEBUSSY 7 iv] from 1886 which might well have been better than Duparc, in his depression, judged it to be.) He is one of the very few composers whose entire vocal output fits comfortably into a single evening's recital (one preferably shared between a number of singers). The inclusion of this duet would sensibly combine two of the evening's voices, as well as giving us a glimpse of the operatic master that Duparc might have been. He was highly conservative by nature, and the music of newly fashionable composers like Debussy, Mahler, or Strauss meant nothing to him. Had his talents remained in his possession, would he have adapted to the spirit of a new age? Probably not, but at least we would have had more songs, settings of Duparc's friends Paul Claudel or Francis Jammes perhaps, men who were too young to have known the composer in his heyday. And one feels certain that Duparc would have found his own way of ensuring that his music, in whatever epoch, remained a faithful mirror of the poet's intentions.

1 *Chanson triste*	*Song of sadness*
(Jean Lahor)	

Dans ton cœur dort un clair de lune,	Moonlight slumbers in your heart,
Un doux clair de lune d'été,	A gentle summer moonlight,
Et pour fuir la vie importune,	And to escape the cares of life
Je me noierai dans ta clarté.	I shall drown myself in your light.

J'oublierai les douleurs passées,
Mon amour, quand tu berceras
Mon triste cœur et mes pensées
Dans le calme aimant de tes bras.*

Tu prendras ma tête malade,
Oh! quelquefois, sur tes genoux,
Et lui diras une ballade
Qui semblera parler de nous;

Et dans tes yeux pleins de tristesses,
Dans tes yeux alors je boirai
Tant de baisers et de tendresses
Que peut-être je guérirai.

I shall forget past sorrows,
My sweet, when you cradle
My sad heart and my thoughts
In the loving calm of your arms.

You will rest my poor head,
Ah! sometimes on your lap,
And recite to it a ballad
That will seem to speak of us;

And from your eyes full of sorrow,
From your eyes I shall then drink
So many kisses and so much love
That perhaps I shall be healed.

2 Soupir

(Sully Prudhomme)

Ne jamais la voir ni l'entendre,
Ne jamais tout haut la nommer,
Mais, fidèle, toujours l'attendre,
    Toujours l'aimer.

Ouvrir les bras et, las d'attendre,
Sur le néant les refermer,
Mais encor toujours les lui tendre,
    Toujours l'aimer.

Ah! ne pouvoir que les lui tendre,
Et dans les pleurs se consumer,
Mais ces pleurs toujours les répandre,
    Toujours l'aimer.

Ne jamais la voir ni l'entendre,
Ne jamais tout haut la nommer,
Mais d'un amour toujours plus tendre
    Toujours l'aimer.

Sigh

Never to see or hear her,
Never to utter her name aloud,
But faithful, always to wait for her,
    Always to love her.

To open my arms and, weary of waiting,
To close them again on a void,
Yet always to hold them out again,
    Always to love her.

Ah, able only to hold them out
And to waste away in tears,
Yet always to shed those tears,
    Always to love her.

Never to see or hear her,
Never to utter her name aloud,
But with a love always more tender,
    Always to love her.

3 Romance de Mignon†

(Victor Wilder, after Goethe)

Le connais-tu, ce radieux pays
Où brille dans les branches d'or des fruits?
Un doux zéphir embaume l'air
Et le laurier s'unit au myrte vert.

Mignon's romance

Do you know it, that radiant land,
Where fruit gleams among golden branches?
A gentle breeze scents the air,
Laurel and green myrtle intertwine.

* A pun is intended here: 'le calme aimant' also translates as 'the calm magnet'
† Cf. 'Kennst du das Land' from *Wilhelm Meisters Lehrjahre*.

Le connais-tu, le connais-tu? Là-bas,
Mon bien-aimé, courons, porter nos pas...

Le connais-tu, ce merveilleux séjour
Où tout me parle encor de notre amour?
Où chaque objet me dit avec douleur:
Qui t'a ravi ta joie et ton bonheur?

Le connais-tu, le connais-tu? Là-bas,
Mon bien-aimé, courons porter nos pas...

Do you know it? Do you know it? There,
My beloved, let us make our way...

Do you know it, that wondrous abode,
Where everything still speaks of our love,
And every object asks me with sorrow:
Who has stolen your delight and joy?

Do you know it? Do you know it? There,
My beloved, let us make our way...

4 Sérénade

(Gabriel Marc)

Serenade

Si j'étais, ô mon amoureuse,
La brise au souffle parfumé,
Pour frôler ta bouche rieuse,
Je viendrais craintif et charmé.

Si j'étais l'abeille qui vole,
Ou le papillon séducteur,
Tu ne me verrais pas, frivole,
Te quitter pour une autre fleur.

Si j'étais la rose charmante
Que ta main place sur ton cœur,
Si près de toi toute tremblante
Je me fanerais de bonheur.

Mais en vain je cherche à te plaire,
J'ai beau gémir et soupirer.
Je suis homme, et que puis-je faire?—
T'aimer... Te le dire... Et pleurer!

If, my beloved, I were
The scented breeze,
I would come, timid and rapt,
To brush your laughing lips.

If I were a bee in flight,
Or a beguiling butterfly,
You would not see me skittishly
Leave you for another flower.

If I were the charming rose
Your hand placed on your heart,
I would, quivering so close to you,
Wither with happiness.

But I seek in vain to please you,
In vain I moan and sigh.
I am a man, and what can I do?
Love you... Confess my love... And cry!

5 Le galop

(Sully Prudhomme)

The gallop

Agite, bon cheval, ta crinière fuyante;
Que l'air autour de nous se remplisse de voix!
Que j'entende craquer sous ta corne bruyante
Le gravier des ruisseaux et les débris des bois!

Flourish, good horse, your flying mane,
That the air about us be filled with voices!
That beneath your clattering hooves I hear
The gravel of streams and the woods' broken
    boughs!

Aux vapeurs de tes flancs mêle ta chaude haleine,

Aux éclairs de tes pieds ton écume et ton sang!

Cours, comme on voit un aigle en effleurant la
    plaine
Fouetter l'herbe d'un vol sonore et frémissant!

'Allons, les jeunes gens, à la nage! à la nage!'
Crie à ses cavaliers le vieux chef de tribu;
Et les fils du désert respirent le pillage,
Et les chevaux sont fous du grand air qu'ils ont bu!

Nage ainsi dans l'espace, ô mon cheval rapide,
Abreuve-moi d'air pur, baigne-moi dans le vent;
L'étrier bat ton ventre et j'ai lâché la bride,

Mon corps te touche à peine, il vole en te suivant.

Brise tout, le buisson, la barrière ou la branche;
Torrents, fossés, talus, franchis tout d'un seul bond;

Cours, je rêve, et sur toi, les yeux clos, je me
    penche...
Emporte, emporte-moi dans l'inconnu profond!

Mingle your hot breath with the steam of your
    flanks,
Your foam and your blood with the sparks from
    your hooves!
Run, like an eagle we see skimming the plain,

Lashing the grass with its quivering loud wings!

'Come, young men, swim your horses across!'
Cries the old tribal chief to his horsemen;
And the sons of the desert are eager for plunder,
And the horses are crazed with the air they have
    drunk!

Swim thus in space, O my swift mount,
Quench my thirst with pure air, bathe me in wind;
The stirrup strikes your belly, I've slackened the
    rein,
My body scarcely touches you, it flies in your wake.

Break down everything, bush, gate, or branch;
Cross torrent, ditch, embankment with a single
    bound;
Race on, I dream, bending over you with closed
    eyes...
Transport me, transport me to the deep unknown!

6 *Au pays où se fait la guerre*

(Théophile Gautier)

To the land where there is war

I

Au pays où se fait la guerre
Mon bel ami s'en est allé;
Il semble à mon cœur désolé
Qu'il ne reste que moi sur terre!
En partant, au baiser d'adieu,
Il m'a pris mon âme à ma bouche.
Qui le tient si longtemps, mon Dieu!
Voilà le soleil qui se couche,
Et moi, toute seule en ma tour,
J'attends encore son retour.

I

To the land where there is war
My handsome lover has gone;
It seems to my desolate heart
That I alone am left on earth!
When we parted with a farewell kiss,
He took my soul from my lips.
Who detains him so long, my God?
See, the sun is setting,
And I, all alone in my tower,
Still await his return.

II

Les pigeons, sur le toit roucoulent,
Roucoulent amoureusement
Avec un son triste et charmant;
Les eaux sous les grand saules coulent.

II

The pigeons on the roof are cooing,
Cooing their songs of love
With a sad, enchanting sound;
Waters flow beneath tall willows.

Je me sens tout près de pleurer;
Mon cœur comme un lis plein s'épanche,
Et je n'ose plus espérer.
Voici briller la lune blanche,
Et moi, toute seule en ma tour,
J'attends encore son retour.

III

Quelqu'un monte à grands pas la rampe:
Serait-ce lui, mon doux amant?
Ce n'est pas lui, mais seulement
Mon petit page avec ma lampe.
Vents du soir, volez, dites-lui
Qu'il est ma pensée et mon rêve,
Toute ma joie et mon ennui.
Voici que l'aurore se lève,
Et moi, toute seule en ma tour,
J'attends encore son retour.

I feel I am near to tears;
My heart unfolds like a full-blown lily
And I dare no longer hope.
See, the white moon is shining,
And I, all alone in my tower,
Still await his return.

III

Someone is bounding up the stairs:
Could it be he, my sweet lover?
It is not he, but only
My little page with my lamp.
Take wing, evening breezes, and tell him
That he is my thought and my dream,
And all my joy and my sorrow.
See, the dawn is breaking,
And I, all alone in my tower,
Still await his return.

7   L'invitation au voyage

(Charles Baudelaire)

Invitation to journey

Mon enfant, ma sœur,
  Songe à la douceur
D'aller là-bas vivre ensemble!
  Aimer à loisir,
  Aimer et mourir
Au pays qui te ressemble!
  Les soleils mouillés
  De ces ciels brouillés
Pour mon esprit ont les charmes
  Si mystérieux
  De tes traîtres yeux,
Brillant à travers leurs larmes.

Là, tout n'est qu'ordre et beauté,
Luxe, calme et volupté.

  Vois sur ces canaux
  Dormir ces vaisseaux
Dont l'humeur est vagabonde;
  C'est pour assouvir
  Ton moindre désir
Qu'ils viennent du bout du monde.
  —Les soleils couchants
  Revêtent les champs,

My child, my sister,
  Think how sweet
To journey there and live together!
  To love as we please,
  To love and die
In the land that is like you!
  The watery suns
  Of those hazy skies
Hold for my spirit
  The same mysterious charms
  As your treacherous eyes
Shining through their tears.

There—nothing but order and beauty dwell,
Abundance, calm, and sensuous delight.

  See on those canals
  Those vessels sleeping,
Vessels with a restless soul;
  To satisfy
  Your slightest desire
They come from the ends of the earth.
  The setting suns
  Clothe the fields,

Les canaux, la ville entière,
   D'hyacinthe et d'or;
   Le monde s'endort
Dans une chaude lumière.

Là, tout n'est qu'ordre et beauté.
Luxe, calme et volupté.

Canals and all the town
   With hyacinth and gold;
   The world falls asleep
In a warm light.

There—nothing but order and beauty dwell,
Abundance, calm, and sensuous delight.

8 *La vague et la cloche*
(François Coppée)

The wave and the bell

Une fois, terrassé par un puissant breuvage,
J'ai rêvé que parmi les vagues et le bruit
De la mer, je voguais sans fanal dans la nuit,
Morne rameur, n'ayant plus l'espoir du rivage...

L'Océan me crachait ses baves sur le front,
Et le vent me glaçait d'horreur jusqu'aux entrailles,
Les vagues s'écroulaient ainsi que des murailles
Avec ce rythme lent qu'un silence interrompt...

Puis, tout changea... la mer et sa noire mêlée

Sombrèrent... sous mes pieds s'effondra le plancher
De la barque... Et j'étais seul dans un vieux clocher,
Chevauchant avec rage une cloche ébranlée.

J'étreignais la criarde opiniâtrement,
Convulsif et fermant dans l'effort mes paupières.
Le grondement faisait trembler les vieilles pierres,
Tant j'activais sans fin le lourd balancement.

Pourquoi n'as-tu pas dit, o rêve, où Dieu nous mène?
Pourquoi n'as-tu pas dit s'ils ne finiraient pas,
L'inutile travail et l'éternel fracas
Dont est faite la vie, hélas, la vie humaine!

Once, laid low by a potent draught,
I dreamed that amid the waves and the roar
Of the sea I drifted without beacon at night,
A bleak oarsman, with no hope of reaching land...

The ocean spat its foam on my brow,
And the wind froze me through with horror,
The waves crashed down like walls about me,
With that slow rhythm a silence severs...

Then everything changed. The sea and its black
   tumult
Subsided. Beneath my feet the floor of the boat
Gave way... And I was alone in an old bell-tower,
Furiously riding a swaying bell.

I doggedly clasped the clamorous metal,
Convulsed, and closing my eyes with the effort.
The booming made the old stones tremble,
So constantly I quickened the heavy swing.

Why did you not say, O dream, where God leads us?
Why did you not say if they will ever end,
The fruitless toil and the endless strife
Of which human life, alas, is made?

9 *Élégie*
(Thomas Moore, trans. Mme Duparc)

*Elegy**

Oh! ne murmurez pas son nom! qu'il dorme dans
   l'ombre,
où froide et sans honneur repose sa dépouille.
Muettes, tristes, glacées, tombent nos larmes,
comme la rosée de la nuit, qui sur sa tête humecte le
   gazon;

Oh! breathe not his name, let it sleep in the shade,

Where cold and unhonoured his relics are laid:
Silent, sad and frozen be the tears that we shed,
As the night-dew that moistens the grass o'er his
   head;

   * See note to Berlioz 1.

mais la rosée de la nuit, bien qu'elle pleure en silence,
fera briller la verdure sur sa couche;

et nos larmes, en secret répandues,
conserveront sa mémoire fraîche et verte dans nos
    cœurs.

But the night-dew, though in silence it weeps,
Shall make the grass green on the grave where he
    sleeps;
And the tear that we shed, though in secret it rolls,
Shall long keep his memory green in our souls.

10 *Extase*

(Jean Lahor)

Sur un lys pâle mon cœur dort
D'un sommeil doux comme la mort:
Mort exquise, mort parfumée
Du souffle de la bien-aimée:
Sur ton sein pâle mon cœur dort...

Rapture

On a pale lily my heart is sleeping
A sleep as sweet as death:
Exquisite death, death perfumed
By the breath of the beloved:
On your pale breast my heart is sleeping...

11 *Le manoir de Rosemonde*

(Robert de Bonnières)

De sa dent soudaine et vorace,
Comme un chien l'Amour m'a mordu;
En suivant mon sang répandu,
Va, tu pourras suivre ma trace.

Prends un cheval de bonne race,
Pars et suis mon chemin ardu,
Fondrière ou sentier perdu,
Si la course ne te harasse.

En passant par où j'ai passé,
Tu verras que, seul et blessé,
J'ai parcouru ce triste monde,

Et qu'ainsi je m'en fus mourir
Bien loin, bien loin, sans découvrir
Le bleu manoir de Rosemonde.

The manor of Rosamonde

With sudden and ravenous tooth,
Love like a dog has bitten me.
By following the blood I've shed—
Come, you'll be able to follow my trail.

Take a horse of fine breeding,
Set out, and follow my arduous course
By quagmire or by hidden path,
If the chase does not weary you.

Passing by where I have passed,
You will see that, solitary and wounded,
I have traversed this sorry world,

And that thus I went off to die
Far, far away, without ever finding
The blue manor of Rosamonde.

12 *Sérénade florentine*

(Jean Lahor)

Étoile, dont la beauté luit
Comme un diamant dans la nuit,
Regarde vers ma bien-aimée,
Dont la paupière s'est fermée,
Et fais descendre sur ses yeux
La bénédiction des cieux.

Elle s'endort: par la fenêtre
En sa chambre heureuse pénètre;
Sur sa blancheur, comme un baiser,
Viens jusqu'à l'aube te poser,
Et que sa pensée alors rêve
D'un astre d'amour qui se lève.

13 *Phidylé*

(Charles-Marie-René Leconte de Lisle)

L'herbe est molle au sommeil sous les frais peupliers,
  Aux pentes des sources moussues
Qui, dans les prés en fleur germant par mille issues,

  Se perdent sous les noirs halliers.

Repose, ô Phidylé! Midi sur les feuillages
  Rayonne, et t'invite au sommeil.
Par le trèfle et le thym, seules, en plein soleil,

  Chantent les abeilles volages.

Un chaud parfum circule au détour des sentiers;
  La rouge fleur des blés s'incline;
Et les oiseaux, rasant de l'aile la colline,

  Cherchent l'ombre des églantiers.

Mais quand l'Astre, incliné sur sa courbe éclatante,
  Verra ses ardeurs s'apaiser,
Que ton plus beau sourire et ton meilleur baiser
  Me récompensent de l'attente!

Florentine serenade

O star whose beauty shines
Like a diamond in the night,
Look down on my beloved
Whose eyelids now are closed,
And let the blessing of heaven
Descend upon her eyes.

She falls asleep: through the window
Enter her happy room;
Alight on her whiteness like a kiss
And linger there till dawn,
And let her thoughts then dream
Of a star of love ascending.

Phidylé

The grass is soft for sleep beneath the cool poplars
  On the banks of the mossy springs
That flow in flowering meadows from a thousand
    sources,
  And vanish beneath dark thickets.

Rest, O Phidylé! Noon on the leaves
  Is gleaming, inviting you to sleep.
By the clover and thyme, alone, in the bright
    sunlight,
  The fickle bees are humming.

A warm fragrance floats about the winding paths,
  The red flowers of the cornfield droop;
And the birds, skimming the hillside with their
    wings,
  Seek the shade of the eglantine.

But when the sun, low on its dazzling curve,
  Sees its brilliance wane,
Let your loveliest smile and finest kiss
  Reward me for my waiting!

14 *Lamento*

(Théophile Gautier)

Connaissez-vous la blanche tombe
Où flotte avec un son plaintif
  L'ombre d'un if?
Sur l'if une pâle colombe,
Triste et seule au soleil couchant,
  Chante son chant.

On dirait que l'âme éveillée
Pleure sous terre à l'unisson
  De la chanson,
Et du malheur d'être oubliée
Se plaint dans un roucoulement,
  Bien doucement.

Ah! jamais plus près de la tombe
Je n'irai, quand descend le soir
  Au manteau noir,
Écouter la pâle colombe
Chanter, sur la branche de l'if,
  Son chant plaintif!

Lament

Do you know the white tomb,
Where the shadow of a yew
  Waves plaintively?
On that yew a pale dove,
Sad and solitary at sundown
  Sings its song;

As if the awakened soul
Weeps from the grave, together
  With the song,
And at the sorrow of being forgotten
Murmurs its complaint
  Most meltingly.

Ah! nevermore shall I approach that tomb,
When evening descends
  In its black cloak,
To listen to the pale dove
On the branch of the yew
  Sing its plaintive song!

15 *Testament*

(Armand Silvestre)

Pour que le vent te les apporte
Sur l'aile noire d'un remord,
J'écrirai sur la feuille morte
Les tortures de mon cœur mort!

Toute ma sève s'est tarie
Aux clairs midis de ta beauté,
Et, comme à la feuille flétrie,
Rien de vivant ne m'est resté;

Tes yeux m'ont brûlé jusqu'à l'âme,
Comme des soleils sans merci!
Feuille que le gouffre réclame,
L'autan va m'emporter aussi...

Mais avant, pour qu'il te les porte
Sur l'aile noire d'un remord,
J'écrirai sur la feuille morte
Les tortures de mon cœur mort!

Testament

That the wind might bear them to you
On the black wing of remorse,
I shall inscribe on the dead leaf
The torments of my dead heart!

All my strength has drained away
In the bright noon of your beauty,
And, like the withered leaf,
Nothing living is left for me.

Your eyes have scorched me to the soul
Like suns devoid of mercy!
The chasm will claim the leaf,
The south wind sweep me away...

But first, that it might bear them to you
On the black wing of remorse,
I shall inscribe on the dead leaf,
The torments of my dead heart!

16 *La vie antérieure*
(Charles Baudelaire)

J'ai longtemps habité sous de vastes portiques
Que les soleils marins teignaient de mille feux,
Et que leurs grands piliers, droits et majestueux,
Rendaient pareils, le soir, aux grottes basaltiques.

Les houles, en roulant les images des cieux,
Mêlaient d'une façon solennelle et mystique
Les tout-puissants accords de leur riche musique
Aux couleurs du couchant reflété par mes yeux.

C'est là que j'ai vécu dans les voluptés calmes,
Au milieu de l'azur, des vagues, des splendeurs
Et des esclaves nus, tout imprégnés d'odeurs,

Qui me rafraîchissaient le front avec des palmes,
Et dont l'unique soin était d'approfondir
Le secret douloureux qui me faisait languir.

A previous life

For long I lived beneath vast colonnades
Tinged with a thousand fires by ocean suns,
Whose giant pillars, straight and majestic,
Made them look, at evening, like basalt caves.

The sea-swells, mingling the mirrored skies,
Solemnly and mystically interwove
The mighty chords of their mellow music
With the colours of sunset reflected in my eyes.

It is there that I have lived in sensuous repose,
With blue sky about me and brightness and waves
And naked slaves all drenched in perfume

Who fanned my brow with fronds of palm,
And whose only care was to fathom
The secret grief which made me languish.

17 *La fuite*
(Théophile Gautier)

KADIDJA
Au firmament sans étoile,
La lune éteint ses rayons;
La nuit nous prête son voile;
    Fuyons! fuyons!

AHMED
Ne crains-tu pas la colère
De tes frères insolents,
Le désespoir de ton père,
De ton père aux sourcils blancs?

KADIDJA
Que m'importent mépris, blâme,
Dangers, malédictions!
C'est en toi que vit mon âme.
    Fuyons! fuyons!

AHMED
Le cœur me manque; je tremble,
Et, dans mon sein traversé,
De leur kandjar il me semble
Sentir le contact glacé!

* Khanjar—an Eastern dagger.

Escape

KADIDJA
In the starless sky
The moon extinguishes its rays;
Night lends us her veil;
    Let us flee! Let us flee!

AHMED
Do you not fear the anger
Of your insolent brothers,
The despair of your father,
Your white-haired father?

KADIDJA
What do I care for scorn, rebuke,
Dangers, imprecations!
My soul lives in you.
    Let us flee! Let us flee!

AHMED
My heart fails me; I tremble,
And in my pierced heart
I seem to feel the icy
Touch of their khanjars!*

KADIDJA
Née au désert, ma cavale
Sur les blés, dans les sillons,
Volerait, des vents rivale.
    Fuyons! fuyons!

AHMED
Au désert infranchissable,
Sans parasol, pour jeter
Un peu d'ombre sur la sable,
Sans tente pour m'abriter...

KADIDJA
Mes cils te feront de l'ombre,
Et, la nuit, nous dormirons
Sous mes cheveux, tente sombre.
    Fuyons! fuyons!

AHMED
Si le mirage illusoire
Nous cachait le vrai chemin,
Sans vivres, sans eau pour boire,
Tous deux nous mourrions demain.

KADIDJA
Sous le bonheur mon cœur ploie;
Si l'eau manque aux stations,
Bois les larmes de ma joie.
    Fuyons! fuyons!

KADIDJA
My desert-born mare
Would fly across the corn,
Along the furrows, vying with winds.
    Let us flee! Let us flee!

AHMED
To the impassable desert,
With no parasol to cast
A little shade on the sand,
With no tent to shelter me...

KADIDJA
My eyelashes shall shade you,
And at night we shall sleep
Beneath the dark tent of my hair.
    Let us flee! Let us flee!

AHMED
If a mirage
Were to hide the true path,
Without food and water to drink,
We would both die tomorrow.

KADIDJA
My heart gives way with happiness;
If there's no water along the route,
Drink the tears of my joy.
    Let us flee! Let us flee!

DUPONT, Gabriel (1878–1914)

A pupil of Massenet and Widor at the Conservatoire, Dupont was already being referred to as 'un musicien trop oublié' in an article written about him in 1921. He died early from a lung disease, and was said to have been obsessed with thoughts of death. On the song platform he is chiefly remembered for a deft little setting of Verlaine's *Mandoline* [FAURÉ 29 i] published in the international Music Company's *40 French songs*. The *Deux poèmes d'Alfred de Musset* (*Chanson* and *Sérénade*) are winning *jeux d'esprit*. Of deeper import is the cycle POÈMES D'AUTOMNE, championed by the tenor John Aler, which boasts a slight setting of Régnier's *Si j'ai aimé*, Rimbaud's *Ophélie*—a fascinating piece this (and a Shakespeare song by proxy)—as well as *La neige* (Verlaine's 'Dans l'interminable | Ennui de la plaine'), a poem which is all but ignored by other composers. *Le silence d'eau* (Gregh) and *La fontaine de pitié* (Bataille) are also fine songs—the piano writing of the latter seems influenced by Koechlin.

DUPRÉ, Marcel (1886–1971)

This great organist, successor to Widor at Saint-Sulpice, and teacher of Messiaen, seems an unlikely composer of mélodies with piano accompaniment. But, like Widor before him, he was attracted to song. A careful reading of the song cycle À L'AMIE PERDUE (Auguste Angellier, 1911) shows him to be an astonishing precursor of Messiaen's style of writing for voice and piano: there is the same style of spiritually influenced text, a similar taste for opulent harmony, the same virtuosic sparkling pianistic flourishes with explosively crushed grace notes, a similar almost static use of ostinato. There is also an other-worldly feel to the exploration of religious themes (the fourth song for example begins 'Ô les profonds les purs et les divins moments') which can seem pretentious to those unsympathetic to such metaphysical elaborations. Interesting from the point of view of repertoire comparisons are the DEUX MÉLODIES TIRÉES DES CHANSONS DE BILITIS (Louÿs, 1920) which are entitled *Sous la pluie* and *Rose dans la nuit*. These are for a higher voice than Debussy's CHANSONS DE BILITIS, but a soprano with a good lower register could manage both sets, and Dupré's fast and glittering songs would make a fine pendant for the Debussy cycle by way of counterbalance and contrast.

DUREY, Louis (1888–1979)

He seems the least likely member of Cocteau's merry band which the critic Henri Collet named Les Six (the others were Auric, Honegger, Milhaud, Poulenc, and Tailleferre). He was the oldest of them by four years, and the first to distance himself from their company. In terms of fame, he always had rather a low profile, and this may have had as much to do with his retiring personality as with his lonely path as a Communist and Maoist—political convictions shared by few of his musical friends. He composed a surprisingly large number of songs, however, and there have been recent signs of a Durey revival. Apart from several Verlaine settings (as yet unpublished), among the first vocal works are the CINQ POÈMES (Francis Jammes) and the L'OFFRANDE LYRIQUE (1914), six songs with texts by Tagore translated by Gide (cf. Casella) and Milhaud's CHILD POEMS. These were inspired by the atonality of Schoenberg's DAS BUCH DER HÄNGENDEN GÄRTEN songs. IMAGES À CRUSOÉ is for piano and seven instruments; the poet was Saint-John Perse, here using one of his other names—Saint Léger Léger. This interesting work, a forerunner of Ravel's CHANSONS MADÉCASSES, was written in 1918 which was Durey's most productive song year. From this period are the ÉPIGRAMMES DE THÉOCRITE (trans. F. Barbier), the TROIS POÈMES DE PETRONIUS, and INSCRIPTIONS SUR UN ORANGER with texts by Évariste Parny (who wrote the poems of the CHANSONS MADÉCASSES). These three works are miniatures, written in the spare, almost minimalist, style which suits classical epigrams, and which was the calling card of all the composers of Les Six at this time. Three works of 1919 are of note. The SIX MADRIGAUX with woodwind and piano accompaniment are extremely well-attuned to Mallarmé's sound world. This almost ranks with Debussy's and Ravel's as a definitive musical portrait of the poet.

LE BESTIAIRE (Apollinaire) is a much bigger cycle. It is fascinating to compare Durey's settings with

Poulenc's, which were dedicated to him. The younger composer's inherent wit and tenderness are hard to beat, but Durey's wider selection of animal poems (elephant, fly, flea, and dove, among many others), supplements Poulenc's much smaller menagerie. The *CHANSONS BASQUES* (1919) is the most miniature cycle of all, and a valuable contribution to the setting of Cocteau to music. The little cycle can stand next to Poulenc's *COCARDES* in this respect. The piano version is just as effective as the various instrumental ensembles suggested by the composer. Durey's later songs include settings of Apollinaire, Éluard, and Rilke. In 1957–8 he provided, a delightful orchestration of his *LE BESTIAIRE* for thirteen instruments—strings, wind, piano, and celesta. Banal agit-prop works like *Les constructeurs* (Seghers, 1966) can disguise, but not eradicate, the wide-ranging achievements of a song composer who is still generally underestimated.

CHANSONS BASQUES	**BASQUE SONGS**
(Jean Cocteau)	
I i *Prière*	*Prayer*
Sainte Vierge Marie, ayez pitié des gens	Holy Virgin Mary, take pity on the people
Qui reviennent de guerre et qui n'ont pas d'argent.	Who return from war and have no money.
Ma femme en aime un autre, elle me rit au nez.	My wife loves another man, she laughs in my face.
Mon chien cherche à me mordre et m'a abandonné.	My dog tries to bite me and has left me.
On me traite d'ivrogne et si je veux du vin,	They call me a drunkard, and if I want wine
On me donne un peu d'eau avec un bout de pain.	They give me a little water and a scrap of bread.
I ii *Polka*	*Polka*
Sirocco, joli vent chaud,	Sirocco, nice warm wind,
Mets tes espadrilles,	Put on your espadrilles,
Entre dans la chambre en chaux	Enter the whitewashed room
De la jeune fille;	Of the young girl.
Fais-la sortir de son lit	Make her leave her bed
Et se chercher un mari,	And look for a husband
Dans la ville de Paris,	In the city of Paris
Loin de sa famille.	Far from her family.

I iii *Attelage*

Deux maisons de travers approchent. On a mis des tapis à fleurs sur les fenêtres. Un grand candélabre les couronne et des lustres ensoleillés traînent de leur bouche triste sur la route.

Harnessing

Two houses draw near askew. Flower carpets have been hung from the windows. A large street-lamp crowns them and sun-kissed chandeliers stretch with sad mouths on the road.

DUTILLEUX, Henri (b. 1916)

Among the very small and concentrated output of this important composer is a handful of songs. The QUATRE MÉLODIES date from 1942, and are dedicated to Charles and Madeleine Panzéra. The first song, *Féerie au clair de lune* (Raymond Genty), is a delicate scherzo, transparent and economical, which evokes moonlight, and the sound of the cricket. *Pour une amie perdue* (Edmond Borsent) is a song of bereavement, a moving and simple elegy of great tenderness. *Regards sur l'infini*, a ravishing setting of Anna de Noailles, is followed by **Fantasio** (André Bellesort), which is in the playful mood of a latter-day *fêtes galantes*, as 'Pauvre Fantasio', who has died in the midst of the festivities, is buried. These are delightful songs which work well as a group. There is also an orchestral version, and the next two vocal works, LA GEÔLE (1944) and the TROIS SONNETS DE JEAN CASSOU (1954), were originally written with orchestral accompaniment. *San Francisco night* (Paul Gilson, 1964) is a single song for voice and piano. Despite its title it has a French text which was also set by Jean Michel Damase.

I *Fantasio*

(André Bellesort), from QUATRE MÉLODIES

La mort t'ayant surpris en travesti de bal,
Pauvre Fantasio, de folles jeunes filles
Te firent un linceul de leurs blanches mantilles,
Et tu fus enterré le soir du carnaval.

Sous un léger brouillard du ciel occidental
Le mardigras folâtre éparpillait ses trilles.
Et ton glas voltigeant sur de lointains quadrilles
Détachait dans la nuit ses notes de cristal.

Des coins du corbillard le feu des girandoles
Éclairait tout un chœur d'étranges farandoles.
Nul n'avait pris le temps de revêtir le deuil,
Et tous faisaient jouer derrière ton cercueil
Une marche funèbre à leurs tambours de basque.

Fantasio

When Death surprised you at the masked ball,
Poor Fantasio, love-crazed young girls
Made you a shroud of their white mantillas,
And you were buried that carnival evening.

Under a light mist of the western sky,
Blithe Shrove Tuesday scattered its trills.
And your knell, flitting across distant quadrilles,
Loosed on the night its crystal notes.

From the hearse's corners, the flare of fireworks
Lit up a whole choir of strange farandoles.
No one had time to put on mourning,
And behind your coffin everyone played
A funeral march on their basque drums.

EMMANUEL, Maurice (1862–1938)

In *Grove 6* Robert Orledge describes Emmanuel as 'one of the few genuine independents in French music . . . deriving his material from sources almost entirely outside the Classical and Romantic tradition'. Such learned treatises as *Essai sur l'orchestique grecque* profoundly influenced his pupil Olivier Messiaen, but also perhaps distanced Emmanuel from the general public. Perhaps this is why his music is not easily to be found in English-speaking countries, for it is easier to fix a composer in the public imagination when he has a lineage. Typically unusual is a work entitled IN MEMORIAM MATRIS (Vallery-Radot, 1908) for male and female voice with piano trio, and written in memory of the composer's mother. The singers are heard in various combinations with solo instruments signifying the voices of the son and, at the work's rapt conclusion, the mother herself. Emmanuel's songs with piano are not many; the most important of these is the cycle MUSIQUES (1908) with poetry by Louis de Launay, the composer's close friend, the death of whose son inspired Emmanuel's First Symphony. There are twelve songs in this collection, including *Le vieux coucou* which prompts memories of Ravel's HISTOIRES NATURELLES, a *Berceuse* which is the expressive centre of the work, and a sinuous *Valse hongroise* which looks forward to Poulenc's *Violon*. The final *Postlude* gathers together the musical and literary themes of this work which, because of its construction, discourages performances of excerpts. At forty minutes' duration, however, it is rather long for recital purposes. The TROIS ODELETTES ANACRÉONTIQUES (Belleau and Ronsard, 1911) for voice, flute, and piano should be mentioned, as well as the TRENTE CHANSONS BOURGUIGNONNES DU PAYS DE BEAUNE (1913) inspired by local songs from five centuries collected from the composer's native region. Sixteen of these simple and often piquant settings were orchestrated by Emmanuel between 1914 and 1936.

ENESCU, George (1881–1955)

This Romanian composer, known also as Georges Enesco, had perhaps the most perfect affinity with the French language of any foreign composer; only Lutoslawski might rival him. This is not so evident in the early *Si j'étais Dieu* (Sully Prudhomme), where he seems to be writing down to salon taste. The TROIS MÉLODIES of Op. 4 (1898) mark a step forward, although *Le désert* (Lemaître) prompts a Rudolph Valentino orientalism which is not the best start to the group. Enescu's attraction to Sully Prudhomme's poetry led him to set *Soupir* and *Le galop*, and the comparisons with Duparc are challenging [DUPARC 2, 5]. Without vanquishing his elder, Enescu emerges unscathed from this test, and both songs make a fine effect in performance. *Soupir* has a brooding intensity that borders on sentimentality, without crossing into it, and *Le galop* is more transparent than Duparc's, although the final pianissimo high A demands a very fine tenor to execute it according to the composer's wishes.

With the SEPT CHANSONS DE CLÉMENT MAROT (1908) Enescu contributed a masterpiece to the French song repertoire; this little cycle is a jewel which deserves to be much better known. The songs, which are worthy of an important French poet, stand effortlessly next to the two settings of Ravel [RAVEL 4 i–ii] where the same Anne we encounter *chez* Enescu is the focal point of Marot's affections. The composer's greatest achievement is in evoking the spirit of sixteenth-century France without recourse to obvious archaisms and laboured pastiche. He manages somehow to retain a style of his own, so that these songs are unlike most of those by other composers attempting the familiar enough occupation of time-travel to distant centuries. The witty flightiness of *Aux damoyselles paresseuses* rubs shoulders with the delicate lyricism of *Estrene de la rose* which leads on to the rollicking humour of *Changeons propos*. *Du conflict en douleur* ends the set with a memorable tone of wistful dignity.

Enescu seems much less happy in his later songs, not only the German settings of Carmen Sylva (the literary pseudonym of the Queen of Romania) but his one remaining French cycle, three songs to the poet Fernand Gregh Op. 19 (1915). These works are infinitely more ambitious and difficult for both performers, and the unremitting complexity of the piano texture is tiring for both singer and listener. Here, unlike the earlier set, the composer seems to be using the mélodie form to express musical ideas beyond its range.

SEPT CHANSONS DE CLÉMENT MAROT

1 i *Estreines à Anne*

Ce nouvel an pour Estreines vous donne
Mon cueur blessé d'une novelle playe.
Contrainct y suis; Amour ainsi l'ordonne,
En qui ung cas bien contraire j'essaye;
Car ce Cueur là, c'est ma richesse vraye;
Le demeurant n'est rien où je me fonde;
Et fault donner le meilleur bien que j'aye
Si j'ay vouloir d'estre riche en ce monde.

1 ii *Languir me fais*

Languir me fais sans t'avoir offensée:
Plus ne m'escriptz, plus de moy ne t'enquiers;
Mais non obstant, aultre Dame ne quiers:
Plus tost mourir que changer ma pensée.

Je ne dy pas t'amour estre effacée,
Mais je me plains de l'ennuy que j'acquiers,
Et loing de toy humblement te requiers
Que loing de moy, de moy ne sois faschée.

SEVEN SONGS OF CLÉMENT MAROT

A gift for Anne

As a New Year gift I offer you
My heart, afflicted with a new wound;
I must, for Love commands me to,
Though I'd rather take a different course:
For this heart of mine is my true wealth,
I've nothing else on which to build;
And I must give my greatest good,
If I'd be rich in this world.

You make me pine

You make me pine, though I've not offended you;
You neither write nor enquire of me;
And yet I desire no other Lady:
I'd sooner die than change my mind.

I do not say your love has died.
But I complain of the grief I suffer,
And far from you I humbly ask
That far from me you be not offended.

I iii *Aux damoyselles paresseuses d'escrire a leurs amys*

Bon jour, et puis, quelles nouvelles?
N'en sçauroit on de vous avoir?
S'en brief ne m'en faictes sçavoir,
J'en feray de toutes nouvelles.

Puis que vous estes si rebelles,
Bon vespre, bonne nuict, bon soir,
     Bon jour!

Mais si vous cueillez des groyselles,
Envoyez m'en; car, pour tout voir,
Je suis gros: mais c'est de vous veoir
Quelcque matin, mes damoyselles;
     Bon jour!

To young ladies too lazy to write to their friends

Good day, and then, what news?
Are we to have none from you?
In short, if you will give me none,
I'll make up my own about you all.

Since you are so obstinate—
Good vespers, good night, good evening,
     Good day!

But if you are picking currants,
Send some to me, for I am eager
To see everything; but mostly you,
One day, my ladies;
     Good day!

I iv *Estrene de la rose*

   La belle Rose à Venus consacrée
L'Œil & le Sens de grand plaisir pourvoit;
Si vous diray Dame qui tant m'agrée
Raison pourquoy de rouges on en voit.
Ung jour Venus son Adonis suyvoit
Parmy Jardins pleins d'Espines & Branches,
Les Piedz tous nudz & les deux Bras sans manches,
Dont d'ung Rosier l'Espine luy mesfeit.
Or estoient lors toutes les Roses blanches,
Mais de son sang de vermeilles en feit.
   De ceste Rose ay ja faict mon proffit
Vous estrenant, car plus qu'à aultre chose
Vostre Visage en doulceur tout confict
Semble à la fresche & vermeillete Rose.

The gift of a rose

   The lovely rose, consecrated to Venus,
Gives great pleasure to the eye and senses;
I shall tell you, lady who delights me so,
The reason why they are red.
One day Venus was following her Adonis
Through gardens full of thorns and branches
With naked feet and arms unsleeved
Which a rose-tree scratched with its thorns;
At that time all roses were white,
But some her blood now coloured crimson.
   I profited from this rose,
By giving it to you, for more than anything,
Your face, steeped in sweetness,
Is like the fresh and crimson rose.

I v *Present de couleur blanche*

   Present, present de couleur de Colombe,
Va où mon Cueur s'est le plus adonné!
Va doulcement, & doulcement y tombe!
Mais au parler ne te monstre estonné!

Dy que tu es pour Foy bien ordonné!
Dy oultreplus (car je te l'abandonne)
Que le Seigneur à qui tu es donné
N'a foy semblable à celle qui te donne.

A white-coloured gift

   O gift the colour of doves,
Go to where my heart has most given itself;
Go gently, and gently alight,
But be not surprised that I speak;

Say that you are well-made for love,
And say further—for I abandon you to him—
That the love of the lord to whom you are given
Cannot match the love of her who gives you.

I vi *Changeons propos, c'est trop chanté d'amours*

Changeons propos, c'est trop chanté d'amours,
Ce sont clamours, chantons de la serpette:
Tous vignerons ont à elle recours,
C'est leur secours pour tailler la vignette;
Ô serpillette, ô la serpillonnette,
La vignollette est par toy mise sus,
Dont les bons vins tous les ans sont yssus!

Le dieu Vulcain, forgeron des haultz dieux,
Forgea aux cieulx la serpe bien taillante,
De fin acier trempé en bon vin vieulx,
Pour tailler mieulx et estre plus vaillante.
Bacchus la vante, et dit qu'elle est seante
Et convenante à Noé le bon hom
Pour en tailler la vigne en la saison.

Bacchus alors chappeau de treille avoit,
Et arrivoit pour benistre la vigne;
Avec flascons Silenus le suyvoit,
Lequel beuvoit aussi droict qu'une ligne;
Puis il trepigne, et se faict une bigne;
Comme une guigne estoit rouge son nez;
Beaucoup de gens de sa race sont nez.

Let's change the subject, enough of lauding love

Let's change the subject, enough of lauding love.
Cacophony! Sing instead of the pruning-knife:
All vine-growers use it
To help them cut the young vines;
O tiny little pruning-knife,
You trim the little vines
That yield good wine each year.

The god Vulcan, blacksmith to the high gods,
Forged in heaven the sharp blade
Of fine steel, tempered in choice old wine,
To dress the vines more valiantly.
Bacchus sings its praises, and says that it is right
And proper for good old Noah
To trim the vine with it in due season.

Bacchus in those days wore a vine-leaf hat
And would arrive to bless the vineyard;
Silenus followed, bearing flagons,
And drank standing bolt upright;
Then he would dance and bruise himself;
His nose was as red as a cherry;
Many are those descended from his race.

I vii *Du confict en douleur*

Si j'ay du mal, maulgré moy je le porte;
Et s'ainsi est qu'aulcun me reconforte,
Son reconfort ma douleur point n'appaise;
Voylà comment je languis en mal aise,
Sans nul espoir de lyesse plus forte.

Et fault qu'ennuy jamais de moy ne sorte,
Car mon estat fut faict de telle sorte,
Dès que fuz né; pourtant ne vous desplaise
        Si j'ay du mal.

Quand je mourray ma douleur sera morte;
Mais ce pendant mon povre cueur supporte
Mes tristes jours en fortune maulvaise,
Dont force m'est que mon ennuy me plaise,
Et ne fault plus que je me desconforte
        Si j'ay du mal.

Steeped in suffering

If I suffer, I suffer despite myself;
And should someone try to comfort me,
His comfort cannot soothe my pain;
Thus do I languish in discomfort,
With no hope of greater joy.

And it is decreed that I shall ever grieve,
For thus was my fate decided
At my birth; yet be not offended
        If I suffer.

When I die, my pain will be dead;
Meanwhile, my heart endures
My sad days in misfortune,
Till I am obliged to enjoy my pain
And no longer be unhappy,
        If I suffer.

FALLA, Manuel de (1876–1946)

This great Spanish composer, snubbed when a student visitor to Paris by Debussy, and encouraged into publication by Paul Dukas, visited the world of the piano-accompanied mélodie only once, but left us with a set of three songs that have a polish and elegance that combines the best of both sides of the Pyrenees. These *TROIS MÉLODIES* (1908–9) to poems of Gautier are a remarkable achievement, and make us regret that Falla wrote nothing else of the kind. Fans of the famous *SIETE CANCIONES ESPAÑOLAS* will recognize here also the transparency of Falla's textures; indeed **Les colombes**, the first song in the group, has an accompaniment that might have been written for guitar. Here and there are Spanish thumbprints, but this beautiful song is hardly a character piece—unlike the remaining two items in the set. *Chinoiserie* shares with Roussel the ability to evoke the Far East with delicacy and economy. The opening page is all but unaccompanied and the fragility of the two-part writing for piano shows Falla at his most fastidious. After this restraint, he lets himself go with *Séguidille*, and, after Bizet's one-off triumph, who but a Spaniard would be able to throw off a song with this title? Here is a sudden burst of sunlight, an imperious stamp of the foot, an earthiness and raw energy which we seldom encounter, even in the best Spanish efforts of the French composers. And yet Falla seems to be amusing himself at our expense because, despite the shouted Alzas and Olàs, this latter-day Carmen is not quite 'la véritable manola', rather a creation for the tourists, the very best of chocolate-box Spain. The song is enormous fun and Falla lavishes on it an accompaniment with moments of delectable contrapuntal ingenuity which energizes a texture already swirling with flounced petticoats. He set one more French poem, G. Jean-Aubry's *Psyché*. This atmospheric song in muted mood from the height of the composer's maturity dates from 1924, and is accompanied by flute, harp, and string trio. There can be no doubt that Falla was influenced by the fashion for writing such works—Ravel's Mallarmé set, the Japanese poems of Stravinsky, and, of course, Schoenberg's *PIERROT LUNAIRE*—but *Psyché* is very much the composer's own, a reflection of Falla's seriousness and austerity, not a note wasted in creating his desired effects. The translation of this song can be found in *The Spanish song companion* (Gollancz).

TROIS MÉLODIES	***THREE MÉLODIES***
(Théophile Gautier)	

1 i *Les colombes*

The doves

Sur le coteau, là-bas où sont les tombes,
Un beau palmier, comme un panache vert
Dresse sa tête, où le soir les colombes
Viennent nicher et se mettre à couvert.

Over there, on the tomb-lined hill,
A beautiful palm, like a green plume,
Raises its crown, when the doves at evening
Come to roost and shelter.

Mais, le matin, elles quittent les branches;
Comme un collier qui s'égrène, on les voit
S'éparpiller dans l'air bleu, toutes blanches,
Et se poser plus loin sur quelque toit.

Mon âme est l'arbre où tous les soirs, comme elles,
De blancs essaims de folles visions
Tombent des cieux, en palpitant des ailes,
Pour s'envoler dès les premiers rayons.

I ii *Chinoiserie*

Ce n'est pas vous, non, madame, que j'aime,
Ni vous non plus, Juliette, ni vous,
Ophélia, ni Béatrix, ni même
Laure la blonde, avec ses grands yeux doux.

Celle que j'aime, à présent, est en Chine;
Elle demeure avec ses vieux parents,
Dans une tour de porcelaine fine,
Au fleuve Jaune, où sont les cormorans.

Elle a des yeux retroussés vers les tempes,
Un pied petit à tenir dans la main,
Le teint plus clair que le cuivre des lampes,
Les ongles longs et rougis de carmin.

Par son treillis elle passe sa tête,
Que l'hirondelle, en volant, vient toucher,
Et, chaque soir, aussi bien qu'un poète,
Chante le saule et la fleur du pêcher.

I iii *Séguidille*

Un jupon serré sur les hanches,
Un peigne énorme à son chignon,
Jambe nerveuse et pied mignon,
Œil de feu, teint pâle et dents blanches;
     Alza! olà!
          Voilà
   La véritable Manola.

Gestes hardis, libre parole,
Sel et piment à pleine main,
Oubli parfait du lendemain,
Amour fantasque et grâce folle;
     Alza! olà!
          Voilà
   La véritable Manola.

But at daybreak they leave the branches;
Like a necklace scattering beads, you see them
Disperse, all white, into the blue air,
And settle on some more distant roof.

My soul is that tree where each evening, like them,
White swarms of wild visions
Fall with fluttering wings from the sky,
To fly away when day first dawns.

Chinoiserie

No, it is not you, madam, whom I love,
Nor you, Juliet, nor you
Ophelia, nor Beatrice, nor even
Fair Laura with her large sweet eyes.

She whom I now love is in China;
She lives with her old parents
In a tower of fine porcelain,
Where cormorants dwell by the Yellow River.

She has eyes that slant toward her temples,
A tiny foot you could hold in your hands,
A complexion clearer than a copper lamp,
Long fingernails of carmine red.

She looks out from her trellis window,
Where a swallow brushes by in flight,
And each evening, like any poet,
She sings of the willow and flowering peach.

Seguidilla

Her skirt clinging to her hips,
In her chignon a huge comb,
Rippling legs and dainty feet,
Eyes ablaze, pale complexion, white teeth;
     Alza! Olà!
          Behold
   A true street-girl of Madrid.

Bold of gesture, free of speech,
Almost too hot to handle,
Utterly oblivious of the morrow,
Explosive love and wild grace;
     Alza! Olà!
          Behold
   A true street-girl of Madrid.

Chanter, danser aux castagnettes,	She sings and dances to castanets
Et, dans les courses de taureaux,	And, in the bull-ring,
Juger les coups des toreros,	Judges the bullfighters' blows,
Tout en fumant des cigarettes;	While smoking her cigarettes;
Alza! olà!	Alza! Olà!
Voilà	Behold
La véritable Manola.	A true street-girl of Madrid.

FAURÉ, Gabriel (1845–1924)

The 'Master of Charms' as Debussy somewhat dismissively called him (at least Duparc's nickname for Fauré—'mon délicieux'—was genuinely affectionate) effortlessly dominates, however diffidently, the history of the mélodie. He is at the heart of this book just as his achievements are at the heart of French song. No other composer's output traverses the years in which the mélodie was at its height with a succession of masterpieces, ranging from tuneful salon trifles in the 1860s to the late cycles, unique in twentieth-century music, which seem as modern and sometimes as unfathomable as anything written by the 1920s avant-garde. Florent Schmitt's verdict on Fauré still seems just: 'Plus profond et plus musicien que Saint-Saëns, plus divers que Lalo, plus spontané que D'Indy, plus classique que Debussy, plus intérieur et plus ému que Chabrier.' The progression from one end of his career to the other is sure-footed and steady, the hard work astonishingly regular (despite the fact that he had to make his living outside composition), the pace of development and self-renewal never forced, yet ineluctable. As a teenager he studied music at the École Niedermeyer where the harmony used by, say, a composer like Saint-Saëns was supplemented and enriched by a study of the church modes. From the beginning he was equipped with a language which was unlike his predecessors' and which quickly became inimitable.

The biographical details of his life seem almost banal in comparison to the importance of the music. No doubt he would have liked to have more money, and to have made a happier marriage. He would have liked to be spared the travel and drudgery as an inspector of conservatoires, and he would have preferred to devote his time to composing rather than take up the reorganization of the Paris Conservatoire, where it surprised everyone that his dreamy manner concealed a reforming zeal—he was nicknamed 'Robespierre'. Success came late, and there was a period in the middle of his life when he doubted that his talent would be truly recognized, but this never stopped the steady flow of music. He was only free to compose in the summer holidays, so we would certainly have had many more works from him had he been financially independent, or given more opportunities to go on working-holidays to inspiring cities (such as the Princesse de Polignac arranged for him in Venice).

But there was something about Fauré which flourished on being inscrutable, and this unexceptional private life is part of his mystery, part of the wonder of his achievement. We know that both women and men were drawn to him with his dark good looks and poetic temperament, but we know far less about his feelings in return, for his romantic life was managed with great discretion. He had a liaison with Emma Bardac, dedicatee of LA BONNE CHANSON, who was later to become the second Mme Debussy, but it took many decades for it to emerge that her first daughter was probably Fauré's. This indication of a lack of fulfilment at home (he always observed the outward proprieties as far as his wife was concerned, and his two sons were devoted to him) affirms the composer as someone with the gentle melancholy of an essentially solitary and secretive man. But this never turned to self-pity, even when old age brought its problems. In his late years Fauré suffered, like Beethoven, from a hearing affliction which left him deaf and aurally confused. But like Beethoven his inner musical mind was as clear as crystal. He pursued his own path to the very end and arrived in regions which transfigured his music, and bewildered his public. In his late songs, he asks no favours of us, and will not be deflected from doing what he has to do. Almost every piece of Fauré derives, from its own implacable sense of direction, a power which is quite out of proportion to its size. In this music we sense the grandeur of the oak in the acorn.

Because the music, and the personality behind it, are of a piece, lovers of Fauré's patrician art find his self-sufficiency almost unbearably poignant. In performers sensitive to its spirit, the music encourages a selflessness which frees them from the need for the normal interpretative apparatus of moulding and 'meaningful' presentation. Fauré's music calls for a transparency both of texture and of approach, and the songs demand a serious devotion from both singer and pianist which places to one side such issues as 'Is this song good for me and my voice?' and concentrates on serving the music in the same spirit of openness and humility in which the composer wrote it. When the performer is able to 'tune in' to Fauré in this way, observing the tempo and dynamic markings, and avoiding gratuitous rubato and histrionics, the surrender to the music's quiet yet imposing momentum brings its own best reward: the elation born of restraint. In any case, this music, even when charming and tuneful, is utterly different from songs which depend on a sales pitch for their effectiveness. Stopping in mid-flight to ponder meaning, or to caress the phrases in passing, disturbs the flow and distorts the musical shape, and is the standard mistake of the inexperienced singer of Fauré. Only right at the end can performers stand back and see (or hear) their work—just as, when an aeroplane has completed its manœuvres and flown away, figures traced in smoke are left suspended for a few moments, a delicate pattern in the sky. Many a singer of the German lied has endeavoured to bestow an 'interesting' performance on a Fauré song which he finds otherwise uneventful and lacking in drama, yet any attempt to force this music into expressive fancy-dress is self-defeating.

The whole of Fauré's career may well seem a failure to those who do not value chamber music and the mélodie. Where are the successful operas, where are the symphonies, and where are the vast choral works which are the mark of an important figure? Actually, a look through a catalogue of Fauré's compositions shows that he wrote a good deal more, and bigger works, than most people realize, but the heart of the music is in those pieces where the humble piano plays some part—piano solos (what riches here are to be found under the innocent titles of nocturne, impromptu, and barcarolle), sonatas for violin and cello, two each of piano quartets and piano quintets, the Piano Trio, and of course the mélodies. Was Fauré's early success in England something to do with the fact that the British were never wont to measure a composer's stature (cf. Mendelssohn, Schubert, and Brahms) by his success in the theatre, or lack of it? Many of his French colleagues found Fauré's music severe and uncompromising, but the English (whose relationship to France is based on the tantalizing exoticism of being at one remove from the culture and language) have embraced his refinement as an improving discipline in an uncouth world. And as the times become even more abrasive, Fauré's music remains one of the great correctives to the self-seeking vulgarity which seeps progressively into the fabric of our artistic life. If we are tempted to challenge him with retrospective accusations ('If you wanted fame, why didn't you push yourself more? What you needed was a publicist!'), the slightly mournful expression in his photographs seems to mock our venal ambitions on his behalf. 'Robespierre' in this case is truly incorruptible, and he reminds us that music is not, as we are often told in modern times, a business, but an art. Fauré's music seems to encourage each one of us to carry on 'doing one's thing', trusting somehow that, with self-discipline, the small voice and great heart will hold its own. After all, for the sake of our sanity alone, we have to continue to believe in a world where it is possible for one tenor gently to sing *Clair de lune* without being drowned by three bellowing *O sole mio*.

There are three *recueils* (published by Hamelle) of twenty songs each. These are the volumes with which all study of the mélodies begins. The songs in the first volume date from between 1861 and 1878. With these works the composer laid the foundation of his reputation as a charmer. Of course not *all* this music is the purest Fauré, for we detect moments of homage to his teacher Saint-Saëns and Gounod, not that this is a bad thing. The composer, helped by the influence of his mentor, Saint-Saëns, was an up-and-coming organist (a path to musical power in the France of those days), hopeful of marriage to Pauline Viardot's daughter Marianne, and the darling of certain influential salons. He was on friendly terms with Lalo, Duparc, Chabrier, and d'Indy, and was a co-founder of the Société Nationale de Musique in 1871. The two Viardot daughters were given to singing together, and two ravishing duets date from this period: Hugo's *Puisqu'ici bas toute âme* [HAHN 3] and an astonishingly tricky *Tarentelle* (Monnier) which gives any two sopranos as much of a vocal workout as they will ever need.

The songs which do not always work in this first set are the ones where the composer aspires to a grandeur of utterance which does not yet suit him. The first mélodie of all, *Le papillon et la fleur* (Hugo, 1861), is a little masterpiece of a salon waltz written by a teenager. It has a perfect scale in every sense—there is something about the élan of the piano's introduction as it rushes up the stave which announces a new and important composer. In *Mai* (Hugo, 1862?) we find another pretty tune supported by those gently rippling broken chords which were to propel forward, in one shape or another, so many Fauré songs. The cadence at 'et l'horizon immense' is especially affecting. Victor Hugo was never Fauré's poet as he was Saint-Saëns's, and *Dans les ruines d'une abbaye* (c.1865) is an example of a fine melody lavished on a curious choice of verse. Fauré is ingenious in accommodating Hugo's prosody, but he has not got the measure of the poem. The influence of the young composer's teacher is obvious when one compares this song to *Enlèvement* by Saint-Saëns. A similar difficulty in capturing the poem's mood may be detected in *Les matelots* (Gautier, c.1870), which strikes a note of religious sublimity out of place in the salon, though to be found there often enough. From a technical viewpoint, however, we note that Fauré is fascinated by the Schubertian technique of building an accompaniment from a single motif. We leaf through the volume and find another Gautier text already familiar from Berlioz's LES NUITS D'ÉTÉ where it is known as *Sur les lagunes* [BERLIOZ 3 iii]. Here it is *La chanson du pêcheur*, a song to be sung in the open air accompanied by rolling arpeggios. (It is not altogether difficult to see why Duparc felt he could do better in his *Lamento*.) We detect here, not for the last time, a leaning towards an Italianate style which is a noticeable feature of the first *recueil*. And then suddenly we open the page at **Lydia,** chaste cousin of Duparc's *Phidylé*, and in their shared poet, Leconte de Lisle, we find a writer whose Parnassian restraint is at one with this composer's temperament. Here Fauré's mastery of the modes of church music enables him to combine austerity with sweetness in a ravishing 'Lydian' manner.

From a completely different world is **Chant d'automne** (*c.*1871), one of the composer's three Baudelaire settings, and important for this reason alone. Fauré would later write better music of brooding drama than we hear in this opening, but the second section of the song ('J'aime de vos longs yeux la lumière verdâtre') is the first Fauré in this *recueil* which permits us to glimpse the master of LA BONNE CHANSON in a flowing arpeggio-accompanied passage typical of his special brand of cantabile serenity. Proust was particularly attached to this passage, hummed it often, and mentioned it in his letters. The melody of **Rêve d'amour** ('S'il est un charmant gazon') wilts in a shy descent of the stave, a feminine cadence which we come to love in this composer as one of his trademarks. Here is an early indication that Saint-Saëns's admiration for Schumann's piano writing had been passed on to Fauré. It is one of many settings of a celebrated lyric. **L'absent** (1871) is the plaint of the self-exiled Hugo, and the fall of Napoleon III made the grand old man's story newsworthy again. From the point of view of the words, this is something of a sentimental tearjerker, but it brings forth a new vein of seriousness in the young song composer who had till now been mainly concerned to write pretty music; here he achieves something deeper. Although he just about brings this song off, there is no doubting that in this period Fauré was more at home in the delicacies of *Aubade* (Pommey, *c.*1873) and the almost café-chanson lilt of Gautier's *Tristesse* (*c.*1873). The intricate weave between voice and piano of **Sylvie** (Choudens, 1878) is justly famous, its accompaniment perhaps the most resourceful so far. Indeed, this song is prophetic of *Nell,* and the fluid piano style of the second *recueil*. **Après un rêve** (Bussine, 1877) boasts a sublime tune which is perhaps better appreciated in the famous arrangement for cello and piano. The poem derives from an anonymous Italian poem; with its long lines and melismas, singers find this very difficult to sing, and even harder to sell the text. One would like to admire the two remaining Baudelaire songs, but in vain: in **Hymne** (1870?) the poet needs greater gravity than Fauré summons up, and Fauré is also ill at ease with the sombre philosophizing of **La rançon** (dedicated to Duparc, but unlikely to shake his supremacy as *the* composer of Baudelaire). The texts of these songs are translated in this book in deference to the greatness of the poet, and because his works are not found often enough in composers' song catalogues. **Au bord de l'eau** to a much less important text (Sully Prudhomme) is a much greater song. It has a calm laziness with a movement of quavers which paints the flowing of a stream on a Sunday afternoon; in this 1875 prequel to *Sunday in the park with George* (or rather, Gabriel), we can almost see the famous impressionists capturing the scene on canvas. One should also mention the beautiful Hugo setting *L'aurore* (WIDOR 2) which was first published in Noske [AFTERWORD 8].

The second Hamelle volume (1878–87) represents a major step forward, partly because Fauré was beginning to find the poets who suited his gifts. Leconte de Lisle, who has already delighted us with *Lydia*, makes a return with **Nell** (1878) from the *Chansons écossaises*, where the poet abandons his Greek assembly of maidens in favour of an anthology of Scottish pulchritude, including *La Fille aux cheveux de lin*, later immortalized by Debussy in a piano piece. For many this song is the quintessential Fauré. The marvellous tune seems to unfold on a long spool of casual invention, and the piano part (as any accompanist will tell you) is seraphically treacherous: each half-beat contains a subtle change of chord, and the constantly moving inner harmonies suffuse the song with a kaleidoscopic glow of colour. Later on in this volume we find *Les roses d'Ispahan* (1884) by the same poet. Here Fauré's mastery is breathtaking; as in Chausson's *La caravane* we are made to feel the sway of the camels as we ride across the desert sands; we also feel the heat and the lassitude and smouldering long-ing—always moderated by Fauréan courtesy, of course. The apostrophized Leïlah is Bizet's Arab host-ess come of age, for here oriental evocation is thoroughly assimilated, deep in the heart of the mélodie.

The composer's first cycle, a triptych entitled *POÈME D'UN JOUR*, is embedded in this volume (Grandmougin, 1878). The poetry has the quality of a serial in a women's magazine, and owes a great deal to Armand Silvestre's 'Poème' cycles (set by Massenet) which were all the rage at the time. The little set is an interesting and effective anthology of the composer's various styles: in *Rencontre* we have a gentle tune moving in small intervals supported by a liquid accompaniment which does not presume much in its own right but which, in the manner of *Nell*, shows a dazzling command of har-monic nuance, a background which enriches the vocal line almost without us noticing; *Toujours* is Fauré appassionato, a mood we find him in more often in his chamber music than his songs, where the harmonic changes in the triplets-on-the-wing fly by far too fast for the comfort of even a fine sight-reader; *Adieu* is the first example of a type of song which we find right up until the compos-er's last cycle—a measured tread in the accompaniment, normally crotchets in $\frac{4}{4}$, that permits the sensual unfolding of a vocal line which flowers into something hypnotically beautiful. The effect is of the pianist supporting the singer in mute adoration, and when we hear an introduction of seem-ingly simple chords of this kind, we know that Fauré has something magical up his sleeve. We find this type of song in *Aurore* (Silvestre, 1884), and again in the beguiling *Le secret* (1880–1) by the same poet, in which we hear the beginnings of the composer's third period. Indeed, much of the rest of the *recueil* is dominated by Silvestre, a civil servant whose verses appealed to composers because they left tactful scope for musical elaboration. Fauré seems to have been attracted to their understated eroticism, and Silvestre inspired Fauré into gentle serenades and wistful evocations. There was a stronger side to the poet, however, which sometimes persuaded the composer into dramatic utter-ance which, for the first time in his mélodies, sounds really convincing. Thus the dark and heavy left-hand octaves of *Automne* (1878) sound an entirely appropriate note of heartache, and the des-peration of the final climax seems unforced. This is also true of *Les berceaux* (Sully Prudhomme, 1879), justly famous for its rocking triplet accompaniment. Where the early *Les matelots* was mawk-ishly sentimental, this great song seems effortlessly to take in the vast horizons scanned by the anx-ious wives of sailors, and to be equal to expressing the longing and the heartache of those left behind. The elegiac mood suggests that it was not lost on Fauré that, for pianists at least, the key of B flat minor is reminiscent of the Chopin sonata in the same key. This new note in Fauré's output also shows the influence of Duparc, whose *L'invitation au voyage* is also water-borne and painted on an epic canvas. It is back to Silvestre for *Notre amour* (c.1879), normally gabbled by young singers, but at the right tempo a gently evocative love song full of harmonic subtlety, and *Chanson d'amour*, one of the first examples of Fauré's madrigal style, and a happy combination of commercial viabil-ity, and true Fauréan feeling. The neglected *La fée aux chansons* (1882) was, rather unexpectedly, one of Gerald Moore's favourites, and he requested it for his 80th birthday concert. This, and another song entitled *Le pays des rêves* (1884), have a lightness and brightness which make it hard to believe that the impassioned and somewhat melodramatic **Fleur jetée** (Silvestre, 1884), resembling the horse-ride of Schubert's *Erlkönig*, comes from the same stable of composer and poet.

There remain three important songs in the second *recueil*. Two of these are settings of a rare and exquisite poet, friend, and admirer of Wagner, Villiers de l'Isle-Adam. **Nocturne** dates from 1886 and **Les présents** from the following year. *Nocturne* requires very fine singing to make its best effect for it has a certain expansiveness which rises to a high tessitura in a forte dynamic, despite its moonlit provenance. *Les présents* on the other hand has to be almost spoken, the semiquavers running off the tongue so as not to disturb the music's hypnotic flow. This song seems so exquisitely planned that not a single note could be added or changed, and we now find this type of lucid perfection increasingly in the mélodies. The final song is the immortal (for no other word will do) **Clair de lune** (1887). Verlaine slips into the volume almost unnoticed, and at the last minute, in order to provide us with an appetizer or a trailer for the third *recueil*. This happiest of marriages between music and text works in a new way—it is an open marriage if you like—in that the composer had the inspired idea to make of this a piano piece with a vocal obbligato. Thus the courtly rituals of life at Versailles (as painted by Watteau, and represented by the piano's minuet) are made to seem all the more detached and at one remove from real life. The accompaniment, a challenge for a pianist's nerve, control of colour, and the reliability of his inner metronome, is imperturbable. Above this music (which is in the composer's 'madrigal' style, but which so far transcends any suggestion of pastiche as to be utterly original) the singer enacts the delicate ballet of courtship weaving in and out of the moonlight. Occasionally voice and piano coalesce in euphonious thirds as if by chance (at 'mode mineur' for example) until they both come into focus together at 'Au calme clair de lune, triste et beau'. As in *Les présents*, the voice and piano are independent of each other and converse freely as the master magician effortlessly juggles the ingredients of his song: every strand floats freely in mid-air it seems, and yet remains very much at his command. The key is B flat minor and it is difficult to imagine the song transposed, so perfectly does this tonality capture the wistful melancholy of a life where happiness is experienced only in the context of etiquette. Was it in this muted tone of gentle ennui that Fauré wooed his mistresses, aware that loyalty to his wife and family prevented the fruitful flowering of any new relationship?

The third *recueil*, which spans the years 1888 to 1904, is perhaps the most extraordinary, for almost every song is a masterpiece. It opens with music in bitter and tempestuous mood, something rarely heard but when experienced not forgotten. What is true of the composer was also true of the man whose temper, rarely provoked, was formidable. The brusque outburst of **Larmes** (Richepin, 1888) is contemporary with Wolf's MÖRIKE LIEDER and we are reminded that a great song composer must have every colour at his disposal, and that the 'master of charms' could be less than charming when necessary. The other songs from this year are **Au cimetière** (also Richepin) and *Spleen* (Verlaine). The first of these has an accompaniment as simple as that for *Larmes* was complicated. It is one of those songs, powerful in its elegiac restraint, which shows the composer's fascination with the sea, and what one of his later poets was to call 'de grands départs inassouvis'. The Verlaine setting is a rival to Debussy's *Il pleure dans mon cœur* and written at about the same time. The composers' accompaniments evoke the falling of rain in different, and equally effective, ways. Fauré's *Spleen* [DEBUSSY 6 vi] has become unfairly neglected for it stands on its own, outside any cycle or set; Debussy's inclusion of his song in the ARIETTES OUBLIÉES ensures its frequent performance. These three dark songs of 1888 are so untypical of Fauré's output that he himself referred to them ironically as 'très gaies!!!'

The next song, *La rose* (Leconte de Lisle, 1890), shows both poet and composer at their grandest. In the past Fauré has built up to a vocal climax of this kind, and the result has been overblown. This rose sustains its freshness and perfume. The song is a masterpiece of organic unity, each phrase unfolding petal-like as part of a whole, the piano writing having a life of its own which twines around the vocal line and provides a mass of colour on the three-staved trellis. The two following songs –*Chanson* and *Madrigal*—were written as incidental music for Edmond Haraucourt's play *Shylock*, modelled on *The Merchant of Venice*, presented at the Odéon in Paris in 1889. They show Fauré's pragmatic skill in writing for less than first-rate singers, but their simplicity seems born of a genuine delight in the madrigal style, which suggests sixteenth-century (and thus Shakespearian) elegance and which the composer was to use to even more subtle effect in his next songs.

These are the celebrated CINQ MÉLODIES 'DE VENISE' (1891). Whereas *Shylock* the play *was* set in Venice, the poems of this cycle have nothing to do with the jewel of the Adriatic. They happen to have been conceived in Venice thanks to the Princesse de Polignac who invited Fauré, overworked and suffering from stress, for a holiday at a particularly opportune time. She had in mind an operatic collaboration with the ailing poet Verlaine, but the fruit of this match-making was a sequence of extraordinary songs. It seems that the composer has been preparing for this set all his life: we find here the fulfilment of ideas that in earlier works have been only a gleam in his eye. Thus **Mandoline** is the greatest of all the serenades, with a suggestion of the plucked lute for accompaniment; the veneer of heartless elegance cracks to reveal deep feeling and real humour, and this reminds us that even the most jaded Versailles courtiers are not made of stone, and long for true love 'parmi les marbres'. In **En sourdine** they find something like it, for here the brittle glitter of the *Fêtes galantes* is cast aside; if there is melancholy here, it is the sadness that the ancients tell us all creatures feel after making love. The accompaniment in fronds of semiquavers makes a shady bower for this languid reverie in the half-light. Who knows what subterfuge has brought these lovers to this assignation, for the intrusion of the word 'désespoir', and the warning song of the nightingale, unmasks an idyll as a stolen moment. In **Green** we have a breathless confession of love (the composer marks it 'haletante'), a tempo and mood strange for a poem which celebrates the aftermath of love-making. We also hear elation in Debussy's enthusiastic and passionate setting; the masochistic devotion of Reynaldo Hahn seems nearer the mark. Nevertheless, Fauré's *Green* is enchanting; just before 'J'arrive tout couvert encore de rosée', the mezzo-staccato quaver accompaniment blossoms into a falling figure enlivened by a pair of semiquavers as light as a caress. This unassuming motif binds the song together, and is heard again in the next two songs, a cyclic feature which bows, in courtly manner, to César Franck. The composer himself summed up the song's paradoxes in acknowledging its interpretative difficulties in a letter to the Princesse de Polignac: 'slow moving but agitated in feeling, happy and miserable, eager and discouraged! What a lot in thirty bars!' *À Clymène* is the only song of the set which is arguably linked to Venice and its barcaroles. It is the least often performed, possibly because it lacks the concision of most of these Verlaine settings, and is more abstract in concept. It is however the purest Fauré, and the final 'Ainsi soit-il!' sums up the art of a man who can only be the thing he is. The style of LA BONNE CHANSON is here announced. The final song of the set is *C'est l'extase*; unlike Debussy who emphasizes the 'langoureuse', Fauré illustrates 'les frissons des bois': the whole mélodie is alive with nervous syncopation and hovering harmony, ever changing and yet staying more or less in the same place—like light dancing before the eyes of an impressionist painter. Artfully concealed within this seamlessly unfolding song, we hear skilfully woven motival echoes of *Green* and *En sourdine*.

There is a certain complexity in the CINQ MÉLODIES 'DE VENISE', where Fauré the creator of absolute music gains the upper hand over another side of his nature—the obliging and considerate setter of verses for famous singers. Although he was never as servile in this respect as Massenet, it is as if he has had enough of the standards and demands of the salon. This is why the later works are undeniably less sung than the early: Fauré ceases to provide singers with what they want, and gives us instead what *he* wants, music which reflects his preoccupations with harmony and form. The song cycle LA BONNE CHANSON (1892–4, nine songs published by Hamelle in a separate volume) is the most substantial Verlaine cycle of all, but it remains an enigma for many, even if it is revered by the Fauré enthusiast. Hugo called the poems a 'flower in a bombshell' when they first appeared, and the same may be said of the settings. The poet declaims his joy in his engagement to Mathilde Mauté, and Bernac used to say that the hard thing about this cycle was that most singers find it easier to express glowering anger or anguish than the unremitting happiness which these texts demand. From the poet's point of view this represents a retreat into fantasy visions of an ideal married life where he is safe from his homosexuality. The musical cycle is a masterpiece, of course, an astonishingly wrought structure with thematic inter-relationships—like the VENISE songs these come to roost in the final song, *L'hiver a cessé*, a blaze of light rendered into music. This unifying device simply reinforces the impression of a work conceived not in parts, but in a single stroke of the pen, the music of a great composer very much in love with its dedicatee Emma Bardac, a work where energy and passion and copious invention abound. Conquering its difficulties exhilarates the performers (who become more devoted to LA BONNE CHANSON the deeper they go into it), but it is frequently received in lukewarm fashion by audiences, and we are reminded what an astonishingly 'modern' piece this is. One could not imagine an art more distant from that of Fauré's teacher Saint-Saëns. The public is bewildered by the constantly changing harmony which passes by too quickly for the average ear to appreciate. Restless music 'on a high' like this, unlike most of the composer's other songs, is too much like quicksilver for many to grasp. (The pianist has a similar feeling as the harmonies fly beneath his fingers.) The whole piece's mercurial quality reflects, whether intentionally or not, Verlaine's sense of fevered unreality, as if the singer/poet protesteth a mite too much his overwhelming happiness. One cannot help remembering that Fauré's relationship with Emma Bardac was as doomed as that of Verlaine and Mathilde Mauté. (The composer was eventually to see Emma, of all bitter things, married to Claude Debussy.) Fauré sought to broaden its appeal by rearranging it for piano quintet accompaniment, but he always much preferred the original version.

When we return to the rest of the third *recueil* we can detect a retreat from this heady complexity. Fauré's last Verlaine setting is *Prison* (1894), which is searingly eloquent; its rhetorical question about the wasting of one's youth more powerful than from any other composer. (This poem was also set to music by Reynaldo Hahn and Déodat de Séverac.) *Soir* (Samain, 1894) is as harmonically complicated as *C'est l'extase*, but the composer now seems to have entered an autumnal phase, and this song is bathed in soft evening light. *Le parfum impérissable* (Leconte de Lisle, 1897) is a suave piece of orientalism, a balm for the wounds of love which prophesies the static glories of the late style to come. And then there is always Fauré the madrigalist, for it seems that he cannot resist this strain of gallant self-effacement: ***Dans la forêt de septembre*** (1902) is a masterpiece, Fauré's only mélodie collaboration with Catulle Mendès, the poet here at his infrequent best. ***Le plus doux chemin*** and *Le ramier* (both Silvestre, 1904) are jewels of transparency, the very quality we had sometimes lost sight of in LA BONNE CHANSON. The performers who give us the settings of Albert Samain—*Arpège* (1897) and *Accompagnement* (1902)—earn our gratitude for rescuing from neglect Fauré's collaborations with a fine poet. The same may be said for his sole setting of Henri de Régnier (*Chanson*—1906), another madrigal of an even sparer texture. This was published as a single item by Heugel, at the same time as Jean Dominique's *Le don silencieux.* These two songs would feature much more in recitals, were it not for their vagrant status outside the shelter of the *recueils.* A glance at the poem for *Le don silencieux* will show why it may be taken to be a perfect summation of this composer's artistic credo, and why a fine performance of this song can be almost unbearably moving for the lover of his music. Also from this period, and published separately, is the duet *Pleurs d'or* (Samain, 1896), where the subtlety of writing for two voices and piano has seldom been surpassed.

There remain four song cycles composed in the so-called late period, which are controversial with performers and audiences alike. This music can be written off as the work of a tired and broken man, deaf and doddering, or it can be heard as the inspired creativity of a Beethoven of the third period. I incline toward the latter school of thought, but most listeners still come down in favour of a judgement somewhere between the two. There will always be those who, in their love for *Nell*, regret the passing of that type of melodious Fauré, and see in the late music only confusion and hardening of the arteries. But the listener who has taken the trouble to follow the composer every step of the way, from entertainer to prophet, rather than simply plundering his cupboard for delectable morsels, will come to revere these late cycles like few other pieces of music. Of course, a work like LA CHANSON D'ÈVE (Van Lerberghe, 1906–10) is daunting, for it is long and deals with the loftiest subject. But once inside the magic garden we find ourselves in a realm like no other. The opening song *Paradis* is nothing less than a masterpiece, absolutely equal to describing such awesome things as the creation of the world and including the (normally impossible) challenge of setting to music the words of God himself. (Alfons Diepenbrock attempts this most unwisely in a poem from Van Lerberghe's set which is avoided by Fauré.) How different all this is from the religious songs of Caplet and Bréville, for in this Eden the Church and its exalted rituals are an anachronism. Eve is a cosmic creature, of course, but she is deeply innocent, as unaware of her own importance as the composer is of his. She simply *is*, as one newly created might be, and Fauré mints a limpid musical language, pared down to essentials, which matches this sense of awesome holiness without religiosity. The cycle, which requires a great span of concentration and a radiant connection with Fauré's wavelength, calls for a very great singer, musician, and human being, and of course it has seldom been granted these things, even in less than complete combination. LE JARDIN CLOS (Van Lerberghe, 1914) is slightly shorter but even more opaque for those without the key to the garden gate. The music is even more spare than LA CHANSON D'ÈVE, and, because it occupies a far less ambitious canvas than the creation of the world, it can make a drier impression. It is in fact far from dry—an old man taking his infinitely moving farewell to the world of female beauty and erotic grace which had mattered so much to him. This is Fauré's *Marienbad Elegy*, perhaps a fitting comparison for some- one who had become the revered old Goethe of French song. Again it is the human quality of the performer, and his or her ability to let go of the normal means of presenting songs in favour of just letting the music shine through them ('how pretentious!' shouts the unconvinced listener, but so be it), which makes a crucial difference. There can be few more vulnerable songs than *Je me poserai sur ton cœur* in the entire *mélodie* repertoire, and *Dans la nymphée* is the apotheosis of the chordal- ly accompanied hymn where the singer floats above the bar-line moving slightly to the left and right, into one key and out of another, permitting us glimpses of undreamed beauty and then leading us onward through the ether. We do not know the final destination, but this music leads us to the heart of whatever distinguishes French music from that of the rest of the world. Those who have heard Hugues Cuenod sing this song can never forget it.

Fauré's wonderful musical journey, like no one else's in the mélodie, ends with two miniature cycles, each one containing four songs. The very fact that these works are shorter than the other two late cycles makes them more accessible to the singer. MIRAGES (Brimont, 1919) seems somehow to have taken on board the epigrammatic spirit of the post-war age, the impatience with large forms which was already informing the work of Les Six. Everything in this cycle is deft, particularly the haunting *Danseuse* with its tripping dotted rhythms which seem to link hands with the antique evo- cations of late Debussy. At the heart of the set is the hauntingly beautiful *Jardin nocturne*. I always play an old 78 of this song to those who need to be shown the greatness of the art of Pierre Bernac: a perfect legato, a strictly controlled tempo without losing those wonderful agogic emphases (a type of rubato-with-words which the French seem to be uniquely capable of in their own language), and a limpid accompaniment from Poulenc who professed himself no fan of Fauré's art, but here seems perfectly to understand it. With this music one is suddenly taken back, as was certainly the com- poser himself, to the young boy growing up in the south of France, in the Ariège, where he used to listen to the sounds of nature in his beloved garden at the monastery of Montgauzy. *Jardin nocturne* is Fauré's final word on that lifelong favourite topic of enchanted gardens, exotic flowers, and their imperishable perfumes.

But he had another theme running though his mélodies, and his farewell to writing songs was also his farewell to the sea, and those intrepid sailors whose wives and mothers we met so long ago in some of the songs of the first *recueil* and in *Les berceaux*. For this cycle he seems to have returned to the real world of singers who, poor vain creatures, need something stirring and impressive to sing. His friendship with the young baritone Charles Panzéra probably had every- thing to do with this last-minute reversion to a more 'public' style in L'HORIZON CHIMÉRIQUE (de La Ville de Mirmont, 1921). It is not as if he entirely abandoned his still, inner world, indeed few songs are more rapt than that hymn to the moon, *Diane, Séléné*. But the other three songs have an element of salty enthusiasm which is all the more stirring for coming from someone who was increasingly physically frail. As he came to the last line of *Vaisseaux, nous vous aurons aimés*, he set words to music which, if taken to come from his own heart, assure us that despite his land- locked limitations he had much to say left in him, many great new departures. But there is a poignancy about the fact that the poet who had dreamed of these journeys had fallen in the war. Grand new departures were not for him. And Fauré too here makes his farewell. Peering into dis- tant horizons he slips from sight, leaving nearly sixty years of songwriting behind him.

1 *Le papillon et la fleur*

(Victor Hugo)

La pauvre fleur disait au papillon céleste:
    Ne fuis pas!
Vois comme nos destins sont différents. Je reste,
    Tu t'en vas!

Pourtant nous nous aimons, nous vivons sans les
        hommes
    Et loin d'eux,
Et nous nous ressemblons, et l'on dit que nous
        sommes
    Fleurs tous deux!

Mais, hélas! l'air t'emporte et la terre m'enchaîne.

    Sort cruel!
Je voudrais embaumer ton vol de mon haleine

    Dans le ciel!

Mais non, tu vas trop loin!—Parmi des fleurs sans
        nombre
    Vous fuyez,
Et moi je reste seule à voir tourner mon ombre
    À mes pieds.

Tu fuis, puis tu reviens; puis tu t'en vas encore
    Luire ailleurs.
Aussi me trouves-tu toujours à chaque aurore
    Toute en pleurs!

Oh! pour que notre amour coule des jours fidèles,
    Ô mon roi,
Prends comme moi racine, ou donne-moi des ailes
    Comme à toi!

2 *Mai*

(Victor Hugo)

Puisque mai tout en fleurs dans les prés nous
    réclame,
Viens! ne te lasse pas de mêler à ton âme
La campagne, les bois, les ombrages charmants,
Les larges clairs de lune au bord des flots dormants,
Le sentier qui finit où le chemin commence,

The butterfly and the flower

The humble flower said to the heavenly butterfly:
    Do not flee!
See how our destinies differ. Fixed to earth am I,
    You fly away!

Yet we love each other, we live without men

    And far from them,
And we are so alike, it is said that both of us

    Are flowers!

But alas! The breeze bears you away, the earth holds
    me fast.
    Cruel fate!
I would perfume your flight with my fragrant
    breath
    In the sky!

But no, you flit too far! Among countless flowers

    You fly away,
While I remain alone, and watch my shadow circle
    Round my feet.

You fly away, then return; then take flight again
    To shimmer elsewhere.
And so you always find me at each dawn
    Bathed in tears!

Ah, that our love might flow through faithful days,
    O my king,
Take root like me, or give me wings
    Like yours!

May

Since full-flowering May calls us to the meadows,

Come! do not tire of mingling with your soul
The countryside, the woods, the charming shade,
Vast moonlights on the banks of sleeping waters,
The path ending where the road begins,

Et l'air et le printemps et l'horizon immense,
L'horizon que ce monde attache humble et joyeux

Comme une lèvre au bas de la robe des cieux!
Viens! et que le regard des pudiques étoiles
Qui tombe sur la terre à travers tant de voiles,
Que l'arbre pénétré de parfums et de chants,
Que le souffle embrasé de midi dans les champs,
Et l'ombre et le soleil et l'onde et la verdure,

Et le rayonnement de toute la nature
Fassent épanouir, comme une double fleur,
La beauté sur ton front et l'amour dans ton cœur!

And the air, the spring and the huge horizon,
The horizon which this world fastens, humble and
    joyous,
Like a lip to the hem of heaven's robe!
Come! and may the gaze of the chaste stars,
Falling to earth through so many veils,
May the tree steeped in scent and song,
May the burning breath of noon in the fields,
And the shade and the sun, and the tide and
    verdure,
And the radiance of all nature—
May they cause to blossom, like a double flower,
Beauty on your brow and love in your heart!

3 *Dans les ruines d'une abbaye*
(Victor Hugo)

In the ruins of an abbey

Seuls tous deux, ravis, chantants!
    Comme on s'aime!
Comme on cueille le printemps
    Que Dieu sème!

Quels rires étincelants
    Dans ces ombres
Jadis pleines de fronts blancs,
    De cœurs sombres!

On est tout frais mariés.
    On s'envoie
Les charmants cris variés
    De la joie.

Frais échos mêlés au vent
    Qui frissonne!
Gaîté que le noir couvent
    Assaisonne!

Seuls tous deux, ravis, chantants!
    Comme on s'aime!
Comme on cueille le printemps
    Que Dieu sème!

Quels rires étincelants
    Dans ces ombres
Jadis pleines de fronts blancs,
    De cœurs sombres!

Alone, together, enraptured, singing!
    How we love each other!
How we reap the springtime
    That God sows!

What sparkling laughter
    In these shadows
Once full of pale faces
    And sombre hearts!

We are newly married.
    We send each other
Charming and varied
    Cries of joy.

Fresh echoes mingling with
    The shivering wind!
Gaiety that the black convent
    Heightens!

Alone, together, enraptured, singing!
    How we love each other!
How we reap the springtime
    That God sows!

What sparkling laughter
    In these shadows
Once full of pale faces
    And sombre hearts!

On effeuille des jasmins
  Sur la pierre
Où l'abbesse joint les mains
  En prière.

On se cherche, on se poursuit,
  On sent croître
Ton aube, amour, dans la nuit
  Du vieux cloître.

On s'en va se becquetant,
  On s'adore,
On s'embrasse à chaque instant,
  Puis encore,

Sous les piliers, les arceaux,
  Et les marbres.
C'est l'histoire des oiseaux
  Dans les arbres.

We pluck the jasmine flowers
  On the stone
Where the abbess joins her hands
  In prayer.

We seek each other, chase each other,
  We feel your dawn
Grow in the night, O love,
  Of the old cloister.

On we go, kissing and cuddling,
  Adoring one another,
Embracing each other every moment,
  Then again,

Beneath the pillars, beneath the vault,
  And the marbles;
Just like all the birds
  In the trees.

4 *Lydia*

(Charles-Marie-René Leconte de Lisle)

Lydia

Lydia, sur tes roses joues,
Et sur ton col frais et si blanc,
Roule étincelant
L'or fluide que tu dénoues.

Le jour qui luit est le meilleur:
Oublions l'éternelle tombe.
Laisse tes baisers de colombe
Chanter sur ta lèvre en fleur.

Un lys caché répand sans cesse
Une odeur divine en ton sein:
Les délices, comme un essaim,
Sortent de toi, jeune déesse!

Je t'aime et meurs, ô mes amours!
Mon âme en baisers m'est ravie.
Ô Lydia, rends-moi la vie,
Que je puisse mourir toujours!

Lydia, onto your rosy cheeks
And your neck so fresh and pale,
The liquid gold that you unbind
Cascades glittering down.

The day that dawns is the best;
Let us forget the eternal tomb.
Let your dove-like kisses
Sing on your flowering lips.

A hidden lily unceasingly sheds
A heavenly fragrance in your breast;
Delights without number
Stream from you, young goddess!

I love you and die, O my love!
My soul is ravished by kisses.
O Lydia, give me back my life again,
That I may ever die!

5 *Chant d'automne*

(Charles Baudelaire)

Bientôt nous plongerons dans les froides ténèbres;
Adieu, vive clarté de nos étés trop courts!
J'entends déjà tomber avec un choc funèbre
Le bois retentissant sur le pavé des cours.

J'écoute en frémissant chaque bûche qui tombe;
L'échafaud qu'on bâtit n'a pas d'écho plus sourd.
Mon esprit est pareil à la tour qui succombe
Sous les coups du bélier infatigable et lourd.

Il me semble, bercé par ce choc monotone,
Qu'on cloue en grande hâte un cercueil quelque part.
Pour qui?—C'était hier l'été; voici l'automne!
Ce bruit mystérieux sonne comme un départ.

J'aime de vos longs yeux la lumière verdâtre,
Douce beauté, mais aujourd'hui tout m'est amer,
Et rien, ni votre amour, ni le boudoir, ni l'âtre,

Ne me vaut le soleil rayonnant sur la mer.

Autumn song

Soon we shall plunge into cold shadows;
Farewell, vivid light of our too-short summers!
Already I hear the funereal thud
Of echoing logs on the courtyard floor.

I listen, trembling, to the fall of each log;
A gallows being built makes no duller sound.
My spirit is like the tower that falls
To the remorseless blows of the battering-ram.

Rocked by those monotone blows, it seems
Somewhere in haste they are nailing a coffin.
But whose? Yesterday summer; autumn now!
This eerie sound rings like some farewell.

I love the emerald glow of your wide eyes,
My sweet, but all today is bitter for me,
And nothing, not your love, the boudoir, or the
     hearth
Can compare with the sunlight on the sea.

6 *Rêve d'amour*

(Victor Hugo)

S'il est un charmant gazon
    Que le ciel arrose,
Où naisse en toute saison
    Quelque fleur éclose,
Où l'on cueille à pleine main
Lys, chèvrefeuille et jasmin,
J'en veux faire le chemin
    Où ton pied se pose!

S'il est un sein bien aimant
    Dont l'honneur dispose,
Dont le tendre dévouement
    N'ait rien de morose,
Si toujours ce noble sein
Bat pour un digne dessein,
J'en veux faire le coussin
    Où ton front se pose!

A dream of love

If there be a lovely lawn
    Watered by the sky,
Where each new season
    Blossoming flowers spring up,
Where lily, woodbine, and jasmine
Can be gathered liberally,
I would strew the way with them
    For your feet to tread!

If there be a loving breast
    Wherein honour dwells,
Whose tender devotion
    Never is morose,
If this noble breast always
Beats with worthy intent,
I would make of it a pillow
    Where your head can rest!

S'il est un rêve d'amour
  Parfumé de rose,
Où l'on trouve chaque jour
  Quelque douce chose,
Un rêve que Dieu bénit,
Où l'âme à l'âme s'unit,
Oh! j'en veux faire le nid
  Où ton cœur se pose!

If there be a dream of love
  With the scent of roses,
Where each day may be found
  Some sweet new delight,
A dream blessed by the Lord
Where soul unites with soul,
Oh! I shall make of it the nest
  Where your heart will rest!

7 L'absent

(Victor Hugo)

—Sentiers où l'herbe se balance,
Vallons, coteaux, bois chevelus,
Pourquoi ce deuil et ce silence?
—Celui qui venait ne vient plus.

—Pourquoi personne à ta fenêtre,
Et pourquoi ton jardin sans fleurs,
Ô maison! où donc est ton maître?
—Je ne sais pas, il est ailleurs.

—Chien, veille au logis.—Pourquoi faire?
La maison est vide à présent.
—Enfant, qui pleures-tu?—Mon père.
—Femme, qui pleures-tu?—L'absent.

—Où donc est-il allé?—Dans l'ombre.
—Flots qui gémissez sur l'écueil,
D'où venez-vous?—Du bagne sombre.

—Et qu'apportez-vous?—Un cercueil.

The absent one

Paths of swaying grass,
Valleys, hillsides, leafy woods,
Why this mourning and this silence?
—He who came here comes no more.

Why is no one at your window,
And why is your garden without flowers,
O house, where is your master?
—I do not know: he is elsewhere.

Dog, guard the home.—For what reason?
The house is empty now.
Child, who is it you mourn?—My father.
Woman, who is it you mourn?—The absent one.

Where has he gone?—Into the shadow.
Waves that moan against the reefs,
From where do you come?—The dark convict
    prison.
And what do you carry?—A coffin.

8 Tristesse

(Théophile Gautier)

  Avril est de retour.
  La première des roses,
  De ses lèvres mi-closes
  Rit au premier beau jour;
  La terre bienheureuse
  S'ouvre et s'épanouit;
  Tout aime, tout jouit.

Hélas! j'ai dans le cœur une tristesse affreuse.

Sadness

  April has returned.
  The first of the roses
  From half-open lips
  Smiles at the first fine day;
  The happy earth
  Opens and blooms:
  All is love and ecstasy.

Alas! a dreadful sadness afflicts my heart.

Les buveurs en gaîté,
Dans leurs chansons vermeilles,
Célèbrent sous les treilles
Le vin et la beauté;
La musique joyeuse,
Avec leur rire clair
S'éparpille dans l'air.

Hélas! j'ai dans le cœur une tristesse affreuse.

En déshabillé blanc,
Les jeunes demoiselles
S'en vont sous les tonnelles
Au bras de leur galant;
La lune langoureuse
Argente leurs baisers
Longuement appuyés.

Hélas! j'ai dans le cœur une tristesse affreuse.

Moi, je n'aime plus rien,
Ni l'homme, ni la femme,
Ni mon corps, ni mon âme,
Pas même mon vieux chien.
Allez dire qu'on creuse,
Sous le pâle gazon,
Une fosse sans nom.

Hélas! j'ai dans le cœur une tristesse affreuse.

The merry drinkers
With their crimson songs
Drink, beneath trellises,
To wine and beauty;
The joyous music
With their bright laughter
Scatters in the air.

Alas! a dreadful sadness afflicts my heart.

In scanty white dresses
Young girls
Pass beneath the arbours
On their lovers' arms;
The languishing moon
Silvers their long
Insistent kisses.

Alas! a dreadful sadness afflicts my heart.

But I love nothing any more,
Neither man nor woman,
Neither my body nor my soul,
Nor even my old dog;
Send for them to dig
Beneath the pallid turf
A nameless grave.

Alas! a dreadful sadness afflicts my heart.

9 *Sylvie*
(Paul de Choudens)

Si tu veux savoir, ma belle,
Où s'envole à tire d'aile
L'oiseau qui chantait sur l'ormeau,

Je te le dirai, ma belle,
Il vole vers qui l'appelle,
Vers celui-là
Qui l'aimera!

Si tu veux savoir, ma blonde,
Pourquoi sur terre et sur l'onde
La nuit tout s'anime et s'unit,

Sylvie

If you wish to know, my sweet,
Where the bird is hastening
That was singing in the elm,

I shall tell you, my sweet,
It flies to the one who calls it,
To the one
Who will love it!

If you wish to know, my fair one,
Why on land and sea
All things at night revive and merge,

Je te le dirai, ma blonde,
C'est qu'il est une heure au monde
Où, loin du jour,
Veille l'amour!

Si tu veux savoir, Sylvie,
Pourquoi j'aime à la folie
Tes yeux brillants et langoureux,

Je te le dirai, Sylvie,
C'est que sans toi dans la vie
Tout pour mon cœur
N'est que douleur!

I shall tell you, my fair one:
There is one hour in the world,
When far from day
Love stands watch!

If you wish to know, Sylvie,
Why I love to distraction
Your bright and yearning eyes,

I shall tell you, Sylvie,
That without you in my life,
My heart feels
Naught but pain!

10 *Après un rêve*

(Romain Bussine, after an anonymous
Tuscan poet)

Dans un sommeil que charmait ton image
Je rêvais le bonheur, ardent mirage,
Tes yeux étaient plus doux, ta voix pure et sonore,
Tu rayonnais comme un ciel éclairé par l'aurore;

Tu m'appelais et je quittais la terre
Pour m'enfuir avec toi vers la lumière,
Les cieux pour nous entr'ouvraient leurs nues,
Splendeurs inconnues, lueurs divines entrevues.

Hélas! hélas, triste réveil des songes,
Je t'appelle, ô nuit, rends-moi tes mensonges;

Reviens, reviens, radieuse,
Reviens, ô nuit mystérieuse!

After a dream

In sleep made sweet by a vision of you
I dreamed of happiness, fervent illusion,
Your eyes were softer, your voice pure and ringing,
You shone like a sky that was lit by the dawn;

You called me and I departed the earth
To flee with you toward the light,
The heavens parted their clouds for us,
We glimpsed unknown splendours, celestial fires.

Alas, alas, sad awakening from dreams!
I summon you, O night, give me back your
     delusions;
Return, return in radiance,
Return, O mysterious night!

11 *Hymne*

(Charles Baudelaire)

À la très-chère, à la très-belle
Qui remplit mon cœur de clarté,
À l'ange, à l'idole immortelle,
Salut en immortalité!

Elle se répand dans ma vie
Comme un air imprégné de sel,
Et dans mon âme inassouvie
Verse le goût de l'éternel.

Hymn

To the dearest one, the fairest one,
Who fills my heart with light,
To the angel, the immortal idol—
I pledge undying love!

She permeates my life
Like a briny breeze,
And into my unsated soul
Pours the taste of the eternal.

Comment, amour incorruptible,
T'exprimer avec vérité?
Grain de musc qui gis, invisible,
Au fond de mon éternité!

À la très-chère, à la très-belle,
Qui remplit mon cœur de clarté,
À l'ange, à l'idole immortelle,
Salut en immortalité!

How, incorruptible love,
Can I express you faithfully?
Grain of musk lying unseen
In the depths of my eternity!

To the dearest one, the fairest one,
Who fills my heart with light,
To the angel, the immortal idol—
I pledge undying love!

12 *La rançon*

(Charles Baudelaire)

L'homme a, pour payer sa rançon,
Deux champs au tuf profond et riche,
Qu'il faut qu'il remue et défriche
Avec le fer de la raison;

Pour obtenir la moindre rose,
Pour extorquer quelques épis,
Des pleurs salés de son front gris
Sans cesse il faut qu'il les arrose.

L'un est l'Art, et l'autre l'Amour.
—Pour rendre le juge propice,
Lorsque de la stricte justice
Paraîtra le terrible jour,

Il faudra lui montrer des granges
Pleines de moissons, et des fleurs
Dont les formes et les couleurs
Gagnent le suffrage des Anges.

The ransom

Man, that his ransom may be paid,
Has two fields of soil, rich and deep,
Which he must till and rake
With the blade of reason;

To grow the merest rose,
To reap but meagre ears of corn,
He must water them night and morn
With salt tears from his ashen brow.

One field is Art, the other Love.
—To propitiate the judge,
When the terrible day
Of strict justice dawns,

He will have to show Him barns abrim
With harvested crops and flowers,
Whose forms and colours gain
The approval of the seraphim.

13 *Au bord de l'eau*

(Sully Prudhomme)

S'asseoir tous deux au bord d'un flot qui passe,
    Le voir passer;
Tous deux, s'il glisse un nuage en l'espace,
    Le voir glisser;
À l'horizon, s'il fume un toit de chaume,
    Le voir fumer;
Aux alentours si quelque fleur embaume,
    S'en embaumer;
Entendre au pied du saule où l'eau murmure

    L'eau murmurer;

At the water's edge

To sit together on the bank of a flowing stream,
    To watch it flow;
Together, if a cloud glides by,
    To watch it glide;
On the horizon, if smoke rises from thatch,
    To watch it rise;
If nearby a flower smells sweet,
    To savour its sweetness;
To listen at the foot of the willow, where water
            murmurs,
    To the murmuring water;

Ne pas sentir, tant que ce rêve dure,
    Le temps durer;
Mais n'apportant de passion profonde
    Qu'à s'adorer,
Sans nul souci des querelles du monde,
    Les ignorer;
Et seuls, tous deux devant tout ce qui lasse,
    Sans se lasser,
Sentir l'amour, devant tout ce qui passe,
    Ne point passer!

Not to feel, while this dream passes,
    The passing of time;
But feeling no deep passion,
    Exccpt to adore each other,
With no cares for the quarrels of the world,
    To know nothing of them;
And alone together, seeing all that tires,
    Not to tire of each other,
To feel that love, in the face of all that passes,
    Shall never pass!

14 *Nell*

(Charles-Marie-René Leconte de Lisle)

Ta rose de pourpre, à ton clair soleil,
    Ô Juin, étincelle enivrée;
Penche aussi vers moi ta coupe dorée:
    Mon cœur à ta rose est pareil.

Sous le mol abri de la feuille ombreuse
    Monte un soupir de volupté;
Plus d'un ramier chante au bois écarté,
    Ô mon cœur, sa plainte amoureuse.

Que ta perle est douce au ciel enflammé,
    Étoile de la nuit pensive!
Mais combien plus douce est la clarté vive
    Qui rayonne en mon cœur charmé!

La chantante mer, le long du rivage,
    Taira son murmure éternel,
Avant qu'en mon cœur, chère amour, ô Nell,
    Ne fleurisse plus ton image!

Nell

Your crimson rose in your bright sun
    Glitters, June, in rapture;
Incline to me also your golden cup:
    My heart is like your rose.

From the soft shelter of shady leaves
    Rises a languorous sigh;
More than one dove in the secluded wood
    Sings, O my heart, its love-lorn lament.

How sweet is your pearl in the blazing sky,
    Star of meditative night!
But sweeter still is the vivid light
    That glows in my enchanted heart!

The singing sea along the shore
    Shall cease its eternal murmur,
Before in my heart, dear love, O Nell,
    Your image shall cease to bloom!

15 *Les roses d'Ispahan*

(Charles-Marie-René Leconte de Lisle)

Les roses d'Ispahan dans leur gaine de mousse,
Les jasmins de Mossoul, les fleurs de l'oranger
Ont un parfum moins frais, ont une odeur moins
        douce,
Ô blanche Leïlah! que ton souffle léger.

* Walled town on the River Tigris, to the N.W. of Baghdad.

The roses of Isfahan

The roses of Isfahan in their mossy sheaths,
The jasmines of Mosul,* the orange blossom
Have a fragrance less fresh and a scent less sweet,

O pale Leilah, than your soft breath!

Ta lèvre est de corail, et ton rire léger
Sonne mieux que l'eau vive et d'une voix plus douce,
Mieux que le vent joyeux qui berce l'oranger,
Mieux que l'oiseau qui chante au bord d'un nid de
　　　mousse...

Ô Leïlah! depuis que de leur vol léger
Tous les baisers ont fui de ta lèvre si douce,
Il n'est plus de parfum dans le pâle oranger,
Ni de céleste arome aux roses dans leur mousse...

Oh! que ton jeune amour, ce papillon léger,
Revienne vers mon cœur d'une aile prompte et douce,
Et qu'il parfume encor les fleurs de l'oranger,
Les roses d'Ispahan dans leur gaine de mousse!

Your lips are of coral and your light laughter
Rings brighter and sweeter than running water,
Than the blithe wind rocking the orange-tree boughs,
Than the singing bird by its mossy nest...

O Leilah, ever since on light wings
All kisses have flown from your sweet lips,
The pale orange-tree fragrance is spent,
And the heavenly scent of moss-clad roses...

Oh! may your young love, that airy butterfly,
Wing swiftly and gently to my heart once more,
To scent again the orange blossom,
The roses of Isfahan in their mossy sheaths!

POÈME D'UN JOUR

(Charles Grandmougin)

POEM OF A DAY

16 i *Rencontre*

J'étais triste et pensif quand je t'ai rencontrée,
Je sens moins aujourd'hui mon obstiné tourment,
Ô dis-moi, serais-tu la femme inespérée
Et le rêve idéal poursuivi vainement?

Ô passante aux doux yeux, serais-tu donc l'amie

Qui rendrait le bonheur au poète isolé,
Et vas-tu rayonner sur mon âme affermie
Comme le ciel natal sur un cœur d'exilé?

Ta tristesse sauvage, à la mienne pareille,
Aime à voir le soleil décliner sur la mer!
Devant l'immensité ton extase s'éveille
Et le charme des soirs à ta belle âme est cher.

Une mystérieuse et douce sympathie
Déjà m'enchaîne à toi comme un vivant lien,
Et mon âme frémit, par l'amour envahie
Et mon cœur te chérit sans te connaître bien.

Meeting

I was sad and pensive when I met you,
Today I feel less my persistent pain;
O tell me, could you be the long hoped-for woman,
And the ideal dream pursued in vain?

O passer-by with gentle eyes, could you be the
　　　friend
To restore the lonely poet's happiness,
And will you shine on my steadfast soul
Like native sky on an exiled heart?

Your timid sadness, like my own,
Loves to watch the sun set on the sea!
Such boundless space awakes your rapture,
And your fair soul prizes the evenings' charm.

A mysterious and gentle sympathy
Already binds me to you like a living bond,
And my soul quivers, overcome by love,
And my heart, without knowing you well, adores
　　　you.

16 ii *Toujours*

Vous me demandez de me taire,
De fuir loin de vous pour jamais
Et de m'en aller, solitaire,
Sans me rappeler qui j'aimais!

Demandez plutôt aux étoiles
De tomber dans l'immensité,
À la nuit de perdre ses voiles,
Au jour de perdre sa clarté!

Demandez à la mer immense
De dessécher ses vastes flots
Et quand les vents sont en démence,
D'apaiser ses sombres sanglots!

Mais n'espérez pas que mon âme
S'arrache à ses âpres douleurs
Et se dépouille de sa flamme
Comme le printemps de ses fleurs!

Forever

You ask me to be silent,
To flee far from you forever
And to go my way alone,
Forgetting whom I loved!

Rather ask the stars
To fall into infinity,
The night to lose its veils,
The day to lose its light!

Ask the boundless sea
To drain its mighty waves,
And the raging winds
To calm their dismal sobbing!

But do not expect my soul
To tear itself from bitter sorrow,
Nor to shed its passion
As springtime sheds its flowers!

16 iii *Adieu*

Comme tout meurt vite, la rose
   Déclose,
Et les frais manteaux diaprés
   Des prés;
Les longs soupirs, les bien-aimées,
   Fumées!

On voit dans ce monde léger
   Changer
Plus vite que les flots des grèves,
   Nos rêves,
Plus vite que le givre en fleurs,
   Nos cœurs!

À vous l'on se croyait fidèle,
   Cruelle,
Mais hélas! les plus longs amours
   Sont courts!

Et je dis en quittant vos charmes,
   Sans larmes,
Presqu'au moment de mon aveu,
   Adieu!

Farewell

How swiftly all things die, the rose
   In bloom,
And the cool dappled mantle
   Of the meadows;
Long-drawn sighs, loved ones,
   All smoke!

In this fickle world we see
   Our dreams
Change more swiftly than waves
   On the shore,
Our hearts change more swiftly than patterns
   Of frosted flowers!

To you I thought I would be faithful,
   Cruel one,
But alas! the longest loves
   Are short!

And I say, taking leave of your charms,
   Without tears,
Almost at the moment of my avowal,
   Farewell!

17 *Le secret*

(Armand Silvestre)

Je veux que le matin l'ignore
Le nom que j'ai dit à la nuit,
Et qu'au vent de l'aube, sans bruit,
Comme une larme il s'évapore.

Je veux que le jour le proclame
L'amour qu'au matin j'ai caché,
Et, sur mon cœur ouvert penché,
Comme un grain d'encens il l'enflamme.

Je veux que le couchant l'oublie
Le secret que j'ai dit au jour
Et l'emporte, avec mon amour,
Aux plis de sa robe pâlie!

The secret

Would that the morn were unaware
Of the name I told to the night,
And that in the dawn breeze, silently,
It would vanish like a tear.

Would that the day might proclaim it,
The love I hid from the morn,
And poised above my open heart,
Like a grain of incense kindle it.

Would that the sunset might forget,
The secret I told to the day,
And would carry it and my love away
In the folds of its faded robe!

18 *Automne*

(Armand Silvestre)

Automne au ciel brumeux, aux horizons navrants,
Aux rapides couchants, aux aurores pâlies,
Je regarde couler, comme l'eau du torrent,
        Tes jours faits de mélancolie.

Sur l'aile des regrets mes esprits emportés,
—Comme s'il se pouvait que notre âge renaisse!—
Parcourent, en rêvant, les coteaux enchantés
        Où jadis sourit ma jeunesse.

Je sens, au clair soleil du souvenir vainqueur
Refleurir en bouquet les roses déliées
Et monter à mes yeux des larmes, qu'en mon cœur,
        Mes vingt ans avaient oubliées!

Autumn

Autumn of misty skies and heart-breaking horizons,
Of swift sunsets and pale dawns,
I watch flow by, like torrential water,
        Your days imbued with melancholy.

My thoughts, borne away on the wings of regret,
—As though our time could come round again!—
Roam in reverie the enchanted hills,
        Where long ago my youth once smiled.

In the bright sun of triumphant memory
I feel untied roses reflower in bouquets,
And tears rise to my eyes, which in my heart
        At twenty had been forgotten!

19 *Les berceaux*

(Sully Prudhomme)

Le long du quai les grands vaisseaux,
Que la houle incline en silence,
Ne prennent pas garde aux berceaux
Que la main des femmes balance.

The cradles

Along the quay the great ships,
Listing silently with the surge,
Pay no heed to the cradles
Rocked by women's hands.

Mais viendra le jour des adieux,
Car il faut que les femmes pleurent,
Et que les hommes curieux
Tentent les horizons qui leurrent.

Et ce jour-là les grands vaisseaux,
Fuyant le port qui diminue,
Sentent leur masse retenue
Par l'âme des lointains berceaux.

But the day of parting will come,
For it is decreed that women shall weep,
And that men with questing spirits
Shall seek enticing horizons.

And on that day the great ships,
Leaving the dwindling harbour behind,
Shall feel their hulls held back
By the soul of the distant cradles.

20 *Notre amour*

(Armand Silvestre)

Notre amour est chose légère,
Comme les parfums que le vent
Prend aux cimes de la fougère
Pour qu'on les respire en rêvant.
—Notre amour est chose légère.

Notre amour est chose charmante,
Comme les chansons du matin
Où nul regret ne se lamente,
Où vibre un espoir incertain.
—Notre amour est chose charmante.

Notre amour est chose sacrée,
Comme le mystère des bois
Où tressaille une âme ignorée,
Où les silences ont des voix.
—Notre amour est chose sacrée.

Notre amour est chose infinie,
Comme les chemins des couchants
Où la mer, aux cieux réunie,
S'endort sous les soleils penchants.

Notre amour est chose éternelle,
Comme tout ce qu'un Dieu vainqueur
A touché du feu de son aile,
Comme tout ce qui vient du cœur,
—Notre amour est chose éternelle.

Our love

Our love is light and gentle,
Like fragrance fetched by the breeze
From the tips of ferns
For us to breathe while dreaming.
—Our love is light and gentle.

Our love is enchanting,
Like morning songs,
Where no regret is voiced,
Quivering with uncertain hopes.
—Our love is enchanting.

Our love is sacred,
Like woodland mysteries,
Where an unknown soul throbs
And silences are eloquent.
—Our love is sacred.

Our love is infinite
Like sunset paths,
Where the sea, joined with the skies,
Falls asleep beneath slanting suns.

Our love is eternal,
Like all that a victorious God
Has brushed with his fiery wing,
Like all that comes from the heart,
—Our love is eternal.

21 *Chanson d'amour*

(Armand Silvestre)

J'aime tes yeux, j'aime ton front,
Ô ma rebelle, ô ma farouche,
J'aime tes yeux, j'aime ta bouche
Où mes baisers s'épuiseront.

J'aime ta voix, j'aime l'étrange
Grâce de tout ce que tu dis,
Ô ma rebelle, ô mon cher ange,
Mon enfer et mon paradis!

J'aime tes yeux, j'aime ton front,
Ô ma rebelle, ô ma farouche,
J'aime tes yeux, j'aime ta bouche
Où mes baisers s'épuiseront.

J'aime tout ce qui te fait belle,
De tes pieds jusqu'à tes cheveux,
Ô toi vers qui montent mes vœux,
Ô ma farouche, ô ma rebelle!

J'aime tes yeux, j'aime ton front,
Ô ma rebelle, ô ma farouche,
J'aime tes yeux, j'aime ta bouche
Où mes baisers s'épuiseront.

Love song

I love your eyes, I love your brow,
O my rebel, O my wild one,
I love your eyes, I love your mouth
Where my kisses shall dissolve.

I love your voice, I love the strange
Charm of all you say,
O my rebel, O my dear angel,
My inferno and my paradise.

I love your eyes, I love your brow,
O my rebel, O my wild one,
I love your eyes, I love your mouth
Where my kisses shall dissolve.

I love all that makes you beautiful
From your feet to your hair,
O you the object of all my vows,
O my wild one, O my rebel.

I love your eyes, I love your brow,
O my rebel, O my wild one,
I love your eyes, I love your mouth
Where my kisses shall dissolve.

22 *Fleur jetée*

(Armand Silvestre)

Emporte ma folie
    Au gré du vent,
Fleur en chantant cueillie
Et jetée en rêvant.
—Emporte ma folie
    Au gré du vent!

Comme la fleur fauchée
    Périt l'amour.
La main qui t'a touchée
Fuit ma main sans retour.
—Comme la fleur fauchée,
    Périt l'amour!

Discarded flower

Bear away my folly
    At the whim of the wind,
Flower, plucked while singing
And discarded while dreaming.
Bear away my folly
    At the whim of the wind!

Like a scythed flower
    Love perishes.
The hand that touched you
Shuns my hand for ever.
Like a scythed flower
    Love perishes!

Que le vent qui te sèche,
  Ô pauvre fleur,
Tout à l'heure si fraîche
Et demain sans couleur!
—Que le vent qui te sèche,
  Sèche mon cœur!

May the wind that withers you,
  O poor flower,
So fresh just now
But tomorrow faded,
May the wind that withers you,
  Wither my heart!

23 *Nocturne*
(Comte de Villiers de l'Isle-Adam)

La nuit sur le grand mystère
Entr'ouvre ses écrins bleus;
Autant de fleurs sur la terre
Que d'étoiles dans les cieux.

On voit ses ombres dormantes
S'éclairer à tous moments
Autant par les fleurs charmantes
Que par les astres charmants.

Moi, ma nuit au sombre voile
N'a pour charme et pour clarté
Qu'une fleur et qu'une étoile,
Mon amour et ta beauté!

Nocturne

Onto a landscape of great mystery
Night half-opens its blue caskets;
As many flowers on earth
As stars in the sky.

Its sleeping shadows are seen
Brightening every moment
As much by charming flowers
As by charming stars.

My own darkly veiled night
Has for charm and light
But one flower and one star—
My love and your beauty!

24 *Les présents*
(Comte de Villiers de l'Isle-Adam)

Si tu demandes quelque soir
Le secret de mon cœur malade,
Je te dirai pour t'émouvoir
Une très-ancienne ballade.

Si tu me parles de tourments,
D'espérance désabusée,
J'irai te cueillir seulement
Des roses pleines de rosée.

Si, pareille à la fleur des morts
Qui fleurit dans l'exil des tombes,
Tu veux partager mes remords,
Je t'apporterai des colombes.

Gifts

If one evening you should ask
The secret of my sick heart—
To move you, I shall relate
A very ancient ballad!

If you speak to me of torments,
Of disillusioned hope,
I shall simply pick for you
Roses decked with dew!

If, like the flower of the dead
That blooms in the exile of tombs,
You wish to share in my remorse...
I shall bring you doves.

25 *Clair de lune*

(Paul Verlaine)

Votre âme est un paysage choisi
Que vont charmant masques et bergamasques
Jouant du luth et dansant et quasi
Tristes sous leurs déguisements fantasques.

Tout en chantant sur le mode mineur
L'amour vainqueur et la vie opportune,
Ils n'ont pas l'air de croire à leur bonheur
Et leur chanson se mêle au clair de lune,

Au calme clair de lune triste et beau,
Qui fait rêver les oiseaux dans les arbres
Et sangloter d'extase les jets d'eau,
Les grands jets d'eau sveltes parmi les marbres.

Moonlight

Your soul is a chosen landscape
Bewitched by masquers and bergamaskers,
Playing the lute and dancing and almost
Sad beneath their fanciful disguises.

Singing as they go in a minor key
Of conquering love and life's favours,
They do not seem to believe in their fortune
And their song mingles with the light of the moon,

The calm light of the moon, sad and fair,
That sets the birds dreaming in the trees
And the fountains sobbing in their rapture,
Tall and svelte amid marble statues.

26 *Larmes*

(Jean Richepin)

Pleurons nos chagrins, chacun le nôtre.
Une larme tombe, puis une autre.
Toi, qui pleures-tu? Ton doux pays,
Tes parents lointains, ta fiancée.
Moi, mon existence dépensée
      En vœux trahis.

Pleurons nos chagrins, chacun le nôtre.
Une larme tombe, puis une autre.
Semons dans la mer ces pâles fleurs.
À notre sanglot qui se lamente
Elle répondra par la tourmente
      Des flots hurleurs.

Pleurons nos chagrins, chacun le nôtre.
Une larme tombe, puis une autre.
Peut-être toi-même, ô triste mer,
Mer au goût de larme âcre et salée,
Es-tu de la terre inconsolée
      Le pleur amer.

Tears

Let us mourn our sorrows, each his own.
One tear falls, another follows.
You, who do you mourn? Your sweet native land,
Your distant family, your betrothed.
And I—my existence, wasted
      On vows betrayed.

Let us mourn our sorrows, each his own.
One tear falls, another follows.
Let us bestrew the sea with these pale flowers.
To our sobbing lament
It will reply with the storm
      Of howling waves.

Let us mourn our sorrows, each his own.
One tear falls, another follows.
Perhaps you yourself, O dismal sea,
That tastes of acrid and salty tears,
Are the inconsolable earth's
      Bitter weeping.

27 *Au cimetière*

(Jean Richepin)

Heureux qui meurt ici
    Ainsi
Que les oiseaux des champs!
Son corps près des amis
    Est mis
Dans l'herbe et dans les chants.

Il dort d'un bon sommeil
    Vermeil
Sous le ciel radieux.
Tous ceux qu'il a connus,
    Venus,
Lui font de longs adieux.

À sa croix les parents
    Pleurants
Restent agenouillés;
Et ses os, sous les fleurs,
    De pleurs
Sont doucement mouillés.

Chacun sur le bois noir
    Peut voir
S'il était jeune ou non,
Et peut avec de vrais
    Regrets
L'appeler par son nom.

Combien plus malchanceux
    Sont ceux
Qui meurent à la mé,
Et sous le flot profond
    S'en vont
Loin du pays aimé!

Ah! pauvres, qui pour seuls
    Linceuls
Ont les goëmons verts
Où l'on roule inconnu,
    Tout nu,
Et les yeux grands ouverts.

In the graveyard

Happy he who dies here
    Even
As the birds of the fields!
His body near his friends
    Is laid
Amid the grass, amid the songs.

He sleeps a good sleep,
    Crimson
Beneath the radiant sky.
All those he has known
    Are come
To bid him a long farewell.

By the cross his weeping
    Parents
Remain kneeling,
And his bones beneath the flowers
    With tears
Are gently watered.

On the black wood all
    Can see
If he was young or not,
And can with true
    Regret
Call him by his name.

How much more unfortunate
    Are they
Who die at sea,
And beneath deep waters
    Drift
Far from their beloved land!

Ah! poor souls! whose only
    Shroud
Is the green seaweed,
Where they roll unknown,
    Unclothed,
And with wide-open eyes.

28 *La rose*

(Charles-Marie-René Leconte de Lisle)

Je dirai la rose aux plis gracieux.
La rose est le souffle embaumé des Dieux,
Le plus cher souci des Muses divines.
Je dirai ta gloire, ô charme des yeux,
Ô fleur de Kypris, reine des collines!
Tu t'épanouis entre les beaux doigts
De l'Aube écartant les ombres moroses;
L'air bleu devient rose, et roses les bois;
La bouche et le sein des vierges sont roses!
Heureuse la vierge aux bras arrondis
Qui dans les halliers humides te cueille!
Heureux le front jeune où tu resplendis!
Heureuse la coupe où nage ta feuille!
Ruisselante encor du flot paternel,
Quand de la mer bleue Aphrodite éclose
Étincela nue aux clartés du ciel,
La Terre jalouse enfanta la rose;
Et l'Olympe entier, d'amour transporté,
Salua la fleur avec la Beauté!

The rose

I shall speak of the rose with its graceful petals.
The rose is the scented breath of the gods,
The most cherished care of the divine Muses.
I shall speak of your glory, O delight of the eyes,
O flower of Cypris,* queen of the hills!
You bloom between the beautiful fingers
Of dawn, brushing gloomy shadows aside;
The blue air turns rose, and rose the woods;
The lips and breasts of virgins are roses!
Happy the virgin with rounded arms
Who gathers you in moist thickets!
Happy the young brow that you adorn!
Happy the cup where your leaves float!
Streaming still from the paternal waters,
When from the blue sea Aphrodite emerged
Glistening naked in the brilliant sky,
Jealous Earth gave birth to the rose:
And all Olympus, transported by love,
Greeted the flower with Beauty!

CINQ MÉLODIES 'DE VENISE'

(Paul Verlaine)

FIVE 'VENETIAN' MÉLODIES

29 i *Mandoline*

Les donneurs de sérénades
Et les belles écouteuses
Échangent des propos fades
Sous les ramures chanteuses.

C'est Tircis et c'est Aminte,
Et c'est l'éternel Clitandre,
Et c'est Damis qui pour mainte
Cruelle fait maint vers tendre.

Leurs courtes vestes de soie,
Leurs longues robes à queues,
Leur élégance, leur joie
Et leurs molles ombres bleues

Mandolin

The gallant serenaders
And their fair listeners
Exchange sweet nothings
Beneath singing boughs.

Tirsis is there, Aminte is there,
And tedious Clitandre too,
And Damis who for many a cruel maid
Writes many a tender song.

Their short silken doublets,
Their long trailing gowns,
Their elegance, their joy,
And their soft blue shadows

* The surname of Venus, who was born on Cyprus.

Tourbillonnent dans l'extase
D'une lune rose et grise,
Et la mandoline jase
Parmi les frissons de brise.

Whirl madly in the rapture
Of a grey and roseate moon,
And the mandolin jangles on
In the shivering breeze.

29 ii *En sourdine*

Calmes dans le demi-jour
Que les branches hautes font,
Pénétrons bien notre amour
De ce silence profond.

Mêlons nos âmes, nos cœurs
Et nos sens extasiés,
Parmi les vagues langueurs
Des pins et des arbousiers.

Ferme tes yeux à demi,
Croise tes bras sur ton sein,
Et de ton cœur endormi
Chasse à jamais tout dessein.

Laissons-nous persuader
Au souffle berceur et doux
Qui vient à tes pieds rider
Les ondes des gazons roux.

Et quand, solennel, le soir
Des chênes noirs tombera,
Voix de notre désespoir,
Le rossignol chantera.

Muted

Calm in the twilight
Cast by lofty boughs,
Let us steep our love
In this deep quiet.

Let us mingle our souls, our hearts
And our enraptured senses
With the hazy languor
Of arbutus and pine.

Half-close your eyes,
Fold your arms across your breast,
And from your heart now lulled to rest
Banish forever all intent.

Let us both succumb
To the gentle and lulling breeze
That comes to ruffle at your feet
The waves of russet grass.

And when, solemnly, evening
Falls from the black oaks,
That voice of our despair,
The nightingale shall sing.

29 iii *Green*

Voici des fruits, des fleurs, des feuilles et des
    branches
Et puis voici mon cœur qui ne bat que pour vous.
Ne le déchirez pas avec vos deux mains blanches
Et qu'à vos yeux si beaux l'humble présent soit
    doux.

J'arrive tout couvert encore de rosée
Que le vent du matin vient glacer à mon front.
Souffrez que ma fatigue à vos pieds reposée
Rêve des chers instants qui la délasseront.

Green

Here are flowers, branches, fruit, and fronds,

And here too is my heart that beats just for you.
Do not tear it with your two white hands
And may the humble gift please your lovely eyes.

I come all covered still with the dew
Frozen to my brow by the morning breeze.
Let my fatigue, finding rest at your feet,
Dream of dear moments that will soothe it.

Sur votre jeune sein laissez rouler ma tête
Toute sonore encor de vos derniers baisers;
Laissez-la s'apaiser de la bonne tempête,
Et que je dorme un peu puisque vous reposez.

On your young breast let me cradle my head
Still ringing with your recent kisses;
After love's sweet tumult grant it peace,
And let me sleep a while, since you rest.

29 iv *À Clymène*

Mystiques barcarolles,
Romances sans paroles,
Chère, puisque tes yeux,
    Couleur des cieux,

Puisque ta voix, étrange
Vision qui dérange
Et trouble l'horizon
    De ma raison,

Puisque l'arome insigne
De ta pâleur de cygne,
Et puisque la candeur
    De ton odeur,

Ah! puisque tout ton être,
Musique qui pénètre,
Nimbes d'anges défunts,
    Tons et parfums,

A, sur d'almes cadences,
En ces correspondances
Induit mon cœur subtil,
    Ainsi soit-il!

To Clymène

Mystical barcarolles,
Songs without words,
Sweet, since your eyes,
    The colour of skies,

Since your voice,
Strange vision that unsettles
And troubles the horizon
    Of my reason,

Since the rare scent
Of your swan-like pallor,
And since the candour
    Of your fragrance,

Ah! since your whole being—
Pervading music,
Haloes of departed angels,
    Sounds and scents—

Has in sweet cadences
And correspondences
Led on my receptive heart—
    So be it!

29 v *C'est l'extase*

C'est l'extase langoureuse,
C'est la fatigue amoureuse,
C'est tous les frissons des bois
Parmi l'étreinte des brises,
C'est, vers les ramures grises,
Le chœur des petites voix.

Ô le frêle et frais murmure!
Cela gazouille et susurre,
Cela ressemble au bruit doux
Que l'herbe agitée expire...
Tu dirais, sous l'eau qui vire,
Le roulis sourd des cailloux.

It is rapture

It is languorous rapture,
It is amorous fatigue,
It is all the tremors of the forest
In the breezes' embrace,
It is, around the grey branches,
The choir of tiny voices.

O the delicate, fresh murmuring!
The warbling and whispering,
It is like the sweet sound
The ruffled grass gives out...
You might take it for the muffled sound
Of pebbles in the swirling stream.

Cette âme qui se lamente	This soul which grieves
Et cette plainte dormante	And this subdued lament,
C'est la nôtre, n'est-ce pas?	It is ours, is it not?
La mienne, dis, et la tienne,	Minc, and yours too,
Dont s'exhale l'humble antienne	Breathing out our humble hymn
Par ce tiède soir, tout bas?	On this warm evening, soft and low?

LA BONNE CHANSON

(Paul Verlaine)

THE GOOD SONG

30 i *Une Sainte en son auréole*

A Saint in her halo

Une Sainte en son auréole,	A Saint in her halo,
Une Châtelaine en sa tour,	A Châtelaine in her tower,
Tout ce que contient la parole	All that human words contain
Humaine de grâce et d'amour;	Of grace and love;
La note d'or que fait entendre	The golden note of a horn
Un cor dans le lointain des bois,	In forests far away,
Mariée à la fierté tendre	Blended with the tender pride
Des nobles Dames d'autrefois;	Of noble Ladies of long ago;
Avec cela le charme insigne	And then—the rare charm
D'un frais sourire triomphant	Of a fresh, triumphant smile,
Éclos dans des candeurs de cygne	Flowering in swan-like innocence
Et des rougeurs de femme-enfant;	And the blushes of a child-bride;
Des aspects nacrés, blancs et roses,	A nacreous sheen of white and pink,
Un doux accord patricien:	A sweet patrician harmony—
Je vois, j'entends toutes ces choses	All these things I see and hear
Dans son nom Carlovingien.	In her Carolingian name.

30 ii *Puisque l'aube grandit*

Since day is breaking

Puisque l'aube grandit, puisque voici l'aurore,	Since day is breaking, since dawn is here,
Puisque, après m'avoir fui longtemps, l'espoir veut bien	Since hope, having long eluded me, would now
Revoler devers moi qui l'appelle et l'implore,	Return to me and my imploring,
Puisque tout ce bonheur veut bien être le mien,	Since all this happiness will truly be mine,

Je veux, guidé par vous, beaux yeux aux flammes
    douces,
Par toi conduit, ô main où tremblera ma main,

Marcher droit, que ce soit par des sentiers de
    mousses
Ou que rocs et cailloux encombrent le chemin;

Et comme, pour bercer les lenteurs de la route,
Je chanterai des airs ingénus, je me dis
Qu'elle m'écoutera sans déplaisir sans doute;
Et vraiment je ne veux pas d'autre Paradis.

I shall, guided by your fair eyes' gentle glow,

Led by your hand in which I place my trembling
    hand,
Walk straight ahead, on mossy paths

Or boulder-strewn and stony tracks;

And while, to ease the journey's languid pace,
I shall sing some simple airs, I tell myself
That she will surely hear me without displeasure;
And truly I crave no other paradise.

30 iii *La lune blanche*

La lune blanche
Luit dans les bois;
De chaque branche
Part une voix
Sous la ramée...

Ô bien-aimée.

L'étang reflète,
Profond miroir,
La silhouette
Du saule noir
Où le vent pleure...

Rêvons, c'est l'heure.

Un vaste et tendre
Apaisement
Semble descendre
Du firmament
Que l'astre irise...

C'est l'heure exquise.

The white moon

The white moon
Gleams in the woods;
From every branch
There comes a voice
Beneath the boughs...

O my beloved.

The pool reflects,
Deep mirror,
The silhouette
Of the black willow
Where the wind is weeping...

Let us dream, it is the hour.

A vast and tender
Consolation
Seems to fall
From the sky
The moon illumines...

Exquisite hour.

30 iv *J'allais par des chemins perfides*

J'allais par des chemins perfides,
Douloureusement incertain.
Vos chères mains furent mes guides.

I walked along treacherous ways

I walked along treacherous ways,
Painfully uncertain.
Your dear hands guided me.

Si pâle à l'horizon lointain
Luisait un faible espoir d'aurore;
Votre regard fut le matin.

Nul bruit, sinon son pas sonore,
N'encourageait le voyageur.
Votre voix me dit: 'Marche encore!'

Mon cœur craintif, mon sombre cœur
Pleurait, seul, sur la triste voie;
L'amour, délicieux vainqueur,

Nous a réunis dans la joie.

So pale on the far horizon
A faint hope of dawn was gleaming;
Your gaze was the morning.

No sound, save his own footfall,
Encouraged the traveller.
Your voice said: 'Walk on!'

My fearful heart, my heavy heart,
Wept, lonely along the sad road;
Love, that charming conqueror,

Has united us in joy.

30 v *J'ai presque peur, en vérité*

J'ai presque peur, en vérité,
Tant je sens ma vie enlacée
À la radieuse pensée
Qui m'a pris l'âme l'autre été,

Tant votre image, à jamais chère,
Habite en ce cœur tout à vous,
Ce cœur uniquement jaloux
De vous aimer et de vous plaire;

Et je tremble, pardonnez-moi
D'aussi franchement vous le dire,
À penser qu'un mot, qu'un sourire
De vous est désormais ma loi,

Et qu'il vous suffirait d'un geste,
D'une parole ou d'un clin d'œil,
Pour mettre tout mon être en deuil
De son illusion céleste.

Mais plutôt je ne veux vous voir,
L'avenir dût-il m'être sombre
Et fécond en peines sans nombre,
Qu'à travers un immense espoir,

Plongé dans ce bonheur suprême
De me dire encore et toujours,
En dépit des mornes retours,
Que je vous aime, que je t'aime!

In truth, I am almost afraid

In truth, I am almost afraid,
So much do I feel my life bound up
With the radiant thoughts
That captured my soul last summer,

So deeply does your ever-dear image
Inhabit this heart that is wholly yours,
This heart, whose sole desire
Is to love you and please you;

And I tremble, forgive me
For telling you so frankly,
To think that one word, one smile
From you is henceforth law to me,

And that one gesture would suffice,
One word, one single glance,
To plunge my whole being in mourning
From its heavenly illusion.

But I would sooner not see you—
However dark the future might be
And full of untold grief—
Could I not, through an immense hope,

Immersed in this supreme happiness,
Repeat to myself again and again,
Despite bleak reversals,
That I love you, I love thee!

30 vi *Avant que tu ne t'en ailles*

Avant que tu ne t'en ailles,
Pâle étoile du matin,
   —Mille cailles
Chantent, chantent dans le thym.—

Tourne devers le poète,
Dont les yeux sont pleins d'amour,
   —L'alouette
Monte au ciel avec le jour.—

Tourne ton regard que noie
L'aurore dans son azur;
   —Quelle joie
Parmi les champs de blé mûr!—

Puis fais luire ma pensée
Là-bas,—bien loin, oh! bien loin!
   —La rosée
Gaîment brille sur le foin.—

Dans le doux rêve où s'agite
Ma mie endormie encor...
   —Vite, vite,
Car voici le soleil d'or.—

Before you fade

Before you fade,
Pale morning star,
   —A thousand quail
Are singing, singing in the thyme.—

Turn to the poet
Whose eyes are full of love,
   —The lark
Soars heavenward with the day.—

Turn your gaze drowned
In the blue of dawn;
   —What delight
Among the fields of ripened corn!—

And make my thoughts gleam
Yonder, far, ah far away!
   —The dew
Glints brightly on the hay.—

Into the sweet dream where still asleep
My love is stirring...
   —Make haste, make haste,
For here's the golden sun.

30 vii *Donc, ce sera par un clair jour d'été*

Donc, ce sera par un clair jour d'été:
Le grand soleil, complice de ma joie,
Fera, parmi le satin et la soie,
Plus belle encor votre chère beauté;

Le ciel tout bleu, comme une haute tente,
Frissonnera somptueux à longs plis
Sur nos deux fronts qu'auront pâlis
L'émotion du bonheur et l'attente;

Et quand le soir viendra, l'air sera doux
Qui se jouera, caressant, dans vos voiles,
Et les regards paisibles des étoiles
Bienveillamment souriront aux époux.

So, on a bright summer day it shall be

So, on a bright summer day it shall be:
The glorious sun, my partner in joy,
Shall make, amid the satin and the silk,
Your dear beauty lovelier still;

The sky, all blue, like a tall canopy,
Shall quiver sumptuously in long folds
Above our two brows, grown pale
With pleasure and expectancy;

And when evening comes, the breeze shall be soft
And play caressingly about your veils,
And the peaceful stars looking down
Shall smile benevolently on man and wife.

30 viii *N'est-ce pas?*

N'est-ce pas? nous irons, gais et lents, dans la voie
Modeste que nous montre en souriant l'Espoir,

Peu soucieux qu'on nous ignore ou qu'on nous voie.

Isolés dans l'amour ainsi qu'en un bois noir,
Nos deux cœurs, exhalant leur tendresse paisible,
Seront deux rossignols qui chantent dans le soir.

Sans nous préoccuper de ce que nous destine
Le Sort, nous marcherons pourtant du même pas,
Et la main dans la main, avec l'âme enfantine

De ceux qui s'aiment sans mélange, n'est-ce pas?

Is it not so?

Is it not so? Happy and unhurried we'll follow
The modest path where Hope directs us with a
   smile,
Little caring if we are neither known nor seen.

Isolated in love as in a dark wood,
Our two hearts, breathing gentle love,
Shall be two nightingales singing at evening.

With no thought of what Destiny
Has in store, we shall walk along together,
Hand in hand, our souls like those of children

Whose love is unalloyed, is that not so?

30 ix *L'hiver a cessé*

L'hiver a cessé: la lumière est tiède
Et danse, du sol au firmament clair.
Il faut que le cœur le plus triste cède
À l'immense joie éparse dans l'air.

J'ai depuis un an le printemps dans l'âme
Et le vert retour du doux floréal,
Ainsi qu'une flamme entoure une flamme,
Met de l'idéal sur mon idéal.

Le ciel bleu prolonge, exhausse et couronne
L'immuable azur où rit mon amour.
La saison est belle et ma part est bonne
Et tous mes espoirs ont enfin leur tour.

Que vienne l'été! que viennent encore
L'automne et l'hiver! Et chaque saison
Me sera charmante, ô Toi que décore
Cette fantaisie et cette raison!

Winter is over

Winter is over, the light is soft
And dances up from the earth to the clear sky.
The saddest heart must surrender
To the great joy that fills the air.

For a year I have had spring in my soul,
And the green return of sweet May,
Like flame encircling flame,
Adds an ideal to my ideal.

The blue sky prolongs, heightens, and crowns
The steadfast azure where my love smiles.
The season is fair and my lot is happy
And all my hopes are at last fulfilled.

Let summer come! Let autumn
And winter come too! Each season
Will delight me, O you graced with
Imagination and good sense!

31 *Prison*

(Paul Verlaine)

Le ciel est, par-dessus le toit,
   Si bleu, si calme!
Un arbre, par-dessus le toit,
   Berce sa palme.

Prison

The sky above the roof—
   So blue, so calm!
A tree, above the roof,
   Waves its crown.

La cloche, dans le ciel qu'on voit,
  Doucement tinte.
Un oiseau sur l'arbre qu'on voit
  Chante sa plainte.

Mon Dieu, mon Dieu, la vie est là,
  Simple et tranquille.
Cette paisible rumeur-là
  Vient de la ville.

—Qu'as-tu fait, ô toi que voilà
  Pleurant sans cesse,
Dis, qu'as-tu fait, toi que voilà,
  De ta jeunesse?

The bell, in the sky that you see,
  Gently rings.
A bird, on the tree that you see,
  Plaintively sings.

My God, my God, life is there,
  Simple and serene.
That peaceful murmur there
  Comes from the town.

O you, what have you done,
  Weeping without end,
Say, what have you done
  With your young life?

32 *Soir*

(Albert Samain)

Voici que les jardins de la Nuit vont fleurir.
Les lignes, les couleurs, les sons deviennent vagues.
Vois, le dernier rayon agonise à tes bagues.
Ma sœur, entends-tu pas quelque chose mourir?...

Mets sur mon front tes mains fraîches comme une
    eau pure,
Mets sur mes yeux tes mains douces comme des fleurs;
Et que mon âme, où vit le goût secret des pleurs,
Soit comme un lys fidèle et pâle à ta ceinture.

C'est la Pitié qui pose ainsi son doigt sur nous;
Et tout ce que la terre a de soupirs qui montent,
Il semble qu'à mon cœur enivré le racontent
Tes yeux levés au ciel, si tristes et si doux.

Evening

Now the gardens of Night begin to flower.
Lines, colours, and sounds begin to blur.
See the last rays fade on your rings.
Sister, can you not hear something die?...

Place your hands, cool as pure water, on my brow,

Place on my eyes your hands as sweet as flowers;
And let my soul, with its secret taste of tears,
Be like a lily at your waist, faithful and pale.

It is Pity that lays thus its finger on us;
And all the sighs that rise from the earth
Seem uttered to my enraptured heart
By your sad sweet eyes raised to the skies.

33 *Le parfum impérissable*

(Charles-Marie-René Leconte de Lisle)

Quand la fleur du soleil, la rose de Lahor,
De son âme odorante a rempli goutte à goutte
La fiole d'argile ou de cristal ou d'or,
Sur le sable qui brûle on peut l'épandre toute.

Les fleuves et la mer inonderaient en vain
Ce sanctuaire étroit qui la tint enfermée:
Il garde en se brisant son arome divin,
Et sa poussière heureuse en reste parfumée.

The imperishable perfume

When the flower of the sun, the rose of Lahore,
Has drop by drop from her scented soul
Filled the phial of clay or crystal or gold,
It can all be scattered on the burning sands.

Rivers and oceans would flood in vain
This narrow sanctuary where it was confined:
On shattering it keeps its heavenly scent,
Which still perfumes its happy dust.

Puisque par la blessure ouverte de mon cœur
Tu t'écoules de même, ô céleste liqueur,
Inexprimable amour, qui m'enflammais pour elle!

Qu'il lui soit pardonné, que mon mal soit béni!
Par delà l'heure humaine et le temps infini
Mon cœur est embaumé d'une odeur immortelle!

Since through the gaping wound of my heart
You likewise flow, O heavenly nectar,
Ineffable love which inflamed me for her,

May she be pardoned and my pain be blessed!
Beyond this world and infinity
My heart is embalmed with immortal fragrance!

34 *Dans la forêt de septembre*
(Catulle Mendès)

In the September forest

Ramure aux rumeurs amollies,
Troncs sonores que l'âge creuse,
L'antique forêt douloureuse
S'accorde à nos mélancolies.

Foliage of deadened sound,
Resonant trunks hollowed by age,
The ancient, mournful forest
Blends with our melancholy.

Ô sapins agriffés au gouffre,
Nids déserts aux branches brisées,
Halliers brûlés, fleurs sans rosées,
Vous savez bien comme l'on souffre!

O fir-trees, clinging to chasms,
Abandoned nests in broken branches,
Burnt-out thickets, flowers without dew,
You well know our suffering!

Et lorsque l'homme, passant blême,
Pleure dans le bois solitaire,
Des plaintes d'ombre et de mystère
L'accueillent en pleurant, de même.

And when man, that pale wanderer,
Weeps in the lonely wood,
Shadowy, mysterious laments
Greet him, likewise weeping.

Bonne forêt! promesse ouverte
De l'exil que la vie implore,
Je viens d'un pas alerte encore
Dans ta profondeur encor verte.

Good forest! Open promise
Of exile that life implores,
I come with a step still brisk
Into your still green depths.

Mais d'un fin bouleau de la sente
Une feuille, un peu rousse, frôle
Ma tête et tremble à mon épaule;
C'est que la forêt vieillissante,

But from a slender birch by the path,
A reddish leaf brushes
My head and quivers on my shoulder—
For the ageing forest,

Sachant l'hiver où tout avorte,
Déjà proche en moi comme en elle,
Me fait l'aumône fraternelle
De sa première feuille morte!

Knowing that winter, when all withers,
Is already close for me as for her,
Bestows on me the fraternal gift
Of its first dead leaf!

35 *Le plus doux chemin*

(Armand Silvestre)

À mes pas le plus doux chemin
Mène à la porte de ma belle,
—Et, bien qu'elle me soit rebelle,
J'y veux encor passer demain.

Il est tout fleuri de jasmin
Au temps de la saison nouvelle,
—Et, bien qu'elle me soit rebelle,
J'y passe des fleurs à la main.

Pour toucher son cœur inhumain,
J'y chante ma peine cruelle,
—Et, bien qu'elle me soit rebelle,
C'est pour moi le plus doux chemin!

The sweetest path

The sweetest path for me
Leads to my fairest's door,
—And though she resists me,
I shall tomorrow pass by once more.

It is all a-bloom with jasmine
When the new season arrives,
—And though she resists me,
I go there bearing flowers.

To touch her inhuman heart
I sing of my cruel pain,
—And though she resists me,
It is for me the sweetest path!

36 *Le ramier*

(Armand Silvestre)

Avec son chant doux et plaintif,
Ce ramier blanc te fait envie:
S'il te plaît l'avoir pour captif,
J'irai te le chercher, Sylvie.

Mais là, près de toi, dans mon sein,
Comme ce ramier mon cœur chante:
S'il t'en plaît faire le larcin,
Il sera mieux à toi, méchante!

Pour qu'il soit tel qu'un ramier blanc,
Le prisonnier que tu recèles,
Sur mon cœur, oiselet tremblant,
Pose tes mains comme deux ailes.

The ring-dove

With its gentle plaintive song,
This white ring-dove makes you envious:
If you want it as a captive,
I'll go and seek it for you, Sylvie.

But there, near you, in my breast,
Like this ring-dove, my heart sings:
If you would like to steal it,
It will be better for you, wicked girl!

For it to be like a white ring-dove,
The prisoner that you conceal,
Place your hands like two wings
On my heart, a trembling little bird.

37 *Arpège*

(Albert Samain)

L'âme d'une flûte soupire
Au fond du parc mélodieux;
Limpide est l'ombre où l'on respire
Ton poème silencieux,

Nuit de langueur, nuit de mensonge,
Qui poses d'un geste ondoyant
Dans ta chevelure de songe
La lune, bijou d'Orient.

Arpeggio

The soul of a flute is sighing
Deep in the melodious park;
The shade is limpid where one breathes
Your silent poem,

Night of langour, night of delusion,
That with a flowing gesture
Sets in your dreamy hair
The moon, that Orient jewel.

Sylva, Sylvie et Sylvanire,
Belles au regard bleu changeant,
L'étoile aux fontaines se mire,
Allez par les sentiers d'argent,

Allez vite—l'heure est si brève!
Cueillir au jardin des aveux
Les cœurs qui se meurent du rêve
De mourir parmi vos cheveux...

Sylva, Sylvie and Sylvanire,
Beauties with eyes of shimmering blue,
Fountains reflect the morning star—
Go along the silvery paths,

Go quickly—time is so short!
To gather in the garden of vows
The hearts which are dying of the dream
Of dying enveloped in your hair...

38 *Accompagnement*

(Albert Samain)

Tremble argenté, tilleul, bouleau...
La lune s'effeuille sur l'eau...

Comme de longs cheveux peignés au vent du soir,
L'odeur des nuits d'été parfume le lac noir.

Le grand lac parfumé brille comme un miroir.

Ma rame tombe et se relève,
Ma barque glisse dans le rêve.

Ma barque glisse dans le ciel
Sur le lac immatériel...

En cadence, les yeux fermés,
Rame, ô mon cœur, ton indolence
À larges coups lents et pâmés.

Là-bas la lune écoute, accoudée au coteau,
Le silence qu'exhale en glissant le bateau...
Trois grands lis frais-coupés meurent sur mon
manteau.

Vers tes lèvres, ô Nuit voluptueuse et pâle,
Est-ce leur âme, est-ce mon âme qui s'exhale?
Cheveux des nuits d'argent peignés aux longs
roseaux...

Comme la lune sur les eaux,
Comme la rame sur les flots,
Mon âme s'effeuille en sanglots!

Accompaniment

Silver aspen, lime, birch...
The moon sheds itself on the water...

Like long hair combed by the evening breeze,
The scent of summer nights perfumes the black
lake.
The great perfumed lake gleams like a mirror.

My oar dips and rises,
My boat glides in the dream.

My boat glides in the sky
On the insubstantial lake...

In cadence, with closed eyes,
Row, O my heart, your indolence
In broad slow swooning strokes.

Over there the moon, against the hillside, listens
To the silence of the gliding boat...
Three large fresh-cut lilies die on my cape.

Is it their soul or mine that reaches out
To your lips, O pale and voluptuous night?
Hair of silver nights combed by tall reeds...

Like the moon on the waters,
Like the oar on the waves,
My soul sheds itself in sobs!

39 *Chanson*

(Henri de Régnier)

Que me fait toute la terre
Inutile où tu n'as pas
En marchant marqué ton pas
Dans le sable ou la poussière!

Il n'est de fleuve attendu
Par ma soif qui s'y étanche
Que l'eau qui sourd et s'épanche
De la source où tu as bu;

La seule fleur qui m'attire
Est celle où je trouverai
Le souvenir empourpré
De ta bouche et de ton rire;

Et, sous la courbe des cieux,
La mer pour moi n'est immense
Que parce qu'elle commence
À la couleur de tes yeux.

40 *Le don silencieux*

(Jean Dominique)

Je mettrai mes deux mains sur ma bouche, pour taire

Ce que je voudrais tant vous dire, âme bien chère!

Je mettrai mes deux mains sur mes yeux, pour
    cacher
Ce que je voudrais tant que pourtant vous cherchiez.

Je mettrai mes deux mains sur mon cœur, chère vie,
Pour que vous ignoriez de quel cœur je vous prie!

Et puis je les mettrai doucement dans vos mains,
Ces deux mains-ci qui meurent d'un fatigant
    chagrin!...

Elles iront à vous pleines de leur faiblesse,
Toutes silencieuses et même sans caresse,

Lasses d'avoir porté tout le poids d'un secret
Dont ma bouche et mes yeux et mon front
    parleraient.

Song

What use to me is all the earth
Where you have not left
The imprint of your steps
In the sand or the dust!

I await no river
To quench my thirst
But the waters that well and flow
From the spring where you have drunk;

The only flower which attracts me
Is that on which I'll find
The crimson memory
Of your lips and your laughter;

And beneath the sweep of the sky,
The sea for me is only immense
Because it begins
With the colour of your eyes.

The silent gift

I shall place my two hands over my mouth, to
    silence
What I so wish to tell you, dearest soul!

I shall place my two hands over my eyes, to hide

What I still so wish you to seek.

I shall place my two hands over my heart, dear life,
That you may not know with how much heart I
    entreat!

And then I shall place them gently in your hands,
These two hands that die of a wearying sorrow!...

They will come to you, full of their weakness,
All silent and even without a caress,

Weary of having borne all the weight of a secret
That my lips and eyes and heart would reveal.

Elles iront à vous, légères d'être vides,
Et lourdes d'être tristes, tristes d'être timides;

Malheureuses et douces et si découragées
Que peut-être, mon Dieu, vous les recueillerez!...

They will come to you, light at being empty,
Heavy at being sad, sad at being shy;

Unhappy and gentle and so downcast
That maybe, my God, you will gather them up!...

41 *Pleurs d'or*

(Albert Samain)

Larmes aux fleurs suspendues,
Larmes aux sources perdues
Aux mousses des rochers creux;

Larmes d'automne épandues,
Larmes de cors entendues
Dans les grands bois douloureux;

Larmes des cloches latines,
Carmélites, Feuillantines...
Voix des beffrois en ferveur;

Larmes des nuits étoilées,
Larmes des flûtes voilées
Au bleu du parc endormi;

Larmes aux grands cils perlées,
Larmes d'amantes coulées
Jusqu'à l'âme de l'ami;

Larmes d'extase, éplorement délicieux,
Tombez des nuits! Tombez des fleurs! Tombez des
yeux!

Tears of gold

Tears clinging to flowers,
Tears from springs lost
In the moss of hollowed rocks;

Tears shed by autumn,
Tears from horns sounding
In great doleful forests;

Tears of church bells,
Of Carmel and Feuillant convents...
Devout belfry voices;

Tears of starlit nights,
Tears of muffled flutes
In the blue of the sleeping park;

Pearly tears on long lashes,
A beloved's tears flowing
To her friend's soul;

Tears of rapture, delicious weeping,
Fall at night! Fall from the flowers! Fall from these
eyes!

LA CHANSON D'ÈVE

(Charles Van Lerberghe)

THE SONG OF EVE

42 i *Paradis*

C'est le premier matin du monde.
Comme une fleur confuse exhalée de la nuit,
Au souffle nouveau qui se lève des ondes,

Un jardin bleu s'épanouit.

Paradise

It is the first morning of creation.
Like an abashed flower breathed on the night air,
With the pristine whisperings that rise from the
waves,

A blue garden blooms.

Tout s'y confond encore et tout s'y mêle,
    Frissons de feuilles, chants d'oiseaux,
      Glissements d'ailes,
Sources qui sourdent, voix des airs, voix des eaux,
    Murmure immense;
    Et qui pourtant est du silence.

Ouvrant à la clarté ses doux et vagues yeux
    La jeune et divine Ève
    S'est éveillée de Dieu.

Et le monde à ses pieds s'étend comme un beau rêve.

    Or Dieu lui dit: Va, fille humaine,
      Et donne à tous les êtres
Que j'ai créés, une parole de tes lèvres,
    Un son pour les connaître.

Et Ève s'en alla, docile à son seigneur,
    En son bosquet de roses,
    Donnant à toutes choses
Une parole, un son de ses lèvres de fleur:

Chose qui fuit, chose qui souffle, chose qui vole...

Cependant le jour passe, et vague, comme à l'aube,
    Au crépuscule, peu à peu,
    L'Éden s'endort et se dérobe
    Dans le silence d'un songe bleu.

La voix s'est tue, mais tout l'écoute encore,
    Tout demeure en attente;
Lorsque avec le lever de l'étoile du soir,
    Ève chante.

Everything is still blurred and indistinct,
    Trembling leaves, singing birds,
      Gliding wings,
Springs that rise, voices of air and water,
    An immense murmuring;
    Which yet is silence.

Opening to the light her soft and vacant eyes,
    Young, heaven-born Eve
    Is awakened by God.

And the world lies at her feet like a lovely dream.

    Now God says to her: Go, daughter of man,
      And bestow on all beings
That I have created a word from your lips,
    A sound that we might know them by.

And Eve went, obedient to her Lord,
    Into her rose grove,
    Bestowing on all things
A word, a sound from her flower-like lips:

On all that runs, that breathes, that flies...

Day meanwhile passes, and hazy, as at dawn,
    Eden sinks slowly to sleep
    In the twilight and steals away
    In the silence of a blue dream.

The voice is hushed, but everything still hearkens,
    Waiting in expectation;
When with the rising of the evening star,
    Eve sings.

42 ii *Prima verba*

Comme elle chante
Dans ma voix,
L'âme longtemps murmurante
Des fontaines et des bois!

Air limpide du paradis,
Avec tes grappes de rubis,
Avec tes gerbes de lumière,
Avec tes roses et tes fruits;

The first words

How it sings
In my voice,
The constantly murmuring soul
Of the springs and woods!

Clear air of paradise
With your ruby grape-clusters,
With your sheafs of light,
With your roses and your fruits;

Quelle merveille en nous à cette heure!
Des paroles depuis des âges endormies
En des sons, en des fleurs,
Sur mes lèvres enfin prennent vie.

Depuis que mon souffle a dit leur chanson,
Depuis que ma voix les a créées,
Quel silence heureux et profond
Naît de leurs âmes allégées!

How we marvel at such a moment!
Words that had slumbered for aeons
Finally come to life on my lips
As sounds, as flowers.

Since my breath uttered their song,
Since my voice created them,
What deep and blissful silence
Is born from their unburdened souls!

42 iii *Roses ardentes*   *Fiery roses*

Roses ardentes
Dans l'immobile nuit,
C'est en vous que je chante,
    Et que je suis.

En vous, étincelles,
À la cime des bois,
Que je suis éternelle,
    Et que je vois.

    Ô mer profonde,
C'est en toi que mon sang
Renaît vague blonde,
    Et flot dansant.

Et c'est en toi, force suprême,
    Soleil radieux,
Que mon âme elle-même
    Atteint son dieu!

Fiery roses
In the motionless night,
It is in you that I sing
    And have my being.

It is in you, gleaming stars
High in the forests,
That I am eternal
    And given sight.

    O deep sea,
It is in you that my blood
Is reborn, white wave
    And dancing tide.

And it is in you, supreme force,
    Radiant sun,
That my very soul
    Reaches its God!

42 iv *Comme Dieu rayonne*   *How radiant is God*

Comme Dieu rayonne aujourd'hui,
Comme il exulte, comme il fleurit
Parmi ces roses et ces fruits!

Comme il murmure en cette fontaine!
Ah! comme il chante en ces oiseaux...
Qu'elle est suave son haleine
Dans l'odorant printemps nouveau!

Comme il se baigne dans la lumière
Avec amour, mon jeune dieu!
Toutes les choses de la terre
Sont ses vêtements radieux.

How radiant is God today,
How he exults and blossoms
Among these roses and fruits!

How he murmurs in this fountain!
Ah! how he sings in these birds...
How sweet is his breath
In the new fragrant spring!

How he bathes in light
With love, my young God!
All earthly things
Are his dazzling raiments.

42 v *L'aube blanche*

L'aube blanche dit à mon rêve:
Éveille-toi, le soleil luit.
Mon âme écoute, et je soulève
Un peu mes paupières vers lui.

Un rayon de lumière touche
La pâle fleur de mes yeux bleus;
Une flamme éveille ma bouche,
Un souffle éveille mes cheveux.

Et mon âme, comme une rose
Tremblante, lente, tout le jour,
S'éveille à la beauté des choses,
Comme mon cœur à leur amour.

The white dawn

The white dawn says to my dream:
Awake, the sun is shining.
My soul listens, and I raise
My eyes a little towards it.

A ray of light touches
The pale flower of my blue eyes;
A flame awakens my mouth,
A breeze awakens my hair.

And my soul, like a rose
That is trembling and listless all day,
Awakens to the beauty of things,
As my heart awakens to their love.

42 vi *Eau vivante*

Que tu es simple et claire,
Eau vivante,
Qui, du sein de la terre,
Jaillis en ces bassins et chantes!

Ô fontaine divine et pure,
Les plantes aspirent
Ta liquide clarté;
La biche et la colombe en toi se désaltèrent.

Et tu descends par des pentes douces
De fleurs et de mousses,
Vers l'océan originel,
Toi qui passes et vas, sans cesse, et jamais lasse
De la terre à la mer et de la mer au ciel.

Spring water

How simple and clear you are,
Spring water,
Who, from the heart of the earth,
Surges into these pools and sings!

O divine, pure fountain,
The plants breathe in
Your liquid limpidity;
The doe and the dove quench in you their thirst.

And you descend by the gentle banks
Of flowers and moss
Towards the primeval ocean,
You who come and go, without cease or fatigue,
From the land to the sea and from the sea to the sky.

42 vii *Veilles-tu, ma senteur de soleil*

Veilles-tu, ma senteur de soleil,
Mon arôme d'abeilles blondes,
Flottes-tu sur le monde,
Mon doux parfum de miel?

La nuit, lorsque mes pas
Dans le silence rôdent,
M'annonces-tu, senteur de mes lilas,
Et de mes roses chaudes?

Are you awake, my fragrant sun?

Are you awake, my fragrant sun,
My scent of bright-coloured bees,
Do you drift across the world,
My sweet aroma of honey?

At night, while my steps
Prowl in the silence,
Do you, who scent my lilacs
And vivid roses, proclaim me?

Suis-je comme une grappe de fruits
Cachés dans les feuilles,
Et que rien ne décèle,
Mais qu'on odore dans la nuit?

Sait-il, à cette heure,
Que j'entr'ouvre ma chevelure,
Et qu'elle respire;
Le sent-il sur la terre?

Sent-il que j'étends les bras,
Et que des lys de mes vallées
Ma voix qu'il n'entend pas
Est embaumée?

Am I like a bunch of fruit
Hidden in the foliage,
That nothing reveals
But whose fragrance is felt at night?

Does he know at this hour
That I am loosening my tresses
And that they are breathing;
Does he sense it on earth?

Does he sense that I reach out my arms,
And that my voice—which he cannot hear—
Is fragrant
With lilies from my valleys?

42 viii *Dans un parfum de roses blanches*

Amid the scent of white roses

Dans un parfum de roses blanches
Elle est assise et songe;
Et l'ombre est belle comme s'il s'y mirait un ange.

L'ombre descend, le bosquet dort;
Entre les feuilles et les branches,
Sur le paradis bleu s'ouvre un paradis d'or.

Une voix qui chantait, tout à l'heure, murmure.
Un murmure s'exhale en haleine, et s'éteint.

Dans le silence il tombe des pétales...

Amid the scent of white roses
She sits and dreams;
And the shade is fair, as if an angel were mirrored there.

Darkness falls, the grove sleeps;
Among the leaves and branches,
A golden paradise opens out over the blue.

A voice which sang but now, now murmurs.
A murmur is breathed, and dies away.

In the silence petals fall...

42 ix *Crépuscule*

Twilight

Ce soir, à travers le bonheur,
Qui donc soupire, qu'est-ce qui pleure?
Qu'est-ce qui vient palpiter sur mon cœur,
Comme un oiseau blessé?

Est-ce une voix future,
Une voix du passé?
J'écoute, jusqu'à la souffrance,
Ce son dans le silence.

Île d'oubli, ô Paradis!
Quel cri déchire, dans la nuit,
Ta voix qui me berce?

This evening, amid the happiness,
Who is it that sighs and what is it that weeps?
What comes to flutter in my heart,
Like a wounded bird?

Is it a premonition,
A voice from the past?
I listen, till it hurts,
To that sound in the silence.

Isle of oblivion, O paradise!
What cry in the night cracks
Your voice that cradles me?

Quel cri traverse Ta ceinture de fleurs, Et ton beau voile d'allégresse?	What cry pierces Your girdle of flowers, And your lovely veil of happiness?

42 x *Ô mort, poussière d'étoiles* — *O death, starry dust*

Ô mort, poussière d'étoiles,
Lève-toi sous mes pas!

Viens, ô douce vague qui brille
Dans les ténèbres;
Emporte-moi dans ton néant!

Viens, souffle sombre où je vacille,
Comme une flamme ivre de vent!

C'est en toi que je veux m'étendre,
M'éteindre et me dissoudre,
Mort, où mon âme aspire!

Viens, brise-moi comme une fleur d'écume.
Une fleur de soleil à la cime
Des eaux,

Et comme d'une amphore d'or
Un vin de flamme et d'arome divin,
Épanche mon âme
En ton abîme, pour qu'elle embaume
La terre sombre et le souffle des morts.

O death, starry dust,
Rise up where I tread!

Come, gentle wave that shines
In the darkness:
Bear me off into your void!

Come, dark sigh in which I tremble,
Like a wind-intoxicated flame!

It is in you that I wish to be absorbed,
To be extinguished and dissolved,
Death, to which my soul aspires!

Come, break me like a flower of foam,
A speck of sun in the crest
Of the waves,

And like a golden amphora's
Flaming wine of heavenly fragrance,
Pour my soul
Into your abyss, that it might perfume
The dark earth and the breath of the dead.

LE JARDIN CLOS — THE WALLED GARDEN
(Charles Van Lerberghe)

43 i *Exaucement* — *Fulfilment*

Alors qu'en tes mains de lumière
Tu poses ton front défaillant,
Que mon amour en ta prière
Vienne comme un exaucement.

Alors que la parole expire
Sur ta lèvre qui tremble encor,
Et s'adoucit en un sourire
De roses en des rayons d'or;

When in your hands of light
You rest your swooning head,
May my love enter your prayer
Like a fulfilment.

When words cxpire
On your still trembling lips,
And mellow into a smile
Of roses and golden rays;

Que ton âme calme et muette,
Fée endormie au jardin clos,
En sa douce volonté faite
Trouve la joie et le repos.

May your calm and silent soul—
Asleep like a fairy in a walled garden—
With its sweet desire now attained,
Find delight and peace of mind.

43 ii *Quand tu plonges tes yeux dans mes yeux*

When you immerse your eyes in mine

Quand tu plonges tes yeux dans mes yeux,
Je suis toute dans mes yeux.

Quand ta bouche dénoue ma bouche,
Mon amour n'est que ma bouche.

Si tu frôles mes cheveux,
Je n'existe plus qu'en eux.

Si ta main effleure mes seins,
J'y monte comme un feu soudain.

Est-ce moi que tu as choisie?
Là est mon âme, là est ma vie.

When you immerse your eyes in mine,
I am wholly in my eyes.

When your lips part mine,
My love is my lips alone.

When you stroke my hair,
I no longer exist but there.

If your hand but brushes my breasts,
I quicken there like a sudden fire.

Is it I that you have chosen?
There is my soul, there is my life.

43 iii *La Messagère*

The Messenger

Avril, et c'est le point du jour.
Tes blondes sœurs qui te ressemblent,
En ce moment, toutes ensemble
S'avancent vers toi, cher Amour.

Tu te tiens dans un clos ombreux
De myrte et d'aubépine blanche:
La porte s'ouvre sous les branches;
Le chemin est mystérieux.

Elles, lentes, en longues robes,
Une à une, main dans la main,
Franchissent le seuil indistinct
Où de la nuit devient de l'aube.

Celle qui s'avance d'abord,
Regarde l'ombre, te découvre,
Crie, et la fleur de ses yeux s'ouvre
Splendide dans un rire d'or.

April, and day has broken.
Your fair sisters who resemble you,
At this moment, all together
Advance towards you, dear Love,

In your shady enclosure
Of myrtle and white hawthorn:
The door opens beneath the branches;
The path is full of mystery.

Slowly, in long gowns,
One by one, hand in hand,
They cross the blurred threshold
Where night becomes dawn.

She who first draws near,
Looks at the shade, discovers you,
Cries out, and her flower-eyes open,
Resplendent in golden laughter.

Et, jusqu'à la dernière sœur,
Toutes tremblent, tes lèvres touchent
Leurs lèvres, l'éclair de ta bouche
Éclate jusque dans leur cœur.

And the sisters without exception
All tremble, your lips touch
Their lips, the brilliance of your mouth
Erupts into their very hearts.

43 iv *Je me poserai sur ton cœur*

Je me poserai sur ton cœur
Comme le printemps sur la mer,
Sur les plaines de la mer stérile
Où nulle fleur ne peut croître,
À ses souffles agiles,
Que des fleurs de lumière.

Je me poserai sur ton cœur
Comme l'oiseau sur la mer,
Dans le repos de ses ailes lasses,
Et que berce le rythme éternel
Des flots et de l'espace.

Je me poserai sur ton cœur
Comme l'oiseau sur la mer.

I shall alight on your heart

I shall alight on your heart
Like springtime on the sea,
On the plains of the barren sea,
Where no flower can grow
In its lithe breezes,
Save flowers of light.

I shall alight on your heart
Like a bird on the sea,
Resting its weary wings
And rocked by the eternal rhythm
Of waves and space.

I shall alight on your heart
Like a bird on the sea.

43 v *Dans la Nymphée*

Quoique tes yeux ne la voient pas,
Pense, en ton âme, qu'elle est là,
Comme autrefois divine et blanche.

Sur ce bord reposent ses mains.
Sa tête est entre ces jasmins;
Là, ses pieds effleurent les branches.

Elle sommeille en ces rameaux.
Ses lèvres et ses yeux sont clos,
Et sa bouche à peine respire.

Parfois, la nuit, dans un éclair
Elle apparaît les yeux ouverts,
Et l'éclair dans ses yeux se mire.

Un bref éblouissement bleu
La découvre en ses longs cheveux;
Elle s'éveille, elle se lève.

In the grotto

Though your eyes do not see her,
Think, in your soul, that she is there,
Divine and pristine, as of old.

Her hands rest on this bank,
Her head is among these jasmine,
There her feet brush the boughs.

She sleeps amid these branches.
Her lips and eyes are closed,
And her mouth is scarcely breathing.

Sometimes, at night, like lightning
She appears with open eyes,
The lightning mirrored in her eyes.

A brief blue glare
Reveals her with her long tresses;
She awakes, she rises.

Et tout un jardin ébloui
S'illumine au fond de la nuit,
Dans le rapide éclair d'un rêve,

And the whole dazzled garden
Is lit up in the depths of night,
In the swift flash of a dream.

43 vi *Dans la pénombre*

À quoi, dans ce matin d'avril,
Si douce et d'ombre enveloppée,
La chère enfant au cœur subtil
Est-elle ainsi tout occupée?

Pensivement, d'un geste lent,
En longue robe, en robe à queue,
Sur le soleil au rouet blanc
À filer de la laine bleue.

À sourire à son rêve encor,
Avec ses yeux de fiancée,
À travers les feuillages d'or
Parmi les lys de sa pensée.

In the half-light

With what, this April morning,
So sweet and swathed in shadow,
Is the dear and tender-hearted girl
So preoccupied?

Pensively and slowly,
In a long flowing robe,
Spinning blue wool
On the sun's white wheel,

Still smiling at her dream
With the eyes of one betrothed,
Across the golden foliage
Among the lilies of her thought.

43 vii *Il m'est cher, Amour, le bandeau*

Il m'est cher, Amour, le bandeau
Qui me tient les paupières closes;
Il pèse comme un doux fardeau
De soleil sur de faibles roses.

Si j'avance, l'étrange chose!
Je parais marcher sur des eaux;
Mes pieds plus lourds où je les pose,
S'enfoncent comme en des anneaux.

Qui donc a délié dans l'ombre
Le faix d'or de mes longs cheveux?
Toute ceinte d'étreintes sombres,
Je plonge en des vagues de feu.

Mes lèvres où mon âme chante,
Toute d'extase et de baiser,
S'ouvrent comme une fleur ardente
Au-dessus d'un fleuve embrasé.

My Love, the blindfold is dear to me

My Love, the blindfold is dear to me
That screens my eyes;
It weighs like a sweet burden
Of sun on languid roses.

If I move forward—how strange!
I seem to walk on water;
Wherever I place my too heavy feet,
They sink as if into rings.

Who, then, has loosened in the shade
The golden weight of my long tresses?
All enclosed by dark embraces,
I plunge into waves of fire.

My lips, where my soul sings
Of naught but rapture and kisses,
Open like an ardent flower
Above a blazing river.

43 viii *Inscription sur le sable*

Toute, avec sa robe et ses fleurs,
Elle, ici, redevint poussière,
Et son âme emportée ailleurs
Renaquit en chant de lumière.

Mais un léger lien fragile
Dans la mort brisé doucement,
Encerclait ses tempes débiles
D'impérissables diamants.

En signe d'elle, à cette place,
Seules, parmi le sable blond,
Les pierres éternelles tracent
Encor l'image de son front.

Inscription on the sand

Entire, with her gown and flowers,
She here became dust once more,
And her soul, borne off elsewhere,
Was reborn in a song of light.

But a light and fragile link,
Gently broken in death,
Encircled her sickly temples
With imperishable diamonds.

As a token of her, in this place,
Alone among the pale sand,
The eternal stones still trace
The image of her brow.

MIRAGES

(Renée de Brimont)

MIRAGES

44 i *Cygne sur l'eau*

Ma pensée est un cygne harmonieux et sage
Qui glisse lentement aux rivages d'ennui
Sur les ondes sans fond du rêve, du mirage,
De l'écho, du brouillard, de l'ombre, de la nuit.

Il glisse, roi hautain fendant un libre espace,
Poursuit un reflet vain, précieux et changeant,
Et les roseaux nombreux s'inclinent quand il passe,
Sombre et muet, au seuil d'une lune d'argent;

Et des blancs nénuphars chaque corolle ronde
Tour à tour a fleuri de désir ou d'espoir...
Mais plus avant toujours, sur la brume et sur l'onde,
Vers l'inconnu fuyant glisse le cygne noir.

Or j'ai dit: 'Renoncez, beau cygne chimérique,
À ce voyage lent vers de troubles destins;
Nul miracle chinois, nulle étrange Amérique
Ne vous accueilleront en des havres certains;

Les golfes embaumés, les îles immortelles
Ont pour vous, cygne noir, des récifs périlleux;
Demeurez sur les lacs où se mirent, fidèles,
Ces nuages, ces fleurs, ces astres et ces yeux.'

Swan on the water

My mind is a gentle, harmonious swan
Gliding slowly along the shores of ennui
On the fathomless waters of dreams and delusion,
Of echo, of mist, of shadow, of night.

He glides, a haughty monarch cleaving a path,
Pursuing a vain reflection, precious and fleeting,
And the countless reeds bow as he passes,
Dark and silent before a silver moon;

And each round corolla of the white water-lilies
Has blossomed by turn with desire or hope...
But ever forward on the mists and the waves,
The black swan glides toward the receding
    unknown.

And I said: 'Renounce, beautiful chimera of a swan,
This slow voyage to troubled destinies;
No Chinese miracle, no exotic America
Will welcome you in safe havens;

The scented gulfs, the immortal isles
Await you, black swan, with their perilous reefs;
Remain on the lakes which faithfully reflect
These clouds, these flowers, these stars, and these eyes.'

44 ii *Reflets dans l'eau*

Étendue au seuil du bassin,
Dans l'eau plus froide que le sein
  Des vierges sages,
J'ai reflété mon vague ennui,
Mes yeux profonds couleur de nuit
  Et mon visage.

Et dans ce miroir incertain
J'ai vu de merveilleux matins...
  J'ai vu des choses
Pâles comme des souvenirs,
Sur l'eau que ne saurait ternir
  Nul vent morose.

Alors—au fond du Passé bleu—
Mon corps mince n'était qu'un peu
  D'ombre mouvante;
Sous les lauriers et les cyprès
J'aimais la brise au souffle frais
  Qui nous évente...

J'aimais vos caresses de sœur,
Vos nuances, votre douceur,
  Aube opportune;
Et votre pas souple et rythmé,
Nymphes au rire parfumé,
  Au teint de lune;

Et le galop des aegypans,
Et la fontaine qui s'épand
  En larmes fades...
Par les bois secrets et divins
J'écoutais frissonner sans fin
  L'hamadryade.

Ô cher Passé mystérieux
Qui vous reflétez dans mes yeux
  Comme un nuage,
Il me serait plaisant et doux,
Passé, d'essayer avec vous
  Le long voyage!...

Si je glisse, les eaux feront
Un rond fluide... un autre rond...
  Un autre à peine...
Et puis le miroir enchanté
Reprendra sa limpidité
  Froide et sereine.

* Goat-footed fawns.   † A wood-nymph.

Reflections in the water

Lying at the pool's edge,
In water more cold than the breasts
  Of wise virgins,
I saw reflected my vague ennui,
My deep and night-dark eyes
  And my face.

And in this uncertain mirror
I have seen wondrous mornings...
  I have seen things
As pale as memories
On the water that no morose wind
  Could mist.

Then on the bed of the blue Past,
My slight body was but a shred
  Of moving shadow;
Beneath the laurel and cypress
I loved the cool breath of wind
  That fanned us...

I loved your sisterly caresses,
Your light and shade, your softness,
  Timely dawn;
And your supple rhythmic step,
You nymphs pale as the moon
  With scented laughter;

And the gallop of the Aegypans,*
And the fountain cascading
  In saltless tears...
In the secret and sacred woods
I heard the hamadryad's†
  Endless quivering.

Cherished, mysterious Past,
Reflected in my eyes
  Like a cloud,
It would be pleasant and sweet for me
To embark with you, O Past,
  On the long voyage!...

If I slip, the waters will ripple
In rings... in rings...
  In rin...
And then the enchanted mirror
Will grow limpid once more,
  Cold and serene.

44 iii *Jardin nocturne*

Nocturne jardin tout rempli de silence,
Voici que la lune ouverte se balance
En des voiles d'or fluides et légers;
Elle semble proche et cependant lointaine...
Son visage rit au cœur de la fontaine
Et l'ombre pâlit sous les noirs orangers.

Nul bruit, si ce n'est le faible bruit de l'onde
Fuyant goutte à goutte au bord des vasques rondes,
Ou le bleu frisson d'une brise d'été,
Furtive parmi des palmes invisibles...
Je sais, ô jardin, vos caresses sensibles
Et votre languide et chaude volupté!

Je sais votre paix délectable et morose,
Vos parfums d'iris, de jasmins et de roses,
Vos charmes troublés de désirs et d'ennui...
Ô jardin muet!—L'eau des vasques s'égoutte
Avec un bruit faible et magique... J'écoute
Ce baiser qui chante aux lèvres de la Nuit.

Nocturnal garden

Nocturnal garden brimming with silence,
Now the full moon is swaying
In light and liquid veils of gold;
Close she seems, yet far away...
Her face is laughing in the heart of the fountain
And shadows pale beneath dark orange-trees.

No sound, save perhaps the whispering wave
Trickling drop by drop from round basins,
Or the blue quiver of a summer breeze,
Furtive among invisible palms...
I know, O garden, your keen caresses
And your languid, torrid voluptuousness!

I know your delicious and sullen peace,
Your scents of iris, of jasmine, of rose,
Your beauty ruffled by desire and ennui...
O silent garden! The waters in the basin drip
With a faint and magical sound... I listen
To this kiss which sings on the lips of Night.

44 iv *Danseuse*

Sœur des Sœurs tisseuses de violettes,
Une ardente veille blémit tes joues...
Danse! Et que les rythmes aigus dénouent
    Tes bandelettes.

Vase svelte, fresque mouvante et souple,
Danse, danse, paumes vers nous tendues,
Pieds étroits fuyant, tels des ailes nues
    Qu'Éros découple...

Sois la fleur multiple un peu balancée,
Sois l'écharpe offerte au désir qui change,
Sois la lampe chaste, la flamme étrange,
    Sois la pensée!

Danse, danse au chant de ma flûte creuse,
Sœur des Sœurs divines.—La moiteur glisse,
Baiser vain, le long de ta hanche lisse...
    Vaine danseuse!

Dancer

Sister of violet-weaving sisters,
A scorching vigil pales your cheeks...
Dance! And let the shrill rhythms unfurl
    Your sashes.

Svelte vase, supple and moving fresco,
Dance with palms outstretched before us,
Slender feet flying like the naked wings
    Which Eros unbinds...

Be the multiple flower swaying a little,
Be the scarf proffered to fickle desire,
Be the chaste lamp, the strange flame,
    Be thought!

Dance, dance to the song of my hollow flute,
Sister of sacred sisters. Moisture trickles,
A vain kiss, along your lithe hip...
    Vain dancer!

L'HORIZON CHIMÉRIQUE

(Jean de La Ville de Mirmont)

THE ILLUSORY HORIZON

45 i *La mer est infinie*

La mer est infinie et mes rêves sont fous.
La mer chante au soleil en battant les falaises
Et mes rêves légers ne se sentent plus d'aise
De danser sur la mer comme des oiseaux soûls.

Le vaste mouvement des vagues les emporte,
La brise les agite et les roule en ses plis;
Jouant dans le sillage, ils feront une escorte
Aux vaisseaux que mon cœur dans leur fuite a suivis.

Ivres d'air et de sel et brûlés par l'écume
De la mer qui console et qui lave des pleurs,
Ils connaîtront le large et sa bonne amertume;
Les goëlands perdus les prendront pour des leurs.

The sea is boundless

The sea is boundless and my dreams are wild.
The sea sings in the sun, as it beats the cliffs,
And my light dreams are overjoyed
To dance on the sea like drunken birds.

The waves' vast motion bears them away,
The breeze ruffles and rolls them in its folds;
Playing in their wake, they will escort the ships,
Whose flight my heart has followed.

Drunk with air and salt, and stung by the spume
Of the consoling sea that washes away tears,
They will know the high seas and the bracing brine;
Lost gulls will take them for their own.

45 ii *Je me suis embarqué*

Je me suis embarqué sur un vaisseau qui danse
Et roule bord sur bord et tangue et se balance.
Mes pieds ont oublié la terre et ses chemins;
Les vagues souples m'ont appris d'autres cadences
Plus belles que le rythme las des chants humains.

À vivre parmi vous, hélas! avais-je une âme?
Mes frères, j'ai souffert sur tous vos continents.
Je ne veux que la mer, je ne veux que le vent
Pour me bercer, comme un enfant, au creux des
    lames.

Hors du port qui n'est plus qu'une image effacée,
Les larmes du départ ne brûlent plus mes yeux.
Je ne me souviens pas de mes derniers adieux...
Ô ma peine, ma peine, où vous ai-je laissée?

I have embarked

I have embarked on a ship that reels
And rolls and pitches and rocks.
My feet have forgotten the land and its ways;
The lithe waves have taught me other rhythms,
Lovelier than the tired ones of human song.

Ah! did I have the heart to live among you?
Brothers, on all your continents I've suffered.
I want only the sea, I want only the wind
To cradle me like a child in the trough of the waves.

Far from the port, now but a faded image,
Tears of parting no longer sting my eyes.
I can no longer recall my final farewells...
O my sorrow, my sorrow, where have I left you?

45 iii *Diane, Séléné*

Diane, Séléné, lune de beau métal,
Qui reflètes vers nous, par ta face déserte,
Dans l'immortel ennui du calme sidéral,
Le regret d'un soleil dont nous pleurons la perte.

* Moon (Gk.).

*Diana, Selene**

Diana, Selene, moon of beautiful metal,
Reflecting on us, from your deserted face,
In the eternal tedium of sidereal calm,
The regret of a sun whose loss we lament.

Ô lune, je t'en veux de ta limpidité
Injurieuse au trouble vain des pauvres âmes,
Et mon cœur, toujours las et toujours agité,
Aspire vers la paix de ta nocturne flamme.

O moon, I begrudge you your limpidity,
Mocking the fruitless commotion of wretched souls,
And my heart, ever weary and ever uneasy,
Longs for the peace of your nocturnal flame.

45 iv *Vaisseaux, nous vous aurons aimés en pure perte*

Ships, we shall have loved you to no avail

Vaisseaux, nous vous aurons aimés en pure perte;
Le dernier de vous tous est parti sur la mer.
Le couchant emporta tant de voiles ouvertes
Que ce port et mon cœur sont à jamais déserts.

La mer vous a rendus à votre destinée,
Au delà du rivage où s'arrêtent nos pas.
Nous ne pouvions garder vos âmes enchaînées;
Il vous faut des lointains que je ne connais pas.

Je suis de ceux dont les désirs sont sur la terre.
Le souffle qui vous grise emplit mon cœur d'effroi,
Mais votre appel, au fond des soirs, me désespère,
Car j'ai de grands départs inassouvis en moi.

Ships, we shall have loved you to no avail,
The last of you all has set sail on the sea.
The sunset bore away so many spread sails,
That this port and my heart are forever forsaken.

The sea has returned you to your destiny,
Beyond the shores where our steps must halt.
We could not keep your souls enchained,
You require distant realms unknown to me.

I belong to those with earthbound desires.
The wind that elates you fills me with fright,
But your summons at nightfall makes me despair,
For within me are vast, unappeased departures.

FERROUD, Pierre Octave (1900–1936)

This pupil of Ropartz and Florent Schmitt (Ferroud wrote a biography of Schmitt) studied in Strasbourg, giving him a feeling for German literature which is reflected in his Goethe cycle DREI TRAUTE GESÄNGE: TROIS POÈMES INTIMES DE GOETHE (1932). This was dedicated to the soprano Lotte Schöne, and includes a gently lyrical setting of *Erster Verlust* (in French translation of course), a poem famous through the music of Schubert. After his studentship, Ferroud was an important advocate of new music in his native Lyons. He moved to Paris in 1923 where he founded Le Triton, an organization which was responsible for the performance of much modern music, including works by Bartók, Hindemith, and Stravinsky, as well as members of Les Six. Ferroud was also a critic of note and his early death (he was decapitated in a driving accident in Hungary) deprived the French musical world of a potentially important figure.

He wrote small song sets of Paul Valéry (1929) and Jules Supervielle (1932), but perhaps his finest set of songs is CINQ POÈMES DE P.J. TOULET (1927), which is worthy of reassessment. The shock of his colleague Ferroud's death was partly responsible for Poulenc's decision to re-evaluate his own music and lifestyle in the light of this intimation of mortality. In his mid-thirties Poulenc allowed a religious dimension to enter his life, and began to write deeply lyrical songs to the texts of Éluard. Thus it was sadly only in his death that Pierre Octave Ferroud exerted his greatest influence on the development of the mélodie.

FRANÇAIX, Jean (1912–1997)

This interesting composer, pupil of Boulanger and a master craftsman within the deliberately contained orbit of his creativity, wrote much vocal music. Of his five operas perhaps *La Princesse de Clèves* (1965) is the best known, and he composed chamber music for voices for a number of delicious combinations: two sopranos and string quartet, four voices and string quintet, four voices and piano duet, as well as various cantatas with string orchestra and different additional instruments. Like Leguerney, Françaix had a marked taste for the poets of the sixteenth to eighteenth centuries, but poets as early as Juvenal and as late as Paul Valéry also make occasional appearances in his work-list. In his songs he set a twentieth-century poet like Louise de Vilmorin (the song *Scherzo impromptu* which appears in the same multi-composer set, MOUVEMENTS DE CŒUR, to which Poulenc contributed a *Mazurka*) but this is the exception.

There are three sets of songs worthy of note, all of which feature Charles d'Orléans, Clément Marot, or a combination of both. (It is significant that he chose a Marot poem to celebrate the 60th birthday of his beloved teacher Nadia Boulanger in 1947—a single song entitled *Marguerite d'Alençon et de soi-même*.) The earliest of these Marot cycles is L'ADOLESCENCE CLÉMENTINE (Marot, 1942), a pithy little succession of songs written for Bernac and Poulenc. Everything is deft and elegant, with never a note wasted. But sometimes one longs for greater lyricism, and for an accompaniment that suggests something more telling than the staccato diffidence of a continuo harpsichord. The fault in Françaix is an elegance so controlled and courtly as to be almost dry. The CINQ POÈMES DE CHARLES D'ORLÉANS (1946) written for Gérard Souzay have a similar clean style but the accompaniments are more difficult to play; one should not forget that the composer was a virtuoso pianist, particularly expert in inventing tricky little figurations which give the songs a wiry nervous energy. This is even more noticeable in the TROIS ÉPIGRAMMES (1961) where the incessant semiquavers of *Une demoiselle malade* (Marot) pose a formidable challenge to the accompanist. In the same set **Belaud, mon petit chat gris** (Joachim du Bellay) is the poet's elegy for his cat. It is a worthy, if technically demanding, addition to the small but distinguished list of cat songs (everything about cats is demanding) in the mélodie repertoire. In 1946 the composer wrote an orchestrally accompanied cycle, again for Souzay, entitled INVOCATION À LA VOLUPTÉ (La Fontaine). The HUIT ANECDOTES DE CHAMFORT (1948) were created by Bernac. Once again, these are cast as pithy musical epigrams, a form which both defines this composer's songs, and sometimes limits their power to touch us.

1 *Belaud, mon petit chat gris*
(Joachim du Bellay)

La tête à la taille pareille,
Une barbelette argentée,
Son musequin damoiselet.
Mon Dieu, quel passetemps c'était
Quand ce Belaud vire-voltait
Folâtre autour d'une pelote!

Belaud, my little grey cat

Such a large head,
A silvery little beard,
An effeminate little snout—
My word, how diverting it was
When Belaud frisked
Around a ball of wool!

Quel plaisir, quand sa tête sotte
Suivant sa queue en mille tours,
D'un rouet imitait le cours!
Ô quel malheur! ô quelle perte,
Qui ne peut être recouverte!
Oui, j'ai perdu depuis trois jours
Mon plaisir, mon bien, mes amours!
Vraiment la mort fut inhumaine,
Si de voir elle eût pris la peine
Un tel chat, son cœur endurci
En eût eu (ce crois-je) merci.
Que plût à Dieu, petit Belaud,
Que j'eusse l'esprit assez bon,
De pouvoir en quelque beau style
Blasonner ta race gentille,
Belaud, dont la beauté fut telle,
Qu'elle est digne d'être immortelle!
Belaud, mon petit chat!
Belaud, mon petit chat gris!

What fun, when his silly head
Chased his tail round and round,
Just like a spinning wheel!
Oh what a tragedy! What a loss,
An irremediable loss!
Yes—for three days now I've lost
My delight, my wealth, my love!
Truly, death was inhumane,
For had it bothered
To behold such a cat, its callous heart
Would, I think, have relented.
I wish to God, my little Belaud,
That I had the skill
To describe in fine style
Your noble race,
Belaud, whose beauty is so great
That it merits immortality!
Belaud, my little cat!
Belaud, my little grey cat!

FRANCK, César (1822–1890)

There can have been few more influential people in French music than this man, one of those Belgians who bring a different strand of perception and temperament to the Gallic cultural tapestry. His experiments with chromatic harmony and cyclical form, combined with an aesthetic which was anchored in an all-pervading religious faith, were an antidote to the simplistic musical fripperies of the Second Empire, and worked as a powerful influence to add a new dimension to what was understood by the term 'French music'.

It is thus something of a let-down to report a comparatively small contribution to the mélodie—eighteen songs and six duets. If, on the other hand, Franck could take credit for his pupils' achievements in this sphere (the young composers known as *la bande à Franck* were avid song composers), almost certainly the longest entry in this book would be under his name. His pupils also played a crucial part in his own career, for their advice to him, as well as their urgings and encouragement, gave him the confidence to continue composing. Henri Duparc was the important name at the beginning of Franck's teaching career, and it was he who introduced his beloved 'Pater Seraphicus' to Alexis de Castillon. Thus was founded the Société Nationale de Musique in 1871 which became an important forum for the performance of new music, including Franck's. The band was later joined by Vincent d'Indy who was a power-house of industry to further the cause, and the roster continues with Ernst Chausson and ends, after many other significant names, with Guillaume Lekeu. In his book on Wagner, Vincent D'Indy wrote that Franck appeared to his pupils as a figure surrounded by a halo, like that of the saints in the fifteenth-century frescoes. Chabrier, speaking at Franck's funeral (an unlikely choice of orator perhaps), spoke of these pupils as a "génération de musiciens robustes, croyants et réfléchis."

If this were a book on piano music, there would be a long list of works which Franck wrote in his late teens and early twenties during his ill-fated career as a piano virtuoso. As an offshoot of these works, there is a much smaller list of early songs which have little interest beyond one's astonishment that a composer later so renowned for serious music should have written them. An example of these is *Ninon* (Musset, 1842–3), a song with a pleasing melody, but which is full of mistakes in prosody, astonishingly clumsy emphases on the wrong words. We thus discover early that the niceties of literature were not as important to this composer as the overall poetic feeling of a text. This enabled him to ignore unhappy imagery (as in the fine song *Nocturne* which contains the unfortunate line 'Mon cœur bouillonne comme une urne') and to concentrate on the main message of the text by which he was moved. There is also a touch of harmonic daring from the early days, and we find this in certain chord progressions in *L'émir de Bengador* (Méry, 1842–3), Franck's contribution to the prevailing fashion for orientalism. In 1844 he transcribed four Schubert songs for solo piano—these were *Die junge Nonne*, *Die Forelle*, *Des Mädchens Klage*, and *Das Zügenglöcklein*. The influence of lieder was thus not surprisingly to be found in some of the songs of the period, *Souvenance* (Chateaubriand, 1842–3) and *Robin Gray* (Florian, 1842–3), the latter song employing an enchanting upper pedal in the Schubertian manner. In *Aimer* (Méry, 1849) we notice for the first time Franck's tendency to write accompaniments where crotchets change to quavers which in turn give way to semiquaver arpeggios. This technique whereby initial simplicity is gradually transformed into a rapturous vision of the sublime is to be found in the two best-known Franck songs from later in his life, *Nocturne* and *La procession*.

Mention should be made of two settings of *S'il est un charmant gazon* (Hugo) [FAURÉ 6]. The first of these dates from 1847 and shows the limitations of the salon with spread chords in rippling attendance; it is less perky than Saint-Saëns's youthful setting from a few years later, but similarly charming in an undemanding way. The second setting (1855–7) is altogether more interesting, both in its richer command of harmony and in the way that the accompaniment now has a life of its own. This is no less than we might have expected from a composer whose writing for solo piano is both demanding and ingenious. After this, Franck did not write songs for some years. He returned to the medium in 1871 with perhaps his most delightful mélodie **Le mariage des roses** (E. David). It is a simple strophic song, but it is winningly graceful with touches of harmonic originality that are completely Franckian. The other mélodies of the middle period of the composer's life (two Hugo settings from 1872—*Roses et papillons*, dedicated to Alexis de Castillon, and *Passez, passez toujours*) are not unattractive, but they lack the inner glow of the little song about roses. *Lied* (Paté, 1873) has the mournful charm of a folksong with its strange augmented intervals.

There are four further songs in the final period of Franck's life, all rather substantial, and now marked out by what we take to be the elevated characteristics of this composer's style. This works for some texts better than others. Thus there seems a mismatch between the emotional music and the rather stiff, patrician words of Sully Prudhomme in *Le vase brisé* (1879). One fears that this song could all too easily sound rather silly on the platform. On the other hand, *Nocturne* (1884, Fourcaud) deserves its reputation, and here we have a mélodie which could only have been written by Franck, its prelude sounding like an organ improvisation. It needs a fine singer, able to meet the demands of the composer, who requires a musical and vocal presence that grows throughout the song, riding the increasingly full accompaniment to elevating effect. This mélodie was later orchestrated by Guy Ropartz. Another song in the same style, this time openly religious, is *La procession* (Brizeux, 1888), a work which was originally written for voice and orchestra, but which works well enough with piano, providing the singer has the inner conviction to carry off the poem about the progress of the Host as it is carried across the fields. Here we even find the use of fugato techniques, and the left hand of the piano, at the entry of the voice, quotes the Lauda Sion chant. The final section shows the composer at his most typical, the whole song takes off into religious ether, flooded with emotion in a way that can sound uplifting or ridiculous, depending on one's cast of mind. Of the composer's own belief in this imagery there is not a shadow of a doubt, nor about the open-hearted personality which made so many different people love and revere him. Not surprisingly, there is a version of this song for voice and organ.

After this, the very last song *Les cloches du soir* (1888, Desbordes-Valmore) is something of a disappointment. The piano writing seems to have been conceived for organ in the first place, and it has the facile emotional tone of late Gounod (the grandly rhetorical 'Pense à moi!' is almost embarrassing). It seems that Franck teetered on the borders of this slightly kitsch style from time to time, but his best songs are saved from that by the force of his personality and musicality, rather than by his feeling for poetry. Indeed, on more than one occasion, it is his choice of texts which scuppers him.

The six duos of 1887–9 are very simple in character although some of the poetry is by interesting writers—Daudet, Desbordes-Valmore, and the composer Guy Ropartz, a Franck pupil of course. We hear, not without pleasure, gentle harmonic turns of phrase and a mood of seraphic contentment which could only have emanated from Franck himself. Of these duets *Les danses de Lormont* (Daudet) and *Soleil* (Ropartz) are the most lively because the least religious, but *La vierge à la crèche* (Daudet) has proved its worth in recital programmes with a Christmas theme.

1 *Le mariage des roses*
  (Eugène David)

Mignonne, sais-tu comment
S'épousent les roses?
Ah! cet hymen est charmant!
Quelles tendres choses
Elles disent en ouvrant
Leurs paupières closes!
Mignonne, sais-tu comment
S'épousent les roses?

Elles disent: aimons-nous!
Si courte est la vie!
Ayons les baisers plus doux,
L'âme plus ravie!
Pendant que l'homme à genoux
Doute, espère ou prie,
Ô mes sœurs, embrassons-nous!
Si courte est la vie!

The marriage of roses

My sweet, do you know how
Roses wed?
Ah! how charming their marriage is!
What tender things
They say, on opening
Their closed eyelids!
My sweet, do you know how
Roses wed?

They say: Let us love each other!
Life is so short!
Let our kisses be sweeter still,
Our souls still more enraptured!
While man on his knees
Doubts, hopes or prays,
O my sisters, let us embrace!
Life is so short!

Croix-moi, mignonne, croix-moi,
Aimons-nous comme elles,
Vois, le printemps vient à toi
Et des hirondelles.
Aimer est l'unique loi,
À leurs nids fidèles.
Ô ma reine, suis ton roi,
Aimons-nous comme elles!

Excepté d'avoir aimé,
Qu'est-il donc sur terre?
Notre horizon est fermé,
Ombre, nuit, mystère!
Un seul phare est allumé,
L'amour nous l'éclaire,
Excepté d'avoir aimé,
Qu'est-il donc sur terre?

Believe me, my sweet, believe me,
Let us love each other as they do,
Look, spring approaches
And swallows too.
To love is the only law
In their faithful nests.
O my queen, follow your king,
Let us love each other as they do!

Apart from having loved,
What else is there on earth?
Our horizon is closed:
Shadow, night, mystery!
One beacon alone is lit,
Lit for us by love.
Apart from having loved,
What else is there on earth?

2 *Nocturne*
(Louis de Fourcaud)

Nocturne

Ô fraîche nuit, nuit transparente,
Mystère sans obscurité,
La vie est noire et dévorante,
Ô fraîche nuit, nuit transparente,
Donne-moi ta placidité.

Ô belle nuit, nuit étoilée,
Vers moi tes regards sont baissés,
Éclaire mon âme troublée,
Ô belle nuit, nuit étoilée,
Mets ton sourire en mes pensers.

Ô sainte nuit, nuit taciturne,
Pleine de paix et de douceur,
Mon cœur bouillonne comme une urne,
Ô sainte nuit, nuit taciturne,
Fais le silence dans mon cœur.

Ô grande nuit, nuit solennelle,
En qui tout est délicieux,
Prends mon être entier sous ton aile,
Ô grande nuit, nuit solennelle,
Verse le sommeil en mes yeux.

O cool night, translucent night,
Mystery without obscurity,
Life is black and life devours,
O cool night, translucent night,
Give me your serenity.

O lovely night, starlit night,
You look down upon me,
Shine your light in my troubled soul,
O lovely night, starlit night,
Light up my thoughts with your smile.

O holy night, silent night,
Full of peace and gentleness,
My heart is seething like a cauldron,
O holy night, silent night,
Bring silence to my heart.

O vast night, solemn night,
Where all things give delight,
Take my whole being beneath your wing,
O vast night, solemn night,
Pour sleep into my eyes.

3 *La procession*

(Auguste Brizeux)

Dieu s'avance à travers les champs!
Par les landes, les prés, les verts taillis de hêtres,
Il vient, suivi du peuple et porté par les prêtres:

Aux cantiques de l'homme, oiseaux, mêlez vos chants!
On s'arrête. La foule autour d'un chêne antique
S'incline, en adorant, sous l'ostensoir mystique:
Soleil, darde sur lui tes longs rayons couchants!
Aux cantiques de l'homme, oiseaux, mêlez vos chants!
Vous, fleurs, avec l'encens exhalez votre arome!
Ô fête! tout reluit, tout prie et tout embaume!
Dieu s'avance à travers les champs.

The procession

God advances across the fields!
Across heath, meadow, and green beech-copse,
He is followed by the people, borne aloft by the
priests:

Mingle your songs, O birds, with the hymns of man!
They halt. The crowd around an ancient oak
Bows in worship beneath the mystic monstrance:
Beam on it, O sun, your long sunset rays!
Mingle your songs, O birds, with the hymns of man!
O flowers, shed your fragrance with the incense!
O festival! All is light, is prayer, is fragrance!
God advances across the fields.

FREITAS BRANCO, Luis de (1890–1955)

This composer was of great significance in the evolution of the cultural life of Portugal. He is normally credited with bringing that country into the twentieth century in terms of musical taste. His songs in French belong to the early part of his career, and the TRILOGIE DE LA MORT (1909) is an astounding achievement for a young composer who had not yet travelled abroad to study (he later worked with Humperdinck and Grovlez). It is a brave man who sets poems of this kind (Baudelaire's *La mort des amants* [DEBUSSY 7 v], *La mort des pauvres*, and *La mort des artistes*) but Freitas brings it off with sincerity and a real melodic gift. More distinguished composers of French birth have stumbled with texts like these, but Freitas keeps the music simple and broad and achieves a real impressionist atmosphere. In 1909 he composed two further Baudelaire songs: *Recueillement* [DEBUSSY 7 iv] and *Élévation*. There is also a set of three Maeterlinck songs, the CICLO MAETERLINCKIANO, as well as an atonal Mallarmé cycle from the same year, 1913. (Freitas was in good company with Ravel and Debussy who also set the poet at precisely this time.) The composer went on to set a great deal of distinguished Portuguese poetry—Camões, Quental, and so on.

GEORGES, Alexandre (1850–1938)

Who today remembers this composer, and his once famous CHANSONS DE MIARKA? These settings of Jean Richepin (they come from a much longer novel) were 'some of the most beautiful of modern French songs' according to *Grove 5*. This is an exaggeration certainly, but the composer does not even figure in the pages of *Grove 6*, and Miarka, the gypsy child from the Thiérache region of northern France, disappears without a trace. The songs from 1899 were part of a vogue for the music of the people, the wave of naturalism that swept through French art as an antidote to *décadence*.

Georges was quite distinguished as a composer of incidental music for the theatre and he also wrote a number of fairly successful operas and oratorios. But the prevalence of MIARKA songs in every second-hand music shop in France shows that this music was wildly popular at about the same time as settings from Kipling's *Jungle book* fascinated a public tired of perfumed high art, and in the mood for a touch of ethnic stiffening in their musical diet. At the same time folksong collectors were busy throughout Europe, and it would not be long before Janáček wrote of the gypsy girl Zefka, Miarka's distant cousin, in his *Diary of one who disappeared*. There are other songs by Georges in a nationalist vein, notably the LÉGENDES NORVÉGIENNES. Of the fourteen songs in the MIARKA set, the most popular were *Hymne au soleil* and *La pluie*, anthologized in American editions. Some of the songs require a chorus of 'Romany' tenors. The poem *L'eau qui coule* was set by Honegger in 1937 under the title *Chanson de l'eau* as part of the music for a film on the Miarka story. Of Georges's other songs, the *Gavotte du masque* (Montjoyeux) is an effective dance in the antique style.

GODARD, Benjamin (1849–1895)

This composer of incidental music and orchestral pieces is best remembered today for the *Berceuse* from *Jocelyn*, one of his six not very successful operas. It is a small-scale piece in the midst of a rather unwieldy work and Godard, great admirer and emulator of Schumann, is at his best when least ambitious. His songs, which number a hundred or more, enjoyed a great vogue in the years leading up to the turn of the century. Perhaps the most wide-ranging of Godard's mélodie projects was a twelve-song cycle entitled CHANSONS DES MOIS. His anthology of poetry for this set includes Coppée and Grandmougin (poet of Fauré's POÈME D'UN JOUR), but the most distinguished text is *Le temps a laissié son manteau* of Charles d'Orléans [DEBUSSY 12 i], which Godard calls *Chanson d'avril*. There are other interesting parallel settings with well-known masterpieces: Godard had the temerity to compose a *L'invitation au voyage* [DUPARC 7], a rather charming setting of the Gautier *Les papillons* [CHAUSSON 3], as well as an under-powered *La captive* [BERLIOZ 6]. There is however a cheekily attractive version of Hugo's *Guitare* [BIZET 2]. His SIX FABLES DE LA FONTAINE include a *La cigale et la fourmi* and *Le corbeau et le renard* [CAPLET 3 ii, 3 i] as well as four other fables less frequently set. Apart from the *Berceuse* from *Jocelyn*, Godard's most famous song is probably the **Chanson d'Estelle** (also known as *Chanson de Florian*), a haunting little bergerette, much ennobled long ago by a recording with Maggie Teyte and Gerald Moore. There are several other Florian songs in the same vein, and some good Hugo settings (*Je ne veux pas d'autres choses*, *Contemplation*, and *Viens!*, the last set by Saint-Saëns and Caplet, among others [CAPLET 4]). He was also inclined to set his own poems to music (*Fleur d'exil* and *Chanson arabe*) from time to time. Godard found considerable favour in the world of late Victorian music-making, and several contemporary English editions of the songs testify to this. His works abound in the sort of grateful charm which was once in vogue, then became very unfashionable, and now seems once again interesting—indeed, music of this kind is now probably overvalued (certainly in Paris's second-hand music stores) because of its rarity, and the elegance of its *fin-de-siècle* overtones. We are no doubt soon due for a Godard revival.

1 *Chanson d'Estelle*

(Jean-Pierre Claris de Florian)

Ah! s'il est dans votre village
Un berger sensible et charmant,
Qu'on chérisse au premier moment,
Qu'on aime ensuite d'avantage,
C'est mon ami: rendez-le-moi;
J'ai son amour, il a ma foi.

Si par sa voix tendre et plaintive
Il charme l'écho de vos bois,
Si les accents de son hautbois
Rendent la bergère pensive,
C'est encore lui: rendez-le-moi;
J'ai son amour, il a ma foi.

Si, passant près de sa chaumière,
Le pauvre, en voyant son troupeau,
Ose demander un agneau,
Et qu'il obtienne encor la mère;
Oh! c'est bien lui: rendez-le-moi;
J'ai son amour, il a ma foi.

Estelle's song

Ah! if there is in your village
A shepherd, tender and charming,
Cherished by all at first sight,
And afterwards loved even more—
That is my friend, return him to me;
I have his love and he my faith.

If with his gentle, plaintive voice
He charms the echo from your woods,
If the playing of his hautboy
Turns the shepherdess to musing—
That is also him, return him to me;
I have his love and he my faith.

If, passing close by his cottage,
A poor man, seeing his flock,
Dares to beg for a lamb
And is given the ewe as well—
Oh! that must be him, return him to me;
I have his love and he my faith.

GOUNOD, Charles (1818–1893)

Ravel dubbed Gounod 'the true founder of the *mélodie* in France'. This question of paternity would be hotly contested by Berlioz partisans whose hero was undoubtedly a greater visionary and pioneer, not to mention composer. But Gounod succeeded in one important respect where a more revolutionary spirit failed: he built bridges between the past and the future rather than burning them. He entertained the French bourgeoisie, but at the same time composed music which was a significant advance on what had gone before in terms of word-setting and harmony. Gounod's gift for singable melody enabled him to smuggle the art song—a high-born and demanding infant—into the homes and hearts of the French middle class where operatic airs, operetta, romance, and chansonnette had previously held sway. Audiences began to judge vocal music in terms of its expressive subtlety rather than as a mere vehicle for a performer's virtuosity. Although he was not the first to effect a civilized marriage between text and music, Gounod's role was to show how poetry and music, and vocal line and accompaniment, could all gracefully interact on a level hitherto only found in the German lied. He acknowledged his debt to Schubert (a composer popular in Paris thanks to the performances of Adolphe Nourrit) by fashioning independently interesting piano parts for his songs, and also by recognizing that even the most beguiling melodies were only the starting point when it came to the overall craft of song composition and performance. The quality of poetry was also taken to be an important factor in this marriage of word and tone, and of the inherited romance and the acquired lied. The child of this union was of enduring beauty; if Gounod was not its parent he was largely responsible for its upbringing.

Gounod himself was born to cultivated parents; his father was a painter and his mother a pianist, and he inherited gifts from both sides. The easy and brilliant progress of his student years and his effortless winning of the Prix de Rome in 1839 are early warning signs of the suave facility which was to characterize a great deal of his output. He was a talented enough painter for Ingres (then director of the Villa Medici in Rome) to offer him an artist's scholarship. There was the soft-grained streak of the dilettante in Gounod's character, and a willingness to please, which at its best produced work which delighted audiences and performers alike, but at its worst encouraged indecisiveness and weakness. In his youth he was human blotting paper, soaking up artistic impressions of Italy: the music of Palestrina inspired a lifelong vocation for religious music. Like Liszt, he was also tempted to enter the priesthood; he lacked the Hungarian's fiery temperament, but both composers were prone to outbursts of piety which inspired their followers, and were dismissed as humbug by their detractors. The people Gounod met in Rome were to influence him for the rest of his life. One of these was Fanny Hensel, Felix Mendelssohn's sister, who introduced him to lieder (her own and her brother's) and the masterpieces of German literature, including Goethe. This was to result some years later in the composition of the celebrated opera *Faust*. After leaving Rome, Gounod travelled to Vienna and to Leipzig where he met Mendelssohn himself. During this period, before he had established his operatic reputation and at the same time that Schumann was producing his greatest songs, Gounod wrote some of the mélodies still considered to be among his very best—*Où voulez-vous aller?* (Gautier, 1839), already set by Berlioz in LES NUITS D'ÉTÉ [BERLIOZ 3 vi], and the astonishingly evocative *Venise* (Musset, 1842) with its turbulent interludes painting that city's ability both to intoxicate and disturb. Two extended songs demonstrate the composer's ability to grapple with the large poetic constructions of Lamartine (despite cutting certain strophes); indeed it would be true to say that this poet has never been better set than in *Le vallon* and *Le soir* (both 1840–2) as well as the touching *Au rossignol*. In these imposing songs we are moved by the religious spaciousness of Gounod's music, here without the sentimentality which would mar some of the later work on metaphysical themes. The famous *Ave Maria* (1852) was also a Lamartine setting at first ('Le livre de la vie est le livre suprême'). It was only in 1859 that the composer adapted the song, first rather clumsily to the Latin text, and then to a French paraphrase of the prayer.

Most of the songs of Gounod were published in six volumes of twenty songs each—four *recueils* by Choudens and two by Lemoine. In the broadest terms the first Choudens volume (perhaps the most useful for the singer of today) contains songs from the 1840s and early 1850s; Volume 2 has songs from the middle 1860s; Volume 3, published after Gounod's three-year-long visit to England, contains the songs from the early 1870s (an exception to this is *Où voulez-vous aller?*—the earliest of the Gounod mélodies). This *recueil* also includes a number of songs composed outside France, and originally in English. Volume 4 of the Choudens collection is almost entirely given over to extracts from the operas. The two Lemoine volumes contain music written between 1871 and 1887, and could safely be said to contain most of the composer's later songs. The list of the poets on the title pages makes fascinating reading, with the earlier volumes showing a higher class of poetic collaborator than the later. In the first Choudens *recueil* for example we see a line-up of Victor Hugo (*Aubade,* the immortal *Sérénade*), Alfred de Musset, Théodore de Banville, and La Fontaine. Gounod's

Lamartine settings were influenced by Louis Niedermeyer: *Le lac* in particular (1821), which has the reputation as the first serious French song; Béranger is a survivor from the days of the romance and chanson, also set by Schumann in *Die Kartenlegerin*; settings of Baïf (***O ma belle rebelle***) and Passerat (***Le premier jour de mai***) show the composer's interest in sixteenth-century poetry and in the use of pastiche 'madrigal' style which was to remain an expressive device for Bizet, Fauré, and Reynaldo Hahn—as well as for Debussy, Ravel, and Poulenc. On the other hand, the later Choudens volumes, apart from a single item from Gautier, show a falling off of literary merit with the increasing appearance of names of men of the theatre such as Émile Augier, and Gounod's faithful librettist Jules Barbier, who became a type of poet and translator-in-residence for the composer. Charming songs are always to be found however: ***Envoi de fleurs, Mignon*** (Gallet, fashioned after Goethe's *Kennst du das Land*), the surgingly energetic ***Chanson de printemps*** (Tourneux), *Ce que je suis sans toi* (Peyre), and so on.

As one turns the pages of these volumes, increasingly filled with extracts from opera and oratorio, it is clear that Gounod's multifarious efforts in the theatre, concert hall, and church increased his sense of artistic mission and self-importance. So much the worse for the mélodie. He had begun his career in the early days of romanticism as a songwriter in the reign of Louis Philippe, but he achieved his greatest operatic successes during the Second Empire, a heavily ornate and artificial era geared to the success of ambitious enterprises instantly grateful to ear and eye. In this period when the operettas of Offenbach and the musical *spectacles* of Meyerbeer were the touchstones of achievement, the uncomplicated sunlight we can feel in the younger man's earlier songs was gradually shut out by the velvet curtains and plush of imperial decadence. This is gradually evident if one sits down to play through the Gounod songs at a sitting. At first the undertaking is unalloyed delight. One is knocked sideways by Gounod's melodic genius, his talent for creating long flowing lines (only surpassed by Fauré), and his instinct for the *harmonie juste*. There is no one else gifted in precisely the same way in the whole genre of French song, and it is here that a comparison comes to mind with his friend Mendelssohn, whose earlier songs also seem more lively and inspired than those of the final years. The more one looks into their later works, one feels that the two composers were not improved by the demands and trappings of fame, and that in both their cases the idolization of the British public was a mixed blessing; both seemed to have adopted a style suitable for the pomposities of gigantic music festivals. Gounod's innate religiosity, which always chimed well with the atmosphere in mid-Victorian England, further encouraged him to see himself as the musical mouthpiece of the age. The seraphic complacency, sentimentality, and overblown emotional tone of some of Gounod's later songs seems to have nothing to do with the flexible and ingenious creations of his twenties and thirties. The freshness of his earlier songwriting years was lost as his music aimed to be significant and sublime, qualities which it could rarely achieve, and never when the composer set out to make a 'pronouncement'. The delicate balance between form and content which is always faultless in the best melodies was increasingly undermined by the same sort of 'grand old man' utterances which rendered the later work of Victor Hugo ponderous in comparison to the earlier writings. It is usually the choice of words which sets the seal on a work's fate. I found the experience of encountering Gounod *en masse* similar to that of playing through the twelve volumes of Parry's *English Lyrics*, where wonderful songs stand shoulder to shoulder with lost causes—good musical ideas are wasted on impossibly portentous poems of an exaltedly religious bent. A song is almost always tied to its poem, and a bad text, hopelessly dated by the facile fervour of another age, can easily drag the music down with it to oblivion.

It is sad that the composer fell into this trap of platitudinous pomposity which marginalizes his place in the French song history of the 1870s and 1880s. In his earlier music, however, we encounter for the first time in the mélodie those qualities of elegance, ingenuity, *sensibilité*, and a concern for literature which together constitute the classic qualities of French song. Gounod's debt to the Germans was a subtle one, and unlike later composers such as Duparc and Chausson there was no Wagner in his pantheon; he was French through and through, although there is no doubt that his broad knowledge of music from other countries and epochs deepened his expressive scope. His influence is to be heard in the songs of Bizet, Saint-Saëns, Fauré, Massenet, and countless others. Satie was to quote him in affectionate parody in *Le chapelier*, and the composers of Les Six admired him (albeit 'self-consciously and as an amusing paradox' as Martin Cooper put it) for his melodic gift and charm of utterance.

The Franco-Prussian War of 1870 marked the watershed in Gounod's creative life. He fled to England and remained there long after his wife returned home. He became caught up in the affairs of the redoubtable singer Mrs Georgina Weldon who ran a girls' orphanage in Tavistock Square in which all the inmates were to be trained to sing; she determined to have Gounod as composer-in-residence for her troupe. His biddable behaviour caused him to be managed, not to mention bullied, by the powerful and increasingly unhinged termagant who regarded Gounod as 'my old man' and who deserves a chapter to herself in a book of English eccentrics. The significance of this sorry episode is that Gounod wrote over sixty songs to English texts which have become virtually a lost part of his legacy. When he returned to France in 1874 his relationships with his English publishers were in tatters, largely thanks to Mrs Weldon. As a conciliatory gesture to his wife he composed an apology in music—the beautiful *L'absent* (1876), one of only two mélodies to his own text (the other is *À la nuit* of 1891). He asked the ever co-operative Barbier and others to set new French words, *post facto*, to these works without acknowledging their original English sources—the English publishers had already paid him (or Mrs Weldon) for the music. Thus it is that words by Byron, Kingsley, Shelley, and lesser Victorian poets are to be found in the *recueils* of Gounod's songs in translation and without reference to their English origins. Two of these appear in the third Choudens collection, and others in the first volume of the Lemoine collection; for example, the celebrated *Viens, les gazons sont verts* (Barbier) started life as *If thou art sleeping, maiden*. In setting this and other poems by Longfellow, Gounod achieved even an American dimension to his songwriting career. In the second Lemoine *recueil* there is a French translation of Byron's celebrated *Maid of Athens* which Hahn later recorded in his delightfully accented English. Although these pieces lie outside the scope of this study, the English-speaking singer will find them well worth investigating—a footnote in the history of the mélodie that is a crucial and fascinating part of the history of Victorian song in England. Judged by the standards of the English composers of the time, Gounod's works shine with daring individuality. His setting of Fred Weatherley's *The worker* (*L'ouvrier* in Lemoine) is a ballad in the English tradition, but superior to almost all the home-grown products of the day. Also outside the scope of this book is Gounod's only song cycle BIONDINA, a set of twelve Italian songs which was strangely enough also composed in England, some thirty years after his residence in Italy. (There are one or two other Italian settings in Lemoine, including the delectable *Quanti mai*.)

Unsurprisingly for an accomplished opera composer, Gounod was also a fine composer of duets, part of his output which is seldom heard in the concert hall. There are two works from the 1850s, comic scenes both, for tenor and baritone: *Deux vieux amis* and *Les châteaux en Espagne*, the castles-in-the-air ambitions of a painter and musician worthy of Puccini's *La bohème*. The majority of the later duets were written during the composer's English sojourn, and reflect the prevailing taste for soprano and contralto (Mrs Weldon's young charges no doubt) joining forces in the drawing room. Apart from settings in English of Palgrave and Wordsworth, these include the expansive *D'un cœur qui t'aime* (Racine, 1872) of which Fauré might have been proud in his more devout moments, and *La siesta*, a delectable Spanish concoction, also singable in French under the title *Sous les feuillages*.

The singer and accompanist of today can still find much in the mélodies of Gounod to captivate their audiences, although performers must be warned that there is no such thing as an easy Gounod song. It is true that the works are very largely strophic and that the vocal lines are memorable and not spiked with enormous learning difficulties, but the singer has to have an impeccable legato with marvellous breath control, and the deft piano writing requires a lightness of touch and a variety of colour—always a necessity in the performing of strophic songs. Like the songs of Schubert, Gounod's mélodies stand halfway between the world of classicism and romanticism. The use of rubato is tempered by a certain *chasteté* and respect for classical shape; the most melting moments in the music are reserved for certain magical modulations and harmonic changes—another affinity with Schubert whose self-effacing *pudeur* in gentle serenades and lullabies as well as songs about children is instinctively emulated by Gounod. It is in this mood of gently contained inward rapture that Gounod can achieve incomparable things. Much of the music is impeccably 'stylish', but on the other hand there are moments where a self-conscious posture is struck as the music shifts its gaze in the direction of the opera house and in the interests of unashamed emotional manipulation. These extremes represent the struggle between two strong sides of the composer's nature, and between two different types of romantic expression—one of which is natural and believable, and the other which seems bogus by today's standards. The skill and taste of the performers can help the composer enormously here, and make all the difference between a moving rendition and a send-up. The worst of the Gounod songs are as bombastic or sanctimonious as the age in which they were written, but the best have an inimitable quality of ingenuity and unforced delight. There is a musical and emotional transparency of texture about them, an air of innocence, which was to delight Poulenc's generation and which continues to delight us. Even if we feel that he was a composer who lost his way, there is no denying that there are at least twenty songs by Gounod without which the French song repertoire would be infinitely the poorer.

1 *Venise*

(Alfred de Musset)

Dans Venise la rouge,
Pas un bateau qui bouge,
Pas un pêcheur dans l'eau,
    Pas un falot.

Venice

In Venice the red,
Not a boat that stirs,
Not a fisherman afloat,
    Not a lantern.

La lune qui s'efface
Couvre son front qui passe
D'un nuage étoilé
　　Demi-voilé.

Tout se tait, fors les gardes
Aux longues hallebardes,
Qui veillent aux créneaux
　　Des arsenaux.

—Ah! maintenant plus d'une
Attend, au clair de lune,
Quelque jeune muguet,
　　L'oreille au guet.

Sous la brise amoureuse
La Vanina rêveuse
Dans son berceau flottant
　　Passe en chantant;

Tandis que pour la fête
Narcisse qui s'apprête,
Met, devant son miroir,
　　Le masque noir.

Laissons la vieille horloge,
Au palais du vieux doge,
Lui conter de ses nuits
　　Les longs ennuis.

Sur sa mer nonchalante,
Venise l'indolente
Ne compte ni ses jours
　　Ni ses amours.

Car Venise est si belle
Qu'une chaîne, sur elle
Semble un collier jeté
　　Sur la beauté.

The waning moon
Hides its fading face
With a starlit cloud,
　　Half-veiled.

All is silent, save the guards
With long halberds,
Keeping watch on the battlements
　　Of the Arsenal.*

Ah! More than one girl
Now waits in the moonlight
For some young gallant,
　　Keenly listening.

Beneath the amorous breeze,
Dreamy Vanina,
Cradled in her gondola
　　Glides singing by.

While for the carnival
Narcissus puts on
Before his mirror
　　The black mask.

Let us leave the old clock
In the old Doge's Palace
To count
　　The tedium of long nights.

On her nonchalant sea,
Indolent Venice
Counts neither her days
　　Nor her loves.

For Venice is so fair
That a chain on her
Seems like a necklace, thrown round
　　Beauty itself.

2 *Le vallon*

(Alphonse de Lamartine)

The valley

Mon cœur, lassé de tout, même de l'espérance,
N'ira plus de ses vœux importuner le sort;
Prêtez-moi seulement, vallons de mon enfance,
Un asile d'un jour pour attendre la mort.

My heart, wearied of all things, even of hope,
No more shall trouble fate with its desires;
Grant me, valleys of my childhood,
One day's refuge to wait for death.

* From the Arabic *darsina' a*—a house of industry. From 1155 onwards, all the galleys of the Republic were built in this dockyard.

D'ici je vois la vie, à travers un nuage,
S'évanouir pour moi dans l'ombre du passé;
L'amour seul est resté: comme une grande image
Survit seule au réveil dans un songe effacé.

Repose-toi, mon âme, en ce dernier asile,
Ainsi qu'un voyageur, qui, le cœur plein d'espoir,
S'assied avant d'entrer aux portes de la ville,
Et respire un moment l'air embaumé du soir.

Tes jours, tristes et courts comme des jours
        d'automne,
Déclinent comme l'ombre au penchant des coteaux;
L'amitié te trahit, la pitié t'abandonne,
Et, seule, tu descends le sentier des tombeaux.

Mais la nature est là qui t'invite et qui t'aime;
Plonge-toi dans son sein qu'elle t'ouvre toujours;
Quand tout change pour toi, la nature est la même,
Et le même soleil se lève sur tes jours.

From here I can see life, across a cloud,
Vanish for me in the darkness of the past;
Love alone has remained—as a great image
Alone survives our waking from a vanished dream.

Rest, my soul, in this final refuge,
Like a traveller who, his heart full of hope,
Sits down before entering the city gates
And breathes for a moment the sweet evening air.

Your days, sad and brief, like autumn days,

Draw in like darkness on the hills;
Friends betray you, compassion deserts you,
And you walk, alone, along the tomb-lined path.

But nature is there, inviting and loving,
Immerse yourself in its ever-open heart;
Though your life change, nature stays the same,
And the same sun rises on your days.

3 *Le soir*

(Alphonse de Lamartine)

Le soir ramène le silence.
Assis sur ces rochers déserts,
Je suis dans le vague des airs
Le char de la nuit qui s'avance.

Vénus se lève à l'horizon;
À mes pieds l'étoile amoureuse
De sa lueur mystérieuse
Blanchit les tapis de gazon.

Tout à coup détaché des cieux,
Un rayon de l'astre nocturne,
Glissant sur mon front taciturne,
Vient mollement toucher mes yeux.

Doux reflet d'un globe de flamme,
Charmant rayon, que me veux-tu?
Viens-tu dans mon sein abattu
Porter la lumière à mon âme?

Descends-tu pour me révéler
Des mondes le divin mystère?
Ces secrets cachés dans la sphère
Où le jour va te rappeler?

Evening

Evening brings silence.
Seated on these lonely rocks
I follow in the vacant air
The chariot of approaching night.

Venus rises above the horizon;
At my feet the star of love
With her mysterious light
Whitens the carpets of lawn.

Suddenly from the heavens
A beam from the evening star,
Gliding across my solemn face,
Softly comes to touch my eyes.

Sweet reflection of a ball of flame,
Charming ray, what is your wish?
Are you come to my despondent heart
To illuminate my soul?

Are you come down to show me
The divine mystery of the world?
Those secrets hidden in the sphere
To which day will recall you?

Viens-tu dévoiler l'avenir
Au cœur fatigué qui t'implore?
Rayon divin, es-tu l'aurore
Du jour qui ne doit pas finir?

Are you come to disclose the future
To this tired heart which implores you?
Divine gleam, are you the dawn
Of the day that has no end?

4 *Au rossignol*

(Alphonse de Lamartine)

To the nightingale

Quand ta voix céleste prélude
Aux silences des belles nuits,
Barde ailé de ma solitude,
Tu ne sais pas que je te suis!

When your heavenly voice ushers in
The silence of the lovely nights,
You are unaware, winged bard
Of my solitude, that I follow you!

Tu ne sais pas que mon oreille,
Suspendue à ta douce voix,
De l'harmonieuse merveille
S'enivre longtemps sous les bois!

You are unaware that my ear,
Spellbound by your gentle voice,
Has revelled for long beneath the trees
In the miracle of your melody!

Tu ne sais pas que mon haleine
Sur mes lèvres n'ose passer,
Que mon pied muet foule à peine
La feuille qu'il craint de froisser!

You are unaware that my breath
Does not dare to pass my lips,
That my soundless feet scarcely tread
The leaves they fear to crush!

Ah! ta voix touchante ou sublime
Est trop pure pour ce bas lieu!
Cette musique qui t'anime
Est un instinct qui monte à Dieu!

Ah! Your voice, touching or sublime,
Is too pure for this base earth!
This music which inspires you
Is an impulse that soars to God!

Tu prends les sons que tu recueilles
Dans les gazouillements des flots,
Dans les frémissements des feuilles,
Dans les bruits mourants des échos,

You gather your melodies
From the murmuring of the waves,
From the rustling of the leaves,
From the echoes' dying cadences,

Et de ces doux sons où se mêle
L'instinct céleste qui t'instruit,
Dieu fit ta voix, ô Philomèle!
Et tu fais ton hymne à la nuit!

And from these sweet sounds, mingled
With the heavenly instinct that instructs you,
God fashioned your voice, O Philomel!
And you sing your hymn to the night!

Ah! ces douces scènes nocturnes,
Ces pieux mystères du soir,
Et ces fleurs qui penchent leurs urnes
Comme l'urne d'un encensoir,

Ah, these sweet nocturnal scenes,
These divine mysteries of evening,
And these flowers which incline their heads
Like a censer's urn,

Et cette voix mystérieuse
Qu'écoutent les anges et moi,
Ce soupir de la nuit pieuse,
Oiseau mélodieux, c'est toi!

And this mysterious voice
That I with angels listen to,
This sigh of divine night—
All this, melodious bird, is you!

Oh! mêle ta voix à la mienne!
La même oreille nous entend;
Mais ta prière aérienne
Monte mieux au ciel qui l'attend!

Ah, mingle your voice with mine!
The same ear hears us both;
But your aerial prayer
Climbs better to heaven which awaits it!

5 *Aubade*

(Victor Hugo)

L'aube naît, et ta porte est close!
Ma belle, ah! pourquoi sommeiller?
À l'heure où s'éveille la rose
Ne vas-tu pas te réveiller?

> Ô ma charmante,
> Écoute ici
> L'amant qui chante
> Et pleure aussi!

Tout frappe à ta porte bénie.
L'aurore dit: Je suis le jour!
L'oiseau dit: Je suis l'harmonie!
Et moi je dis: Je suis l'amour!

> Ô ma charmante,
> Écoute ici
> L'amant qui chante
> Et pleure aussi!

Aubade

Dawn breaks, and your door is closed!
O sweet, why do you sleep?
At the hour when the rose awakes,
Will you not also waken?

> O my dearest,
> Listen to your lover
> Singing here
> And weeping too!

All things knock at your sacred door.
Dawn says: I am the day!
Birds say: I am harmony!
And I say: I am love!

> O my dearest,
> Listen to your lover
> Singing here
> And weeping too!

6 *Sérénade*

(Victor Hugo)

Quand tu chantes, bercée
Le soir entre mes bras,
Entends-tu ma pensée
Qui te répond tout bas?
Ton doux chant me rappelle
Les plus beaux de mes jours...—
    Ah! chantez, ma belle,
    Chantez toujours!

Quand tu ris, sur ta bouche
L'amour s'épanouit,
Et soudain le farouche
Soupçon s'évanouit.

Serenade

When you sing, cradled
In my arms at evening,
Do you hear my thoughts
Softly answering you?
Your sweet song recalls
The loveliest days of my life...
    Ah! sing, my fair one,
    Sing on!

When you laugh, your lips
Blossom with love,
And instantly, wild
Suspicion vanishes.

Ah! le rire fidèle
Prouve un cœur sans détours...—
   Ah! riez, ma belle,
   Riez toujours!

Quand tu dors, calme et pure,
Dans l'ombre, sous mes yeux,
Ton haleine murmure
Des mots harmonieux.
Ton beau corps se révèle
Sans voile et sans atours...—
   Ah! dormez, ma belle,
   Dormez toujours!

Ah! That faithful laughter
Shows a sincere heart...
   Ah! laugh, my fair one,
   Laugh on!

When you sleep, calm and pure,
In the shade beneath my gaze,
Your breath murmurs
Melodious words.
Your body is revealed in its beauty
Without veil or finery...
   Ah! sleep, my fair one,
   Sleep on!

7 *O ma belle rebelle*

(Jean-Antoine de Baïf)

O my rebellious belle

O ma belle rebelle,
Las! que tu m'es cruelle!
Ou quand d'un doux souris,
Larron de mes espris,
Ou quand d'une parolle
Mignardetement molle,
Ou quand d'un regard d'yeux
Fierement gracieux,
Ou quand d'un petit geste,
Tout divin, tout celeste,
En amoureuse ardeur
Tu plonges tout mon cœur.
   O ma belle rebelle,
Las! que tu m'es cruelle!
Quand la cuisante ardeur
Qui me brusle le cœur
Fait que je te demande
A sa bruslure grande
Un rafraichissement
D'un baiser seulement!
   O ma belle rebelle,
Las! que tu m'es cruelle!
Quand d'un petit baiser
Tu ne veux m'apaiser.
Me puissé-je un jour, dure,
Vanger de ton injure,
Mon petit maistre Amour
Te puisse outrer un jour!
Et pour moy langoureuse
Il te face amoureuse,

O my rebellious belle,
Alas, how cruel you are,
When with a sweet smile
You steal my soul,
Or with a soft
Seductive word,
Or with a proud
And winning glance,
Or with a little gesture,
So heavenly and divine,
You plunge my heart
Into ardent rapture.
   O my rebellious belle,
Alas, how cruel you are,
When the burning desire
That consumes my heart
Compels me to beg of you
A single kiss
To quench
Its conflagration!
   O my rebellious belle!
Alas, how cruel you are,
When with a little kiss
You will not soothe me.
May I one day, O callous one,
Return the harm you caused me,
May my little master, Cupid,
Pierce your heart one day
And make you
Pine for me,

Comme il m'a langoureux
Pour toy fait amoureux!
Alors par ma vengeance
Tu auras connoissance
Quel mal fait, du baiser
Un amant refuser.

As he made me pine
With love for you!
By my revenge
You then shall know
The harm you cause
In refusing a lover a kiss.

8 *Le premier jour de mai*

(Jean Passerat)

May day

Laissons le lit et le sommeil
   Cette journée:
Pour nous l'Aurore au front vermeil
   Est déjà née.
Or que le ciel est le plus gai
En ce gracieux mois de mai,
   Aimons, mignonne;
Contentons notre ardent désir:
En ce monde n'a du plaisir
   Qui ne s'en donne.

Let us leave our beds and throw off sleep
   On this day,
For us the crimson dawn
   Has already broken.
Now the sky is at its brightest
In this kindly month of May,
   Let us love, my sweet!
Let us slake our ardent desire,
There's no pleasure in this world
   For those who do not yield to it.

Viens, belle, viens te promener
   Dans ce bocage,
Entends les oiseaux jargonner
   De leur ramage.
Mais écoute comme sur tous
Le rossignol est le plus doux,
   Sans qu'il se lasse.
Oublions tout deuil, tout ennui,
Pour nous réjouir comme lui:
   Le temps se passe.

Come, my fair one, and walk with me
   In these woods,
Listen to the birds warbling
   From their branches,
But hark how the nightingale
Sings sweetest of all,
   Without ever tiring.
Let us forget all grief and all ennui
And like her let us rejoice:
   Time passes.

Laissons les regrets et les pleurs
   À la vieillesse;
Jeunes, il faut cueillir les fleurs
   De la jeunesse.

Let us leave regret and tears
   Till we grow old.
When young, we must gather the flowers
   Of youth.

9 *Envoi de fleurs*

(Émile Augier)

A gift of flowers

Si l'on veut savoir qui m'envoie
Ces belles fleurs,
Elles me viennent d'où la joie
Et les douleurs,

If you would know who sends me
These beautiful flowers,
They come to me from where
Joy and sorrow dwell,

Elles me viennent d'où ma vie
Pend désormais,
De celle-là pour qui j'oublie
Ceux que j'aimais!

Si l'on cherche pourquoi je l'aime
À cet excès,
Hélas! je n'en sais rien moi-même,
Ce que je sais,
C'est que dans ses yeux on voit luire
Tout son esprit,
Et qu'au coin de son fin sourire
Mon cœur se prit!

Comme un oiseau qui s'effarouche,
Et fuit dans l'air,
Plus je le cherche sur sa bouche,
Plus il se perd.
C'est pourquoi celle qui m'envoie
Ces belles fleurs
Est celle d'où me vient la joie
Et les douleurs!

They come to me from one
On whom my life depends,
From her for whom I forget
All those that I once loved!

If you should wonder why I love her
So excessively,
Alas, myself, I do not know,
I only know
That in her eyes I see
Her whole spirit gleaming,
And that the corners of her pretty smile
Have carried off my heart!

Like a startled bird
That flies into the air,
The more I seek her smile,
The more it hides.
That is why she who sends me
These beautiful flowers
Is the cause of my joy
And my sorrow!

10 Mignon*

(Louis Gallet, after Goethe)

Mignon

Connais-tu le pays où dans l'immense plaine
Brille comme de l'or le fruit des orangers,
Où sous des cieux bénis une amoureuse haleine
Recueille et porte au loin le parfum des vergers?
Ce pays où le jour plus radieux se lève,
Le connais-tu, dis-moi, le connais-tu?
C'est là, mon bien-aimé, que m'emporte mon rêve!
Ah, c'est là!, c'est là! que je voudrais m'en aller avec
    toi!

Connais-tu la maison toute blanche et posée
Dans les bosquets de myrte aimés des papillons
Et les champs lumineux où la fraîche rosée
Sème ses diamants dans l'herbe des sillons?
Ce pays où le jour plus radieux se lève,
Le connais-tu, dis-moi, le connais-tu?
C'est là, mon bien-aimé, que m'emporte mon rêve!
Ah, c'est là!, c'est là! que je voudrais m'en aller avec
    toi!

Do you know the land, where in the vast plain
The fruit of the orange-trees gleam like gold,
Where beneath blest skies a loving breeze
Gathers the fragrance of orchards and wafts it away?
That land, where day more radiantly dawns,
Do you know it, O tell me, do you?
It is there, my love, that my dream transports me!
It is there that I would go with you!

Do you know the whitewashed house
Among thickets of myrtle that butterflies love,
And the translucent fields, where fresh dew
Strews diamonds in the grassy furrows?
That land, where day more radiantly dawns,
Do you know it, O tell me, do you?
It is there, my love, that my dream transports me!
It is there that I would go with you!

* See note to DUPARC 3.

11 *Chanson de printemps*

(Eugène Tourneux)

Viens, enfant, la terre s'éveille
Le soleil rit au gazon vert!
La fleur au calice entr'ouvert
Reçoit les baisers de l'abeille.
Respirons cet air pur!
Enivrons-nous d'azur!
Là-haut sur la colline,
Viens cueillir l'aubépine!
La neige des pommiers
Parfume les sentiers.

Viens, enfant, voici l'hirondelle
Qui passe en chantant dans les airs.
Ouvre ton âme aux frais concerts
Éclos sous la feuille nouvelle.
Un vent joyeux, là-bas,
Frémit dans les lilas,
C'est la saison bénie,
C'est l'amour, c'est la vie!
Qu'un fleuve de bonheur
Inonde notre cœur!

Viens, enfant, c'est l'heure charmante
Où l'on voudrait rêver à deux,
Mêlons nos rêves et nos vœux
Sous cette verdure naissante.
Salut, règne des fleurs,
Des parfums, des couleurs!
Les suaves haleines
Voltigent sur les plaines,
Le cœur épanoui
Se perd dans l'infini!

Spring song

Come, child, the earth's awakening,
The sun is smiling on the green grass!
With its calyx half-opened
The flower receives the bee's kiss.
Let us breathe this pure air!
Let us get drunk on blue sky!
Up there on the hill
Come let us gather hawthorn!
The snow of apple-trees
Fills the paths with fragrance.

Come, child, there's the swallow
Singing on the wing,
Open your soul to the fresh strains
Bursting from beneath young leaves.
A joyful wind over there
Rustles in the lilac,
It is the blest season,
It is love, it is life!
Let a stream of rapture
Flood our hearts!

Come, child, it is the charmed hour,
When we would dream together,
Let us mingle our dreams and our vows
Beneath this greening foliage.
Hail to the kingdom of flowers,
Of scent and colour!
Gentle breezes
Move over the plains,
The radiant heart
Loses itself in infinity!

12 *L'absent*

(Charles Gounod)

Ô silence des nuits dont la voix seule est douce,
Quand je n'ai plus sa voix,
Mystérieux rayons, qui glissez sur la mousse
Dans l'ombre de ses bois,

Dites-moi si ses yeux, à l'heure où tout sommeille
Se rouvrent doucement
Et si ma bien-aimée, alors que moi je veille,
Se souvient de l'absent.

The absent one

O silence of the nights, whose voice alone is sweet,
When I hear her voice no more,
Mysterious rays, that glide across the moss
In the shade of her woods—

Tell me if her eyes, at the hour when all are sleeping,
Once more gently open,
And if, as I lie awake, my beloved
Remembers the absent one.

Quand la lune est aux cieux, baignant de sa lumière
Les grands bois et l'azur;
Quand des cloches du soir qui tintent la prière
Vibre l'écho si pur,

Dites-moi si son âme, un instant recueillie,
S'élève avec leur chant,
Et si de leurs accords la paisible harmonie
Lui rappelle l'absent!

When the moon is in heaven, bathing in its light
The great woods and the sky,
When vesper bells, tolling for prayer,
Awaken so pure an echo—

Tell me if her soul, musing for a moment,
Quickens with their song,
And if the serene harmony of their strains
Reminds her of the absent one!

13 *Viens, les gazons sont verts*
(Jules Barbier, after Longfellow)

Come, the lawns are green

Si tu dors, jeune fille,
Debout, debout! voici le soleil!
Chasse de tes yeux l'indolent sommeil!
C'est l'heure du réveil!

Suis moi, vive et gentille!
Pieds nus, viens! Les gazons sont verts!
Les ruisseaux jaseurs par les bois déserts
Promènent leurs flots clairs!

If you are sleeping, my girl,
Rise up, rise up, the sun is here!
Brush idle sleep from your eyes,
It is time to awake!

Follow me quickly and sweetly,
Barefoot, come, the lawns are green!
The babbling brooks in the empty woods
Flow with limpid water!

GRIFFES, Charles (1884–1920)

This accomplished American composer is experiencing something of a revival in the concert hall and recording studio. In terms of songs his greatest debt is to the German lied and he composed some thirty settings of such poets as Heine, Eichendorff, Geibel, and Lenau. His earliest song (1901) was Hugo's *Si mes vers avaient des ailes*, followed by *Sur ma lyre l'autre fois* of Sainte-Beuve. The remaining songs with such French titles as *Le jardin*, *Impression du matin*, *La mer*, *Les ballons*, and *Le réveillon* (1912–15) are deceptive for lovers of mélodie, for they are in fact songs in English to the poems of Oscar Wilde who gave them atmospheric titles in French. Many of the musical turns of phrase might have come from an album of songs by Debussy. Thus Griffes is something like Whistler, an American, owing a great deal to French impressionism, painting the Thames (as in *Impression du matin*) rather than, as we might have first expected, the Seine.

GROVLEZ, Gabriel (1879–1944)

This gifted conductor, critic, and teacher was an important figure in French musical life between the wars. Fauré was one of his teachers at the Conservatoire, and he taught piano at the Schola Cantorum for ten years. His most active period as a conductor at the Paris Opére (1914–1933) was a crucial one for the revival of an interest in early French opera, and he edited volumes of arias from these works which greatly influenced the understanding of the age of Rameau in England. Grovlez was so much of an all-rounder, as well as a busy international conductor, that he was not taken very seriously as a composer. But his abilities in this direction stand up to scrutiny, and many of his fifty-or-so songs make an elegant and sometimes whimsical effect on the platform. A good example of his style at its best is *TROIS MÉLODIES SUR DES POÈMES DE JACQUES HEUGEL* with its delicious *Si j'étais Charles d'Orléans*. *PAROLES À L'ABSENTE* (1918) is a set of two songs to words by the critic G. Jean-Aubry (a poet also set by Roussel and Caplet). The second of these, *Vestiges*, is particularly effective, as is Grovlez's setting of *Guitares et mandolines* (1913), a poem by Saint-Saëns which had earlier been set by its author [SAINT-SAËNS 7]. The *TROIS BALLADES DE PAUL FORT* (1927) are more simple down-to-earth settings of this poet than the better-known Caplet songs. Grovlez had a strong connection with the English market, through his interest in music for children. His *L'ALMANACH AUX IMAGES* was once a popular work among aspiring British pianists. His Jean-Aubry cycle was published by Chester, and the firm of Augener published such works as *PETITES LITANIES DE JÉSUS* (Klingsor, 1911), and his *CHANSONS ENFANTINES* (1912) issued as *LITTLE PEOPLE'S SONGBOOK*.

HAHN, Reynaldo (1875–1947)

In this book there are a number of greater composers with shorter entries. The purist may raise his eyebrows when he sees so much space allocated to a so-called minor figure, but there has been a Hahn revival in the last twenty years, and an ever-widening range of his mélodies is to be heard regularly on the recital platform. This composer knew perfectly well that he himself was a *petit maître*; at times he aspires to be more, and there are a number of bigger works where he almost convinces us that he deserves a greater *appellation*. But the qualities that he did have in plenty, literary sensibility and boundless charm not precluding deep feeling, are precious ones—although non-admirers would call Hahn precious in the pejorative sense. Mallarmé, no less, dedicated these lines to the composer: 'Le pleur qui chante au langage | Du poète Reynaldo |Hahn tendrement le dégage | Comme en l'allée un jet d'eau' (The tear which sings in the language | Of the poet, Reynaldo | Hahn tenderly releases it | Like a fountain in the avenue).

Hahn's music evokes a Paris, indeed a way of life, forever gone and, like Proust's world, retrievable only at special moments where taste, sight, or the sound of a musical phrase provoke the memory, or even perhaps the collective unconscious. Those who lived in the *belle époque* at the same time as realizing its transience and cherishing its atmosphere, like Proust, found the muse of Reynaldo an indispensable vade-mecum. That Hahn's mélodies can continue to open the doors of that Parisian past is the reason why these songs have never lost their audience, and why Reynaldo is regarded by his devotees as an enchanting guide with whom to discover the *décadence* and the sunset of a voluptuous century. It is not surprising that we find ourselves using his first name when affectionately talking about him.

Although he wrote and spoke exquisite French, Reynaldo Hahn's first language was Spanish, and his surname was German. His mother was a Venezuelan Catholic. His Jewish father, Carlos Hahn, was born in Hamburg and had moved to Caracas as a young man to make his fortune in Latin America. (The family name is thus pronounced *with* the aspirate H, not in the French manner as 'Ahn'.) The youngest of twelve children, he was only 3 years old when his family left Caracas to settle in Paris. At the age of 10, he entered the Paris Conservatoire, where Cortot and Ravel were among his fellow students in the piano class. The venerable Gounod gave him composition lessons, and some of this composer's songs remained part of Reynaldo's repertory when, some years later, he sang to such memorable effect in the grand salons of Paris. (*Maid of Athens* sung in Hahn's deliciously accented English, to his own piano accompaniment, is one of the classic recordings of French song.) Apart from Gounod, Reynaldo was in touch with many other famous musicians; his professor of composition at the Conservatoire was Massenet, a man to whom he was to stay loyal throughout his life, long after that composer's music ceased to be fashionable.

It was at the home of Alphonse Daudet in 1893 that the famous singer Sybil Sanderson performed Hahn's songs to the texts of Verlaine. These were the CHANSONS GRISES, and Verlaine himself was present. Although prematurely aged and ill, he was able to hear these old verses of his given a musical life which he could understand. Indifferent to Fauré's more musically demanding settings of his poems, Verlaine wept to hear Hahn's songs. This set opens with a *Chanson d'automne* where mélodie crosses the border into the world of *chanson*, with a prophetic whiff of Trenet. *En sourdine,* which murmurs voluptuously on repeated notes, too dreamy to move too far around the stave, is less of a masterpiece than Fauré's, but just as loveable. In *L'heure exquise* (where Hahn would almost certainly win an audience prize if his song were to compete with Fauré's) he demonstrates his ability to use time and space (rather than melody and harmony alone) as essential ingredients in the creation of magic. Somehow these 'songs in grey' evoke vistas of calm space and twilight grandeur.

By the age of 19, Reynaldo had set many texts about love, but his worldly sophistication in the fields of music, literature, and painting hid a great shyness about his private feelings. In 1894 at Réveillon, the home of the painter Madeleine Lemaire, he met Marcel Proust, three years older, highly strung and snobbish. People doubted whether the writer would ever do anything worthwhile with his life, let alone become one of the greatest of all French novelists. The two men shared a love of painting; Reynaldo knew about literature, Marcel was an avid fan of music, particularly Fauré's. They collaborated on a work for reciter and piano about painters, they went on holiday together in Brittany and to Venice where the composer wrote his enchanting VENEZIA. Although these Italian songs fall outside the scope of this book, it seems fair to say that *La barcheta* from this set is one of the composer's most beloved songs. Also interesting, though from a later date, are Hahn's five songs in English, settings of Robert Louis Stevenson which include *The swing*, once famous in England in another version by Liza Lehmann.

During this period Hahn developed his own literary skills. He was to become, and remain, one of the best of all writers about music and musicians, particularly in the field of vocal studies. (His books *Du chant, Thèmes variés,* and *L'oreille au guet* still make fascinating reading, not to mention his memoir of Sarah Bernhardt to whom he became a devoted friend.) Proust and Hahn became lovers: If the trouble with Verlaine was that he was always chasing Rimbauds (as Dorothy Parker averred), Hahn was a chicken who was always coming home to Proust—at least for the two years the affair lasted. The friendship, however, endured until the novelist's death twenty-eight years later. Hahn was later to form a partnership with the singer Guy Ferrant, but neither novelist nor composer were to know a friendship to match theirs. The rest of Hahn's life was not without distinction, but there is a decided feeling of musical and personal anticlimax. He became a note-worthy conductor (Maggie Teyte judged him the greatest of all Mozartians), and was willing to accompany the handful of singers he admired as correctly schooled (his books on singing show a merciless impatience with anything but the highest technical accomplishment). He made a number of fascinating gramophone records, singing his own music and accompanying himself, and he had a famous duo partnership with the great soprano Ninon Vallin, also preserved in classic recordings.

As there seemed to be less and less interest in his own serious music, he broadened his composi-tional thrust and concentrated on the world of operetta which has a timeless appeal and turns the clock back with impunity. He had some of his greatest successes in the 1920s and 1930s collaborat-ing with famous names like Sacha Guitry and Yvonne Printemps, but nothing could bring back the times when great poets had likened him to a young Apollo. Modern life seemed increasingly to fill him with bile; nothing could match the achievements and standards of his youth. For him Fauré was the last of the great composers; even Debussy was not above stringent criticism. He was too intelligent to confuse commercial success with the artistic respect given to great creators, an artistic respect that he had taken for granted, and so enjoyed, in his youth. Forced to flee France during the Nazi occupation because he was half Jewish, he made a brief return to the public arena in 1945 when he was appointed the first director of the Paris Opéra after the war. He died soon afterwards with-out being able to execute the necessary reforms which were well within the scope of his formidable abilities as an administrator. This might have been a grand new phase in his career.

There are twenty songs in Hahn's first *recueil* (1895)—the most famous of his collections of mélodies. Like every other composer of the time, Reynaldo was drawn to the poetry of Victor Hugo. ***Si mes vers avaient des ailes*** seems to have become the composer's motto song. It has a perfection about it which makes the youthfulness of the composer (he was 13) seem all the more extraordinary. The distinguishing marks of Hahn's style are all there: an accompaniment which undulates in the background like the slow unfurling of a skein of sumptuous material, a background of seemingly little import which nevertheless shapes the melody in the manner of the lightest of hands on a pot-ter's wheel; a vocal line which is derived from the intimacy of speech but which contains it in the seeds of a wonderful melody truly to be *sung*; the use of unexpected intervals and cadences (the leaps are sometimes large) which transport us suddenly from a conversational tone in the middle of the stave to the swoon-inducing delight of a cunningly placed mezza voce. Although the composer's debts to Massenet are obvious, this music has a depth of feeling, a sense of pain and longing, which that composer was seldom to attain in his songs. ***Rêverie*** is another Hugo setting. The theme is unforced, dreamy charm; the piano's vamping (alternating legato with staccato) at first seems almost comic in its accommodating will to please, and then strikes us as ever so slightly risqué—an anti-dote to the romanticism of the words.

The Verlaine settings outside the CHANSONS GRISES (which are published in a separate volume) include *L'incrédule,* a charming trifle in conversational style, and *Offrande,* one of Hahn's great mélodies. Although the composer was only 16, it stands as a proud alternative to the settings of both Debussy and Fauré, both with the title *Green* [DEBUSSY 6 v; FAURÉ 29 iii]. It is unlikely that Hahn knew either of those songs when he wrote his setting. A footnote to the edition states that the song is published with the permission of MM—the poet's ex-wife, Mathilde Mauté. However great the Fauré and Debussy songs are as pieces of music (more complex than *Offrande* by far), Hahn, despite his tender years (the song is mysteriously dedicated 'to ***'), has profoundly understood the poem's background: the melancholy and masochism inherent in Verlaine's homosexual passion for Arthur Rimbaud. Debussy and Fauré, with the confidence of men destined to win their fair ladies, composed songs which offer baskets of fruit and bouquets of flowers with breathless delight. In Hahn's empty accompaniment of listless minims, and a vocal line that is all but a monotone, we hear the helplessness of a man who knows that he will be treated unkindly by the object of his passion, who knows his offering will be scornfully rejected, and that nowhere will he find sympathy for his plight. Here is the state of depression which descends when love dares not speak its name.

D'une prison was composed in 1892. Fauré's immortal setting of this poem (*Prison* [FAURÉ 31]) was not published until 1896, so we cannot blame Hahn for *lèse-majesté* in deciding to set it. The Fauré song contains all the pent-up anguish and regret which is missing here. Instead of a man who sees his life ruined, Hahn gives us the gentle and regretful musings of a gentleman temporarily down on his luck. We can be sure that these thoughts of a misspent youth were vocalized as the composer-singer-accompanist's cigarette smoke, spiralling gently to the salon ceiling. *Fêtes galantes* is another Verlaine poem which many a French composer has felt obliged to tackle. Hahn's song combines attributes of Fauré's *Mandoline* [FAURÉ 29 i] with its Watteau-like elegance, and Debussy's breathless and piquant song of the same name, without quite being as successful as either. In his hands there is something (deliberately?) banal about these exchanges of courtly pleasantries. Despite these drawbacks, the song is a useful one to enliven a typically languid group of songs by this composer. Another lively song is the earthy *Trois jours de vendange,* one of the very few settings by Alphonse Daudet in the mélodie repertoire, and testimony to the composer's closeness to the Daudet family—above all as a protégé of Alphonse, the grand old man of French literature. The son, Lucien Daudet, was destined to replace Reynaldo as the lover of Marcel Proust.

Of the remaining songs in the first volume, *Infidélité* (Gautier) is a perfect pastel, like *Offrande* a portrait of a tentative love that is doomed to disappointment and incomprehension. The vocal line seems caught within a small circle of notes as if to reflect the unchanging constancy of the narrator. The calm atmosphere of the evening is beautifully caught, and sets up the small but oh-so-poignant change of harmony (which mirrors the change of the lover's feeling) on the cooly distant 'vous' at the end. *L'enamourée* is built upon the charm of a descending sequence of exquisite sighs, but what would in other hands be cheap musical manipulation somehow achieves a moving dignity of utterance in Hahn's hands.

The second *recueil* (1921) opens, like the first, with a setting of Victor Hugo. *Quand la nuit n'est pas étoilée* is an earlier work than many other songs in this collection. Its low tessitura suggests the laconic crooning style of the composer himself (at least in the opening pages). Hugo's poem is immense in its imagery and this rhapsodic setting rises to the challenge. As in *Les étoiles* (discussed later) he takes his brush to a larger canvas and succeeds. *Le rossignol des lilas* (Dauphin) is another rondel. This song is one of Hahn's loveliest creations—and most unusual, in that the vocal line and the piano are welded together throughout (the one frequently doubling the other). The shape of the song shows beyond doubt Hahn's experience in the world of operetta where the voice has to carry the main melody, and that melody has to be memorable. *À Chloris* (de Viau) is the summit of Reynaldo Hahn's art as a pasticheur, and it ranks as perhaps the most successful musical time-travelling in the French mélodie (if one excludes that peerless masterpiece of the madrigal style, Fauré's *Clair de lune*). The fact that it is based on the striding bass line of Bach's Air on the G String seems irrelevant: one smiles at the composer's audacity at the beginning, but one stays to listen to the music, *Hahn's* music, in its own right. It uses one of his favourite devices where the accompaniment is a piano piece with its own momentum; over this the voice embroiders an inspired overlay which seems half sung and half spoken, moving with conversational grace between whispered confidences and declarations of love in full voice.

Probably inspired by the work of Charles Koechlin with some of the same texts, Hahn composed a set of twelve RONDELS to the poetry of Charles d'Orléans and Théodore de Banville. At least three of these are worthy of note, and are actually included in the second *recueil*. *Le printemps* (Banville) ranks as one of the composer's most exuberant songs. At the top of the music Hahn writes the words 'Viens enfant, la terre s'éveille'—the opening lines from Gounod's *Chanson de printemps* [GOUNOD 11]. From that mélodie he adopts the ceaseless semiquavers of the accompaniment. This is truly a song for a high voice of some power and both singer and pianist are challenged by its élan. *Quand je fus pris au pavillon* (Charles d'Orléans) is one of Hahn's most celebrated pastiches of the Renaissance style, with its leaping staccato basses, and the cheeky melisma on the word 'belle' in the second verse. *Les étoiles* (Banville) is the composer at his most sumptuous. The piano writing consists of alternating chords in both hands spaced a semiquaver apart. When these chords are played softly enough, and smoothly between the hands, they produce a shimmering effect of amplitude and heavenly repose. The melody is long-breathed and spacious and makes its effect over a long span. Towards the end there is an imposing climax at 'ces fournaises de diamants' which is probably the grandest moment in any of the composer's mélodies.

The *ÉTUDES LATINES* is a group of eighteen poems by Leconte de Lisle, ten of which Hahn chose to set for his cycle of the same name published in 1900. Like the collections of RONDELS, a number of these songs involve a chorus and are thus not suitable for the recital repertoire. The concluding song *Phidylé* for example (not the same text as the Duparc song) requires bass soloist, mixed chorus, and piano duettists. Although Hahn dedicated *Phidylé* to Proust, the jewel of the cycle is undoubtedly *Tyndaris* for tenor and piano. It is here that Hahn finds the perfect means to evoke this dream of distant antiquity. The limpidity of the quasi-modal accompaniment (who else would make something so beautiful of a simple downward scale at the song's opening?) and the unforced prosody of a vocal line which seems to flow from the heart combine to ravishing effect. Here is a song as fresh and unspoiled as Hahn imagined the civilization to be which inspired it. Distance has truly lent enchantment.

CHANSONS GRISES

I i *Chanson d'automne*

Les sanglots longs
Des violons
   De l'automne
Blessent mon cœur
D'une langueur
   Monotone.

Tout suffocant
Et blême, quand
   Sonne l'heure,
Je me souviens
Des jours anciens
   Et je pleure;

Et je m'en vais
Au vent mauvais
   Qui m'emporte
Deçà, delà,
Pareil à la
   Feuille morte.

I ii *Tous deux*

Donc, ce sera par un clair jour d'été:
Le grand soleil, complice de ma joie,
Fera, parmi le satin et la soie,
Plus belle encor votre chère beauté;

Le ciel tout bleu, comme une haute tente,
Frissonnera somptueux à long plis
Sur nos deux fronts heureux qu'auront pâlis
L'émotion du bonheur et l'attente;

Et quand le soir viendra, l'air sera doux
Qui se jouera, caressant, dans vos voiles,
Et les regards paisibles des étoiles
Bienveillamment souriront aux époux.

SONGS IN GREY

Autumn song

With long sobs
The violins
   Of autumn
Wound my heart
With languorous
   Monotony.

All choking
And pale, when
   The hour sounds,
I remember
Departed days
   And I weep;

And I go
Where ill winds blow,
   Buffeted
To and fro,
Like a
   Dead leaf.

Both of us

So, on a bright summer day it shall be:
The great sun, my partner in joy,
Shall make, amid the satin and the silk,
Your dear beauty lovelier still;

The sky, all blue, like a tall canopy,
Shall quiver sumptuously in long folds
Above our two happy brows, grown pale
With pleasure and expectancy;

And when evening comes, the breeze shall be soft
And play caressingly about your veils,
And the peaceful stars looking down
Shall smile benevolently on man and wife.

I iii *L'allée est sans fin*

L'allée est sans fin
Sous le ciel, divin
D'être pâle ainsi:
Sais-tu qu'on serait
Bien sous le secret
De ces arbres-ci?

Le château, tout blanc
Avec, à son flanc,
Le soleil couché,
Les champs à l'entour:
Oh! que notre amour
N'est-il là niché!

The path is endless

The path is endless
Beneath the sky, divine
In being so pale:
Do you know how at ease
We could be
Beneath the secret of these trees?

The castle, all white,
Flanked by
The sun now set,
Encircled by fields:
Oh! that our love
Were hidden there!

I iv *En sourdine*

Calmes dans le demi-jour
Que les branches hautes font,
Pénétrons bien notre amour
De ce silence profond.

Fondons nos âmes, nos cœurs
Et nos sens extasiés,
Parmi les vagues langueurs
Des pins et des arbousiers.

Ferme tes yeux à demi,
Croise tes bras sur ton sein,
Et de ton cœur endormi
Chasse à jamais tout dessein.

Laissons-nous persuader
Au souffle berceur et doux
Qui vient à tes pieds rider
Les ondes de gazon roux.

Et quand, solennel, le soir
Des chênes noirs tombera,
Voix de notre désespoir,
Le rossignol chantera.

Muted

Calm in the twilight
Cast by lofty boughs,
Let us steep our love
In this deep quiet.

Let us mingle our souls, our hearts,
And our enraptured senses
With the hazy languor
Of arbutus and pine.

Half-close your eyes,
Fold your arms across your breast,
And from your heart now lulled to rest
Banish forever all intent.

Let us both succumb
To the gentle and lulling breeze
That comes to ruffle at your feet
The waves of russet grass.

And when, solemnly, evening
Falls from the black oaks,
That voice of our despair,
The nightingale shall sing.

I v *L'heure exquise*

La lune blanche
Luit dans les bois;
De chaque branche
Part une voix
Sous la ramée...

Ô bien-aimée.

L'étang reflète,
Profond miroir,
La silhouette
Du saule noir
Où le vent pleure...

Rêvons, c'est l'heure.

Un vaste et tendre
Apaisement
Semble descendre
Du firmament
Que l'astre irise...

C'est l'heure exquise.

Exquisite hour

The white moon
Gleams in the woods;
From every branch
There comes a voice
Beneath the boughs...

O my beloved.

The pool reflects,
Deep mirror,
The silhouette
Of the black willow
Where the wind is weeping...

Let us dream, it is the hour.

A vast and tender
Consolation
Seems to fall
From the sky
The moon illumines...

Exquisite hour.

I vi *Paysage triste*

L'ombre des arbres dans la rivière embrumée
    Meurt comme de la fumée
Tandis qu'en l'air, parmi les ramures réelles,
    Se plaignent les tourterelles.

Combien, ô voyageur, ce paysage blême
    Te mira blême toi-même,
Et que tristes pleuraient dans les hautes feuillées
    Tes espérances noyées!

Mournful landscape

The shadow of trees in the river mist
    Expires like smoke,
While up above, in the real branches,
    The turtle-doves lament.

How this faded landscape, O traveller,
    Watched you yourself fade,
And how sadly in the lofty leaves
    Your drowned hopes wept!

I vii *La bonne chanson*

La dure épreuve va finir:
Mon cœur, souris à l'avenir.

Ils sont finis les jours d'alarmes
Où j'étais triste jusqu'aux larmes.

The good song

The harsh ordeal is about to end:
Greet the future with a smile, O heart.

The days of fear are finished,
When I was wretched even to tears.

J'ai tu les paroles amères
Et banni les sombres chimères.

Mes yeux exilés de la voir
De par un douloureux devoir,

Mon oreille avide d'entendre
Les notes d'or de sa voix tendre,

Tout mon être et tout mon amour
Acclament le bienheureux jour

Où, seul rêve et seule pensée,
Me reviendra la fiancée!

I have silenced bitter words
And banished dark imaginings.

My eyes, exiled from her sight
By a painful duty,

My ears, eager to hear
The golden notes of her tender voice,

All my soul and all my love
Acclaim the blessed day

When—my one thought and dream—
My betrothed will return to me!

2 *Si mes vers avaient des ailes*

(Victor Hugo)

Mes vers fuiraient, doux et frêles,
Vers votre jardin si beau,
Si mes vers avaient des ailes,
Comme l'oiseau.

Ils voleraient, étincelles,
Vers votre foyer qui rit,
Si mes vers avaient des ailes,
Comme l'esprit.

Près de vous, purs et fidèles,
Ils accourraient nuit et jour,
Si mes vers avaient des ailes,
Comme l'amour.

If my verses had wings

My verses would flee, sweet and frail,
To your garden so fair,
If my verses had wings,
Like a bird.

They would fly, like sparks,
To your smiling hearth,
If my verses had wings,
Like the mind.

Pure and faithful, to your side
They'd hasten night and day,
If my verses had wings,
Like love.

3 *Rêverie*

(Victor Hugo)

Puisqu'ici-bas toute âme
    Donne à quelqu'un
Sa musique, sa flamme,
    Ou son parfum;

Puisqu'ici toute chose
    Donne toujours
Son épine ou sa rose
    À ses amours;

Reverie

Since here on earth each soul
    Gives someone
Its music, its ardour,
    Or its perfume;

Since here all things
    Will always give
Their thorns or roses
    To those they love;

Puisque l'air à la branche
 Donne l'oiseau;
Que l'aube à la pervenche
 Donne un peu d'eau;

Puisque, lorsqu'elle arrive
 S'y reposer,
L'onde amère à la rive
 Donne un baiser;

Je te donne, à cette heure,
 Penché sur toi,
La chose la meilleure
 Que j'aie en moi!

Reçois donc ma pensée,
 Triste d'ailleurs,
Qui, comme une rosée,
 T'arrive en pleurs!

Reçois mes vœux sans nombre,
 Ô mes amours!
Reçois la flamme et l'ombre
 De tous mes jours!

Mes transports pleins d'ivresses,
 Purs de soupçons,
Et toutes les caresses
 De mes chansons!

Since the breeze gives
 To the branch the bird;
And dawn to the periwinkle
 Gives of its dew;

Since when they come
 To settle there,
The briny waves
 Give the shore a kiss;

I give you, at this hour,
 Inclining over you,
The finest things
 I have in me!

Accept, then, my thoughts,
 Sad though they be,
Which like drops of dew
 Come to you as tears!

Accept my countless vows,
 O my loves!
Accept the flame and the shade
 Of all my days!

My frenzied rapture,
 Devoid of all distrust,
And all the caresses
 Of my songs!

4 *L'incrédule*

(Paul Verlaine)

 Tu crois au marc de café,
  Aux présages, aux grands jeux:
Moi je ne crois qu'en tes grands yeux.

 Tu crois aux contes de fées,
  Aux jours néfastes, aux songes,
Moi je ne crois qu'en tes mensonges.

 Tu crois en un vague Dieu,
  En quelque saint spécial,
En tel *Ave* contre tel mal.

 Je ne crois qu'aux heures bleues
  Et roses que tu m'épanches
Dans la volupté des nuits blanches!

The unbeliever

 You believe in coffee grains,
  In omens, in high stakes:
But I believe only in your large eyes.

 You believe in fairy-tales,
  In ill-starred days, in dreams,
But I believe only in your lies.

 You believe in some vague god,
  In some special saint,
In the power of Aves to counter evil.

 I believe only in the blue-pink
  Hours you lavish on me
In the ecstasy of sleepless nights!

Et si profonde est ma foi
Envers tout ce que je croi
Que je ne vis que pour toi.

And so deep is my faith
In all I believe,
That I live for you alone.

5 *Trois jours de vendange*

(Alphonse Daudet)

Je l'ai rencontrée un jour de vendange,
La jupe troussée et le pied mignon;
Point de guimpe jaune et point de chignon:
L'air d'une bacchante et les yeux d'un ange.

Suspendue an bras d'un doux compagnon,
Je l'ai rencontrée aux champs d'Avignon,
    Un jour de vendange.

Je l'ai rencontrée un jour de vendange.
La plaine était morne et le ciel brûlant;
Elle marchait seule et d'un pas tremblant,
Son regard brillait d'une flamme étrange.

Je frissonne encore en me rappelant
Comme je te vis, cher fantôme blanc,
    Un jour de vendange!

Je l'ai rencontrée un jour de vendange,
Et j'en rêve encor presque tous les jours.

.   .   .   .   .   .

Le cercueil était couvert en velours,
Le drap noir portait une double frange.
Les sœurs d'Avignon pleuraient tout autour...
La vigne avait trop de raisin; l'Amour
    Avait fait la vendange.

Three days of vintaging

During the vintage I met her one day,
Skirt tucked in and dainty feet;
No yellow veil and no coiled-up hair:
A maenad with an angel's eyes.

She was leaning on a sweet friend's arm,
When I met her at Avignon in the fields,
    During the vintage one day.

During the vintage I met her one day.
The plain was bleak and the sky ablaze;
She was walking alone and with faltering steps,
Her face was lit by a curious glow.

I still shudder as I remember
How I saw you, dear white spectre,
    During the vintage one day!

During the vintage I met her one day,
And still almost daily I dream of it.

.   .   .   .   .   .

The coffin was draped in velvet,
The black shroud had a double fringe.
The Avignon nuns wept all around it...
The vine had too many grapes; Love
    Had gathered its harvest.

6 *Infidélité*

(Théophile Gautier)

Voici l'orme qui balance
Son ombre sur le sentier;
Voici le jeune églantier,
Le bois où dort le silence;
Le banc de pierre où le soir
Nous aimions à nous asseoir.

Infidelity

Here is the elm that sways
Its shadow on the path;
Here is the young wild rose,
The wood where silence sleeps;
The stone bench where, at evening,
We would love to sit.

Voici la voûte embaumée
D'ébéniers et de lilas,
Où, lorsque nous étions las,
Ensemble, ô ma bien-aimée!
Sous des guirlandes de fleurs,
Nous laissions fuir les chaleurs.

L'air est pur, le gazon doux...
Rien n'a donc changé que vous.

Here is the fragrant canopy
Of ebony and lilac trees,
Where, when we were tired,
Together, my beloved,
Beneath garlands of flowers,
We would let the heat waft by.

The air is pure, sweet the grass...
Nothing has changed but you.

7 *L'enamourée*
(Théodore de Banville)

The loved one

Ils se disent, ma colombe,
Que tu rêves, morte encore,
Sous la pierre d'une tombe:
Mais pour l'âme qui t'adore,
Tu t'éveilles ranimée,
Ô pensive bien-aimée!

They say, my dove,
That, though dead, you dream
Beneath the headstone of a grave:
But for the soul that adores you,
You waken, restored to life,
O pensive beloved!

Par les blanches nuits d'étoiles,
Dans la brise qui murmure,
Je caresse tes longs voiles,
Ta mouvante chevelure,
Et tes ailes demi-closes
Qui voltigent sur les roses!

During sleepless, starlit nights,
In the murmuring breeze,
I caress your long veils,
Your billowing hair,
And your half-folded wings
That flutter over roses!

Ô délices! je respire
Tes divines tresses blondes!
Ta voix pure, cette lyre,
Suit la vague sur les ondes,
Et, suave, les effleure,
Comme un cygne qui se pleure!

Oh delight! I inhale
Your divine blonde tresses!
Your pure voice, this lyre,
Follows the waves across the water,
And softly ripples them,
Like a lamenting swan!

8 *Quand la nuit n'est pas étoilée*
(Victor Hugo)

When night is not studded with stars

Quand la nuit n'est pas étoilée,
Viens te bercer aux flots des mers;
Comme la mort elle est voilée,
Comme la vie ils sont amers.

When night is not studded with stars,
Come, rock yourself on the ocean waves;
Night, like death, is veiled,
Waves, like life, are bitter.

L'ombre et l'abîme ont un mystère
Que nul mortel ne pénétra;
C'est Dieu qui leur dit de se taire
Jusqu'au jour où tout parlera!

The dark and the abyss hold mysteries
Unfathomed by human kind;
It is God who bids them be silent
Until the day when all shall speak!

D'autres yeux de ces flots sans nombre
Ont vainement cherché le fond!
D'autres yeux se sont emplis d'ombre
À contempler ce ciel profond!

Toi, demande au monde nocturne
De la paix pour ton cœur désert!
Demande une goutte à cette urne!
Demande un chant à ce concert!

Plane au-dessus des autres femmes,
Et laisse errer tes yeux si beaux
Entre le ciel où sont les âmes
Et la terre où sont les tombeaux!

Other eyes have vainly
Sought to sound these depths!
Other eyes have been filled with darkness
In scanning the deep sky.

O ask the nocturnal world
To shed peace on your forsaken heart!
Entreat a drop from this urn,
From this harmony entreat a song!

Soar above all other women,
And let your beautiful eyes roam
Between heaven with its souls
And earth with its tombs!

9 Le rossignol des lilas

(Léopold Dauphin)

The nightingale among the lilac

Ô premier rossignol qui viens
Dans les lilas, sous ma fenêtre,
Ta voix m'est douce à reconnaître!
Nul accent n'est semblable au tien!

Fidèle aux amoureux liens,
Trille encore, divin petit être!
Ô premier rossignol qui viens
Dans les lilas, sous ma fenêtre!

Nocturne ou matinal, combien
Ton hymne à l'amour me pénètre!
Tant d'ardeur fait en moi renaître
L'écho de mes avrils anciens,
Ô premier rossignol qui viens!

O first nightingale to appear
Among the lilac beneath my window,
How sweet to recognize your voice!
There is no song like yours!

Faithful to the bonds of love,
Trill away, divine little being!
O first nightingale to appear
Among the lilac beneath my window!

Night or morning—O how
Your hymn to love strikes at my heart!
Such ardour reawakens in me
Echoes of my Aprils past,
O first nightingale to appear!

10 À Chloris

(Théophile de Viau)

To Chloris

S'il est vrai, Chloris, que tu m'aimes,
Mais j'entends que tu m'aimes bien,
Je ne crois pas que les rois mêmes
Aient un bonheur pareil au mien.
Que la mort serait importune
À venir changer ma fortune
Pour la félicité des cieux!
Tout ce qu'on dit de l'ambroisie
Ne touche point ma fantaisie
Au prix des grâces de tes yeux.

If it be true, Chloris, that you love me,
(And I'm told you love me dearly),
I do not believe that even kings
Can match the happiness I know.
Even death would be powerless
To alter my fortune
With the promise of heavenly bliss!
All that they say of ambrosia
Does not stir my imagination
Like the favour of your eyes!

11 *Le printemps*
    (Théodore de Banville)

Spring

Te voilà, rire du Printemps!
Les thyrses des lilas fleurissent.
Les amantes qui te chérissent
Délivrent leurs cheveux flottants.

Smiling Spring, you have arrived!
Sprays of lilac are in bloom.
Lovers who hold you dear
Unbind their flowing hair.

Sous les rayons d'or éclatants
Les anciens lierres se flétrissent.
Te voilà, rire du Printemps!
Les thyrses des lilas fleurissent.

Beneath the beams of glistening gold
The ancient ivy withers.
Smiling Spring, you have arrived!
Sprays of lilac are in bloom!

Couchons-nous au bord des étangs,
Que nos maux amers se guérissent!
Mille espoirs fabuleux nourrissent
Nos cœurs émus et palpitants.
Te voilà, rire du Printemps!

Let us lie alongside pools
That our bitter wounds may heal!
A thousand fabled hopes nourish
Our full and beating hearts.
Smiling Spring, you have arrived!

12 *Quand je fus pris au pavillon*
    (Charles d'Orléans)

When I was caught in the pavilion

Quand je fus pris au pavillon
De ma dame, très gente et belle,
Je me brûlay à la chandelle,
Ainsi que fait le papillon.

When I was caught in the pavilion
Of my most beautiful and noble lady,
I burnt myself in the candle's flame,
As the moth does.

Je rougis comme vermillon,
À la clarté d'une étincelle,
Quand je fus pris au pavillon
De ma dame, très gente et belle.

I flushed crimson
In the brightness of a spark,
When I was caught in the pavilion
Of my most beautiful and noble lady.

Si j'eusse été esmerillon
Ou que j'eusse eu aussi bonne aile,
Je me fusse gardé de celle
Qui me bailla de l'aiguillon,
Quand je fus pris au pavillon.

If I had been a merlin
Or had wings as strong,
I should have shielded myself
From her who pierced me with her arrows,
When I was caught in the pavilion.

13 *Les étoiles*
    (Théodore de Banville)

Stars

Les cieux resplendissants d'Étoiles
Aux radieux frissonnements,
Ressemblent à des flots dormants
Que sillonnent de blanches voiles.

The heavens resplendent with Stars,
Glittering and shimmering,
Are like slumbering waves
Streaked with white sails.

Quand l'azur déchire ses voiles,	When the azure breaks through its veils,
Nous voyons les bleus firmaments,	We see the blue firmament,
Les cieux resplendissants d'Étoiles	The heavens resplendent with Stars,
Aux radieux frissonnements.	Glittering and shimmering.
Quel peintre mettra sur ses toiles,	What painter will capture on canvas,
Ô Dieu! leurs clairs fourmillements,	O God, this limpid teeming,
Ces fournaises de diamants	These diamantine furnaces
Qu'à nos yeux ravis tu dévoiles,	You unveil to our enraptured eyes,
Les cieux resplendissants d'Étoiles?	The heavens resplendent with Stars?

14 *Tyndaris*   *Tyndaris*

(Charles-Marie-René Leconte de Lisle), from *ÉTUDES LATINES*

Ô blanche Tyndaris, les Dieux me sont amis:	O white Tyndaris, the Gods are friends to me:
Ils aiment les Muses Latines;	They love the Latin Muses;
Et l'aneth, et le myrte et le thym des collines	And dill and myrtle and thyme from the hills
Croissent aux prés qu'ils m'ont soumis.	Thrive in the meadows they gave me.
Viens! mes ramiers chéris, aux voluptés plaintives,	Come! My beloved ring-doves, delighting in grief,
Ici se plaisent à gémir;	Here are pleased to moan;
Et sous l'épais feuillage il est doux de dormir	And beneath dense leaves it is sweet to sleep
Au bruit des sources fugitives.	To the sound of running springs.

HENZE, Hans Werner (b. 1926)

This important German composer, like almost all of his compatriots, has not had a great link with French culture—Italy has been more his field. He did, however, write the incidental music to *Les caprices de Marianne*, a play by Musset, and he made a significant contribution to the setting of the poetry of Arthur Rimbaud in *BEING BEAUTEOUS* (1963) [BRITTEN 1 viii]. This cantata for coloratura soprano, harp, and four cellos is of unearthly beauty, and bears easy comparison with Britten's setting of the same poem in *LES ILLUMINATIONS*. The soprano writing is extremely high and technically demanding and this, as well as the unusual forces required, perhaps helps explain why the work is relatively seldom performed.

HILLEMACHER, Paul (1852–1933) and Lucien (1860–1909)

These brothers were both winners of the Prix de Rome (1876 and 1880). They were music's answer to the *frères* Goncourt, and no doubt their decision to collaborate was partly based on the glamour surrounding those famous literary siblings. Paul seems to have been the more talented composer, but he achieved little after his brother's early death. They were relatively successful in writing stage works, but their inclusion in this book rests on their VINGT MÉLODIES which is an anthology of remarkable grace and accomplishment, and is also distinguished for its choice of poets. The *recueil* opens with *Ici-bas* (Sully Prudhomme), a song which was discovered among the papers of Alexander von Meck in Moscow, and published in the early 1930s by Eschig as the recently unearthed work of the young Debussy. This suggests that Debussy, when he visited Moscow in 1881 as part of the musical retinue of Mme von Meck, possibly passed this song off as his own in order to please his employer. It is a charming waltz in the Tchaikovsky manner, and Debussy (who cared little for Tchaikovsky's music) may well have chosen it to ingratiate himself with Mme von Meck; he had made her acquaintance, and sized up her musical tastes, the previous year. It is a pity that memories of the Hillemachers as song composers should rest on this rather bizarre incident. There are three settings of Armand Silvestre, a lively Gautier *Noël*, two songs to texts by Henri Murger (author of *Scènes de la vie de bohème*), and two songs to Hugo texts, one of them *S'il est un charmant gazon* [FAURÉ 6] which was also set by Liszt, Franck, and others. Of other well-known lyrics there is a *L'invitation au voyage* [DUPARC 7] in something of the manner of Chabrier, and a *Soupir* of Sully Prudhomme [DUPARC 2]. Other poets in this collection are Banville, Passerat (a charming *Villanelle*), and André Chénier. Almost every aspect of the salon mélodie of the 1870s is captured here, and if originality is lacking, there is a definite melodic gift and a stylish way with word-setting.

HOIBY, Lee (b. 1926)

This most genial and approachable of American song composers (a pupil of Menotti) has published one set of French songs. The TROIS POÈMES DE RIMBAUD (1982) were written for the late William Parker, an important young baritone cut off in his prime, whose enthusiasm for French music (he recorded Poulenc alongside Souzay) was a driving force behind the popularization of the French repertoire in the United States. The poems set are *Le cœur volé*, *L'éternité*, and *Rêve pour l'hiver*. Rimbaud is a poet largely ignored by native-born French composers (for reasons of awe as much as anything), so these songs are a useful addition to the repertoire for baritones denied the beauties of Britten's tenor cycle LES ILLUMINATIONS.

HOLMÈS, Augusta (1847–1903)

A larger-than-life character, Holmès was born of Irish parentage, and brought up in the town of Versailles. She remained an impassioned Irish patriot to the end of her days. Her godfather was Alfred de Vigny, and right from the beginning of her life she was used to moving centre-stage in French artistic circles. She was a pupil of César Franck, and in her teens heard a performance of *Das Rheingold* which placed her firmly in the Wagner camp for the rest of her life. She had a passion for Wagnerian scale, and her music often founders because her aspirations to the grand gesture are not matched by technical command. Augusta made light of her musical shortcomings, which were forgotten in the presence of her celebrated *allure*; many famous men of the day fell under her spell, although she did not hesitate to sign her work with the pseudonym Hermann Zenta, when it suited her. Working within the realistic boundaries of her talent, Cécile Chaminade was a more successful composer, as was Holmès's gifted English contemporary Maude Valérie White. White in particular was a connoisseur of literature, but Holmès had a fearless belief in her own abilities as a poet and librettist which undermined her songs, not to mention her attempts at works for the stage. She might have sought the help of her long-standing lover Catulle Mendès; but he was such a disastrous collaborator for composers like Chabrier and Debussy that a cynic might aver that she would have been even worse off with his poetic help.

One hardly ever encounters a song by Holmès which is not a setting of her own words; a rare example is *La chanson du Jean Prouvaire* from Hugo's *Les misérables*. The lack of stimulus from another creative spirit makes her mélodies less varied and interesting than they might otherwise have been, although at least none of her settings is in competition with more distinguished rivals. The music often has an enthusiastic and singable vocal line, but banal piano writing (the spread chord of the sublime minstrel, often Irish in inspiration, a vamp to match her reputation as a seductress) is commonplace in her work. Holmès had a tendency to write songs in large series—such as the 1882 cycle LES SEPT IVRESSES (a *fin-de-siècle* catalogue of seven deadly sins consisting of songs about love, wine, glory, hate, dreams, desire, and gold), LES SÉRÉNADES (1883), CONTE DE FÉES (1892), and so on. Other titles of shorter series were BALLADES HÉROÏQUES and RÊVES PARISIENS (1886–92). It was as if she found the song form itself somewhat unworthy of her talents and was only happy to write mélodies if they were part of a bigger scheme. Her best songs are those in which she has taken the time to work on pianistic detail, avoiding a tendency to double the vocal line. Effective examples are *Les griffes d'or* and *Chanson catalane*, both of which are Spanish in inspiration. The latter has a melody which recalls the famous violin *Havanaise* of Saint-Saëns (a composer who allegedly proposed to her). *Les chevaliers du ciel* has an epic sweep to it which suggests someone infatuated with Wagner's *Parsifal*. The song *L'éternelle idole* is a quasi-pagan hymn to a goddess of stone; the wittiest thing about this song is its apposite dedication to the sculptor Rodin. Holmès is more successful when less ambitious. Thus a delicate little evocation of eighteenth-century France (and the composer's home town) entitled *À Trianon* is delightful. In the end another woman composer's verdict on Holmès's music seems more than fair: Ethel Smyth gallantly spoke of 'jewels wrought by one who was evidently not among the giants, but for all that knew how to cut a gem'.

HONEGGER, Arthur (1892–1955)

Few would now deny that Poulenc was the songwriting genius of Les Six, but opinions have always been divided as to who in the group was the next most interesting composer of mélodies. Early on it was Auric with his wide general culture and knowledge of poetry (as well as a sizeable output) whose music tended to be taken even more seriously than Poulenc's. Now the palm of *proxime accessit* seems to belong to Milhaud, whose mélodies, aided by the tireless advocacy of his widow Madeleine, are becoming better known, and are generally accepted to be next in line to Poulenc's in terms of songwriting achievement. There are certainly a great many items to explore in Milhaud's catalogue, but it would be no surprise to see his place usurped by Honegger, whose songs are arguably better written for the voice and seem shamefully neglected and ripe for re-evaluation. The same is true of the surprisingly unknown songs of Louis Durey.

Honegger was an admirer of Wagner and Debussy, but also of the modern world of steam engines and rugby teams. He was as interested in jazz as in Gregorian chant or Protestant hymns, and unlike many mélodies of the post-Debussy period his songs are not over-written, indeed they seem models of lucidity. Sympathy for German and Swiss culture (Honegger was nicknamed 'Beethoven' by some of his composer friends) adds a certain weight and seriousness to the music, particularly in the earlier songs, but they remain French to the core with an economy of means which now strikes the listener as not that far removed from the aesthetic of Les Six—although Honegger was always said to be only a nominal member of this group. His choice of poets reflects his own tastes and cultivated literary sympathies which appear complementary to Poulenc's, though they shared an enthusiasm for Apollinaire and Cocteau. His songs illustrate the importance of such writers as Jules Laforgue, Paul Fort, Paul Claudel, and Francis Jammes, writers whose work is also identified with Milhaud.

The first songs were QUATRE POÈMES, with poems by Fontainas, Laforgue, Jammes, and Archag Tchobanian. The cycle for medium voice (1914–16) was published by Chester and dedicated to Jane Bathori, the indefatigable interpreter of so much music by young composers of the day. The third song in the cycle, the simple *Prière* (Jammes), was considered by the composer to be the best mélodie he ever wrote. This music, indeed all the vocal music from 1916, shows us Honegger still in love with the Debussian world of mysterious atmospheres and pedalled bell-like sonorities. The forest of the opening of *Pelléas et Mélisande* is evoked in the horn music which resounds through *Le chasseur perdu dans la forêt*, the first of TROIS POÈMES DE PAUL FORT (1916). The composer's interest in bell music is reaffirmed in *Cloche du soir*, the second of this set; the concluding *Chanson de fol*, with its fairies and after-dark spirits, is also a nocturne of sorts.

An impressionistic tone is still very much in evidence in the SIX POÈMES DE GUILLAUME APOLLINAIRE to words from the poet's *Alcools* (1915–17). It is astonishing how these songs reflect an entirely different Apollinaire from the one revealed to the world of music by Poulenc's LE BESTIAIRE composed only a year later. From Honegger's set, *À la Santé* is this poet's latter-day equivalent of Verlaine's *Prison*. The song is about the poet's incarceration in the Santé prison in 1911 when he was accused of receiving stolen goods. In setting only part of a much longer text on a single page of music, Honegger finds suitably lugubrious music for the slow passing of the hours. *Saltimbanques* seems particularly successful in capturing the saucy yet deeply poetic mood of the poem; and the subject matter of *Les cloches* by now almost seems a Honegger trademark. *Nature morte* (Vanderpyl, 1917) is a haunting little song, with a static quality ideally suited to a still-life, and is one of the few works from this period which shows a composer's interest in the world of the visual arts.

In 1920 Honegger wrote TROIS FRAGMENTS for soprano and string quartet. The beautiful text was taken from LES PÂQUES À NEW YORK by Blaise Cendrars (an important literary figure of the time all but ignored by song composers.) This poignant work, unafraid of a depth of religious feeling, could claim to be the first 'real' Honegger, and it awaits rediscovery by a new generation of interpreters. This was the period of the composer's liaison with the great mélodie singer Claire Croiza who bore Honegger a son, and it was Croiza who created the SIX POÉSIES DE JEAN COCTEAU (1920–3). *Le nègre* from this set reveals his fascination with jazz and is laced with a suggestion of Bach, prophecy of Jacques Loussier and the Swingle Singers. In *Souvenirs d'enfance* from the same set we hear a link with COCARDES, Poulenc's Cocteau settings. The poem of the fifth song (here entitled *Une danseuse*) was set by Érik Satie at about the same time [SATIE 5 ii]. Despite Honegger's reputed dislike for that composer's work, some of the songs in this set make a Satiean impression, perhaps in a spirit of deliberate parody. Five of the Apollinaire settings, as well as the three Paul Fort songs, were later orchestrated by Arthur Hoérée.

The other songs from the Croiza period (Honegger was soon to leave her and marry Andrée Vaurabourg who was to become a leading exponent of his piano music) include the composer's contribution to the Ronsard *recueil* organized and published by the *Revue musicale* to celebrate the 400th anniversary of the poet's birth. This *Chanson de Ronsard* ('Plus tu connais que je brûle') evokes the past in very much Honegger's own way, a feeling for what the French might call 'le parfum d'archaïsme' which was to reappear in the SALUSTE DU BARTAS cycle. The original accompaniment was for string quartet. Croiza also gave the first performance of songs written for a marionette version of Hans Andersen's *The little mermaid*. These TROIS CHANSONS DE LA PETITE SIRÈNE (René Morax, 1926) are tiny vocal fragments, but they evoke the fairy-tale mood of the story in masterly fashion. The *Berceuse de la sirène* from this set was recorded by Croiza and the composer. Two settings of Shakespeare (DEUX CHANTS D'ARIEL) written as part of the incidental music for a production of *The tempest* also belong to the 1920s and are remarkably atmospheric miniatures. Both *Venez jusqu'à ces sables d'or* ('Come unto these yellow sands') and *Où butine l'abeille* ('Where the bee sucks') have a madcap other-worldly quality which was unmatched by any composer until Tippett's settings some forty years later. The songs are even more effective in the composer's luminous orchestration.

The songs of the 1930s are more chanson than mélodie, songs in popular vein like *Chanson des quatre* and *Chanson de l'émigrant* (both J. R. Bloch, 1937) written for the drama *La construction d'une cité*. Two settings from Jean Richepin's *Miarka*, the character made famous in mélodie by Alexandre Georges in an earlier generation, were composed for a film in the same year: these are *Chanson de la route* and *Chansons de l'eau*. Numerous chansons were written for films made during the war years. In 1939–40 the composer wrote a set of mélodies (TROIS POÈMES DE CLAUDEL) for Pierre Bernac. There is a solid majesty about these songs which somehow captures the character of their dedicatee. The composer seems to abandon melody in favour of recitative, a type of heightened speech which suits the words of this patrician and intellectual poet particularly well. Another rather austere work is the TROIS PSAUMES (translations from the Psalms of David by Théodore de Bèze and Clément Marot, 1940–1), modelled on the rigours of Protestant church music. In *Psaume CXL*, the second song of the set, the repeated line 'Ô dieu donne-moi délivrance de cet homme pernicieux' seems as eloquent a plea for France's safety from Hitler as could be penned. The Marot setting which concludes the cycle shares some of its thematic material with Honegger's Second Symphony.

Also from 1941 is a cycle which seems removed as far as possible from the events of the war, although it does look towards England with a fond affection which seems to be born of memories of better times. The words are from Jean Giraudoux's *Suzanne et le Pacifique*, and the title of the cycle is PETITS COURS DE MORALE, another work conceived for Bernac and Poulenc. These five miniatures (with the titles **Jeanne, Adèle, Cécile, Irène**, and **Rosemonde**) invoke 'Londres', 'Douvres', 'Lancastre', 'Édimbourg', and the exile of one 'Spencer'. They are examples of the quintessential Honegger in his maturity—pithy, witty, and with a serious undertone which is typical of this composer. A tone of cheeky insouciance is even more noticeable in SALUSTE DU BARTAS, six villanelles of Bédat de Monlaur. Bartas was a historical figure, one of the knights in the service of Marguerite de Navarre, the same Margot who inspired a play by Édouard Bourdet, and thus songs from both Auric and Poulenc. Sixteenth-century France is evoked here in a manner unlike that of any other composer given to the writing of historical pastiche. Honegger's idiom remains modern and very much his own, yet manages effortlessly to suggest the swashbuckling gallantry in the time of the Valois kings (only Enescu's Marot settings are a similarly happy blend of ancient and modern). Most notable are the swagger of the first song, **Le château du Bartas**, the infectious gaiety of **Nérac en fête**, and the beautiful **Duo** (in fact a solo song) with which the cycle closes; as the poet meets the queen we hear the name 'Marguerite' sung three times, music which is haunting and exquisite. Here Honegger matches Poulenc in terms of heartfelt lyricism, and yet he achieves his effects in an entirely individual manner. The cycle was created by its dedicatee, Noémie Pérugia, in 1942, but it is a work more recent listeners will associate with the artistry of Hugues Cuenod. While listening to such music we regret that this composer had had no strong and permanent working relationship with a singer since the 1920s. This is no doubt the reason why Honegger did not compose more songs in later life.

There are a few other vocal works from the 1940s apart from the film music: DEUX ROMANCES SENTIMENTALES (B. Zimmer, 1943) are rather fetching chansons in popular style; *Ô temps, suspends ton vol* (Henri Martin, 1945) is a serious essay in Honegger's hieratic style, its static nature expertly reflecting the words. The last cycle was written between 1940 and 1945. This is QUATRE CHANSONS POUR VOIX GRAVE. For the opening number, *La douceur de tes yeux*, Honegger returns to the Armenian poet of his first songs, Archag Tchobanian. He also joins the ranks of Verlaine's composers with a mesmeric *Un grand sommeil noir* [RAVEL 2] and contributes another Ronsard song—a rather fast and tricky one (*La terre les eaux va buvant*)—to the catalogue. The last single song dates from 1946 and marks a return to the biblical psalms of an earlier cycle. This setting of Psalm 130 is entitled *Mimaamaquim*, and in choosing a Hebrew text the composer shows a sympathy for Zionism, a burning issue of the time. The work has an orchestration for woodwind, horn, harp, and strings. The last nine years of Honegger's life are sadly lacking in secular mélodies. There is a *Panis Angelicus* for voice and piano (1950) in a style which still suggests the rigours and economies of the war years.

PETIT COURS DE MORALE

(Jean Giraudoux)

A LITTLE COURSE IN MORALS

I i *Jeanne*

Dans Londres, la grande ville,
Il est un être plus seul
Qu'un naufragé dans son île
Et qu'un mort dans un linceul.
Grand badaud, petit rentier.
Jeanne, voilà son métier.

Jeanne

In London, that great city,
There is a creature more alone
Than a castaway on his island
And a dead man in his shroud.
A great idler, with a life of leisure.
That, Jeanne, is his métier.

I ii *Adèle*

À Douvres un original
Tombe un jour dans le chenal.
Il appelle au sauvetage.
Il se cramponne au récif.
Mais vers lui nul cœur ne nage...
Adèle, ainsi meurt l'oisif.

Adèle

In Dover an eccentric
Falls one day into the channel.
He calls the lifeguard.
He clings to the reef.
But not a soul swims out to him...
Idlers die like that, Adèle.

I iii *Cécile*

Le grand Chinois de Lancastre
Vous attire avec des fleurs...
Puis vous inonde d'odeurs...
Bientôt sa pipe est votre astre!
Du lys au pavot, Cécile,
La route, hélas! est docile.

Cécile

The great Chinaman of Lancaster
Attracts you with flowers...
Then smothers you with fragrances...
Soon his pipe's your guiding star!
From lilies to poppies, Cécile,
The path, alas, is an easy one.

I iv *Irène*

Le lord prévôt d'Édimbourg
Dit que l'amour est chimère.
Mais un jour il perd sa mère...
Ses larmes coulent toujours.
Irène, petite Irène.
L'Amour c'est la grande peine.

Irène

The Lord Provost of Edinburgh
Says that love's a chimera.
But one day he loses his mother...
And still his tears are flowing.
Irène, little Irène,
Love is the great sorrow.

I v *Rosemonde*

Qu'as-tu vu dans ton exil?
Disait à Spencer sa femme,
À Rome, à Vienne, à Pergame,
À Calcutta?—Rien!... fit-il...
Veux-tu découvrir le monde
Ferme tes yeux, Rosemonde.

Rosemonde

What did you see in exile?
His wife would ask Spencer,
In Rome, in Vienna, in Pergamum,
In Calcutta?—Nothing!... he would say
If you wish to discover the world
Close your eyes, Rosemonde.

SALUSTE DU BARTAS *

(Pierre Bédat de Monlaur)

SALUSTE DU BARTAS

2 i *Le château du Bartas*

Un Gascon à mine fière
Écrit de beaux vers pompeux
Dans cette gentilhommière.

Il ressemble comme un frère
À Monluc,[†] illustre preux,
Un Gascon à mine fière.

Le jeune poète espère
Un jour revenir fameux
Dans cette gentilhommière.

Gloire! descends sur la terre
Élire au dessus des dieux
Un Gascon à mine fière
Dans cette gentilhommière.

Château du Bartas

A Gascon of proud mien
Writes beautiful high-flown poesy
In this country-seat.

He could be taken for a brother
Of Monluc, that illustrious knight,
A Gascon of proud mien.

The young poet hopes
To return famous one day
To this country-seat.

O Glory! Descend to earth
And elevate above the gods
A Gascon of proud mien
In this country-seat.

2 ii *Tout le long de la Baïse*[‡]

Tout le long de la Baïse
C'est Saluste du Bartas
Qui sans cesse poétise.

All along La Baïse

All along La Baïse,
Behold Saluste du Bartas
Ever penning poesy.

---

* A Gascon poet who, in 1556, took up arms in the service of Henri of Navarre.
† Blaise de Montluc (1502–77), Marshall of France, and one of the bravest soldiers of all time; it is said that scars covered almost his entire body.
‡ A river that waters Nérac and flows into the Garonne.

Il songe à sa Cidalyse*
En marchant à petits pas
Tout le long de la Baïse.

C'est la souveraine exquise,
Marguerite aux doux appas
Qui sans cesse poétise.

Reine, quelqu'un vous courtise.
Ne l'aimeriez-vous pas?
Tout le long de la Baïse,
Qui sans cesse poétise.

He dreams of his Cidalyse,
While promenading
All along La Baïse.

Behold the exquisite sovereign,
Marguerite with her sweet charm
Ever penning poesy.

Someone is courting you, O Queen,
Might you not love him?
All along La Baïse
Ever penning poesy.

2 iii *Le départ*

Avec sa belle prestance,
Lèvre rouge, regard noir,
Quel modèle d'élégance!

Il part pour courir sa chance
Loin des tours du vieux manoir,
Avec sa belle prestance.

Sur son chapeau se balance
La plume au souffle du soir,
Quel modèle d'élégance!

Tous! admirez sa fringance,
Venez vite, venez voir,
Avec sa belle prestance
Quel modèle d'élégance!

The departure

With his noble bearing,
Red lips, scowling gaze,
What matchless elegance!

He departs to seek his fortune
Far from the towers of the ancient manor,
With his noble bearing.

The plume on his hat
Sways in the evening breeze.
What matchless elegance!

Let all admire his dashing looks,
Come quickly, come and see!
With his noble bearing
What matchless elegance!

2 iv *La promenade*

Marguerite de Navarre
Par un jour brûlant d'été
À promener se prépare.

Sa toilette est du plus rare;
Elle aime tant sa beauté,
Marguerite de Navarre.

Dans Nérac† quel tintamarre!
La princesse en vérité
À promener se prépare.

The promenade

Marguerite de Navarre,
One sweltering summer's day,
Prepares to promenade.

She wears exquisite finery;
She loves her beauty so,
Marguerite de Navarre.

Pandemonium in Nérac!
The Princess, verily,
Prepares to promenade.

---

* See note to Auric 2 iii.
† A town, 24 km S.W. of Agen, where Henri of Navarre held court.

Page, laisse ta guitare,
Puisque en son parc enchanté
Marguerite de Navarre
À promener se prépare.

Page—leave your guitar,
For in her delightful park
Marguerite de Navarre
Prepares to promenade.

2 v *Nérac en fête*

Qu'est-ce donc sur la garenne?
Le peuple danse gaîment.
On accourt lorgner la Reine.

Mais que voit-on? C'est à peine
Comme un mirage charmant.
Qu'est-ce donc sur la garenne?

Des couples vont par centaines
Enlacés étroitement.
On accourt lorgner la Reine!

Amour! c'est toi qui les mène.
Mais chut, elle vient vraiment.
Qu'est-ce donc sur la garenne...
On accourt lorgner la Reine.

Nérac celebrates

What's happening in the castle grounds?
The subjects are dancing merrily.
All run up to gaze on the Queen.

But what do they see? Hardly more
Than a charming mirage.
What's happening in the castle grounds?

Couples come in their hundreds,
Fondly arm in arm.
All run up to gaze on the Queen.

Love! It is you who guides them!
But hush! In truth she comes.
What's happening in the castle grounds...
All run up to gaze on the Queen.

2 vi *Duo*

L'amour auquel tout invite
Va réunir à la fin
Le poète et Marguerite.

Telle en songe elle palpite,
Captive d'un beau destin,
L'amour auquel tout invite.

Avec la ferveur d'un rite
Ils se tiennent par la main,
Le poète et Marguerite.

Éros qui tout facilite,
Allume donc dans leur sein
L'amour auquel tout invite.
Le poète et Marguerite.

Duo

Love all-engaging
Will finally unite
The poet and Marguerite.

As in a dream she palpitates,
Fair destiny's captive,
Love all-engaging.

With a sacred fervour
They hold each other's hand,
The poet and Marguerite.

Eros, who makes all things possible,
Kindle in their breasts
Love all-engaging,
The poet and Marguerite.

HOPKINS, Antony (b. 1921)

This celebrated broadcaster and music educationalist is an accomplished composer, particularly of chamber opera. Two items are published by Chester which are of interest to explorers of settings in French. *FIVE FRENCH FOLKSONGS* includes a pair of songs dedicated to Sophie Wyss, the Swiss soprano who is the link between Britten and Hopkins in this field; we are reminded that Britten is not the only English composer to have arranged folksongs from France (Rawsthorne is another). Hopkins also composed a setting of Baudelaire's *Recueillement* (1952) [DEBUSSY 7 iv] which is one of the most ambitious attempts by an English composer to tackle a text of this import.

HÜE, Georges (1858–1948)

There is a period charm to the music of this Prix de Rome winner of 1879. His operas have vanished without trace, but his songs find their way into anthologies from time to time, and are always well made and sometimes a great deal more than that. Like Saint-Saëns, Hüe was an inveterate traveller, and *CROQUIS D'ORIENT* (Tristan Klingsor), at one time a well-known oriental cycle, reflects this, as do the *ESQUISSES MAROCAINES*. The *TROIS POÈMES MARITIMES* (André Lebey, 1904) paint the sea in three different moods—*Mer grise, Mer païenne*, and *Mer sauvage*. Another well-known cycle of the time was Hüe's *CHANSONS PRINTANIÈRES* (Jean Bénédict), which includes the much-anthologized song *Les clochettes des muguets* with its ingeniously dancing accompaniment. Probably the best cycle is *VERSAILLES* (the composer's home-town incidentally—he must have known Augusta Holmès, another native of the region), four songs where the effect of the music is immeasurably enriched by the fine poetry of Albert Samain. (Nadia Boulanger was attracted to the same group of poems.) Of Hüe's separately published mélodies the most interesting setting is of Heine's *J'ai pleuré en rêve* ('Ich hab' im Traum geweinet') a poem immortalized by Schumann in his *DICHTERLIEBE*. The *recueil* of *VINGT MÉLODIES* published by Leduc includes settings by such poets as Armand Silvestre, Hugo, Coppée, and Leconte de Lisle, as well as a *L'invitation au voyage* (Baudelaire) [DUPARC 7] which is not entirely devoid of interest in a strong field dominated by such names as Duparc and Chabrier.

IBERT, Jacques (1890–1962)

This composer was, in his own rather understated way, an important part of French musical life. Winner of the Prix de Rome in 1919, he returned to Rome in 1937 as director of the Académie de France, a post he held until 1960. His most profound work is probably his String Quartet, but his catalogue is full of useful, even celebrated pieces like the Flute Concerto, and the delectable *Le petit âne blanc* for piano (which is also available as a song). Though he wrote some twenty-five mélodies, only the *QUATRE CHANSONS DE DON QUICHOTTE* (1932) appear with any regularity on the concert stage.

These had the distinction of being chosen above Ravel's songs on the same theme for a film starring Chaliapin. It is of course the Ravel settings (to different poems) which remain famous, but Ibert's songs (to poems by Ronsard and Alexandre Arnoux) are useful additions to the repertoire. They gave the great Russian singer more leeway with interpretation than Ravel's songs allow (a number of unaccompanied or free recitative passages) and there was a nobly pathetic *Chanson de la mort* which Chaliapin must have seized on with relish. A single hearing of these songs shows how very difficult it must have been to choose between the two composers' work.

Ibert's first songs date from 1910. Both *Le jardin du ciel* (Mendès) and *Chanson* (Maeterlinck) have a Fauréan calm, the latter song something of a companion piece for Fauré's only song in English, *Chanson de Mélisande.* This is the writing of a young man who has soberly absorbed the lessons of the past. The TROIS CHANSONS DE CHARLES VILDRAC (1919–21) show quite an advance in style (elaborate flute-like piano writing, a vocal line in speech rhythms) and it is obvious that late Debussy and Ravel have come into the young composer's pantheon, although there is not a trace of the minimalism of Les Six. In the time-honoured tradition of duets for women's voices there is Ibert's realization (1922) of Francesco Milani's (1645) *Canzone madrigalesca* with French words. Apart from the Flute Concerto, the composer's interest in this instrument is also evident from the DEUX STÈLES ORIENTÉES (Ségalen, 1925) for voice and flute without piano. This music of cryptic simplicity suggests the rigours of a distant culture; the work is a Chinese counterpart of Ravel's CHANSONS MADÉCASSES which date from more or less the same time.

Perhaps the most typical set of Ibert's mélodies is the QUATRE CHANTS (1926-7) to poems by Jean-Aubry and Philippe Chabaneix. In a song from this set like *Familière* we find the tender elegance and understated melancholy of the mélodie at its most transparent. The sad little envoi as the lover leaves for Colombo has the hallmarks of an Albert Roussel epilogue. Thus it is with Ibert: impeccable craftsmanship, but almost always the echo of another man's voice. Also worthy of mention is an extra song from the *Don Quichotte* film—a charming *Chanson de Sancho*—a melodious *Chanson de Fortunio* (from Musset's play *Le chandelier*), and a pretty little pair of songs composed in 1943 for Ibert's radio opera entitled *Barbe bleue.* These DEUX CHANSONS DE MELPOMÈNE (William Aguet) may be accompanied by either piano or harpsichord, and are pleasant trifles for soprano. From the same opera and the same poet there is also a charming little ensemble for two sopranos, alto, tenor, and baritone: *Quintette de la peur.*

QUATRE CHANSONS DE DON QUICHOTTE

FOUR DON QUIXOTE SONGS

I i *Chanson du départ de Don Quichotte*

(Pierre de Ronsard)

The song of Don Quixote's parting

Ce Chasteau-neuf, ce nouvel edifice
Tout enrichy de marbre et de porphire,
Qu'Amour bastit chasteau de son empire,
Où tout le Ciel a mis son artifice,
  Est un rempart, un fort contre le vice,
Où la Vertu maistresse se retire,
Que l'œil regarde, et que l'esprit admire,
Forçant les cœurs à luy faire service.
  C'est un Chasteau fait de telle sorte,
Que nul ne peut approcher de la porte,
Si des grands Rois il n'a sauvé sa race,
  Victorieux, vaillant et amoureux.
Nul Chevalier, tant soit aventureux,
Sans estre tel, ne peut gaigner la place.

This new castle, this new edifice,
Enriched with marble and porphyry
That Love built to guard his empire,
To which all heaven has lent its skill,
  Is a rampart, a stronghold against evil,
Where Mistress Virtue can take refuge,
Whom the eye observes and the spirit admires,
Compelling hearts to pay her homage.
  This castle is fashioned in such a way
That no one can approach its gate,
Unless he is descended from great Kings,
  With victory, valour, and love.
No knight, however bold,
Without such merit, can enter here.

I ii *Chanson à Dulcinée*

(Alexandre Arnoux)

Song to Dulcinea

Un an me dure la journée
Si je ne vois ma Dulcinée.

Mais, amour a peint son visage,
Afin d'adoucir ma langueur,
Dans la fontaine et le nuage,
Dans chaque aurore et chaque fleur.

Un an me dure la journée
Si je ne vois ma Dulcinée.

Toujours proche et toujours lointaine,
Étoile de mes longs chemins,
Le vent m'apporte son haleine
Quand il passe sur les jasmins.

Un an me dure la journée
Si je ne vois ma Dulcinée.

A day seems like a year
If I do not see my Dulcinea.

But to sweeten my languishing,
Love has painted her face
In fountains and clouds,
In every dawn and every flower.

A day seems like a year
If I do not see my Dulcinea.

Ever near and ever far,
Star of my weary journeying,
Her breath is brought me on the breeze,
As it passes over jasmine flowers.

A day seems like a year
If I do not see my Dulcinea.

I iii *Chanson du duc*

(Alexandre Arnoux)

Je veux chanter ici la dame de mes songes
Qui m'exalte au-dessus de ce siècle de boue.
Son cœur de diamant est vierge de mensonges,
La rose s'obscurcit au regard de sa joue.
Pour elle j'ai tenté les hautes aventures:
Mon bras a délivré la princesse en servage,
J'ai vaincu l'enchanteur, confondu les parjures
Et ployé l'univers à lui rendre l'hommage.
Dame par qui je vais, seul dessus cette terre,
Qui ne soit prisonnier de la fausse apparence,
Je soutiens contre tout chevalier téméraire
Votre éclat non pareil et votre précellence.

The Duke's song

I wish now to praise the Lady of my dreams,
Who lifts me above this squalid age.
Her diamond heart is devoid of deceit,
The rose grows dim beside her cheeks.
For her I've embarked on great adventures:
Princesses in thrall I've freed with my arm,
I've vanquished sorcerers, confounded perjurers,
And compelled the universe to pay her homage.
Lady, for whom I travel this earth alone,
Who is not deceived by false pretences,
Against any rash knight I shall uphold
Your peerless beauty and perfection.

I iv *Chanson de la mort de Don Quichotte*

(Alexandre Arnoux)

Ne pleure pas, Sancho,
Ne pleure pas, mon bon,
Ton maître n'est pas mort,
Il n'est pas loin de toi,
Il vit dans une île heureuse
Où tout est pur et sans mensonge,
Dans l'île enfin trouvée
Où tu viendras un jour,
Dans l'île désirée,
Ô mon ami Sancho.

Les livres sont brûlés
Et font un tas de cendres,
Si tous les livres m'ont tué,
Il suffit d'un pour que je vive;
Fantôme dans la vie
Et réel dans la mort—
Tel est l'étrange sort
Du pauvre Don Quichotte. Ah!

Song of Don Quixote's death

Weep not, Sancho,
Weep not, good fellow,
Your master is not dead,
He is not far from you,
He lives on a happy isle,
Where all is pure and truthful,
On this isle that he has finally found,
Where you shall also come one day,
On this longed-for isle,
O Sancho, my friend.

Books have been burnt
To a heap of ashes.
If all those books have caused my death,
It will take but one to make me live;
A phantom in life
And real in death.
Such is the strange fate
Of poor Don Quixote. Ah!

INDY, Vincent d' (1851–1931)

Like his teacher César Franck, this important figure in the history of French music contributed relatively little to the mélodie in his own right, certainly in comparison to his friends and contemporaries Duparc and Chausson. His pupils Roussel, Magnard, and Satie were also to have a strong influence on the song form, far exceeding that of their teacher. As founder of the Schola Cantorum, however, d'Indy's educational beliefs were of incalculable influence on at least two generations of young composers. But despite d'Indy's undeniable stature, there is something rather dry and mirthless about his reputation (unjustly, supporters claim) and d'Indy's formidable personality seems not to have been song-friendly: a sheerly melodic gift was not a strong point, unlike a gift for variation form, for example, for which he was renowned. He was almost too strong in terms of his personality: blazing conviction, impeccable morals, patriotism bordering on chauvinism, wholehearted dedication to duty. All these things (which are, dare one say, not typical of every French composer) have made this fascinating man somewhat unattractive to those who value the Gallic muse for its easy *laissez-faire*. He is a figure of many contradictions: a gallant fighter in the Franco-Prussian War, he was conquered by German art and took the advice of Wagner to adapt the principles of Bayreuth to a French subject. Thus we have *Fervaal*, one of the operas least likely to be revived in modern times, but one which contains some fine music. On the other hand, and despite this Germanic bias, d'Indy was an avid collector of French folk music (there are some 180 piano-accompanied folksong arrangements from the Vivarais and Vercors regions) and one of his finest works, the *Symphonie sur un chant montagnard français* is based on folk music from the Ardèche. In this respect d'Indy is a real pioneer, the link between the partially invented folksong arrangements of Brahms, for example, and the more modern and scrupulously researched work of Bartók, Kodály, and Janáček. Without d'Indy's example neither Emmanuel nor Canteloube would have made their arrangements.

Some of d'Indy's early songs seem rather lifeless affairs, including some Hugo and Baudelaire poems (of the latter poet, d'Indy set *L'amour et le crâne*). An example of the composer's less than complete identification with words is a setting of *L'attente* (Hugo, 1871) [SAINT-SAËNS 2], which both Wagner and Saint-Saëns turned into exciting scherzo movements. D'Indy decides to accompany the opening verse in quavers, the next verse in triplets, and the final strophe in sextuplets. Tension is supposed to mount according to this tidy scheme, but the composer has ignored the fact that the rhythm of Hugo's verse shows excitement right from the beginning. By the time d'Indy's music takes this on board the power and drive of the poetic conception is lost. *Madrigal* (Bonnières, 1872), on the other hand, to a more static poem, is a delightful evocation of early music. The melody of the second strophe is the same as the first but the accompaniment, like music for a chest of viols, proliferates into four parts in a manner which shows that this composer knew a great deal about sixteenth-century music. From a slightly later period is the *Plainte de Thécla* (1880); Bonnières's translation of Schiller's *Des Mädchens Klage* is an offshoot of the triptych of symphonic overtures entitled *Wallenstein*. (The original poem was set three times by Schubert, as well as by the young Mendelssohn.) The somewhat cumbersome *La chevauchée du Cid* (Bonnières, 1876) is a scène for baritone, chorus, and orchestra in the Spanish-Moorish manner beloved by so many French song composers.

A marked progress in d'Indy's song style is shown with the *Lied maritime* (1896) to the composer's own text. The song's German and English versions (*Meereslied, Song of the sea*) were published simultaneously with the original. The melody has the honest and hearty strength of folksong, and the increasingly elaborate accompaniment is written in such a way to suggest the freedom of improvisation, arpeggios surging like waves over the stave. Here d'Indy achieves something genuinely inventive; at first glance it has a touch of Chausson about it, but remains very much his own. And just when we have pigeon-holed him into someone earnestly worthy but lacking in humour and tenderness, we discover *La première dent* (J. de La Laurencie, 1898), a *berceuse enfantine* of Fauréan simplicity, full of a father's affection and gentleness, a companion piece to Loewe's *Der Zahn* (on the same toothy subject) and Séverac's *Ma poupée chérie*. There is a later setting of Paul Gravollet (*Mirage*, 1903) and *Les yeux de l'aimée* (1904), unexpectedly sensual love music coloured by Tristan-like harmony, to the composer's own poem. His last song is a duet—*Madrigal à deux voix* (Charles d'Orléans, 1928) for soprano and cello.

Despite a handful of approachable songs, the problems which d'Indy still poses for the musical world cannot be resolved by championing his mélodies alone. His long-overdue reassessment, if it is ever to take place, must be based on his larger works.

1 *Lied maritime*

(Vincent d'Indy)

Au loin, dans la mer, s'éteint le soleil,
Et la mer est calme et sans ride;
Le flot diapré s'étale sans bruit,
Caressant la grève assombrie;
Tes yeux, tes traîtres yeux sont clos,
Et mon cœur est tranquille comme la mer.

Au loin, sur la mer, l'orage est levé,
Et la mer s'émeut et bouillonne;
Le flot jusqu'aux cieux s'érige superbe,
Et croule en hurlant vers les abîmes.

Tes yeux, tes traîtres yeux si doux
Me regardent jusqu'au fond de l'âme,
Et mon cœur torturé, mon cœur bien heureux
S'exalte et se brise comme la mer!

Song of the sea

Afar, in the sea, the sun is fading,
And the sea is calm and smooth;
The bespangled waves stretch silently
And caress the darkened shore;
Your eyes, your treacherous eyes are closed,
And my heart is as still as the sea.

Afar, on the sea, the storm has broken,
And the sea is seething and boiling;
The mighty waves rear up to heaven,
And crash howling down into the depths.

Your eyes, so sweet and treacherous,
Gaze right into the depths of my soul,
And my tortured and so happy heart
Exults and breaks like the sea!

IVES, Charles (1874–1954)

There are four French songs published together as Nos. 76–9 in the celebrated collection *114 SONGS* by a composer who was an astonishing pioneer of the modern, and perhaps America's most innovative musician. Three French songs date from 1897–8. The first of them is *Rosamunde* ('J'attends hélas dans la douleur'), which is a translation by Béranger of a German poem by Wilhelmine von Chézy. Ives had already set (in the original German) another poem from *Rosamunde*—'Der Vollmond strahlt' which is famous in Schubert's setting. *Qu'il m'irait bien* (it is not certain who wrote the text) has a dance-like naivety although the final effect, as in all these songs, is of a modernity that not only borders on the eccentric, but enters that realm with wholehearted determination. The very title of the *Chanson de Florian* gives the name of the poet away; it too is a sprightly ditty ('Tempo di scherzo') and perhaps the easiest of the Ives songs in French to bring off in performance. Ives no doubt took the words from the once-famous setting of the same text by Benjamin Godard [GODARD 1]. The last and longest of Ives's forays into French song dates from 1901 and is an amazingly static version of Gallet's *Élégie*, a poem which was enormously popular in another setting [MASSENET 2]. Ives's song does not resemble the French composer's in the slightest, but the poem seems to have been lifted from that score rather than traced back to its poetic source.

   It is pointless to complain about the hair-raising prosody of these songs, for Ives is always unashamedly Ives. Is it merely inept clumsiness to give a dotted semibreve (in largo tempo) to the words 'le' and 'et' in *Élégie*, or a deliberate distortion to create a poetic effect very much the composer's own? He simply did not care about rules of this kind. What seems beyond dispute is that Ives, judging by his choice of models and texts, was better acquainted with good songs from the lieder repertoire than with the best of contemporary French mélodies. This is in marked contrast to other cultivated American composers of the epoch (Carpenter, Griffes, and Loeffler) who seem to have felt greater affinity with France. With Ives we have strangely individual French songs without French polish.

JACOB, Maxime (1906–1977)

An astonishingly prolific composer (Grove refers to *c.*400 songs but does not list them), Maxime Jacob is completely forgotten. This is a great pity for those who value the mélodie between the wars for its accessibility and stylish understatement. Jacob (no relation to the poet Max Jacob) was a pupil of Koechlin and a member of the École d'Arcueil, the group of young composers who gathered around Érik Satie towards the end of his life. In 1929, in surprisingly similar fashion to his near-namesake Max Jacob, he took holy orders. His new name of Dom Clément OSB is to be found on some of the editions of his songs. These appeared in various sets, the biggest of which are two *recueils* entitled simply *CHANSONS D'AMOUR* (1928–9). The lettering on the cover, and the phrase 'se vend à Paris chez Jean Jobert', immediately suggest an eighteenth-century publication, and these songbooks are a veritable anthology of literature from Molière's time, including a number of settings of the great playwright himself. Such devotion to an earlier epoch prefigures Leguerney's devotion to the poets of the Pléiade, and seldom has a French song composer given himself over to the pastiche style with greater thoroughness.

The *DEUX CHANSONS DE MEZZETIN* add two rare Verlaine poems to the musical lists—*Puisque tout n'est rien que fables* and *Va! Sans nul autre souci*. There are also two Cocteau cycles (*CARTES POSTALES*, which evoke Marseilles, Lourdes and Aix, and *SIX POÈMES*), a tuneful Musset set, one of Lamartine (a strange choice for the time), and the whimsical René Chalupt cycle *LE DÉPOT EST OBLIGATOIRE*. Two elegant settings of Georges Duret about spring and autumn (entitled *PROMENADES*) were written for Hugues Cuenod, and the Poulenc enthusiast will discover with great interest the *DEUX POÈMES DE CHARLES D'ORLÉANS*. The first of these is a gentle little setting of *Priez pour paix* [POULENC 9] which was composed some time before the setting by the more famous composer. Despite the fact that Poulenc was somewhat disparaging about Jacob, perhaps we owe the famous composer's setting (one of his best) to the example of the earlier song?

JAUBERT, Maurice (1900–1940)

Jaubert was mainly known for his many film scores from the 1930s. He worked with such directors as Vigo, Clair, and Carné, and with Giraudoux in the theatre. It is only now that Jaubert, killed on active service, is beginning to be reassessed as a composer of serious music. The *CHANTS SAHARIENS* (1924) is a set of five songs for voice, oboe, tambourine, and string quartet. Two songs from Giraudoux's novel *Elpénor* (1927) on the theme of Ulysses—*Chanson de la sirène rousse* and *Chanson du pilote*—were given their first performance by Jane Bathori. The *TROIS SÉRÉNADES* (1928) are settings of Apollinaire, Jammes, and Supervielle, and the latter poet was also set in a substantial cycle of four songs entitled *SAISIR*. Jaubert seems to have been attracted to vocal music with instrumental ensemble (in the manner of Delage's *QUATRE POÈMES HINDOUS* and the Ravel of the *CHANSONS MADÉCASSES*), but he was also interested in piano-accompanied song. Interesting examples of his writing for voice and piano alone are: *QUATRE ROMANCES* (Toulet, 1924), an attractive set of miniatures; *LE TOMBEAU DE L'AMOUR* (Demoustier, 1925), a collection of short letter-like songs to eighteenth-century texts, including the haunting *Exilée au sein de Paris*; and the *DEUX POÈMES DE MALHERBE* (1927), where sixteenth-century verse gives rise to songs of gravity and vivacity. In music of this kind, Jaubert suggests musical archaisms in a manner which does not preclude modern dissonance. A later set of songs is *Ô MES FRÈRES PERDUS* (Éluard) which comprises *Novembre 1936* and *Sans âge*. Jaubert was killed on 19 June 1940, exactly a day before the death in action of another fine French composer, Jehan Alain.

JOLIVET, André (1905–1974)

This composer was only six years younger than Poulenc, but he inhabited a different musical world. He was only in his early twenties when Schoenberg visited Paris, but it was an experience that left its mark on him. Jolivet was to become a member of La Jeune France, a group which also included Olivier Messiaen, Yves Baudrier, and Daniel-Lesur. Unlike Messiaen, he was not destined to create his own world of sound and aesthetics; rather he was forced by circumstance into a greater flexibility of approach. The somewhat severe esoteric early style of a young lion of the avant-garde yielded to a more unbuttoned attitude in the war years. Jolivet wrote an *opéra bouffe* entitled *Dolorès*, and his LES TROIS COMPLAINTES DU SOLDAT (to his own poems, 1940) were sung by Bernac in the orchestral version in 1943. These are moving and unusual songs in monologue style which draw on the composer's own experiences of anguish and disillusionment in the vanquished French army. The last song, *La complainte à Dieu*, finds religious consolation in the debacle of war. Another substantial cycle from this period is the POÈMES INTIMES (L. Emié, 1944), written to celebrate the composer's tenth wedding anniversary; here the tone of exalted love in its mystical forms seems to lie somewhere between the mood of Poulenc's Éluard settings and Messiaen's POÈMES POUR MI. Almost every song that Jolivet composed in his maturity was orchestrated. In recent years there has been something of a revival of interest in his single songs with piano from earlier in his career which had been all but forgotten. These include numerous settings of François Villon as well as songs with texts by Jammes and Reverdy, and have been reissued by the publisher Gérard Billaudot. They show the versatility and wide range of interests of a man who was practical enough to be director of music at the Comédie Française for sixteen years (1943–59), and intellectual enough to be a serious scholar of French Renaissance polyphony. Jolivet's interest in this period of musical history is shown by his Villon setting *Rondel* ('Au retour de dure prison'), by his beautiful *Sonnet de Ronsard* (1929) for three unaccompanied women's voices, and by a most approachable set of songs, QUATRE MÉLODIES SUR DES POÉSIES ANCIENNES, which also dates from 1929. Interesting in the same way, but from a much later date, are the TROIS POÈMES GALANTS (Saint-Gellais, Bucher, and Père le Moyne, 1951). His comic gift is well illustrated by the early *Chewing gum* (Claude Sernet, 1928), where the voice is told to sound like 'un mauvais saxophone', as well as a racy Max Jacob setting entitled *La mule de Lord Bolingbroke*. Despite a very different musical language, it is here that Jolivet seems to link hands with the Poulenc of LE BAL MASQUÉ. The last of this composer's vocal works is SONGE À NOUVEAU RÊVÉ (1971), in effect a symphony for soprano and orchestra in three movements. The texts are by the music critic Antoine Goléa, but the composer makes full use of vocalise techniques and onomatopoeic effects in a manner reminiscent of Messaien.

JONGEN, Joseph (1873–1953)

This composer is still popular in his native Belgium, where his songs are frequently performed by enterprising Conservatoire students, although they deserve better than relegation to the classroom. Being a writer of mélodies in Belgium was never easy. Cut off from mainstream Parisian musical contacts (a composer had to be well-regarded in Paris itself to find a publisher) a long list of musicians, some of them gifted in the field of song, languished in parochial obscurity, and without the means to distribute their work. Those few musicians who are acquainted with the unknown reaches of Belgian mélodie talk of an unexplored treasure trove. At least Jongen was published, locally in Belgium, and sometimes abroad. *Quand ton sourire me surprit* (Silvestre), for example, was issued by Senart in Paris, and is an attractive exercise in the Fauré manner. Those of his mélodies which he allowed to survive were composed between 1902 and 1923. *Calmes, aux quais déserts* (Samain) for voice and string quartet, and a useful addition to works for these forces, was published by Chester. Perhaps the most interesting songs are those to Belgian poets not otherwise well served in the world of mélodie: *Les pauvres* (Émile Verhaeren), *Les cadrans* (Frans Hellens), and *Dans son écrin* (Roger Audoin) are fine settings of distinguished texts in rather sombre mood. There is a musical personality here that seems similar to that of Jongen's compatriot Guillaume Lekeu. In the madrigal style suggesting an earlier century is *Villanelle* (Gauthier-Villars, Colette's 'Willy'). This, and the more light-hearted *Bal de fleurs* (A. Hardy), are perhaps Jongen's most immediately appealing songs, and the *Chanson roumaine* (Hélène Vacaresco) with its wordless melismas has great charm. A curiosity is a setting of *Après un rêve* (Bussine, 1902) [FAURÉ 10] where the text is taken rather more seriously than it is by Fauré, whose beautiful melody somewhat overshadows the words. Jongen's song seems rather Chaussonesque in style, and shows his affiliation to the Franck school.

KOECHLIN, Charles (1867–1950)

He is one of the strangest anomalies in French song. Respected as a teacher, widely influential as a writer and musical authority (on the mélodie itself among other things), he was uncompromisingly incorruptible, but also strangely unworldly. He came from a good Alsace bourgeois family, but leant heavily towards the Left, supporting, though never joining, the Communist Party. Such people are seldom able, or interested enough, to negotiate the networking and political side of the world of music. In his day, Koechlin was dismissed as an eccentric, the Parisian equivalent of a strangely dressed Hampstead intellectual, a musical Michael Foot, admired for his integrity at the same time as raising a smile. There is no doubt that he created his own sound-world, though some audiences may prefer to visit this realm only for a short while. Koechlin's music can ramble, sometimes inventively, often charmingly, usually alarmingly as far as the performers are concerned. His delight in his own harmonies (where chords of the fourth and fifth are piled on top of each other) sometimes makes him forget that he has an audience whose patience can wear thin. One has the impression that his music was written largely for himself. His seeming lack of self-criticism, and his disinclination to revise any of his works, make many of them too long and seemingly disorganized. But as more of his output has become known to the world at large, audiences have come to see the eccentric side of him to be as truly inventive as, say, in Charles Ives, and there is much about his music which confirms his vision, originality, and startling modernity. We find traces of almost everyone in Koechlin's output, which is unashamedly eclectic: his beloved Fauré and Debussy without doubt, but also Bach, Chopin, Schumann, Massenet, Satie, and Milhaud, and other composers less known such as Sauguet. As is usually the case when tracing musical lineage, it is difficult to say who copied whom, and in some cases the influence worked in both directions.

The big drawback of the Koechlin songs is the composer's lack of a memorable melodic gift. The fascination of his work rests with its harmonic adventurousness, its ability to create atmosphere and its often delightful quirkiness. Koechlin's vocal lines approximate to speech, but they lack the glamour of Debussy's when he is on the same tack. The effect is often of accompanied recitation or chant rather than melody. And yet there are certain poets, and one thinks especially of Albert Samain, whose entire aesthetical world is re-created for us in Koechlin's long and complex settings of his texts. In these songs, one cannot say that any one phrase is revelatory because of a cunning marriage of word and tone, but the effect of the whole is as true, in its own way, to the spirit of this poet as anything created by Fauré in his Samain songs, and a great deal more ambitious.

The earlier songs remain the most accessible, and they are also Koechlin's first work as a composer (because he deliberately approached the art of composition through this medium). There are no less than twenty-one *rondels* to the poetry of Banville, spread over three opus numbers. It may have been these which fired Reynaldo Hahn to set some of the same texts a few years later, albeit in a completely different way. *La nuit*, the first rondel of Op. 1 (1890–4), had already been set by Chausson as a duet. Here we can still find traces of salon style; sometimes Koechlin resorts to the trick of a suddenly high note or unexpectedly luscious cadence to create an exquisite effect. *Le thé* (1890) is more original and, lifted out of the set of rondels, remains one of the most widely performed of Koechlin's songs. It has a trace of chinoiserie appropriate to the teacup's provenance, but the overwhelming impression is of Massenet crossed with the English gentility of Miss Ellen, who pours the tea. It is also a prophecy of minimalism in music with its repetitive tune, and its deliberately banal background ostinato.

Another song along these minimalist lines is once again a Banville rondel, *L'hiver* (1895), which is built entirely on a pianistic background of glissandos up and down the keyboard. The other celebrated song which has something of the automatic and repetitive about it is **Si tu le veux** (de Marsan, 1894). This might be described as a triumph of non-melody aided by adept harmony and sweeping arpeggios in the accompaniment; the result is something which manages to sound both offhand and exquisite.

Returning to the Banville rondels, *Le printemps* seems rather tame in comparison with Hahn's ecstatic setting [HAHN 11] and the same could be said of *L'air*, where the younger composer is more imaginative. But there are many other fine and unusual things in these Banville songs: *La pêche*, despite competition from Hahn, has a robust individuality; and both *La lune* (a mock minuet which deliciously captures the point of 'Elle est absurde, elle est charmante') and *Le matin* would grace any programme. *La paix*, set as a gentle duet, is a useful item for two women's voices. The third set of

RONDELS (1896–9) includes *Le midi*, which is dedicated to Hahn; it is a poem suitable for a programme about painters which mentions Fragonard, Boucher, and Watteau. *Les métaux* is a moonscape of a song, with thick chords widely spaced in both hands, and a sneaky Wagnerian quotation (from *Das Rheingold*) hidden in the texture. *Les étoiles* [HAHN 13] is dedicated to Duparc and has nothing of the melodic sweep of Hahn's famous setting; with its static harmony it is an appropriately unearthly evocation of starlight. Although some of this composer's piano writing is extremely demanding, he himself was no great pianist.

The CINQ MÉLODIES Op. 5 (1893–7) begin with *Promenade galante* (also Banville), a fine song for women's chorus dedicated to the muse of both Fauré and Debussy—Emma Bardac; here Koechlin exceeds Hahn's efforts in the piano-accompanied choral medium. Almost every composer of the time had a go at pastiche, but Koechlin's *Menuet* (Gregh) is more original than most. Problems arise when the length of a poem encourages the composer to ramble, and it has to be admitted that there are a number of his songs which outstay their welcome for reasons of length alone. Sometimes the composer, aided by a good poem, carries it off, and among the successes of this period are *Déclin d'amour* (Sully Prudhomme, 1894) from the POÈMES D'AUTOMNE which builds into a song of considerable grandeur without embracing the more impractical of Koechlin's flights of fancy. *Le nénuphar* (Haraucourt) from the same set might be explored by those interested in the repertoire of songs with obbligato instruments, although the singer might object to standing through two pages of slow flute and piano music after having reached her fortissimo musical climax. But then this is typical of Koechlin who courts the unusual as a matter of course, and who, in the manner of Berlioz, sometimes seems impervious to the practical side of music-making, and the limitations of both singers and their patience. It is little wonder that Massenet's songs received many more performances. One of the most manageable sets of songs (in terms of length and vocal demands) is QUATRE POÈMES DE E. HARAUCOURT (1890–95). There are moments of virtuosity (as always in Koechlin) but this cycle, in either its piano or orchestral version, makes a good case for the composer's best qualities.

The turn of the century produced some fine songs. The most substantial work from this time was TROIS POÈMES (1899–1901), the words taken from Kipling's *Jungle book*, large choral settings with vocal soloists and orchestra, including a *Berceuse phoque* much admired by Satie. The composer published a version with piano which is all but unplayable. (The *Jungle book* was to occupy Koechlin, on and off, for some thirty years from 1899–1939.) For those interested in comparative settings, Koechlin's *Le colibri* (1898–9) [CHAUSSON 6] is worthy of study, as is the Samain setting *Accompagnement*, a poem also tackled by Fauré [FAURÉ 38]. As fine a set of songs that Koechlin ever wrote was his Op. 22, QUATRE MÉLODIES (1900–1), which includes three valuable Verlaine settings. *La chanson des ingénues* and *Mon rêve familier*, both from the poet's *Poèmes saturniens*, are indispensable additions to Verlaine's song-list, the first cheekily capricious, the other a superb murmured confession of loneliness which displays for the first time in this composer's songs the obsessive longing for the female ideal which will pervade his later work. The third Verlaine song is *Il pleure dans mon cœur* [DEBUSSY 6 ii], where Koechlin's familiar vocal monotones and floatingly anonymous chords are ideally suited to the poem. The fourth item in the set is a gem: *Novembre* (the poet is Paul Bourget who had been a favourite of the young Debussy) is a song as prophetic of Poulenc as any we will find in the repertoire, a Debussy *Spleen* for a new century. The world of the smoky nightclub and the seventh and ninth chords which announce jazz are here to be found long before this particular tone had found its way into the mélodies of other composers. (It is surprising, therefore, to discover that Koechlin loathed jazz itself when he finally heard some in the 1920s, although he was a willing orchestrator for Cole Porter's *Within the quota,* danced by the Ballet Suédois in 1923.) At first the singer seems almost too languid and depressed by the autumn blues to do anything but waver around one or two notes low on the stave, but the music builds to an impassioned climax before returning to the first mood with subtle harmonic modifications. There are four further Verlaine settings published as Op. 24 (1901–2), all taken from *La bonne chanson.* Three of these use different poems from Fauré's set. The one duplication is *N'est-ce pas?* [FAURÉ 30 viii], which Koechlin has conceived as a homage to his old *maître* by modelling its rhythm on *Une Sainte en son auréole* [FAURÉ 30 i], the opening song of Fauré's cycle.

It is at this point in his work that the composer enters a new phase of complexity and difficulty. This period is typified by Koechlin's concentration on the poetry of Albert Samain and Pierre Louÿs. The mood is that of Debussy's CHANSONS DE BILITIS writ large, as if Koechlin has taken his main inspiration from that cycle of miniatures and expanded it to an epic canvas which strives to show a broader vista of the antique world. Samain's poems from his collection *Aux flancs du vase* yield such large and spacious songs as *Le cortège d'Amphitrite* and *Amphise et Melitta* (1905–7). These are rather daunting for listeners and performers but they are highly impressive in their way; after listening to them one has to admit that nowhere else in the mélodie is there anything quite like this music, infinitely fluid yet as static as an ancient frieze. Between 1898 and 1908 Koechlin composed his own CINQ CHANSONS DE BILITIS (Louÿs) which further explore this vein of misty antique evocation ideally suited to the blur of Koechlin's music, but without the essential understatement and grace which makes Debussy's cycle immortal. Indeed, the opening song *Hymne à Astarté,* with its fortissimo invocation 'Astarté!', achieves a pagan vehemence which appears almost crude by comparison. With *Le repas préparé* (Samain) from Op. 31 we can hear something of the tone of Ravel's SHÉHÉRAZADE, and it comes as no surprise that Koechlin embarked on a vast survey of the Tristan Klingsor poems from which Ravel had selected the three songs for his cycle. In this frank purloining of the poetry of Klingsor and Louÿs, Koechlin was doing nothing underhand; rather was his theft of ideas an act of naive and open-hearted homage to composers whom he acknowledged were greater than himself. In any case, his SHÉHÉRAZADE songs (13 in all from Opp. 56 and 84) avoid the texts used by Ravel. *Le voyage,* from the second collection of 1922–3, takes us to the heart of Koechlin's mature, multi-layered harmonic world, and the heart of his belief that dreams were more beautiful than reality.

The final chapter in the story of Koechlin songs is perhaps the most bizarre. It concerns his passion for a film actress of the 1930s called Lilian Harvey. This was an infatuation of an ageing man for an enchanting image on the silver screen and it produced an amazing amount of music. Koechlin wrote many letters to this now-forgotten star (though she only replied to the first), and this muse of the early talkies inspired over 100 of his best cameos. The first *ALBUM DE LILIAN* (1934) contains two songs (most of the music inspired by her is for piano solo or for flute and piano) which are typical of the composer in this mood. ***Keep that school girl complexion*** is based on the Palmolive advert Koechlin saw on his American travels. The text (in French despite the song's title) is by the composer himself. *Tout va bien* is a waltz of great charm made all the more whimsical by the words of a besotted admirer. He flirts with Lilian and teases her through his music which provokes an ambivalent response: we do not know whether to be amused by a *jeu d'esprit,* or feel sad for the loneliness of a 66-year-old man. Whatever the truth of the matter, this must be the only example of the 'stalking' of an idol, however innocently meant, that has ever taken a musical form.

The SEPT CHANSONS POUR GLADYS (1935) are named after a role played by Lilian Harvey in the Anatol Litvak film *Calais-Douvres*, and once again the composer has provided his own words—a very eccentric undertaking indeed. In one song, **Le cyclone**, Koechlin lovingly draws attention to the fact that the English 'savant' who had discovered the circulation of the blood was also named Harvey. Koechlin has emerged from a period when he was preoccupied with harmonic concoctions of linear complexity, and has developed his interest in counterpoint and modality (we hear a fragment of sixteenth-century music quoted at the beginning of *Tu croyais le tenir*). The music is concise and witty without losing that moonstruck, diaphanous quality which is the composer's hallmark. From the practical point of view this cycle is the ideal length for inclusion in a recital, something that cannot be said for some of Koechlin's other opus numbers. As a matter of interest, Koechlin was not entirely faithful to Lilian—later in the 1930s he wrote DANSES POUR GINGER [Rogers], and a sensuous instrumental *Épitaphe de Jean Harlow*. The time of songwriting, however, was over.

1 *Le thé*

(Théodore de Banville)

Miss Ellen, versez-moi le Thé
Dans la belle tasse chinoise,
Où des poissons d'or cherchent noise
Au monstre rose épouvanté.

J'aime la folle cruauté
Des chimères qu'on apprivoise:
Miss Ellen, versez-moi le Thé
Dans la belle tasse chinoise.

Là sous un ciel rouge irrité,
Une dame fière et sournoise
Montre en ses longs yeux de turquoise
L'extase et la naïveté:
Miss Ellen, versez-moi le Thé.

Tea

Miss Ellen, pour me tea
In the beautiful China cup,
Where goldfish pick quarrels
With the terrified rose-red monster.

I like the crazed cruelty
Of chimaeras* one seeks to tame:
Miss Ellen, pour me tea
In the beautiful China cup.

There, beneath an angry red sky,
A lady, proud and sly,
Reveals in her wide turquoise eyes
Ecstasy and innocence:
Miss Ellen, pour me tea.

---

* Fabled fire-breathing monster with a lion's head, goat's body, and serpent's tail, that was killed by Bellerophon in Greek mythology.

2 *Si tu le veux*
(Maurice de Marsan)

Si tu le veux, ô mon amour,
Ce soir dès que la fin du jour
Sera venue,
Quand les étoiles surgiront,
Et mettront des clous d'or au fond
Bleu de la nue,
Nous partirons seuls tous les deux
Dans la nuit brune en amoureux,
Sans qu'on nous voie,
Et tendrement je te dirai
Un chant d'amour où je mettrai
Toute ma joie.

Mais quand tu rentreras chez toi.
Si l'on te demande pourquoi,
Mignonne fée,
Tes cheveux sont plus fous qu'avant,
Tu répondras que seul le vent
T'a décoiffée,
Si tu le veux, ô mon amour.

If you so desire

If you so desire, O my love,
This evening, as soon as day
Has ended,
When the stars appear
And stud with gold
The blue of the skies,
We two shall set out alone
As lovers into the dark night,
Without being seen,
And tenderly I shall sing you
A love-song into which I'll pour
All my joy.

But if, when you return home,
They ask you why,
Sweet elfin creature,
Your hair is more tousled than before,
Tell them that the wind alone
Dishevelled you,
If you so desire, O my love.

3 *Keep that school girl complexion*
(Charles Koechlin)

Gardez ce teint de jeune fille,
Gardez ce teint.
La savon Palmolive vous le conservera.
Gardez ce teint de jeune fille,
Gardez ce teint.

Le savon Palmolive est à base d'huile de palme
Et d'huile d'olive.
On pourrait s'en servir pour la salade,
Mais il vaut mieux s'en servir pour la peau,
Pour la peau des dames.

Il leur donne un velouté merveilleux,
Et tel que le peut désirer
Le plus exigeant amoureux.
Gardez ce teint de jeune fille.

Keep that school girl complexion

Keep that school girl complexion,
Keep that complexion.
Palmolive soap will preserve it for you.
Keep that school girl complexion,
Keep that complexion.

Palmolive soap is palm-oil
And olive-oil based.
You could use it for salads,
But it's better to use it for skin,
For ladies' skin.

It imparts a wonderful softness,
That even the most demanding
Of lovers could desire.
Keep that school girl complexion.

4 *Le cyclone*   *The cyclone*

(Charles Koechlin), from SEPT CHANSONS POUR GLADYS

'Un cyclone?'	'A cyclone?'
La mer était calme, et le soleil radieux.	The sea was calm, and the sun radiant.
Un cyclone?	A cyclone?
Ce n'était qu'un prétexte inventé par le fidèle Jean,	It was merely a pretext invented by faithful old John,
le merveilleux et ridicule serviteur.	that wonderful and ridiculous servant.
Un cylcone?	A cyclone?
'Il n'y en avait pas plus que dans le creux de la main' dites-vous?	'No more than there was in the palm of your hand', you say?
Mais le cyclone était dans ton cœur où le sang bouillonnait	But the cyclone was in your heart where the blood was boiling
avec frénésie.	wildly.
Et comme cela se trouve!	And how very apposite!
La circulation du sang fut découverte par un savant d'Angleterre,	The circulation of the blood was discovered by an English scientist,
qui s'appelait Harvey, ô Lilian!	whose name was Harvey,* O Lilian!

KOSMA, Joseph (1905–1969)

The world of the French popular chanson lies outside the scope of this book, but Kosma, compos-er of the popular *Feuilles mortes* (Prévert), is a figure who bridges two genres. Just as mélodie com-posers have flirted with popular styles and have occasionally written smash hits (Ravel's *Fascination,* and Auric's *Moulin Rouge* theme for example) popular chansonniers have occasionally approached the seriousness of the mélodie. Kosma, a pupil of Hanns Eisler, was a Hungarian who lived in Paris from 1933; his gift for melody and a taste for the best poetry were ideally suited to serious song-writing. Although he wrote such operas as *Les canuts* and *Les hussards,* he made his name by writing film scores, perhaps the most famous of which was for *Les enfants du paradis.* It was his songs, how-ever, music with a social conscience, which made Kosma a darling of the French intellectual Left. His music combined a popular laid-back musical style with an often surprising vehemence of utter-ance, and a well-informed choice of texts by fine writers. Kosma's popular *Verlaine,* for example, is a setting of that poet's celebrated *Chanson d'automne* [HAHN 1 i]. This marriage of literary intellect with musical 'street cred' seems typically Parisian, although John Dankworth tried the same thing (without the political overtones) with his jazz settings of Shakespeare.

Kosma began his collaboration with Jacques Prévert (who also wrote the script of *Les enfants du paradis*) in 1935. The first fruit of this was *À la belle étoile,* a laconic evocation of Parisian prostitutes, tramps, and beggars; one thinks of the contemporary photographs of Kosma's fellow Hungarian Brassaï. The song appeared in Renoir's film *Le crime de M. Lange.* Prévert was without doubt

---

* William Harvey (1578–1657).

Kosma's special poet: *21 CHANSONS* appeared in 1946, and *25 AUTRES CHANSONS* in 1947. Well-known examples of enduring popular classics by this team are *Barbara*, *Cet amour*, *La pêche à la baleine*, and, most memorable of all, *Feuilles mortes*. But Kosma also composed his own *LES CHANSONS DE BILITIS* (after Pierre Louÿs, 1954) and he set the words of Aragon, Anouilh, and Sartre among others. An example of a more politically motivated set of songs is *À L'ASSAUT DU CIEL* (Henri Bassis, 1951), which celebrated the Parisian Commune of 1871. There is a faux-naïf sophistication here (not to mention a political viewpoint) which stems from Eisler. The concentration on melody at the expense of the piano writing almost defiantly separates this work from the mélodie mainstream, although it is true that there is not many a piano to be found on a street march, and much of Kosma's political work deliberately eschews the bourgeois overtones of this instrument.

For the conventional recitalist, Kosma's most successful songs are perhaps those which were composed much later (1965) to texts by Robert Desnos, fertile poetic ground for Witold Lutoslawski at exactly the same time. There are two cycles to this poet: a latter-day *BESTIAIRE* entitled *LA MÉNAGERIE DE TRISTAN* (which includes such delights as *L'oiseau du Colorado*, *Le poisson sans souci*, and *L'araignée à moustaches*), and the shorter *LE PARTERRE D'HYACINTHE*, which includes *L'arbre qui boit du vin* and *La rose à voix de soprano*. Much of this composer's work needs the very special skills of a Piaf, Trenet, or Brel. But the Desnos cycles show Kosma belatedly willing to compromise with the classical concert world which he had earlier found elitist. Here he shows that he is easily able to write developed and interesting piano accompaniments. With this support on the platform, rather than the strummed chords of many of the chansons, art-song singers can add Kosma to their recital programmes with splendid effect.

LALO, Édouard (1823–1892)

There are only twenty-three songs by this highly gifted song composer and yet they are an indispensable part of French musical history. He had a melodic gift of course—perhaps not as individual as that of Bizet—but his main contribution to the genre was his impeccable feeling for the architecture of a song as a fully integrated collaboration between voice and piano. He was one of the French composers who was influenced by Schubert and Schumann, and we can hear this in a certain weight of utterance which betokens a dose of German seriousness, as well as in the independence and vitality of the piano parts. Lalo was a string player by training, yet his accompaniments are always highly idiomatic. They glitter and sparkle and are feather-light, glinting in apposition to the vocal line with a piquant (and frequent) use of staccato. There is a certain classical 'dryness' about the piano writing which is an antidote to the lush, pedalled haze of the accompaniments of composers from the Franck school. Lalo has something in common with Saint-Saëns whose sound is similarly deft (avoiding gush and openly romantic gestures), and favouring clarity and lucidity. This type of pianism from an earlier age valued evenness of finger work where each note was in its exact place—the so-called *jeu perlé*, where runs and scales sounded like strings of exquisite pearls. An extreme example of such technical challenges can be found in the astonishingly florid *Si j'étais petit oiseau* (Béranger, 1849). The vocal writing is rather ordinary and would fail to take wing on its own, but the pianistic flights of fancy recall the most demanding études of Kalkbrenner, and announce a composer determined to use whatever means he has at his disposal, including keyboard extravagances reminiscent of the early Liszt, to illustrate the text. Indeed the colourful flair of that composer, thoroughly assimilated into the French style, can be numbered among Lalo's influences.

Si j'étais petit oiseau is one of the SIX ROMANCES POPULAIRES of 1849. The scholarly edition of Lalo's works in the Le Pupitre series chooses to ignore these early works as untypical. The first 'proper' Lalo songs, the SIX MÉLODIES (Hugo, 1856), are among the most successful debuts in the history of the genre—there is not one among them which seems weaker than the rest. Nevertheless, Lalo himself was not satisfied with the work, and issued a second version of it in 1885. The first five of the songs were revised only in small details, but the last of them was completely rewritten. This accounts for there being two quite different versions of Hugo's *Chanson à boire* ('Amis, vive l'orgie!'). *Guitare* is perhaps better known in Bizet's setting [BIZET 2] but Lalo's song is a gem. We hear the twang of plucked strings throughout, and there is a momentum to this music which has a tightly sprung energy which we will come to recognize as a Lalo trademark. *Puisqu'ici-bas tout âme* is better known as the poem of Hahn's *Rêverie* [HAHN 3], but the fluent charm of that delicious trifle seems rather superficial when measured next to this serious song. Even more exceptional is *L'aube naît* [GOUNOD 5], where we see something of the influence of Berlioz. The middle section suddenly has a gently tripping accompaniment. Dawn knocks on the door, and Lalo gracefully compliments Schubert when he quotes that dancing figure of two semiquavers and a quaver that we recognize from the Shakespeare *Ständchen* ('Horch, horch! die Lerch'). The fourth song, *Dieu qui sourit*, is full of rumbustious masculine swagger, but it nevertheless retains its elegance. This type of celebration of life and beauty (with a glass of wine never far away) was much favoured by Lalo when he wrote for tenor voice. (A number of the composer's songs were written for his wife, who was an accomplished mezzo.) One of his favourite devices is alternating chords between the hands in triple time so that sometimes the strong first beat in the bar falls in the right hand, sometimes in the left. This gives a devil-may-care nonchalance to the music. The fifth of the set is *Oh! quand je dors* which Liszt set in 1842 [LISZT 1]. Lalo's song is not as rhapsodic and erotic, but its gently flowing semiquavers and many harmonic subtleties are part of a remarkably suave interpretation of a great lyric. It is here that we notice how the accompaniment provides a unity to the musical structure in a manner which seems entirely inspired by the German lied. The first version of *Amis, vive l'orgie!* (and published under that name) is demanding and exciting, but somewhat over-written in comparison to the second—*Chanson à boire*—which generates the same excitement without the noisy doublings of vocal line and piano. What is remarkable about this music is its panache, which has something of the same quality of Chabrier's polonaise in *Le roi malgré lui*. Indeed Lalo's music often suggests Chabrier; the two composers share a quirky delight in the offbeat (both literally and metaphorically), the sudden insinuation of a rhythmic or melodic tic which transforms the commonplace into the poetic, the same delight in the tiny musical insurrections which tease the ear and tickle the senses.

These songs are the prototypes of all subsequent Lalo mélodies, and we revisit the same types of songs in later opus numbers. Of the set of three songs to poems by Musset (*c*.1870), **La Zuecca** is an Italian character piece (the poem also set by Massenet as both solo and duet) and *À une fleur* an affecting romance, much more concise than Bizet's setting of the poem which opens that composer's

*FEUILLES D'ALBUM. **Ballade à la lune*** (also a Musset poem) is another of his tenor serenades, and a thoroughly delightful one. Occasionally Lalo invents a new type of song—for example the *Chant breton* (Delpit, 1884) where the piano substitutes for the flute and oboe in recitative-like interjections. This has the freedom of an adventurous folksong arrangement from a much later age. In 1879 Schott in Mainz published CINQ LIEDER. (Lalo was one of the very few composers whose work was taken seriously in Germany, another was Saint-Saëns.) Of these 'lieder' a beautiful *Tristesse* (Armand Silvestre) shows the composer at his most simple and eloquent, and *La chanson de l'alouette* (Laprade) contains the most adventurous and original piano writing of all, a veritable aviary of twittering birdsong. Another song from much later, *Le rouge-gorge* (Theuriet, 1887), explores this same ornithological territory. Of the later sets, the most rewarding is the TROIS MÉLODIES (1887). *La fenaison* (Stella) is a bucolic idyll which has the simplicities and strong contours of country music; *L'esclave* (Gautier) is a beautiful and deeply felt orientalism (Massenet's setting of this is good, but not as perfect as this); and the tenderly evocative *Souvenir* (Hugo), simple on the page, is deeply affecting in performance. At one time *Marine* (Theuriet, 1884) was the most celebrated of Lalo's songs; it has a certain dark power, but unfortunately it becomes untypically grandiloquent—something usually avoided by this most balanced of sensibilities.

There are a few other songs which do not strictly rank as mélodies, but which are included in the older *recueils*. *Humoresque* (Beauquier) with its amusingly philosophical text is actually taken from *Fiesque*, an early opera. There are two beautiful duets: *Au fond des halliers* (Theuriet, 1887) for baritone and mezzo also from *Fiesque*, and *Dansons* (1884), a substantial and jolly piece for soprano and mezzo, which derives from the ballet *Namouna*, a work much admired by Debussy.

1 *La Zuecca**

(Alfred de Musset)

À Saint-Blaise, à la Zuecca,
Vous étiez bien aise
   À Saint-Blaise.
À la Zuecca,
   Nous étions bien là.

Mais de vous en souvenir
   Prendrez-vous la peine?
Mais de vous en souvenir
   Et d'y revenir,

À Saint-Blaise, à la Zuecca,
Dans les prés fleuris cueillir la verveine,
   À Saint-Blaise, à la Zuecca,
   Vivre et mourir là!

The Zuecca

At Saint-Blaise, on the Zuecca,
You were well content
   At Saint-Blaise.
On the Zuecca,
   We were happy there.

   But will you trouble
   To remember?
To remember
   And return,

To Saint-Blaise, on the Zuecca,
Oh! to gather vervain in flowery meadows,
   At Saint-Blaise, on the Zuecca,
   There to live and die!

* Venetian dialect for the Giudecca, a series of eight little islands, linked by bridges, next to San Giorgio Maggiore.

2 *Ballade à la lune*
(Alfred de Musset)

Ballad to the moon

C'était, dans la nuit brune,
Sur le clocher jauni,
   La lune,
Comme un point sur un i.

Lune, quel esprit sombre
Promène au bout d'un fil,
   Dans l'ombre,
Ta face et ton profil?

Es-tu l'œil du ciel borgne?
Quel chérubin cafard
   Nous lorgne
Sous ton masque blafard?

N'es-tu rien qu'une boule?
Qu'un grand faucheux bien gras
   Qui roule
Sans pattes et sans bras?

Rends-nous la chasseresse,
Diane, au sein virginal,
   Qui presse
Quelque cerf matinal!

Phœbé qui, la nuit close,
Aux lèvres d'un berger
   Se pose,
Comme un oiseau léger.

Lune, en notre mémoire,
De tes belles amours
   L'histoire
T'embellira toujours.

Et toujours rajeunie,
Tu seras du passant
   Bénie,
Pleine lune ou croissant.

T'aimera le pilote
Dans son grand bâtiment,
   Qui flotte,
Sous le clair firmament!

There, in the dark night,
On the sere steeple,
   The moon,
Like a dot on an i!

Moon, what dark spirit
Leads you on a leash
   Through the gloom,
Face and profile?

Are you the heavens' single eye?
What spying cherub
   Gazes on us
Beneath your pale mask?

Are you merely a ball?
A big fat daddy-long-legs
   Rolling along
Without legs and arms?

Give us back the huntress,
Diana with her pure breast,
   Hunting
Some morning stag!

Phoebe* who, after dark
Alights on a shepherd's
   Lips,
Like a delicate bird.

Moon, in our minds,
The stories of your fair
   Loves,
Makes you ever fairer.

And ever restored to youth,
You shall be blessed by
   Passers-by,
Either full or waxing.

The sailor will love you
In his great ship,
   Floating
Beneath the clear sky!

* A name given to Diana or the moon.

Et qu'il vente ou qu'il neige,
Moi-même, chaque soir,
     Que fais-je,
Venant ici m'asseoir?

Je viens voir à la brune,
Sur le clocher jauni,
     La lune
Comme un point sur un i.

And I, come wind or snow,
What do I do each evening,
     When I come
To sit here?

At dusk I come to see,
On the sere steeple,
     The moon
Like a dot on an i.

3 L'esclave

(Théophile Gautier)

Captive et peut-être oubliée,
Je songe à mes jeunes amours,
     À mes beaux jours,
Et par la fenêtre grillée
Je regarde l'oiseau joyeux,
     Fendant les cieux.

Auprès de lui, belle Espérance,
Porte-moi sur tes ailes d'or,
     S'il m'aime encor,
Et, pour endormir ma souffrance,
Suspends mon âme sur son cœur
     Comme une fleur!

The slave girl

Imprisoned and perhaps forgotten,
I dream of my young love,
     Of my halcyon days,
And through the barred window
I see the joyous bird
     Cleave the skies.

Take me to his side, fair Hope,
On your wings of gold,
     If he loves me still,
And, to quieten my pain,
Fasten my soul to his heart
     Like a flower!

4 Souvenir

(Victor Hugo)

Comme un ange qui se dévoile,
Tu me regardais, dans ma nuit,
Avec ton beau regard d'étoile,
     Qui m'éblouit.

Mon bras pressait ta taille frêle
Et souple comme le roseau;
Ton sein palpitait comme l'aile
     D'un jeune oiseau.

Longtemps muets, nous contemplâmes
Le ciel où s'éteignait le jour.
Que se passait-il dans nos âmes?
     Amour! Amour!

Remembrance

Like an angel unveiling,
You gazed on my benightment,
With your sweet star-filled gaze,
     Which dazzled me.

I held you round your frail waist
As supple as a reed,
Your breast quivered like the wing
     Of some young bird.

For long we were silent, and watched
The sky where day was fading.
What was stirring in our souls?
     Love! Love!

LAZZARI, Sylvio (1857–1944)

Born in Austria, Lazzari came to the Paris Conservatoire at the age of 25 to study with Gounod and Franck, and he soon became completely assimilated into French musical life. As a song composer he favoured such poets as Tristan Klingsor and Maeterlinck. In 1912 he wrote *La lépreuse*, an opera with a libretto by Henri Bataille which was much admired by Fauré, who took the younger composer under his wing. Bataille, not often set to music, was the poet of a number of Lazzari mélodies including *La fontaine de pitié* and *Le nouveau Christ*, as well as being a gifted artist and portraitist.

The song enthusiast of today will perhaps be more interested to discover Lazzari's long-forgotten settings of Verlaine: the song cycle À L'ABSENTE (1892) is a collection of six songs two of which are to the words of this poet. The work opens with *Apaisement* [HAHN 1 v], a setting of the famous *La lune blanche* lyric which pre-dates that of Fauré, but which is influenced by the style of the older master. There is also a worthwhile *En sourdine* in this cycle [HAHN 1 iv]. Of the Jean Lahor settings which make up the rest of the cycle, the best is *Air de Schumann*, where the interplay between voice and piano seems modelled, not surprisingly, on the style of DICHTERLIEBE. A gently undemonstrative, but hypnotically effective *Green* [DEBUSSY 6 v] dates from 1919.

LECOCQ, Charles (1832–1918)

This famous composer of operettas such as *La fille de Mme Angot* was also an indefatigable writer of songs. His allusive and witty style is ideally suited to parody, and the elegant SIX FABLES DE LA FONTAINE are to be recommended. Of course they are not on the same level as Caplet's settings, but they are more pithy than Offenbach's, and often just as entertaining. *Le corbeau et le renard* [CAPLET 3 i] and *La chauve-souris et les deux belettes* are particularly successful. There is also a surprisingly elaborate setting of Hugo's *Guitare* [BIZET 2], written in the gently rocking barcarole rhythm of Fauré's *Les berceaux*.

LEGUERNEY, Jacques (1906–1997)

There is so much character and vitality in this music that its neglect is difficult to explain. One must conclude that Leguerney was born at the wrong time. He was just too young to be a member of Les Six, and the circumstances of his life (he was forced into business to support his family) only enabled him to concentrate on composing from the 1940s. He was thus a part-time composer and a late starter, and nothing new was heard from him after 1964; in this comparatively short period he composed his songs, works which are an important achievement, however slowly they take their rightful place in the mainstream repertoire.

His talent was at its height during Messaien's ascendancy, and the fashion for mélodies (apart from the public's enthusiasm for that handful of composers who had already established themselves) was already becoming a thing of the past. Because he was largely self-educated in music he lacked the network of friends and colleagues on which careers are built, although he was championed by Gérard Souzay and his sister Geneviève Touraine who have left some superb recordings of Leguerney's work. His great misfortune was to be working at the same time as Francis Poulenc who, in the field of the mélodie at least, seems to have said all that was worth saying at the time. At first glance, and at superficial hearing, these songs seem to be sub-Poulenc, and they have sometimes been written off as such. But the truth is that although Leguerney's art is not as broad and all-encompassing as the more famous composer's, it has a colour, above all an energy, all of its own. For someone who never went through the conventional channels of music education, Leguerney's command of harmony is a wonder. More extraordinary is the fluency of his piano writing—much of it extremely demanding—when he himself was no real pianist. Perhaps this is why the accompaniments seldom seem to get stuck in a rut of familiar patterns; this composer is always inventing new pianistic figurations to challenge his hard-working accompanists.

Throughout French song we notice a strong tendency towards time-travel and graceful pastiche. Indeed this exploration of nostalgia is part and parcel of almost every composer of the mélodie. Leguerney takes this tendency to its logical conclusion. He turns to sixteenth-century poetry, his almost exclusive poetic domain, and thinks himself into the past so convincingly that his music is effortlessly coloured by the era of Ronsard without needing extraneous touches of obvious archaic harmonic colouring to emphasize the fact. If anyone deserves to be remembered as the composer of this great poet it is Leguerney. There are some sixty songs arranged into various *recueils*, and of these over a third are by Ronsard. The most important single set is the POÈMES DE LA PLÉIADE which are published in eight volumes containing songs mainly written between 1942 and 1954. (The grouping of the songs in the original Rouart Lerolle edition of six *recueils* is slightly different from the arrangement of the more recent Eschig publications which adds further works.) Although it may be invidious to select songs from an output which deserves serious consideration in its entirety, personal favourites include: *Je me lamente* and *Bel aubépin* (both Ronsard) from the first *recueil*; three delicious songs from the second *recueil*—the irresistibly lilting *À sa maîtresse*, the rumbustious and insouciant *À son page* (again both Ronsard), which is a more successful setting than Poulenc's of a different version of the same poem, and *Ma douce jouvence est passée*, as simple and moving a picture of the tribulations of old age as can be found in the song repertoire. Also delectable, this time from the third *recueil*, is *Ode anacréontique* which is the purest Leguerney moto perpetuo, as is *La fontaine d'Hélène*, water music in translucent semiquavers (the poet is Ronsard yet again). In the fourth *recueil* there is the grave and statuesque *Invocation* (Ronsard) written for Germaine Lubin; in the fifth, *Villanelle* (Desportes), another very typical scherzo (as well as Bertaud's *Chanson triste* where the influence of Poulenc is to be heard soft and clear); and in the sixth, as a *coup de grâce* for the whole of this extraordinary set, *Sonnet pour Hélène* (Ronsard), a passionate and turbulent outburst which finds its resolution on a perfect final page, the whole piece wonderfully sung incidentally by the young Souzay on disc (Lys 053/4). Another fine Ronsard setting from the original sixth set (reallocated to the second) is the scuttling and vehement *Épipalinodie*, a desperate hymn to the poet's lover Denise whom he accused of sorcery, claiming she had cast a spell over him.

A high baritone and very good pianist might consider tackling the SEPT POÈMES DE FRANÇOIS

MAYNARD (1948–9) which are vintage Leguerney and were dedicated to Souzay whose voice seems written into the set. This varied and carefully constructed cycle ends with one of the rudest, if not the most rude, song in the repertoire: the insults throughout **Compliments à une duègne** (and particularly the one on the last page) make this a valuable, if not particularly gallant, comic song.

Other poets set by Leguerney include Racine (a short set of four songs entitled LE PAYSAGE, OU DESCRIPTION DE PORT-ROYAL DES CHAMPS (1951–2), the unfortunate Théophile de Viau, languishing in prison accused of homosexuality (a strong and rather sombre cycle entitled LA SOLITUDE from 1950 which was also orchestrated), and Apollinaire (Leguerney composed a *Clotilde* as well as Honegger). *Le présent* (Louise Lalanne) invites comparison with Poulenc's song to the same text, although the settings are quite different, and Leguerney's is arguably more revealing. In fact he also set such poets as Moréas, Toulet, and Fombeure, as if to refute the charge that he was uninterested in nineteenth- and twentieth-century poetry. Nevertheless it cannot be disputed that it is the writing of an earlier age which brings out the best in him. The baroque poet and musician Marc Antoine Girard, sieur de Saint-Amant, inspired two sets of three short songs each—LA NUIT (1951), where a single poem is treated cyclically as a sequence of connected movements, and LE CARNAVAL (1952), a work of striking originality which contains little that might have been written by another composer. In *Le grotesque*, for example, the piquancy of harmonic wit disguises a darker and more dangerous maliciousness than anything in Poulenc. The final song of the set—*Le carnaval*—is one of those dizzily fast pieces with the tripping 'la, la las' which are one of the hallmarks of Leguerney's use of the voice (the inebriated ending of *À son page* is similarly delectable). In 1954 Poulenc wrote to Leguerney saying he thought these were among the best of his songs. Also by Saint-Amant is *La caverne d'Écho*, published in the seventh PLÉIADE volume. Here, as the poet's voice echoes to the sound of his lute accompaniment, an effect admirably captured in the accompaniment, we are reminded of the dark mystery of Debussy's *La grotte*.

A closing word about two favourite Ronsard settings which are included in the last two volumes of the PLÉIADE cycle, a final tidying-up of Leguerney's output from earlier years. These are a touching *Le tombeau de Ronsard, composé par lui-même* from the eighth *recueil* which dates from as early as 1928 and, from the seventh, a song from 1942 which is entitled **Nous ne tenons.** This dates from the darkest days of the war in 1942, and is as moving and pithy a lament in times of human barbarity as any that has been written. It almost deserves to stand next to Poulenc's *C,* and it is this qualifying 'almost'—only sometimes justified, and possibly not even here—that has overshadowed this music for so long. There is much in Leguerney's music which stands on its own two (sometimes very nimble) feet. In the later years of the composer's life it was taken up and recorded by a group of much younger performers guided by the teaching enthusiasm of Dalton Baldwin, Lorraine Nubar, and the pianist Mary Dibbern. (It is astonishing how often the mélodie, when neglected, has been nourished and protected by transatlantic enthusiasm.) But this music is too good to remain a rarity. It would certainly repay the championing of a new generation of interpreters, and Leguerney's name deserves to be seen on concert programmes as a matter of course.

1 *À sa maîtresse*

(Pierre de Ronsard)

Ma petite colombelle,
Mon petit œil, baisez-moi,
Ma petite toute belle,
Mon petit œil, baisez-moi.
D'une bouche toute pleine
D'amour, chassez-moi la peine
De mon amoureux émoi.

    Quand je vous dirai: Mignonne,
Approchez-vous; qu'on me donne
Neuf baisers tout à la fois,
Donnez m'en seulement trois.

To his mistress

My little dove,
My little sweet, kiss me,
My lovely lovely little one.
Kiss me, my little sweet.
With lips abrim
With love, banish the sorrows
That love causes me.

    When I say: My love,
Draw near to give me
Nine kisses all at once,
Or simply give me three.

2 *À son page*

(Pierre de Ronsard)

    Rafraîchis-moi le vin, de sorte
Qu'il soit aussi frais qu'un glaçon;
Fais venir Janne, qu'elle apporte
Son luth pour dire une chanson;
Nous ballerons tous trois au son;
Et dis à Barbe qu'elle vienne,
Les cheveux tors à la façon
D'une folâtre Italienne.

    Ne vois-tu que le jour se passe?
Je ne vis point au lendemain;
Page, reverse dans ma tasse,
Remplis-moi ce verre tout plein.
Maudit soit qui languit en vain!
Les Philosophes je n'appreuve:
Le cerveau n'est jamais bien sain
Que l'Amour et le vin n'abreuve.

To his page

    Chill my wine, that it might be
As cool as an icicle;
Send for Janne, that she might bring
Her lute to sing a song to me;
The three of us will dance along;
And tell Barbe that she should come
With her hair coiled archly
À l'italienne.

    Can you not see how the day is dying?
Tomorrow I shall be no more;
Page, pour me another glass,
Fill it to the very brim.
Cursed be he who languishes in vain!
I do not approve of Philosophers:
The brain is only ever sound
When watered by Love and wine.

3 *Compliments à une duègne*

(François Maynard)

Cache ton corps sous un habit funeste;
Ton lit, Margot, a perdu ses chalands
Et tu n'es plus qu'un misérable reste
Du premier siècle et des premiers Galants.

Compliments to a duenna

Hide your body beneath deadly weeds;
Your bed, Margot, attracts no more custom
And you are merely now the wretched remains
Of the first century and the first lovers.

Il est certain que tu vins sur la terre
Avant que Rome eut détrôné ses Rois
Et que tes yeux virent naître la guerre
Qui mit les Grecs dans un cheval de bois.

La Mort hardie et sous qui tout succombe
N'ose envoyer ta carcasse à la tombe
Et n'est pour toi qu'un impuissant Démon.

Veux-tu savoir quel siècle t'a portée?
Je te l'apprends. Ton corps est du limon
Qui fut pétri des mains de Prométhée.

It is certain that you appeared on earth
Before Rome had dethroned its kings
And that your eyes beheld the war break out
Which placed the Greeks in a wooden horse

Audacious death, before whom all succumb,
Dares not dispatch your carcass to the tomb
And is for you but a powerless devil.

Would you care to know which century bore you?
I shall tell you: your body issued from the clay
That Prometheus moulded with his hands.

4 *Nous ne tenons*

(Pierre de Ronsard)

Nous ne tenons en nostre main
Le temps futur du lendemain:
La vie n'a point d'assurance:
Et pendant que nous désirons
La faveur des Rois, nous mourons
Au milieu de nostre espérance.
   L'homme après son dernier trépas
Plus ne boit ni mange là-bas,
Et sa grange qu'il a laissée
Pleine de blé devant sa fin,
Et sa cave pleine de vin
Ne luy viennent plus en pensée.

We do not hold

We do not hold
The future in our hands:
Life has no security:
And while we crave
The favour of kings, we die
In the midst of hope.
   Man, after his final departure,
Neither drinks nor eats in the beyond,
And the barn he left behind
Brimming with corn before he died,
And his cellar full of wine
No longer cross his mind.

LEKEU, Guillaume (1870–1894)

This Belgian composer decided to study with Franck and d'Indy after a visit to Bayreuth in 1889. He achieved success when Ysaÿe commissioned the Violin Sonata (1892) which remains Lekeu's most celebrated work. He died only two years later from typhoid fever and his posthumous reputation has been burnished by the widely held belief that his youthful promise would have led to great achievements in every genre. His chamber works are still played, but he also wrote a quantity of orchestral and piano music.

   He began to write songs at the age of 17, at the same time as he was working on *Les Burgraves*, a Victor Hugo opera, now lost. The first two songs are settings of Lamartine, *La fenêtre de la maison paternelle* and *Les pavots* (both 1887). The first of these shows considerable ability, a long tune built over rather conventional throbbing triplets; the second from a few months later is more solemn and static—it looks on the page as if it has been conceived for string quartet accompaniment, a prophecy of a future musical penchant. The theme of both songs is death and the transient nature of beauty, typical enough of a young man's literary tastes, but eerily appropriate in the case of the composer's own fate (Lili Boulanger, who was to die at the same age as Lekeu, was also drawn to deathly texts).

After this, Lekeu preferred to write his own poems. *L'ombre plus dense* (1893) and *Quelque antique et lente danse* (1889) are both drawn from all that remains of plans for a much larger LIEDERKREIS. That title is significant of a Belgian approach to songwriting, where Brussels recognized German influence more readily than did Paris. In any case this openness to influences across the Rhine was a feature of Franck's teaching. The opening of the first song is starkly reminiscent of Schubert's *Der Doppelgänger*, the second makes some concessions to the minuet style. Both are effective songs, but not nearly as accomplished as the four remaining mélodies which represent the legacy of the composer's maturity. *Chanson de mai* (1891) is a setting of words by the composer's uncle Jean Lekeu. It has a steady, even massive, swing to it, a serenade with universal implications, the piano almost orchestral in its lusciousness. This confident amplitude and generosity of heart is thoroughly Franckian, of course, but the music sounds very much Lekeu's own.

The *TROIS POÈMES* (1892) are a fine group; the superscriptions to each song are quotations from Lamartine, Verlaine, and Hugo, but once again the composer prefers to set his own poems. The least exceptional is the first, *Sur une tombe*, where Lekeu continues to dwell on what appears to be a death fixation in a harmonic language typical of the Franckists. *Ronde*, on the other hand, is a song rondo with a returning episode—light, clear, vivacious, the writing transparent and harmonically adventurous. It is a song in the 'gather ye rosebuds while ye may' mould which ends on a note of ominous warning with mention of 'crazed lovers' and 'happiness that knows no morrow'. Will these sexual pleasures be paid for in the manner of the illness which pervades Schnitzler's *Reigen*, later known on film in France as *La ronde*? The third and final song of the *TROIS POÈMES* is *Nocturne*, where Lekeu added an optional string quartet to the accompaniment. (Chausson was to take up this idea for the accompaniment of his *Chanson perpétuelle* in 1898; it is notable that in 1888 Lekeu had written *Noël* for two sopranos, string quartet, and piano, and in 1891 he arranged for the same forces *Plaint d'Andromède*, an extract from his cantata written for the Prix de Rome.) There is an amplitude and lyricism about the *Nocturne* which brings to mind Debussy's *Recueillement*; on these pages we hear most clearly Lekeu's flirtation with impressionism. He had all the passionate intensity of the followers of Franck, but he had too much vivacity and humour to become another d'Indy or Ropartz. Permitted his full span, he would probably have been further enriched by Debussy's influence, as well as that of Ravel, or even Stravinsky.

1 *Ronde*

(Guillaume Lekeu)

Venez, mêlez-vous à la ronde
Qui chante dans la clarté blonde,
Tombant du ciel étoilé.
Ne restez pas à regarder la danse,
Rhytme troublant qui se balance
Sous votre œil songeur et voilé.

The dance

Come, come, join the dance
Resounding in the golden light
That falls from the starry sky.
Do not just gaze at the dance—
Its heady rhythm sways
Beneath your blurred and dreamy eyes.

Venez, apportez-nous votre divin sourire,
Votre douce beauté;
Près de nous vous entendrez bruire
Les murmures d'amour de ce beau soir d'été.

Venez, venez, mêlez-vous à la ronde;
Il n'est pas de peine profonde
À votre âge ensoleillé.
Vous savez bien que tout ici vous aime,
Que vous êtes la joie suprême
De l'univers émerveilleé.
Laissez se ranimer, ô ma belle oublieuse,
Votre cœur endormi:
Avec nous veuillez être heureuse,
Et soyez infidèle à l'infidèle ami.

Venez, venez, mêlez-vous à la ronde,
Qui tourbillonne comme l'onde
Dans le parfum des baisers;
Venez goûter notre amoureuse ivresse:
Tout l'infini de la caresse
Palpite en vos yeux baissés.

Les amantes viendront, folles, l'une après l'une,
Vous prendre par la main,
Et vous verrez fuir, dans le clair de lune,
Votre bonheur sans lendemain.

Come, bring us your heavenly smile,
Your gentle beauty;
Alongside us you shall hear love murmuring
On this beautiful summer evening,

Come, come, join the dance;
Deep sorrow does not exist
At your sunlit age.
You know that here you are loved by all,
That you are the greatest joy
Of the marvelling world.
Let your slumbering heart, O my oblivious sweet,
Be rekindled once again:
Be content in our midst,
And be unfaithful to your unfaithful friend.

Come, come, join the dance
That swirls like the tide
In the fragrance of kisses.
Come and savour our lovers' rapture;
The boundless bliss of embraces
Quiver in your lowered eyes.

Crazed lovers, one by one,
Will take you by the hand,
And in the moonlight you shall see
Your short-lived happiness slip away.

LEONCAVALLO, Ruggero (1857–1919)

This celebrated composer of verismo operas, as well as the Caruso gramophone hit *Mattinata*, was a true cosmopolitan. He ambitiously kept operatic projects going in London and New York, as well as his native Italy, and in the field of song it is no surprise to find a handful of English songs and mélodies for the London and Paris markets. In 1893, for example, he composed *Tonight and tomorrow* (Weatherley) and also *Déclaration* (Silvestre). This French song was one of two published under the misleading title DUE LIRICHE—the second is a setting of Andrea Chénier entitled *La chanson des jeux*. Both songs were conceived for tenor. Another favourite poet was Musset, but Leoncavallo was also quite capable of writing his own French texts. The most engaging of the French songs are LES DEUX SÉRÉNADES (E. Collet, 1903). *Sérénade française* (with either mandolin or violin obbligato) is given over to Pierrot, and *Sérénade napolitaine* is a real find, full of melody and swaggering charm, for those who like a touch of Italianate cantilena translated into the less vocally ambitious French salon style.

LEROUX, Xavier (1863–1919)

A pupil of Massenet, Leroux won the Prix de Rome in 1885. He was chiefly a composer for the theatre (his operas have all but disappeared) and in the field of song he enjoyed a great vogue. His best-known mélodie was *Le Nil* to a poem by Armand Renaud whose *Nuits persanes* was the basis for Saint-Saëns's MÉLODIES PERSANES [SAINT-SAËNS 4 (*Tournoiement*)]. Among a number of cycles, Leroux composed LES SÉRÉNADES, a set of ten songs to the poems of Catulle Mendès. Other favourite poets were Théodore de Banville (*Le jour* and *La nuit*, cf. Koechlin's settings) and Armand Silvestre (*Chrysanthème* and *Pensées de printemps*). Leroux was an adept pasticheur and a song like *Le baiser dérobé* from TROIS MÉLODIES DANS LE STYLE ANCIEN is a coy monologue from a shy Versailles beauty shocked to be asked for a kiss. On the other hand his setting of *Offrande* (Ronsard) from the same set returns to the composer's own harmonic vocabulary. His inspiration is limited when compared with his greatest contemporaries, but the songs are typical of their time, and never less than the work of a highly professional tunesmith.

LIPATTI, Dinu (1917–1950)

Grove 6 mentions that this great Romanian pianist had lessons with Paul Dukas and Nadia Boulanger, but lists none of his compositions. In actual fact Lipatti was a reasonably prolific composer with works for piano (including two pieces with orchestra), chamber music, and music for winds. His first set of songs was written in 1941—CINQ MÉLODIES SUR DES POÈMES DE PAUL VERLAINE, published in Romania as CINCI LIEDURI PE VERSURI DE VERLAINE. These songs are a valuable addition to the Verlaine catalogue, and it is a pity that they are almost unknown. The opening piece *À une femme*, marked 'agitato', is written for tenor; with references to 'ma détresse violente', it is much more passionate than the typical Verlaine setting. Lipatti keeps the excitement going through the swirling accompaniment, but it is never in danger of becoming merely a piano piece, which leads the voice and swamps it. *Green* [FAURÉ 29 iii, DEBUSSY 6 v] has the character of a measured gavotte, and *Il pleure dans mon cœur* [DEBUSSY 6 ii] provides a novel yet simple piano figuration to suggest the sound of gentle drizzle. *Le piano que baise une main frêle* (a poem also set movingly by Bordes [BORDES 1]) is gently evocative, the meaning of the poem's title reflected in the accompaniment's insouciant manner, as if a hand were brushing the keys absent-mindedly, searching for an old melody. The composer provides this, a delightfully lilting tune in 6/8 which the singer hums at the end of the song. The final song, *Sérénade*, is more ambitious, with an opening piano figuration which recalls Fauré's *Mandoline*. The mood here, though, is much more bitter and malicious. The mixture of speech and song is unusual and not completely successful. Nevertheless, this is an imaginative response to the poem.

The second of Lipatti's vocal works is QUATRE MÉLODIES, an exquisite little group which shows a fine feeling for the well-chosen texts, more modern this time. These are *Sensation* (Rimbaud), *L'amoureuse* (Éluard), *Capitale de la douleur* (Éluard)—a particularly lovely song, this—and *Les pas*

(Valéry), which was also set by Mompou. No one could guess that the composer of these accompaniments was a world-class virtuoso, so spare in texture are they, so concerned to match the luminosity of the words. In this music we hear the self effacement of a great artist searching for the truth. This, of course, is also evident in Lipatti's piano playing—a quality which made listeners, even, reputedly, a tough man like the recording supremo Walter Legge, weep.

LISZT, Franz (1811–1886)

In the history of song Liszt is an outsider and part of no tradition. His lack of fluency in the German language is evident in his cavalier treatment of fine poems like Lenau's *Die drei Zigeuner*, where all literary considerations are sacrificed to the musical effect of the moment. This gypsy evocation gives much musical pleasure, however, and it cannot be denied that Liszt wrote some very beautiful lieder which have held their place on the recital platform, because of the size and warmth of their composer's personality. In this sphere, as in others, he was a great communicator. The same may be said of his French songs which are neither lieder, nor strictly speaking mélodies. It is clear that they stand outside any established French tradition, but in their way they mirror the extravagances of the era perfectly. They all seem white-hot and newly minted, a spontaneous combustion between word and tone which, if not always perfectly under control (particularly in the songs' earlier versions), suggests a man at the centre of the volcano of erupting romanticism. The ascendancy of French over German as an international language is shown by the way the composer seems more at home in this literature. For his texts he goes to Victor Hugo without hesitation, and we sense how well he knew all his fellow artists on the Parisian scene, most of whom had been stunned by his playing. Indeed it may be argued that because Liszt is a foreigner, he is free of the baggage of the past, in this case the strophic style of the French romance which continued to influence Berlioz. In comparison to that master, his choice of poetry is far more representative of the new romantic *Zeitgeist*.

Because Liszt was a pianist, and a great one, it is hardly surprising that his accompaniments should lead the voice. And it is because of the piano writing, of course, that these songs have such a strong character. The first is a setting of Hugo's *Comment, disaient-ils* [BIZET 2] where the strumming of guitar strings is brilliantly suggested—to hear the composer himself play this must have been magical. The first version of 1842 with its cadenza reaching a high C for the voice is hardly ever performed. Liszt revised it some seventeen years later into a slimmer shape, both more economical and more practical. These revisions, where youthful enthusiasm was replaced by the sobriety of middle age, are typical of how his songwriting changed with the years. In the Italian settings of Petrarch it must be admitted that the original versions, if the performers can handle the vocal and pianistic demands, are more exciting. On the whole however Liszt's second thoughts on the French settings are more singer-friendly. A good example of this is the famous *Oh! quand je dors* (Hugo), where the 1842 version is far too fussy. By 1859 Liszt had learned to leave the spinning of magic to the singer, who needs to be unhectored by the accompaniment to weave the necessary spell. If Liszt had never written any other song than this he would have a place of honour in the annals of Hugo's musicians, and of French mélodie in general; the music has an elevated sweep and exaltation that matches the words to perfection, a grand manner which is very much of its time, but which does not preclude the intimacy the poem also demands. This is love music which encourages biographical parallels: the exalted relationship between Petrarch and Laura seems mirrored by that of the composer and Marie d'Agoûlt.

From 1844 comes another Hugo setting, and again in two versions—*Enfant, si j'étais roi.* The early version shows a downright lack of knowledge of the capabilities and limitations of the human voice when pitted against pianistic virtuosity. The later arrangement (1859), much pruned, thunders quite enough and is still an exciting and stirring song. Once again there are two versions of *S'il est un charmant gazon* (Hugo, 1844 and 1859) [FAURÉ 6], where the second is more light and deft, a miniature which is surely more in the spirit of the poem. The first version is great fun, however, given a virtuoso pianist able to listen to his singer and redress problems of balance. Hugo's *La tombe et la rose* (1844) needed no revision because it is eminently practical, not too long, and a good choice for those inclined to melodramatic songs where the grave itself is given a singing voice. *Gastibelza: boléro* (Hugo, 1844) on the other hand is an unmitigated monster. Perhaps Liszt had heard the modest mélodie on this text by Hippolyte Monpou (1841) and decided to write a barn-stormer in comparison. Fischer-Dieskau and Barenboim can attempt this music, but it requires that level of accomplishment to get anywhere near this fiendish bolero. Voice and piano slug it out in battle for hegemony, only to join together in a unison chromatic scale towards the end to depict the howling of the wind. Impossible and impractical certainly, vulgar perhaps, but also undeniably impressive in the very rare right hands and larynx. This *coup de foudre* finishes the Victor Hugo period of Liszt's life.

There are, again, two versions of *Jeanne d'Arc au bûcher* (Dumas, 1845 and 1874) where Liszt goes far beyond the boundaries of song and writes what the French would have termed a scène. This is not the best Liszt (Rossini did better on the same theme) and the piano writing seems rather stiff and conceived for orchestra. Far more impressive, for those interested in this grandiose type of statement, is *Le vieux vagabond* (Béranger, 1848) which somehow captures the egalitarian spirit of that tumultuous year, and foreshadows *Les préludes* and the 'Dante' Symphony. (Lalo also set this text as one of his SIX ROMANCES POPULAIRES of 1849.) Liszt cannot make us forget that this is a strophic song which outstays its welcome, although the piano writing, which becomes increasingly heated, somewhat disguises the fact. The last but one of the French songs is a setting of Alfred de Musset from 1872—*J'ai perdu ma force et ma vie.* This is Liszt in his self-lacerating confessional mood and the song is not free of self-indulgent religiosity. But with late Liszt this is rather to be expected, and with a performance of conviction the song is moving within its own parameters. The last French song of all is half mélodie, half church music; the composer specifies a contralto as if he had a Bach passion in mind, and he designates the accompaniment for piano or harmonium. *Le crucifix* (Musset, 1884) reflects the deeply religious aspect of this composer's later years and is divided into four sections depicting various stations of the cross. The spiritual journey between the sensuality of *Oh! quand je dors* and this sombre and anguished music describes the extraordinary trajectory of Liszt's life. There is not a trace of the high-living piano virtuoso of yore.

Robert and Clara Schumann, and many other musicians, both past and present, have raised an eyebrow at Liszt's extravagances. Reactions to his work and his person have extended to downright animosity. But we must confess that much of the fun and excitement in Liszt's music stems from this very ability to become carried away by the passion of the moment. If Liszt cavorts on a long leash, it is only his poet-collaborator who can rein him in. Fritz Noske prints a little-known song by Liszt entitled *Élégie* (Monnier, 1844). This is harmonically audacious, but undermined by a weak poem and by Liszt's tendency to repeat the final lines seemingly *ad infinitum*. It serves to remind us that in terms of his French songs Liszt was fortunate to have found in Victor Hugo a giant of romantic literature to match the mood and amplitude of his own spirit and aspirations. And apart from these mélodies of course we owe to the same poet Liszt's *Mazeppa*, *Ce qu'on entend sur la montagne*, *Après une lecture de Dante*, and even—via Verdi—the paraphrase on *Rigoletto*. In the field of literature, only the profundities of Goethe influenced Liszt more, but it may be argued that the composer was far better temperamentally suited to Hugo's French-speaking muse.

1 *Oh! quand je dors*
(Victor Hugo)

Oh! quand je dors, viens auprès de ma couche,
Comme à Pétrarque apparaissait Laura,
Et qu'en passant ton haleine me touche...—
　　Soudain ma bouche
　　S'entr'ouvrira!

Sur mon front morne où peut-être s'achève
Un songe noir qui trop longtemps dura,
Que ton regard comme un astre s'élève...—
　　Soudain mon rêve
　　Rayonnera!

Puis sur ma lèvre où voltige une flamme,
Éclair d'amour que Dieu même épura,
Pose un baiser, et d'ange deviens femme...—

　　Soudain mon âme
　　S'éveillera!

Ah, while I sleep!

Ah, while I sleep, come close to where I lie,
As Laura once appeared to Petrarch,
And let your breath in passing touch me...
　　At once my lips
　　Will part!

On my sombre brow, where a dismal dream
That lasted too long now perhaps is ending,
Let your countenance rise like a star...
　　At once my dream
　　Will shine!

Then on my lips, where a flame flickers—
A flash of love which God himself has purified—
Place a kiss and be transformed from angel into
　　　woman...
　　At once my soul
　　Will wake!

2 *Enfant, si j'étais roi*
(Victor Hugo)

Enfant! si j'étais roi, je donnerais l'empire,
Et mon char, et mon sceptre, et mon peuple à
　　　genoux,
Et ma couronne d'or, et mes bains de porphyre,
Et mes flottes, à qui la mer ne peut suffire,
　　Pour un regard de vous!

Child, if I were king

Child, if I were king—I'd give my realm,
And my chariot and my sceptre and my prostrate
　　　people,
And my golden crown and my porphyry baths,
And my fleets that the ocean cannot contain,
　　For a single look from you!

Si j'étais Dieu, la terre et l'air avec les ondes,	If I were God—the earth and the air and the waves,
Les anges, les démons courbés devant ma loi,	The angels, the devils, bowed before my law,
Et le profond chaos aux entrailles fécondes,	And the fertile womb of profound chaos,
L'éternité, l'espace, et les cieux, et les mondes,	Eternity, space, and the heavens and the worlds,
Pour un baiser de toi!	For a single kiss from you!

LOEFFLER, Charles (1861–1935)

This career is from the epoch of Henry James and Edith Wharton when the interchange between Europe and the United States shaped the artistic life of the younger nation. Loeffler was a composer born in Alsace who spent much of his life in America. He studied in Berlin, with Joachim among others, but developed an antipathy to Germany, the land of his fathers. Instead the young composer cultivated a passionate attachment to France, a country where he felt at home, and which he frequently visited. Thus his considerable work-list has a decidedly French flavour: there is only a handful of songs in German, his mother tongue, in comparison to a long list of mélodie titles. Loeffler became an American citizen in 1897 and was a popular solo violinist, playing the American premières of concerti by Bruch, Saint-Saëns, and Lalo. He was attracted to the idea of voice and piano with obbligato instruments (particularly strings), and an early passion was to include the viola in his songs, perhaps inspired by the example of Brahms. *Chanson des ingénues*, *La lune blanche*, *Rêverie en sourdine*, and *Le rossignol* are all Verlaine titles. These, as well as Baudelaire's *Harmonie du soir* [DEBUSSY 76 ii], date from 1893–7, and include a viola obbligato.

QUATRE POÈMES Op. 5 (written in 1893, published in 1904) are the composer's own pick of the viola songs of the period. These include interesting settings of Baudelaire's *La cloche fêlée* (also set by Caplet), and three Verlaine songs: *Dansons la gigue* [BORDES 2], *Le son du cor s'afflige vers les bois* [DEBUSSY 9 ii], which was dedicated to Ysaÿe, and *Sérénade* ('Comme la voix d'un mort qui chanterait'). There are problems of balance between voice and instruments in these songs where the constant presence of the viola is in danger of obscuring the text, a defect that could be remedied in the recording studio perhaps. From 1899 comes a cycle for voice and piano alone, *QUATRE MÉLODIES* Op. 10, where the poet is Gustave Kahn. The extravagant final song of the set, *Les paons*, is dedicated to John Singer Sargent who painted Loeffler's portrait in 1903. Verlaine's *À une femme* (1904) is set for voice and piano with an optional violin obbligato and Samain's *Ton souvenir est comme un livre bien-aimé* (1911) for voice and piano alone.

Loeffler was an important and influential figure in American life, and was also recognized by France with the Légion d'honneur. His songs are extremely sophisticated in the transatlantic manner of the time, although his delight in 'decadent' impressionistic harmony (the mark of an outsider who is naughtily playing at being French) can sound mannered and something of a cliché to modern ears. The later settings of English poetry, and of that of W. B. Yeats, seem more individual in that they are less Debussy-influenced. On the other hand, some of the harmonies in a late French setting like *Vieille chanson d'amour* (1925) seem prophetic of Messiaen.

LUTOSLAWSKI, Witold (1913–1994)

The old historical link between Poland and France (the libretto of Chabrier's opera *Le roi malgré lui*, for example, is based on the Poles' invitation to Henri of Valois to be their king) is perfectly illustrated by the enthusiasm with which Lutoslawski adopted French for the majority of his important vocal music. He also chose French titles for much of his instrumental work. Of all twentieth-century composers working outside France, it is his ear that was the most keenly attuned to the French language: his music is very much in accord with Gallic ideals of self-control, refinement, and economy. There are, however, moments of grandeur, and even savagery, in the song cycles (apart from the deliberately childlike *CHANTEFLEURS ET CHANTEFABLES*) which show Lutoslawski to be far from a mere pasticheur of the elegant manners of a foreign culture. He was of course a greater composer than his fellow Poles featured in this book—Poldowski and Paderewski. One would have to look as far back as Frédéric Chopin to find a similarly distinguished blend of Polish passion and French sensibility.

Lutoslawski's sympathies with France are evident from the early years of his maturity: the *FIVE SONGS* with Polish texts (1956–7) are dedicated to Marya Freund (a Polish-French singer who was an early interpreter of Schoenberg and Poulenc) and Nadia Boulanger. It was not long before he was drawn to French poetry: one of his most important pieces, *TROIS POÈMES D'HENRI MICHAUX POUR CHOEUR ET ORCHESTRE* (1962–3), is a semi-aleatoric work conceived for two separate ensembles, each with a conductor. The three movements are *Pensées, Le grand combat,* and *Repos dans le malheur.* Although the composer claimed that his choice of text came only after he had conceived his musical ideas (an obvious reverse of the usual trend of inspiration) it is clear that he already associated the resonances of the French language with those of his own instrumental music. When the great English tenor Peter Pears commissioned a new orchestral song cycle from Lutoslawski, the composer proposed France as a geographical compromise between their two cultures; he must also have been aware of Benjamin Britten's earlier excursion into French stylization, *LES ILLUMINATIONS* [BRITTEN I i–x]. In *PAROLES TISSÉES* (1965), the 'woven words' of Jean-François Chabrun pose no less of a challenge to Lutoslawski than that faced by Britten in coming to grips with Rimbaud's allusive texts. The work is in four movements which correspond to Chabrun's *Quatre tapisseries pour la châtelaine de Vergy.* The poetry was inspired by the illicit love affair between the Duke of Burgundy and the Lady of Vergi, although this biographical background is scarcely obvious from a reading of the words. The score is for string orchestra, harp, piano, and percussion. The first two sections are colourful and lively, the last drained of energy and descriptive of sleep—'dormez cette blancheur est chaque jour nouvelle'. The third movement is a violent contrast; images of cats in the first two 'tapisseries' are replaced by those of a thousand horses carrying the poet's pain, a thousand cocks crowing his misery. Angular counterpoint here takes over from the aleatoric freedom of the other three sections.

Some ten years later, Lutoslawski wrote a work at the request of another great singer of the twentieth century—Dietrich Fischer-Dieskau—and once again he proposed France as neutral territory, the meeting-ground between Germany and Poland. Having attempted to find a German text, Lutoslawski heard Fischer-Dieskau perform Debussy and Ravel and was immediately reassured that French would be an appropriate language for their collaboration. It was also perhaps no coincidence that the poet chosen by Lutoslawski for this project, Robert Desnos, was a member of the French Resistance who died in a Nazi concentration camp. (One of Poulenc's most touching late songs is a setting of Desnos's *Dernier poème* [POULENC 18], lines which were said to have been written in Theresienstadt and addressed to the poet's wife Youki.) In this way **Les espaces du sommeil** (1975) assumes something of the quality of Britten's *War Requiem* as a work of post-war reconciliation and a celebration of love as a mightier force than evil; the work has the quality of an Éluard-like liturgy with the recurring refrain 'Il y a toi' which puts us in mind of Poulenc's Éluard settings, *Tu vois le feu du soir*, for example. Here the poet's beloved is numbered as one of the seven wonders of the world. Like *Paroles tissées* the score is subdivided into four sections, the third of which contains the grand musical climax, the voice silenced in the overwhelming orchestral commentary. The poetry of Desnos is framed by a large and imposing array of instruments: strings, wind and brass, and a large percussion section including marimba, tom-toms, bongos, tam-tam, cymbals, vibraphone, harp, and piano.

For the text of his final vocal cycle Lutoslawski once again turned to the work of Robert Desnos. CHANTEFLEURS ET CHANTEFABLES (1989–90) is a set of nine small songs for soprano and small orchestra; the first performance was conducted by the composer at a BBC Promenade Concert in 1991. The texts are taken from two Desnos collections (also set to music in two separate sets by Jean Wiener), the first about flowers (CHANTEFLEURS), the second about animals (CHANTEFABLES) in the manner of a latter-day La Fontaine. In these miniatures, the composer shows a perfect understanding for the world of childhood wonder and simplicity. Beside the exquisitely drawn portraits of plants and flowers (*La belle-de-nuit, La véronique, La rose*) Lutoslawski's virtuosic orchestrations are especially apt in capturing the sounds of the grasshoppers in *La sauterelle* and, in the concluding song *Le papillon*, the shimmering colours of butterflies in flight.

I *PAROLES TISSÉES*

(Jean-François Chabrun)

Première tapisserie

Un chat qui s'émerveille
une ombre l'ensorcelle
blanche comme une oreille

Le cri du bateleur et celui de la caille
celui de la perdrix celui du ramoneur
celui de l'arbre mort celui des bêtes prises

Une ombre qui sommeille
une herbe qui s'éveille
un pas qui m'émerveille

WOVEN WORDS

First tapestry

A marvelling cat
A shadow bewitches her
white as an ear

The tumbler's cry and the quail's
the partridge's and the chimney-sweep's
the dead tree's the captured beasts'

A shadow that sleeps
grass that awakes
a step I marvel at

Deuxième tapisserie

Quand le jour a rouvert les branches du jardin
un chat qui s'émerveille
le cri du bateleur et celui de la caille
une herbe qui s'éveille
celui de la perdrix celui du ramoneur
une ombre l'ensorcelle
celui de l'arbre mort celui des bêtes prises
au dire des merveilles
l'ombre en deux s'est déchirée

Troisième tapisserie

Mille chevaux hors d'haleine
mille chevaux noirs portent ma peine
j'entends leurs sabots sourds
frapper la nuit au ventre
s'ils n'arrivent s'ils n'arrivent
avant le jour ah la peine perdue

Le cri de la perdrix celui du ramoneur
au dire des merveilles une herbe qui s'éveille
celui de l'arbre mort celui des bêtes prises
Mille coqs hurlent ma peine

mille coqs blessés à mort
un à un à la lisière des faubourgs
pour battre le tambour de l'ombre
pour réveiller la mémoire des chemins
pour appeler une à une
s'ils vivent s'ils vivent
mille étoiles toutes mes peines

Quatrième tapisserie

Dormez cette pâleur nous est venue de loin
le cri du bateleur et celui de la caille
dormez cette blancheur est chaque jour nouvelle
celui de la perdrix celui du ramoneur
ceux qui s'aiment heureux s'endorment aussi pâles

celui de l'arbre mort celui des bêtes prises

n'endormiront jamais cette chanson de peine
que d'autres ont repris d'autres la reprendront

Second tapestry

When day has reopened the garden's branches
A marvelling cat
The tumbler's cry and the quail's
grass that awakes
the partridge's and the chimney-sweep's
a shadow bewitches her
the dead tree's the captured beasts'
speaking of marvels
the shadow is torn in two.

Third tapestry

A thousand horses out of breath
A thousand black horses bear my sorrow
I hear their heavy hooves
strike the midriff of the night
If they do not come if they do not come
before day dawns ah all will have been in vain

The partridge's cry and the chimney-sweep's
speaking of marvels grass that awakes
the dead tree's the captured beasts'
A thousand cocks scream my pain

a thousand cocks wounded to death
one by one at the suburb's edge
to beat the shadow's drum
to wake the memory of streets
to call one by one
if they live if they live
a thousand stars all my sorrows

Fourth tapestry

Sleep this pallor has reached us from afar
the tumbler's cry and the quail's
sleep this paleness is new each day
the partridge's and the chimney-sweep's
those who love each other happily fall asleep and
     pale
the dead tree's the captured beasts'

will never quieten this song of sorrow
that others have repeated others will repeat

2 *Les espaces du sommeil*

(Robert Desnos)

Dans la nuit il y a naturellement les sept merveilles du monde et la grandeur et le tragique et le charme.

Les forêts s'y heurtent confusément avec des créatures de légende cachées dans les fourrés.

Il y a toi.

Dans la nuit il y a le pas du promeneur et celui de l'assassin et celui du sergent de ville et la lumière du réverbère et celle de la lanterne du chiffonnier.

Il y a toi.

Dans la nuit passent les trains et les bateaux et le mirage des pays où il fait jour. Les derniers souffles du crépuscule et les premiers frissons de l'aube.

Il y a toi.

Un air de piano, un éclat de voix.

Une porte claque. Une horloge.

Et pas seulement les êtres et les choses et les bruits matériels.

Mais encore moi qui me poursuis ou sans cesse me dépasse.

Il y a toi l'immolée, toi que j'attends.

Parfois d'étranges figures naissent à l'instant du sommeil et disparaissent.

Quand je ferme les yeux, des floraisons phosphorescentes apparaissent et se fanent et renaissent comme des feux d'artifice charnus.

Des pays inconnus que je parcours en compagnie de créatures.

Il y a toi sans doute, ô belle et discrète espionne.

Et l'âme palpable de l'étendue.

Et les parfums du ciel et des étoiles et le chant du coq d'il y a 2,000 ans et le cri du paon dans des parcs en flamme et des baisers.

Des mains qui se serrent sinistrement dans une lumière blafarde et des essieux qui grincent sur des routes médusantes.

Il y a toi sans doute que je ne connais pas, que je connais au contraire.

Mais qui, présente dans mes rêves, t'obstines à s'y laisser deviner sans y paraître.

Toi qui restes insaisissable dans la réalité et dans le rêve.

Toi qui m'appartiens de par ma volonté de te posséder en illusion mais qui n'approches ton visage du mien que mes yeux clos aussi bien au rêve qu'à la réalité.

Sleep's spaces

In the night there are of course the seven wonders of the world and greatness and tragedy and mystery.

The forests collide tangling with legendary beasts hidden in the thickets.

There is you.

In the night there is the wayfarer's step and the assassin's and the policeman's and the light of the street-lamp and the ragman's lantern.

There is you.

In the night trains pass by and boats and the mirage of lands where day is dawning. The last breath of twilight and the first tremors of dawn.

There is you.

A piano melody, a voice's cry.

A door bangs. A clock.

And not only beings and things and sounds of nature.

But also me pursuing or endlessly overtaking myself.

There is you the sacrificed, you whom I await.

Sometimes strange shapes loom up at the moment of sleep and disappear.

When I close my eyes, phosphorescent flowers appear and wither and reappear like fireworks of flesh.

Unknown lands I traverse in the company of creatures.

There is you no doubt, discreet and beautiful spy.

And the palpable soul of the universe.

And the scents of the sky and the stars and the cock-crow of 2,000 years ago and the cry of the peacock in the blazing park and kisses.

Hands ominously clasped in a wan light and axles grating on petrified roads.

There is you no doubt, whom I do not know, whom on the contrary I know.

But who, present in my dreams, persist in being prophesied without appearing.

You who remain elusive in reality and in dreams

You who belong to me because of my desire to possess you in illusion, though you only bring your face close to mine when my eyes are closed as much to dreams as to reality.

Toi qu'en dépit d'une rhétorique facile où le flot meurt sur les plages, où la corneille vole dans des usines en ruines, où le bois pourrit en craquant sous un soleil de plomb.

Toi qui es à la base de mes rêves et qui secoues mon esprit plein de métamorphoses et qui me laisses ton gant quand je baise ta main.

Dans la nuit il y a les étoiles et le mouvement ténébreux de la mer, des fleuves, des forêts, des villes, des herbes, des poumons de millions et millions d'êtres.

Dans la nuit il y a les merveilles du mondes.

Dans la nuit il n'y a pas d'anges gardiens mais il y a le sommeil.

Dans la nuit il y a toi.

Dans le jour aussi.

You who despite a facile rhetoric where waves die on beaches, where the crow flies in ruined factories, where wood cracks as it rots beneath a leaden sun.

You on whom my dreams are founded and who rouse my spirit filled with metamorphoses and who leave me her glove when I kiss her hand.

In the night there are the stars and the dark movement of the sea, rivers, forests, cities, plants, the lungs of millions and millions of beings.

In the night there are the wonders of the world.

In the night there are no guardian angels but there is sleep.

In the night there is you.

In the day also.

LUTYENS, Elizabeth (1906–1983)

This indomitably avant-garde English composer has a vast work-list of vocal music of every kind. She was always something of a Francophile, and one of her most distinguished pieces represented a turning point in her career. This work, written with twelve-tone technique, was *Ô saisons, ô châteaux!* (Rimbaud, 1946) for soprano, mandolin, guitar, harp, and string orchestra. Her catalogue of works also includes a *Cantata* (Baudelaire, 1979) for soprano, contralto, and baritone and instrumental ensemble, and *Fleur du silence* (Rémy de Gourmont, 1980) for tenor and string ensemble. *THAT SUN* is a song cycle for contralto and piano (1979) to words by Flaubert in the translation of J. Cohen.

MAGNARD, Albéric (1865–1914)

Magnard was born into a well-to-do family. His father was editor of *Le Figaro*, and he could easily have opted for an easy life in journalism. He was made of much sterner stuff, however, and, after a period at the Conservatoire, was introduced to César Franck and his circle by Guy Ropartz. After that he became a pupil of d'Indy. Magnard was a difficult man with a large chip on his shoulder concerning his background and career. All the virtues and faults of the Franck circle seem united in him: hard work, integrity, idealism, seriousness, ivory-tower values, lack of humour, inflexibility, and grandiloquence of utterance. Added to this was a real element of tragedy. He was killed by enemy cavalry on his own estate at Baron during the German advance on Paris. He fired from an upstairs window killing two men, was killed in the resulting fracas, and his house was burned to the ground. This impetuous and foolhardy behaviour seems less surprising when one hears Magnard's setting of Musset's *Le Rhin allemand* (Musset, 1915)—a virulently anti-German poem from the

Franco-Prussian war, unearthed for a new conflict. Magnard's song, with its echoes of *La Marseillaise*, is marked 'Avec insolence', and is eerily prophetic of Samuel Barber's music for Joyce's *I hear an army*. It is said that the only manuscript of *DOUZE POÈMES EN MUSIQUE* (1913–14), a new collection of songs, was destroyed in the blaze. These were settings of André Chénier and Marceline Desbordes-Valmore. As such they represented a new departure for the composer who had hitherto set mainly his own words to music. We might evaluate his songwriting differently in the light of the music which went up in smoke.

As it is, he left two collections: *SIX POÈMES EN MUSIQUE* (1887-90) where the unlikely combination of Musset and Guy Ropartz join the composer as poets, and *QUATRE POÈMES DE MUSIQUE* (1902). If any of Magnard's works have held the concert stage it is the latter set—a noble and heroic group for a particularly heroic baritone. Anything less would not be the Magnard ideal, and this is the problem with the songs: they expect too much of both performers and audience, indeed of life itself. There is nothing as frivolous as titles here, the four songs are listed in the catalogue by their tempo markings 'Assez lent', 'Doucement', 'Vif', and 'Modéré'. We wonder whether the texts represent the composer's confessional. The first song begins 'Je n'ai jamais connu les baisers d'une mère' and continues with revelations in imitation of *Les fleurs du mal* which refer to dallying with 'vendeuses d'amour aux caresseses serviles'. This is all placed into relief by the description of the hoped-for beloved ('Révèle-toi . . . reine de mes désirs'). The music moves from stillness to excited grandeur and back to a seraphic postlude. This is impressive if the singer and pianist can carry it off, but Duparc did it all better in *Phidylé* which, despite its phoney classical Greek frame, seems more real. Even in the second song, which is a much simpler love lyric, this impression of 'me and my loved ones against the world' continues. The third song 'Enfant rieuse' is no laughing matter, and the fourth 'Quand la mort viendra' is all one would expect from such a beginning. The music has the melancholy Franckian chromaticism of Ropartz but much more passion, indeed an alarming amount of it which suggests the vehement frustration of a volcanic temperament only able to express emotions through music.

Magnard remains a problematic figure. His talent is vaunted by those sympathetic to his courting of the sublime, but the destroyed set of songs might have shown a new ability to step back from himself and, in serving the literary ideas of others, achieve a sense of proportion lacking elsewhere in his vocal music. Apart from the two extant sets of *POÈMES EN MUSIQUE*, there is a single love song for tenor, *À Henriette* (1892). The poem is by the composer, of course, and there are moments of sensual beauty, Duparc-like, which show the songwriting abilities of Magnard at his best. Nevertheless, the newcomer to this composer might be better served by getting to know his Violin Sonata or the last two symphonies.

MALIPIERO, Gian Francesco (1882–1973)

The six French songs by this important Italian composer number among his earlier works and show the influence of Malipiero's visits to Paris just before the First World War. He was at the first performance of *Le sacre du printemps* in 1913 with his friend Casella, another composer who made occasional excursions into the realm of mélodie. The CINQ MÉLODIES are a varied collection of songs written between 1914 and 1916, and were completed in Asolo in the Veneto, the home of the composer until his death. The first three songs (*Chanson Morave*, *Les yeux couleur du temps*, and *Pégade*) have texts by Victor Margueritte, a writer best known at the time for his collaborations with his brother Paul. *Ariette* has a text by Jean Moréas, and the last song, *L'archet*, is to a poem by Charles Cros, in the hothouse manner of Chausson's *Chanson perpétuelle*. The choice of texts does not imply a great knowledge of French literature. The piano writing of this work is quasi-orchestral, though never impossibly so, and seems more influenced by Debussy and Ravel than Stravinsky. The other song in French is entitled *Keepsake*; the poet is G. Jean-Aubry whom, like so many other composers of the epoch, Malipiero met through his dealings with the publishing house of Chester. In any event, this handful of French settings is merely a curtain-raiser to a distinguished career of song composition in the composer's native language that extended to the *Abracadabra* of 1962.

MANZIARLY, Marcelle de (1899–1989)

This pupil of Nadia Boulanger was a French composer who had a strong connection with America. She was also a conductor and pianist as well as a teacher of composition in Paris and New York. Her main achievements were perhaps in the field of instrumental music and she came to prominence with an orchestral piece, *Sonate pour Notre-Dame de Paris*, which marked the liberation of the French capital in 1944. In terms of song, Manziarly is best remembered by her first substantial vocal composition, the TROIS FABLES DE LA FONTAINE (1935). These are extremely accomplished pieces, beautifully written for the piano, witty and elegant, certainly the best La Fontaine settings since Caplet's. The pieces are the often set-to-music *La cigale et la fourmi* [CAPLET 3 ii], and two further fables that are not easily to be found elsewhere—*L'oiseau blessé d'une flèche* and *La grenouille qui veut se faire aussi grosse que le bœuf*. The second of these is marked 'Très lent' and ranks as the most concise of all La Fontaine settings. The third with its incessant right-hand semiquavers supported by spiky left-hand quavers is reminiscent of the clockwork style of Jean Françaix. The first and last of the set are obviously the work of a very adept professional pianist. Later Manziarly works include POÈMES EN TRIO (1940), settings of Louise de Vilmorin for three female voices (her brother Alexandre was one of the numerous lovers of the poetess), and DEUX ODES DE GRÉGOIRE DE NAREK (1955) for contralto and piano.

MARTIN, Frank (1890–1974)

The most famous vocal works by this Swiss composer were in German—DIE WEISE VON LIEBE UND TOD DES CORNETS CHRISTOPH RILKE, and SECHS MONOLOGE AUS JEDERMANN. However he did write vocal music in French, which, after all, was his mother tongue. From as early as 1910 there is a song cycle for baritone and orchestra—TROIS POÈMES PAÏENS to texts of Leconte de Lisle. In 1921 he wrote

QUATRE SONNETS À CASSANDRE, which are settings of Ronsard for mezzo-soprano, flute, viola, and cello. There is only one work where the accompaniment is for piano alone—the beautiful *Dédicace* for tenor (1945), the text also by Ronsard. The best songs in French however are undoubtedly the *TROIS CHANTS DE NOËL* (Rudhardt, 1947) for soprano (they were written for the composer's 15-year-old daughter), piano, and flute. These are in Martin's modal style, but are anything but pastiches of traditional carolling commonplaces. The music is lively, ingenious, and touching—merry, as is appropriate to the seasonal mood, but with a serious centre of piety as can be seen by the text for *Les bergers*. Christmas songs by such composers as Gounod, and even Fauré, tend to mawkishness, and both Debussy and Ravel wrote strange somewhat anti-seasonal mélodies to their own texts. Difficult as it is to believe, good Christmas songs are few and far between in the song repertoire, which makes this set especially valuable.

1 *Les bergers*   *The shepherds*

(Albert Rudhardt), from *TROIS CHANTS DE NÖEL*

Il n'était pas encor minuit	Midnight had not yet arrived
Que la nouvelle étoile a lui	When the new star shone
Pour éclairer la terre;	To light up the earth;
Puis soudain le ciel s'entrouvrit,	Then suddenly the skies parted,
Et vêtus de lumière,	And clothed in light,
On pouvait voir en Paradis	All the angels in Paradise
Tous les anges réunis	Could be seen
En prière.	At prayer.
Par les déserts, marchant pieds nus,	Across deserts, barefoot,
Tous les bergers étaient venus	All the shepherds had come
Jusqu'à la pauvre hutte.	To the lowly shed.
Ils amusaient l'Enfant Jésus	They were entertaining the Infant Jesus,
Avec des airs de flûte.	Playing tunes on their flutes.
Les anges chantaient: Gloria!	The angels were singing: Gloria!
Et les pâtres: Hosanna!	And the herdsmen: Hosanna!
Alleluia, Alleluia,	Alleluia, Alleluia,
Alleluia, Alleluia.	Alleluia, Alleluia!

MARTINI, Johann Paul (1741–1816)

It comes as something of a surprise to many people that the composer of the immortal *Plaisir d'amour* was not the celebrated Padre Martini, the Italian composer so admired by Mozart. Johann (or Jean) Paul Martini was a German composer who spent most of his career in France. He left Germany and arrived destitute in Nancy in 1760 without knowing the language. He dropped his pseudonym of 'Schwarzendorf' and became known as 'Martini il tedesco'. He moved to Paris where he became a well-known opera composer, and much concerned with the reform of French military music. He eventually became almost as celebrated as Monsigny, Grétry, and Philidor, and Fétis credits him with the special distinction as being the first composer in France to compose songs with piano accompaniment rather than continuo. *Plaisir d'amour* was composed in Nancy in 1784. It was originally published as a supplement to the novella *Célestine* where it appeared as *Romance de chevrier*. The poem is by Jean-Pierre Claris de Florian, an important figure in the early history of the romance and mélodie, whose poems were set by such disparate composers as Benjamin Godard and Charles Ives.

1 *Plaisir d'amour*

(Jean-Pierre Claris de Florian)

Plaisir d'amour ne dure qu'un moment;
Chagrin d'amour dure toute la vie.
J'ai tout quitté pour l'ingrate Sylvie:
Elle me quitte et prend un autre amant.
　Plaisir d'amour ne dure qu'un moment;
Chagrin d'amour dure toute la vie.

Tant que cette eau coulera doucement
Vers ce ruisseau qui borde la prairie,
Je t'aimerai, me répétait Sylvie:
L'eau coule encore; elle a changé pourtant.
　Plaisir d'amour ne dure qu'un moment;
Chagrin d'amour dure toute la vie.

The joys of love

The joys of love last but a moment;
The sorrows of love endure a whole life.
I abandoned all for ungrateful Sylvie:
She abandons me for another lover.
　The joys of love last but a moment;
The sorrows of love endure a whole life.

As long as this water gently flows
Towards this stream that bounds the plain,
I shall love you, Sylvie used to say:
The water still flows, but she has changed.
　The joys of love last but a moment;
The sorrows of love endure a whole life.

MASCAGNI, Pietro (1863–1945)

The opera *Amica*, composed in 1905, and given its first performance in Monte Carlo, was one of many works that Mascagni composed in the years following the success of *Cavalleria rusticana*. It was one of the composer's many futile attempts to recapture the popularity of that early work. *Amica* had a French libretto by the publisher Paul de Choudens. It was perhaps natural that some of the music should reappear in mélodie guise (published by Choudens of course). *Tous les jours de l'année* and *Plus près du ciel et plus loin de la terre* are arias masquerading as songs (as are a number of items in the Choudens *recueils* of such composers as Gounod and Bizet). Mascagni wrote many songs in Italian, of course, but many of these remain unpublished and almost all of them are operatic in character.

MASSÉ, Victor (1822–1874)

Andrew Lamb succinctly states in *Grove 6* that Massé was 'inclined to aim above his talents'. His unassuming *Les noces de Jeanette* is known and appreciated by aficionados of *opéra comique*, but most of his theatre music was more ambitious and failed to find its mark. His music is little heard today, despite the fact that during his lifetime he steadily climbed the ladder of official honours and celebrity. As one of the early mélodistes, and the composer of over 100 songs (including three *recueils* of romances published in 1868, 1874, 1877), his name cannot be omitted from any history of the medium, but composers can always be found who had a more vivid and imaginative response to texts, a greater melodic gift, a better sense of the piano, and so on. However beautiful his songs must have seemed to audiences at the time of their composition, Massé now strikes us as ill at ease with the new emerging medium of the mélodie. His penchant was for Renaissance texts, but he lacked the easy ability of Gounod, and subsequent pasticheurs like Hahn, to transport us to another epoch by deft imaginative touches; instead his music seems either overblown and melodramatic, or simple to the point of plainness. Among the better Massé songs are *Mignonne* (Ronsard, from the collection entitled LES CHANTS D'AUTREFOIS, 1849), *La chaumière* and *La chanson de Marie* from LES CHANTS BRETONS (1853), and, above all, *Ninon* (Musset) from LES CHANTS DU SOIR (1850), a large song in five sections which has the structure of an operatic aria, but which nevertheless expresses considerable tenderness and lyricism.

MASSENET, Jules (1842–1912)

There can be no more potent illustration in French musical history of the transitory nature of fame. Although a number of Massenet's operas have held the stage, it is rare indeed to hear his songs on the recital platform. And yet in their day they were the height of fashion, published almost as soon as they were written, and sung in every salon in the land. They were what would be now termed a 'market leader'. Of course this composer was unusually aware of the market. An astute businessman (he has been compared to Strauss and Puccini in this respect), he believed in giving his audiences what they wanted to hear. As a result he tended to stick to winning formulae once he had found them, and in his song output we are not aware of a great change in musical style from the first works of the 1860s until the final set from 1912: the experiments with declamation which are such a feature of his last set, the EXPRESSIONS LYRIQUES, are to be found in less sophisticated form in the early POÈME D'AVRIL.

Indeed, Massenet was perhaps the most prolific French mélodie composer of all, with about 260 songs to his credit published in eight *recueils* and in numerous separate collections. This makes it especially astonishing that so very few of the songs have survived today. They are defended and promoted by some enthusiasts who insist on their excellence, but like the Schubert operas, and despite any number of well-meaning amateur performances to rescue them, they fail to catch fire in the minds and hearts of world-class artists and their audiences. Massenet was a master-craftsman who had an instinct for the theatre which amounted to genius. What is in question here, however, is his status as a song composer.

Perhaps Massenet's cause would have been better served if he had composed fewer songs. Although reprints of some of them have become more recently available, the scores are not always easy for modern-day performers to find, and when they come to light, the sheer amount of music is overwhelming. There are no short cuts in discovering the best of the output, for the weakest songs are liable to stand next to the strongest in the collections and cycles, and patient study is need to assemble a programme consisting of Massenet's most interesting mélodies. His attainment of excellence seems haphazard; just when you have decided, on playing through a pile of music, that he does not have much to say, he suddenly writes something which is charming, moving, and skilful. Too often he tends to neglect the piano, and this is the gravest charge to be laid against some of his songs. It is not that he cannot write inventively for the instrument, but his passion for singers, and his desire to please them, leads to undue reticence. After all, the piano part in the entire mélodie repertoire represents the collaborative voice of the composer himself, but in these songs the piano writing often seems an afterthought rather than an organic part of the whole. Massenet's songs come to life on the occasions when the piano writing interacts productively with the voice rather than walking three steps behind it in a spirit of deference to the singer's importance. Good examples of songs enlivened by their piano parts are *Les alcyons* (J. Autran, 1887), where the keyboard writing is modelled on Chopin's *Fantasie-impromptu*), and the *Chanson juanesque* (Félicien Champsaur, 1905), where the accompaniment is a delicate little scherzo with a life of its own.

In the least interesting of the Massenet songs, everything seems slavishly framed to the singer's needs. Richard Strauss comes to mind as another composer fascinated by divas and strong female personalities, above all his wife, the redoutable Pauline de Ahna; his piano writing however is never self-effacing. With Massenet, nothing must upstage the star, and this includes the lyrics which often seem manufactured in a word factory that churns out all-purpose lyrics of love in every hackneyed manifestation. The quality of a song composer's output is governed by the quality of the poems which he sets, and no composer can completely avoid being dragged down by less than successful texts; Massenet is the classic example of someone who is all too often scuppered by his collaborators. Another is his English contemporary Hubert Parry who also wrote fine pieces of music to some terrible Victorian poetry. Massenet seems to have been moved by sentimental literature where platitudes and commonplaces are no substitute for strong imagery. A song like *Les mains* (1899, Noël Bazan) contains some fine music, but it is literally ruined by an execrable poem.

Massenet's song catalogue is hardly a roster of literary distinction. Admittedly there is one Verlaine solo song published posthumously entitled *Je mourrai plus que toi*, a setting where this poet is far from his best. The beautiful duet *Rêvons, c'est l'heure* (1871), known as *L'heure exquise* in other settings, is also a Verlaine text [FAURÉ 30 iii], and has the distinction of being among the very first musical setting of that poet's work. But why did Massenet not follow this success up, and why was he not drawn to the rest of Verlaine's poetry when the field was still free of composing rivals? The answer must be that his literary taste did not match his musical skill. He preferred to compose songs to the sort of pseudo-poetic gush published in popular magazines of the time with an eye on immediate success. The literary nonentities in this composer's œuvre is daunting, the potential subject of a thesis. Many of them were famous in their time no doubt, but how faded their lyrics now appear!

Admittedly here and there we find Hugo and Ronsard and it is significant that the better the poet, the better the song. This is illustrated by the settings of Armand Silvestre, who was a close friend of the composer, and who won his own celebrity at the same time as Massenet was fighting for his. Silvestre was admittedly no Verlaine, Baudelaire, Leconte de Lisle, or Albert Samain (the list of poets more important than Silvestre is a long one), but his gifts attracted many composers, including Fauré. The Massenet songs that enlist Silvestre's collaboration start life with a stronger chance of survival. There are Silvestre settings from the beginning of Massenet's career (a good example is *Il pleuvait* from 1871 which has a Fauré-like accompaniment of running semiquavers which admirably evoke rain), until 1905 when he bids farewell to this poet with the hypnotic little lullaby *Dors, Magda*.

The first songs are more or less contemporary with Fauré's earliest attempts. *Souvenir de Venise* (Musset, 1865) is a charmingly Italianate serenade which was arranged as a duet in 1872. The same text was set by Lalo as *La Zuecca* [LALO 1]. The first cycle is the *POÈME D'AVRIL* (1866, Silvestre), and here we see the hand of an innovator, indeed the work is astonishingly adventurous for the height of the Second Empire. The composer was always fascinated by the thespian side of singers' natures, and the cycle includes declaimed poems and piano solos. This hybrid genre, where the piano might be used to accompany speech as well as song, was to be much imitated (Massenet's pupil Reynaldo Hahn wrote a piece for declamation, *PORTRAITS DE PEINTRES*, to the prose poems of Marcel Proust, no less), and the older composer returned to this idea at the end of his life. Although *POÈME D'AVRIL* is hardly performed today, it is an important milestone in French song, for it is a real cycle, and it is meant to be heard as a whole in the same way as Schumann's *DICHTERLIEBE* or *FRAUENLIEBE UND -LEBEN*, cycles which no doubt played their part in influencing Massenet in the first place. As in all works of this type by Massenet, the inspiration is uneven, but the good is very good indeed. The piano interlude before *Riez-vous?* shows just how well he could write for the instrument when he chose, *Que l'heure est donc brève* is most affecting, and *Sur la source* is a charming piece of water music. The more interesting and worked-out the accompaniment, and the more the vocal line is forced to engage with it, the less the music strikes an attitude of *fin-de-siècle* bathos.

The next set of songs was published as Op. 12 (1868) and are among his very best. Gautier's *L'esclave* was set to music by Lalo a few years later [LALO 3], and *Sérénade aux mariés* (Ruelle) is surely one of the most attractive of the Massenet songs, almost the equal in charm of the celebrated *Sérénade* of Gounod. *La vie d'une rose* is a pleasantly lively song (we tire of the languid Massenet all too easily—it is a relief to hear a quick tempo). *Le portrait d'un enfant* (Ronsard) is as fine an evocation of the madrigal style as we will hear from any composer of the time. It is unusual however for Massenet to publish songs under an opus number. He preferred the 'Poème' formula he had established earlier. Thus we have the cycles *POÈME DU SOUVENIR* (again Silvestre, 1868), *POÈME PASTORAL* (Silvestre, 1872), *POÈME D'OCTOBRE* (Collin, 1876), *POÈME D'AMOUR* (Robiquet, 1879), and so on. *POÈME D'HIVER* (Silvestre, 1882) is undoubtedly one of the better cycles; the first song, *C'est au temps de la chrysanthème*, is a counterpart to Chausson's *Le temps des lilas*; the accompaniment depicts the blooming of a flower, heavy on its stalk, with swooning arpeggio figures in contrary motion. The most famous offshoot of this cyclic idea was a piece published by Fauré in 1878, the *POÈME D'UN JOUR* [FAURÉ 16 i–iii], a mini-cycle of three songs which attempts something of a narrative and musical unity, and employs more than a hint of Massenet's sentimental style.

The single songs also contain treasures if one knows where to look. Many (though not all) of these were published in the eight *recueils* of Massenet's work which were issued by Heugel. Apart from the eighth, which offers a selection of posthumous works, these collections appeared one by one through the years, almost as if they were musical journals. The first includes songs 1864–75; the second 1869–*c*.1871; the third 1881–91; the fourth 1891–6; the fifth 1897–9; the sixth 1900–2. Sometimes Massenet held songs back for revision: volume vii, effectively the composer's last mélodie publication, contains some songs from earlier years but extends to 1912. The task of burrowing amongst the dross to rescue the best things is what has always daunted anyone except the devoted Massenet disciple. Only a few songs can be mentioned here, but these will all repay study.

It is often the earlier songs which are the freshest. *Nouvelle chanson sur un vieil air* (Hugo, 1869) [FAURÉ 6] is a serenade remarkable for the clever pianistic evocation of a plucked and strummed lute. The world-famous song *Élégie* started life as one of the DIX PIÈCES for piano, published in 1866. After its reincarnation as a song (*c*.1869, poem by Gallet) it was used again by Massenet, this time without words, as part of his incidental music to Leconte de Lisle's play *Les Érinnyes* (1873). The song was published in no less than four keys, and there was a popular version with cello obbligato. There were other songs written to include this instrument—for example *Amours bénis* (Alexandre, 1899) and *Oh! si les fleurs avaient des yeux* (Buchillot, 1903). The popular *Si tu veux, Mignonne* (Boyer), full of life and movement and tender passion, dates from 1876. From 1880 comes a fascinating peculiarity, a song in English entitled *Come into the garden, Maud* (also published as *Viens, sous les ombrages, Maud*) which was this composer's contribution to the book of musical settings published to honour Alfred, Lord Tennyson. *Le poète et le fantôme* (1891) does not acknowledge an author, but is a useful song for singers who are able to suggest a colloquy between two characters. Massenet seems at his best when his songs require him to invoke his dramatic skills. They are at their most colourless when they retreat into a faded world of solitary, self-indulgent contemplation. Character pieces bring out the best in him, and he thrives when there is a background scenario, a *raison d'être* for action. *Première danse* (Normand, 1899) conjures a scene of a little girl dancing under the watchful eyes of adults who see that she is already as coquettish and aware of her beauty as any young woman. Massenet handles this as carefully as if it had been a scene in an opera. And it can be no surprise that the composer of *Manon* was brilliant at stylizations which evoke the past. Among the best are *Le verger* (Distel, 1868), *Marquise* (again Silvestre, 1888), and *L'éventail*, subtitled 'vieille chanson française' (Morel-Retz, 1892).

As early as 1872 Massenet evoked Spanish music in *Nuits d'Espagne* (Gallet, 1872), which was derived from the orchestral suite SCÈNES PITTORESQUES. Other songs in this vein include a setting of the celebrated *Guitare* (Hugo, 1886) which had so appealed to other composers [BIZET 2], the elegant farandole *Pitchounette* (J. Normand, 1897), and the very last of his posthumous songs published as late as 1933 entitled *La verdadera vida* (Guillot de Saix). A rare note in his vocal music with piano is struck by *Chant de guerre cossaque* (Vacaresco, 1893), which suggests raw pagan power.

Also bordering on the world of opera are Massenet's works for more than one voice which are almost always well written. The cycle LUI ET ELLE (Maquet, 1891) is a set of two linked songs for lovers where his jealous fears are answered by her soothing reassurances. Apart from *Rêvons, c'est l'heure* already mentioned above, there are charmingly lightweight duets with the titles *Joie* and *Marine* (both Camille Distel, 1868), an atmospheric *L'heure solitaire* for two voices (J. Ader, 1908), and another colloquy in the *LUI ET ELLE* mould, this time to a gently risqué poem by Musset after Horace entitled *Horace et Lydie* (1893). *Matinée d'été* (Distel, 1868) is for a trio of women's voices, and *Le temps et l'amour* (Ludana, 1907) is for the more unusual combination of tenor and baritone. *CHANSONS DES BOIS D'ARAMANTHE* (Marc Legrand, translating Oskar Redwitz, 1900) is a suite for soprano, alto, tenor, and bass which includes trios, duets, and quartets. This reflects the taste for such concerted cycles at the turn of the century (Reynaldo Hahn wrote a number of such works, as did the English women composers Liza Lehmann and Amy Woodforde-Finden. The French taste for the form no doubt goes back to Schumann with his *MINNESPIEL* and *SPANISCHES LIEDERSPIEL* cycles.)

At the end of his life, Massenet could look around at other song composers, not only his contemporaries like Saint-Saëns, but his juniors like Fauré, and those twenty years younger than him like Debussy, and know, with some satisfaction, that his work had influenced them all. This is quite apart from such a composer as Reynaldo Hahn who unashamedly acknowledged Massenet as his master. The blooming of a gracious and pleasing melodic line, first curvaceously erotic, and then tending to wilt and fade away, was Massenet's special trade mark—this is to be found hidden, and unacknowledged, in certain passages of works as revolutionary as *Pelléas et Mélisande*. Time and time again we find this fingerprint appropriated by composers who have borrowed his exquisite musical manners when they need an injection of charm in their work. That this same melodic gift can also seem unctuous, exuding a perfume that is sickly sweet and which can outstay its welcome, is part of the price one has to pay for keeping company with this highly talented man whose song catalogue is prolix and uneven.

The last songs, like all the rest, have both *longueurs* and splendours. Who would be prepared for the sombre and majestic Hugo setting (who else was still setting Hugo in 1912?) entitled *Soleil couchant*? This achieved publication only in the posthumous eighth *recueil*, and some of the more adventurous songs are to be found in the seventh which contains, perhaps, the most representative selection of the composer at his mature best. Indeed, it is as if Massenet was thinking less of success and more of his reputation as a serious musician as he got older. In this volume two Buchillot settings, in particular, both with violoncello obbligato, are worthy of investigation: *Oh! Si les fleurs avaient des yeux* (1903) and *Les yeux clos* (1905). Among other good songs are *La lettre* (Jane Mendès, 1907) and *C'est l'amour* (Hugo, 1908). *Rêverie sentimentale* (Peyre, 1910) is more effective than its title suggests, and *La mort de la cigale* (Faure, 1911) is a useful and atmospheric animal portrait in contrast to the cicada songs of Chabrier and Chausson.

Of the half-sung, half-recited *EXPRESSIONS LYRIQUES* from 1912, the most interesting, considering that Massenet is famous for the opera *Werther*, are a reworking of Werther's suicide in song terms (*La dernière lettre de Werther*—R. de Gontant Biron), and a sinuous waltz, *Mélancolie*, by the same poet. And just when we have tired of the Massenet mannerisms with many pages written on a sort of musical autopilot, he ends the set magnificently with *Feux-follets d'amour* (Madeleine Grain) where the piano writing seems more energetic and innovative than any he has given us. It is entirely typical of this old charmer that he should have something up his sleeve to surprise and seduce us at the last minute, just when we think he has nothing more to offer. The reader of this article will have gathered that there is more than enough of interest to be found in Massenet's output to encourage singers to include his work, from time to time, in their recitals. The selection of suitable and effective items will take time and care, but total neglect seems far too high a price to exact from this composer because of his failure to limit his song publications to his best work. In this context, the seemingly over-rigorous self-censorship of Duparc seems to have been prudent and wise.

POÈME D'AVRIL

(Armand Silvestre)

APRIL POEM

1 i Prélude

Prelude

Une rose frileuse, au cœur noyé de pluie,
Sur un rameau tremblant vient de s'épanouir,
Et je me sens repris de la douce folie
De faire des chansons et de me souvenir!

A chilly rose, its heart drenched with rain,
Has just blossomed on a trembling bough.
And I feel the sweet folly assail me once more
To create songs and recall the past!

Les amours trépassés qui dormaient dans mon âme,
Doux Lazare sur qui j'ai tant versé de pleurs,
Soulèvent, en riant, leur suaire de fleurs
Et demandent le nom de ma nouvelle dame.

All the dead loves asleep in my soul,
Gentle Lazarus, on whom I shed so many tears,
Laughingly raise their shroud of flowers,
And ask me the name of my new love.

Ma Mignonne aux yeux bleus, mets ta robe et fuyons
Sous les bois remplis d'ombre et de mélancolie.
Chercher le doux remède à la douce folie.
—Le soleil m'a blessé de ses premiers rayons!

O my blue-eyed darling, dress and let us flee
Through woods filled with melancholy and shade,
To seek a sweet cure for our sweet folly.
—The sun has wounded me with its first rays!

1 ii Sonnet matinal

Morning sonnet

Les étoiles effarouchées
Viennent de s'envoler des cieux.
J'en sais deux qui se sont cachées,
Mignonne, dans vos jolis yeux;

The affrighted stars
Have just fled the skies.
I know of two that hid,
My love, in your pretty eyes;

À l'ombre de vos cils soyeux
Et sous vos paupières penchées:
Attendez!—mes baisers joyeux
Les auront bientôt dénichées!

In the shade of your silky lashes
And beneath your drooping lids:
Wait!—my joyous kisses
Will soon ferret them out!

Vous feignez de dormir encor:
Éveillez-vous, mon doux trésor!
—L'aube pleure sous les feuillées,

You pretend to be still asleep:
Wake up, my sweetest treasure!
—Dawn weeps beneath the leafy boughs,

Le ciel désert est plein d'ennui.
—Ouvrez les yeux et rendez-lui
Les deux étoiles envolées!

The forsaken sky is full of distress.
Open your eyes and give back to it
The two stars that have taken flight!

I iii *Voici que les grands lys*

Voici que les grands lys ont vêtu leur blancheur;
Sur les gazons tremblants l'aube étend sa fraîcheur.
—C'est le printemps! c'est le matin! Double jeunesse!

Ma mie, en s'éveillant, m'a dit: 'Le beau soleil!
Le temps est donc venu que tout charme renaisse.
Partout des chants! Partout des fleurs! Double réveil!'

Mais la tiédeur de l'air la rendant moins farouche,
Je me penchai vers elle et je posai ma bouche
Sur son front et sur ses cheveux, double trésor!

Now the large lilies

Now the large lilies have dressed in their white,
Dawn spreads its cool on the shivering lawns.
—It is spring. It is morning. Youth twice over!

My love, as she woke, said to me: 'the beautiful sun!
The time has finally come when all beauty's reborn.
Songs everywhere! Everywhere flowers! Awakening
    twice over!'

But with the warmth of the air making her less shy,
I leant forward, and placed my lips
On her brow and on her hair, delight twice over!'

I iv *Riez-vous?*

Riez-vous? Ne riez-vous pas?
—Quand vous l'avez dit tout à l'heure,
Ce mot!—Vous l'avez dit si bas!...
Je n'ai pas compris, mais je pleure.
—Riez-vous?—Ne riez-vous pas?

Pitié! votre bouche m'effleure.
Ce bruit! vous l'avez fait si bas!...
Si c'est un baiser, que je meure!
—Riez-vous? Ne riez-vous pas?

Si c'est un baiser, que je meure!
—Sur mon cou je sens votre bras...
Vous m'avez baisé tout à l'heure!
Je n'ose y croire, mais je pleure.
—Riez-vous?—Ne riez-vous pas!

Are you jesting?

Are you jesting? Or are you not?
—When you uttered that word just now,
You whispered it so softly!...
I did not understand, but I am weeping.
—Are you jesting? Or are you not?

Have pity! Your lips brush mine.
That sound—you whispered it so softly!...
If it is a kiss, let me die!
—Are you jesting? Or are you not?

If it is a kiss, let me die!
—I feel your arm about my neck...
You kissed me just a moment ago!
I dare not believe it, but I am weeping.
—Are you jesting?—Surely you are not!

I v *Vous aimerez demain*

Le doux printemps a bu, dans le creux de sa main,
Le premier pleur qu'au bois laissa tomber l'aurore;
Vous aimerez demain, vous qui n'aimiez encore,
Et vous qui n'aimiez plus, vous aimerez demain!

—Le doux printemps a bu dans le creux de sa main.

You shall love tomorrow

Sweet spring has drunk from the hollow of her hand
The first tear that dawn shed in the wood.
You who have not yet loved, shall love tomorrow,
And you shall love tomorrow, who love no
    longer!
—Sweet spring has drunk from the hollow of her
    hand.

Le printemps a cueilli, dans l'air, des fils de soie,
Pour lier sa chaussure et courir par les bois;
Vous aimerez demain pour la première fois,
Vous qui ne saviez pas cette immortelle joie!
—Le printemps a cueilli, dans l'air, des fils de soie.

Le printemps a jeté des fleurs sur le chemin
Que Mignonne remplit de son rire sonore;
Vous aimerez demain, vous qui n'aimiez encore,
Et vous qui n'aimiez plus, vous aimerez demain!

—Le printemps a jeté des fleurs sur le chemin.

Spring has gathered threads of silk in the air
For her to lace her shoes and fly through the woods;
You shall love tomorrow for the first time,
You who have not known this imperishable joy!
—Spring has gathered threads of silk in the air.

Spring has strewn flowers along the path
That my love fills with her ringing laughter;
You who have not yet loved, shall love tomorrow,
And you shall love tomorrow, who love no
      longer!
—Spring has strewn flowers along the path.

I vi *Que l'heure est donc brève*

Que l'heure est donc brève
Qu'on passe en aimant!
—C'est moins qu'un moment,
Un peu plus qu'un rêve.

Le temps nous enlève
Notre enchantement.
—Que l'heure est donc brève
Qu'on passe en aimant!

Sous le flot dormant
Soupirait la grève;
M'aimas-tu vraiment?
Fut-ce seulement
Un peu plus qu'un rêve?...
—Que l'heure est donc brève
Qu'on passe en aimant!

How brief the time

How brief the time
We spend in loving!
—It is less than a moment,
A little more than a dream.

Time robs us
Of our enchantment.
How brief the time
We spend in loving!

The shore sighed
Beneath the sleeping waves;
Did you really love me?
Was it merely
A little more than a dream?...
—How brief the time
We spend in loving!

I vii *Sur la source*

Sur la source elle se pencha;
La source doubla son image,
Et ce fut un charmant mirage
Qu'un peu de vent effaroucha.

Sous les grands bois elle chanta:
L'oiseau doubla son chant sauvage,
Et ce fut un charmant ramage
Que le vent lointain emporta.

At the spring

She leant over the spring,
The spring reflected her face—
A charming mirage,
Ruffled by a gust of wind.

She sang beneath the great trees:
The bird repeated her wild song,
And it was a delightful warbling
The wind bore far away.

Quand j'effleurai son doux visage,
Sa bouche ma bouche doubla.
—Le vent peut balayer la plage,
Mignonne, que me fait l'orage?
—Ton baiser reste toujours là!

When I touched her sweet face,
Her lips responded to my lips.
—Though the wind sweep the shore,
My love, what is the storm to me?
—Your kiss will always remain!

1 viii *Complainte*

Nous nous sommes aimés trois jours;
Trois jours elle me fut fidèle.
—Trois jours!—La constance éternelle
Et les éternelles amours!

Je pars! Adieu, ma chère âme,
Garde bien mon souvenir!
—Quoi! sitôt partir, ma Dame!
Ne devez-vous revenir?

—Si—je reviendrai peut-être...
Si—bien sûr je reviendrai...
Va m'attendre à la fenêtre;
De plus loin te reverrai.

J'attendis à la fenêtre
Le retour tant espéré,
Mais, ni bien sûr, ni peut-être,
Ni jamais la reverrai!

Bien fol qui croit quand sa Dame
Lui jure de revenir.
Je meurs!—Adieu, ma chère âme!
J'ai gardé ton souvenir.

Lament

We loved each other for three days;
Three days she was faithful.
—Three days.—Eternal constancy
And eternal love!

I depart! Farewell, my love,
Remember me well!
—What! Parting so soon, my lady!
Will you not return?

—Yes—I shall return perhaps...
Yes—of course I shall return...
Go and wait for me at the window;
I shall see you from afar.

I waited at the window
For the cherished return,
But, neither of course, nor perhaps,
Nor ever shall I see her!

Foolish the man who believes his Lady
When she vows to return.
I am dying!—Farewell, my dear love!
I have preserved your memory.

2 *Élégie*
(Louis Gallet)

Ô doux printemps d'autrefois, vertes saisons, vous avez fui pour toujours! Je ne vois plus le ciel bleu, je n'entends plus les chants joyeux des oiseaux! En emportant mon bonheur, ô bien-aimé, tu t'en es allé! Et c'est en vain que revient le printemps! Oui! Sans retour, avec toi, le gai soleil, les jours riants sont partis! Comme en mon cœur tout est sombre et glacé, tout est flétri pour toujours!

Elegy

O sweet Spring of yesteryear, green seasons, you have fled forever! I no longer see the blue sky, I no longer hear the joyous songs of the birds! You have fled, my love, and with you has fled my happiness. And it is in vain that the spring returns! For along with you, the cheerful sun, the laughing days have gone! As my heart is dark and frozen, so all is withered for evermore!

3 *Si tu veux, Mignonne*
(Abbé Claude Georges Boyer)

If you wish, Mignonne

Si tu veux, Mignonne, au printemps
Nous verrons fleurir l'aubépine,
Qui sème dans les prés naissants
La neige de sa tête fine,
Si tu veux, Mignonne, au printemps
Nous verrons fleurir l'aubépine!

If you wish, Mignonne, in the spring
We shall see the hawthorns flower,
Bestrewing the wakening fields
With snow from their graceful crowns,
If you wish, Mignonne, in the spring
We shall see the hawthorns flower!

Si tu veux, quand viendra l'été,
Nous écouterons dans les branches
Les chants d'amour et de gaîté
Des petites colombes blanches,
Si tu veux, quand viendra l'été,
Nous écouterons dans les branches!

If you wish, when summer comes
We shall listen among the boughs
To the songs of love and mirth
The small white doves will sing,
If you wish, when summer comes,
We shall listen among the boughs!

Nous irons dans les bois jaunis,
Si tu veux, quand viendra l'automne,
Pour qu'elles aient chaud dans leurs nids
Leur porter des brins d'anémone,
Si tu veux, Mignonne,
Nous irons dans les bois jaunis
Quand viendra l'automne...

We shall walk in the yellowing woods,
If you wish, when autumn comes,
To make them warm inside their nests
We'll bring them sprigs of anenome,
If you wish, Mignonne,
We shall walk in the yellowing woods
When autumn comes...

Et puis, quand reviendra l'hiver...
Nous nous ressouviendrons des roses,
Du printemps, et du sentier vert
Où tu m'as juré tant de choses!
Alors... quand reviendra l'hiver...
Nous nous ressouviendrons des roses!
Si tu veux, Mignonne!

And then, when winter comes once more,
Once more we shall remember the roses
Of spring, once more the verdant path,
Where you vowed to me so many things!
Then... When winter comes once more...
Once more we shall remember the roses!
If you wish, Mignonne!

MAURICE, Pierre (1868–1936)

This Swiss composer was a pupil of Massenet and a disciple of Fauré. At the same time he was attracted to Wagner, which led him to write large operas to his own texts. During the First World War, the composer's Swiss neutrality and French-speaking background placed him in an ambivalent relationship with the German opera houses, but his *Misé Brun* achieved some success in 1917. Maurice's music for the stage stands between the French and German traditions, but in his songs he inhabits the world of the mélodie rather than the Lied. His songs have a delicate and understated melancholy, and it is through these works that he is remembered in Switzerland. One of the best is

Vierges mortes (Haraucourt), which has the gentle contemplative hallmarks of his style, and is dedicated to Koechlin. Also worthy of investigation are *Le petit port* and *Soir de neige* (both Antoinette Maurice), *Coucher de soleil à Kerazur* (Tiercelin), *Couche-toi sur la grève* (Régnier), as well as *La chanson de quatre saisons* (Paul Labbé).

MENASCE, Jacques de (1905–1960)

Like a modern-day Loeffler, Menasce was an American composer by adoption. He was born in Switzerland of Franco-Egyptian and German descent. His training was in Vienna, where he was a pupil of Berg, but his musical predilections seem to have been French. His epigramatic style is typified by *DEUX LETTRES D'ENFANTS* (1954), settings of thank-you letters from the two children of the composer Daniel-Lesur. The first of these, **Lettre de Béatrice**, has a delicately feminine ring to it, while the **Lettre de Christian** is more boisterous and proud (he signs off with his full name which is faithfully set to music). These miniatures, which have the humour of Mussorgsky's *NURSERY* cycle, are as good as any songs in the repertoire at depicting through music the varying voices and characters of children. There are also two small-scale cycles, *POUR UNE PRINCESSE* (including settings of Tristan l'Hermite and Ronsard) and *QUATRE CHANSONS*, for tenor and string orchestra (Molière, Clément Marot, Villon (*Ballade des femmes de Paris*, also set by Debussy [DEBUSSY 15 iii]), and Charles d'Orléans). The little set *DEUX POÈMES D'ANNE FONTAINE* includes *Vaucluse*, a lyrical evocation of the south of France.

DEUX LETTRES D'ENFANTS	***TWO LETTERS FROM CHILDREN***
1 i *Lettre de Béatrice*	*Béatrice's letter*
Monsieur, Merci pour le bonhomme qui joue avec des balles. Il est tellement drôle qu'il me fait rire, c'est effrayant.	Monsieur, Thank you for the little man who juggles with balls. He's so funny that he makes me laugh, it's tremendous.
Béatrice	Béatrice

I ii *Lettre de Christian*

Le 8 mars 1953

Monsieur,
Nous avons été ravis tous les deux des jolis jouets que vous avez donnés à Papa et à Maman pour nous, et vous en remercions beaucoup.

Mon motocycliste prend des virages formidables toute la journée, cela m'amuse énormément. Veuillez croire, Monsieur, ainsi que Madame,

à mes sentiments respectueux,
    Christian Daniel Lesur

Christian's letter

8 March 1953

Monsieur,
We were both delighted with the lovely toys you gave Mummy and Daddy to give to us, and we thank you very much.

My motorcyclist's terrific at taking bends all day long, it's enormous fun.

Yours sincerely
    Christian Daniel Lesur

MESSAGER, André (1853–1929)

Messager's career as a composer was overtaken by his work as a conductor. He was no fool and this was perhaps a wise decision, for he had his limits, as his mélodies show. There is no doubting the charm and memorability of his finest operettas (*Les p'tites Michu*, *Véronique*, *Monsieur Beaucaire*, and so on) as well as his ballet *Les deux pigeons*. There is also no doubt that he was respected everywhere for his knowledge of music, Wagner's in particular. Fauré admired Messager, and Debussy dedicated *Pelléas et Mélisande* to him, entrusting the first performance to Messager's baton. One might have thought that such a musical personality would be drawn to the best literature, but a glance through Messager's song-list shows poets like Mendès and Silvestre (both already very old hat by the time Messager came to set them) rather than immortals like Baudelaire, Verlaine, and Mallarmé, or newer poets like Samain. The single songs (the most important of which are to be found in QUINZE MÉLODIES, published in 1912) are unaffectedly melodic, but the piano writing all too often disappoints the professional accompanist. On the other hand this simplicity probably suited the salon pianists of the time, and in this way Messager, like Massenet, seems to have been very aware of the market. The most substantial work for voice and piano is the Massenet-inspired cycle AMOUR D'HIVER (1911). These six songs have charming touches, but the wit of the operettas is lacking, and there is a disappointing lack of passion. Perhaps the most interesting song in the set is *Quand tu passes, ma bien-aimée*, the mood of which is poised between elation and self-doubt reminiscent of Fauré's LA BONNE CHANSON. There is little stylistic difference between these songs and the much earlier NOUVEAU PRINTEMPS, a set of five Heine translations from 1885. Sometimes Messager published numbers from earlier operas (*Isoline* and *La fauvette du temple*) rearranged as songs, and these at least have charming tunes. The Silvestre setting *Notre amour* is an interesting comparison with Fauré's [FAURÉ 20]. Try as Messager might, the inner, word-inspired animation of the real mélodiste is lacking; he needed the theatre to bring his art to life. The songs with piano of Franz Lehár are disappointing in the same way.

MESSIAEN, Olivier (1908–1992)

It is a paradox that this composer who towered over his generation, and the musical life of France, seems out of place in a book of this kind. There is certainly no other composer remotely like him in these pages. Even like-minded contemporaries, members of La Jeune France for example, made some concessions in later life to the mainstream traditions of mélodie. Apart from a childhood admiration for Debussy and a high regard for the music of Berlioz (a composer who was also something of an outsider in the mélodie tradition) Messiaen seems to have created almost unaided his own world of music and aesthetics. In actual fact he took inspiration from a dazzling array of sources, but the result is so singular, and single-minded, that it seems to have come about by parthenogenesis. Of collaboration with others, the essential *raison d'être* of the mélodie composer who enters a poet's world in order to give it a new depth and dimension, there is scarcely a sign. It is not as if Messiaen was insensitive to others, or uninterested in them (he was a remarkably kind and open-minded teacher); it was simply that he had created a musical universe of his own making where nature, ethnomusicology, and birdsong impressed him more than anything written by a mere poet or librettist. It is true that he read and admired the work of the surrealist poet André Breton, but he did not set him to music. He was not easily influenced, even by what fascinated him. He was the only student at the Paris Conservatoire (he claimed) to know Schoenberg's *Pierrot lunaire*; the score of Berg's *Lyric suite* accompanied his wartime captivity in Silesia—but these Austrian masters never became his models. When he looked outwards for inspiration it was to other times and other civilizations: his interests as a self-styled 'rythmicien' were awoken with Greek metre and Hindu rhythms (here the teaching of Marcel Dupré and Maurice Emmanuel played its part). His famous analyses of the works of Le Jeune, Mozart, Beethoven, Chopin, and Stravinsky departed from the norms of study at the time, and concentrated on the rhythmic nature of their works. Messiaen learned and took from these composers what no one else had seen or heard. His canvas was broader and his aspirations more lofty than those of his contemporaries, whom he puzzled and sometimes enraged. His creative impulses were just as likely to be aroused by the cultures of such countries as Peru, Japan, and Indo-China as by anything that France had to offer. Indeed he found the bird life of France infinitely more to his taste than the literary. His own brand of Roman Catholicism permeated everything he did. This, and his predilection for organ music, places him nearer by far to the serious and elevated world of Franck and his disciples (like Lekeu and Magnard, Messiaen wrote his own song texts) than to the urbane song-composing typified by Poulenc.

From this it is clear that Messiaen did not write mélodies in the accepted sense of the term. He has a place in this book because he wrote important songs for voice and piano in the French language, but they have little to do with the mélodie tradition. Messiaen's vocal music does not represent the meeting of the musical world with the literary, but the creation of a world apart, strange and wonderful certainly, but an acquired taste. Not everyone succumbs ecstatically to this exalted mysticism. For some musicians it is endlessly fascinating and profoundly moving, for others it is impersonal and divorced from life, nothing to do with the human condition as they understand it. (Some of this depends on the listener's sympathy with the religious background to the music, but perhaps the most important thing is a fascination with Messiaen's musical language which can be the most heady of harmonic stimulants.) For doubting listeners, one piece seems very like another; the words do not make much of a difference to what happens; there is a curious sensation of endless variations on the same mystical text, a repetitive litany, fixed as faith, which is fashioned to fit all of Messiaen's music in one way or another. These texts (the composer's own) were mostly conceived at the same time as the music, so it is impossible for the music to change as a result of their unexpected influence—something which is the delight of the more conventional song composer. Words seem suspended on the musical line like decorative jewels, as inevitable as the vestments of time-honoured ritual. And of course difficulty always repels performers, and the difficulty of much (but not all) of this music has, until recently, placed it beyond the reach of all but the dedicated specialist; singers of the new millennium will perhaps find the challenges less redoubtable. After all, some of this music is more than sixty years old. Messiaen makes no concessions at all—neither to his performers nor his audiences. He terminates the tradition of captivating the salon and currying favour with its sheet-music-buying clientele. We find ourselves standing before a succession of supremely authoritative pieces of music, unquestionably created by a master, which still resist incorporation into the everyday life of the recital platform. Their colourful splendours provoke admiration and awe rather than the affection born of familiarity. Of course, this will almost certainly change with the passage of time, but the POÈMES POUR MI (1936), remain as steadfastly modern and challenging as on the day that they were written.

The 13-year-old Messiaen began his songwriting career with DEUX MÉLODIES DE VILLON (1921) which are unpublished. By 1930 he had progressed to the TROIS MÉLODIES which are usually counted his first set of songs. At the time he was still a pupil of Paul Dukas at the Conservatoire. These are undoubtedly his most accessible group in that they are the shortest and easiest. The music is still governed by bar-lines. Even here Messiaen elects to write two of the three poems (for the first song, *Pourquoi?*, and the last, *La fiancée perdue*). His mother Cécile Sauvage provides the text for the single-page song *Le sourire*, one of the simplest of the composer's creations and one of his loveliest. From almost the first note of the first song of this group we are taken into the antechamber of the harmonic world of Messiaen's maturity. Already his style and his uniquely prismatic colours seem dependent on no one else for their origins. From 1930 dates *La mort du nombre* for soprano, tenor, violin, and piano. This is the only one of Messiaen's song works which includes the male voice. The poem is by the composer himself and the conventional duet possibilities between two voices are eschewed in favour of a formula (prophetic of *Quatuor pour la fin du temps*) where the performers combine in unexpected ways: after a violin solo, and episodes for soprano/piano and piano/violin, the work culminates in a dialogue between the singers, the tenor representing love's torment, the soprano answering in radiant assurance. One is reminded, almost despite oneself, of the similar dialogue in Brahms's *Von ewiger Liebe*.

There are two books of POÈMES POUR MI (1936), Messiaen's single most celebrated work for voice and piano (or orchestra). In these, the composer celebrates his marriage to Claire Delbos with a large suite of poems set to music which give voice to the various moods of the husband as he contemplates the joining of man and woman in the sight of God. Although the words are written from the man's viewpoint, Messiaen has conceived the cycle, like almost all his other works for voice and piano, for soprano. There are four songs in the first set. Of these the first, *Action de grâces*, and the last, *Épouvante*, pose formidable difficulties for both singer and pianist. Since Purcell, there has never been a more extraordinary and extended 'alleluia' in song than at the end of *Actions de grâces*. The repeated phrases—'ha, ha, ho!'—of *Épouvante* seem comical on paper, but are magisterial in performance, a haunting landscape of mystical dreams. ***Paysage*** and ***La maison*** are more intimate songs. Some of these texts read like the surrealism of Éluard where that poet's celebration of the harmony between man, woman, and nature (in the *LA FRAÎCHEUR ET LE FEU* poems set by Poulenc, for example) seem, for a moment, to be related to Messiaen's. The *POÈMES POUR MI* were given their première in the same year as Poulenc's *TEL JOUR TELLE NUIT*, and there are passages in the latter cycle (*Figure de force brûlante et farouche* for example [POULENC 6 viii]) where the music has a similar sense of mystical exaltation. In the context of Messiaen's unswerving faith, we are reminded that *TEL JOUR TELLE NUIT* was composed soon after Poulenc's pilgrimage to the shrine of the Black Virgin in Rocamadour which reconverted him to the Catholicism of his fathers.

The second book of *POÈMES POUR MI* has the remaining five songs. There is a similar mix here between radiant simplicity (still very difficult to sing and play), and music of coruscating grandeur where the composer unleashes the formidable forces of his imagination at full pelt. Thus we have the gentle ***L'épouse*** and the bewitching ***Ta voix*** in contrast to ***Les deux guerriers***, a battle-cry and exhortation to live on this earth before reaching the Holy City. ***Le collier*** is one of Messiaen's most beautiful songs, in heartfelt praise of the simple joys of marriage. The concluding ***Prière exaucée*** is remarkable for its extraordinary evocations of bells ('Carillonne, mon cœur!'), and a melismatic setting of 'La joie' which blazes with a sense of intoxicating delirium. The power to write visionary music of this kind belongs to Messiaen alone, although we find similar flights of exalted melismatic grandeur in the work of Sir Michael Tippett.

If we encounter *POÈMES POUR MI* rather seldom on the concert platform, their appearance before the public seems regular in comparison to Messiaen's next cycle, *CHANTS DE TERRE ET DE CIEL* (1938). In practical terms this is hardly surprising, since this work is even more demanding as far as singer and pianist are concerned. Once again Messiaen has written poems which celebrate his private happiness, uniting this theme with meditations on his faith. Thus the title refers to both earthly and divine marriage; the composer's son has been born, and the music also hymns the joys of paternity. (His mother Cécile Sauvage had celebrated his own birth with a cycle of poems.) Once again he chooses the female voice to express his thoughts. The third song in the set, by far the longest, has the title of *Danse du bébé-Pilule* to which is added *pour mon petit Pascal*. There are moments of great tenderness in this cycle, particularly in the opening *Bail pour Mi (pour ma femme)* and the fourth song, *Arc-en-ciel d'innocence*, which ends with a disarming 'Bonjour, petit garçon'. The fifth song, *Minuit pile et face (pour la mort)*, is amongst the most ferocious of all Messiaen's songs, and the closing *Résurrection (pour le jour de Pâques)* is remarkable for the grandeur of its many repeated 'alleluias', the piano punctuating unaccompanied vocal passages with terrifically virtuosic flourishes.

Those performers (and their audiences) who have emerged unscathed from the two large cycles from the 1930s will now want to tackle a work even more formidable. This is *HARAWI (CHANT D'AMOUR ET DE MORT)* (1945), the first of a *Tristan and Isolde* trilogy of works which was later to include the *Turangalîla-symphonie* (1948) and the *CINQ RECHANTS* (1949) for twelve mixed voices. *HARAWI* is scarcely less than a *Tristan und Isolde* in song, inspired by the old myth but modelled on the folk traditions of Peru and that country's traditional music. The composer even studied Quechua, the language spoken by Peruvians before the Spanish occupation, in order to write his texts which are partly in an invented language of his making. (For example in the song *Syllabes* there are no less than five tumultuous pages of music around the sound 'pia'.) The work is still for one singer, of course—the familiar Messiaen soprano of untiring voice and imperturbable brain. (The composer himself paid tribute to Marcelle Bunlet who was his vocal ideal, a singer capable of Isolde, Kundry, and Brünnhilde, and whose voice was the model for all his vocal writing. It was she who gave the first performance of this work with the composer.)

The rhythmical complexity of *HARAWI* is amazing, and the piano writing is an anthology of this composer's preoccupations: birdsong, huge chords, glittering arpeggio figurations, rhythmic canons, and so on. No pianist should undertake this work who is not already familiar with the *VINGT REGARDS*, and other Messiaen solo piano works. The last song *Dans le noir* is one of the most exceptional vocal pieces in French music. The silence of eternal sleep and death is caught in sounds and silences as old as time itself, and which seem to fossilize before our very ears. Although this is a work meant to be experienced as a whole, I have heard the fifth movement (*L'amour de Piroutcha*) stand successfully, and movingly, on its own in recital. Messiaen's music for this colloquy between 'la jeune fille' and 'le jeune homme' seems to evoke the exotic colours and static grandeur of a canvas by Gauguin. (At the same time Poulenc was absorbed in writing his cycle *LE TRAVAIL DU PEINTRE*, depicting painters as diverse as Picasso and Klee.)

Students of Messiaen songs should familiarize themselves with as much of his music as possible before embarking on these works. The vocal music for solo voice and piano discussed here is merely a part of the composer's overall vision (which included the surprise of an opera written towards the end of his life—*Saint François d'Assise*, 1983). It is perhaps impossible to acquire a total comprehension of this man's musical and internal world, but a well-informed sympathy for his visions and aims will engender the sort of fervid and heated performances which the works merit. This is music like no other, not something to render the conventional mélodie obsolete as some of Messiaen's followers might suggest, but the challenge of writing for voice and piano taken up from a completely new angle. These songs are not merely the province of the iron-willed singer (absolute pitch also helps), and the virtuoso pianist with steely fingers; they require a combination of mind, heart, and inner conviction which is unique in twentieth-century song.

TROIS MÉLODIES

1 i *Pourquoi?*
(Olivier Messiaen)

Pourquoi les oiseaux de l'air,
Pourquoi les reflets de l'eau,
Pourquoi les nuages du ciel,
Pourquoi?
Pourquoi les feuilles de l'Automne,
Pourquoi les roses de l'Été,
Pourquoi les chansons du Printemps,
Pourquoi?

THREE MÉLODIES

Why?

Why are the birds of the air,
Why are the gleaming waters,
Why are the clouds of heaven,
Why?
Why are the leaves of autumn,
Why are the roses of summer,
Why are the songs of spring,
Why?

Pourquoi n'ont-ils pour moi de charmes, | Why for me are they devoid of charm,
Pourquoi? | Why?
Pourquoi, Ah! Pourquoi? | Why? Ah, why?

I ii *Le sourire*

(Cécile Sauvage)

The smile

Certain mot murmuré | A certain word whispered
Par vous est un baiser | By you is a kiss,
Intime et prolongé | Intimate and lingering,
Comme un baiser sur l'âme. | Like a kiss on the soul.
Ma bouche veut sourire | My mouth wishes to smile
Et mon sourire tremble. | And my smile flickers.

I iii *La fiancée perdue*

(Olivier Messiaen)

The lost fiancée

C'est la douce fiancée, | She is the gentle fiancée,
C'est l'ange de la bonté, | She is the angel of kindness,
C'est un après-midi ensoleillé, | She is a sun-drenched afternoon,
C'est le vent sur les fleurs. | She is the wind on the flowers.
C'est un sourire pur comme un cœur d'enfant, | She is a smile as pure as a child's heart,
C'est un grand lys blanc comme une aile, très haut | She is a tall lily, white as a wing, towering in a gold
    dans une coupe d'or! | vase!
O Jésus, bénissez-la! | O Jesus, bless her!
Elle! | Her!
Donnez-lui votre Grâce puissante! | Bestow on her your powerful Grace!
Qu'elle ignore la souffrance, les larmes! | May she never know pain and tears!
Donnez-lui le repos, Jésus! | Bestow peace of mind on her, O Jesus!

POÈMES POUR MI

(Olivier Messiaen)

PREMIER LIVRE

2 i *Action de grâces*

Le ciel
Et l'eau qui suit les variations des nuages,
Et la terre, et les montagnes qui attendent toujours,
Et la lumière qui transforme.
Et un œil près de mon œil, une pensée près de ma
    pensée,
Et un visage qui sourit et pleure avec le mien,
Et deux pieds derrière mes pieds
Comme la vague à la vague est unie.
Et une âme,
Invisible, pleine d'amour et d'immortalité,
Et un vêtement de chair et d'os qui germera pour la
    résurrection,
Et la Vérité, et l'Esprit, et la Grâce avec son héritage
    de lumière.
Tout cela, vous me l'avez donné.
Et vous vous êtes encore donné vous-même,
Dans l'obéissance et dans le sang de votre Croix,
Et dans un Pain plus doux que la fraîcheur des
    étoiles,
Mon Dieu.
Alleluia, alleluia.

2 ii *Paysage*

Le lac comme un gros bijou bleu.
La route pleine de chagrins et de fondrières,
Mes pieds qui hésitent dans la poussière,
Le lac comme un gros bijou bleu.
Et la voilà, verte et bleue comme le paysage!
Entre le blé et le soleil je vois son visage:
Elle sourit, la main sur les yeux.
Le lac comme un gros bijou bleu.

POEMS FOR MI

FIRST BOOK

Thanksgiving

Sky
And water, following the changes of cloud,
And earth and mountains, ever waiting,
And light, transforming.
And an eye close to my eye, a thought close to my
    thought,
And a face that smiles and weeps with mine,
And two feet behind my feet
As wave to wave is joined.
And a soul,
Invisible, full of love and immortality,
And garments of flesh and bone to germinate for
    the resurrection,
And Truth, and Spirit, and Grace with its luminous
    heritage.
All that, you have given me.
And you have given yourself too,
In the obedience and blood of your Cross,
In Bread sweeter than the coolness of stars,

My God.
Alleluia, alleluia.

Landscape

The lake like a big blue jewel.
The road full of sorrows and pot-holes,
My feet faltering in the dust,
The lake like a big blue jewel.
And there she is, green and blue like the landscape!
Between corn and sun I see her face:
She smiles, one hand shading her eyes.
The lake like a big blue jewel.

2 iii *La maison*

Cette maison nous allons la quitter:
Je la vois dans ton œil.
Nous quitterons nos corps aussi:
Je les vois dans ton œil.
Toutes ces images de douleur qui s'impriment dans
        ton œil,
Ton œil ne les retrouvera plus:
Quand nous contemplerons la Vérité,
Dans des corps purs, jeunes, éternellement lumineux.

The house

We shall be leaving this house:
I can see it in your eye.
We shall be leaving our bodies too:
I can see them in your eye.
All these images of pain imprinted on your eye,

Your eye shall not find them again:
When we come to gaze on Truth
In bodies pure, young, and ever luminous.

2 iv *Épouvante*

Ha, ha, ha, ha, ha, ha, ha, ho!
N'enfouis pas tes souvenirs dans la terre, tu ne les
        retrouverais plus.
Ne tire pas, ne froisse pas, ne déchire pas.
Des lambeaux sanglants te suivraient dans les
        ténèbres
Comme une vomissure triangulaire,
Et le choc bruyant des anneaux sur la porte
        irréparable
Rythmerait ton désespoir
Pour rassasier les puissances du feu.
Ha, ha, ha, ha, ha, ha, ha, ho!

Terror

Ha, ha, ha, ha, ha, ha, ha, ho!
Don't bury your memories in earth, you will not
        find them again.
Don't pull, don't crease, don't tear.
The bloodied shreds would pursue you in the dark

Like a triangular lump of vomit,
And the clanging of rings on the door beyond repair

Would beat time to your despair
To satiate the powers of fire.
Ha, ha, ha, ha, ha, ha, ha, ho!

DEUXIÈME LIVRE

2 v *L'épouse*

Va où l'Esprit te mène,
Nul ne peut séparer ce que Dieu a uni,
Va où l'Esprit te mène,
L'épouse est le prolongement de l'époux,
Va où l'Esprit te mène,
Comme l'Église est le prolongement du Christ.

SECOND BOOK

The bride

Go whither the Spirit lead you,
No one can put asunder what God has united,
Go whither the Spirit lead you,
The bride is the extension of the bridegroom,
Go whither the Spirit lead you,
As the Church is the extension of Christ.

2 vi *Ta voix*

Fenêtre pleine d'après-midi,
Qui s'ouvre sur l'après-midi,
Et sur ta voix fraîche
(Oiseau de printemps qui s'éveille).
Si elle s'ouvrait sur l'éternité
Je te verrais plus belle encore.

Your voice

Window brimming with afternoon,
Opening onto the afternoon,
And onto your fresh voice
(Awakening bird of spring).
Were it to open on eternity,
I'd see you fairer yet.

Tu es la servante du Fils,
Et le Père t'aimerait pour cela.
Sa lumière sans fin tomberait sur tes épaules,
Sa marque sur ton front.
Tu complèterais le nombre des anges incorporels.

À la gloire de la Trinité sainte
Un toujours de bonheur élèverait ta voix fraîche
(Oiseau de printemps qui s'éveille):
Tu chanterais.

You are the maidservant of the Son,
And for that the Father would love you.
His unending light would fall on your shoulders,
His sign on your brow.
You would complete the number of incorporeal
    angels.
To the glory of the Holy Trinity,
A joyous ever-after would raise up your fresh voice
(Awakening bird of spring):
You would sing.

2 vii *Les deux guerriers*

De deux nous voici un. En avant!
Comme des guerriers bardés de fer!
Ton œil et mon œil parmi les statues qui marchent,
Parmi les hurlements noirs,
Les écroulements de sulfureuses géométries.
Nous gémissons: ah! écoute-moi,
Je suis tes deux enfants, mon Dieu!
En avant, guerriers sacramentels!
Tendez joyeusement vos boucliers.
Lancez vers le ciel les flèches du dévouement
        d'aurore:
Vous parviendrez aux portes de la Ville.

The two warriors

The two of us now are one. Onwards!
Like iron-clad warriors!
Your eye and mine among walking statues,
Among black shrieking,
Among sulphurous geometries tumbling down.
We moan: ah! listen to me,
I am your two children, my God!
Onwards, sacramental warriors!
Joyfully hold up your shields!
Cast to the heavens the arrows of dawn devotion:

You shall reach the City gates.

2 viii *Le collier*

Printemps enchaîné, arc-en-ciel léger du matin,
Ah! mon collier! Ah! mon collier!
Petit soutien vivant de mes oreilles lasses,
Collier de renouveau, de sourire et de grâce,
Collier d'Orient, collier choisi multicolore
Aux perles dures et cocasses!
Paysage courbe, épousant l'air frais du matin,
Ah! mon collier! Ah! mon collier!
Tes deux bras autour de mon cou, ce matin.

The necklace

Spring enchained, light rainbow of morning,
Ah! my necklace! Ah! my necklace!
Small living support of my weary ears,
Necklace of renewal, of smiles, of grace,
Oriental necklace, chosen, multicoloured
With hard, whimsical pearls!
Curving landscape, espousing the fresh morning air,
Ah! my necklace! Ah! my necklace!
Your two arms round my neck, this morning.

2 ix *Prière exaucée*

Ébranlez la solitaire, la vieille montagne de douleur,
Que le soleil travaille les eaux amères de mon cœur!
Ô Jésus, Pain vivant et qui donnez la vie,
Ne dites qu'une seule parole, et mon âme sera guérie.

A prayer granted

Shake up the solitary, ancient mountain of pain,
May the sun work over the bitter waters of my heart!
O Jesus, living bread, giver of life,
Say but one word and my soul shall be healed.

Ébranlez la solitaire, la vieille montagne de douleur,	Shake up the solitary, ancient mountain of pain,
Que le soleil travaille les eaux amères de mon cœur!	May the sun work over the bitter waters of my heart!
Donnez-moi votre grâce,	Give me your grace,
Donnez-moi votre grâce!	Give me your grace!
Carillonne, mon cœur!	Ring out, my heart!
Que ta résonnance soit dure, et longue et profonde!	May your ringing resound hard, long, and deep!
Frappe, tape, choque pour ton roi!	Strike, knock, smite for your king!
Frappe, tape, choque pour ton Dieu!	Strike, knock, smite for your God!
Voici ton jour de gloire et de résurrection!	Behold the day of your glory and resurrection!
La joie est revenue.	Bliss has returned.

MEYERBEER, Giacomo (1791–1864)

Meyerbeer's songs are the products of a truly cosmopolitan career. His mélodies were translated into German by Schubert's collaborators Ignaz Castelli and Ludwig Rellstab, and the German songs were translated into French: the best of both worlds for a man whose fame was international. So Meyerbeer could be said to have contributed to both the lied and the mélodie with everything he wrote (not to mention his excursions into the Italian repertoire), although some detractors would say he had nothing much to say in either language. In the German settings there are some attractive Heine, Rückert, and Goethe songs which make amusing comparisons with lieder by Schubert and Schumann on the same texts. Here Meyerbeer was competing with genius working in a long-established art form; it is hardly surprising that his efforts in this sphere are charming rather than revelatory. But the mélodie was a much younger phenomenon. In the Parisian musical world which was still attached to the vacuous romance, Berlioz led the struggle to accustom the public to vocal music of deeper feeling and significance, and in this respect he welcomed Meyerbeer as an ally. Both composers agreed that song with piano could be a serious thing. In Meyerbeer there was a German sensibility at work—a depth of response to words which was considered highly original at the time, although not exceptional by the French standards of fifty years later. As an accomplished pianist and experienced accompanist, his piano writing is an integral part of the conception, and there are signs of a man who is not unacquainted with Schubert. (The most inventive accompaniment in Meyerbeer's songs is probably that for *La fille de l'air*—Méry, 1837—which flies to the top of the keyboard and stays there in a shimmer of demi-semiquavers, hovering well above the vocal line.)

Meyerbeer's songs incline, not unnaturally in an opera composer, to the dramatic. As the majority of songs were written before he enjoyed his greatest operatic successes, one feels that with the captive audience in the salon, he was sometimes trying to prove himself as a composer for the stage. When a song becomes a scène it is likely to be long, vocally demanding, and with a touch of bathos which is very much of its time. There have always been larger-than-life singers who can handle music with these attributes—indeed they revel in them—and it is these artists who find Meyerbeer attractive today. That he wrote for extremely accomplished vocalists is evident from the technical demands of his music. *Le ranz de vaches d'Appenzell* (Scribe, 1828), for example, is not content with an imaginary colloquy between two voices (using instrumental obbligato) as in Schubert's *Der Hirt auf dem Felsen* (and incidentally written at exactly the same time); two singers are needed, and soprano and mezzo compete in melismatic confrontation as if this were an excerpt from an opera. Another song with two characters is *Nella* (Deschamps, *c.*1839), where the singer is expected to play the role of the serenader as well as the loyal girl who has promised her heart to a lowly page. In *Rachel à Nephtali* (Deschamps, 1834) a biblical scenario is played out as Rachel rebuffs her brother-in-law's advances. The song is addressed to him exactly as one character in grand opera might address another on the stage ('Pitie, pitié, je suis ta sœur'). *Mère grand* (Betourné, 1830) is another lengthy duet, and is so ornately written for the two female voices that Norma and Adalgisa would feel at home with it.

More restrained is the *Ballade* (Marguerite de Navarre, 1829) which is nearer to the romance in its strophic form and delicate melancholy. *Le moine* (Émilien Pacini, 1834) is written for bass as a grand scena; directions scattered throughout the score include 'avec angoisse', 'avec onction', 'avec délire', and so on. Along the same lofty lines of tortured abstention from the pleasures of life is the *Cantique du trappiste* (1842). Grander than either of these is *Le poète mourant* (Millevoye, 1836) for tenor. This includes a high C towards the end which surely contributes to the protagonist's death. The title page has a picture of a dying man lying in bed holding a rather heavy-looking lyre. The singer of today has to muster all his conviction to take us with him 'over the top' to join composer and poet. (Niedermeyer's setting of this poem is also not without interest.)

Meyerbeer seems to have had a penchant for Henri Blaze (not a great poet but a powerful critic—we are somehow not surprised that this composer was an adept politician!) and sometimes good musical ideas are scuppered by the lyrics, as in *Fantaisie* (1836) where we have to endure the inelegant lines 'j'attends Hermann, Hermann, Hermann mon jeune époux' no less than six times. Other Blaze settings are more fortunate, for piano-accompanied Meyerbeer is more believable in a light-hearted *Ständchen* than doleful monastic abstention: *Chant de mai* (1837) with an accompaniment reminiscent of Schubert's *Hark, hark the lark* has a delicate touch and pretty melody (although it is a long song which somewhat outstays its welcome). On the other hand *La Marguerite du poète* (1837) is an effective miniature, and **La chanson de maître Floh** (1839–40) is an ideal vehicle for a good buffo baritone. Deftly turned character pieces suit the salon better than narrative effusions, and *Sicilienne* (Méry, *c.*1845), with its piquant charm, ingenious modulations and reasonable vocal demands seems to me the perfect Meyerbeer song (compare the impossibly high vocal line of *Sur le balcon*—Thierry, 1845). The question of a song's length and scale depends on the poem, of course, and the Heine settings, not under consideration here, seem in perfect proportion as a result of the pithy lyrics. Indeed, one must come to the conclusion that Meyerbeer was better served by his German poets (many of them great literary names) than by the procession of hacks and dilettante poetasters with whom he collaborated in his French songs, often for reasons of expediency and musical politics.

1 *La chanson de maître Floh*

(Henri Blaze)

Un jour qu'on faisait vendange,
La cruche de maître Floh
Se gorgea de vin nouveau,
Et sur le soir, chose étrange,
Fut ivre comme un bedeau.

Alors elle se remue,
Et d'un pas lent et peu sûr
Saute et va battant le mur,
Et s'échauffe, et court et sue
D'amples gouttes de vin pur.

Elle rit, et tourne et danse,
Fait tant d'éclat et de bruit,
Que, sur la fin de la nuit,
Voilà que sa grosse panse
Est trouée et qu'elle fuit.

Pourtant maître Floh arrive,
Se signe et dit un Pater
Pour sauver son vin d'hier,
Qu'en son ivresse lascive
La cruche emporte dans l'air.

Ensuite, pour que nul n'entre,
Il ferme la porte à clé;
Et, prenant le pot fêlé,
Il engloutit dans son ventre
Le vin rouge encor troublé,

En s'écriant: 'Sur ma tête,
Amis, voilà le seul pot
Qui ne soit point en défaut,
Et la seule cruche faite
Pour garder le vin nouveau.'
Ainsi disait maître Floh.

The song of Master Floh

One grape-harvest day
Master Floh's own pitcher
Gorged itself with new wine,
And towards evening, strange to relate,
Was drunk as a lord!

It then bestirs itself,
And slowly and unsteadily
Jumps up and knocks against the wall,
Gets hot and bothered and runs and sweats
Drop after drop of pure wine.

It laughs and spins and dances,
Creates such a din and such a stir
That, as night draws to a close—
Lo and behold! Its great paunch
Is breached, and springs a leak.

Master Floh, however, now appears,
Crosses himself and says a prayer
To salvage yesterday's wine
Which the jug, wantonly drunk,
Was hurling into the air.

Then, so that none might enter,
He locks the door
And, picking up the cracked jug,
He gulps into his paunch
The red and still unsettled wine,

Exclaiming: 'Upon my word, my friends,
This is the only pot
Without defect,
And the only pitcher
Designed to store new wine.'
Quoth Master Floh.

MIGOT, Georges (1891–1976)

Migot's reputation as a prolific composer of mélodies has not travelled far outside his own country. The same is true of many a composer of English song, Gerald Finzi for example, but neither merits the indifference of international recital audiences. In the case of Migot, pupil of Widor,

Emmanuel, and d'Indy, this may be because he is difficult to categorize from a stylistic point of view. Migot is not a purveyor of that easily exportable musical atmosphere that is recognizably impressionistic or Parisian. Like his teacher Maurice Emmanuel, he soon had a reputation for being entirely his own man with music to match. He was a real polymath—an exhibited painter, and a published poet and aesthetician with a penchant for writing religious music (no less than ten oratorios). Not exactly a member of the avant-garde, he was untouched by neo-classicism, or indeed any of the 'isms' of the time: distant from the ethics of both Les Six and La Jeune France, his music is characterized by long musical lines, more modal than tonal, which are allowed to interact freely to richly polymelodic effect. This chimes with the composer's enthusiasm for (and expert knowledge of) the church polyphony of the distant past, although the result is far from time-travelling pastiche. If it were, it might be more popular.

Migot wrote some 150 mélodies. Of these the *SEPT PETITES IMAGES DU JAPON* (translations of the 9th century poems of Heian, 1917) and the *TROIS MÉLODIES* (Tristan Darème, 1923), love songs in a high-flown ecstatic style, are the earliest significant achievement. By far his most important work in this field is *POÈMES DE BRUGNON* (Tristan Klingsor, 1933), which the composer subtitled *LES AMOURS DU MUSICIEN*. Although Klingsor is much set (by Ravel among many others), it is sometimes claimed that the poet, who was himself a published composer of songs, never found a better collaborator than Migot, and certainly Klingsor himself was overwhelmed by the music. The symbol of this work, in which Klingsor attempts to hide the desperation of love with a brave smile, is found in the title: the nectarine with its 'skin of a plum and flesh of a peach'. Although the poems are written from a male viewpoint, Migot conceived the cycle for woman's voice; in this respect he is at one with Messaien whose *POÈMES POUR MI*, male love songs for soprano voice, were written only three years later. The Migot cycle, no less than seventeen songs of varied mood, often complex for both performers, also shares something of Messaien's epic sense of scale. Migot displays the full range of his musical resources: dance movements and sombre chorales are cleverly juxtaposed throughout to signify the duality of mood; deliberately varied vocal styles are employed, as well as the spoken word. *POÈMES DE BRUGNON*, a wide-ranging anthology of a lover's emotions, is counted a masterpiece by some French commentators, a cycle almost as important as *LA BONNE CHANSON* in the history of the mélodie. The English-speaking listener, perhaps less well attuned to the refinements of prosody, will probably take this to be special pleading. We should remember, however, how many English composers, highly admired by local audiences, fail to make an effect across the Channel.

MILHAUD, Darius (1892–1974)

One cannot help feeling rather sorry for Milhaud, the mélodiste. He was such a nice man, so generous to all his colleagues, so open-hearted in his music-making which unites Jewish warmth and Mediterranean colour, that it seems unfair that his old friend Poulenc should have swept the board. Singers flock to Poulenc, but it seems Milhaud is yet to find the interpreters, singers, and pianists who are prepared to go through the large output (some of it very difficult to sing and play) in search of the best. Christopher Palmer writes of sifting through 'vast quantities of chaff in search of the isolated grain of wheat'. This seems unduly harsh, but there are moments when we tire of Milhaud's note-spinning. Other composers waited for inspiration; when Milhaud was waiting, he was composing the while. This applies to all the genres for which he wrote, orchestra, choral, and chamber, but it is perhaps the singer who feels most intimidated by a corpus of music that can seem rather uninviting on the printed page. Even the look of Milhaud on the stave can seem casual and inconsequential, as if written for an instrument rather than the human voice. Added to this, his accompaniments, though not at all easy, do not always make the best of the instrument's possibilities. Neither do they lie gratefully under the hands in the manner of most song composers in this repertoire who habitually played their own songs. He seems seldom to have received stern advice from a singer about his writing for the voice, which can be curiously un-vocal in shape.

There are times when Milhaud is possessed by such a bout of composing enthusiasm (and one can tell that the notes are coming thick and fast by their appearance on the page) that he actually forgets to allow any time for the singer to breathe. The vocal line on these occasions can seem curiously shapeless. Another problem is that his sets of mélodies are sometimes too long for practical purposes. Composers like Britten and Poulenc knew that seven or eight was an optimum number of songs for a cycle. It is nothing for Milhaud to have a group of twenty-four songs in a single set, such as *TRISTESSES*, the Jammes suite for baritone and piano from 1956. It would take a rare performer to give up an entire recital to this work of *WINTERREISE* length. Pierre Bernac's advice often moderated and honed Poulenc's craft, but Milhaud had no such singer in his immediate circle.

On the other hand, one can only admire the tireless spirit of invention that seems never to have left Milhaud throughout his life, despite exile from his own country and crippling infirmity. Many of the songs are novel precisely because they explore unfamiliar pianistic and vocal patterns, although it must be said that on the whole Milhaud's gift, something like Koechlin's (an important model for him, incidentally) was harmonic rather than melodic. What the songs need above all is frequent performances by good singers so that they begin to sound familiar to the ears of listeners. Only then will the best of Milhaud take its rightful place in the repertoire, and its composer become valued for his real achievements in the genre.

Milhaud's first songs date from as early as 1910, settings of the poet Francis Jammes (who was set at about the same time by Lili Boulanger). Another favourite poet was Paul Claudel, the man whom Milhaud admired almost more than any other. *SEPT POÈMES EXTRAITS DE 'LA CONNAISSANCE DE L'EST'* (1912–13) were the first fruit of this friendship. The cycle begins with the Chinese-inspired *La nuit à la véranda* which is rather influenced by Debussy; elsewhere one is astonished that the young composer already sounds very much like himself. On the whole it is a strange spectacle—a Jewish composer setting the profoundly religious words of two Catholic mystics—Jammes and Claudel. Milhaud seems to have felt the responsibility almost too keenly; exalted texts about man's destiny and inner spiritual life do not bring out the best in him as a composer of mélodies. He tends to lose his sense of proportion, and the songs wander as a result—particularly if he chooses to set prose, a tricky challenge for anyone. On occasion, however, prose without a strong metre suits the Koechlin-like meander of Milhaud's musical style, as in the more concise *TROIS POÈMES EN PROSE DE LUCILE DE CHATEAUBRIAND*, particularly in the second song, *À la lune*.

Also from 1913 is the song cycle *ALISSA* with words taken from *La porte étroite* by André Gide (a rare instance of a cycle that Milhaud did revise, in 1931). Towards the end of the cycle there is a large

Prélude for piano, and at over thirty minutes the work may seem too long for the aphoristic character of Gide's writing. Nevertheless this is genuine, vintage Milhaud in half-melodic, half-speech style. Although the cycle contains two characters (Jérôme and Alissa herself) it is conceived for a single female voice. The work had its fervent admirers: as a monologue the critic Collaer compared it to Monteverdi's *Lamento d'Arianna*. This period was one of the composer's most productive, or rather a period where a high standard of inspiration was maintained (Milhaud was always productive!) One of his best cycles is QUATRE POÈMES DE LÉO LATIL (1914), where the texts themselves dictate the right length for a successful cycle. These four substantial songs make up an excellent group; the two bird songs *Le rossignol* and the final **La tourterelle** are genuinely lyrical, and the whole set seems touched by the sunlight and warmth of Aix where it was composed. Latil was killed at Verdun in 1915 and was a close, and greatly mourned, friend of the composer. Another work with a connection to Latil is the cycle of three songs dedicated to his memory: D'UN CAHIER INÉDIT DU JOURNAL D'EUGÉNIE DE GUÉRIN (1915). The texts are taken from the jottings of an otherwise unknown woman with mystical leanings who was brought up in solitude at the chateau of Cazay where she died at an early age. The set is remarkable for its polytonality, its sense of suppressed anguish (in the second song *Nous voilà donc exilés*), and its use of fugal techniques in the final *À mesure qu'on avance*.

In 1916 Paul Claudel invited Milhaud to be his secretary, when he was appointed French minister to Brazil. It was natural that the young official should have set further texts by his distinguished employer. The QUATRE POÈMES DE PAUL CLAUDEL (1915–17) are well written for baritone; however noble they might have sounded at the time, it is unlikely today that a singer would feel comfortable with all this exaltation and philosophy, not to mention a punishing vocal line. The truth is that these intense and private meditations are simply not the best material for musical setting. Milhaud even followed his mentor's interest in Catholic verse in other languages by setting DEUX POÈMES DE COVENTRY PATMORE (1915) in Claudel's translations, as curious a choice of Victorian poetry as might be imagined for a young French composer. This set is remarkable for Milhaud's decision to set both the translation and the original language at the same time, changing the accentuation for the English version; thus songs with the titles *Departure* and *The azalea* enter the French song repertoire. The five CHILD-POEMS (Tagore, 1916) are further examples of the composer's fluent and sophisticated interest in a language that he would have to adopt much later in life during his American exile. Milhaud no doubt got to know these poems first through Gide's translations, as did both Casella and Durey. The POÈMES JUIFS are also from 1916. Once again there are perhaps too many in the set for a complete performance, but a judicious selection from this cycle, where the words are translated from the Hebrew, shows the earthy side of Milhaud's composing personality to great advantage; in this music he espouses Zionism some thirty years before the establishment of the Jewish state. This is among the first of a large number of works which Milhaud was to write devoted to his ancestral faith.

At the other extreme of song length is the tiny song miniature. The first set of these was CHANSONS BAS DE STÉPHANE MALLARMÉ (1917), vivid little evocations of working people and their trades which show a different side of this great poet from that explored by Debussy and Ravel. More serious, but equally epigrammatic, are the DEUX PETITS AIRS (Mallarmé, 1918), where Milhaud's polytonal sound world reflects the strangeness of the words to interesting effect. For two years Milhaud lived in South America, where there were rich musical pickings for him in instrumental music. He returned home in time to be drawn into the circle of Les Six.

The songs of the 1920s are influenced by the aesthetic of the composer's new colleagues. It is also true that such works as the epigrammatic Mallarmé settings and the ballet *Le bœuf sur le toit* influenced them in turn. The songs of this period are short miniatures of a zany character rather than attempts to storm the citadels of philosophy. *LES SOIRÉES DE PÉTROGRADE* (1919) is a cycle to words by that talented wordsmith René Chalupt, a constant presence in the mélodies of such composers as Roussel, Satie, and Ravel among others. Twelve tiny songs are divided into two series of six songs each, subtitled *L'ancien régime* and *La révolution*. These are picture-postcard views of life in Russia before and after the upheaval of 1917: old St Petersburg versus the new Petrograd. Even the assassination of Rasputin is cryptically referred to, and the songs owe something to the pithy and witty aspect of Mussorgksy. Jane Bathori remembered that the aristocratic Russian refugees in Paris at the time of the first performance were decidedly underwhelmed by the songs' ironic (and typically French) handling of recent political events. Also planned as a set of miniatures in cheekily anti-sublime mood was the droll *MACHINES AGRICOLES* (1919) for voice and seven instruments; each of the six songs about farm machinery is dedicated to a different member of Les Six and to Cocteau. In 1920 that poet inspired the *TROIS POÈMES DE JEAN COCTEAU*, a short and lively sequence of songs (*Fumée*, *Fête de Bordeaux*, and *Fête de Montmartre*), conceived at more or less the same time as Poulenc's Cocteau trilogy *COCARDES*. After the notoriety engendered by *MACHINES AGRICOLES*, it is hardly surprising that Milhaud planned a sequel—*CATALOGUE DE FLEURS* (1920) for the same instrumental combination. By the very nature of the material this music is more perfumed than its predecessor. These snippets of song remain charmingly fresh with touches of real humour and poetry—even if the texts were said to have been taken from a flower catalogue they are, of course, artful and witty constructions of catalogue style by Lucien Daudet, the son of Alphonse. The work can be easily performed in the version with piano. The *QUATRE POÈMES DE CATULLE* (1923) for voice and violin have an exact sense of balance and proportion (as is appropriate to these classical texts) and emphasize what we have already guessed—the composer does not need (or value) piano sonority for its own sake in the way that Poulenc does, for example.

From 1925 there is a set of *CHANTS POPULAIRES HÉBRAÏQUES* written for the Jewish singer Madeleine Grey and conceived with both piano and orchestral accompaniment. These are Milhaud's answer to the Jewish folksong arrangements in a similar vein which Ravel had made for the same singer the year before. Because he was competing with such a predecessor, Milhaud took a great deal of trouble with these songs, and it shows. This set, with its intensity and colourful vitality, should re-enter the regular repertoire as soon as possible. In this connection, mention should be made of two other substantial vocal works on Jewish themes. The first of these, *PRIÈRES JOURNALIÈRES À L'USAGE DES JUIFS DU COMTAT VENAISSAN* (1927), is a cycle of three prayers (morning, afternoon, and evening) with words taken from the services of the ancient synagogue of Carpentras with its congregation protected by papal edict since the fifteenth century. How soon things would change! In the ominous year of 1933 Milhaud wrote the *LITURGIE COMTADINE*, five liturgical songs for the Jewish New Year which can be sung in either French or Hebrew. There are also a number of single songs on Jewish themes: in 1925 alone *Israël est vivant* and *Hymne à Sion*.

The 1930s saw various new experiments, including the writing of music for children which was then not such a popular preoccupation with composers as it was later to become. Milhaud wrote a number of works in this genre which do not strictly qualify as mélodies, but which are piano accompanied and might be adapted for concert performance. *UN PETIT PEU DE MUSIQUE* (Armand Lunel) is subtitled *JEU POUR ENFANTS* and was commissioned by Mrs Elizabeth Sprague Coolidge. To the right of the stage sit the good pupils, and to the left the naughty ones. Milhaud wrote this music for children participating in musical education schemes devised by André Gédalge. Even though these songs have been conceived for choral performance, a number of them could work as duets and even as solos in the manner of Britten's *FRIDAY AFTERNOON* songs. They are a rich source of interest for those searching the repertoire for comic numbers with which to end recitals. A similar project from the same period is *À PROPOS DE BOTTES*, a piece which is this time called *CONTE MUSICAL POUR ENFANTS*. The texts (rather good ones) are by René Chalupt; *Chanson du chinois* and *Chanson du cinéaste* are particularly appealing.

The year 1937 produced at least three worthwhile sets of songs. The first of these is really another piece of children's music (*Les quatre petits lions,* and so on), published with amusing illustrations. These *CINQ CHANSONS DE CHARLES VILDRAC* are easy-to-listen-to pieces; the only thing against them for English-speaking singers is that they are basically strophic—a form of songwriting which can expose the linguist lapses of the foreign singer in merciless fashion. The *TROIS CHANSONS DE TROUBADOUR* (Valmy-Baisse) were written for Bernac, and are an attractive set for baritone with a touch of the antique madrigal style so beloved of French composers. Once again Milhaud seems to have worked hard on the piano parts, and the vocal line (despite a demanding high A flat at the end of the third song) shows signs of consultation with a good singer. The *TROIS CHANSONS DE NÉGRESSE* (Supervielle, 1935–6) are the composer's answer to Ravel's *CHANSONS MADÉCASSES*. The poems come from Supervielle's *Bolivar* for which Milhaud wrote the incidental music; in the play the songs are sung by the slave Précipitation. These songs have become more frequently performed in recent years, and justifiably so. The first, **Mon histoire,** is a catchy potted history of the protagonist from slavery to freedom. This is a gift of a cycle for a low mezzo, particularly one of Afro-Caribbean origin. It has its sombre side, but it is also celebratory and the use of jazz dance rhythms is irresistible.

No sooner had Milhaud written about the slavery of oppressed people than he was to experience for himself the horror and heartbreak of having to leave France in the wake of the Nazi terror. Fortunately he found refuge, like so many other European artists, in California. One of the last pieces to be written in France was the cycle *LE VOYAGE D'ÉTÉ* (Camille Paliard, 1940) which is the opposite of Schubert's *WINTERREISE* in every way. It is light and charming and childlike—a holiday diary of fifteen short songs. Not quite children's music, this is a cycle about a child's reactions to an enchanting summer and the music is suffused with the sunlight of happier times. Not all the songs are equally good and here, as elsewhere in Milhaud, one must be ruthless enough to prune the set for practical performance. It is surely better to present excerpts from such a long cycle than to ignore it altogether.

In America, Milhaud continued to write unabated and there is some evidence that the composer benefited from the interest in French vocal music that has always been a feature of teaching institutions in the United States. From 1940 dates *CHANSON DU CARNAVAL DE LONDRES*, Milhaud's arrangements of items from John Gay's *The beggar's opera*. It seems to be an oblique compliment to Britain's wartime spirit and famous humour as it faced the Blitz. It is possible that these thirty-four numbers could be rescued by performances of humour and vitality, and the tunes themselves are, after all, tested by time. But it is difficult to be enthusiastic about this project in comparison to Britten's dazzling display of re-creative genius with the same material. With Milhaud the piano accompaniments are all rather dull, and seem ruthlessly to double the vocal line.

The *QUATRE CHANSONS DE RONSARD* also date from 1940, and are among the composer's most successful vocal works. They suggest the epoch of Ronsard without recourse to obvious archaisms. The titles are *À une fontaine, À Cupidon* (a poem also set by Jacques Leguerney), *Tay toy, babillarde Arondelle,* and *Dieu vous gard'.* They were written for Lily Pons and exploit the coloratura range with virtuosity and élan. Although the set was conceived with orchestral accompaniment, the piano reduction is eminently playable, and this ranks as one of the composer's best song cycles in every respect. For the less stratospheric soprano voice, the cycle *RÊVES* (1942, to anonymous twentieth-century words) is to be recommended, a product of a composer homesick for his beloved Provence. At six songs, this is the perfect length for a work of this kind. Most effective in the set are *'Long distance'* (note the influence of Milhaud's adopted home) and *Jeunesse.*

In this (more or less) chronological survey there are two more works to be mentioned, both from 1956, and both to the poetry of Milhaud's old favourite, Francis Jammes. The long cycle *TRISTESSES* takes forty minutes to perform, and was mentioned at the beginning of this article: numbers 3, 5–7, 10, 12, 13, 15, 17, 19–21, and 24 are settings of poems which, over forty years earlier, had been part of Lili Boulanger's *CLAIRIÈRES DANS LE CIEL* [BOULANGER 1–13]. The other cycle is *FONTAINES ET SOURCES* (1956), a pleasing anthology of six water songs in various moods and tempi. After the composer had returned to France, he continued his affiliations with American musical life. The cycle *L'AMOUR CHANTE* (1964) is dedicated to the remarkable New York singer, and patroness of song composers, Alice Esty. This is as interesting a group as the composer ever wrote, particularly from the point of view of texts. With such a wide brief as the title implies, Milhaud could include such a mixture of poets and centuries as Joachim du Bellay, Alfred de Musset, Louise Labé, and Ronsard. The curiosity of the set is a beautiful Verlaine setting *Nevermore*, for this is not a poet that one associates at all with this composer. The next song *Veillées* (Rimbaud) is also a surprise. It seems that the cultivated Miss Esty had some hand in the choosing of this remarkable anthology of texts, and it brings home once again how much more the composer might have accomplished in the field of mélodie if he had had the benefit of a guiding hand that was experienced in both literary and vocal matters.

A passion for intractable poems (by writers whom he admired, but whom he should have left alone as a musician) sometimes led him astray. These were honest miscalculations, the result of a surfeit of affection rather than a want of feeling or sensitivity. When he finds the right poetry and a fine singer, the framework for a harmonious and practical whole, Milhaud is capable of writing fine mélodies. Although his reputation as a composer has never rested on this repertoire to any great extent, there is much that needs to be discovered in his vocal music, and he awaits new and persuasive performers as his advocates. An astonishing recent revival of *Christophe Colomb* in Berlin notwithstanding, the world seems less impressed by the gigantic Milhaud works than it was some fifty years ago and now it is surely time to reappraise the smaller works; some of the very best of Milhaud is to be found among these many songs. Despite the inevitable chaff, there is, after all, enough wheat to provide a hearty repast.

1 *La tourterelle,*

(Léo Latil), from QUATRE POÈMES DE LÉO LATIL

Ma colombe, ô ma tourterelle,
Est-ce vous dont j'entends la voix plaintive qui gémit
dans les rameaux de ces ormeaux qui s'assombrissent?
Dans cette fin du jour l'air du soir était
caressé par vos ailes,
et maintenant, dans l'arbre balancé
votre voix chante grave et pure,
se mêlant au confus murmure des eaux.
Ah! quelles tempêtes et quels orages
vous ont emporté dans leur vaste univers,
mon bel oiseau si fier, conduisant votre course
avec celle des grands nuages vagabonds.

Qu'il est pur le ciel à son zénith!
Se peut-il que les vents calmés
vous aient abandonné dans les rameaux
de ces grands arbres?
Leur feuillage hautain est confus sur le firmament.
Que vous vous plaignez tristement!
Quelle flèche vous a blessé,
mon bel oiseau si doux?
C'est ici la vallée de mes larmes.
Voici ces tendres coteaux, ces fleurs
jamais cueillies, ces rives nébuleuses
qui cheminent vers l'horizon.
Le soleil a laissé ses rayons dans le ciel, dans un ciel
pur où palpite le vol d'autres
colombes invisibles.
Vous chantez sur cet arbre au pied duquel je pleure.
Ma colombe, ô ma tourterelle,
demeurez avec moi, dans ma vallée.

.

The turtle-dove

My dove, O my turtle dove,
is it yours, the plaintive voice I hear moaning
in the branches of these darkening elms?
At the close of this day the evening air was
caressed by your wings,
and now, in the swaying tree,
your voice sings low and clear,
mingling with the indistinct murmur of the waters.
Ah! What tempests and what storms
have swept you into their vast universe,
my bird so proud and beautiful, merging your path
with that of the great nomadic clouds.

How clear the sky at its zenith!
Could it be that the now calm winds
have deserted you in the branches
of these tall trees?
Their lofty leaves are blurred against the firmament.
How sadly you moan!
What arrow has wounded you,
my bird so sweet and beautiful.
This is the vale of my tears,
these are the gentle hills, the never-gathered
flowers, the misty river-banks
that move toward the horizon.
The sun has left its rays in the sky, in a clear sky
quivering with the flight of other
unseen doves.
You sing in this tree at whose base I weep.
My dove, O my turtle-dove,
stay with me in my valley

CATALOGUE DE FLEURS

(Lucien Daudet)

A CATALOGUE OF FLOWERS

2 i *La violette*

La violette cyclope se force admirablement d'un beau rouge Solférino. Elle est très parfumée, hâtive et vigoureuse.

Violets

The Cyclops Violet blooms a lovely Solferino red. It is highly scented and a strong early flowerer.

2 ii *Le bégonia*

Bégonia Aurora, fleur très double; abricot mêlé de corail, coloris très joli, rare et curieux.

Begonias

The Aurora Begonia has a full double blossom; apricot, tinged with coral—a most pretty colour. It is rare and unusual.

2 iii *Les fritillaires*

Les fritillaires aiment les endroits exposés au soleil et à l'abri du vent et des gelées printanières. Pendant l'hiver on les couvre. On les appelle aussi Œufs de Vanneau et Couronnes Impériales.

Fritillaries

Fritillaries favour ground exposed to sunlight and shelter from winds and spring frosts. During the winter they should be covered. They are also known as Lapwing Eggs and Crown Imperials.

2 iv *Les jacinthes*

Albertine blanc pur. Lapeyrouse mauve clair. Roi des Belges carmin pur, Roi des bleus, bleu foncé. Mademoiselle de Malakoff jaune vif à bouquet.

Hyacinths

Pure white 'Albertine'. Light mauve 'Lapeyrouse'. Pure carmine 'King of the Belgians'. Dark blue 'King of the Blues'. 'Mademoiselle de Malakoff'—bright yellow clusters of flowers.

2 v *Les crocus*

Les Crocus se forcent en potées ou dans des soucoupes, sur de la mousse humide. À la pleine terre, seuls ou mêlés à d'autres plantes printanières, ils font un très bel effet.

Crocuses

Crocuses can be forced in pots or saucers with damp moss. Outside, alone or mixed with other spring flowers, they make a lovely effect.

2 vi *Le brachycome*

Brachycome iberidifolia; étoile bleue. Nouveauté, plante naine charmante couverte de fleurs bleues, d'un bleu vif.

The brachycome

Brachycome iberidifolia is a blue-starred novelty, a charming dwarf plant covered with bright blue flowers.

2 vii *L'eremurus*

Eremurus isabellinus, sa floraison est garantie. La hampe de cette magnifique espèce atteint parfois deux mètres; ses fleurs sont d'un beau coloris entre jaune et rose et d'une longue durée. Vous recevrez les prix par correspondance.

The eremurus

Eremurus isabellinus is guaranteed to bloom. The stem of this magnificent species sometimes reaches a height of two metres. Its flowers are a lovely shade between yellow and pink, and last for a long time. Price list on application.

CHANTS POPULAIRES HÉBRAÏQUES   POPULAR HEBREW SONGS

3 i   *La séparation*

Celui qui distingue le sacré du profane,
nous pardonne nos péchés.
Il multipliera comme le sable et les astres
notre argent et nos enfants,
Bonne semaine.

Que faire? ça ne va pas.
Des enfants il y en a,
mais de l'argent il n'y en a pas
et le pain s'obtient péniblement.
Bonne semaine.

Le jour tombe, le Sabbat s'éloigne
comme l'ombre d'un arbre.
Dans les plats plus une miette
et bientôt arrive la semaine heureuse.
Bonne semaine.

Separation

He who distinguishes the sacred from the profane
will pardon us our sins.
He will multiply, as he does the sand and stars,
our money and our children,
A good week.

What can be done? This won't do.
There are children all right,
but there is no money
and bread can only be got with difficulty.
A good week.

Daylight fades, the Sabbath retreats
like the shadow of a tree.
Not a single crumb on the plates
and soon the happy week will arrive.
A good week.

3 ii   *Le chant du veilleur*

Holà! Qui va là?
Triste veilleur, pauvre sentinelle,
je traverse la nuit,
le sommeil me fuit terriblement.
Suis-je donc fait de fer?
Tout le monde dort et repose en paix
et oublie le tracas du jour.
Moi seul, je cherche en vain du repos sur la pierre.
Holà! Qui va là?

The watchman's song

Stop! Who goes there?
Sad watchman, wretched sentry,
I walk through the night,
sleep shuns me most horribly.
Am I then made of iron?
Everyone sleeps and rests in peace
and forgets the trials of the day.
I alone seek rest in vain on stone.
Stop! Who goes there?

3 iii   *Chant de délivrance*

Pour la grâce de mon ami,
mon cœur se consume en amour craintif,
je supplie Dieu pour qu'il apaise ma douleur.
Si j'appelle, il m'entendra,
lui mon épée, mon bouclier, ma cuirasse.
Tout mon être s'élance vers lui.
Et je prierai le jour et la nuit
pour qu'il apporte la consolation à tout son peuple;
alors, j'oublierai toutes mes douleurs
et je me mettrai au service de Dieu.

Song of deliverance

For the sake of my friend,
my heart pines away in fearful love,
I beseech God to assuage my pain.
If I call, he will hear me,
he my sword, my shield, my breast-plate.
My whole being flies towards him.
And I shall pray both day and night
that he might bring consolation to all his people;
I shall then forget all my griefs
and place myself in the service of God.

Vois, Isaac ne désespère plus,
ses ennemis s'enfuient devant lui.
La bénédiction de Dieu me protège et me soutient.
L'envoyé de Dieu viendra.
Oui, le voici. Il apportera à mon deuil
le soulagement que je demandais,
sa droite me soutiendra
tous les jours et toutes les nuits.
Et déjà voici la délivrance.

Behold, Isaac no longer despairs,
his enemies take flight from him.
The blessing of God protects me and sustains me.
God's messenger will come.
Here he is. He will bring to my mourning
the solace that I asked for,
his right hand will sustain me
through all the days and all the nights.
And behold! deliverance is already nigh.

3 iv *Berceuse*

Dors, dors, dors,
ton papa ira au village
et rapportera une pomme
et caressera ta petite tête.

Dors, dors, dors,
ton papa ira au village
et rapportera une noix
et caressera ton petit pied.

Dors, dors, dors,
ton papa ira au village
et rapportera un canard
et caressera tes petites mains.

Dors, dors, dors,
ton papa ira au village
et rapportera la soupe
et caressera ton petit ventre.
Dors, dors, dors.

Cradle-song

Sleep, sleep, sleep,
your daddy will go to the village
and bring back an apple
and stroke your little head.

Sleep, sleep, sleep,
your daddy will go to the village
and bring back a walnut
and stroke your little foot.

Sleep, sleep, sleep,
your daddy will go to the village
and bring back a duck
and stroke your little hands.

Sleep, sleep, sleep,
your daddy will go to the village
and bring back some soup
and stroke your little tummy.
Sleep, sleep, sleep.

3 v *Gloire à Dieu*

Mon Dieu est ma force et ma tour
et moi je suis si pauvre!

Tout mon espoir en Dieu
et toute ma confiance en toi,
mon Dieu, Dieu Zébaoth.

Je suis brûlé à vif,
transpercé par une flèche de feu
de mon Seigneur, de mon Dieu.

Glory to God

My God is my strength and my tower
and I am so poor!

All my hope is in God
and all my faith is in you,
my God, God of Sabaoth.

I am burnt to the quick,
pierced by an arrow of fire
of my Lord, of my God.

Il m'a percé le cœur
et il a brûlé dans mon cœur
mon arrogance et ma fierté,
Dieu Zebaoth!

He has pierced my heart
and in my heart he has burnt
my arrogance and my pride,
God of Sabaoth!

3 vi *Chant hassidique*

Que te dirai-je et que te raconterai-je?
Qui peut te dire et t'expliquer
ce que signifie un, deux, trois, quatre, cinq, six, sept?
Sept c'est le Sabbat et six les parts du Talmud*
et cinq les parties de la Bible et quatre les aïeux
et trois les patriarches et deux les tables de la loi

et un c'est notre Dieu, c'est notre Dieu unique,
il n'a pas son pareil, notre Dieu est un.
Un c'est notre Dieu et deux les tables de la loi
et trois les patriaches et quatre les aïeux
et cinq les parties de la Bible et six les parts du
    Talmud
et sept c'est le Sabbat.
Mais un c'est notre Dieu,
et un c'est notre Dieu.

Hassidic song

What shall I tell you and what shall I recount?
Who can say and explain to you
the meaning of one, two, three, four, five, six, seven?
Seven is the Sabbath and six the parts of the Talmud
and five the parts of the Bible and four our ancestors
and three the patriarchs and two the tables of the
    law
and one is our God, our only God,
he is without equal, our God is one.
One is our God and two the tables of the law
and three the patriarchs and four our ancestors
and five the parts of the Bible and six the parts of
    the Talmud
and seven is the Sabbath.
But one is our God,
and one is our God.

TROIS CHANSONS DE NÉGRESSE

(Jules Supervielle)

THREE NEGRESS SONGS

4 i *Mon histoire*

J'étais toute petite
Quand un grand négrier,
Cachant la vérité,
Me fit venir d'Afrique.

On nous entassa toutes
Dans une barque à voiles
Et je compris en route
Que j'étais une esclave!

Devant la vérité
Pauvre de moi, mes frères,
Voyez cette misère,
Horrible à constater.

My story

I was a very small girl
When a big slave-trader,
Hiding the truth,
Sent for me from Africa.

They crammed all us women
Into a sailing boat
And I learned en route
That I was a slave!

Faced with the truth,
Wretched me, O my brothers,
Observe this misery,
A terrible sight.

---

* Hebrew word meaning 'Study', an abbreviation of 'Talmud Torah' ('Study of the Torah'). It was a collection of Jewish books, containing traditions, laws, rules and institutions.

Ah! je n'étais plus même
Précipitation,
J'étais calamité
Et indignation.

Maintenant on est libre
De tous ses mouvements,
On a beau être nègre,
On est comme les Blancs.

La jambe par devant,
La jambe par derrière,
Nous sommes des enfants
Libres et volontaires.

Ah! My name was no longer
Precipitation,
I was calamity
And indignation.

Now we are free
In all our movements,
Despite being black,
We are like the Whites.

One leg in front,
One leg behind,
We are free
And self-willed children.

4 ii *Abandonnée*

En attendant je serai
À la maison toute seule,
Sans avoir un seul baiser
À me mettre sous la gueule.

J'aurai tout plaisir gâté,
Comme une pauvre orpheline,
Le cœur pâle d'anxiété
Je ferai triste cuisine.

Je salerai mes repas
Avec des larmes brûlantes,
Je m'en irai pas à pas
Vers les solutions violentes.

Mais, mon petit, voici l'heure
De ton alimentation.
Étant femme, avec pudeur,
J'irai derrière un buisson
Donner mon sein de couleur
À notre petit garçon.

Abandoned

While waiting I shall be
Utterly alone at home,
Without being kissed
A single time.

All pleasures will be marred,
Like a poor orphan girl,
Heart pale with worry,
I shall cook meagre meals.

I shall salt my food
With burning tears,
I shall gradually resort
To violent solutions.

But, little man, it's time
For your feed.
Being a woman of modesty,
I shall go behind a bush
And give my coloured breast
To our little boy.

4 iii *Sans feu ni lieu*

Pour les enfants sans feu ni lieu
Faudrait une chanson si belle
Qu'elle puisse leur tenir lieu
De demeure très naturelle.

Without hearth or home

For children without hearth or home
You would need a song so beautiful
That it could take the place
Of the most natural abode.

Tout ce dont ils auraient besoin,	Everything that they might want,
Un peu de lait, un peu d'étoffe,	A little milk, a little fabric,
Ainsi que tous les autres soins,	As well as all other needs,
Ils les trouveraient dans les strophes,	They would find in verse,
Afin de leur faire comprendre	In order to make them understand
Qu'ils sont moins seuls qu'ils n'en ont l'air,	They are less alone than they seem,
Même au milieu de la montagne	Even in the midst of the mountain
Et de la guerre et de l'hiver.	And of winter and war.

QUATRE CHANSONS DE RONSARD

FOUR SONGS OF RONSARD

5 i *À une fontaine*

To a fountain

Écoute moi, Fontaine vive,	Hearken to me, O spring water,
En qui j'ai rebu si souvent,	Where I've so often slaked my thirst,
Couché tout plat dessus ta rive,	Reclining alongside your bank
Oisif à la fraîcheur du vent,	Idly in the refreshing breeze,
Quand l'été ménager moissonne	While thrifty summer reaps the harvest
Le sein de Cérès dévêtu,	From Ceres' bared breast,
Et l'aire par compas résonne	And the threshing floor resounds,
Gémissant sous le blé battu.	Groaning beneath the flailed corn.
Ainsi toujours puisses-tu être	Thus may you remain forever
En religion à tous ceux	A sacred place for all those
Qui te boiront ou fairont paître	Who shall drink from you and lead their oxen
Tes verts rivages à leurs bœufs.	To graze on your green meadows.
Ainsi toujours la lune claire	And may the moonlight always
Voie à minuit au fond d'un val	Glimpse at midnight down in the valley
Les Nymphes près de ton repaire	The Nymphs around your retreat
À mille bonds mener le bal!	Leaping as they lead the dance!

5 ii *À Cupidon*

To Cupid

Le jour pousse la nuit	The day expels the night
Et la nuit sombre	And sombre night
Pousse le jour qui luit	Expels the day, glimmering
D'une obscure ombre.	In dim shadow.
L'Automne suit l'Été	Autumn follows Summer,
Et l'âpre rage	And the bitter blast
Des vents n'a point été	Of the winds blew not at all,
Après l'orage.	The storm once past.

Mais la fièvre d'amours
   Qui me tourmente
Demeure en moi toujours
   Et ne s'alente.
Ce n'était pas moi, Dieu,
   Qu'il fallait poindre;
Ta flèche en d'autre lieu
   Se devait joindre.
Poursuis les paresseux
   Et les amuse,
Mais non pas moi, ni ceux
   Qu'aime la Muse...

Yet Love's feverish ill
   That torments me
Inhabits me still
   Nor will let be.
It was not I, O God,
   At whom you should have aimed;
Your arrow should have sped
   To some other mark.
Pursue the idle
   And amuse them,
But not myself, nor those
   Beloved by the Muse...

5 iii *Tay toy, babillarde Arondelle*

   Tay toy, babillarde Arondelle,
Ou bien, je plumeray ton aile
Si je t'empongne, ou d'un couteau
Je te couperay la languette,
Qui matin sans repos caquette
Et m'estourdit tout le cerveau.
   Je te preste ma cheminée,
Pour chanter toute la journée,
De soir, de nuict, quand tu voudras.
Mais au matin ne me reveille,
Et ne m'oste quand je sommeille
Ma Cassandre d'entre mes bras.

Hush, you chattering swallow

   Hush, you chattering swallow,
Or else I shall pluck off your wing
If I can catch you, or with a knife
Cut off your little tongue,
That prattles each morning on and on
And makes my head go round and round.
   I'll lend you my chimney
Where you can sing throughout the day,
The evening, the night, and when you will.
But do not wake me in the morning,
And when I'm slumbering do not steal
My Cassandra from my embrace.

5 iv *Dieu vous gard'*

   Dieu vous gard', messagers fidèles
Du Printemps, gentes hirondelles,
Huppes, coucous, rossignolets,
Tourtres, et vous oiseaux sauvages
Qui de cent sortes de ramages
Animez les bois verdelets.
   Dieu vous gard', belles pâquerettes,
Belles roses, belles fleurettes,
Et vous boutons jadis connus
Du sang d'Ajax et de Narcisse,
Et vous thym, anis et mélisse,
Vous soyez les bien revenus.

God shield you

   God shield you, faithful messengers
Of Spring, gentle swallows,
Hoopoes, cuckoos, nightingales,
Turtle-doves, and you wild birds,
Who with your hundred varied words
Gladden the greening woods.
   God shield you, lovely daisies
Lovely roses, lovely flowerets,
And you buds that once were named
After the blood of Ajax and Narcissus,
And you thyme, anise, and balm,
All be welcome back again.

Dieu vous gard', troupe diaprée	God shield you, O spangled flight
Des papillons, qui par la prée	Of butterflies, who flit across the meadow
Les douces herbes suçotez;	Drinking from the sweet grasses;
Et vous, nouvel essaim d'abeilles,	And you, new-born swarm of bees
Qui les fleurs jaunes et vermeilles	Who nibble at the yellow
De votre bouche baisotez.	And vermilion flowers.
Cent mille fois je resalue	A hundred thousand times your sweet
Votre belle et douce venue.	And beauteous coming I greet again.
Ô que j'aime cette saison	Oh how I love this season
Et ce doux caquet des rivages,	And the voices along the river bank,
Au prix des vents et des orages	More than the winds and storms
Qui m'enfermaient en la maison!	That confined me to my home!

MOMPOU, Frederic (1893–1987)

This Catalan composer, a master of miniature forms, was much influenced by Fauré and Satie. He is one of the few Spanish composers to have had a regular French publisher (Salabert) and he spent a great deal of time in France—as a student between 1911 and 1914, and then for twenty years (1921–41), returning to Spain only at the time of the Nazi occupation. We encounter the French language in 1926 in a modest way in TRES COMPTINES, which have something of both Satie and Poulenc about them. Here there is a deliberately bilingual format with a French song, *Margot la pie*, sandwiched between two Catalan texts. It is significant that Mompou next set French in 1943 when he was living in Spain, as if homesick for the language of a country in which he had lived for so long. This is another set of TRES COMPTINES with the same formula of a middle movement in French. This time it is poignantly entitled *Petite fille de Paris*; we feel as if the composer has left behind those he loved in his sudden exodus. In 1948 two further songs were added, both of them exceedingly brief— *Rossignol joli* and *Frédéric tic, tic*. The critic Jankélévitch compared these to Stravinsky's miniature PRIBAOUTKI songs.

The most substantial of the songs in French dates from 1951. This is *Le nuage* to a poem by Mathilde Pomès, and we might have believed this was the last of the Mompou songs to be composed in a language other than his own. Thus it is something of a surprise that in 1973 the composer wrote CINQ MÉLODIES SUR DES TEXTES DE PAUL VALÉRY (*La fausse morte, L'insinuant, Le sylphe, Le vin perdu*, and *Les pas*) which come from that poet's collection entitled CHARMES, the texts of which can be found in *The Spanish Song Companion* (Gollancz). The fantasy of these texts (the composer knew the poet personally) admirably matches Mompou's style where he appears to invent the next turn in his music on the spur of the moment. Particularly beautiful is the aptly named *L'insinuant*, while the almost minimalist *Le vin perdu* and the Debussian *Les pas* (also set by Dinu Lipatti) show the composer's interest in repetitive rhythmic figurations.

MONPOU, Hippolyte (1804–1841)

Monpou's name is unknown today, but it is an important one in the history of French song as the early nineteenth-century romance evolves into the mélodie as we know it. His life story reads like something from *La bohème*, always short of money and surviving on the edge of poverty by a last-minute sale of a song. But it was the unruly and daring side of his nature and a lack of respect for the inhibited social conventions of the time which gave him a niche in musical history: he was the first to have the audacity to set his great contemporaries, the romantic poets, to music. He wrote over ninety songs among which are settings of Hugo, Musset, Gautier, as well as Goethe and Bürger in translation. His taste for German literature gave him the nickname 'le roi de la ballade'. Harmonically the music is far from adventurous, but it has a certain élan about it, particularly if the composer is writing something in the Spanish style. His most resounding success was with Musset's *L'andalouse*. Apparently the words which refer to this woman's breasts, and to the fact that she is the poet's 'lionne', were too indelicate for salon consumption, and had to be altered for the blushing ladies. But this move away from shepherds and shepherdesses towards a literary world of flesh and blood was an important turning point in the musical life of Paris. Other successful Monpou songs included *Le lever* (also Musset) and four Hugo settings: the melodramatic *La juive*; *À genoux* (a setting of Hugo's *Puisqu'ici-bas toute âme* [HAHN 3]; *La captive* [BERLIOZ 6] and *Gastibelza*, a song as simple as Liszt's setting of the same text is virtuosic.

MOZART, Wolfgang Amadeus (1756–1791)

To Mozart belongs the distinction of having written the two earliest French songs to find a regular place in the recital repertoire. He composed them in Mannheim in the winter of 1777–8 when he was on his way to Paris to broaden his reputation and hopefully find fame and fortune. He dallied in the German city, however, for five months, very much to his father's exasperation. The reason for this unwillingness to leave for the French capital was Aloysia, the eldest daughter of the Weber family who lived in Mannheim, and with whom Mozart had fallen desperately in love. Leopold Mozart was terrified by signs of his son slipping out of paternal control.

Oiseaux, si tous les ans K307 (Ferrand) and ***Dans un bois solitaire*** K308 (Houdar de La Motte) were composed as a result of the composer's friendship with another musical family in the same city—the Wendlings. (The roles of Ilia and Electra in *Idomeneo* were to be created by women from this family.) Mozart wrote to his father: 'The Wendlings are all of the opinion that my compositions would be extraordinarily popular in Paris. I have no fears on that score, for as you know I can more or less adopt and imitate any kind and any style of composition. Shortly after my arrival I composed a French song for Madame Augusta (the daughter) who gave me the words; and she sings it incomparably well. At the Wendlings it is sung every day.'

This household success was probably the second of the songs, and Mozart sent a copy to his father who maintained that his son's success in the French style was all the more reason for hurrying on to Paris. Despite faults in the prosody these are perfect little romances of the epoch; they might be by Phildor or Grétry, except that they are far more interesting than their models. In *Dans un bois solitaire* we glimpse Mozart the opera composer capable of turning even a cardboard Cupid into a living character. There is a flexibility and a fluidity to this music with its subtle mixture of aria and arioso (Schubert was to learn much from this side of Mozart's songwriting), and there is an equally charming vivacity in the tripping dotted rhythms of *Oiseaux, si tous les ans.* All this shows how deeply Mozart had assimilated the French style. It is also a reminder how well German-speaking composers of the time understood and accepted that musical taste in France was different from that of other countries. The history of the mélodie could not have asked for a more distinguished composer at its inauguration, albeit one who was unaware of the historical significance of his two small songs, *jeux d'esprit* written to impress the ladies with his versatility.

1 *Oiseaux, si tous les ans*

(Antoine Houdar de La Motte)

Oiseaux, si tous les ans
Vous quittez nos climats,
Dès que le triste hiver
Dépouille nos bocages;
Ce n'est pas seulement
Pour changer de feuillages,
Ni pour éviter nos frimats;
Mais votre destinée
Ne vous permet d'aimer,
Qu'à la saison des fleurs.
Et quand elle est passée,
Vous la cherchez ailleurs,
Afin d'aimer toute l'année.

If yearly, birds

If yearly, birds,
You leave our clime,
The moment sad winter
Strips bare our woods,
It is not solely
For change of foliage,
Nor to escape our winter;
It is because your destiny
Only permits you to love
In the season of flowers.
And when that season is past,
You search for it elsewhere,
That you might love throughout the year.

2 *Dans un bois solitaire*

(Antoine Ferrand)

Dans un bois solitaire et sombre
Je me promenais l'autr' jour,
Un enfant y dormait à l'ombre,
C'était le redoutable Amour.

J'approche, sa beauté me flatte,
Mais je devais m'en défier;
J'y vis tous les traits d'une ingrate,
Que j'avais juré d'oublier.

In a lonely wood

In a dark and lonely wood
I walked a while ago,
A child was sleeping in its shade—
It was fearsome Cupid himself.

I drew near, his beauty charmed me,
But I had to be on my guard;
I saw all the looks of a faithless maid
Whom I had sworn to forget.

Il avait la bouche vermeille,	His lips were bright red,
Le teint aussi beau que le sien,	His complexion as beautiful as hers,
Un soupir m'échappe, il s'éveille;	A sigh escapes me, he awakes;
L'Amour se réveille de rien.	Cupid wakes at anything.
Aussitôt déployant ses ailes et saisissant	Spreading at once his wings and seizing
Son arc vengeur,	His vengeful bow,
D'une de ses flèches cruelles, en partant,	Unleashing one of his cruel shafts
Il me blesse au cœur.	He wounds me to the heart.
Va! va, dit-il, aux pieds de Sylvie,	'Go!' he said, 'at Sylvie's feet
De nouveau languir et brûler!	To languish and to burn anew!
Tu l'aimeras toute ta vie,	You shall love her all your life
Pour avoir osé m'éveiller.	For having dared to wake me.'

NIEDERMEYER, Louis (1802–1861)

This composer of Swiss birth was often credited with writing the first 'real' French song, although this honour belongs to many people: the birth of the mélodie was accomplished over a number of years with a number of composers claiming paternity, or acting as midwives. Nevertheless, according to Saint-Saëns, Niedermeyer was the 'first to break the mould of the antiquated and insipid French romance . . . The resounding success of *Le lac* paved the way for Gounod and all those who followed this path.' Noske points out, though, that however superior they were to the work of his contemporaries, Niedermeyer's works were not really innovative: the texts were of a higher quality, the accompaniments were more worked out, there were structural changes to mirror the mood of the music, but the songs were still a mixture of romance and scène. In **Le lac** (Lamartine, 1821), the composer hits on a particularly felicitous way of differentiating the rhetorical and meditative parts of the poem, the first with recitative and tremolando, the second with a section which is actually labelled 'Romance', and consists of three couplets in the old-fashioned manner. There are other Lamartine settings to be found in the *recueil* of ten mélodies published by Pacini in 1851. These are even longer and more pianistically elaborate—*L'isolement* (the last four lines of which Satie set in the first of his QUATRE PETITES MÉLODIES [SATIE 5 i]), *L'automne*, and *La voix humaine*. It is easy to see how these songs might be thought to lead directly to Gounod's Lamartine mélodies *Le soir* and *Le vallon*, for they have a similar scale and seraphic expansiveness.

Also worthy of investigation is Niedermeyer's *Le poète mourant* (Millevoye), which is at least as interesting as Meyerbeer's setting championed in recent years by Thomas Hampson. There are appealing shorter strophic songs like *Jane Gray* (Pacini) about the nine-day queen who was also the subject of a song by Schoenberg of all composers. *Le fou de Grenade* (Charlemagne, 1859) is a reply to Monpou's Victor Hugo setting *Gastibelza, le fou de Tolède* (1840). Also for bass voice is Hugo's *La mer* (published 1862), where the left-hand aquatic rumblings become an irritating commonplace. Much more beautiful is a haunting little *Puisqu'ici-bas toute âme* [HAHN 3], which deserves to be better known as a precursor to so many other settings. Also exquisite is *O ma belle rebelle!* (Baïf), so different from Gounod's song [GOUNOD 7] but no less poised. Niedermeyer adopts here a pointed little accompanying figure which is reminiscent of *Letzte Hoffnung* from Schubert's WINTERREISE. The two duets *Vois l'aurore* and *Ne parlons pas d'amour* are charming salon pieces. This type of characterful piano writing almost in the lied manner is a reminder that German song was unquestionably the influence which enabled the romance to deepen its response to words. Niedermeyer wrote his songs at a time when an injection of his Swiss seriousness into this ageing form, dying as a result of a lifetime of superficiality and frivolity, played an essential role in the metamorphosis which would lead to the mélodies of Gounod and beyond. His place in song history is further assured by his founding of the École Niedermeyer for church music, the institution where the musical personality and harmonic vocabulary of Gabriel Fauré evolved under the watchful eye of Saint-Saëns.

1 *Le lac*

(Alphonse de Lamartine)

Ainsi, toujours poussés vers de nouveaux rivages,
Dans la nuit éternelle emportés sans retour,
Ne pourrons-nous jamais sur l'océan des âges
    Jeter l'ancre un seul jour?

Ô lac! l'année à peine a fini sa carrière,
Et près des flots chéris qu'elle devait revoir,
Regarde! je viens seul m'asseoir sur cette pierre
    Où tu la vis s'asseoir!

Tu mugissais ainsi sous ces roches profondes;
Ainsi tu te brisais sur leurs flancs déchirés;
Ainsi le vent jetait l'écume de tes ondes
    Sur ses pieds adorés.

Un soir, t'en souvient-il? nous voguions en silence;
On n'entendait au loin, sur l'onde et sous les cieux,
Que le bruit des rameurs qui frappaient en cadence
    Tes flots harmonieux.

Ô lac! rochers muets! grottes! forêt obscure!
Vous que le temps épargne ou qu'il peut rajeunir,
Gardez de cette nuit, gardez, belle nature,
    Au moins le souvenir!

Que le vent qui gémit, le roseau qui soupire,
Que les parfums légers de ton air embaumé,
Que tout ce qu'on entend, l'on voit ou l'on respire,
    Tout dise: 'Ils ont aimé!'

The lake

Thus, driven ever on toward new shores,
Carried beyond return into eternal night,
Can we never cast anchor in the ocean of time
    For just a single day?

O lake! the year has scarcely run its course,
And, by the dear waves she was to see again,
Behold, I come by myself to sit on this stone
    Where you once saw her sit!

Thus you moaned beneath these steep rocks;
Thus you broke against their jagged sides;
Thus the wind hurled the foam of your waves
    Onto her cherished feet.

One evening, do you remember, we sailed in silence;
We only heard afar, on the water and beneath the skies,
The rowers beating time with falling oars
    On your melodious waves.

O lake! Silent rocks! Caves! Dark forest!
You whom time spares or makes young once more,
Keep, fair nature, keep at least,
    The memory of that night!

Let the moaning wind, the sighing reed,
Let the delicate scent of your fragrant air,
Let all that is heard, seen, or breathed,
    Let everything say: 'They loved!'

OFFENBACH, Jacques (1819–1880)

For those who love this composer's operettas and *Les contes d'Hoffmann*, the mélodies come as rather a disappointment. Like Meyerbeer, another essentially French composer of German origin, Offenbach wrote a number of songs in both his native and adopted languages. Unlike Meyerbeer's songs, however, Offenbach's efforts in this genre come nowhere near to capturing the authority that he enjoyed in his theatrical works. It is significant that the modern reprints of the songs have not originated in France but in Germany; much of the material conforms to an old-fashioned German idea (no longer prevalent among younger artists) of what French song should be—trivial, entertaining, and undemanding harmonically. Paradoxically, what comes across in the songs is a certain dogged determination to be funny where, surprisingly enough, the legendary light touch of France is scarcely discernible. These are shaggy-dog songs where whatever delight we have experienced in the first few pages is dissipated by the end. At the same time the music lacks any depth of German feeling in the lieder style: typical of neither one nation nor the other, as we sometimes feel with Meyerbeer. Almost all the Offenbach songs are too long for the musical ideas, and the piano writing is banal (the composer was a virtuoso cellist and not at all interested in writing keyboard works).

The first set was SIX FABLES DE LA FONTAINE (1842), the earliest of the various song cycles prompted by these celebrated fables. The songs are: *Le berger et la mer, Le corbeau et le renard* [CAPLET 3 i]*, La cigale et la fourmi* [CAPLET 3 ii], *La laitière et le pot au lait, Le rat de ville et le rat de champs, Le savetier et le financier*. This work was not well received even at the time, and the critic Bourges wrote of 'skimming, dismembering, and breaking into pieces the fables of La Fontaine. Ideas of this sort would never have entered a French brain.' This is rather harsh, for one or two of these fables can make a pleasantly amusing impression despite the composer's vandalizing the texts. A performance of the entire set cannot be recommended however: the effect of a long stretch of this music is dull, and the editor of the modern German edition frankly admits to adapting the piano writing to make it more interesting. The two other cycles were LE LANGAGE DE FLEURS (Plouvier, 1846), a *belle époque* (and lengthier) counterpart of Milhaud's CATALOGUE DE FLEURS, and the relatively ambitious LES VOIX MYSTÉRIEUSES (1852). In the latter cycle, the most interesting songs are those to familiar texts: *Chanson de Fortunio* (Musset, also set by Albéniz), *Ma belle amie est morte* (Gautier) [BERLIOZ 3 iii], and *Barcarolle* (Gautier), which is none other than *Où voulez-vous aller?* [BERLIOZ 3 vi]. There is also a Heine setting in French entitled *Sur la grève*, a rather heavy-handed comic military number, *Le sergent recruteur* (Plouvier), and another Gautier song, this time a Spanish evocation entitled *Sérénade du toréro*.

Offenbach is a comic genius in his way, and on paper these songs promise much in terms of subject matter and appeal. But recitalists cannot take on trust their efficacy on the platform. They were written to satisfy the taste of the time (a source of frustration to a number of Offenbach's contemporaries who were struggling to educate audiences for better things), and modern ears yearn for more harmonic diversity. The songs work best one or two at a time in the hands of skilled singing actors with perfect timing, and as part of a mixed group (an array of La Fontaine settings by various composers for example) when the limitations of the style do not outstay their welcome.

OLLONE, Max d' (1875–1959)

Occasionally one will come across this name when sorting through music in a second-hand music shop in France. I long resisted buying the music, fairly certain that a composer so unknown to me, and without any reputation on the concert platform (in Britain at least), would not be interesting. How wrong I was; d'Ollone was no dilettante whose parents had paid to have his works published, but a composer of ten works for the theatre, as well as symphonic and chamber music. His output has simply been lost in the welter of accomplished music by other composers published in his life-time; too young to be of Debussy's generation, too old to belong to Poulenc's, not a member of the Schola Cantorum, his plight as a composer without a school, and attempting to find his own voice, is fairly typical of the struggles faced by composers when the mélodie was at its apogee.

The refined quality of much of his output, his skilful use of the voice and of pianistic resources (he was a pupil of Massenet though his style owes as much to Chausson and Fauré), might have led to greater fame in another country. That d'Ollone's music has been all but ignored testifies to the highly competitive nature of mélodie composition in the early years of the twentieth century—the period of his first songs (settings of Hugo, Sully Prudhomme, Silvestre, Verlaine, and so on). In 1910 he wrote *In memoriam*, a setting, in French translation, of five strophes from Tennyson's mighty poem. The intensity of these pieces, where the religious convictions of the poet seem matched by those of the composer, gives the work a Franckian seriousness. D'Ollone seems to have read widely in foreign languages: other settings include a Tagore cycle (*DEUX POÉSIES*, 1935), *Chanson nocturne* to a Stefan George text, as well as songs taken from poems by Nekrasov and Apukhtin. Like Ropartz, Lekeu, and Magnard, d'Ollone was also fond of setting his own poems (eighteen of his sixty-seven songs are to his own texts), and he was also a distinguished musicologist and writer. The cycle *PAYSAGES GRECS* (1923) has a touch of the neo-classicism of Roussel, a much cooler work than the *IMPRESSIONS D'AUTOMNE,* a stormily romantic set of three songs composed some twenty years earlier. His selection of texts by French poets includes works by Anna de Noailles (*Le vent*, 1922, *Enfant Éros*, 1928), Maeterlinck, Bouchor, and Klingsor.

PADEREWSKI, Ignacy (1860–1941)

This great Polish musician, had he not entered politics and led a punishing life as a virtuoso pianist, might have become a much greater composer. The accomplishment of his piano music is relatively well known, but his songs have failed to find a place in the repertoire. He wrote two sets of Polish songs (Opp. 7 and 18) but by far the most important is a cycle of *DOUZE MÉLODIES* (Catulle Mendès) which were published in Paris in 1903. It is a paradox that one of the greatest works of this supreme-ly Polish musician should have been in French, and sadly not to the greatest French poet. Nevertheless the words serve well enough for this composer's moods which range from gentle melancholy to stronger and more dramatic *Weltschmerz*. Touches of impressionism show the sub-liminal influence of composers like Debussy and Ravel, and these combine with a nobly

Chopinesque neo-classicism. There is an indefinable Polish quality in these songs, which at their best have an epic and visionary quality without a sense of bombast. There is an occasional delightfully lighter touch as in the capricious *Querelleuse*. They fit well into one's image of the sort of music written by a great man who was later to shoulder the cares of his country. The last song in the set is ominously entitled *L'ennemie*; it was a different enemy which was to be his main preoccupation. In any case, no other prime minister, president, or monarch (*pace* Henry VIII and Prince Albert) of any country has come anywhere near to creating music as persuasive as this.

PALADILHE, Émile (1844–1926)

This winner of the 1860 Prix de Rome is a good example of someone who contributed little of lasting value to the stage or in chamber music, but who was nevertheless a gifted and interesting composer of mélodies. In this field he does not deserve his neglect. His *Mandolinata* (Bussine), composed when he was still in Rome (and which he incorporated into a later opera), was once very famous. Another song in this genre is *Sérénade napolitaine* (Pradels), which has a similarly delicious sense of poise, where popular success is courted without sacrifice of refinement. The first collection of VINGT MÉLODIES contains many a *trouvaille*. The *recueil* opens with *La lune de mai*, a delicate setting of a translation of Thomas Moore's *The young May moon*. A melodic gift and a deft sense of counterpoint are combined with a real ability to write interestingly for the piano. This is confirmed by *Ballade* ('Si tu veux, faisons un rêve'), a turbulent Hugo setting where the composer copes seemingly effortlessly with the size and range of the poem. *Désespérance* is a setting of Sully Prudhomme's *Soupir* [DUPARC 2]; of the many songs attempting to rival Duparc's setting, this is unquestionably one of the best. It was written for Mme Lalo, who was a noted singer as well as the composer's wife. *Les papillons* (Gautier) is similarly not at all a disappointment in comparison to Chausson's setting [CHAUSSON 3]. A spirited *Havanaise* (translated from the Spanish by Wilder) is followed by Gautier's *Chanson du pêcheur* [BERLIOZ 3 iii], which is certainly the equal of either Gounod's setting or Fauré's. *Le vase brisé* (Sully Prudhomme) outdoes Franck's song in terms of an imaginative response to the text. *La chanson des blondes* (Jean Aicard) is in Bizet's best farandole manner. Paladilhe was obviously at home in the company of poets, something which is emphasized by the dedication of this song to Henri de Régnier. The volume concludes with *Danse indienne* (Lahor)—a campy evocation of the east reminiscent of the once famous *Ballet égyptien* by Alexandre Luigini and a counterpart to Lahor's *Danse macabre* set by Saint-Saëns.

The second *recueil* of VINGT MÉLODIES seems rather less distinguished, but it includes *Sonnet de Pétrarque*, a French translation of 'Benedetto sia'l giorno, e'l mese, e l'anno' famous in Liszt's setting, and a beautiful duet version of Sully Prudhomme's *Au bord de l'eau* [FAURÉ 13]. This is not the only time that Paladilhe chose the same poem as Fauré. His cycle of six CHANSONS ÉCOSSAISES (Leconte de Lisle, 1877) includes *Nell* [FAURÉ 14] side by side with *Nanny* [CHAUSSON 1] as well as *La fille aux cheveux de lin* which was first a Debussy song, then a piano piece, and *Chanson du rouet* which was later to be set by Ravel [RAVEL 5]. In this set, Paladilhe changes his harmonic vocabulary completely and attempts (largely successfully) to re-create the simple yet heartfelt style of Scottish folksong. The most famous Paladilhe mélodie of all was Corneille's *Psyché* (also set by Koechlin), where old-fashioned formal verse in the grand manner is subjected to every trick in the salon book of rubato, pathos, and apposite modulation in order to enchant us. Maggie Teyte made a recording of this song with the nobility of a Sarah Bernhardt (and the over-the-top sentiment too), and earned for it an enduring affection with English-speaking listeners. But it is clear that Paladilhe was very far from being a one-song composer.

1 *Psyché*	*Psyche*
(Pierre Corneille)	

Je suis jaloux, Psyché, de toute la nature:	I am jealous, Psyche, of all nature:
Les rayons du soleil vous baisent trop souvent;	The rays of the sun kiss you too often;
Vos cheveux souffrent trop les caresses du vent:	Your hair suffers too often the wind's caresses:
Quand il les flatte, j'en murmure;	The moment he strokes them, I demur;
L'air même que vous respirez	The very air you breathe
Avec trop de plaisir passe par votre bouche;	Passes your lips with too much pleasure;
Votre habit de trop près vous touche;	Your garment clings to you too closely;
Et sitôt que vous soupirez,	And the instant you sigh,
Je ne sais quoi qui m'effarouche	Something which frightens me
Craint parmi vos soupirs des soupirs égarés.	Fears that your sighs are not all for me.

PESSARD, Émile (1843–1917)

He won the Prix de Rome in 1866, and he is now only remembered as Ravel's harmony teacher at a less than happy time at the Conservatoire for that composer. Nevertheless, his songs (like those of other winners of this prize, the Hillemacher brothers and Paladilhe) do not deserve extinction, for they were written by a skilled craftsman of imagination and taste. Debussy thought highly enough of *Chanson d'un fou* (Alphonse Daudet) to copy it out and take it to Russia with him in 1881. Thus it came about (like the Hillemacher song *Ici-bas*) that it was republished in 1932 and attributed to Debussy. Other interesting Pessard songs are *Renovare* (Murger), *Le lever* (Musset), *Le premier jour de mai* (Passerat), which was also set by Lennox Berkeley and Gounod [GOUNOD 8], and *Bonjour, Suzon* (Gautier) [DELIBES 2], which is reminiscent of Dvořàk's *Humoresque*. Rather more audaciously, Pessard set Gautier's *Le spectre de la rose* [BERLIOZ 3 ii]; if one can forget the world-famous setting of these words, Pessard's is an effective song. Less successful is his riposte to Liszt in *Oh! quand je dors!* (Hugo) where the difference between inspiration on the highest level and solid craftsmanship is too marked for comfort. If we wish to find an alternative to Liszt's setting we turn to Lalo.

PIERNÉ, Gabriel (1863–1937)

This pupil of Franck and Massenet won the Prix de Rome in 1882. He was a fine organist, a talented conductor always interested in championing new music (such composers as Stravinsky and Milhaud). His own work was a combination of the serious (the church music tradition represented by his teacher Franck) and the more light-hearted (his operas *Sophie Arnould* (1927) and *Fragonard* (1934) owe much to Massenet). He was also a composer of ballets, as well as symphonic, choral, and chamber music. He was held in high esteem by his contemporaries, and even today his is a name that appears from time to time on concert programmes, though almost never in song recitals. His *recueil* of VINGT MÉLODIES (published in 1890) contains interesting and accomplished settings of such poets as Coppée, Hugo, Gautier, the ubiquitous Armand Silvestre (a *Bonsoir* worthy of Hahn), but also a fair amount of disappointing poetry by Blanchecotte, Grandmougin, Guinand, and the like. Two famous texts are included in the volume: *Les trois chansons* is a pleasing version of Hugo's 'Viens!—une flûte invisible' [CAPLET 4], which Pierné probably knew from one of Saint-Saëns's settings of the lyric; *Les filles de Cadix* (Musset) [DELIBES 1] is lively enough, but no competition for its famous rival, although there is a winning *Mimi Pinson* by the same poet. *Villanelle*, a setting of the sixteenth-century poet Desportes, is an exercise in pastiche, and *Chanson de berger* (Gauthier-Villars), written for Emma Calvé, is a strophic romance and a rather charming revisiting of the old-fashioned tradition of the bergerette. *Sérénade* (Adenis) was once a popular hit, arranged for every conceivable instrument and combination (piano 6 hands, organ, saxophone etc.) The cycle SOIRS DE JADIS (Jean Lorrain) is in more serious style and requires an off-stage chorus and flute for the final number.

Other important poets later set by this composer were Tristan Klingsor and Paul Fort, the latter poet an enthusiasm shared with André Caplet, who composed his CINQ BALLADES FRANÇAISES DE PAUL FORT in 1919. In writing his SIX BALLADES FRANÇAISES DE PAUL FORT (1921), Pierné selects *La vie, Les baleines, Complaintes des arches de Noé, Le petit rentier, Les dernières pensées,* and *La ronde autour du monde.* These are different poems from the rival cycle with one exception—*La ronde* [CAPLET 2 ii] (the poem calls on all nations to link hands in friendship), which is the second song of Caplet's set. Pierné, on the other hand, uses it for the jubilant C major conclusion to his cycle. The music is rather less complicated than Caplet's, aiming rather for a childlike directness. TROIS CHANSONS DE MÉTIER (Guillot de Saix, published in 1933) are settings of quasi-folksong texts orchestrated in the manner of Canteloube, although they can also be accompanied by piano.

POLDOWSKI (Lady Dean Paul) (1880–1932)

She was the daughter of the famous violinist Wieniawski and his English wife. 'Poldowski' was a pseudonym for Irena Regina Wieniawska. After study with Gevaert in Brussels and Gédalge and d'Indy in Paris, she married Sir Aubrey Dean Paul and lived in London, where some of her music was published by Chester. She was firmly Francophile in her musical sympathies, and the most important of her thirty or so songs were sixteen Verlaine settings (composed between 1915 and 1920) which enjoyed a great vogue with singers and audiences in the 1920s. These include settings of familiar poems like *Mandoline* [FAURÉ 29 i], *En sourdine* [FAURÉ 29 ii], *L'heure exquise* [HAHN 1 v], *Spleen* [DEBUSSY 6 vi], *Fantoches* [DEBUSSY 8 ii], *Le faune* [DEBUSSY 13 ii], and *Sur l'herbe* [RAVEL 13]. *Dansons la gigue* had been set by Bordes and Loeffler [BORDES 2], and *Dimanches d'avril* is another version of *L'échelonnement des haies* [DEBUSSY 9 iii]. These songs are always written with an awareness of what her more distinguished predecessors had done with a lyric, and a firm determination to have her own say. *Bruxelles* is a setting of Verlaine's 'La fuite est verdâtre et rose' which was not set by any of her famous rivals.

Poldowski enters the spirit of the French style at the same time as reserving the right to think differently from her male colleagues. There is a mannered *fin-de-siècle* decadence about these songs, that atmosphere of wilting exquisiteness which English-speaking audiences, and those who have come to love Paris at a distance, take to be the very essence of French culture. In its desire to please and to ravish with luxurious harmonic surprises, her work has something in common with Hahn, lacking the stature, or individuality, to compete with Debussy. It would, however, be wrong to accuse her of lacking originality. *Colombine* (Verlaine, 1913) has the raffish quality of Debussy's QUATRE CHANSONS DE JEUNESSE, which Poldowski could not have known or imitated. Of her French songs to other poets, the most interesting are *Dans une musette* (Jean Dominique), *Nocturne* (Moréas), and *Pannyre aux talons d'or* (Samain), poets (although not poems) set by Fauré and Chausson. There is no doubt that Poldowski was widely read in French literature; she was typical of the close affinity with France felt by a great many Polish artists, not only of her own time (Paderewski) but of the future (Lutoslawski). Her songs almost always work in performance, and are worthy of occasional revival. They are particularly useful in a mixed group of Verlaine songs where audiences are delighted to discover new settings of familiar lyrics.

POULENC, Francis (1899–1963)

He is the most loveable of composers, not because he is a joker (which most of the time, contrary to his reputation, he is not) but because he is not afraid to yield to his emotions and follow his heart. Poulenc seems unafraid to share his feelings with us because he has nothing to lose: no mantle was promised him at an early age, and the institutional rigours and formalities of French musical life passed him by. Because he never had to earn his living, he was spared the youthful panic of the student desperate to make his way. He learned as he went along, and he was never expected to win the race—the tortoise to Auric's hare. He was not tipped to succeed Debussy and Ravel as France's most famous song composer (even his close friends would have laughed at such an idea at the beginning of his career) and he never had an image of himself being anything other than himself. He gave up on posterity because there was a depressive side to his nature that was fairly sure that posterity would give up on him. (When he died, after all, the world seemed to belong to Boulez and his followers.) For him, great composers were people like Monteverdi, Bach, Mozart, Debussy, and Stravinsky. He felt he was on the sidelines in comparison to such masters, but he continued to sing his song, building his reputation slowly, and almost despite himself. One says 'almost' because there was another side to Cerberus-Poulenc which was very *mondaine*; when in buoyant mood he was perfectly capable of self-promotion, and he was always well connected to the people who mattered in artistic Paris. But this was only 'playing the game'. At heart he was humble, and he remained miraculously open to change, allowing himself to be moulded by influences that came into his life by chance (the works of Apollinaire and Éluard were guiding stars). The more his music absorbed many and various inspirations from outside, the more utterly Poulencian it became. At the end of his life he could look back with a certain surprise on an important body of work, surpassing that of most of his contemporaries. The size and range of his output is that of a self-confessedly lazy man who is astounded to discover that he has been surprisingly productive. Singers (to quote W. H. Auden on Edward Lear) 'swarmed to him like settlers. He became a land.' His reputation as a great classic seems unassailable now, but it is more poignant for the fact that he basks posthumously in love and understanding, while during his lifetime he failed to receive comfort and support from a long-term relationship. In this and a few other respects, there is something Schubertian about Francis Poulenc.

He was born into a well-to-do Parisian family. His father was strictly religious, his mother a city-dweller through-and-through, fascinated by music and the theatre. And there was Uncle Papoum, her brother, a bachelor dandy, who initiated Poulenc into an appreciation of music hall and cabaret in smoke-filled *boîtes*. Deep down in his nature there was a pull between the serious side, inherited from his father, and the hedonistic pleasures of Paris, both *beau monde* and *demi-monde*. In the first half of his life it was the search for pleasure which was in the ascendant. One cannot deny that Poulenc was part of the *jeunesse dorée*, with never a money worry, and a light-hearted need to show off and entertain. This joker phase of his life is the one remembered by all those who know his music only superficially, for it is all too easy to typecast a composer as 'Leg-Poulenc' (a pun he himself enjoyed) and expect him never to change. The first piece for voice and piano is the *Intermède vocal* from the RHAPSODIE NÈGRE (1917), dedicated to Érik Satie. This is a po-faced chant with ridiculous words ('Honoloulou, poti lama!') credited to one Makoko Kangourou (now thought to be the poet Marcel Ormoy). In this way Poulenc jumps head-first into the anarchies of the twentieth century; not for him adolescent songs modelled on Ravel or Roussel. This is followed by the chanson *Toréador* with a text by Cocteau (a high-spirited *capriccio* which places a bull-fight in the middle of Venice). This might have been written for the music hall. So in his late teens we have a very precocious young man indeed; not really *musically* precocious, because these pieces show as yet no real command of composition, and skilfully disguise the fact, but sophisticated beyond his years in the manner of a rich undergraduate, a French Sebastian Flyte. Early music for winds and brass also cocks a snook at the world of old fogeys.

The composer found himself reaping the rewards of being young in the era of intellectual ferment following the First World War. Always at ease with fellow artists, he was taken under the wing of Cocteau, and became one of Les Six, the group of strangely assorted young Turks whose fun and games announced that the serious era of establishment music typified by Saint-Saëns and Duparc was now at an end. But seriousness of another kind was beginning. The first sign of genius is in the first song cycle LE BESTIAIRE (1919). Poulenc had heard Apollinaire, shortly before his death, reading his verse aloud at Les Amis du Livre, Adrienne Monnier's bookshop in the rue de l'Odéon. These six tiny animal fragments have an astonishing power, grave and gay, witty and serious, and they have remained effortlessly in the repertoire. Musically the cycle is a patchwork quilt of two-bar phrases stitched together, for this composer thought in blocks and seldom sought to develop his material organically. Like Satie, genius seems not to have been hampered by a mere lack of advanced technique. Each of these miniatures stays in the mind: high-points are the loping dromedaries of Don Pedro d'Alfaroubeira, the gambolling dolphins, and the mysterious carp in their deep dark pool. If the composer had written only this latter page he would have been remembered; the rise and fall of the vocal line on 'Poissons de la mélancolie' reveals a tenderness which is the wistful voice of Poulenc himself (we will come to love it more and more) as he signs off from his first masterpiece. In 1956 Poulenc returned to the *Bestiaire* poems in honour of one of the cycle's first interpreters Marya Freund. The single-page song *La souris* is a moving evocation of old times. What has happened, he asks, to those golden years gnawed away by the mouse of time?

The next cycle is also delightful, but it fails to strike the same deep chords as LE BESTIAIRE. This is COCARDES (1919), Poulenc's only Cocteau cycle. Here the poet's stream-of-consciousness imagery seems ideally suited to the composer's correspondingly small stretches of musical inspiration, colourful ideas skilfully sewn together. It is a nostalgic work, such as can only be written by someone still very young, in memory of his vanished youth. It is seminal Poulenc and rewarding in fine performance, but it is above all an insider's piece, full of references to popular culture of the time, and the effect is bewildering unless the work has been thoroughly studied, or the composer already holds you in his thrall. The piano version is a contemporary arrangement of the original scoring for cornet, trombone, bass drum, triangle, cymbal, and violin. More problematic are the five POÈMES DE RONSARD (1924–5), despite a marked effort to write in longer paragraphs. They are the result of composition lessons with Charles Koechlin which were beneficial in some ways, particularly in regard to choral music and counterpoint. But they were not useful for Poulenc the song composer. Here we find him attempting to write 'significant', complex music that will impress others. The composer opens the door on avant-garde musical life in the Paris of 1924, and, after the PROMENADES for piano and the POÈMES DE RONSARD, slams it shut again the better to preserve his own kingdom of sounds and ideas. Never again in his songs do we hear Poulenc lose touch with his essential self, and seldom in the future do we hear him set poetry from the distant past. Of course there is much here to please obdurate Poulenc fans who will argue how fine the Ronsard songs are, but they make a bad introduction to the composer's work and do not really sound like his music. Poulenc arranged the work for orchestra in 1934 but the version was unpublished in his lifetime. Jaques Leguerney was later to set the fifth and last text of the cycle, *À son page*, with rather more success [LEGUERNEY 2].

There was something about Poulenc which was like a little boy who delighted in shocking and scandalizing more prudish sensibilities. The eight CHANSONS GAILLARDES (1925–6) are the epitome of the devil-may-care songwriting of the 1920s in Paris, riotous living of the present combined with a bow to the scabrous living of the past. Anonymous seventeenth-century texts serve the composer's sexual iconoclasm well; adultery, promiscuity, and drunken licence (one must not forget that this was more topical in a world of American prohibition, and that Poulenc's choral *Chanson à boire* was banned at Harvard) are openly apostrophized in *La maîtresse volage, Madrigal, Couplets bachiques*, and *La belle jeunesse.* And one does not have to read very deeply between the lines to see sly references to man's endowment at the hand of the Fates (*Invocation aux Parques*), and a virgin's use of a candle (*L'offrande*) if such an endowment does not come readily to hand. And if it does, literally, one might sing the closing *Sérénade* in the hope that the audience will not fumble to the fact that a mélodie could have *such* a meaning—despite the vocal portamenti which slide back and forth to give Onan a musical voice. The pianist is likely to be more shocked by the accompaniments than the poems: they are among the composer's most hair-raising in terms of sheer technical difficulty. The seventeenth-century bonhomie of the style is at one with the neo-classicism of the time when new wine is poured into old bottles. These songs, and the manner in which Poulenc had set them, seemingly to *épater les bourgeois*, did not amuse the young baritone Pierre Bernac and, impatient of such *pudeur*, Poulenc dropped him as a collaborator. They were to re-find each other only a decade later.

The *AIRS CHANTÉS* (Moréas, 1927–8) are a fascinating attempt by a composer to write anti-music, an illustration of the fact that parody is the hardest of musical arts. When Schubert sets out to lampoon Italian opera he writes such effective and beautiful songs, despite himself, that the joke is on the perpetrator of the prank: the composer himself. And when Poulenc so disliked the Parnassian tone of Moréas's lofty poetry that he wrote music not *for* the text but *against* it, the joke falls flat because the resulting songs are so attractive: sopranos discovered an elegant and eminently singable cycle. The composer was doomed for the rest of his life to hear his deliberate guying of Moréas's poetry taken at face value by generations of singers who thought a charming musical effect more important than scoring sly points against a forgotten poet. And so indeed it is.

It seems incredible that after the success of *LE BESTIAIRE* it should have taken Poulenc thirteen years to return to Apollinaire. The *TROIS POÈMES DE LOUISE LALANNE* (1931) are not by a female poet of that name, but neither are they all by Apollinaire as the composer thought when he set them. The central song *Chanson* is indeed by Apollinaire, but the outer songs of the set are by his mistress, the painter Marie Laurencin, who only later revealed her authorship to Poulenc. The whole story, right up to the posthumous revelation of authorship, has something about it which is akin to the affectionate collaboration of Goethe and Marianne von Willemer. The opening song *Le présent* has the 'wind blowing over a grave' feel of the last movement of Chopin's B flat minor Piano Sonata, and *Chanson* is the purest music-hall nonsense. But in *Hier* we hear something for the first time: lyricism tinged with the melancholy of the smoke-filled room, and the popular song of a chanteuse in a blue mood. How different this is from the Rabelaisian knees-up of the *CHANSONS GAILLARDES* six years before. Poulenc is coming to the end of his youth, and perhaps he sensed that the loneliness of his late twenties was never really to be assuaged. The pulse is that floating movement of quavers which, like a heartbeat, gently propels some of his greatest and most heartfelt songs, and saves them from wallowing in sentimentality.

Also from 1931 come the *QUATRE POÈMES*, enchanting Apollinaire miniatures. The first of these (*L'anguille*) is a pithy evocation of Parisian low life in valse-musette style (one can almost hear the accordion), 'The Eel' something of a Parisian counterpart to a character from the New York underworld of Damon Runyon. *Carte postale* is more of a bourgeois interior ('Misia Sert at the piano, painted by Bonnard,' Poulenc wrote in his *Journal de mes mélodies*) which has a delicate air of imperturbable grace. Few, if any, composers could have set *Avant le cinéma* so well. It is a subtle summation of linguistic snobbery in a fast-changing modern world, the social assumptions of the old order challenged by the arrival of new-fangled twentieth-century inventions. It is one of the composer's most comical songs, although the mood is wry rather than uproarious. The music of the postlude has a touch of Laurel and Hardy about it, the triplets illustrative of the slightly shaky turning of a reel of film on the projector of a provincial cinema. And *1904* is sheer Maurice Chevalier, French music-hall style enlisted to compact the memories of the young Kostrowiski (Apollinaire's real name) into a torrent of voluble memories. And all this is to set up the poem's last line, a magical yet understated fifteen seconds of poetic regret. The mood of this postlude reminds us of Poulenc's unsuccessful attempt to win the hand of Raymonde Linossier; she had died suddenly in January 1930.

Recently published for the first time are the quirky Koechlin-like QUATRE POÈMES DE MAX JACOB (1921) with wind quintet accompaniment. But it was not until 1931 that the composer made a complete portrait of the 'moine et voyou', the monk and street-urchin which is often the epithet applied to the double-edged personality of Poulenc himself. Jacob is the poet of Poulenc's astonishing *cantate profane* for baritone and instrumental ensemble entitled LE BAL MASQUÉ. In that work, all of Jacob's wild extravagance is revealed and revelled in. It is a piece which would have merited a film by Pasolini, and if Max Jacob himself were alive, that director, with his nose for the bizarre, would have placed the poet in a starring role. The CINQ POÈMES of Max Jacob on the other hand show a gentler, less spectacular side to this enigmatic writer, the dreamer and folklorist from Brittany. There are here some touchingly simple portraits of women: in *Chanson bretonne* a peasant girl sings of her misfortunes, and *La petite servante* hopes for a good husband who will not beat her; in *Berceuse* the nursemaid is an impatient rogue, but Poulenc lavishes on her one of his divine waltzes. Perhaps the child (whose father is at mass, and whose mother is at a cabaret) is the composer himself, for these tastes sound comically like those of his own parents. At the end of *Souric et Mouric*, which is a reasonably abrasive song, there is a magical page which evokes the night in a burst of Poulencian lyricism. We shall hear this mood of calm nocturnal ecstasy again, notably in the closing pages of *Babar, le petit éléphant*, and the Apollinaire songs *Dans le jardin d'Anna*, and *Sanglots*.

The CINQ POÈMES DE PAUL ÉLUARD date from 1935. They announce the arrival of a great and influential new poet in the composer's life, but he does not invent an Éluard style easily or quickly. There is a sense, as Poulenc himself noted, of the key turning in the lock, and we can hear the grating of the mechanism. The last three songs *Plume d'eau claire*, *Rôdeuse au front de verre*, and *Amoureuses* find the composer progressively at ease—the last of these is racy and delectable. These are the most Parisian of Poulenc's Éluard songs, and he quickly came to realize that when Éluard's poetry suggested a key turning in the musical lock, the doors opened out onto different landscapes and loftier regions. For Poulenc, the real Éluard was the poet of love and humanity, the poet of the big issues that were emerging in his own life in the middle to late 1930s, issues that seemed especially relevant in a world threatened by Fascism and war. The fact is that the 1920s were only a distant memory and the composer was changing as the world changed. Poulenc had encountered Pierre Bernac again and accompanied him at the Salzburg Festival of 1934. He quickly realized that he had found not only an ideal interpreter, but an invaluable friend and ally. (He never addressed Bernac as 'Tu', regarding such intimate usage as inappropriate for the depth of their friendship which was based on professional and personal admiration.) In August 1936 Pierre Octave Ferroud, a young composer who was also a critic, died in a grisly motoring accident in Hungary. This shocked the composer to the core, and reminded him on what a slender thread human life depends. Accompanied by Bernac and the choral conductor Yvonne Gouverné, Poulenc visited the shrine of the Black Virgin in the mountainous region of Rocamadour in the Uzerche. Here he had a mystical experience which returned him to the faith of his fathers. For the rest of his life he was a practising Catholic, erratic perhaps in terms of certain observations of the letter, but true to the spirit of a believer, particularly in terms of a great deal of religious music written in his own mind for the greater glory of God. There was a side to Poulenc's nature which had the simple faith of a Bruckner.

It is at this point that the Poulenc enthusiast begins to talk about certain pieces of his music being profound. This is a matter of non-comprehension as far as many more casual listeners are concerned. Profound Poulenc? Those who prefer their French music light and undemanding would regard that phrase as ridiculous. But yes, Poulenc's music in conjunction with Éluard, and with the collaboration of a singer like Bernac, *is* profound and takes its place among the deepest experiences that French music has to offer. This is particularly true of his greatest song cycle, TEL JOUR TELLE NUIT (Éluard, 1936–7). The surrealist poetry is not easy to understand, but it has a strength, even a majesty, which is a perfect complement to the composer's new-found lyricism, a human warmth far removed from the style of the cheeky young tearaway of the 1920s. The cycle is a compendium of various styles: the hushed nocturne of *Une ruine coquille vide*; three songs (*Le front comme un drapeau perdu, À toutes brides,* and *Figure de force brûlante et farouche*) which are what Poulenc called 'trampoline' songs, swift scherzo-like movements which lead in and out of more lyrical numbers; the sinister single-paged horror of *Une roulotte couverte en tuiles*; the exquisite *Une herbe pauvre*, simple and fresh as mountain snow; the romantic heart-on-sleeve of *Je n'ai envie que de t'aimer.* The two outer pillars supporting the cycle at either end are the opening *Bonne journée* and the concluding *Nous avons fait la nuit*, in C major/minor. The opening song, dedicated to Picasso, is a genial reaffirmation of friendship and human companionship, and the last is quite simply one of the greatest love songs in the French repertoire. The poet writes of his love for his wife Nusch. As he lies next to her in the dark, at the moment before sleep where love awakens in all its forms, he finds himself thinking about what she means to him. Éluard uses rich imagery to describe how Nusch continues to fascinate him: the freshness of her perceptions and the originality of her childlike nature are what he needs in order to comprehend a world which continually renews itself in his eyes, thanks to her mediation. The final cadence in the vocal line ('Qui est toujours nouveau') is a moment of spine-tingling wonder. It takes a lonely homosexual composer (whom many would have accused of emotional immaturity) to write one of the most moving musical paeans to the deepening nature of love between two human beings that has ever been written. In this song we glimpse (not without being moved by the poignant gap between idealism and reality) the type of relationship that was to be denied Poulenc, as well as Bernac, his great interpreter who gave the first performance of this work, and so many others. The moving postlude, longer than in any other of his songs, seems to bring the threads of the cycle together in the manner of Schumann's DICHTERLIEBE.

In 1937 Poulenc began to set the poetry of Louise de Vilmorin whom he had known since 1934. This was in accordance with his desire to write not just for Bernac's baritone, but for a woman's voice too. His feeling that music for the female voice would gain in interest from the poetry of a woman is an interesting indication of how deeply he responded to the atmosphere of his songs which at this period, his most productive, were subtle conjunctions of word and tone equal to any in the entire repertoire. The first fruits of this collaboration were the TROIS POÈMES, elegant songs all, and worthy of more frequent performance. *Le garçon de Liège* is as light and buoyant as cork, *Au-delà* a roaming fantasy for the roaming hand, and *Aux officiers de la garde blanche* a noble hymn to the angels, full of humility and piety, a surprising conclusion to a *recueil* which had begun in a mood of such levity. Such is the composer's mastery of turning a poet's voice into an almost physically delineated musical portrait ('C'est ton portrait, c'est ainsi que tu es,' as Poulenc and Vilmorin would say together in another song) that we almost feel that Vilmorin herself has materialized before our eyes.

The other Vilmorin cycle is much more celebrated—the FIANÇAILLES POUR RIRE of 1939. This is a wonderful set of six songs which finds much favour with sopranos. It seems that the composer is concerned to avoid profundity almost as much as he courts it with Éluard: everything has its place and Vilmorin has been enlisted to enchant us. The mixture of styles in the cycle is familiar, and Poulenc is a practical musician, an accompanist at many recitals of his own music, who knows exactly how a set of songs should be put together. Thus we have a gently flowing introduction (*La dame d'André*) followed by a statuesque and moving slow movement of chaste and disembodied purity (*Dans l'herbe*). This mood returns for *Mon cadavre est doux comme un gant,* but not before the intervention of a devilish scherzo, *Il vole,* which froths with excitement and the racing pulses of sexual innuendo. *Violon* is one of Poulenc's most popular songs, a perfect evocation of a Hungarian nightclub complete with gypsy violinist. This was included because Louise de Vilmorin had married an Hungarian count and spent the war years on his estates. The cycle ends with *Fleurs,* one of those magical Poulenc songs, very slow on first hearing and almost minimalist in means, which is actually faster than one thinks. It breathes at the tempo of a heartbeat and moves forward as a living, feeling thing, the plaint of a real person with real needs. This is simply a sign that Poulenc is in touch with the expressive needs of singers, and as a result they love him like few other twentieth-century composers.

The years 1938 to early 1939 were a wonderful period for mélodies, perhaps because so much seemed at stake in the world in this last period of uneasy peace. Eight songs were written, at least six of which were masterpieces. The remaining two, *Le portrait* (Colette) and the angry *Je nommerai ton front* (a 'trampoline' song if ever there was one) are fine but not in the same class as three Apollinaires and other Éluards, a tidy balance sheet for the year's output. The first of the DEUX POÈMES (Apollinaire) is the spectacular but difficult *Dans le jardin d'Anna,* a fantasy about the life of a landowning aristocrat in eighteenth-century France, where the composer achieves miracles of cohesion despite his familiar difficulties of conjuring short phrases into an homogeneous whole. *Allons plus vite* is one of the most Parisian of all Poulenc's songs. It begins as abstract and elevated as Baudelaire and then, when the music changes from A minor to A major, we find ourselves cruising a Parisian pavement, looking for love. Poulenc confessed to understanding the footfall of the nocturnal hunter all too well. Apollinaire depicts Pauline the prostitute with her cupid's-bow lips, and the policeman who moves her on who does not believe for a moment that she had only been speaking to her brother. Here is a piece of Parisian low-life which has a poetry and purity amidst sordidity which is worthy of Jean Genet. Another Apollinaire song is *La Grenouillère,* a portrait of the Froggery, an island in the Seine where the impressionist painters used to go with their girls. The poet depicts it abandoned and sad; boats bump together in the current with an end-of-season atmosphere at a once-busy resort. Poulenc unerringly comes up with music which somehow suggests a place that is haunted by memories; this is a Proustian madeleine in song, and very much about the remembrance of things past. At the same time as fears of a second world catastrophe loom in the hieratical fragment of prayer *Priez pour paix* (Charles d'Orléans), the composer takes us back to the First World War, as a presentiment of events to come. The nickname for soldiers was 'Bleuet', after the cornflower blue of their uniform. This *Bleuet* is Poulenc's only song for tenor (it was slightly too high for Bernac and the composer seems to have had a lighter, more innocent voice in mind) and it is one of his most moving. His tenderness for the young man who is doomed to go 'over the top' at 1700 hours is almost palpable. And we also hear the musician's compassion for the poet whom he never really got to know, and who died in 1918 in the influenza epidemic of that year, no doubt weakened by his war-wounds. The last page of this song has those enigmatic lines 'Ô douceur d'autrefois | Lenteur immémoriale' which are only equalled by Mörike's 'alte unnennbare Tage' in Wolf's *Im Frühling*, an envoi which sums up mankind's impossible longing for the joys and securities of times that are now beyond reach. For this passage Poulenc writes music noble yet ethereal; in the calm movement of the piano's quavers we can sense the relentless trickle of sand in time's hourglass.

The three Éluard songs from this period could not be more different, both from the contemporary Apollinaire settings, and from each other. *Tu vois le feu du soir* is one of the grandest of the Poulenc mélodies, a hymn of love (the words again were conceived with Nusch in mind) which rises magnificently to the challenge of finding music for a text which seems to be written in the stars rather than with mere paper and ink. When Poulenc is in this elevated mood he can surprise even his most hardened detractors; the composer of the opera *Dialogues des Carmélites* here shows himself for the first time. Despite his notorious short phrase-lengths Poulenc was capable of writing music of a greater breadth and scale than anyone would have thought possible fifteen years earlier. Profound Poulenc? Indubitably. *Je nommerai ton front* (January 1939), the second song in this set published under the title MIROIRS BRÛLANTS, is a vituperative firework, a piece of musical anger written as a contrast to *Tu vois le feu du soir*, and meant to offset that song's sustained mood, the better to proceed with something serious afterwards. *Ce doux petit visage* (1939) is one of those perfect little songs which this composer was capable of writing to a text which moved him profoundly. The secret is the use of modest, even humble, musical means which ensures that the clarity of the lyric is not obscured. Not a note could be different here for fear of disturbing the carefully judged complicity between word and tone.

The next important set of songs for baritone (though it can equally be sung by female voice) is entitled BANALITÉS (Apollinaire, 1940). This is amongst the composer's most popular works and it is easy to see why. He has taken care to write a superbly balanced group of mélodies in which he can display almost every facet of his songwriting art. *Chanson d'Orkenise* is a home-made folksong, rough around the edges. *Hôtel* is the laziest song in the world, a smoker's daydreaming from an epoch when smoking was still an elegant pastime. A justly famous encore, this. *Fagnes de Wallonie* is one of those amiable fast movements, not awash with fleeting semiquavers, as when the composer is in his presto mood, but gently pressing forward—a single musical thought described in a graceful arch of sound. The pleasing shape of this mélodie represents a technical hurdle triumphantly surmounted, and it cost Poulenc more effort than one would think. *Voyage à Paris* is another famous encore. Bernac and the composer used to sing it as their ever-so-slightly malicious farewell to audiences on provincial gigs. Madcap gaiety and hilarity combine with a poetic love of Paris which no other composer of the mélodie has felt so intensely. Mind you, unlike many of the others, Poulenc was a native of the city; although he had a beautiful house in the Touraine, he preferred the excitement of life in the capital and eagerly returned to his tiny apartment overlooking the Jardins du Luxembourg. The final song of *BANALITÉS* is **Sanglots** which is the counterpart to *Tu vois le feu du soir*. It has the same broad canvas and serious tone, an oration of a song; it is philosophical in a way that we find nowhere else in Poulenc's Apollinaire songs.

The *CHANSONS VILLAGEOISES* (1942) is an infectiously rumbustious cycle, rather seldom performed in its entirety, which was also orchestrated. These are the composer's own home-made folksongs (from a collection of *Chansons de la grande hune* by Maurice Fombeure). *Les gars qui vont à la fête* could not be bettered as a vivid evocation of the hoopla among working folk which Poulenc had observed as a young boy at the fun-fairs of Nogent-sur Marne, where his grandparents had a house. The swagger of young men dressed up for a night with their girls is irresistibly conveyed in a song which would have done Maurice Chevalier proud. *C'est le joli printemps,* with its short spring-like melody repeated with slight modifications is a cousin of Carl Orff's *Carmina burana* (the same air of primeval peasantry and homage to the rising sap of spring) but with much more heart. In *Le mendiant* we hear the dark and powerful influence of Mussorgsky, a disturbing, almost revolutionary, song from a composer not noted for his interest in social realism. The whirlwind of **Chanson de la fille frivole** is a patter song of the giddiest kind; both the girl and the music are fast. *Le retour du sergent* is the only song in the set which reminds us that the cycle was written in France's dark hours. The plight of the old soldier, and the horrors of war over which he has no control, are admirably caught in one of Poulenc's most serious songs, a sort of pendant to *Bleuet*. But Poulenc's most famous mélodies about the war were yet to come: *DEUX POÈMES* (Louis Aragon, 1943). Has there ever been a better patriotic song than *C*? Aragon's view of history produces words which mention an insane duke and the false glories of château life on the Loire; these are softened by the humanity of Poulenc's music. Goodness knows how *C* avoids banality and sentimentality with all those heart-rending sequences, as one luscious chord falls on another. But providing the performers remember how desperate the composer's intent is, the effect is of the greatest nobility. Of course it is the words (where all the lines end in the rhyme 'cé') which provide a strong backbone, eloquent and angry, as Aragon the Marxist despairs of the rotten progress of French history, as much as lashing out at the Boches. A collaboration of this kind where two great artists balance each others' qualities, and modify each others' excesses, is useful in music of this genre; songs of patriotism written in times of war normally cause toe-curling embarrassment, once hostilities are over. But *C*, like France, survives; it seems as true and as moving as it did on the day of its composition. And with unerring programme-building panache, the composer set up all this emotion only to knock it down in the song which is its companion. *Fêtes galantes* is as loaded a title as you could ever find: memories of the studied elegance of Watteau and Verlaine immortalized by Fauré and Debussy in a more civilized age are swept away without any ceremony. Instead we have a *chanson-scie* from the *caf' conc'*, a genre which traditionally expresses joy and humour. To understand the deliberate irony, imagine a mixture of Londoners, some with Rolls-Royces and others with hand carts, fleeing the Germans, as Gracie Fields sings about it with a smile and a wink. Here we have black comedy and a type of gallantry. If you have to flee for your life, perhaps the greatest defiance you can show to the invader is to laugh, rather than mope and weep.

From 1943 comes another group of songs which is often found on the concert platform today.

The texts are by the composer's 'resident' woman poet Louise de Vilmorin, although these three MÉTAMORPHOSES can be performed by both male and female singers. The outer movements are both fast: the first of these, *Reine des mouettes*, is as light and frothy as sea foam while the tricky accompaniment gives the impression (if well played) of gentle insouciance; *Paganini* is a madcap waltz, terrifically fast, to a stream-of-consciousness poem built around the imagery of the violin. The central panel of the set is *C'est ainsi que tu es*, which is the most famous of the three and melts the heart. It owes something to Chopin with its languorous rubato; one can hear the composer improvising in an empty room with a tear in his eye (there is a Poulenc piano piece, *Mélancolie*, which conjures the same atmosphere). Weaving in and out of the accompaniment the vocal line has a confessional air and is suffused with the most tender regret culminating in the final words 'Que je t'ai bien connue'. Here is someone whose farewells to lovers are neither violent nor acrimonious, simply sad and philosophical. No one has better understood the tenderness of the promiscuous, the sad inevitability of 'moving on', than Poulenc. And in this respect, as in others, Vilmorin is a kindred spirit.

For three years after the war (1945–8) Poulenc more or less abandoned the idea of cycles in favour of single songs. The greatest of these are *Montparnasse* (Apollinaire, 1945), *Main dominée par le cœur* (Éluard, 1947), and *Le disparu* (Desnos, 1947). There has never been a greater song written about Paris than *Montparnasse*. It pictures the city through the eyes of the young Apollinaire for whom it was the most glamorous place on earth, and we feel the composer's affection for the city in music which almost aches with nostalgia, and affectionate understanding for the mistakes of youth. The setting of 'Il fait un peu lourd et vos cheveux sont longs, | Ô bon petit poète un peu bête et trop blond' strikes me as amongst the most loving lines in all French music; on the recording (which I first heard on a red-labelled HMV 78) one can hear and *feel* the poet caressing his younger alterego in nostalgic affection; this physical gesture is translated into music by Poulenc's left hand which stretches the chord of a tenth under 'blond', while Bernac lingers on the consonant like no one else. One would rush to be a friend of a man who could compose like this, and of course many did. Poulenc had no shortage of friends of both sexes who adored him, but the search for the suitable companion of a lifetime was another matter. In the absence of emotional continuity, Poulenc looked to his religion, to the consolation of his professional duo with Bernac (who was increasingly his confidant and counsellor), and to the poetry of Éluard which always seems to have reminded him of the shining idealism that might have been tarnished by a life of fleeting encounters (however poetic they may have been made to appear in *Allons plus vite*). The Éluard song *Main dominée par le cœur* reminds us of this altruism, and it produces from the composer something approaching absolute music in song terms. It is cleverly constructed to move inevitably from the home key of C major back to C major after a series of arabesques and excursions. It is over in a moment, but it gives an impression of grace and inevitability. The song's title is as good a summing-up of Poulenc's own talent in a single phrase as could be imagined. *Le disparu* was inspired by another aspect of the war—the bravery of members of the Resistance who were tortured and murdered by the Gestapo. This is another Poulencian waltz rendered deadly serious by its subject. The melody has this composer's familiar mix of melancholy and insouciance—one of those tunes, incomprehensible to the Boches, which might have been whistled by a hunted man to warn his colleagues of mortal danger. The poet of this song was Robert Desnos; that he was among these heroes' number is obvious from the text. Another Desnos setting, *Dernier poème* was written towards the end of Poulenc's life. The poem was conceived as early as 1926, and in this form was said to have been smuggled out of Treblinka, written on a match-box.

Not everything Poulenc touched turned to gold. Like Schubert he never wrote a completely uninteresting song, but some were more successful than others. Thus one does not look to the *TROIS CHANSONS DE F. GARCIA-LORCA* (1947) for the most typical Poulenc, but he was not disgraced by this set either. The next major cycle, *CALLIGRAMMES* (Apollinaire, 1948), was once again inspired by the poems the poet wrote during the First World War. This is a difficult work, not really suitable in its subject matter for the female voice, but mightily challenging for any baritone. It is a work that was written for Bernac at the height of his powers, and every note bears witness to the grandeur and pathos of utterance that was at this singer's command, as well as that droll quality which was also uniquely his. The poems are among the most complex that the composer ever set, and on the whole he succeeds yet again in opening a door into Apollinaire's world. A glance at the original poems arranged and printed, according to their subject matter, as a combination of fanciful calligraphy and elusive diagram (as in the trench amidst an encampment of words in the war poem *Bleuet* [POULENC 10]) makes one respect Poulenc's achievement even more; through music he deciphers Apollinaire's intentions, bringing order and illumination to texts which are, in some cases, a seemingly random jumble of words and images. The poetry has an autobiographical slant, and refers to the poet's life as a soldier from 1914 when he was far away from his mistress Marie Laurencin. The coexistence of love and war results in music sometimes lyrical (as in *L'espionne*, *Vers le sud*, and *La grâce exilée*) and sometimes abrasive (the heartless waltz *Mutation*, and *Aussi bien que les cigales*, conceived in the mud of the trenches). The latter song is on a scale seldom attempted, angry and ecstatic in turns, painted with the broadest possible brush. The closing song *Voyage* is another leave-taking, but this time more permanent, for it is the 'journey of Dante' which is described. The composer was now almost 50 and entering that generation which begins to lose friends as a matter of course. The phrase 'C'est ton visage que je ne vois plus' is one of those magical lines (like 'C'est ton portrait' in *C'est ainsi que tu es*) which no other composer could have written. It is full of heart, *almost* sentimental, but also almost unbearably noble and reticent. Who can explain this musical alchemy? Poulenc's imitators sometimes had one or other of his qualities, but it was the combination of them all which produced the inimitable magic.

There are two more song cycles to the words of Éluard. *LA FRAÎCHEUR ET LE FEU* (1950) contains seven relatively short songs. Here a composer of great personal inner contrasts writes a cycle which uses the interplay of slow and fast tempi, and major and minor tonalities, to embody the extremes of the work's title: the contrasts between water and fire, coolness and heat, light and dark are encapsulated by the human polarity of man and woman, difficult and puzzling certainly, but essential for the miracle of life. A theme which is a never-ending source of inspiration for the very heterosexual poet is taken up enthusiastically by a composer whose manifold personal experiences had surprisingly, and unexpectedly, included the birth of a daughter in 1946. The work is remarkable for its sense of unity (the last song recapitulates material from the first), the passionate virtuosity of much of the piano writing, sometimes uncharacteristically reminiscent of Rachmaninov, the quotation from Stravinsky's Serenade in A in the third song, and the hypnotic beauty of the litany which lies at the centre of the work, *Homme au sourire tendre.* If anyone needs convincing that Éluard's poetry had an elevating effect on Poulenc's music they need look no further than this. *LE TRAVAIL DU PEINTRE* (1956) is almost the composer's farewell to this poet (there is a fragile *Une chanson de porcelaine* from 1958). The song texts were taken from *Voir*, an illustrated Éluard anthology which collected together a number of poems about painters which had first appeared in earlier books. Poulenc's music adds yet another dimension—a fascinating mixture of disciplines where one art form attempts to pay tribute to another. This work (devoted to musical sketches of seven painters) would be ideally presented with the aid of back-projections which would enable the audience to see details of the paintings during a performance. It is sad that Éluard did not share Poulenc's enthusiasm for Matisse. Nevertheless we have a monumental *Pablo Picasso*, a capriciously whimsical *Marc Chagall*, a lyrical *Georges Braque*, and so on. The most beautiful song in my opinion is the gravely touching *Jacques Villon*, an artist not nearly as well known as some of the other names in this cycle like *Joan Miró* and *Paul Klee.* In between these works of Éluard, Poulenc returned to Max Jacob for the two songs of *PARISIANA* (1954) which live up to their names in terms of atmosphere, particularly *Vous n'écrivez plus?*—a wickedly witty portrait of a writer down on his luck and attempting to shrug off his temporary employment as bottle-washer at the Café de la Paix.

Poulenc's last song cycle dates from 1960. Bernac had retired in 1959 (both composer and singer had turned 60 within days of each other) and the composer established a duo with the soprano Denise Duval. For her (and dedicated to her young son) he wrote *LA COURTE PAILLE* (Carême), seven short songs which are not quite children's music but about children—rather like the *Kinderszenen* of Schumann. These songs have many of the familiar Poulenc thumbprints (they are popular recital items) but their style seems to indicate a composer who no longer has the energy to tussle with the complexities of great poetry. Especially affecting are the third, fifth, and seventh songs: *La reine de cœur* is a haunting little waltz-like fragment, *Les anges musiciens* has Mozartian echoes (the 'Romanze' from the D minor Piano Concerto K466), and *Lune d'avril* voices the concern of parents for the violence of the modern world. Carême here strikes a CND note from the 1960s which conjures up images of Bertrand Russell marching in the midst of the mélodie, but the poet's misgivings about war and violence remain topical, and always will. The last work which Poulenc wrote for Denise Duval is too long to be considered a conventional song, too short for an opera; it is one of the few modern equivalents of the old nineteenth-century scène. This is *LA DAME DE MONTE-CARLO* (Cocteau, 1961) which is an effective recital piece; given a sympathetic pianist, one does not miss the orchestration to any great extent. (The same cannot be said of that other Cocteau monologue *LA VOIX HUMAINE* for orchestra which is more opera than song; the publishers and composer's heirs seem implacably opposed to performances of this work with piano.)

There are a handful of songs which stand apart from the main body of the mélodies (135 in number) but as some of these pieces are often to be heard on the concert platform they should be mentioned. In 1935 Poulenc published four little comic chansons to the words of Jean Nohain who wrote under the pseudonym Jaboune. Especially delectable if the singer has excellent (and fast) French and an imperturbable memory are *Nous voulons une petite sœur* (a splendid song for Christmas programmes), and *Le petit garçon bien portant.* On a more serious note, but also written for somewhere more commercial than the recital hall, was *À sa guitare* (Ronsard, 1935). This was created for Yvonne Printemps and was performed in Bourdet's play *Margot* about Queen Marguerite of Navarre. *Les chemins de l'amour* (1940) was written for the same singer and appeared in Jean Anouilh's *Léocadia*;

it is a pretty enough waltz, but its success with certain singers in the last fifteen years or so has often been at the expense of the composer's other mélodies which are passed over in favour of an easy hit with the public. There is no doubt that this music has contributed to a general impression of Poulenc as a lightweight; its rightful place is as an encore at a recital where something more serious from the composer has already been heard. A dessert after all is meant to be preceded by a main course. There is one magical song in English where even the composer's mistakes in English prosody ('or in *the* heart') seem more charming than disturbing: this is a setting of Shakespeare's *Tell me where is fancy bred?* (it is dedicated to Miles and Flora, the child characters in Britten's opera *The turn of the screw*). A stray duet entitled *Colloque* (Valéry, 1940) is hardly a typical work; the poet does not appear elsewhere in the composer's output, and it is not really a duet as the two voices never sing together. We often find this type of dialogue song in Schubert who, like Poulenc, seems to have disliked the idea of recital songs for combined voices.

LE BESTIAIRE OU *CORTÈGE D'ORPHÉE*	*THE BOOK OF BEASTS* *OR PROCESSION OF ORPHEUS*

(Guillaume Apollinaire)

I i *Le dromadaire*

	The dromedary
Avec ses quatre dromadaires Don Pedro d'Alfaroubeira Courut le monde et l'admira. Il fit ce que je voudrais faire Si j'avais quatre dromadaires.	With his four dromedaries Don Pedro d'Alfaroubeira Roamed the world and admired it. He did what I would like to do If I had four dromedaries too.

I ii *La chèvre du Thibet*

	The Tibetan goat
Les poils de cette chèvre et même Ceux d'or pour qui prit tant de peine Jason, ne valent rien au prix Des cheveux dont je suis épris.	The hair of this goat and even The golden hair that so preoccupied Jason, cannot match The head of hair I'm smitten with.

I iii *La sauterelle*

	The grasshopper
Voici la fine sauterelle, La nourriture de saint Jean. Puissent mes vers être comme elle, Le régal des meilleures gens.	Behold the delicate grasshopper, The food Saint John was wont to eat. May my verses likewise be A feast for the elite.

1 iv *Le dauphin*

Dauphins, vous jouez dans la mer,
Mais le flot est toujours amer.
Parfois, ma joie éclate-t-elle?
La vie est encore cruelle.

The dolphin

Dolphins, you play in the sea,
Though the waves are briny.
Does my joy at times erupt?
Life is still cruel.

1 v *L'écrevisse*

Incertitude, ô mes délices
Vous et moi nous nous en allons
Comme s'en vont les écrevisses,
À reculons, à reculons.

The crayfish

Uncertainty, O! my delights
You and I we progress
As crayfish progress,
Backwards, backwards.

1 vi *La carpe*

Dans vos viviers, dans vos étangs,
Carpes, que vous vivez longtemps!
Est-ce que la mort vous oublie,
Poissons de la mélancolie.

The carp

In your pools, in your ponds,
Carp, how you live for aeons!
Does death forget you,
Fish of melancholy?

2 *La souris*

(Guillaume Apollinaire)

Belles journées, souris du temps,
Vous rongez peu à peu ma vie.
Dieu! Je vais avoir vingt-huit ans,
Et mal vécus, à mon envie.

The mouse

Lovely days, mouse of time,
Little by little you gnaw at my life.
God! I'll soon be twenty-eight,
Years that are wasted, I fear.

CHANSONS GAILLARDES

(textes anonymes du XVIIe siècle)

NAUGHTY SONGS

(anonymous 17th century poems)

3 i *La maîtresse volage*

Ma maîtresse est volage,
Mon rival est heureux;
S'il a son pucelage,
C'est qu'elle en avait deux.

Et vogue la galère,
Tant qu'elle pourra voguer.

The fickle mistress

My mistress is fickle
My rival fortunate;
If he takes her virginity,
She must have had two.

Let's ride our luck
As long as it lasts!

3 ii *Chanson à boire*

Les rois d'Égypte et de Syrie,
Voulaient qu'on embaumât leurs corps,
Pour durer plus longtemps morts.
   Quelle folie!

Buvons donc selon notre envie,
Il faut boire et reboire encore.
Buvons donc toute notre vie,
Embaumons-nous avant la mort.
   Embaumons-nous;
   Que ce baume est doux.

Drinking song

The kings of Egypt and Syria
Wished to have their bodies embalmed
To last longer dead
   What folly!

So let's drink as we wish,
We must drink and drink again.
So let's drink throughout our life,
Embalm ourselves before we die.
   Embalm ourselves;
   Since this balm is sweet.

3 iii *Madrigal*

Vous êtes belle comme un ange,
Douce comme un petit mouton;
Il n'est point de cœur, Jeanneton,
Qui sous votre loi ne se range.
Mais une fille sans têtons
Est une perdrix sans orange.

Madrigal

You are as beautiful as an angel,
Gentle as a little lamb;
There is not a heart, Jeanneton,
That can resist your spell.
But a girl without tits
Is a partridge without orange.

3 iv *Invocation aux Parques*

Je jure, tant que je vivrai,
De vous aimer, Sylvie.
Parques, qui dans vos mains tenez
Le fil de notre vie,
Allongez, tant que vous pourrez,
Le mien, je vous en prie.

Invocation to the Fates

I swear, as long as I live,
To love you, Sylvie.
Fates, who hold in your hands
The thread of our life,
Make mine as long as you can,
I pray.

3 v *Couplets bachiques*

Je suis tant que dure le jour
Et grave et badin tour à tour.
Quand je vois un flacon sans vin,
Je suis grave, je suis grave,
Est-il tout plein, je suis badin.

Je suis tant que dure le jour
Et grave et badin tour à tour.

Bacchic verses

Throughout the livelong day
I'm sad and merry in turn.
When I see a flagon without wine
I'm sad, I'm sad,
When it's brimful I'm merry.

Throughout the livelong day
I'm sad and merry in turn.

Quand ma femme me tient au lit,
Je suis sage, je suis sage,
Quand ma femme me tient au lit
Je suis sage toute la nuit.

Si catin au lit me tient
Alors je suis badin.
Ah! belle hôtesse, versez-moi du vin.
Je suis badin, badin, badin.

When I'm in bed with my wife,
I behave, I behave,
When I'm in bed with my wife,
I behave all night long.

If I'm in bed with a whore,
Then I'm merry.
Ah! fair hostess, pour me some wine,
I'm merry, merry, merry.

3 vi *L'offrande*

Au dieu d'Amour une pucelle
Offrit un jour une chandelle,
Pour en obtenir un amant.
Le dieu sourit de sa demande
Et lui dit: Belle, en attendant,
Servez-vous toujours de l'offrande.

The offering

A virgin to the god of Love
Offered one day a candle
That she might acquire a lover.
The god smiled at her request
And said to her: while you wait, my pretty thing,
Avail yourself of the offering.

3 vii *La belle jeunesse*

Il faut s'aimer toujours
Et ne s'épouser guère.
Il faut faire l'amour
Sans curé ni notaire.

Cessez, messieurs, d'être épouseurs,
Ne visez qu'aux tirelires,
Ne visez qu'aux tourelours,
Cessez, messieurs, d'être épouseurs,
Ne visez qu'aux cœurs.
Cessez, messieurs, d'être épouseurs,
Holà, messieurs, ne visez plus qu'aux cœurs.

Pourquoi se marier,
Quand les femmes des autres
Ne se font pas prier
Pour devenir les nôtres.
Quand leurs ardeurs,
Quand leurs faveurs,
Cherchent nos tirelires,
Cherchent nos tourelours,
Cherchent nos cœurs.

Gilded youth

You should always love
And seldom marry.
You should make love
Without priest or notary.

Cease, good sirs, your wooing,
Aim only at the you-know-twats,
Aim only at the you-know-twats,
Cease, good sirs, your wooing,
Aim only at the heart,
Cease, good sirs, your wooing,
Enough, aim henceforth only at the heart.

Why marry,
When others' wives
Need no persuading
To become ours.
When their ardours,
when their favours
Seek our you-know-twats,
Seek our you-know-twats,
Seek our hearts.

3 viii *Sérénade*

Avec une si belle main,
Que servent tant de charmes,
Que vous devez du dieu malin
Bien manier les armes!
Et quand cet enfant est chagrin
Bien essuyer ses larmes.

Serenade

With so fair a hand,
Possessed of such charms,
You should easily handle the arrows
Of Cupid, that god-cum-imp!
And when this child is limp
Wipe away his tears.

QUATRE POÈMES

(Guillaume Apollinaire)

FOUR POEMS

4 i *L'Anguille*

Jeanne Houhou la très gentille
Est morte entre des draps très blancs
Pas seule Bébert dit l'Anguille
Narcisse et Hubert le merlan
Près d'elle faisaient leur manille*

Et la crâneuse de Clichy
Aux rouges yeux de dégueulade
Répète Mon eau de Vichy
Va dans le panier à salade
Haha sans faire de chichi

Les yeux dansants comme des anges
Elle riait elle riait
Les yeux très bleus les dents très blanches
Si vous saviez si vous saviez
Tout ce que nous ferons dimanche

The Eel

Jeanne Houhou the very demure
Died between the whitest of sheets
Not alone Bébert alias the Eel
Narcissus and Hubert the whiting
Played manille close by her side

And the swanky Clichy woman
With the vomit-red eyes
Throws up my Vichy water
Goes in the Black Maria
Haha without a fuss

Eyes dancing like angels
She laughed and laughed
Her eyes very blue her teeth very white
If only you knew if only you knew
Just what we'll do on Sunday

4 ii *Carte postale*

† └'ombre de la très douce est évoquée ici,
└ ndolente, et jouant un air dolent aussi:
Ν octurne ou lied mineur qui fait pâmer son âme

⊃ ans l'ombre où ses longs doigts font mourir une
   gamme
⋏ u piano qui geint comme une pauvre femme

Postcard

└ o, the shade of the sweetest being is here evoked,
└ ndolent and playing a doleful air too:
Ν octurne or Lied in the minor key making her soul
   swoon
⊃ own beneath her long fingers in the shade a scale is
   dying
⋏ t the piano which whimpers like a poor woman.

* A card-game, also a cheroot.
† The sixteen year-old sister of Fernand Molina da Silva, whom Apollinaire tried in vain to seduce.

4 iii *Avant le cinéma*

Et puis ce soir on s'en ira
Au cinéma

Les Artistes que sont-ce donc
Ce ne sont plus ceux qui cultivent les Beaux-Arts
Ce ne sont pas ceux qui s'occupent de l'Art
Art poétique ou bien musique
Les Artistes ce sont les acteurs et les actrices

Si nous étions des Artistes
Nous ne dirions pas le cinéma
Nous dirions le ciné

Mais si nous étions de vieux professeurs de province
Nous ne dirions ni ciné ni cinéma
Mais cinématographe

Aussi mon Dieu faut-il avoir du goût

Before the cinema

And then this evening we'll go
To the cinema

But who are these Artistes
No longer those who cultivate the Fine Arts
Nor those concerned with Art
The art of poetry or even music
The Artistes are actors and actresses

If we were Artistes
We would not say the cinema
We would say the ciné

But if we were old professors from the provinces
We would say neither ciné nor cinema
But cinematograph

My word we must have taste and how

4 iv *1904*

À Strasbourg en 1904
J'arrivai pour le lundi gras
À l'hôtel m'assis devant l'âtre
Près d'un chanteur de l'Opéra
Qui ne parlait que de théâtre

La Kellnerine rousse avait
Mis sur sa tête un chapeau rose
Comme Hébé qui les dieux servait
N'en eut jamais ô belles choses
Carvaval chapeau rose Ave!

À Rome à Nice et à Cologne
Dans les fleurs et les confetti
Carnaval j'ai revu ta trogne
Ô roi plus riche et plus gentil
Que Crésus Rothschild et Torlogne

Je soupai d'un peu de foie gras
De chevreuil tendre à la compote
De tartes flans etc.
Un peu de kirsch me ravigote

Que ne t'avais-je entre mes bras

1904

In Strasbourg in 1904
I arrived for Shrove Monday
At the hotel sat down by the fireside
Next to a singer from the Opéra
Who spoke only of theatre

The red-haired Kellnerin had
Put a pink hat on her head
Such as Hebe who served the gods
Never possessed O lovely things
Carnival pink hat all hail!

At Rome Nice and Cologne
In flowers and confetti
Carnival I've seen your fat face again
O king richer and kinder
Than Croesus Rothschild and Torlonia*

I dined on a little foie gras
On tender venison with compote
On baked-custard tarts etc.
A little kirsch jazzes me up

If only I'd had you in my arms

* A wealthy Roman family, ennobled by Pope Pius VII at the start of the 19th century.

TEL JOUR TELLE NUIT
(Paul Éluard)

AS THE DAY SO THE NIGHT

5 i *Bonne journée*

Bonne journée j'ai revu qui je n'oublie pas
Qui je n'oublierai jamais

Et des femmes fugaces dont les yeux
Me faisaient une haie d'honneur
Elles s'enveloppèrent dans leurs sourires

Bonne journée j'ai vu mes amis sans soucis
Les hommes ne pesaient pas lourd
Un qui passait
Son ombre changée en souris
Fuyait dans le ruisseau

J'ai vu le ciel très grand
Le beau regard des gens privés de tout
Plage distante où personne n'aborde

Bonne journée qui commença mélancolique
Noire sous les arbres verts
Mais qui soudain trempée d'aurore
M'entra dans le cœur par surprise.

A good day

A good day again I've seen those I do not forget
Shall never forget

And fleeting women whose eyes
Formed for me a line of honour
They wrapped themselves in their smiles

A good day I've seen my friends free of care
The men did not weigh much
One who was passing by
His shadow metamorphosed into a mouse
Fled into the gutter

I've seen the great wide sky
The beautiful look of the utterly bereft
Distant shores where no man lands

A good day which began mournfully
Black beneath the green trees
But which suddenly drenched with dawn
Invaded my unsuspecting heart.

5 ii *Une ruine coquille vide*

Une ruine coquille vide
Pleure dans son tablier
Les enfants qui jouent autour d'elle
Font moins de bruit que des mouches

La ruine s'en va à tâtons
Chercher ses vaches dans un pré
J'ai vu le jour je vois cela
Sans en avoir honte

Il est minuit comme une flèche
Dans un cœur à la portée
Des folâtres lueurs nocturnes
Qui contredisent le sommeil.

A ruin empty shell

A ruin empty shell
Weeps into its apron
Surrounded by children at play
Making less noise than flies

The ruin gropes along
Seeking her cows in a meadow
I have seen the day I see that
Without feeling shame

It is midnight like an arrow
In a heart within reach
Of the lively nocturnal glimmerings
Which deny sleep.

5 iii *Le front comme un drapeau perdu*

Le front comme un drapeau perdu
Je te traîne quand je suis seul
Dans des rues froides
Des chambres noires
En criant misère

Je ne veux pas les lâcher
Tes mains claires et compliquées
Nées dans le miroir clos des miennes

Tout le reste est parfait
Tout le reste est encore plus inutile
Que la vie

Creuse la terre sous ton ombre

Une nappe d'eau près des seins
Où se noyer
Comme une pierre.

My forehead like a surrendered flag

My forehead like a surrendered flag
I drag you when I am alone
Through cold streets
Dark rooms
Destitute

I will not let them go
Your light and intricate hands
Born in the darkened mirror of my own

All else is perfect
All else is vainer still
Than life

Hollow the earth under your shadow

A sheet of water close to your breasts
To drown in
Like a stone.

5 iv *Une roulotte couverte en tuiles*

Une roulotte couverte en tuiles
Le cheval mort un enfant maître
Pensant le front bleu de haine
À deux seins s'abattant sur lui
Comme deux poings

Ce mélodrame nous arrache
La raison du cœur.

A tiled gypsy wagon

A tiled gypsy wagon
The horse dead a child master
Thinking his forehead blue with hate
For the two breasts beating down on him
Like two fists

This melodrama rips from us
The heart's sanity.

5 v *À toutes brides*

À toutes brides toi dont le fantôme
Piaffe la nuit sur un violon
Viens régner dans les bois

Les verges de l'ouragan
Cherchent leur chemin par chez toi
Tu n'es pas de celles
Dont on invente les désirs

Viens boire un baiser par ici
Cède au feu qui te désespère.

Riding full tilt

Riding full tilt you whose ghost
Prances at night on a violin
Come and reign in the woods

The lashing hurricane
Seeks its path by way of you
You are not of those
Whose desires can be imagined

Come drink a kiss over here
Surrender to the fire that drives you to despair.

5 vi *Une herbe pauvre*

Une herbe pauvre
Sauvage
Apparut dans la neige
C'était la santé
Ma bouche fut émerveillée
Du goût d'air pur qu'elle avait
Elle était fanée.

A meagre blade of grass

A meagre blade of grass
Wild
Appeared in the snow
Health itself
My mouth marvelled
At its taste of pure air
It was withered.

5 vii *Je n'ai envie que de t'aimer*

Je n'ai envie que de t'aimer
Un orage emplit la vallée
Un poisson la rivière

Je t'ai faite à la taille de ma solitude
Le monde entier pour se cacher
Des jours des nuits pour se comprendre

Pour ne plus rien voir dans tes yeux
Que ce que je pense de toi
Et d'un monde à ton image

Et des jours et des nuits réglés par tes paupières.

I long only to love you

I long only to love you
A storm fills the valley
A fish the river

I have formed you to fit my solitude
The whole world to hide in
Days nights to understand each other

To see nothing more in your eyes
But what I think of you
And of a world in your image

And of days and nights ruled by your eyelids.

5 viii *Figure de force brûlante et farouche*

Figure de force brûlante et farouche
Cheveux noirs où l'or coule vers le sud
Aux nuits corrompues
Or englouti étoile impure
Dans un lit jamais partagé

Aux veines des tempes
Comme au bout des seins
La vie se refuse
Les yeux nul ne peut les crever
Boire leur éclat ni leurs larmes
Le sang au-dessus d'eux triomphe pour lui seul

Intraitable démesurée
Inutile
Cette santé bâtit une prison.

Image of force fiery and wild

Image of force fiery and wild
Black hair in which gold flows south
Towards corrupt nights
Gold engulfed tainted star
In a bed never shared

To temple veins
And tips of breasts
Life is denied
No one can blind the eyes
Drink their brilliance or their tears
The blood above them triumphs for itself alone

Obstinate immoderate
Useless
This health builds a prison.

5 ix *Nous avons fait la nuit*

Nous avons fait la nuit je tiens ta main je veille
Je te soutiens de toutes mes forces
Je grave sur un roc l'étoile de tes forces
Sillons profonds où la bonté de ton corps germera

Je me répète ta voix cachée ta voix publique

Je ris encore de l'orgueilleuse
Que tu traites comme une mendiante
Des fous que tu respectes des simples où tu te
    baignes
Et dans ma tête qui se met doucement d'accord avec
    la tienne avec la nuit
Je m'émerveille de l'inconnue que tu deviens
Une inconnue semblable à toi semblable à tout ce
    que j'aime
Qui est toujours nouveau.

We have created night

We have created night I hold your hand I lie awake
I sustain you with all my strength
I engrave on a rock the star of your strength
Deep furrows where your body's goodness will
    germinate
I repeat to myself your hidden voice your public
    voice
I still laugh at the haughty woman
You treat as a beggar
At the fools you respect the simple folk in whom
    you steep yourself
And in my head which gently begins to harmonize
    with yours with the night
I marvel at the stranger you become
A stranger resembling you resembling all I love

Which is ever new.

FIANÇAILLES POUR RIRE

(Louise de Vilmorin)

LIGHT-HEARTED BETROTHAL

6 i *La dame d'André*

André ne connaît pas la dame
Qu'il prend aujourd'hui par la main.
A-t-elle un cœur à lendemains
Et pour le soir a-t-elle une âme?

Au retour d'un bal campagnard
S'en allait-elle en robe vague
Chercher dans les meules la bague
Des fiançailles du hasard?

A-t-elle eu peur, la nuit venue,
Guettée par les ombres d'hier,
Dans son jardin lorsque l'hiver
Entrait par la grande avenue?

Il l'a aimée pour sa couleur
Pour sa bonne humeur de Dimanche.
Pâlira-t-elle aux feuilles blanches
De son album des temps meilleurs?

André's ladyfriend

André does not know the woman
Whose hand he takes today.
Has she a heart for the future,
And for evening has she a soul?

Returning from a country dance,
Did she in her loose-fitting gown
Go and seek in the haystacks
The ring of random betrothal?

Was she afraid, when night fell,
Watched by the ghosts of the past,
In her garden, when winter
Entered by the wide avenue?

He loved her for her complexion,
For her Sunday good humour.
Will she fade on the blank pages
Of his album of better days?

6 ii *Dans l'herbe*

Je ne peux plus rien dire
Ni rien faire pour lui.
Il est mort de sa belle
Il est mort de sa mort belle
Dehors
Sous l'arbre de la Loi
En plein silence
En plein paysage
Dans l'herbe.

Il est mort inaperçu
En criant son passage
En appelant, en m'appelant
Mais comme j'étais loin de lui
Et que sa voix ne portait plus
Il est mort seul dans les bois
Sous son arbre d'enfance
Et je ne peux plus rien dire
Ni rien faire pour lui.

In the grass

I can say nothing more
Do nothing more for him.
He died for his fair one
He died a fair death
Outside
Beneath the tree of Justice
In utter silence
In open country
In the grass.

He died unnoticed
Crying out as he passed away
Calling, calling me
But since I was far from him
And since his voice no longer carried
He died alone in the woods
Beneath his childhood tree
And I can say nothing more
Do nothing more for him.

6 iii *Il vole**

En allant se coucher le soleil
Se reflète au vernis de ma table:
C'est le fromage rond de la fable
Au bec de mes ciseaux de vermeil.

—Mais où est le corbeau?—Il vole.

Je voudrais coudre mais un aimant
Attire à lui toutes mes aiguilles.
Sur la place les joueurs de quilles
De belle en belle passent le temps.

—Mais où est mon amant?—Il vole.

C'est un voleur que j'ai pour amant,
Le corbeau vole et mon amant vole,
Voleur de cœur manque à sa parole
Et voleur de fromage est absent.

—Mais où est le bonheur?—Il vole.

Je pleure sous le saule pleureur
Je mêle mes larmes à ses feuilles
Je pleure car je veux qu'on me veuille
Et je ne plais pas à mon voleur.

—Mais où donc est l'amour?—Il vole.

Stealing away

The sun as it sets
Is reflected in my polished table—
It is the round cheese of the fable
In the beak of my silver scissors.

But where's the crow? Stealing away on its wing.

I'd like to sew but a magnet
Attracts all my needles.
In the square the skittle-players
Pass the time playing game after game.

But where's my lover? Stealing away on his wing.

I've a stealer for lover,
The crow steals away and my lover steals,
The stealer of my heart breaks his word
And the stealer of cheese is absent.

But where is happiness? Stealing away on its wing.

I weep under the weeping willow
I mingle my tears with its leaves
I weep because I want to be wanted
And because my stealer doesn't care for me.

But where can love be? Stealing away on its wing.

* 'Voler' = to fly and to thieve, an almost untranslatable double meaning.

Trouvez la rime à ma déraison
Et par les routes du paysage
Ramenez-moi mon amant volage
Qui prend les cœurs et perd ma raison.

Je veux que mon voleur me vole.

Find the sense in my nonsense
And along the country ways
Bring me back my wayward lover
Who steals hearts and robs me of my senses.

I want my stealer to steal me.

6 iv *Mon cadavre est doux comme un gant*

My corpse is as soft as a glove

Mon cadavre est doux comme un gant
Doux comme un gant de peau glacée
Et mes prunelles effacées
Font de mes yeux des cailloux blancs.

Deux cailloux blancs dans mon visage,
Dans le silence deux muets
Ombrés encore d'un secret
Et lourds du poids mort des images.

Mes doigts tant de fois égarés
Sont joints en attitude sainte
Appuyés au creux de mes plaintes
Au nœud de mon cœur arrêté.

Et mes deux pieds sont les montagnes,
Les deux derniers monts que j'ai vus
À la minute où j'ai perdu
La course que les années gagnent.

Mon souvenir est ressemblant.
Enfants emportez-le bien vite,
Allez, allez, ma vie est dite.
Mon cadavre est doux comme un gant.

My corpse is as soft as a glove
Soft as a glove of glacé kid
And my hidden pupils
Make two white pebbles of my eyes.

Two white pebbles in my face
Two mutes in the silence
Still darkened by a secret
Laden with the dead weight of what they've seen.

My fingers that roved so often
Are joined in a saintly pose
Resting on the hollow of my sorrows
At the centre of my arrested heart.

And my two feet are mountains,
The last two hills I saw
At the very moment I lost the race
That the years always win.

Your memory of me is true—
Children, bear it swiftly away,
Go, go, my life is over.
My corpse is as soft as a glove.

6 v *Violon*

Violin

Couple amoureux aux accents méconnus
Le violon et son joueur me plaisent.
Ah! j'aime ces gémissements tendus
Sur la corde des malaises.
Aux accords sur les cordes des pendus
À l'heure où les Lois se taisent
Le cœur, en forme de fraise,
S'offre à l'amour comme un fruit inconnu.

Loving couple of misapprehended sounds
Violin and player please me.
Ah! I love these long wailings
Stretched on the string of disquiet.
To the sound of strung-up chords
At the hour when Justice is silent
The heart, shaped like a strawberry,
Gives itself to love like an unknown fruit.

6 vi *Fleurs*

Fleurs promises, fleurs tenues dans tes bras,
Fleurs sorties des parenthèses d'un pas,
    Qui t'apportait ces fleurs l'hiver
    Saupoudrés du sable des mers?
Sable de tes baisers, fleurs des amours fanées
Les beaux yeux sont de cendre et dans la cheminée
    Un cœur enrubanné de plaintes
    Brûle avec ses images saintes.

Flowers

Promised flowers, flowers held in your arms,
Flowers from a step's parentheses,
    Who brought you these flowers in winter
    Sprinkled with the sea's sand?
Sand of your kisses, flowers of faded loves
Your lovely eyes are ashes and in the hearth
    A moan-beribboned heart
    Burns with its sacred images.

DEUX MÉLODIES

(Guillaume Apollinaire)

TWO MÉLODIES

7 i *Dans le jardin d'Anna*

Certes si nous avions vécu en l'an dix-sept cent
    soixante

Est-ce bien la date que vous déchiffrez Anna sur ce
    banc de pierre

Et que par malheur j'eusse été allemand
Mais que par bonheur j'eusse été près de vous
Nous aurions parlé d'amour de façon imprécise
Presque toujours en français
Et pendue éperdument à mon bras
Vous m'auriez écouté vous parler de Pythagoras
En pensant aussi au café qu'on prendrait
Dans une demi-heure

Et l'automne eût été pareil à cet automne
Que l'épine-vinette et les pampres couronnent

Et brusquement parfois j'eusse salué très bas

De nobles dames grasses et langoureuses

J'aurais dégusté lentement et tout seul
Pendant de longues soirées
Le tokay épais ou la malvoisie
J'aurais mis mon habit espagnol
Pour aller sur la route par laquelle
Arrive dans son vieux carrosse
Ma grand-mère qui se refuse à comprendre
    l'allemand

In Anna's garden

Of course had we lived in the year seventeen
    hundred and sixty

That is I take it the date you decipher Anna on this
    stone bench

And had I by misfortune been German
But had by good fortune been by your side
We would have spoken darkly of love
Almost always in French
And hanging infatuated on my arm
You would have listened to me talk of Pythagoras
While thinking also of the coffee we'd take
In half an hour

And the autumn would have resembled this autumn
Garlanded with berberis and vine

And sometimes I'd have bowed abruptly and very
    low
To corpulent languorous noblewomen

I'd have sipped slowly and quite alone
Through long evenings
Rich tokay or malmsey
I'd have donned my Spanish coat
To go out on the road on which
Will arrive in her ancient carriage
My grandmother who refuses to understand
    German

J'aurais écrit des vers pleins de mythologie
Sur vos seins la vie champêtre et sur les dames
Des alentours

J'aurais souvent cassé ma canne
Sur le dos d'un paysan

J'aurais aimé entendre de la musique en mangeant
Du jambon

J'aurais juré en allemand je vous le jure
Lorsque vous m'auriez surpris embrassant à pleine
    bouche

Cette servante rousse

Vous m'auriez pardonné dans le bois aux myrtilles

J'aurais fredonné un moment
Puis nous aurions écouté longtemps les bruits du
    crépuscule

I'd have written lines full of mythology
On your breasts on pastoral life and on the ladies
Of the neighbourhood

I'd have often broken my walking-stick
On a peasant's back

I'd have liked to hear music while eating
Ham

I'd have sworn in German I swear
When you caught me kissing on the lips

This red-haired servant-girl

You would have forgiven me in the myrtle wood

I'd have hummed for a moment
Then we'd have listened long to the sounds of
    twilight

7 ii *Allons plus vite*

Et le soir vient et les lys meurent
    Regarde ma douleur beau ciel qui me l'envoies
        Une nuit de mélancolie

                Enfant souris ô sœur écoute
Pauvres marchez sur la grand-route
        Ô menteuse forêt qui surgis à ma voix
                Les flammes qui brûlent les âmes

    Sur le Boulevard de Grenelle*
Les ouvriers et les patrons
        Arbres de mai cette dentelle
        Ne fais donc pas le fanfaron
    Allons plus vite nom de Dieu
        Allons plus vite

Tous les poteaux télégraphiques
Viennent là-bas le long du quai
Sur son sein notre République
A mis ce bouquet de muguet
Qui poussait dru le long du quai
        Allons plus vite nom de Dieu
            Allons plus vite

* A street in Montmartre notorious for its prostitution.

Move along

And evening comes and lilies die
    See my suffering beautiful sky you who send me
        A night of melancholy

                Smile child O sister listen
Walk wretches on the high road
        O false forest summoned by my voice
                The flames that burn souls

    On the boulevard de Grenelle
Workers and employers
        Maytime trees this lace
        Don't flaunt it
    Move along for God's sake
            Move along

All the telegraph poles
Stretch there along the quay
Our Republic has placed on her breast
This lily-of-the-valley bouquet
That grew thick and fast along the quay
        Move along for God's sake
            Move along

La bouche en cœur Pauline honteuse
        Les ouvriers et les patrons
Oui-dà oui-dà belle endormeuse
Ton frère
      Allons plus vite nom de Dieu
        Allons plus vite

Shameful Pauline with Cupid's bow lips
        Workers and employers
Yes indeed yes indeed dissembling beauty
Your brother
      Move along for God's sake
        Move along

8 *La Grenouillère**
(Guillaume Apollinaire)

The Froggery

Au bord de l'île on voit
Les canots vides qui s'entre-cognent
Et maintenant
Ni le dimanche ni les jours de la semaine
Ni les peintres ni Maupassant ne se promènent
Bras nus sur leurs canots avec des femmes à grosses
        poitrines
      Et bêtes comme chou
Petits bateaux vous me faites bien de la peine
Au bord de l'île

By the island's shore you see
The empty boats knock against each other
And now
Neither on Sundays nor weekdays
Neither painters nor Maupassant go boating
Bare-armed with their big-breasted women

        as stupid as cabbages
Little boats you make me truly sad
By the island's shore

9 *Priez pour paix*
(Charles d'Orléans)

Pray for peace

Priez pour paix, douce Vierge Marie,
Reyne des cieulx et du monde maîtresse,
Faictes prier, par vostre courtoisie,
Saints et Saintes et prenez vostre adresse
Vers vostre fils, requérant sa haultesse
Qu'il Lui plaise son peuple regarder,
Que de son sang a voulu racheter,
En déboutant guerre qui tout desvoye;
De prières ne vous veuillez lasser:
Priez pour paix, le vrai trésor de joye!

Pray for peace, sweet Virgin Mary,
Queen of heaven and Mistress of this world,
Cause, by your courtesy, all the saints
To pray, and address
Your Son, beseeching his high Majesty
To deign to look upon his people,
Whom he wished to redeem with his blood,
Banishing war which disrupts all;
Pray untiringly, we beg of you:
Pray for peace, the true treasure of joy!

---

* A riverside bathing and boating resort, popular among artists, writers, and weekend trippers. It was situated on the Île de Croissy and had a floating restaurant, seen in paintings by Monet and Renoir.

10 *Bleuet**

(Guillaume Apollinaire)

Jeune homme
De vingt ans
Qui as vu des choses si affreuses
Que penses-tu des hommes de ton enfance

Tu   Tu
   as
      vu   connais
      la
         mort   la bravoure et la ruse
            en
               face
                  plus
                     de
                        cent
                           fois
                              tu
                                 ne
                                    sais
Transmets ton intrépidité   pas
                                          ce
À ceux qui viendront   que
                                               c'est
      Après toi   que
                                                 la
                                                 vie

Jeune homme
Tu es joyeux ta mémoire est ensanglantée
      Ton âme est rouge aussi
            De joie
Tu as absorbé la vie de ceux qui sont morts près de toi

      Tu as de la décision
Il est 17 heures et tu saurais
            Mourir
Sinon mieux que tes aînés
      Du moins plus pieusement
      Car tu connais mieux la mort que la vie
      Ô douceur d'autrefois
            Lenteur immémoriale

Rookie

Young man
Of twenty
You who have seen such terrible things
What do you think of the men from your childhood

You   You
   have
      faced   know
         death
            more   what bravery is and cunning
               than
                  a
                     hundred
                        times
                           you
                              do
                                 not
                                    know
                                       what
Hand down your fearlessness   life
                                              is
To those who shall come

      After you

      Young man
You are joyous your memory is steeped in blood
      Your soul is red also
            With joy
You have absorbed the life of those who died beside you

      You are resolute
It is 1700 hrs and you would know
            How to die
If not better than your elders
      At least with greater piety
      For you are better acquainted with death than life
      O sweetness of bygone days
            Slow-moving beyond all memory

---

* An untranslatable conflation of ideas. 'Un bleu' is a raw recruit; 'un bleuet' (or 'bluet') a cornflower.

BANALITÉS

(Guillaume Apollinaire)

BANALITIES

II i   *Chanson d'Orkenise**

Par les portes d'Orkenise
Veut entrer un charretier.
Par les portes d'Orkenise
Veut sortir un va-nu-pieds.

Et les gardes de la ville
Courant sus au va-nu-pieds:
'—Qu'emportes-tu de la ville?'
'—J'y laisse mon cœur entier.'

Et les gardes de la ville
Courant sus au charretier:
'—Qu'apportes-tu dans la ville?'
'—Mon cœur pour me marier.'

Que de cœurs dans Orkenise!
Les gardes riaient, riaient,
Va-nu-pieds la route est grise,
L'amour grise, ô charretier.

Les beaux gardes de la ville
Tricotaient superbement;
Puis, les portes de la ville,
Se fermèrent lentement.

Song of Orkenise

Through the gates of Orkenise
A waggoner wants to enter.
Through the gates of Orkenise
A vagabond wants to leave.

And the sentries guarding the town
Rush up to the vagabond:
'What are you taking from the town?'
'I'm leaving my whole heart behind.'

And the sentries guarding the town
Rush up to the waggoner:
'What are you carrying into the town?'
'My heart in order to marry.'

So many hearts in Orkenise!
The sentries laughed and laughed:
Vagabond, the road's not merry,
Love makes you merry, O waggoner!

The handsome sentries guarding the town
Knitted vaingloriously;
The gates of the town then
Slowly closed.

II ii   *Hôtel*

Ma chambre a la forme d'une cage
Le soleil passe son bras par la fenêtre
Mais moi qui veux fumer pour faire des mirages
J'allume au feu du jour ma cigarette
Je ne veux pas travailler je veux fumer

Hotel

My room is shaped like a cage
The sun slips its arm through the window
But I who want to smoke to make mirages
I light my cigarette on daylight's fire
I do not want to work I want to smoke

II iii   *Fagnes de Wallonie*

Tant de tristesses plénières
Prirent mon cœur aux fagnes désolées
Quand las j'ai reposé dans les sapinières
Le poids de kilomètres pendant que râlait
Le vent d'ouest

* A road in Autun leading to the Roman gate.

Walloon moss-hags

So much utter sadness
Seized my heart in the desolate upland moss-hags
When weary I set down in the fir plantation
The weight of kilometres to the roar
Of the west wind

J'avais quitté le joli bois	I had left the pretty wood
Les écureuils y sont restés	The squirrels stayed there
Ma pipe essayait de faire des nuages	My pipe tried to make clouds
Au ciel	In the sky
Qui restait pur obstinément	Which stubbornly stayed clear
Je n'ai confié aucun secret sinon une chanson	I confided no secret but an enigmatic song
énigmatique	
Aux tourbières humides	To the dank peat-bogs
Les bruyères fleurant le miel	The honey-fragrant heather
Attiraient les abeilles	Attracted the bees
Et mes pieds endoloris	And my sore feet
Foulaient les myrtilles et les airelles	Crushed bilberries and whortleberries
Tendrement mariée	Tenderly united
Nord	North
Nord	North
La vie s'y tord	Life is gnarled there
En arbres forts	In strong trees
Et tors	And twisted
La vie y mord	Life there bites
La mort	Death
À belles dents	Voraciously
Quand bruit le vent	When the wind howls

II iv *Voyage à Paris*   *Trip to Paris*

Ah! la charmante chose	Oh! how delightful
Quitter un pays morose	To leave a dismal
Pour Paris	Place for Paris
Paris joli	Charming Paris
Qu'un jour	That one day
Dut créer l'Amour	Love must have made
Ah! la charmante chose	Oh! how delightful
Quitter un pays morose	To leave a dismal
Pour Paris	Place for Paris

II v *Sanglots*

Notre amour est réglé par les calmes étoiles
Or nous savons qu'en nous beaucoup d'hommes
    respirent
Qui vinrent de très loin et sont un sous nos fronts

C'est la chanson des rêveurs
Qui s'étaient arraché le cœur
Et le portaient dans la main droite
    Souviens-t'en cher orgueil de tous ces souvenirs

    Des marins qui chantaient comme des
        conquérants
    Des gouffres de Thulé* des tendres cieux d'Ophir†
    Des malades maudits de ceux qui fuient leur
        ombre
    Et du retour joyeux des heureux émigrants
De ce cœur il coulait du sang
Et le rêveur allait pensant
À sa blessure délicate
    Tu ne briseras pas la chaîne de ces causes
Et douloureuse et nous disait
    Qui sont les effets d'autres causes
Mon pauvre cœur mon cœur brisé
Pareil au cœur de tous les hommes
    Voici voici nos mains que la vie fit esclaves
Est mort d'amour ou c'est tout comme
Est mort d'amour et le voici   Ainsi vont toutes
    choses
Arrachez donc le vôtre aussi
    Et rien ne sera libre jusqu'à la fin des temps
    Laissons tout aux morts
    Et cachons nos sanglots

Sobs

Our love is governed by the calm stars
Now we know that in us many men have their
    being
Who came from afar and are one beneath our
    brows
It is the song of the dreamers
Who tore out their hearts
And carried them in their right hands
    Remember dear pride all these memories

    The sailors who sang like conquerors

    The chasms of Thule the gentle Ophir skies
    The accursed sick those who flee their shadows

    And the joyous return of happy emigrants
This heart ran with blood
And the dreamer kept thinking
Of his delicate wound
    You shall not break the chain of these causes
Of his painful wound and said to us
    Which are the effects of other causes
My poor heart my broken heart
Like the hearts of all men
    Here here are our hands that life enslaved
Has died of love or so it seems
Has died of love and here it is   Such is the fate of
    all things
So tear out yours too
    And nothing will be free till the end of time
    Let us leave all to the dead
    And conceal our sobs

CHANSONS VILLAGEOISES

(Maurice Fombeure)

12 i *Chanson du clair-tamis*

Où le bedeau a passé
Dans les papavéracées
Où le bedeau a passé
Passera le marguillier

VILLAGE SONGS

Song of the fine sieve

Where the verger has gone
Among the poppies
Where the verger has gone
The churchwarden too will go

---

* An unidentified island in the North Sea, called 'Ultima' by the ancients, because of its great distance from the continent.
† An unidentified region celebrated in ancient times and the Old Testament for its gold and precious stones.

Notre vidame est mort
Les jolis yeux l'ont tué
Pleurons son heureux sort
En terre et enterré
Et la croix de Lorraine
Sur son pourpoint doré

Ils l'ont couché dans l'herbe
Son grand sabre dessous
Un oiseau dans les branches
A crié: 'Coucou'

C'est demain dimanche
C'est fête chez nous

Au son de la clarinette
Le piston par en-dessous
La piquette, la musette
Les plus vieux sont les plus saoûls

Grand'mère à cloche-lunettes
Sur ses jambes de vingt ans
Vienne le printemps mignonne
Vienne le printemps

Où la grenouille a passé
Sous les renonculacées
Où la grenouille a passé
Passera le scarabée.

Our lord and master is dead
Pretty eyes have killed him
Let us bewail his happy lot
In earth and interred
And the cross of Lorraine
On his gilded doublet

They have laid him in the grass
His great sword beneath him
A bird in the branches
Cried: 'Cuckoo'

It's Sunday tomorrow
It's the day of our fair

To the sound of the clarinet
And the cornet in the bass
Coarse wine accordion
The oldest are the drunkest

Grandmother with specs askew
On her twenty-year-old legs
Let the springtime come my sweet
Let the springtime come

Where the frog has gone
In amongst the buttercups
Where the frog has gone
The beetle too will go.

12 ii *Les gars qui vont à la fête*

Les gars qui vont à la fête
Ont mis la fleur au chapeau

Pour y boire chopinette
Y goûter le vin nouveau

Y tirer la carabine
Y sucer le berlingot

Les gars qui vont à la fête
Ont mis la fleur au chapeau

Sont rasés à la cuiller
Sont raclés dessous la peau

The lads who're off to the fair

The lads who're off to the fair
Have stuck flowers in their hats

They're off to booze
And taste new wine

To fire rifles
To suck sweets

The lads who're off to the fair
Have stuck flowers in their hats

They've shaved their faces down to the skin
They've scraped beneath the skin

Ont passé la blouse neuve	And put on new smocks
Le faux-col en cellulo	And detachable collars of celluloid
Les gars qui vont à la fête	The lads who're off to the fair
Ont mis la fleur au chapeau	Have stuck flowers in their hats
Y faire danser les filles	They'll dance with the girls
Chez Julien le violoneur	At Julian the fiddler's
Des polkas et des quadrilles	Polkas and quadrilles
Et le pas des patineurs	And the skaters' dance
Le piston la clarinette	Cornet and clarinet
Attendrissent les costauds	Move the machos
Les gars qui vont à la fête	The lads who're off to the fair
Ont mis la fleur au chapeau	Have stuck flowers in their hats
Quand ils ont bu, se disputent	When they've drunk they argue
Et se cognent sur la peau	And beat each other up
Puis vont culbuter les filles	And go to tumble girls
Au fossé sous les ormeaux	In the ditch beneath the elms
Les gars qui vont à la fête	The lads who're off to the fair
Ont mis la fleur au chapeau	Have stuck flowers in their hats
Reboivent puis se rebattent	They drink again and fight again
Jusqu'au chant du premier jô	Till the dawn chorus is heard
Le lendemain on en trouve	The next day some are found
Sont couchés dans le ruisseau	Sleeping in the ditch
Les gars qui vont à la fête	The lads who're off to the fair
Ont mis la fleur au chapeau.	Have stuck flowers in their hats.

12 iii *C'est le joli printemps* — *It's the sweet springtime*

C'est le joli printemps	It's the sweet springtime
Qui fait sortir les filles	That lures the lasses out
C'est le joli printemps	It's the sweet springtime
Qui fait briller le temps	That brings the fine weather
J'y vais à la fontaine	I'm off to the fountain
C'est le joli printemps	It's the sweet springtime
Trouver celle qui m'aime	To find the girl who loves me
Celle que j'aime tant	The girl I love so much

C'est dans le mois d'avril
Qu'on promet pour longtemps
C'est le joli printemps
Qui fait sortir les filles

La fille et le galant
Pour danser le quadrille
C'est le joli printemps
Qui fait briller le temps

Aussi profitez-en
Jeunes gens, jeunes filles
C'est le joli printemps
Qui fait briller le temps

Car le joli printemps
C'est le temps d'une aiguille
Car le joli printemps
Ne dure pas longtemps.

It's in the month of April
That lasting vows are made
It's the sweet springtime
That lures the lasses out

The lass and her lover
To dance the quadrille
It's the sweet springtime
That brings the fine weather

So make the most of it
Young lads and young lasses
It's the sweet springtime
That brings the fine weather

For the sweet springtime
Is over in a trice
For the sweet springtime
Does not last for long.

12 iv *Le mendiant*

Jean Martin prit sa besace
Vive le passant qui passe
Jean Martin prit sa besace
Son bâton de cornouiller

S'en fut au moutier mendier
Vive le passant qui passe
Va-t-en dit le père moine
N'aimons pas les va-nu-pieds

S'en fut en ville mendier
Vive le passant qui passe
Épiciers et taverniers
Qui mangez la soupe grasse
Et qui vous chauffez les pieds
Puis couchez près de vos femmes
Au clair feu de la veillée

Jean Martin l'avez chassé
Vive le passant qui passe
On l'a trouvé sur la glace
Jean Martin a trépassé

Tremblez les gros et les moines
Vive le passant qui passe
Tremblez ah! maudite race
Qui n'avez point de pitié

The beggar

Jean Martin picked up his sack
Good health to travellers all
Jean Martin picked up his sack
And his dogwood staff

Off to the monastery he went to beg
Good health to travellers all
Away with you the friar said
We do not care for tramps

And off to the town he went to beg
Good health to travellers all
Grocers and publicans
Who eat meat soup
And warm your feet
Then sleep with your wives
By the evening fire

You've driven away Jean Martin
Good health to travellers all
They found him lying on the ice
Jean Martin passed away

May friars and fat men shake with fear
Good health to travellers all
Tremble ah! accursed tribe
Devoid of all compassion

Un jour prenez garde ô race
Les Jean Martin seront en masse
Aux bâtons de cournouiller

Il vous crè'ront la paillasse
Puis ils violeront vos garces
Et chausseront vos souliers

Jean Martin prends ta besace
Ton bâton de cornouiller.

One day O tribe be on your guard
The Jean Martins will all rise up
With their dogwood staffs

They'll stab you in the gut
Then rape your women
And put on your shoes

Jean Martin pick up your sack
And your dogwood staff.

12 v *Chanson de la fille frivole*

Song of the flighty girl

Ah dit la fille frivole
Que le vent y vire y vole
Mes canards vont sur l'étang
Belle lune de printemps

Ah dit la fille frivole
Que le vent y vire y vole
Sous les vergers éclatants
Belle lune de printemps

Ah dit la fille frivole
Que le vent y vire y vole
Et dans les buissons chantants
Belle lune de printemps

Ah dit la fille frivole
Que le vent y vire y vole
Je vais trouver mes amants
Sous la lune de printemps

Ah dit la fille frivole
Que le vent y vire y vole
L'âge vient trop vitement
Sous la lune de printemps

Ah dit la fille frivole
Que le vent y vire y vole
Plus tard soucis et tourments
Sous la lune de printemps

Ah dit la fille frivole
Que le vent y vire y vole
Aujourd'hui guérissez-m'en
Belle lune de printemps

Ah said the flighty girl
Let the wind veer round and blow
My ducks are swimming on the pond
Lovely springtime moon

Ah said the flighty girl
Let the wind veer round and blow
Beneath the burgeoning orchards
Lovely springtime moon

Ah said the flighty girl
Let the wind veer round and blow
And in the singing bushes
Lovely springtime moon

Ah said the flighty girl
Let the wind veer round and blow
I'm off to find my lovers
Beneath the springtime moon

Ah said the flighty girl
Let the wind veer round and blow
Old age comes too quickly
Beneath the springtime moon

Ah said the flighty girl
Let the wind veer round and blow
Leave cares and torments till later
Beneath the springtime moon

Ah said the flighty girl
Let the wind veer round and blow
Cure me of them now today
Lovely springtime moon

Ah dit la fille frivole
Que le vent y vire y vole
Baisez-moi bien tendrement
Sous la lune de printemps.

Ah said the flighty girl
Let the wind veer round and blow
Kiss me very tenderly
Beneath the springtime moon.

12 vi *Le retour du sergent*

The return of the sergeant

Le sergent s'en revient de guerre
Les pieds gonflés sifflant du nez
Le sergent s'en revient de guerre
Entre les buissons étonnés

The sergeant returns from the war
Feet swollen nose sniffling
The sergeant returns from the war
Along the astonished bushes

A gagné la croix de Saint-Georges
Les pieds gonflés sifflant du nez
A gagné la croix de Saint-Georges
Son pécule a sous son bonnet

He's won the Saint George Cross
Feet swollen nose sniffling
He's won the Saint George Cross
Gratuity beneath his cap

Bourre sa pipe en terre rouge
Les pieds gonflés sifflant du nez
Bourre sa pipe en terre rouge
Puis soudain se met à pleurer

He fills his pipe of red clay
Feet swollen nose sniffling
He fills his pipe of red clay
Then suddenly begins to cry

Il revoit tous ses copains morts
Les pieds gonflés sifflant du nez
Il revoit tous ses copains morts
Qui sont pourris dans les guérets

He sees again all his dead mates
Feet swollen nose sniffling
He sees again all his dead mates
Who have rotted in the fields

Ils ne verront plus leur village
Les pieds gonflés sifflant du nez
Ils ne verront plus leur village
Ni le calme bleu des fumées

They shall not see their village again
Feet swollen nose sniffling
They shall not see their village again
Nor the smoke of peaceful blue

Les fiancées va marche ou crève
Les pieds gonflés sifflant du nez
Envolées comme dans un rêve
Les copains s'les sont envoyées

Their sweethearts struggle on or snuff it
Feet swollen nose sniffling
Put to flight as in a dream
Their mates have ravished them

Et le sergent verse une larme
Les pieds gonflés sifflant du nez
Et le sergent verse une larme
Le long des buissons étonnés.

And the sergeant sheds a tear
Feet swollen nose sniffling
And the sergeant sheds a tear
By the astonished bushes.

DEUX POÈMES DE LOUIS ARAGON   TWO POEMS OF LOUIS ARAGON

13 i   C*   C

J'ai traversé les ponts de Cé   I have crossed the bridges of Cé
C'est là que tout a commencé   It is there that everything began

Une chanson des temps passés   A song of bygone days
Parle d'un chevalier blessé   Tells of a knight who injured lay

D'une rose sur la chaussée   Of a rose upon the carriage-way
Et d'un corsage délacé   And a bodice with an unlaced stay

Du château d'un duc insensé   And the castle of an insane duke
Et des cygnes dans les fossés   And swans in castle moats

De la prairie où vient danser   And of the meadow where
Une éternelle fiancée   An eternal fiancée comes to dance

Et j'ai bu comme un lait glacé   And I have drunk the long lay
Le long lai des gloires faussées   Of false glories like icy milk

La Loire emporte mes pensées   The Loire bears my thoughts away
Avec les voitures versées   With the overturned jeeps

Et les armes désamorcées   And the unprimed arms
Et les larmes mal effacées   And the ill-dried tears

Ô ma France ô ma délaissée   O my France O my forsaken one
J'ai traversé les ponts de Cé   I have crossed the bridges of Cé

13 ii   Fêtes galantes   Fêtes galantes

On voit des marquis sur des bicyclettes   You see fops on cycles
On voit des marlous en cheval-jupon   You see pimps in kilts
On voit des morveux avec des voilettes   You see whipper-snappers with veils
On voit les pompiers brûler les pompons   You see firemen burning their pompoms

On voit des mots jetés à la voirie   You see words hurled on the garbage heap
On voit des mots élevés au pavois   You see words praised to the skies
On voit les pieds des enfants de Marie   You see the feet of orphan children
On voit le dos des diseuses à voix   You see the backs of cabaret singers

On voit des voitures à gazogène   You see cars run on gazogene
On voit aussi des voitures à bras   You see handcarts too
On voit des lascars que les longs nez gênent   You see sly fellows hindered by long noses
On voit des coïons de dix-huit carats   You see unmitigated idiots

---

* Les Ponts-de-Cé, near Angers, have been the scene of repeated conflicts from the Roman period on. In May 1940 thousands of French men and women fled over the bridge to escape the advancing Germans.

On voit ici ce que l'on voit ailleurs
On voit des demoiselles dévoyées
On voit des voyous On voit des voyeurs
On voit sous les ponts passer des noyés

On voit chômer les marchands de chaussures
On voit mourir d'ennui les mireurs d'œufs
On voit péricliter les valeurs sûres
Et fuir la vie à la six-quatre-deux

You see here what you see everywhere
You see girls who are led astray
You see guttersnipes you see Peeping Toms
You see drowned corpses float beneath bridges

You see out-of-work shoemakers
You see egg-candlers bored to death
You see securities tumble
And life rushing pell-mell by

MÉTAMORPHOSES

(Louise de Vilmorin)

MÉTAMORPHOSES

14 i *Reine des mouettes*

Reine des mouettes, mon orpheline,
Je t'ai vue rose, je m'en souviens,
Sous les brumes mousselines
    De ton deuil ancien.

Rose d'aimer le baiser qui chagrine
Tu te laissais accorder à mes mains
Sous les brumes mousselines
    Voiles de nos liens.

Rougis, rougis, mon baiser te devine
Mouette prise aux nœuds des grands chemins.

Reine des mouettes, mon orpheline,
Tu étais rose accordée à mes mains
Rose sous les mousselines
    Et je m'en souviens.

Queen of seagulls

Queen of seagulls, my little orphan,
I recall you blushing pink,
Beneath the muslin mists
    Of your ancient sorrow.

Blushing pink at the kiss which provokes you,
You surrendered to my hands
Beneath the muslin mists,
    Veils of the bond between us.

Blush, blush, my kiss finds you out,
Seagull caught where great highways meet.

Queen of seagulls, my little orphan,
You blushed pink, surrendered to my hands,
Pink beneath the muslin
    And I recall the moment.

14 ii *C'est ainsi que tu es*

Ta chair, d'âme mêlée,
Chevelure emmêlée,
Ton pied courant le temps,
Ton ombre qui s'étend
Et murmure à ma tempe.
Voilà, c'est ton portrait,
C'est ainsi que tu es,
Et je veux te l'écrire
Pour que la nuit venue,
Tu puisses croire et dire,
Que je t'ai bien connue.

That is how you are

Your flesh, mingled with soul,
Your tangled hair,
Your feet pursuing time,
Your shadow which stretches
And whispers close to my temple.
There, that is your portrait,
That is how you are,
And I shall write it down for you
So that when night comes,
You may believe and say
That I knew you well.

14 iii *Paganini*

Violon hippocampe et sirène
Berceau des cœurs cœur et berceau
Larmes de Marie Madeleine
Soupir d'une Reine
     Écho

Violon orgueil des mains légères
Départ à cheval sur les eaux
Amour chevauchant le mystère
Voleur en prière
     Oiseau

Violon femme morganatique
Chat botté courant la forêt
Puits des vérités lunatiques
Confession publique
     Corset

Violon alcool de l'âme en peine
Préférence muscle du soir
Épaules des saisons soudaines
Feuille de chêne
     Miroir

Violon chevalier du silence
Jouet évadé du bonheur
Poitrine des mille présences
Bateau de plaisance
     Chasseur.

Paganini

Violin sea-horse and siren,
Cradle of hearts heart and cradle
Tears of Mary Magdalene
A queen's sigh
     Echo

Violin pride of delicate hands
Departure on horseback over the waters
Love astride mystery
Thief at prayer
     Bird

Violin morganatic wife
Puss-in-Boots ranging the forest
Well of capricious truths
Public confession
     Corset

Violin alcohol of the troubled soul
Preference muscle of the evening
Shoulders of sudden seasons
Oak-leaf
     Mirror

Violin knight of silence
Toy escaped from happiness,
Breast of a thousand presences
Pleasure-boat
     Hunter.

15 *Montparnasse*

(Guillaume Apollinaire)

Ô porte de l'hôtel avec deux plantes vertes
Vertes qui jamais
Ne porteront de fleurs
Où sont mes fruits Où me planté-je
Ô porte de l'hôtel un ange est devant toi
Distribuant des prospectus
On n'a jamais si bien défendu la vertu
Donnez-moi pour toujours une chambre à la
     semaine
Ange barbu vous êtes en réalité
Un poète lyrique d'Allemagne
Qui voulez connaître Paris

Montparnasse

O hotel door with two green plants
Green which shall never
Bear any flowers
Where are my fruits Where did I plant myself
O hotel door an angel stands before you
Distributing prospectuses
Virtue has never been so well defended
Give me for ever a room by the week

Bearded angel you are in reality
A lyric poet from Germany
Who wants to know Paris

Vous connaissez de son pavé
Ces raies sur lesquelles il ne faut pas que l'on marche
       Et vous rêvez
D'aller passer votre Dimanche à Garches*

Il fait un peu lourd et vos cheveux sont longs
Ô bon petit poète un peu bête et trop blond
Vos yeux ressemblent tant à ces deux grands ballons
Qui s'en vont dans l'air pur
À l'aventure

You know its pavements'
Lines where you must not step
       And you dream
Of spending your Sunday at Garches

It's somewhat oppressive and your hair is long
O good little poet rather stupid and too blonde
Your eyes so resemble those two big balloons
Which float away in the pure air
Haphazardly

16 Main dominée par le cœur
(Paul Éluard)

Hand ruled by the heart

Main dominée par le cœur
Cœur dominé par le lion
Lion dominé par l'oiseau

L'oiseau qu'efface un nuage
Le lion que le désert grise
Le cœur que la mort habite
La main refermée en vain

Aucun secours tout m'échappe
Je vois ce qui disparaît
Je comprends que je n'ai rien
Et je m'imagine à peine

Entre les murs une absence
Puis l'exil dans les ténèbres
Les yeux purs la tête inerte.

Hand ruled by the heart
Heart ruled by the lion
Lion ruled by the bird

The bird a cloud obliterates
The lion the desert intoxicates
The heart where death abides
The hand closed in vain

No succour all escapes me
I see what vanishes
I realize I have nothing
And I barely imagine myself

Between the walls an absence
Then exile into darkness
The eyes pure the head inert.

17 Le disparu
(Robert Desnos)

Gone missing

Je n'aime plus la rue Saint-Martin
Depuis qu'André Platard l'a quittée.
Je n'aime plus la rue Saint-Martin,
Je n'aime rien, pas même le vin.

Je n'aime plus la rue Saint-Martin
Depuis qu'André Platard l'a quittée.
C'est mon ami, c'est mon copain.
Nous partagions la chambre et le pain.
Je n'aime plus la rue Saint-Martin.

I no longer care for rue Saint-Martin
Since André Platard left it.
I no longer care for rue Saint-Martin,
I care for nothing not even wine.

I no longer care for rue Saint-Martin
Since André Platard left it.
He's my friend, he's my mate,
We used to share a room and bread.
I no longer care for rue Saint-Martin.

* A residential suburb of Paris.

C'est mon ami, c'est mon copain.
Il a disparu un matin,
Ils l'ont emmené, on ne sait plus rien.
On ne l'a plus revu dans la rue Saint-Martin.

Pas la peine d'implorer les saints.
Saints Merri, Jacques, Gervais et Martin,
Pas même Valérien qui se cache sur la colline.
Le temps passe, on ne sait rien.
André Platard a quitté la rue Saint-Martin.

He's my friend, he's my mate,
He went missing one morning,
They took him away, no more is known,
He was seen no more in rue Saint-Martin.

No point in imploring the saints,
Saints Merri, Jacques, Gervais, and Martin,
Not even Valérien who hides on the hill.
Time passes, nothing is known,
André Platard has left rue Saint-Martin.

18   *Dernier poème*

(Robert Desnos)

J'ai rêvé tellement fort de toi,
J'ai tellement marché, tellement parlé,
Tellement aimé ton ombre,
Qu'il ne me reste plus rien de toi.
Il me reste d'être l'ombre parmi les ombres
D'être cent fois plus ombre que l'ombre
D'être l'ombre qui viendra et reviendra
          dans ta vie ensoleillée.

Final poem

I have dreamt of you so,
I have walked so, talked so,
Loved your shadow so,
That nothing more of you remains for me—
But to be the shadow among shadows
To be a hundred times more shadow than shadow
To be the shadow that will come and come again
          into your sun-drenched life.

19   *Voyage*

(Guillaume Apollinaire), from CALLIGRAMMES

Adieu amour nuage qui fuit et n'a pas chu pluie
          féconde
Refais le voyage de Dante

Télégraphe
Oiseau qui laisse tomber ses ailes partout

Où va donc ce train qui meurt au loin
Dans les vals et les beaux bois frais du tendre été si
          pâle?

La douce nuit lunaire et pleine d'étoiles
C'est ton visage que je ne vois plus

Journey

Farewell love cloud that flees and has not shed
          fertile rain
Go on Dante's journey again

Telegraph
Bird that lets its wings fall everywhere

Where is this train going that dies in the distance
In the valleys and lovely fresh woods of tender
          summer so pale?

Sweet moonlit night and full of stars
It is your face I no longer see

LA FRAÎCHEUR ET LE FEU	*THE COOLNESS AND THE FIRE*
(Paul Éluard)	

20 i *Rayons des yeux et des soleils*

Beams of eyes and suns

Rayons des yeux et des soleils	Beams of eyes and suns
Des ramures et des fontaines	Of branches and of fountains
Lumière du sol et du ciel	Light of earth and sky
De l'homme et de l'oubli de l'homme	Of man and man's oblivion
Un nuage couvre le sol	A cloud covers the earth
Un nuage couvre le ciel	A cloud covers the sky
Soudain la lumière m'oublie	Suddenly the light forgets me
La mort seule demeure entière	Death alone remains entire
Je suis une ombre je ne vois plus	I am a shadow I no longer see
Le soleil jaune le soleil rouge	The yellow sun the red sun
Le soleil blanc le ciel changeant	The white sun the changing sky
Je ne sais plus	I no longer know
La place du bonheur vivant	Where living joy abides
Au bord de l'ombre sans ciel ni terre.	At the shadow's edge with neither earth nor sky.

20 ii *Le matin les branches attisent*

The branches fan each morning

Le matin les branches attisent	The branches fan each morning
Le bouillonnement des oiseaux	The flurry of the birds
Le soir les arbres sont tranquilles	Each evening the trees are tranquil,
Le jour frémissant se repose.	The quivering day's at rest.

20 iii *Tout disparut même les toits même le ciel*

All vanished even the roofs even the sky

Tout disparut même les toits même le ciel	All vanished even the roofs even the sky
Même l'ombre tombée des branches	Even the shade fallen from the branches
Sur les cimes des mousses tendres	Onto the tips of soft mosses
Même les mots et les regards bien accordés	Even the words and harmonious glances
Sœurs miroitières de mes larmes	Sisters mirroring my tears
Les étoiles brillaient autour de ma fenêtre	Stars shone round my window
Et mes yeux refermant leurs ailes pour la nuit	And my eyes closing once more their wings for the night
Vivaient d'un univers sans bornes.	Lived in a limitless universe.

20 iv *Dans les ténèbres du jardin*

Dans les ténèbres du jardin
Viennent des filles invisibles
Plus fines qu'à midi l'ondée
Mon sommeil les a pour amies
Elles m'enivrent en secret
De leurs complaisances aveugles.

Into the darkness of the garden

Into the darkness of the garden
Some invisible maidens enter
More delicate than the midday shower
My sleep has them for friends
They intoxicate me secretly
With their blind complaisance.

20 v *Unis la fraîcheur et le feu*

Unis la fraîcheur et le feu
Unis tes lèvres et tes yeux
De ta folie attends sagesse
Fais image de femme et d'homme.

Unite the coolness and the fire

Unite the coolness and the fire
Unite your lips and your eyes
From your folly await wisdom
Make an image of woman and man.

20 vi *Homme au sourire tendre*

Homme au sourire tendre
Femme aux tendres paupières
Homme aux joues rafraîchies
Femme aux bras doux et frais
Homme aux prunelles calmes
Femme aux lèvres ardentes
Homme aux paroles pleines
Femme aux yeux partagés
Homme aux deux mains utiles
Femme aux mains de raison
Homme aux astres constants
Femme aux seins de durée

Il n'est rien qui vous retient
Mes maîtres de m'éprouver.

Man with the tender smile

Man with the tender smile
Woman with the tender eyelids
Man with the freshened cheeks
Woman with the sweet fresh arms
Man with the calm eyes
Woman with the ardent lips
Man with abundant words
Woman with the shared eyes
Man with the useful hands
Woman with the hands of reason
Man with the steadfast stars
Woman with the enduring breasts

There is nothing that prevents you
My masters from testing me.

20 vii *La grande rivière qui va*

La grande rivière qui va
Grande au soleil et petite à la lune
Par tous chemins à l'aventure
Ne m'aura pas pour la montrer du doigt

Je sais le sort de la lumière
J'en ai assez pour jouer son éclat
Pour me parfaire au dos de mes paupières
Pour que rien ne vive sans moi.

The great river that flows

The great river that flows
Vast beneath the sun and small beneath the moon
In all directions randomly
Will not have me to point it out

I know the spell of the light
I've enough of it to play with its lustre
To perfect myself behind my eyelids
To ensure that nothing lives without me.

LE TRAVAIL DU PEINTRE

(Paul Éluard)

THE WORK OF THE PAINTER

21 i *Pablo Picasso*

Entoure ce citron de blanc d'œuf informe
Enrobe ce blanc d'œuf d'un azur souple et fin
La ligne droite et noire a beau venir de toi
L'aube est derrière ton tableau

Et des murs innombrables croulent
Derrière ton tableau et toi l'œil fixe
Comme un aveugle comme un fou
Tu dresses une haute épée dans le vide

Une main pourquoi pas une seconde main
Et pourquoi pas la bouche nue comme une plume
Pourquoi pas un sourire et pourquoi pas des larmes
Tout au bord de la toile où jouent les petits clous

Voici le jour d'autrui laisse aux ombres leur chance

Et d'un seul mouvement des paupières renonce

Pablo Picasso

Surround this lemon with formless egg-white
Coat this egg-white with a supple and delicate blue
Though the straight black line stems from you
Dawn lies behind your picture

And innumerable walls crumble
Behind your picture and you staring
Like a blind man like a madman
You raise up a tall sword in the void

A hand why not a second hand
And why not a mouth unadorned like a quill
Why not a smile and why not tears
At the very edge of the canvas where tiny nails are
    fixed

This is the day of others leave their good fortune to
    the shadows
And with a single movement of the eyelids
    renounce

21 ii *Marc Chagall*

Âne ou vache coq ou cheval
Jusqu'à la peau d'un violon
Homme chanteur un seul oiseau
Danseur agile avec sa femme

Couple trempé dans son printemps

L'or de l'herbe le plomb du ciel
Séparés par les flammes bleues
De la santé de la rosée
La sang s'irise le cœur tinte

Un couple le premier reflet

Et dans un souterrain de neige
La vigne opulente dessine
Un visage aux lèvres de lune
Qui n'a jamais dormi la nuit.

Marc Chagall

Ass or cow cock or horse
Even a violin's skin
Singing man single bird
Agile dancer with his wife

Couple steeped in their springtime

The gold of the grass the lead of the sky
Divided by the blue flames
Of health of dew
The blood grows iridescent the heart rings

A couple the first reflection

And in a cavern of snow
The luxuriant vine traces
A face with moon-like lips
Which has never slept at night.

21 iii *Georges Braque*

Un oiseau s'envole,
Il rejette les nues comme un voile inutile,
Il n'a jamais craint la lumière,
Enfermé dans son vol,
Il n'a jamais eu d'ombre.

Coquilles des moissons brisées par le soleil.
Toutes les feuilles dans les bois disent oui,
Elles ne savent dire que oui,
Toute question, toute réponse
Et la rosée coule au fond de ce oui.

Un homme aux yeux légers décrit le ciel d'amour.

Il en rassemble les merveilles
Comme des feuilles dans un bois,
Comme des oiseaux dans leurs ailes
Et des hommes dans le sommeil.

Georges Braque

A bird flies off,
It discards the clouds like a useless veil,
It has never feared the light,
Enclosed in its flight
It has never had a shadow.

Sun-split husks of harvest grains.
All the forest leaves say yes,
Yes is all they know how to say,
Every question, every answer
And the dew flows in the depth of this yes.

A man with carefree eyes describes the heaven of
love.
He gathers together its wonders
Like leaves in a wood,
Like birds in their wings
And men in sleep.

21 iv *Juan Gris**

De jour merci de nuit prends garde
De douceur la moitié du monde
L'autre montrait rigueur aveugle

Aux veines se lisait un présent sans merci
Aux beautés des contours l'espace limité
Cimentait tous les joints des objets familiers

Table guitare et verre vide
Sur un arpent de terre pleine
De toile blanche d'air nocturne

Table devait se soutenir
Lampe rester pépin de l'ombre
Journal délaissait sa moitié

Deux fois le jour deux fois la nuit
De deux objets un double objet
Un seul ensemble à tout jamais

Juan Gris

Give thanks by day beware by night
One half of the world sweetness
The other showed blind harshness

In the veins a relentless present could be read
In the beauties of the contours limited space
Cemented together all familiar objects

Table guitar and empty glass
On an acre of full earth
Of white canvas of night air

Table had to support itself
Lamp remain a pip of the shadow
Newspaper shed a half of itself

Twice the day twice the night
Of two objects one double object
A single whole for evermore

* Juan Gris (1887–1927), Spanish artist who settled in Paris and lived near Picasso; painted Cubist pictures and also used *collage*; worked for Diaghileff in 1922–3.

21 v *Paul Klee*

Sur la pente fatale, le voyageur profite
De la faveur du jour, verglas et sans cailloux,
Et les yeux bleus d'amour, découvre sa saison
Qui porte à tous les doigts de grands astres en bague.

Sur la plage la mer a laissé ses oreilles
Et le sable creusé la place d'un beau crime.
Le supplice est plus dur aux bourreaux qu'aux
        victimes
Les couteaux sont des signes et les balles des larmes.

Paul Klee

On the fatal slope, the traveller profits
From the day's favour, frost-glazed and pebbleless,
And eyes blue with love, he discovers his season
Which wears on each finger great stars as rings.

The sea has left its ear-shells on the shore
And the hollowed sand the site of a noble crime.
Executioners agonize more than victims

Knives are omens and bullets tears.

21 vi *Joan Miró*

Soleil de proie prisonnier da ma tête,
Enlève la colline, enlève la forêt.
Le ciel est plus beau que jamais.

Les libellules des raisins
Lui donnent des formes précises
Que je dissipe d'un geste.

Nuages du premier jour,
Nuages insensibles et que rien n'autorise,
Leurs graines brûlent
Dans les feux de paille de mes regards.

À la fin, pour se couvrir d'une aube
Il faudra que le ciel soit aussi pur que la nuit.

Joan Miró

Sun of prey prisoner of my head
Remove the hill, remove the forest.
The sky is lovelier than ever.

The grapes' dragonflies
Give it precise forms
That I with one gesture dispel.

Clouds of primeval day,
Indifferent clouds sanctioned by nothing,
Their seeds burn
In the straw fires of my glances.

At the last, to cloak itself with dawn
The sky must be as pure as night.

21 vii *Jacques Villon**

Irrémédiable vie
Vie à toujours chérir

En dépit des fléaux
Et des morales basses
En dépit des étoiles fausses
Et des cendres envahissantes

En dépit des fièvres grinçantes
Des crimes à hauteur du ventre
Des seins taris des fronts idiots
En dépit des soleils mortels

Jacques Villon

Irremediable life
Life to be cherished always

Despite scourges
And base morals
Despite false stars
And encroaching ashes

Despite creaking fevers
Belly-high crimes
Desiccated breasts foolish faces
Despite mortal suns

---

* Jacques Villon (1875–1963) was the brother of Marcel Duchamp; he went to Paris in 1895, where he befriended Toulouse-Lautrec. Became a Cubist in 1911.

En dépit des dieux morts
En dépit des mensonges
L'aube l'horizon l'eau
L'oiseau l'homme l'amour

Despite dead gods
Despite the lies
Dawn horizon water
Bird man love

L'homme léger et bon
Adoucissant la terre
Éclaircissant les bois
Illuminant la pierre

Man light-hearted and good
Sweetening the earth
Clearing the woods
Illuminating the stone

Et la rose nocturne
Et le sang de la foule.

And the nocturnal rose
And the blood of the crowd.

LA COURTE PAILLE

(Maurice Carême)

THE SHORT STRAW

22 i *Le sommeil*

Sleep

Le sommeil est en voyage,
Mon Dieu! où est-il parti?
J'ai beau bercer mon petit,
Il pleure dans son lit-cage,
Il pleure depuis midi.

Sleep has gone on his travels.
Good gracious! Where to?
In vain I've rocked my little man,
He's crying in his folding cot,
He's been crying since midday.

Où le sommeil a-t-il mis
Son sable et ses rêves sages?
J'ai beau bercer mon petit,
Il se tourne tout en nage,
Il sanglote dans son lit.

Where's the sandman put
His sand and gentle dreams?
In vain I've rocked my little man,
Drenched in sweat he kicks and turns,
He's sobbing in his bed.

Ah! reviens, reviens, sommeil,
Sur ton beau cheval de course!
Dans le ciel noir, la Grande Ourse
A enterré le soleil
Et rallumé ses abeilles.

Ah! Sleep, come back, come back,
Astride your handsome race-horse!
The Great Bear in the black sky
Has buried the sun
And lit again his bees.

Si l'enfant ne dort pas bien,
Il ne dira pas bonjour,
Il ne dira rien demain
À ses doigts, au lait, au pain
Qui l'accueillent dans le jour.

If the child doesn't sleep soundly,
He'll never say 'good day',
And have nothing to say tomorrow
To his fingers, his milk and bread
That greet him in the morning.

22 ii *Quelle aventure*

Une puce, dans sa voiture,
Tirait un petit éléphant
En regardant les devantures
Où scintillaient les diamants.

—Mon Dieu! mon Dieu! quelle aventure!
Qui va me croire, s'il m'entend?

L'éléphanteau, d'un air absent,
Suçait un pot de confiture.
Mais la puce n'en avait cure,
Elle tirait en souriant.

—Mon Dieu! mon Dieu! que cela dure
Et je vais me croire dément!

Soudain, le long d'une clôture,
La puce fondit dans le vent
Et je vis le jeune éléphant
Se sauver en fendant les murs.

—Mon Dieu! mon Dieu! la chose est sûre.
Mais comment le dire à maman?

What goings-on!

A flea, aboard its carriage,
Was drawing an elephant calf along,
Gazing at shop windows
Where diamonds sparkled.

'My goodness, my goodness, what goings-on!
Who'll ever believe me, if I tell?'

The elephant calf, distractedly,
Was licking a pot of jam.
But the flea took no notice
And smiling drew him along.

'My goodness, my goodness! if this goes on,
I think I'll go insane!'

Suddenly, as they passed a fence,
The flea was blown away by the wind,
And I saw the elephant calf make off,
Crashing away through walls.

'My goodness! My goodness! It's perfectly true,
But how shall I tell Mummy?'

22 iii *La Reine de Cœur*

Mollement accoudée
À ses vitres de lune,
La reine vous salue
D'une fleur d'amandier.

C'est la Reine de Cœur,
Elle peut, s'il lui plaît,
Vous mener en secret
Vers d'étranges demeures.

Où il n'est plus de portes,
De salles ni de tours
Et où les jeunes mortes
Viennent parler d'amour.

La reine vous salue,
Hâtez-vous de la suivre
Dans son château de givre
Aux doux vitraux de lune.

The Queen of Hearts

Leaning lightly on her elbows
At her window-panes of moon,
The queen waves to you
With an almond bloom.

She's the Queen of Hearts
And can, if she desires,
Lead you secretly
To strange places,

Where there are no more doors
Or rooms or towers,
And where girls who have died
Come to speak of love.

The queen waves to you,
Make haste and follow
Into her hoar-frosted castle
With its lovely lead windows of moon.

22 iv *Ba, be, bi, bo, bu*

Ba, be, bi, bo, bu, bé!
Le chat a mis ses bottes,
Il va de porte en porte
Jouer, danser, chanter.

Pou, chou, genou, hibou.
'Tu dois apprendre à lire,
À compter, à écrire',
Lui crie-t-on de partout.

Mais rikketikketau,
Le chat de s'esclaffer,
En rentrant au château:
Il est le Chat botté!

Ba, be, bi, bo, bu

Ba, be, bi, bo, bu, boo!
The cat's put on his boots,
He goes from door to door,
Playing, dancing, singing.

Pou, chou, genou, hibou.*
'You must learn to read,
To count, to write',
They scream at him from every side.

But rikketikketau,
The cat explodes with laughter,
Returning to the castle:
His name is Puss-in-Boots!

22 v *Les anges musiciens*

Sur les fils de la pluie,
Les anges du jeudi
Jouent longtemps de la harpe.

Et sous leurs doigts, Mozart
Tinte délicieux,
En gouttes de joie bleue.

Car c'est toujours Mozart
Que reprennent sans fin
Les anges musiciens,

Qui, au long du jeudi,
Font chanter sur la harpe
La douceur de la pluie.

The angel musicians

On threads of rain
The Thursday angels
Play their harps for hours on end.

And beneath their fingers, Mozart
Tinkles deliciously
In drops of blue joy.

For it's always Mozart
That's perpetually played
By the angel musicians;

All Thursday long
They sing on their harps
The sweetness of the rain.

22 vi *Le carafon*

'Pourquoi, se plaignait la carafe,
N'aurais-je pas un carafon?
Au zoo, madame la Girafe
N'a-t-elle pas un girafon?'
Un sorcier qui passait par là,
À cheval sur un phonographe,
Enregistra la belle voix
De soprano de la carafe
Et la fit entendre à Merlin.

The baby carafe

'Why?' complained the carafe,
'Can't I have a baby carafe?
At the zoo, hasn't Mrs Giraffe
Got a baby giraffe?'
A wizard who was passing by
Riding on a phonograph
Recorded the lovely soprano voice
Of the carafe,
And played it for Merlin to hear.

* Nouns that form their plural in -*x*.

'Fort bien, dit celui-ci, fort bien!'
Il frappa trois fois dans les mains
Et la dame de la maison
Se demande encore pourquoi
Elle trouva, ce matin-là,
Un joli petit carafon
Blotti tout contre la carafe
Ainsi qu'au zoo, le girafon
Pose son cou fragile et long
Sur le flanc clair de la girafe.

'Most fine', said he, 'most fine!'
Thrice he clapped his hands,
And the lady of the house
Still wonders why
She found that very morning
A pretty baby carafe
Snuggling close to the carafe,
Just as at the zoo the baby giraffe
Lays his long and fragile neck
Against the pale flank of the giraffe.

22 vii *Lune d'avril*

Lune,
Belle lune, lune d'Avril,
Faites-moi voir en mon dormant
Le pêcher au cœur de safran,
Le poisson qui rit du grésil,
L'oiseau qui, lointain comme un cor,
Doucement réveille les morts
Et surtout, surtout le pays
Où il fait joie, où il fait clair,
Où soleilleux de primevères,
On a brisé tous les fusils.
Belle lune, lune d'Avril,
Lune.

April moon

Moon,
Beautiful moon, April moon,
Let me see in my sleep
The peach tree with the saffron heart,
The fish who laughs at the sleet,
The bird that, distant as a hunting horn,
Gently wakens the dead,
And above all, above all, the land
Where there is joy, where there is light,
Where sunlit with primroses
All the guns have been destroyed.
Beautiful moon, April moon,
Moon.

23 *À sa guitare*

(Pierre de Ronsard)

Ma guitare, je te chante
Par qui seule je déçois,
Je déçois, je romps, j'enchante
Les amours que je reçois.

Au son de ton harmonie
Je rafraîchis ma chaleur,
Ma chaleur flamme infinie
Naissante d'un beau malheur.

To his guitar

My guitar, I sing of you,
Through whom alone I delude,
I delude, break off, enchant
The loves that I receive.

At the sound of your harmony
I rekindle my ardour,
The infinite flame of my ardour
Born of a beautiful sorrow.

24 *Les chemins de l'Amour* — *The paths of love*

(Jean Anouilh)

Les chemins qui vont à la mer	The paths that lead to the sea
Ont gardé de notre passage	Have retained from our passing
Des fleurs effeuillées	The flowers that shed their petals
Et l'écho sous leurs arbres	And the echo beneath their trees
De nos deux rires clairs.	Of our clear laughter.
Hélas! des jours de bonheur,	Alas! no trace of those happy days,
Radieuses joies envolées,	Those radiant joys now flown,
Je vais sans retrouver traces	Can I find again
Dans mon cœur.	In my heart.
Chemins de mon amour,	Paths of my love,
Je vous cherche toujours,	I search for you ceaselessly,
Chemins perdus, vous n'êtes plus	Lost paths, you are no more
Et vos échos sont sourds.	And your echoes are muted.
Chemins du désespoir,	Paths of despair,
Chemins du souvenir,	Paths of memory,
Chemins du premier jour,	Paths of our first day,
Divins chemins d'amour.	Divine paths of love.
Si je dois l'oublier un jour,	If one day I must forget,
La vie effaçant toute chose,	Since life obliterates everything,
Je veux dans mon cœur qu'un souvenir	I wish for my heart to remember one thing,
Repose plus fort que l'autre amour.	More vivid than the other love,
Le souvenir du chemin,	To remember the path
Où tremblante et toute éperdue,	Where trembling and quite distracted,
Un jour j'ai senti sur moi brûler tes mains.	I one day felt on me your passionate hands.

PUGET, Loïsa (1810–1889)

In Frits Noske's standard work *French song from Berlioz to Duparc*, the name of Loïsa Puget is regularly invoked as being representative of the worst banalities of the salon romance at the time of Louis Philippe and Napoleon III. At one time a student of Adolphe Adam, her career waned as a result of the new-found interest in the mélodie, a more sophisticated form of song than she had been wont to compose. She was a singer herself, of course, as were Pauline Viardot, and later the English women composers Maude Valérie White and Liza Lehmann. The tradition of writing one's own material for performance was deeply ingrained in the pianistic tradition (one thinks of the piano music of Clara Schumann and Cécile Chaminade for example) and, in the same way, songwriting was an opening for woman composers who were vocally gifted. Female singers can never be replaced or rivalled by male ones, and this gave women song composers a foothold in a male preserve which they could claim by right. Puget's success was not lost on her successors like Augusta Holmès, and there was a tradition of women composers making songs their special preserve for the next hundred years. Puget composed more than 300 romances, many of which were also published in Germany and England. Many of the volumes of her songs are collectors' items on account of the accompanying illustrative plates. Most of her texts were written by the poet Gustave Lemoine whom she married in 1842. The subject matter of the songs ranges from genteel seduction in the guise of consolation (*Appelle-moi ta mère*—for baritone!) to *Morte d'amour*, a song adaptation of a true story about a jilted girl who drowned herself in the Seine. Sometimes Puget can write reasonably interesting accompaniments (as in *Le postillon de Séville*) but they are normally extremely simple, bordering on the banal. Her popular romance *Mon rocher de Saint-Malo* formed the basis for the first of the *Embryons desséchés for piano* (1913) by Érik Satie.

RAVEL, Maurice (1875–1937)

There has always been a tendency, on the part of their admirers, to make opponents of Ravel and Debussy. In the same way, we are sometimes asked to play the game of choosing between Bach and Handel, Haydn and Mozart, Britten and Tippett. In all these cases, two contemporaries, both with undeniable genius, attract adherents who fight for their idols at the expense of a so-called rival. The rest of the world may confuse the talents of men generally taken to be as indistinguishable as Tweedledum and Tweedledee, but these experts believe that they have every good reason to raise one above the other. It is, of course, true that Debussy and Ravel were very different (in temperament, taste, and the direction of their talents), but the making of a competition between them is a waste of time: recital audiences delight in them both as great and indispensable song composers. Musical history is often as complicated as fugue, and the simultaneous existence of two such great subjects is an illustration of the richness of the contrapuntal fabric of French musical life at the turn of the century.

Both composers had certain shared points of reference: they acknowledged the influence of Chabrier, for example, as well as the help and encouragement of Satie. It is true that we hear a Debussian flavour in some of Ravel's music (how could it be otherwise?—he attended the first thirty performances of *Pelléas et Mélisande*) but the opposite was also true. In a private letter to the critic Pierre Lalo, Ravel gently pointed out that before his piano piece *Jeux d'eau* (1901), Debussy had only published *Pour le piano*, which breaks no new ground, and that certain technical innovations exploited by Debussy in writing for the instrument were in fact Ravelian (as his 1895 *Habanera* confirms). Lalo indiscreetly published the letter, and this, combined with Ravel's support for Debussy's first wife at the time of the marriage break-up, strained the relationship between the two composers after years of respectful coexistence (though more hostility emanated from Debussy than from Ravel). Ultimately we have to acknowledge Debussy was a greater innovator with a wider emotional range; he had a larger catalogue of works, and his status as a pioneer is unique. But as Poulenc put it (according to an interview he once gave in America): 'Some composers *innove*, but some great composers do not *innove*. Schubert does not *innove*. Wagner, Monteverdi, they *innove*. Debussy *innove*; Ravel does not *innove*. It is not necessary that one *innove*.'

Ravel's ear for beauty of sonority is apparent from the very first things he wrote. He found his songwriting feet quicker than Debussy, although his studentship at the Conservatoire was counted far from successful. Not for him romantic effusions in the style of Massenet written for his mistress, an older woman and a singer (how far apart the two composers seem, even from the beginning, for Ravel owed nothing to Massenet and, as far as we know, never had a mistress, or lover of any kind). His first song, the *Ballade de la reine morte d'aimer* (Roland de Marès, 1893) shows the influence of the medievalism of Érik Satie whom he had met and befriended in Montmartre, and who was then at the height of his 'Rose+Croix' phase. It is startlingly modern in its exploration of antiquity: the time-travelling tradition of nostalgic musical pastiche here takes on an austere new slant. Ravel was to retreat into the past on a number of occasions (most famously in the *Menuet antique* and the *Pavane pour une infante défunte*) as if in search of the hieratic disciplines of past times, a past which included the magic kingdoms of fairy-tale. He seemed to feel safer when the formalities of ritual (and compositional technique, after all, is a ritual of a kind) placed a certain distance between composer and public. In this music we encounter a sense of inscrutable mystery; but at the same time we hear the germ of Stravinsky's neo-classical style. Ravel's Swiss father was an unhymned inventor of the internal combustion engine, and the composer inherited the precision of an engineer in everything he did. Stravinsky actually described Ravel as a 'Swiss watch-maker', but unashamedly learned from him about the poetry inherent in well-oiled mechanisms. The favourite theme of chiming bells, which Ravel was to explore in various pieces for piano, also makes an important appearance at the end of the song—indeed it was probably the references to 'les grosses cloches de Bohème | Et les cloches de Thulé' which attracted him to this poem in the first place. Perhaps a taste for bells was inspired by the same Balinese gamelan orchestra which had enchanted Debussy at the World's Fair in Paris in 1889. *Un grand sommeil noir* (1895) is one of the bleakest of all Verlaine settings, closer to Stravinsky and Varèse (who later set the same poem) than to Fauré or Debussy. Or so it seems at first, with its sombre landscape hardly enlivened by repeated growling low G sharps, and a use of the bottom regions of the piano which emphasize, to an almost grotesque extent, that this is a 'mélodie noire'. On second hearing, we must admit Debussy's influence: the opening chords are reminiscent of *De fleurs* from the PROSES LYRIQUES, and the sudden outburst at 'Ô! la triste histoire' adopts the Debussian trick of contrasting music of quiet depression with sudden hysteria, and a flight to the top of the stave (cf. *C'est l'extase*, and, above all, *Spleen*, from the ARIETTES OUBLIÉES). Apart from anything else, the resulting vocal range of over two octaves makes the song rather impractical in performance. Ravel, the perfectionist, chose not to publish either of these songs in his lifetime.

At this point, he was forced to leave the Conservatoire temporarily, having failed to pass the obligatory examinations. His friend Ricardo Viñes (later a famous virtuoso and Poulenc's piano teacher) felt that he was somehow destined for musical greatness, but it was clear that this was not going to be through a career as a pianist. Ravel returned to the Conservatoire to study composition with Gabriel Fauré who had been newly appointed to the staff on the departure of Massenet. Ravel wrote two songs in 1896, indeed these represent his entire musical output for the year. *Sainte* (Mallarmé) is a hymn to St Cecilia which is once again indebted to Satie, with modal chords suggestive of medieval church music—a fine match of text and mystical musical atmosphere. The song's coda explores the paradox of sound-in-silence ('Musicienne du silence') that we have already encountered in *Un grand sommeil noir* which has 'silence' as its final repeated phrase, as if the composer delights in fading from the scene with the self-effacement of a vanishing magician. Also from 1896 is **D'Anne jouant de l'espinette** (Clément Marot), which is one of the greatest of the many French songs in the antique manner. The text is a gift to a composer (Schubert's *Laura am Klavier* is a Schiller setting with the same scenario), and the music shows Ravel's sympathy with the clavecinistes well before the harpsichord revival spearheaded by Wanda Landowska. In style it is prophetic of such works for solo piano as the *Sonatine* and *Le tombeau de Couperin*. The accompaniment, light and dry, is contained within the small keyboard compass of a seventeenth-century instrument. The composer's punctilious use of articulation and phrasing adds to the feel of early music, and it is more historically accurate in its texture than most such evocations (compare the plush sound-world of Hahn's *À Chloris*). Also typical of Ravel is the devilish hemiola at 'J'ay du plaisir, et d'oreilles et d'yeulx' where piano (suddenly on three staves) and voice are in grave danger of losing each other in an Elizabethan maze of displaced rhythms that have perplexed all this song's performers.

In 1899 Ravel prefaced this song with another Marot setting—**D'Anne qui me jecta de la neige.** This is another little miracle which somehow evokes the epoch of the poet without needing to resort to the sonority of the spinet. There is a grave and courtly beauty to this music, as cool as snow and somehow aflame with passion—we encounter for the first time the white heat of Ravel, quite different in nature from Debussy's fiery red glow. The song is reminiscent of Chabrier in the doubling of vocal line with piano, as well as the use of swooning triplets and pedal points. Unlike Chabrier, however, this music is too serious for a smile. Every afflicted lover will recognize in this song the mixture of pain and rapture as time stands still at a turning point in a longed-for relationship. These two songs were published together as ***DEUX ÉPIGRAMMES DE CLÉMENT MAROT*** in 1900, and were later orchestrated by Maurice Delage. Together with Enescu's Marot cycle, they are a fitting memorial to a great sixteenth-century poet.

There were two further songs in 1898, neither of which Ravel published, but which are both worthy of comment. **Chanson du rouet** (Leconte de Lisle) displays a carpet-bag of influences: in the strophic simplicity of the vocal line, folk music (appropriate for a text from a collection of poems entitled *Chansons écossaises*); Schubert's *Gretchen am Spinnrade*, of course, in the use of a spinning-wheel motif; Duparc, in the way the semiquaver oscillations support the voice, reminiscent of *L'invitation au voyage*; Chopin and Chabrier, in the harmonic language, and also because a song at the spinning wheel is central to Chabrier's opera *Gwendoline*; Gregorian chant, in the ominous quotation of Dies Irae at 'Quand, près de mourir' when the girl sings of weaving her own winding sheet. The eclectic mixture of simple melody and highly sophisticated accompaniment makes the piece sound like one of Britten's folksong arrangements, a cross between *The Miller of the Dee*, and *Il y a quelqu'un sur terre*, another spinning song which becomes more intense with each verse. Perhaps it is the Basque side of Ravel's nature which makes him sympathetic to folk music, for he was one of the first great masters (unlike Debussy) to be interested in providing new accompaniments for old tunes.

The other 1898 song, **Si morne!** (Verhaeren), is unlike any other in this composer's output. As Gerald Larner points out, it is one of two Ravel mélodies which we are tempted to interpret as confessional in nature. Verhaeren's gloomy poem is something which might have been set by Lekeu, Magnard, or one of the other Franck disciples. Apart from its use of the whole-tone scale, it might almost have been composed by one of them, for it is written in a rambling 9/8 with thick textures and dark colours—like much of their music. It speaks of depression, suppression, and an illness of the spirit, and Ravel sets it with an intensity that allows us to glimpse a struggle, almost certainly of a sexual nature, which was going on behind his tantalizing mask of elegant indifference. This music, as austere as d'Indy, is as far from Ravel the dandy as might be imagined: at its climax—ferociously difficult to sing—it is distressingly impassioned in a way that we will not hear again in his mélodies. It is little wonder that the composer, more obsessively discreet than any of his contemporaries, did not allow this song to be published in his lifetime.

The next period of songwriting is dominated by the effect on Ravel of hearing so many performances of Debussy's *Pelléas et Mélisande* in 1902, although once Debussy's influence is filtered through the prism of Ravel's genius, the result is a kaleidoscope of musical colour that is his alone. In 1903 the publisher Hamelle commissioned a number of composers to set poems from a collection by Paul Gravollet, entitled *Les frissons*. Ravel's contribution was **Manteau de fleurs**, decried by most of the commentators because of the text, both pretentiously symbolist and sentimental, but which actually marks a step forward in the composer's song-style. The vocal line of this song has a sensuous fluidity which shows the influence of the Debussy opera, as well as such songs as the CHANSONS DE BILITIS. The climax is a sumptuous flowering of passion at 'Du printemps et de l'été', which is remarkably reminiscent of the high-point of Debussy's *La chevelure*. The only trouble with this song is that the text seems hardly worthy of the extravagant musical means lavished upon it, but there may be a reason for this, as we shall see later. In any case, Ravel thought well enough of this song to orchestrate it.

The other Debussy-influenced work is one of Ravel's greatest achievements: the orchestral song cycle SHÉHÉRAZADE, the culmination of a long-standing project based on *The Thousand and One Nights*, and which included an overture for orchestra of the same name as early as 1898. The poems in free verse are by Tristan Klingsor (the pseudonym of the poet Léon Leclère), a frequently encountered name in the annals of the mélodie. Klingsor never achieved greater fame than for his part in these remarkable songs, where Ravel draws on every aspect of his own skills to depict the Orient. We also hear, in no uncertain terms, the important place of the great Russian composers (Rimsky-Korsakov, Borodin, Balakirev) in Ravel's list of enthusiasms. Right from the beginning of the first song, *Asie*, we feel ourselves in the hands a master tour-guide, for this is magic-carpet music, second to none. We fly over one exotic sight after the other—a bird's-eye view of an entire continent. One seems to be viewing a filmed travelogue, so vivid and strongly defined are the musical images. The music picks up the listener in a tornado of sound, and lands him, light years from Kansas, in an Oz of Ravelian enchantment. The boldness to attempt something on this scale comes from Debussy—there is a certain *Pelléas*-like way with the vocal line. But as we follow Ravel on his journeys, we acknowledge that his powers as a wizard of sound are unlike anyone else's.

The rest of the cycle comprises two much shorter songs. **La flûte enchantée** is a beguiling relative of Debussy's *La flûte de Pan* from the BILITIS set. The theme here is thwarted love, because this is a serenade to a slave-girl who dares not go out for fear of waking her master. She has to make do with only the sound of her suitor's melodies to caress her, so this is love at one remove, a dream of passion rather than its reality. (The elaborate music of the sexually frustrated god Pan before the bacchanal in *Daphnis et Chloé* was also consigned to the flute.) Even more thought-provoking, as a song of hopeless longing for fulfilment, is *L'indifférent.* Here the singer tries in vain to interest a passing stranger in her hospitality. He is a young man of feminine beauty, and has other tastes, it seems. At 'comme ceux d'une fille' (and similar passages) there is a surge of sound from pianissimo to mezzo forte and back again—a triumph of orchestration. The surge of sexual desire, as sudden and magical as tumescence, is doomed to inevitable let-down. The musical sigh tapers away like the ache of regret felt by those denied the object of their heart's desire—the reason for the narrator's disappointment is something as irrefutable as the young man's sexual orientation, which, incidentally, was also that of the poet Klingsor. Jean-Michel Nectoux avers that the song was a warning to its dedicatee, Emma Bardac: she had left Fauré, had not yet married Debussy, and it seems that her attentions had turned to the young dandy Ravel. Perhaps *L'indifférent* was a coded message, letting Mme Bardac know that she was wasting her time. Interesting, and not often remarked upon, is that Ravel borrows the music from *Manteau de fleurs* for the unaccompanied lines 'mais non, tu passes | Et de mon seuil je te vois éloigner.' Going back to that flower song we see that the composer had written the same music, note for note, for the following lines in Gravollet's poem: 'Seul, dans tout ce rose un peu troublant, | Les lys ont le droit d'être blancs.' Following this clue, we see that perhaps Ravel regarded himself as lily-white in the troubling world of rosy sexual spectacles. After all, we cannot be certain that *L'indifférent* is on his way to visit a virile, Valentino-like sheikh; the young man may be celibate or asexual. Somewhere deep in his composing consciousness, Ravel seems to be saying that not everyone *has* to be sexually active: like the virginally white lilies, one has the right to be in the pink without being classified as a rose—or even a pansy. The SHÉHÉRAZADE cycle is published in a vocal score with piano reduction, but it seems unwise to perform it as such in concert. Only the most redoubtably gifted pianist can cope with *Asie* in concert (I have heard it brought off with distinction by Jessye Norman with Mark Markham), but the composer himself made a version for *La flûte enchantée* with accompaniment for flute and piano.

The next song is something of an oddity—*Noël des jouets* (1905) to the composer's own text, a strange forerunner of *Noël des enfants qui n'ont plus de maisons*—Debussy's Christmas song (also to his own text) of ten years later. Here we see Ravel's fascination with all things mechanical. This is not like Debussy's *La boîte à joujoux* where the toys come to life; in Ravel's song they remain automatons, whirring and whizzing like Hoffmann's doll Olympia (a subject which had fascinated the young composer enough for him to sketch the beginnings of an opera). Here Ravel proves himself the son of an inventor—on a yachting holiday which took him to Aarhus, he had been fascinated by a gigantic iron foundry, and wrote of a 'marvellous symphony of conveyor belts, whistles and massive hammer blows'. There is a certain angularity and stiffness built into this song which shows the composer's delight in a world free of human feelings where gleaming and functional artificiality is all that matters—whether in the toy-cupboard, or in the workings of the many clocks in his opera *L'heure espagnole.* The Christ child is made of sugar according to Ravel's words, and the mechanically repetitive bleating of the toy cattle ('Noël! Noël!') could easily be read as a baleful comment on Christmas by an agnostic composer.

The CINQ MÉLODIES POPULAIRES GRECQUES represents a selection of the best of eight Greek folksong settings made by Ravel between 1904 and 1906. He apparently composed the first group of them astonishingly quickly, and the critic M.-D. Calvocoressi, himself of Greek descent, commissioned the remainder, and made the translations into French. The songs have remained in the repertoire with great tenacity, and it is easy to see why: the tunes are good ones, and the accompaniments are within the capabilities of most pianists. The catchy *Le réveil de la mariée* (the printed title of *Chanson de la mariée* is a mistake—it is the bridegroom who sings) is supported by a delicate shimmer of sound; the moving *Là-bas, vers l'église*, a funeral chant for war heroes, achieves a doleful grandeur with the greatest economy of means; *Quel galant m'est comparable?* is a saucy song for a boastful Jack-the-lad whose pistols and sharp sabres are not all that hang below the belt—the cheeky interlude and postlude illustrate shameless flirting with 'Dame Vasiliki', a woman of experience who does not believe for a minute the outrageously insincere 'Et c'est toi que j'aime'; *Chanson des cueilleuses de lentisques* is a song where the heavy swaying of the women's bodies, as they work in the fields, is built into the music—performers come adrift when they turn the song into free recitative, and fail to observe minutely the composer's notated rhythms; *Tout gai!* (*Be gay!* according to the old-fashioned English translation, although nothing to do with what was once termed the Greek vice) is a rumbustious dance which alternates between 2/4 and 3/4 with the earthy simplicity of a real peasants' knees-up. Ravel orchestrated the first and last of the set; in 1935, Manuel Rosenthal did the same for the remaining songs. A further item in this manner, *Tripatos*, was written in 1909 and published posthumously.

We now come to the most important, and the most individual, contribution that Ravel made to the song repertoire. These are the *HISTOIRES NATURELLES* (1906), five settings of the jewelled and pointed texts of Jules Renard, and a fitting continuation of the grand tradition of animal music from French composers which goes back to Rameau and Janequin and continues to Poulenc, and beyond. Today, it seems difficult to understand the scandal that the first performance of this music provoked. Much of this was to do with the composer's decision to import the mute 'e' of spoken Frency into sung music. All serious French mélodies up to this point had honoured the prosodic tradition that even if certain word-endings were not spoken in everyday speech, they were to be sung, or at least allowed for in the scanning and setting of texts. Because Renard's pieces are prose rather than poetry (and because they would certainly be read aloud with none of the mute 'e's sounding), Ravel was bold enough to translate this into song—to the horror of even old friends, like Fauré. The result is disarmingly natural and casual: the poet's observations are voiced in the most spontaneous way. It is as if Ravel himself is speaking to us, and the piano's purpose is to heighten that speech, underlining the wry humour of the commentary, and assisting the singer to cross a magical threshold when the music unexpectedly plunges into some of the most poetic moments that this composer ever created. And yet, some of the most uncomfortable minutes I ever spent on a concert platform were with these songs some twenty years ago—during a performance in Spoleto where this music provoked a disturbance in the theatre. The music requires ears that can appreciate voice and piano as a single descriptive entity; the lack of discernible vocal melody seemed to be taken as a personal affront by the Italian audience who, in the absence of Italian opera, would have much preferred lieder. (The centuries-old split between French and Italian musical taste is still apparent.)

Each of the animals in this masterpiece is astonishingly evoked in the opening bars of the accompaniment. The pomposity of the self-regarding peacock (*Le paon*—Handelian dotted rhythms); the fastidious cricket (*Le grillon*—delicately oscillating semiquavers); the languidly gliding swan (*Le cygne*—liquid septuplets in an impressionistic haze which links, somewhat ironically, these vain royal birds with Debussy, king of composers; there is also a suggestion, in the shape of the melody, of *Le cygne* by Saint-Saëns); the kingfisher, stunningly beautiful as it sits on a branch (*Le martin-pêcheur*—a prophecy of Messiaen's music of stasis, where magical chord sequences are suspended in time); the querulous guinea fowl (*La pintade*—hammered repeated notes which pierce the air like the bird's cry): all these animals are introduced to us by piano music which is both complex and immediate, sophisticated, yet conceived with the gimlet eye of a devoted naturalist. This distillation of the essence of a song into its piano writing could not have been bettered by Schubert. And there is something else which places Ravel in the same league as the great lieder composers (where Debussy also belongs): with each poet whom he tackles, he changes something of his musical character. Thus, in the *HISTOIRES NATURELLES*, he becomes a precise observer of nature because Renard leads him in that direction. The voice keeps its analytical cool throughout (except when imitating the cries of peacock and guinea fowl). The drama of the cycle centres in the piano where, in each of these magical songs, there is a least one moment where Ravel produces an extra-special effect. In *Le paon*, who else would have depicted the dazzling spectacle of an opening peacock tail by means of a contrary motion glissando on the black keys, a kaleidoscope of notes to summon up a kaleidoscope of colour?

Sometimes it is the postludes which make us catch our breath: in *Le grillon*, the clock-like whirrings and meticulous machinations of the insect (whom Renard depicts as an anally retentive fuss-pot) are counterbalanced by a coda ('Dans la campagne muette, les peupliers se dressent commes des doigts en l'air et désignent la lune') which seems to emerge from the depths of the earth, dissolving the tension, and suffusing the picture with a peace redolent of a fragrant countryside bathed in moonlight. The next postlude works in the opposite direction. At the end of *Le cygne* we have had enough of the creature's beauty and grace; indeed Ravel, rather wickedly, builds this up as an impressionistic cliché, only to knock the whole picture into perspective with a wry sentence which reveals the swan as greedy, self-serving, and overweight. *Le martin-pêcheur* (marked 'On ne peut plus lent'—one cannot be slower) is a sacred moment, above all for its remarkable depiction of the true nature-lover's humility (and ability to be utterly still) when confronted by the majestic beauties of creatures in the wild. The fishing rod which the bird takes to be the branch of a tree, and on which he perches for a few awe-inspiring moments, seems to have been invented to appeal to Ravel: it successfully appears to be something which it is not. The composer seems as thrilled by the idea of a real bird on a false branch, as much as he would have adored a clockwork bird in a real tree. *La pintade* is the hardest of the songs for the pianist; its most engaging innovation is a musical depiction of the Doppler effect. After the bird has gone away, and all creatures breathe a sigh of relief, it returns in a virtuoso flurry of repeated piano notes; these start softly at the top of the stave as the guinea fowl's cry is heard in the distance, and descend in pitch as the troublesome creature gets nearer—similar to an approaching ambulance, and not nearly as reassuring. This song is a real tour de force, and a vivid and peremptory end to the cycle.

It is inevitable that these settings should be compared to Chabrier's farmyard songs. Ravel's are greater mélodies of course—they are more profound, and much more clever. If they lack Chabrier's good nature, and his love for whatever meets his gaze, we cannot castigate one composer for not being another, although we can fantasize about what we should have had if Ravel, lonely and complex, had been given Chabrier's openness of heart. The songs annoyed Debussy, a sign of a real parting of the ways; he reproved the critic Louis Laloy for favourably comparing this cycle to

Mussorgsky's NURSERY cycle, and dismissed Ravel's songs as Americanisms, 'conjuring tricks', empty of real emotion. But he would have been incapable of the crystalline detachment which is the glory of this music, and which, like the later songs of Fauré, is capable of moving us intensely precisely because of its aristocratic *pudeur*. This music is inimitable precisely because it is the reflection of a personality unlike any other in French musical history.

Ravel would never again attempt anything like these songs. Two further single items date from 1907. *Les grands vents venus d'outre-mer* was Ravel's only setting of his friend Henri de Régnier, the poet who had inspired *Jeux d'eau*, and who provided the superscription to that work for piano, in his own hand, on Ravel's manuscript. The song belongs to that handful of works (such as *Si morne!* and *Un grand sommeil noir*) where the composer allows his depressive side to surface. Alan Hollinghurst recently used this poem to preface his novel *The folding star*—a tale of hopeless homosexual love for a young man played out on a colourless Belgian background. Like the other 'confessional' songs of Ravel, the music begins in sombre manner and rises to an agitated state of anguish. The effect is masterful and bleak. The depiction of the dead clock ('l'horloge est morte') is typical of the composer: whirring demisemiquavers give way to lugubrious triplets with an offbeat accent in the right hand, like machinery going terribly wrong. Like the crucial passage of rejection in *L'indifférent*, mention of the 'adolescents amers' is mournfully unaccompanied; this is altogether the music of a loner.

Completely different is *Sur l'herbe*, Ravel's second setting of Verlaine and an important addition to the significant body of Verlaine songs by great composers. With Fauré and Debussy we have a number of songs which describe the dreamy, other-worldly side of the *Fêtes galantes*. Like Debussy's second set of these poems (1904), Ravel exploits something more sinister than the idylls of elegant courtship. *Sur l'herbe* stars a pair of old roués, an abbé and a marquis, whose 'noirceur', we are somehow led to believe, could lead to a sequel straight from the pages of the Marquis de Sade. Ravel, so diffident in writing about love, seems to find no difficulty in writing about sexual licence—further proof of this was *L'heure espagnole*, which took a long time to reach the stage because of its risqué plot. Here we have Verlaine, well known for the catholicity of his sexual tastes, hinting at an open-air *partouze*. The composer relishes the chance faithfully to transcribe the notes of the *solfège* in such a way as to suggest wandering fingers (one for each note mounting the stave, *faute de mieux*), as well as a conversation which switches mercurially between the men and the girls who make half-hearted attempts to protect their honour. The final 'Hé! bonsoir la Lune!' (which gives a certain dignity to 'mooning') swoons with delight, and takes us back to the nocturnal atmosphere which closes *Le grillon*.

Further essays in folksong setting date from 1910. The background story to the four CHANTS POPULAIRES is rather a bizarre one, in that Ravel, at the height of his fame, and while he was composing *Daphnis et Chloé*, was not ashamed to enter a competition for songs of this type run by the Maison du Lied in Moscow. (We are reminded that Ravel was never wealthy, and often short of money.) He won in four categories out of seven, and these songs were duly published. They are useful recital items, but seem diluted Ravel, less individual by far than the Greek songs. *Chanson espagnole* has women saying farewell to their men going to war—the all-purpose Iberian style at the composer's command throughout his career was later to yield more memorable songs; *Chanson française* is a delicate bergerette in neo-classical style; the verismo *Chanson italienne* is oddly ambiguous—one wonders whether to take the sudden Puccini evocation at the end seriously, or whether the composer is laughing at its heart-on-sleeve emotion; *Chanson hébraïque* is probably the best of the set, a song in Yiddish ('Mejerke, main Suhn') worthy of the other Hebrew arrangements of later years. Ravel took the trouble to orchestrate this in 1923–4. The *Chanson écossaise* won no prize in Moscow, so it was only published posthumously. This is an evocative setting of Burns's 'Ye banks and braes of bonnie Doon'. It seems prophetic of Britten's folksong settings in its transparent use of piano sonorities, and the marriage of age-old melody with gently modern harmony; indeed this is only one of a number of times that Ravel's ear and fastidious craftsmanship bring to mind the sound-world of the master of Aldeburgh.

The *TROIS POÈMES DE STÉPHANE MALLARMÉ* are the songs which stake Ravel's claim to be considered as a completely modern, twentieth-century master, for this is the cycle which is the link between the second Viennese school and *PLI SELON PLI* of Boulez. It dates from 1913, and was conceived during a stay in Switzerland (paid for by Diaghilev) where Ravel collaborated with Stravinsky in the orchestration of Mussorgsky's *Khovanshchina*. Stravinsky had recently heard Schoenberg's *Pierrot lunaire* in Berlin, and was impressed enough with the work (in its version with mixed instrumental accompaniment) to write his *THREE JAPANESE LYRICS* for the same combination: voice, two flutes, two clarinets, string quartet, and piano. Stravinsky dedicated the last of the *JAPANESE LYRICS* to Ravel. And thus it came about that Ravel was influenced, albeit at one remove, by Schoenberg, and wrote two of his Mallarmé songs, the first of which, **Soupir**, is dedicated to Stravinsky. According to Ravel's droll analysis, Schoenberg avoided charm 'to the point of asceticism, martyrdom even'. So there was no question of his being influenced by that composer's harmonic theories; rather was he made doubly bold and open to experimentation by Schoenberg's daring, and Stravinsky's enthusiasm for it. Ravel's work is beguiling and lyrical, a velvet glove thrown down to his younger colleague to show him that he was as capable of creating something new as any of the avant-garde composers still in their twenties, without sacrificing a jot of his established musical personality. It served to remind Stravinsky, moreover, that Ravel was still a relatively young man in a way Debussy was not.

From the very opening of *Soupir* with its arpeggio harmonics depicting the white fountain soaring towards the October sky, we enter a new world of sound, and word-to-music relationships; and yet this autumnal scene is as completely typical of Ravel as we could wish. Just as he found a style and a manner appropriate to Jules Renard, he now finds the key to enter Mallarmé's world as if it were his own. When we hear music such as this, and the opening of **Placet futile** (which Stravinsky copied in the *Pastorale* of the *L'histoire du soldat*) we can only agree with Debussy's verdict on Ravel's musical ear—'the most refined there has ever been'. In *Placet futile* we are a thousand miles from Verlaine's Abbé in *Sur l'herbe*, apart from the fact that both songs are revelations of the private lives of men sworn to chastity at a time when appearing 'nu sur le Sèvre' was as much a disaster as being caught with your pants down in the moonlight by the *Sun*. There is something immensely touching and lyrical about this song which has echoes of *Daphnis et Chloé*—the last line ('Princesse, nommez-nous berger de vos sourires') is as lovely a phrase as Ravel ever wrote. And who else would have been interested in lavishing his time on a plea for love that was doomed to failure before it had begun? Or so the composer no doubt thought himself. Imagine his surprise when he heard from the publisher Durand that, exactly at the same time, and purely by chance, Debussy had set *Soupir* and *Placet futile* as songs with piano. A major new edition of Mallarmé's *Poésies* had been published by the Nouvelle revue française, and both composers had obviously bought copies at the same time. The texts had been originally promised by the holders of the copyright to Ravel, who immediately interceded to ensure that Debussy was allowed to publish his songs as well. Debussy's set, also entitled *TROIS POÈMES DE STÉPHANE MALLARMÉ*, included a third song, *Éventail* [DEBUSSY 16], which encouraged Ravel to amplify his two-song set into a cycle of three. With the completion of his Mallarmé songs, Ravel entered the avant-garde lists in a way that he had never done before, showing Debussy that he was moving in a new (albeit Stravinskian) direction. Almost defiantly, it seems, he chose one of the most inscrutable poems (Ravel himself called it 'hermetic') in Mallarmé's collection—*Surgi de la croupe et du bond*. In this work about the emptiness of a vase without flowers, he all but abandons tonality: this easily stands as the most 'advanced' music that he ever composed.

Only two further songs date from this period, as different as can be imagined from the Mallarmé complexities. These are the *DEUX MÉLODIES HÉBRAÏQUES* (1914), which became famous in the eloquent performances of the Jewish singer Madeleine Grey. Both the *Kaddisch* and *L'énigme éternelle* are extremely simply harmonized, and yet, in the hands of the right performers, they make a powerful impact, the first song the most solemn of all liturgical utterances in the Jewish faith, the second a gentle and haunting evocation, not without a touch of a smile and shrug, of the Hebraic view of the riddles of the universe. Ravel orchestrated both songs in 1919.

The First World War (during which Ravel had a thwarted ambition to join the air force), the death of his mother, and his loss of Diaghilev's confidence were to change the composer's career forever. His friendship with Stravinsky was not to survive the debacle over the ballet *La valse*. (Diaghilev, when hearing the work played by Ravel, rejected it on the spot in the presence of the Russian composer who failed to raise a single word in its defence.) The main work of the post-war years was the opera *L'enfant et les sortilèges* to a libretto by Colette. Songs are now to be found only here and there in Ravel's catalogue, indeed there is a ten-year gap between the *DEUX MÉLODIES HÉBRAÏQUES* and *Ronsard à son âme*, written in 1924 as part of the celebrations of the 400th anniversary of the poet's birth. This is an extremely spare song (the piano writing is on one stave only) which makes a bleakly moving effect. Ravel boasted that he could play the accompaniment with his left hand, while smoking a cigarette with his right. Fauré had been attracted by the same text, but abandoned the idea of setting it when he heard that his former pupil had done so—a matter of great regret for all admirers of late Fauré. In the same style of simplicity taken to its most spare form, is the song *Rêves* (1927), the only setting by Ravel of his old friend Léon-Paul Fargue, a poet also set by Érik Satie. Some commentators have named Fargue (because he went through a homosexual phase) as a possible lover of Ravel's youth, but attempting to unravel Ravel's life in this respect is of little help to the performer; indeed, the music seems to thrive on an air of ambiguity and mystery.

There is one more unequivocal masterpiece—the *CHANSONS MADÉCASSES* of 1926. This was written as a result of a commission from that great American patroness of the arts Mrs Elizabeth Sprague Coolidge. She stipulated that the voice should be accompanied by flute, cello, and piano, but allowed the composer to choose his own texts. Given the instrumental combination, Ravel's choice of poems written in 1787 by Évariste Parny, a Creole poet domiciled in France who had never visited Madagascar, seems particularly inspired. He was proud of these songs and with reason; less abstract than the Mallarmé cycle, they evoke yet another Ravelian sound-world, this time of African 'luxe, calme et volupté'. Just as the composer had effortlessly transported us to the fantasy world of

Schéhérazade, we now enter, from the very first notes, a primitive yet noble pre-colonial world, where passions and climate are equally steamy. *Nahandove* is a love song very much in the equivocal tradition of this composer's output. Protected by the barrier of characterization which called for a depiction of a different, less inhibited sexuality (as in *L'heure espagnole*), Ravel seems both unbuttoned and inscrutable. The song is the tantalizingly inexplicit description of an encounter between lovers; we get some of the torrid details, but not enough to be sure what is happening. The narrator (a man, but, in a twist typical of this composer, sung by a woman) awaits the visit of the beautiful Nahandove; accompanied only by a sinuous cello line, he repeats her name obsessively like a magic spell; she arrives, she dallies, she leaves. 'Stop or I shall die', he says to her in the middle of their embrace, but there is an accelerando in the music which betokens—what?—sexual congress? a lapse of time? In any case, 'le plaisir passe comme un éclair', and we hear his pleasure slipping away without having come to grips with it. She will return that night, but what has actually passed between man and woman is almost as ambiguous and understated as in *L'indifférent*. We never hear Nahandove herself during this monologue, so perhaps this is all the dream of a lonely man who chants the name of the beloved the better to encourage the gods to bring her to his side. *Aoua!* shows a completely different side of Ravel: here we discover the left-wing, anti-colonial agnostic who has little respect for the benefits of Christian civilization. There is real menace here (the full force of piano sonority comes into its own, having kept a very low profile in the first song), and the composer has caught to perfection the brooding anger of occupied peoples, and the dangers of a volcanic island that can erupt into violence at any time. The final song, *Il est doux*, is an *Invitation au voyage* for the twentieth century, an African *Under the greenwood tree*. Who can resist the picture painted here of a life in the sun; the magic of the flute combining with cello harmonics and tiny splashes of colour from the piano? The effect of gentle drum-beats from the cello half-way through is a masterstroke. The coda is a combination of that for *Le grillon* and *Le cygne*: first a rapt nocturnal evocation at 'le vent du soir se lève', and then, to prick the poetic bubble—just as Strauss does at the end of his last opera, *Capriccio*, with 'Frau Gräfin, das Souper ist serviert'—the descent into bathos for 'allez, et préparez le repas'.

The last songs have something in common with Fauré's, in that both composers suddenly developed something of a popular touch. In *L'HORIZON CHIMÉRIQUE*, Fauré recaptures the approachability and earthiness of an earlier period (if such an epithet can be applied to seafaring songs), and *DON QUICHOTTE À DULCINÉE* (Morand, 1932–3) is performed by baritones everywhere, including such mélodie-unfriendly countries as Germany. They were written for Chaliapin in the hope that they would be used for a film; in the event Ibert was the successful composer for this project (Marcel Dellanoy and Darius Milhaud had also been approached). But Ravel provides music that is accessible and charming, and the musically demanding experiments of the pre-war years seem far away. Spanish atmosphere comes easily to this composer with Basque blood: so we have in *Chanson romanesque* a bewitching *guajira* where two in a bar alternates with three; in *Chanson épique* a rapt prayer, where the serious religious manner of Don Quixote's Spanish Catholicism is caught to perfection in the grave 5/4 metre of the *zorzica*; and in *Chanson à boire*, a turbulent and melismatic *jota*, where the piano crashes down the keyboard in inebriated manner, and even the drinker's hiccup is incorporated into the lively music.

There are only a few curiosities left to mention. Manuel Rosenthal maintained that Ravel was the composer of the famous ballad *Fascination* (1904)—this was published as the work of the popular composer F. D. Marchetti. Serious composers sometimes wrote songs of this kind and sold them as a means of paying the rent—they did not wish to lose their serious reputations by entering the commercial world. A close examination of the song shows a number of Ravelian thumbprints, including the accompaniment in unharmonized octaves. The shape of the main melody is also, by chance, to be found concealed in *Sur l'herbe*. Almost as famous is the *Vocalise-étude en forme de habanera*, one of the most celebrated tunes ever written, and best known in transcription for cello and piano. Only its lack of text relegates it to a footnote in a book on the mélodie. It should also be mentioned that Ravel allowed the publication of TROIS CHANSONS (1914–15), which are transcriptions for solo voice and piano of *Nicolette, Trois beaux oiseaux de paradis*, and *Ronde*. These songs (to the composer's own texts) were originally conceived for mixed chorus, and although they sound best as such, the Ravel enthusiast might do worse than to bring them from the cupboard for an occasional airing.

1 *Ballade de la reine morte d'aimer*

(Roland de Marès)

En Bohême était une Reine,
Douce sœur du Roi de Thulé,
Belle entre toutes les Reines,
Reine par sa toute Beauté.

Le grand Trouvère de Bohême
Un soir triste d'automne roux
Lui murmura le vieux: 'Je t'aime'!
Âmes folles et cœurs si fous!...

Et la Très Belle toute blanche
Le doux Poète tant aima
Que sur l'heure son âme blanche
Vers les étoiles s'exhala...

Les grosses cloches de Bohême
Et les clochettes de Thulé
Chantèrent l'Hosanna suprême
De la Reine morte d'aimer.

Ballad of the queen who died of love

In Bohemia there lived a Queen,
The King of Thule's* gentle sister,
There was never a queen more beautiful,
She reigned through beauty alone.

The great Troubadour of Bohemia,
One sad russet autumn evening,
Murmured: 'I love you', that old refrain!
Crazed souls and such crazed hearts!...

And the white-skinned beauty
Was so loved by the gentle poet,
That of a sudden her white soul
Gave up the ghost and fled to the stars...

The great bells of Bohemia
And the little bells of Thule
Sang the last Hosanna
Of the Queen who died of love.

* See note to POULENC II v.

2 *Un grand sommeil noir*
(Paul Verlaine)

Un grand sommeil noir
Tombe sur ma vie:
Dormez, tout espoir,
Dormez, toute envie!

Je ne vois plus rien,
Je perds la mémoire
Du mal et du bien...
Ô la triste histoire!

Je suis un berceau
Qu'une main balance
Au creux d'un caveau:
Silence, silence!

3 *Sainte*
(Stéphane Mallarmé)

À la fenêtre recélant
Le santal vieux qui se dédore
De la viole étincelant
Jadis selon flûte ou mandore,

Est la Sainte pâle, étalant
Le livre vieux qui se déplie
Du Magnificat ruisselant
Jadis selon vêpre et complie:

À ce vitrage d'ostensoir
Que frôle une harpe par l'Ange
Formée avec son vol du soir
Pour la délicate phalange

Du doigt que, sans le vieux santal
Ni le vieux livre, elle balance
Sur le plumage instrumental,
Musicienne du silence.

A vast dark sleep

A vast dark sleep
Falls on my life:
Slumber, all hope,
Slumber, all desire!

I have lost my sight,
All memories fail
Of good and evil...
Oh dismal tale!

I am a cradle
Rocked by a hand
In a hollow vault:
Silence, silence!

Saint

At the window that harbours
The old sandalwood of flaking gilt
Of the viol that sparkled
Once to flute or mandola,

Stands the pale saint, displaying
The ancient unfolded book
Of the Magnificat that glistened
Once to vespers and compline:

At this monstrance-glass
Brushed by a harp the Angel
Forms in his evening flight
For the delicate finger-

Tip that, lacking the old sandalwood
And the ancient book, she poises
On the instrumental plumage,
Musician of silence.

DEUX ÉPIGRAMMES DE CLÉMENT MAROT

4 i *D'Anne qui me jecta de la neige*

Anne par jeu me jecta de la neige,
Que je cuidoys froide, certainement:
Mais c'estoit feu, l'expérience en ay je,
Car embrasé, je fus soudainement.
   Puis que le feu loge secretement
Dedans la neige, où trouveray je place
Pour n'ardre point? Anne, ta seule grace
Estaindre peult le feu que je sens bien,
Non point par eau, par neige ne par glace,
Mais par sentir un feu pareil au mien.

4 ii *D'Anne jouant de l'espinette*

Lors que je voy en ordre la brunette,
Jeune, en bon poinct, de la ligne des dieux,
Et que sa voix, ses doits et l'espinette
Meinent un bruyct doulx et mélodieux,
J'ay du plaisir et d'oreilles et d'yeulx
Plus que les sainctz en leur gloire immortelle,
Et autant qu'eulx je deviens glorieux
Dès que je pense estre un peu aymé d'elle.

5 *Chanson du rouet*
(Charles-Marie-René Leconte de Lisle)

Ô mon cher rouet, ma blanche bobine,
Je vous aime mieux que l'or et l'argent!
Vous me donnez tout, lait, beurre et farine,
Et le gai logis, et le vêtement.
Je vous aime mieux que l'or et l'argent,
Ô mon cher rouet, ma blanche bobine!

Ô mon cher rouet, ma blanche bobine,
Vous chantez dès l'aube avec les oiseaux;
Été comme hiver, chanvre ou laine fine,
Par vous, jusqu'au soir, charge les fuseaux.
Vous chantez dès l'aube avec les oiseaux,
Ô mon cher rouet, ma blanche bobine.

TWO EPIGRAMS OF CLÉMENT MAROT

On Anne who threw snow at me

Anne in play threw snow at me,
Which I certainly thought cold:
But what I felt from it was fire,
For suddenly I was all aflame.
   Since fire dwells secretly
In the snow, where shall I find a place
Where I'll not burn? Anne, your favour alone
Can quench the flame I so keenly feel,
Not water nor snow nor ice,
But by feeling a fire which matches mine.

On Anne playing the spinet

When I see my neat and dark-haired lady,
Young, comely, of divine lineage,
And when her voice, her fingers, and the spinet
Make a sweet melodious sound,
My ears and eyes know greater pleasure
Than the saints in their immortal glory:
And I become as glorious as they,
The moment I feel she loves me a little.

Song of the spinning-wheel

O my dear spinning-wheel, my white bobbin,
I love you more than silver and gold!
You give me all: milk, butter and flour,
A happy home, and clothing too.
I love you more than silver and gold,
O my dear spinning-wheel, my white bobbin!

O my dear spinning-wheel, my white bobbin,
You sing at daybreak with the birds;
In summer and winter, hemp or fine wool
Load through you the spindle till nightfall.
You sing at daybreak with the birds,
O my dear spinning-wheel, my white bobbin!

Ô mon cher rouet, ma blanche bobine,
Vous me filerez mon suaire étroit,
Quand, près de mourir et courbant l'échine,
Je ferai mon lit éternel et froid.
Vous me filerez mon suaire étroit,
Ô mon cher rouet, ma blanche bobine!

O my dear spinning-wheel, my white bobbin,
You shall spin me my narrow shroud,
When, near death and stooping low,
I'll make my eternal and freezing bed.
You shall spin me my narrow shroud,
O my dear spinning-wheel, my white bobbin!

6 *Si morne!*
(Émile Verhaeren)

So bleak!

Se replier toujours sur soi-même, si morne!
Comme un drap lourd, qu'aucun dessin de fleur
     n'adorne.

So bleak to retreat within oneself!
Like a heavy cloth, unadorned by flowers.

Se replier, s'appesantir et se tasser
Et se toujours, en angles noirs et mats, casser.

To retreat, be weighed down and to cower
And always, in dark and dull corners, to snap.

Si morne! et se toujours interdire l'envie
De tailler en drapeaux l'étoffe de sa vie.

So bleak! And always to disallow oneself the desire
Of slicing into rags the fabric of one's life.

Tapir entre les plis ses mauvaises fureurs
Et ses rancœurs et ses douleurs et ses erreurs.

To crouch between the folds with one's evil rages,
One's bitternesses, griefs, and mistakes.

Ni les frissons soyeux, ni les moires fondantes
Mais les pointes en soi des épingles ardentes.

With neither silky shimmers nor melting moire,
But burning pins to pierce one's flesh.

Oh! le paquet qu'on pousse ou qu'on jette à l'écart,
Si morne et lourd, sur un rayon, dans un bazar.

Oh! the package you push or cast aside,
So bleak and heavy, on a shelf in some cheap store.

Déjà sentir la bouche âcre des moisissures
Gluer, et les taches s'étendre en leurs morsures.

Already to feel your mouth, acrid with mould,
Gluing up, and the stains spreading in their bites.

Pourrir, immensément emmaillotté d'ennui;
Être l'ennui qui se replie en de la nuit.

To putrefy, hugely swathed in ennui,
To be that ennui retreating into night.

Tandis que lentement, dans les laines ourdies,
De part en part, mordent les vers des maladies.

While slowly, in warped wool,
The worms of disease gnaw their way right through.

7 *Manteau de fleurs*
(Paul Gravollet)

Cloak of flowers

Toutes les fleurs de mon jardin sont roses,
Le rose sied à sa beauté.
Les primevères sont les premières écloses,
Puis viennent les tulipes et les jacinthes roses,
Les jolis œillets, les si belles roses,

All the flowers in my garden are pink,
Pink becomes her beauty.
The primroses are the first to bloom,
Then come pink tulips and hyacinths,
Pretty carnations, such lovely roses,

Toute la variété des fleurs si roses,	The full variety of the pinkest flowers
Du printemps et de l'été!	Of springtime and of summer!
Le rose sied à sa beauté!	Pink becomes her beauty!
Toutes mes pivoines sont roses,	All my peonies are pink,
Roses aussi sont mes glaïeuls,	My gladioli too are pink,
Roses mes géraniums; seuls,	Pink my geraniums; only lilies,
Dans tout ce rose un peu troublant,	Amid this rather heady pink,
Les lys ont le droit d'être blancs.	Only they have the right to be white.
Et quand elle passe au milieu des fleurs	And when she walks amid the flowers
Emperlées de rosée en pleurs,	Beaded with weeping dew
Dans le parfum grisant des roses,	In the reeling fragrance of the roses
Et sous la caresse des choses,	And beneath the caress of nature,
Toute grâce, amour, pureté!	The embodiment of grace, love, and purity,
Les fleurs lui font un manteau rose	The flowers fashion a pink cloak for her
Dont elle pare sa beauté.	With which she adorns her beauty.

SHÉHÉRAZADE *   /   SCHEHERAZADE

(Tristan Klingsor)

8 i Asie   /   Asia

Asie, Asie, Asie,	Asia, Asia, Asia,
Vieux pays merveilleux des contes de nourrice,	Ancient wonderland of fairy tales,
Où dort la fantaisie	Where fantasy sleeps
Comme une impératrice	Like an empress
En sa forêt tout emplie de mystères,	In her mystery-filled forest,
Asie,	Asia,
Je voudrais m'en aller avec la goélette	I long to set sail with the schooner
Qui se berce ce soir dans le port,	Which rocks this evening in the harbour,
Mystérieuse et solitaire,	Mysterious and solitary
Et qui déploie enfin ses voiles violettes	And which spreads at last its violet sails
Comme un immense oiseau de nuit dans le ciel d'or.	Like a huge night-bird in the golden sky.
Je voudrais m'en aller vers des îles de fleurs	I long to set sail for isles of flowers
En écoutant chanter la mer perverse	As I listen to the song of the wayward sea
Sur un vieux rythme ensorceleur;	With its old bewitching rhythm;
Je voudrais voir Damas et les villes de Perse	I long to see Damascus and the cities of Persia
Avec les minarets légers dans l'air;	With their airy minarets;
Je voudrais voir de beaux turbans de soie	I long to see beautiful silken turbans
Sur des visages noirs aux dents claires;	Above black faces with white teeth;
Je voudrais voir des yeux sombres d'amour	I long to see eyes dark with love
Et des prunelles brillantes de joie	And pupils sparkling with joy
En des peaux jaunes comme des oranges;	Sunk in skins as yellow as oranges;
Je voudrais voir des vêtements de velours	I long to see velvet raiments
Et des habits à longues franges;	And long-fringed robes;

* In the *Arabian nights*, she married King Shahriyar who, instead of killing her—the usual fate of his wives—allowed her to tell the tales that compose that work. Klingsor entitles his collection *Schéhérazade*.

Je voudrais voir des calumets entre des bouches
Tout entourées de barbe blanche;
Je voudrais voir d'âpres marchands aux regards
    louches,
Et des cadis et des vizirs
Qui du seul mouvement de leur doigt qui se penche
Accordent vie ou mort au gré de leur désir.

Je voudrais voir la Perse et l'Inde et puis la Chine,
Les mandarins ventrus sous les ombrelles,
Et les princesses aux mains fines
Et les lettrés qui se querellent
Sur la poésie et sur la beauté;

Je voudrais m'attarder au palais enchanté
Et comme un voyageur étranger
Contempler à loisir des paysages peints
Sur des étoffes en des cadres de sapin
Avec un personnage au milieu d'un verger;

Je voudrais voir des assassins souriant
Du bourreau qui coupe un cou d'innocent
Avec son grand sabre courbé d'Orient;
Je voudrais voir des pauvres et des reines;
Je voudrais voir des roses et du sang;
Je voudrais voir mourir d'amour ou bien de haine,
Et puis, m'en revenir plus tard
Narrer mon aventure aux curieux de rêves,

En élevant comme Sindbad
Ma vieille pipe arabe
Du temps en temps jusqu'à mes lèvres
Pour interrompre le conte avec art...

8 ii *La flûte enchantée*

L'ombre est douce et mon maître dort,
Coiffé d'un bonnet conique de soie,
Et son long nez jaune en sa barbe blanche.
Mais moi je suis éveillée encore
Et j'écoute au-dehors
Une chanson de flûte où s'épanche
Tour à tour la tristesse ou la joie,
Un air tour à tour langoureux ou frivole
Que mon amoureux chéri joue,
Et quand je m'approche de la croisée,
Il me semble que chaque note s'envole
De la flûte vers ma joue
Comme un mystérieux baiser.

I long to see calumets* in mouths
Fringed about with white beards;
I long to see grasping merchants with shifty looks,

And cadis† and viziers
Who with a single crook of the finger
Dispense life or death on a whim.

I long to see Persia, and India, and then China,
Portly mandarins beneath their sunshades,
And princesses with delicate hands,
And learned men disputing
About poetry and beauty;

I long to linger in enchanted palaces,
And like a foreign traveller
Gaze at leisure on landscapes painted
On fabrics in pinewood frames,
With a figure in the midst of an orchard;

I long to see assassins smiling,
As the executioner cuts off an innocent head
With his great curved Oriental scimitar;
I long to see beggars and queens;
I long to see roses and blood;
I long to see death for love or else for hate,
And then to return later
And recount my adventures to those intrigued by
    dreams,
While raising like Sinbad
My old Arabian pipe
From time to time to my lips,
Artfully to interrupt the tale...

The enchanted flute

The shade is soft and my master sleeps,
A cone-shaped silken cap on his head,
And his long yellow nose in his white beard.
But I am still awake,
Listening to the song
Of a flute outside that pours forth
Sadness and joy in turn,
A tune now languorous now lively,
Which my dear lover plays.
And when I draw near the casement,
Each note seems to fly
From the flute to my cheek
Like a mysterious kiss.

* A tobacco-pipe with a bowl of clay or stone, and a long reed stem carved and ornamented with feathers.
† A Cadi is a civil judge, usually Turkish, Arabian or Persian.

8 iii *L'indifférent*

Tes yeux sont doux comme ceux d'une fille,
Jeune étranger,
Et la courbe fine
De ton beau visage de duvet ombragé
Est plus séduisante encore de ligne.

Ta lèvre chante
Sur le pas de ma porte
Une langue inconnue et charmante
Comme une musique fausse;
Entre! et que mon vin te réconforte...

Mais non, tu passes
Et de mon seuil je te vois t'éloigner
Me faisant un dernier geste avec grâce
Et la hanche légèrement ployée
Par ta démarche féminine et lasse.

The indifferent one

Your eyes are soft like a girl's,
Young stranger,
And the delicate curve
Of your handsome down-shaded face
Is still more attractively shaped.

Your lips sing
At my door
An unknown charming tongue,
Like music off-pitch;
Enter! And let my wine refresh you...

But no, you pass by
And I see you leaving my threshold,
Gracefully waving farewell,
Your hips lightly swaying
In your languid feminine way.

9 *Noël des jouets*

(Maurice Ravel)

Le troupeau verni des moutons
Roule en tumulte vers la crèche.
Les lapins tambours, brefs et rêches,
Couvrent leurs aigres mirlitons.
Vierge Marie, en crinoline,
Ses yeux d'émail sans cesse ouverts,
En attendant Bonhomme hiver,
Veille Jésus qui se dodine.
Car, près de là, sous un sapin,
Furtif, emmitouflé dans l'ombre
Du bois, Belzébuth, le chien sombre,
Guette l'Enfant de sucre peint.
Mais les beaux anges incassables
Suspendus par des fils d'archal
Du haut de l'arbuste hiémal
Assurent la paix des étables.
Et leur vol de clinquant vermeil
Qui cliquette en bruits symétriques
S'accorde au bétail mécanique
Dont la voix grêle bêle:
'Noël! Noël! Noël!'

The toys' Christmas

The painted flock of sheep
Trundles towards the Crib.
The rabbit drummers, sharp and harsh,
Drown their shrill hewgags'* sound.
The Virgin Mary in crinoline,
Her enamel eyes ever open,
Waits for good old winter to come,
Watching over Jesus who lies abed.
For nearby, skulking beneath a fir-tree
And muffled in the forest's shadow,
Beelzebub, the sinister dog,
Lies in wait for the coloured-sugar Child.
But the beautiful unbreakable angels,
Hanging by wires of brass
From the top of the Christmas tree
Guarantee the stables' peace.
And their tinselled vermilion flight,
Jingling in symmetrical sounds
Harmonizes with the mechnical cattle,
Whose harsh voices bellow:
'Noël! Noël! Noël!'

---

* A toy musical instrument for children, made of a wooden tube with a hole near one end, the other end being closed by a piece of parchment, whose vibration produces a wailing sound.

CINQ MÉLODIES POPULAIRES GRECQUES	FIVE GREEK FOLKSONGS

(traditional, trans. M. D. Calvocoressi)

10 i *Le réveil de la mariée*
The bride's awakening

Réveille-toi, réveille-toi, perdrix mignonne.
Ouvre au matin tes ailes.
Trois grains de beauté, mon cœur en est brûlé.
Vois le ruban, le ruban d'or que je t'apporte
Pour le nouer autour de tes cheveux.
Si tu veux, ma belle, viens nous marier:
Dans nos deux familles, tous sont alliés.

Wake up, wake up, pretty partridge,
Spread your wings to the morning.
Three beauty spots—and my heart's ablaze.
See the golden ribbon I bring you
To tie around your tresses.
If you wish, my beauty, let us marry!
In our two families all are related.

10 ii *La-bàs, vers l'église*
Down there by the church

Là-bas, vers l'église,
Vers l'église Ayio Sidero,
L'église, ô Vierge sainte,
L'église, Ayio Costanndino
Se sont réunis, rassemblés en nombre infini,
Du monde, ô Vierge sainte!
Du monde tous les plus braves!

Down there by the church,
By the church of Saint Sideros,
The church, O Holy Virgin,
The church of Saint Constantine,
Are gathered together, buried in infinite numbers,
The bravest people, O Holy Virgin,
The bravest people in the world!

10 iii *Quel galant m'est comparable?*
What gallant can compare with me?

Quel galant m'est comparable,
D'entre ceux qu'on voit passer?
Dis, dame Vassiliki?
Vois, pendus, pendus à ma ceinture,
Pistolets et sabre aigu...
Et c'est toi que j'aime!

What gallant can compare with me
Among those seen passing by?
Tell me, Mistress Vassiliki?
See, hanging at my belt,
Pistols and sharp sword...
And it's you I love!

10 iv *Chanson des cueilleuses de lentisques*

Ô joie de mon âme,
Joie de mon cœur, trésor qui m'est si cher;
Joie de l'âme et du cœur.
Toi que j'aime ardemment,
Tu es plus beau qu'un ange.
Ô lorsque tu parais, ange si doux,
Devant nos yeux,
Comme un bel ange blond,
Sous le clair soleil,
Hélas, tous nos pauvres cœurs soupirent!

Song of the lentisk gatherers

O joy of my soul, joy of my heart,
Treasure so dear to me;
Joy of the soul and of the heart,
You whom I love with passion,
You are more beautiful than an angel.
Oh when you appear, angel so sweet,
Before our eyes,
Like a lovely, blond angel
Under the bright sun—
Alas, all our poor hearts sigh!

10 v *Tout gai!*

Tout gai,
Ha, tout gai;
Belle jambe, tireli qui danse,
Belle jambe, la vaisselle danse.
Tra-la-la.

So merry!

So merry,
Ah, so merry;
Lovely leg, tireli, that dances,
Lovely leg, the crockery dances,
Tra la la.

HISTOIRES NATURELLES

(Jules Renard)

NATURAL HISTORIES

11 i *Le paon*

Il va sûrement se marier aujourd'hui.

Ce devait être pour hier. En habit de gala, il était prêt. Il n'attendait que sa fiancée. Elle n'est pas venue. Elle ne peut tarder.

Glorieux, il se promène avec une allure de prince indien et porte sur lui les riches présents d'usage. L'amour avive l'éclat de ses couleurs et son aigrette tremble comme une lyre.

La fiancée n'arrive pas.

Il monte au haut du toit et regarde du côté du soleil. Il jette son cri diabolique:

Léon! Léon!

C'est ainsi qu'il appelle sa fiancée. Il ne voit rien venir et personne ne répond. Les volailles habituées ne lèvent même point la tête. Elles sont lasses de l'admirer. Il redescend dans la cour, si sûr d'être beau qu'il est incapable de rancune.

The peacock

He will surely get married today.

It was to have been yesterday. In full regalia he was ready. It was only his bride he was waiting for. She has not come. She cannot be long.

Proudly he processes with the air of an Indian prince, bearing about his person the customary lavish gifts. Love burnishes the brilliance of his colours, and his crest quivers like a lyre.

His bride does not appear.

He ascends to the top of the roof and looks towards the sun. He utters his devilish cry:

Léon! Léon!

It is thus that he summons his bride. He can see nothing drawing near, and no one replies. The fowls are used to all this and do not even raise their heads. They are tired of admiring him. He descends once more to the yard, so sure of his beauty that he is incapable of resentment.

Son mariage sera pour demain.

Et, ne sachant que faire du reste de la journée, il se dirige vers le perron. Il gravit les marches, comme des marches de temple, d'un pas officiel.

Il relève sa robe à queue toute lourde des yeux qui n'ont pu se détacher d'elle.

Il répète encore une fois la cérémonie.

His marriage will take place tomorrow.

And, not knowing what to do for the rest of the day, he heads for the flight of steps. He ascends them, as though they were the steps of a temple, with a formal tread.

He lifts his train, heavy with eyes that have been unable to detach themselves.

Once more he repeats the ceremony.

II ii *Le grillon*

C'est l'heure où, las d'errer, l'insecte nègre revient de promenade et répare avec soin le désordre de son domaine.

D'abord il ratisse ses étroites allées de sable.

Il fait du bran de scie qu'il écarte au seuil de sa retraite.

Il lime la racine de cette grande herbe propre à le harceler.

Il se repose.

Puis, il remonte sa minuscule montre.

A-t-il fini? Est-elle cassée? Il se repose encore un peu.

Il rentre chez lui et ferme sa porte.

Longtemps il tourne sa clef dans la serrure délicate.

Et il écoute:

Point d'alarme dehors.

Mais il ne se trouve pas en sûreté.

Et comme par une chaînette dont la poulie grince, il descend jusqu'au fond de la terre.

On n'entend plus rien.

Dans la campagne muette, les peupliers se dressent comme des doigts en l'air et désignent la lune.

The cricket

It is the hour when, weary of wandering, the black insect returns from his outing and carefully restores order to his estate.

First he rakes his narrow sandy paths.

He makes sawdust which he scatters on the threshold of his retreat.

He files the root of this tall grass likely to annoy him.

He rests.

Then he winds up his tiny watch.

Has he finished? Is it broken? He rests again for a while.

He goes inside and shuts the door.

For an age he turns his key in the delicate lock.

And he listens:

Nothing untoward outside.

But he does not feel safe.

And as if by a tiny chain on a creaking pulley, he lowers himself into the bowels of the earth.

Nothing more is heard.

In the silent countryside the poplars rise like fingers in the air, pointing to the moon.

II iii *Le cygne*

Il glisse sur le bassin, comme un traîneau blanc, de nuage en nuage. Car il n'a faim que des nuages floconneux qu'il voit naître, bouger, et se perdre dans l'eau. C'est l'un d'eux qu'il désire. Il le vise du bec, et il plonge tout à coup son col vêtu de neige.

Puis, tel un bras de femme sort d'une manche, il le retire.

The swan

He glides on the pond like a white sledge, from cloud to cloud. For he is hungry only for the fleecy clouds that he sees forming, moving, dissolving in the water. It is one of these that he wants. He takes aim with his beak and suddenly immerses his snow-clad neck.

Then, like a woman's arm emerging from a sleeve, he draws it back up.

Il n'a rien.

Il regarde: les nuages effarouchés ont disparu.

Il ne reste qu'un instant désabusé, car les nuages tardent peu à revenir, et, là-bas, où meurent les ondulations de l'eau, en voici un qui se reforme.

Doucement, sur son léger coussin de plumes, le cygne rame et s'approche...

Il s'épuise à pêcher de vains reflets, et peut-être qu'il mourra, victime de cette illusion, avant d'attraper un seul morceau de nuage.

Mais qu'est-ce que je dis?

Chaque fois qu'il plonge, il fouille du bec la vase nourrissante et ramène un ver.

Il engraisse comme une oie.

He has caught nothing.

He looks about: the startled clouds have vanished.

Only for a second is he disappointed, for the clouds are not slow to return, and, over there, where the ripples fade, there is one reappearing.

Gently, on his soft cushion of down, the swan paddles and approaches...

He exhausts himself fishing for empty reflections, and perhaps he will die, a victim of that illusion, before catching a single shred of cloud.

But what am I saying?

Each time he dives, he burrows with his beak in the nourishing mud and brings up a worm.

He's getting as fat as a goose.

II iv *Le martin-pêcheur*

Ça n'a pas mordu, ce soir, mais je rapporte une rare émotion.

Comme je tenais ma perche de ligne tendue, un martin-pêcheur est venu s'y poser.

Nous n'avons pas d'oiseau plus éclatant.

Il semblait une grosse fleur bleue au bout d'une longue tige. La perche pliait sous le poids. Je ne respirais plus, tout fier d'être pris pour un arbre par un martin-pêcheur.

Et je suis sûr qu'il ne s'est pas envolé de peur, mais qu'il a cru qu'il ne faisait que passer d'une branche à une autre.

The kingfisher

Not a bite, this evening, but I had a rare experience.

As I was holding out my fishing rod, a kingfisher came and perched on it.

We have no bird more brilliant.

He was like a great blue flower at the tip of a long stem. The rod bent beneath the weight. I held my breath, so proud to be taken for a tree by a kingfisher.

And I'm sure he did not fly off from fear, but thought he was simply flitting from one branch to another.

II v *La pintade*

C'est la bossue de ma cour. Elle ne rêve que plaies à cause de sa bosse.

Les poules ne lui disent rien: brusquement, elle se précipite et les harcèle.

Puis elle baisse sa tête, penche le corps, et, de toute la vitesse de ses pattes maigres, elle court frapper, de son bec dur, juste au centre de la roue d'une dinde.

Cette poseuse l'agaçait.

Ainsi, la tête bleuie, ses barbillons à vif, cocardière, elle rage du matin au soir. Elle se bat sans motif, peut-être parce qu'elle s'imagine toujours qu'on se moque de sa taille, de son crâne chauve et de sa queue basse.

Et elle ne cesse de jeter un cri discordant qui perce l'air comme une pointe.

The guinea-fowl

She is the hunchback of my barnyard. She dreams only of wounding, because of her hump.

The hens say nothing to her: suddenly, she swoops and harries them.

Then she lowers her head, leans forward, and, with all the speed of her skinny legs, runs and strikes with her hard beak at the very centre of a turkey's tail.

This poseuse was provoking her.

Thus, with her bluish head and raw wattles, pugnaciously she rages from morn to night. She fights for no reason, perhaps because she always thinks they are making fun of her figure, of her bald head and drooping tail.

And she never stops screaming her discordant cry, which pierces the air like a needle.

Parfois elle quitte la cour et disparaît. Elle laisse aux volailles pacifiques un moment de répit. Mais elle revient plus turbulente et plus criarde. Et, frénétique, elle se vautre par terre.

Qu'a-t-elle donc?

La sournoise fait une farce.

Elle est allée pondre son œuf à la campagne.

Je peux le chercher si ça m'amuse.

Elle se roule dans la poussière, comme une bossue.

Sometimes she leaves the yard and vanishes. She gives the peace-loving poultry a moment's respite. But she returns more rowdy and shrill. And in a frenzy she wallows in the earth.

Whatever's wrong with her?

The cunning creature is playing a trick.

She went to lay her egg in the open country.

I can look for it if I like.

And she rolls in the dust, like a hunchback.

12 Les grands vents venus d'outre-mer

(Henri de Régnier)

The great ultramarine winds

Les grands vents venus d'outre-mer
Passent par la Ville, l'hiver,
Comme des étrangers amers.

Ils se concertent, graves et pâles,
Sur les places, et leurs sandales
Ensablent le marbre des dalles.

Comme des crosses à leurs mains fortes
Ils heurtent l'auvent et la porte
Derrière qui l'horloge est morte;

Et les adolescents amers
S'en vont avec eux vers la Mer!

The great ultramarine winds
Pass through the City in winter,
Like bitter strangers.

Solemn and pale, they scheme together
In the squares, and their sandals
Strew with sand the marble flagstones.

As though holding crooks in their strong hands,
They ram the porch-roof and the door,
Behind which the clock has died;

And the bitter adolescents
Make off with them toward the Sea!

13 Sur l'herbe

(Paul Verlaine)

On the lawn

L'abbé divague.—Et toi, marquis,
Tu mets de travers ta perruque.
—Ce vieux vin de Chypre est exquis
Moins, Camargo,* que votre nuque.

—Ma flamme...—Do, mi, sol, la, si.
L'abbé, ta noirceur se dévoile!
—Que je meure, Mesdames, si
Je ne vous décroche une étoile!

—Je voudrais être petit chien!
—Embrassons nos bergères l'une
Après l'autre.—Messieurs, eh bien?
—Do, mi, sol.—Hé! bonsoir, la Lune!

The abbot rambles on.—'And you, Marquis,
You've got your wig on all askew.'
'This old Cyprus wine's exquisite,
But less so, Camargo, than the nape of your neck.'

'My love...'—'Do, mi, so, la, ti.
Abbot, you're baring your base soul!'
'May I die, ladies, if
I don't detach a spangle from your hair!'

'I'd like to be a little dog!'
'Let's kiss our shepherdesses, one
By one.' 'Well, gentlemen?'
'Do, mi, sol.' 'Hey! Good evening, Moon!'

* A dancer (1710–70), she was the subject of a famous painting by Lancret.

TROIS POÈMES DE STÉPHANE MALLARMÉ

14 i *Soupir*

Mon âme vers ton front où rêve, ô calme sœur,
Un automne jonché de taches de rousseur,
Et vers le ciel errant de ton œil angélique
Monte, comme dans un jardin mélancolique,
Fidèle, un blanc jet d'eau soupire vers l'Azur!
—Vers l'Azur attendri d'Octobre pâle et pur

Qui mire aux grands bassins sa langueur infinie
Et laisse, sur l'eau morte où la fauve agonie
Des feuilles erre au vent et creuse un froid sillon,

Se traîner le soleil jaune d'un long rayon.

14 ii *Placet futile*

Princesse! à jalouser le destin d'une Hébé
Qui poind sur cette tasse au baiser de vos lèvres,
J'use mes feux mais n'ai rang discret que d'abbé

Et ne figurerai même nu sur le Sèvres.

Comme je ne suis pas ton bichon embarbé,
Ni la pastille ni du rouge, ni jeux mièvres
Et que sur moi je sais ton regard clos tombé,
Blonde dont les coiffeurs divins sont des orfèvres!

Nommez-nous... toi de qui tant de ris framboisés

Se joignent en troupeau d'agneaux apprivoisés
Chez tous broutant les vœux et bêlant aux délires,

Nommez-nous... pour qu'Amour ailé d'un éventail
M'y peigne flûte aux doigts endormant ce bercail,

Princesse, nommez-nous berger de vos sourires.

THREE POEMS OF STÉPHANE MALLARMÉ

Sigh

My soul rises toward your brow where, calm sister,
An autumn strewn with russet spots is dreaming,
And toward the restless sky of your angelic eye,
As in some melancholy garden
A white fountain faithfully sighs toward the Azure!
—Toward the tender Azure of pale and pure
October
That mirrors its infinite languor in the vast pools,
And, on the stagnant water where the tawny agony
Of leaves wanders in the wind and digs a cold
furrow,
Lets the yellow sun draw itself out in one long ray.

Futile supplication

Princess! In envying the fate of a Hebe
Who appears on this cup at the kiss of your lips,
I expend my ardour but have only the modest rank
of abbé
And shall not figure even naked on the Sèvres.*

Since I am not your bearded lap-dog,
Nor lozenge, nor rouge, nor affected games,
And know you look on me with indifferent eyes,
Blonde, whose divine coiffeurs are goldsmiths—

Appoint me... you whose many laughs like
raspberries
Are gathered among flocks of docile lambs
Grazing through all vows and bleating at all
frenzies,

Appoint me... so that Love winged with a fan
May paint me there, fingering a flute and lulling this
fold,
Princess, appoint me shepherd of your smiles.

* The town of Sèvres, near Paris, has been famous since 1756 for its porcelain, mosaic-work and painted glass.

14 iii *Surgi de la croupe et du bond*

Surgi de la croupe et du bond
D'une verrerie éphémère
Sans fleurir la veillée amère
Le col ignoré s'interrompt.

Je crois bien que deux bouches n'ont
Bu, ni son amant ni ma mère,
Jamais à la même Chimère,
Moi, sylphe de ce froid plafond!

Le pur vase d'aucun breuvage
Que l'inexhaustible veuvage
Agonise mais ne consent,

Naïf baiser des plus funèbres!
À rien expirer annonçant
Une rose dans les ténèbres.

Risen from the crupper and leap

Risen from the crupper and leap
Of an ephemeral ornament of glass,
Without garlanding the bitter vigil,
The neglected neck stops short.

I truly believe that two mouths never
Drank, neither her lover nor my mother,
From the same Chimera,
I, sylph of this cold ceiling!

The vase pure of any draught
Save inexhaustible widowhood
Though dying does not consent—

Naive and most funereal kiss—
To breathe forth any annunciation
Of a rose in the shadows.

DEUX MÉLODIES HÉBRAÏQUES

15 i *Kaddisch*

Que ta gloire, ô Roi des rois, soit exaltée, ô toi qui
dois renouveler le Monde et ressuciter les trépassés.
Ton règne, Adonaï,* soit proclamé par nous, fils
d'Israël, aujourd'hui, demain, à jamais. Disons tous:
Amen. Qu'il soit aimé, qu'il soit chéri, qu'il soit loué,
glorifié ton nom radieux. Qu'il soit béni, sanctifié;
qu'il soit adoré, ton nom qui plane sur les cieux, sur
nos louanges, sur nos hymnes, sur toutes nos béné-
dictions. Que le ciel clément nous accorde la vie
calme, la paix, le bonheur. Ah! ah! ah! ah! ah! Disons
tous: Amen.

TWO HEBREW SONGS

Kaddish

May thy glory, O King of Kings, be exalted, O thou
who art to renew the world and resurrect the dead.
May thy reign, Adonaï, be proclaimed by us, the sons
of Israel, today, tomorrow, forever. Let us all say:
Amen. May thy radiant name be loved, cherished,
praised, glorified. May it be blessed, sanctified, exalted, thy name which soars above the heavens, above
our praises, above our hymns, above all our benisons.
May merciful heaven grant us tranquillity, peace,
happiness. Ah! Let us all say: Amen.

15 ii *L'énigme éternelle*

Monde tu nous interroges:
Tra la tra la la la la
L'on répond:
Tra la la...
Si l'on ne peut te répondre:
Tra la la...
Monde tu nous interroges:
Tra la la...

* God.

The eternal enigma

World, you question us:
Tra la...
The answer comes:
Tra la...
If you cannot be answered:
Tra la...
World, you question us:
Tra la...

16 *Ronsard à son âme*

(Pierre de Ronsard)

Amelette Ronsardelette,
Mignonnellette, doucelette,
Très chère hôtesse de mon corps,
Tu descends là-bas faiblelette,
Pâle, maigrelette, seulette,
Dans le froid Royaume des morts:
Toutefois simple, sans remords
De meurtre, poison, et rancune,
Méprisant faveurs et trésors
Tant enviés par la commune.
    Passant, j'ai dit, suis ta fortune,
Ne trouble mon repos, je dors.

Ronsard to his soul

Dear little Ronsardian soul,
Little sweet one, little soft one,
My body's dearest denizen,
You go so weakly down to the depths,
So pale, so meagre, so lonely,
To the cold kingdom of the dead:
Simple withal, unburdened by remorse
For murder, poison, and bitterness,
Scorning favours and riches,
So greatly envied by the common man.
    Passer-by, I have done: follow your fortune,
Do not disturb my rest, I sleep.

17 *Rêves*

(Léon-Paul Fargue)

Un enfant court
Autour des marbres...
Une voix sourd
Des hauts parages...

Les yeux si tendres
De ceux qui t'aiment
Songent et passent
Entre les arbres...

Aux grandes orgues
De quelque gare
Gronde la vague
Des grands départs...

Dans un vieux rêve
Au pays vague
Des choses brèves
Qui meurent sages...

Dreams

A child runs
Round marble statues...
A voice issues from
High places...

The oh so tender eyes
Of those who love you
Dream and flit by
Between the trees...

In the mighty blare
Of some station
Roars the wave
Of great departures...

All this in an old dream,
In the indistinct land
Of ephemeral things
That die discreetly...

CHANSONS MADÉCASSES
(Évariste Parny)

MADAGASCAN SONGS

18 i *Nahandove*

Nahandove, ô belle Nahandove! L'oiseau nocturne a commencé ses cris, la pleine lune brille sur ma tête, et la rosée naissante humecte mes cheveux. Voici l'heure; qui peut t'arrêter, Nahandove, ô belle Nahandove!

Le lit de feuilles est préparé; je l'ai parsemé de fleurs et d'herbes odoriférantes; il est digne de tes charmes, Nahandove, ô belle Nahandove!

Elle vient. J'ai reconnu la respiration précipitée que donne une marche rapide; j'entends le froissement de la pagne qui l'enveloppe; c'est elle, c'est Nahandove, la belle Nahandove!

Reprends haleine, ma jeune amie; repose-toi sur mes genoux. Que ton regard est enchanteur! Que le mouvement de ton sein est vif et délicieux sous la main qui le presse! Tu souris, Nahandove, ô belle Nahandove!

Tes baisers pénètrent jusqu'à l'âme; tes caresses brûlent tous mes sens; arrête, ou je vais mourir. Meurt-on de volupté, Nahandove, ô belle Nahandove!

Le plaisir passe comme un éclair. Ta douce haleine s'affoiblit, tes yeux humides se referment, ta tête se penche mollement, et tes transports s'éteignent dans la langueur. Jamais tu ne fus si belle, Nahandove, ô belle Nahandove!

Tu pars, et je vais languir dans les regrets et les désirs. Je languirai jusqu'au soir. Tu reviendras ce soir, Nahandove, ô belle Nahandove!

Nahandove

Nahandove, O lovely Nahandove! The nocturnal bird has begun its cries, the full moon shines overhead, and the new-born dew moistens my hair. Now is the hour; who can be delaying you, Nahandove, O lovely Nahandove!

The bed of leaves is prepared; I have strewn it with flowers and sweet-smelling herbs; it is worthy of your charms, Nahandove, O lovely Nahandove!

She comes. I recognized her breathing, quickened by her rapid walk; I hear the rustle of the loin-cloth wrapped around her; it is she, it is Nahandove, lovely Nahandove!

Take breath, my little love; rest on my lap. How bewitching your gaze is! How quick and delightful is the motion of your breast beneath a caressing hand! You smile, Nahandove, O lovely Nahandove!

Your kisses reach right into my soul; your caresses set all my senses ablaze: stop, or I shall die. Can one die of delight, Nahandove, O lovely Nahandove?

Pleasure passes like lightning. Your sweet breath falters, your moist eyes close, your head falls gently forwards, and your ecstasy dies, giving way to languor. Never were you so lovely, Nahandove, O lovely Nahandove!

You leave, and I shall languish in sorrow and desire. I shall languish until evening. You will return tonight, Nahandove, O lovely Nahandove!

18 ii *Aoua!*

Aoua! Aoua! Méfiez-vous des blancs, habitans du rivage. Du tems de nos pères, des blancs descendirent dans cette île. On leur dit: Voilà des terres, que vos femmes les cultivent; soyez justes, soyez bons, et devenez nos frères.

Les blancs promirent, et cependant ils faisoient des retranchemens. Un fort menaçant s'éleva; le tonnerre fut renfermé dans des bouches d'airain; leurs prêtres voulurent nous donner un Dieu que nous ne

Aoua!

Aoua! Aoua! Beware of white men, dwellers of the shore. In our fathers' time, white men landed on this island; they were told: here is land, let your women work it; be just, be kind, and become our brothers.

The white men made promises, and yet they made entrenchments too. A menacing fort was built; thunder was stored in muzzles of cannon; their priests pressed on us a God we did not know; they spoke

connoissons pas; ils parlèrent enfin d'obéissance et d'esclavage. Plutôt la mort! Le carnage fut long et terrible; mais malgré la foudre qu'ils vomissoient, et qui écrasoit des armées entières, ils furent tous exterminés. Aoua! Aoua! Méfiez-vous des blancs.

Nous avons vu de nouveaux tyrans, plus forts et plus nombreux, planter leur pavillon sur le rivage. Le ciel a combattu pour nous. Il a fait tomber sur eux les pluies, les tempêtes et les vents empoisonnés. Ils ne sont plus, et nous vivons, et nous vivons libres. Aoua! Aoua! Méfiez-vous des blancs, habitans du rivage.

finally of obedience and slavery. Sooner death! The carnage was long and terrible; but despite the thunder they spewed and which crushed whole armies, they were all wiped out. Aoua! Aoua! Beware of white men.

We have seen new tyrants, stronger and more numerous, setting their tents on the shore: heaven has fought on our behalf; has hurled rains upon them, storms and poisoned winds. They are no more, and we live, and live in freedom. Aoua! Aoua! Beware of white men, dwellers of the shore.

18 iii *Il est doux*

Il est doux de se coucher, durant la chaleur, sous un arbre touffu, et d'attendre que le vent du soir amène la fraîcheur.

Femmes, approchez. Tandis que je me repose ici sous un arbre touffu, occupez mon oreille par vos accens prolongés. Répétez la chanson de la jeune fille, lorsque ses doigts tressent la natte, ou lorsqu'assise auprès du riz, elle chasse les oiseaux avides.

Le chant plaît à mon âme. La danse est pour moi presque aussi douce qu'un baiser. Que vos pas soient lents; qu'ils imitent les attitudes du plaisir et l'abandon de la volupté.

Le vent du soir se lève; la lune commence à briller au travers des arbres de la montagne. Allez, et préparez le repas.

It is sweet

It is sweet to lie in the heat beneath a leafy tree, and wait for the coolness of the evening wind.

Women, draw near! While I rest here beneath a leafy tree, fill my ear with your long-drawn tones. Sing the song of the young girl, who when her fingers braid her plaits, or when she sits beside the rice, chases off the greedy birds.

Song pleases my soul; dance is for me almost as sweet as a kiss. Let your steps be slow; let them mime the gestures of pleasure and the abandon of passion.

The evening breeze begins to stir; the moon begins to gleam through trees on the mountainside. Go, prepare the meal.

DON QUICHOTTE À DULCINÉE
(Paul Morand)

DON QUIXOTE TO DULCINEA

19 i *Chanson romanesque*

Si vous me disiez que la terre
À tant tourner vous offensa,
Je lui dépêcherais Pança:
Vous la verriez fixe et se taire.

Si vous me disiez que l'ennui
Vous vient du ciel trop fleuri d'astres,
Déchirant les divins cadastres,
Je faucherais d'un coup la nuit.

Romantic song

Were you to tell me that the earth
Offended you with so much turning,
I'd dispatch Panza to deal with it:
You'd see it still and silenced.

Were you to tell me that you are wearied
By a sky too studded with stars—
Tearing the divine order asunder,
I'd scythe the night with a single blow.

Si vous me disiez que l'espace
Ainsi vidé ne vous plaît point,
Chevalier dieu, la lance au poing,
J'étoilerais le vent qui passe.

Mais si vous disiez que mon sang
Est plus à moi qu'à vous, ma Dame,
Je blêmirais dessous le blâme
Et je mourrais, vous bénissant.

    Ô Dulcinée.

Were you to tell me that space itself,
Thus denuded was not to your taste—
As a god-like knight, with lance in hand,
I'd sow the fleeting wind with stars.

But were you to tell me that my blood
Is more mine, my Lady, than your own,
I'd pale at the admonishment
And, blessing you, would die.

    O Dulcinea.

19 ii *Chanson épique*

Bon Saint Michel qui me donnez loisir
De voir ma Dame et de l'entendre,
Bon Saint Michel qui me daignez choisir
Pour lui complaire et la défendre,
Bon Saint Michel, veuillez descendre
Avec Saint Georges sur l'autel
De la Madone au bleu mantel.

D'un rayon du ciel bénissez ma lame
Et son égale en pureté
Et son égale en piété
Comme en pudeur et chasteté:
    Ma Dame.

(Ô grands Saint Georges et Saint Michel)
L'ange qui veille sur ma veille,
Ma douce Dame si pareille
À Vous, Madone au bleu mantel!
    Amen.

Epic song

Good Saint Michael who gives me leave
To behold and hear my Lady,
Good Saint Michael who deigns to elect me
To please her and defend her,
Good Saint Michael, descend, I pray,
With Saint George onto the altar
Of the Madonna robed in blue.

With a heavenly beam bless my blade
And its equal in purity
And its equal in piety
As in modesty and chastity:
    My Lady.

(O great Saint George and great Saint Michael)
Bless the angel watching over my vigil,
My sweet Lady, so like unto Thee,
O Madonna robed in blue!
    Amen.

19 iii *Chanson à boire*

Foin du bâtard, illustre Dame,
Qui pour me perdre à vos doux yeux
Dit que l'amour et le vin vieux
Mettent en deuil mon cœur, mon âme!

Je bois
À la joie!
La joie est le seul but
Où je vais droit... lorsque j'ai... bu!

Drinking song

A pox on the bastard, illustrious Lady,
Who to discredit me in your sweet eyes,
Says that love and old wine
Are saddening my heart and soul!

I drink
To joy!
Joy is the only goal
To which I go straight... when I'm... drunk!

Foin du jaloux, brune maîtresse,	A pox on the jealous wretch, O dusky mistress,
Qui geind, qui pleure et fait serment	Who whines and weeps and vows
D'être toujours ce pâle amant	Always to be this lily-livered lover
Qui met de l'eau dans son ivresse!	Who dilutes his drunkenness!
Je bois	I drink
À la joie!	To joy!
La joie est le seul but	Joy is the only goal
Où je vais droit... lorsque j'ai... bu!	To which I go straight... when I'm... drunk!

RAWSTHORNE, Alan (1905–1971)

This English composer, always a fastidious craftsman, was drawn into the world of French song, like a number of other British composers, by the fashion for folksong arrangements. THREE FRENCH NURS-ERY SONGS written for Gemma Blech were published in 1938, with the subtitle TROIS CHANSONS DE NOURRICE. Although there is an English singing translation, the songs—*Je suis un pepit poupon, Il pleut, il pleut, bergère*, and *Fais do-do, Pierrot*—were set in the original French. These are attractive arrangements where the vocal line, despite its connection with real folksong, has been cleverly reworked. The second song might seem to have been influenced by Britten's French arrangements had it not pre-dated them. More characteristic of Rawsthorne's piquant harmonic style is the dance-like *Nous étions trois filles*, dedicated to Sophie Wyss who did a great deal to encourage British composers to work in this language. *Two fish* is a song from the end of the composer's life, a wry meditation on adultery and marital constancy. This is a French song at one remove: the text is by the sixteenth-century French poet Guillaume du Bartas, translated into English by one Joshua Sylvester as early as 1641.

REBER, Henri (1807–1880)

Saint-Saëns described this composer as something of a musical anachronism, as if he were 'a contemporary of Mozart's, astonished and somewhat shocked by our music and manners'. As this was also more or less said of Saint-Saëns by his contemporaries, we can detect that Reber's neo-classicism, his love of the Viennese masters (particularly Schubert), and his penchant for setting old texts were all influential on the younger composer. But Reber played a more general role in the history of the mélodie, and his solid craftsmanship (he was the author of a famous treatise on harmony), his fastidious attention to the accompaniments of his song, and his concern for literature were all recognized, and emulated, by such composers as Gounod and Delibes. Some of his favourite poets were Charles d'Orléans, Marot, and Malherbe—to be set in the twentieth century by, respectively, Debussy, Ravel, and Poulenc. It might be argued that the French taste for polished evocations of the antique style, a genre which accounts for a large number of distinguished French mélodies, was something established by Reber. One has only to listen to *L'ermite* (Marot) to hear an unmistakable forerunner of Fauré's Henri de Régnier setting *Chanson*, and the whole of that composer's celebrated madrigal style. The fact that there are no fewer than fourteen Victor Hugo settings composed from 1845 on makes Reber something of a Hugo pioneer. These include *La captive* [BERLIOZ 6], *Le papillon et la fleur* [FAURÉ 1], an ingratiating *Si mes vers avaient des ailes* [HAHN 2], *Guitare* [BIZET 2], and *Si vous n'avez rien à me dire*, also set by Saint-Saëns. In addition Reber also set Gautier's *Villanelle* and *Absence* [BERLIOZ 3 i, 3 iv]. Reber is worthy of reassessment. A group of his songs, simple, yet lacking sentimentaility and bathos (the besetting sin of his period), would make an unusual and appropriate beginning to a mélodie recital.

REYER, Ernest (1823–1909)

As a composer of mélodies, Reyer has not held the recital stage (with some justification, for there is a stiffness about both the vocal and the piano writing), but his name was once an important one in French music—particularly in the field of opera (*Sigurd*, *Salammbô*). His friendship with such poets as Gautier and Méry encouraged him to write mélodies. He composed his first songs in the 1840s, and fifty years later there seems no appreciable change of style. Thus *Sous les tilleuls* (Pierre Dupont, 1858) does not seem very different from the TROIS SONNETS DE CAMILLE DU LOCLE (1896–9), where a song like *Le dernier rendez-vous* has a pleasing salon elegance. Reyer's music is typical of an epoch which could take seriously, and savour, the eroticism of the opening lines of his song *Rédemption* (1853)—'Je ne suis pas le Christ, ô pâle Madeleine.'

RIVIER, Jean (1896–1987)

A member of Le Groupe du Triton which had been founded by Pierre Octave Ferroud, Rivier was prolific in all spheres of composition, and an accomplished mélodiste. Between 1925 and 1944 he was drawn to Apollinaire, and there are at least ten settings of this poet, some of them orchestrated. Probably his best set of songs, however, is the group entitled TROIS POÈMES DE RONSARD ET UN DE CLÉMENT MAROT (1945). This comprises a mellifluous *Bel aubépin* (also set memorably by Leguerney), a dancingly light *Rossignol mon mignon* (set by Roussel for voice with flute [ROUSSEL 6]), a gently elegiac *Le tombeau de Ronsard*, and the jewel of the set, *Dedans Paris, ville jolie*, which recalls the neo-classical staccato style of Jean Françaix. This Marot poem is a delight, and provides Rivier with the chance of apostrophizing the capital city in song, something which Debussy does, tongue in cheek, in his *Ballade des femmes de Paris*, but which otherwise seems to belong almost exclusively to Poulenc in collaboration with Apollinaire. A later song cycle, written for Irène Joachim, is QUATRE POÈMES DE RENÉ CHALUPT (1949), which includes the fox trot *Cartomancie*, the polka *'À traduire en estonien'*, and the waltz *Hommage à Valery-Larbaud*.

RODRIGO, Joaquín (1901–1999)

This famous composer of Spanish song was a pupil of Dukas in the 1920s, and spent a great deal of time in Paris in the years between the wars. His music was much influenced by the French style, and he acknowledged his debt to Debussy with LA GROTTE (1962), a miniature cycle of three songs to words by Louis Emié, the poet from Bordeaux who was a friend of Henri Sauguet. This takes as its musical starting point the unmistakable Scotch-snap rhythm of the opening of Debussy's setting of Tristan l'Hermite, *La grotte* ('Auprès de cette grotte sombre' [DEBUSSY 12 ii]), and it is this motif which links all three songs. The first two explore a Debussian world of recitative, mainly unaccompanied; the third is more lively where the piano briefly plays a more important role.

ROPARTZ, Guy (1864–1955)

Ropartz defected from the Conservatoire, where he had studied with Massenet, in order to study with Franck, and this affiliation is audible in almost every note of his music. It is not that it sounds like that of his master, but Ropartz has embraced the aesthetic of the Franck circle utterly: music is a serious and noble thing, to be used to describe the deepest emotions. Arthur Hoérée writes of his conducting as sober and profound, and these words might also be applied to his music. His Breton temperament (and his choice of Breton poets) inclined to the serious, and consequently his songs are almost always slow and meaningful, as well as lengthy. It is seldom we hear in Ropartz the calm radiance and beatific optimism of his teacher which is an antidote to melancholy introspection. The earlier songs are somewhat lighter than the later: of these *Lever d'aube* and *Berceuse* (both 1894) are probably the most interesting, as well as *Si j'ai parlé de mon amour* (1897) which has the benefit of a poem by Henri de Régnier.

Ropartz's finest set is probably the QUATRE POÈMES D'APRÈS L'"INTERMEZZO' D'HENRI HEINE (translated by the composer himself, 1899), but even these imposing songs cling to one mood too tenaciously. The first thing we hear in the substantial introduction are the four ominous notes of the Dies Irae which pervade the cycle in typically Franckian manner. There has probably never been a more intense evocation of Heine's bitterness and disappointment, but Schumann better understood how this dark mood had to be placed in relief with lighter, brighter conceits and fantasies in order to get the true measure of the poet. (The work was conceived with orchestral accompaniment but the piano version comes more readily to hand.) The cycle VEILLES DE DÉPART (Guérin, 1902) is a succession of five melancholy songs, each beautiful and finely written, but rather too monochrome as a group. Although few composers have evoked better the profound and disturbed world of Baudelaire than Ropartz in *Chant d'automne* (1905) [FAURÉ 5], this song is similarly sunk in the darkest autumnal depression. The music is highly impressive until we reach the words 'J'aime de vos longs yeux la lumière verdâtre', where Ropartz lacks the ability to flood the music with light and warmth as Fauré does in a song which is otherwise no match for this in its scale and intensity. This work was also originally conceived orchestrally.

Ropartz is occasionally capable of fast, dramatic music. *Chanson de bord* (Le Braz, 1907) is part of a cycle inspired by Brittany. This is the plaint of a seaman far from home, a companion piece to Duparc's *La vague et la cloche*, and worthy of exploration by a strong-voiced baritone. The preceding song in this Breton set, *Tout le long de la nuit*, is a perfect little jewel, Ropartz at his unforced best. Also very approachable are the simple *La route* (1913), a farewell song where the composer is once again the poet, and the late cycle *LES HEURES PROPICES* (Mercier, 1927), a touchingly simple set of three songs about an old married couple returning to their native region to spend the rest of their days. On the whole, however, Ropartz favours less tranquil moods, and almost always in the minor key—as in *Il pleut* (Gregh, 1907), where the piano writing is demanding and evocative. If Roussel's *Le jardin mouillé* comes to mind at first, the scale of this piece exceeds anything in Roussel with a grandeur that borders on grandiloquence and seems to strain the boundaries of the song form itself, the subject matter out of proportion with the scale of its treatment. In complete contrast is a very rare example of the composer letting his hair down in a captivating (and concise) chanson entitled *Si j'étais roi* (de Kerfott).

ROREM, Ned (b. 1923)

Rorem writes: 'Frustration awaits the American composer impelled to write songs in French, for those songs will seldom be heard. The rare French recitalist who programs an American song will make an effort to learn one in English. Meanwhile American singers will find it more "legitimate" for their French group to be by Frenchmen.' Despite this frustration, there have always been foreigners tempted into setting French as a kind of homage to an admired civilization. This most articulate and literary of American song composers has more than usual grounds for such homage, as he had a long and deep connection with France. He first went there in 1949 to study with Honegger, and after spending a period of time in Morocco settled in 1952 in Paris, where he lived until 1958. Thanks to the patronage of the formidable Marie-Laure de Noailles, he was one of the few Americans, or indeed young composers of any nationality, at home in the highest milieux of Parisian cultural life during a golden age of mélodie—its Indian summer, in fact. Cocteau, Poulenc, and Auric and many others were regular visitors to the Noailles household, and Rorem met them all constantly, as his celebrated published diaries testify.

Although he was much influenced by various aspects of French style, particularly the songwriting of Satie and Poulenc, and although there were various unpublished settings of Cocteau and Apollinaire dating from as early as 1945, Rorem has been basically loyal to poetry in English, regarding it the duty of a composer to set his mother tongue. The only exception to this among the published cycles is *POÈMES POUR LA PAIX* (1953), which he wrote in Paris and orchestrated in 1956. The texts were taken from Éluard's *Anthologie vivante de la poésie du passé*. The composer introduces the songs thus: 'Having been raised a Quaker and a pacifist, I found this fifteenth century verse close to my heart; it is no less close to the heart of our own century. Created as it was in a period of constant war, of surfeited anguish, of poetic terror.' The song are *Lay* (Jehan Regnier), **Ode** (a Ronsard poem which begins 'Je te salue, heureuse paix'), *Sonnet I* and *II* (Olivier de Magny), another *Sonnet*

(Jean Daurat), and a final solemn chorale—*Hymne de la paix* (Jean Antoine de Baïf). Songs celebrating peace (as opposed to praying for that rare commodity, as in Poulenc's *Priez pour paix*) are in short supply. They were not among the most successful works of Fauré (*C'est la paix*, 1919) and Hahn (*La paix* from the *DOUZE RONDELS*), so Rorem has the field to himself with music which, however impassioned, is always written with Gallic clarity and lucidity.

The only other published French setting is the single song *Jack l'Éventreur* (Jack the Ripper), with a text by Marie-Laure de Noailles, and a vocal range of more than two octaves. Mention should also be made of settings of French poetry in English translation: *SWORDS AND PLOUGHSHARES* for four solo voices and orchestra to a text of Rimbaud, and *THREE POEMS OF BAUDELAIRE*, including a setting of *L'invitation au voyage* (in translation *The invitation to the voyage*), written for the BBC singers in 1986. A most touching song is *For Poulenc* (1963) with a poem by Frank O'Hara, an elegy written to mourn that composer's sudden death. And as we have allowed an English poem into this discussion, why not another? Rorem's ravishing song *The early morning* (Robert Hillyer) is as poignant a song-portrait of Paris ('I was breakfasting on croissants | And café au lait | Under greenery like scenery | Rue François Premier') as any that exists in our own language.

1 *Ode*

(Pierre de Ronsard)

Je te salue heureuse Paix,
Je te salue et re-salue:
Toy seule Déesse tu fais
Que la vie soit mieux voulue.
Ainsi que les champs tapissez
De pampre, ou d'espics herissez
Desirent les filles des nues
Apres les chaleurs survenues,
Ainsi la France t'attendoit,
Douce nourriciere des hommes,
Douce rosee qui consommes
La chaleur qui trop nous ardoit.

Tu as esteint tout l'ennuy
Des guerres injurieuses,
Faisant flamber aujourd'huy
Tes graces victorieuses.
En lieu du fer outrageux,
Des menaces et des flammes,
Tu nous ramènes les jeux,
Le bal et l'amour des Dames,
Travaux mignards et plaisants
À l'ardeur des jeunes ans.

Ode

I greet thee, O happy peace,
I greet thee and greet thee again:
Thou alone, O goddess, canst make
Our life a better thing.
Just as fields carpeted
With vine or bristling corn
Long for laughing rain-clouds
After all the heat,
So France awaited thee,
Sweet nurse of men,
Sweet dew that absorbs
The heat that burned us so.

Thou hast extinguished all the ills
Of harmful wars,
Letting today the flame
Of thy triumphs blaze.
In place of desecrating sword,
Of threats and flames,
Thou bringeth us entertainment,
Dance and the love of noble Ladies,
Sweet and pleasant employment
For us in our fervent youth.

ROSENTHAL, Manuel (b. 1904)

This celebrated conductor, friend of Ravel (in the news again in recent years as an untiring veteran, conducting *Der Ring* to great acclaim in Seattle), was a skilled composer of mélodies. Because of his inside knowledge of the orchestra, almost all of his songs also exist in orchestral versions. He showed astonishing precocity with his first cycle, *RONSARDISES* (1927), songs from which should feature on any song programme devoted to this poet, for a mature and attractive style is already formed. There are five songs, the first three of which are epitaphs of various kinds, an idea for a cycle which was taken up by the American composer Theodore Chanler, and Pierre Vellones among others. The composer's sense of humour, and a certain audacity, is shown by the fact that he casts the third song, *Épitaphe pour luy-mesme*, as a blues, an anachronistic triumph. The final song in this set, *L'arondelle*, has the energy and vivacity (a moto perpetuo in semiquavers) which we associate with Jacques Leguerney's settings of this poet. The three *POÈMES D'AMOUR* (anonymous and Jehannot de Lescurel) from 1941 show a similar taste for neo-classical style inspired by fourteenth- and sixteenth-century poetry.

CINQ CHANSONS JUIVES (1928) post-date the Jewish songs of both Ravel and Milhaud. Rosenthal is more ambitious than either composer in this regard, and his cycle exploits pianistic resources, as well as the full range of the soprano voice, much more boldly than either of his seniors. From the opening *Chanson du gardien de la vigne* to the final *Bacchanale* (inspired by Psalm 149), the work cries out for revival. The *TROIS MÉLODIES SUR DES POÈMES DE MARIE ROUSTAN* (1933–4) are a fine set, typical of Rosenthal's refined understanding of the voice, and a Ravelian feel for the keyboard. The final *Sérénade* of this set is particularly graceful and supple.

The most often performed Rosenthal songs are *CHANSONS DU MONSIEUR BLEU* (Nino, 1934; 'Nino' was Michel Veber, brother-in-law of Jacques Ibert). 'Le monsieur bleu' is the composer himself: he had a bright blue suit of which he was very proud, and the poet's children gave him this nickname. These delightful songs, almost for children, but not quite, include **La souris d'Angleterre**, a must for any English singer adept at self-parody, or a French one who likes to send up English manners. Others in this set, which consists of nursery ditties and animal portraits, include **L'éléphant du Jardin des Plantes** (who 'fait pipi dans sa culôte'), *Fido, Fido, Grammaire, Le petit chat est mort*, and so on. Probably too long to be programmed in its entirety, a group selected from these twelve songs would enliven any recital. The same light-hearted poet provided texts for another cycle, *SIX CHANSONS COLONIALES* (1942). Typical of his graceful output is a very useful set of duets for soprano and contralto from the same year. These are *TROIS CHANTS DE FEMMES BERBÈRES* (1942), latter-day orientalisms which, despite their affinity with Bizet's *Adieux de l'hôtesse arabe*, strike an original note in the duet repertoire. At the same time as being an entertainer Rosenthal attempted more serious things. Also from 1942, his response to the horrors of the war years was *DEUX PRIÈRES POUR LE TEMPS MALHEUREUX* (1942), a work for a heroic baritone with words from the prophet Jeremiah and Psalm 76. Only in music of this kind, which has to touch the sublime to be taken seriously, does Rosenthal show his limitations. On the other hand, anything requiring urbanity and charm is his natural province.

1 *La souris d'Angleterre*

(Nino)

C'était une souris qui venait d'Angleterre,
Yes, Madame, yes, my dear,
Ell' s'était embarquée au port de Manchester
Sans même savoir où s'en allait le navire.
No, Madam', no, my dear.
Elle avait la dent longu' comme une vieille Anglaise,
S'enroulait dans un plaid à la mode écossaise
Et portait une coiffe en dentelle irlandaise.

Dans le port de Calais, elle mit pied à terre,
Yes, Madame, yes, my dear,
Elle s'en fut bien vite à l'hôtel d'Angleterre,
Et grimpe l'escalier tout droit sans rien leur dire,
No, Madam', no, my dear,
Le grenier de l'hôtel lui fut un vrai palace,
La souris britannique avait là tout sur place,
Du whisky, du bacon, du gin, de la mélasse.

Chaque soir notre miss faisait la ribouldingue,
Yes, Madame, yes, my dear,
C'était toute la nuit des gigues des bastringues,
Les bourgeois de Calais ne pouvaient plus dormir,
No, Madam', no, my dear,
En vain l'on remplaçait l'appât des souricières,
Le Suiss' par le Holland', le Bri' par le Gruyère,
Rien n'y fit, lorsqu'un soir on y mit du Chester.

C'était une souris qui venait d'Angleterre,
Yes, Madame, yes, my dear.

2 *L'éléphant du Jardin des Plantes*

Ah! savez-vous pourquoi, ma tante,
L'éléphant du Jardin des Plantes
Traîne son nez d'un air gêné,
Comme s'il était pris en faute?

Cela ne se dit pas, ma tante,
Dans le monde à voix haute.
L'éléphant du Jardin des Plantes
A fait pipi dans sa culôte.

The English mouse

There was once an English mouse,
Yes, Madame, yes, my dear,
Who embarked from the port of Manchester,
Not knowing even where the ship was bound.
No, Madame, no, my dear.
She was long in the tooth like an old English maid,
In Scottish mode was wrapped in a plaid
And wore a head-dress of Irish lace.

In the port of Calais she set foot on land,
Yes, Madame, yes, my dear,
Booked quickly in at the Angleterre,
And without a word went straight upstairs,
No, Madame, no, my dear,
The hotel loft was a sumptuous palace,
Where the British mouse had all on tap,
Whisky, bacon, gin, molasses.

Each evening our miss went out on a spree,
Yes, Madame, yes, my dear,
At low-dive dances all night long,
The burghers of Calais could sleep no more,
No, Madame, no, my dear,
In vain they changed the mousetrap bait,
Swapped Swiss with Dutch, Brie with Gruyère,
Till one evening they put down some Chester.

There was once an English mouse,
Yes, Madame, yes, my dear.

The Botanical Garden elephant

Oh auntie, do you know why
The Botanical Garden elephant
Drags his nose all ill at ease,
As though guilty of a crime?

The answer, auntie, must not be
Cried to all and sundry.
The Botanical Garden elephant
Has wee-wee'd in his pants.

ROSSINI, Gioachino (1792–1868)

The songs of Rossini are unlike any others, and it seems to make little difference in what language they are written. Like that other famed international composer Meyerbeer, whose German lieder have much the same characteristics as his French mélodies and romances, many of the hallmarks of Rossini's Italian songs seem to apply also to those in French—the languages seem interchangeable. This was, after all, also in the established tradition of Donizetti's works for voice and piano. The first Rossini song in French is a tenor solo with piano or harp accompaniment entitled *Les adieux à Rome* (Delavigne, 1827). After this, two large collections were issued. The first of these, the *SERATE MUSICALI* or *SOIRÉES MUSICALES*, was published in 1835 and contains only songs and duets in Italian. The *PÉCHÉS DE VIEILLESSE* or *SINS OF OLD AGE*, on the other hand, is a compendium of music of all kinds— an extensive collection arranged into thirteen volumes, six of which are devoted to piano solos ('morceaux semi-comiques' with titles like *Quatre hors d'œuvres* which prophesy Satie) and one to chamber music. The remaining six volumes are devoted to vocal music. Of these, three collections contain songs in French: the *ALBUM FRANÇAIS*, the *MORCEAUX RÉSERVÉS*, and the *MISCELLANÉE DE LA MUSIQUE*. This music written between 1857 and 1868 had not at first been intended for publication, but these alluringly humorous pieces became well known, even notorious, at the salons held by the composer in the town of Passy, or at his Parisian apartment in the chaussée d'Antin. Artists were soon clamouring to get hold of them, and some of the pieces were published later in the nineteenth century. In the 1950s the Fondazione Rossini Pesaro published a selection of this music; but Rossini admirers have had to wait until the 1990s for the complete edition to appear.

The *ALBUM FRANÇAIS* begins with an octet (two singers of each voice type) in praise of the New Year— *Toast pour le nouvel an*. Then *Roméo*, an extended and difficult aria for a tenor who mourns his Juliette—the text is a very poor paraphrase of Shakespeare. The main poet of this collection is Émilien Pacini, a willing accomplice for Rossini's ironic sense of humour. He furnishes the text for the soprano's camp effusion *La grande coquette (Ariette Pompadour)* and much else besides: *Le dodo des enfants* (for mezzo); *Le lazzone: chanson de cabaret* (a song in praise of Naples, for baritone); *Soupirs et sourire* (a duet for soprano and tenor). Most of these pieces have surprisingly sophisticated piano parts: each song is almost always preceded by an extended introduction. An exception to this is the *Chœur de chasseurs démocrates* for unaccompanied male quartet.

It is difficult to know how seriously to take the music when it is heart-rending, for this composer has a way of making us think something is in earnest when it is a joke, and vice versa. *Adieux à la vie: élégie sur une seule note* (Pasini again) is a case in point. The text of this song which ends 'Ma mère, ma mère adieu' is full of the pathetic farewells of a dying man—it is sung on a single note which gives the idea of 'croaking' a double meaning—and here the song dies as well as the singer. How can we marry the idea of such a poignant farewell with a vocal line (or lack of it) which seems increasingly ridiculous with each bar? Similarly the tenor and baritone duet entitled *Un sou: complainte à deux voix* is a heartfelt description of poverty; but surely the rhyming lines 'nous errons, hélas, sans savoir où, | Donnez-leur un sou, un sou' can only bring a smile to our faces despite the sad circumstances of father and son forced to beg. Rossini has a cruel streak and seems to relish this with *Schadenfreude*. He savours the penury of his duettists at the same time as the audience's discomfort. Another such song is *L'orpheline du Tyrol: ballade élégie*, where the poor orphan is made to yodel her distress, no less. Once again a strophe like 'Ma mère, ton adieu, | en ce lieu, | m'inspire mon seul vœu, | au bon Dieu' is very hard to take when a pious prayer heavenwards suddenly changes into a yodel. The little beast should be removed from the mountain immediately. On the other hand, even this composer's sense of humour is not ghoulish enough to make an intentional joke of *Le dodo des enfants*, when a mother sings a lullaby to her dead child. *Chanson de Zora: la petite bohémienne* is almost touching, and presents a cameo of a singing gypsy girl who says, 'Il faut vous plaire | gagner mon salaire.' Once again, doggerel can raise, all too easily, an involuntary giggle. In *L'amour à Pékin*, Rossini makes fun of the whole-tone scale (many years before Debussy was to adopt this device), and he also mocks Wagner's prelude to *Tristan und Isolde*. Six solo piano pieces entitled *Montée, Descente, Montée, Descente, Montante et descendante* (I and II) preface *Petite mélodie sur la gamme chinoise*. This song contains the clearest illustration of the whole-tone scale—Rossini could not have guessed that this would be taken deeply seriously within twenty-five years. He would have howled with laughter at the thought.

The collection entitled MORCEAUX RÉSERVÉS is a mixture of French and Italian items. All the French pieces have lyrics by Pacini with the exception of *Ariette à l'ancienne* which boasts a text by Jean-Jacques Rousseau. The first has the imposing title of *Chœur: quelques mesures de chant funèbre: à mon pauvre Meyerbeer*. This funeral tribute is for large male chorus with drum accompaniment. *Les amants de Séville* is an effective exercise in the Spanish manner, written for the useful (and seldom encountered) combination of contralto and tenor. The pretty bergerette *Le sylvain* begins with a long and tender piano prelude, but as soon as the vocal line begins, the rhymes 'blonde', 'profondes', and 'fécondes', quickly followed by 'solitaire', 'se taire', and 'mystère', give the song an air of 'Pyramus and Thisbe' by Shakespeare's mechanicals. Can this be intentional, one asks, and the answer with Rossini is 'Yes, it can'. If there is any doubt about the composer's humorous intention, then the 'mad' cadenza on the word 'non' repeated many times (like Thisbe's cadenza in Britten's *A Midsummer Night's Dream*) lays all doubts to rest.

The MISCELLANÉE DE LA MUSIQUE contains several delectable things. **La chanson du bébé** is a comic masterpiece and extremely gratifying to perform for a tenor who is not easily embarrassed. The baby might as well be the truculent composer himself, reverting to a second childhood. Never had Pacini served his composer in more risqué fashion—or perhaps the word scatological would be more accurate. At one point Rossini changes the text from harmless sneezing onomatopoeia ('Atchi!') to 'Maman, Papa | Pipi, caca'—these are merely 'nonsense words' according to the tactful author of *The Master Musicians* volume on Rossini, but they seem quite explicit enough for those who have potty-trained an infant. The child's sense of triumph at having finally delivered what is required of him is brilliantly caught in the strains of the music.

The music of all these French songs is much more droll than that of Offenbach or Meyerbeer (there is something curiously leaden and German about their lighter songs), but it requires careful performance. Most, though not all, of the songs are too long for deliberately arch or send-up performances—the joke cannot be sustained by guying the music, which is seldom uproariously amusing, only gently so. On the other hand, earnest performances which fail to take account of the malicious glint in the composer's eye are also less than truthful to the mordant style of Rossini's last years. A born comedian with a light touch, an unobtrusively raised eyebrow, and a subtle sense of self-parody could bring this music off. But it can defeat all but the most intrepid, because apart from the knife-edged interpretation, these songs are often devilishly difficult to sing. Rossini would have been delighted that he had given singers such a problem to solve. 'Serve them right,' he would have said. And audiences are still left wondering how to react. After all, it takes great courage to start cackling from the stalls in the middle of an orphan's plaint (Tyrolean or otherwise) or, as in *Un sou: complainte à deux voix*, at the distress of a father and son reduced to the humiliation of the sou kitchen.

1   *La chanson du bébé*

(Émilien Pacini)

Maman, le gros Bébé t'appelle, il a bobo:
Tu dis que je suis beau, quand je veux bien faire
    dodo.
Je veux de confitures, c'est du bon nanan;
Les groseilles sont mûres, donne-m'en, j'en veux,
    maman,
Je veux du bon nanan, j'ai du bobo, maman.
Atchi! Papa, maman, ca-ca.

Bébé voudrait la chanson du sapeur
Dans *Barbe-bleue,** un air qui fait bien peur.
Maman, ta voix si douce en chantant ça,
Enfoncerait Schneider† et Thérésa.‡
Atchi! Pipi, maman, papa, ca-ca.

Ma bonne, en me berçant, m'appelle son bijou,
Un diable, un sapajou, si j'aime mieux faire joujou.
Quand je ne suis pas sage, on me promet le fouet!
Moi, je fais du tapage, le moyen réussit bien.
Je veux du bon nanan, j'ai du bobo, maman.
Atchi! Papa, maman, caca.

Baby's song

Mummy, diddums wants you, ouch it hurts,
You say I'm beautiful when I want bye-byes.

I want some jam, jam is yummy,
Give me ripe redcurrants, I want some, Mummy.

Want something yummy, ouch it hurts, Mummy.
Atishoo! Papa, Mummy, pooh.

Diddums wants the 'sapper's song'
From *Bluebeard*, a terrifying tune.
Mummy, when you sing it so sweetly
You put Schneider and Thérésa to shame.
Atishoo! Wee-wee, Mummy, Papa, pooh.

Nanny, when she rocks me, calls me her treasure—
And devil and monkey when I'd sooner play.
When I'm naughty, they say they'll whip me!
But I make a din, and that does the trick.
I want something yummy, ouch it hurts, Mummy.
Atishoo! Papa, Mummy, look—pooh-pooh!

ROUSSEL, Albert (1869–1937)

It is not only the world-famous composers whose songs define the boundaries of this form: there is something about Roussel's music which is the quintessence of the mélodie at its most lean and understated, retaining nevertheless a certain wiry muscular strength. Just as Caplet's *Forêt* seems an

---

* Operetta by Offenbach (1866).
† Hortense Schneider (1833–1920 or 1922), celebrated French soprano who created the role of Boulotte in *Barbe-bleu*.
‡ Thérésa [Emma Valadon (1837–1913)] was the most famous of all the café-concert singers; much admired by Offenbach, she was also frequently drawn and painted by Degas. The song 'Rien n'est sacré pour un sapeur!' was by A. de Villebichot, and must have been sung by Thérésa in many of her guest appearances in operettas of the time.

indispensable benchmark of sumptuous impressionism, Roussel's *Le jardin mouillé*—a song of delicate refinement and incomparable atmosphere—demonstrates sensuality under wraps: the languorous legacy of Debussy and Ravel is adapted to the harder edges of the new century. The great soprano Claire Croiza summed up Roussel's art thus: 'Mélancolie sans drame—mesure, jamais d'"effet" sentimental, jamais rien en "trop"—ce "trop" qui, dans l'art comme dans la vie, détruit si souvent, au fond de nous-mêmes, toute sensibilité.' (Melancholy, without drama—moderation, never a sentimental 'effect', never any of that excess which, in life as in art, so often destroys within ourselves every trace of sensitivity.) Roland-Manuel called him 'un aristocrate timide'.

The composer had originally intended to have a career in the navy, but, unlike Jean Cras who persevered as a sailor, Roussel slowly realized that he would have to abandon ships (not before he had seen a great deal of the world) in order to concentrate on his music. He was one of the most well travelled of composers; the journey which influenced him the most from a musical point of view was probably his extensive tour of south-east Asia in 1909. Of all the men in French music, he had one of the highest moral reputations in every sense: despite his penchant for composing unhappy love songs, his marriage was idyllic and a constant source of inspiration to his work; he was famously fair as a teacher (even Satie found him so, and much later Martinů adored him); he was incorruptible as a competition juror, and generous (to the point of damaging his own interests) with talented colleagues who deserved encouragement. The personal and professional esteem in which he was held in France is shown by the celebrations for his 60th birthday in 1929, which included a celebratory issue of *La revue musicale*. The supplement to this opened with *À Roussel*, a song by Delage (text by Chalupt), accompanied by flute and piano, which began 'Roussel, marin favorisé'. There were also piano pieces by Honegger, Ibert, and Poulenc. The poem of Francis Jammes, *Quatrain*, set by Milhaud in Roussel's honour, is another character sketch with suitably marine overtones:

Des noms sont exaltés un à un qui s'effacent,	Exalted names vanish one by one,
Tels que des flots ailés repris par l'océan;	Like airborne waves the ocean reclaims;
Mais un vrai nom résiste à la mode qui passe:	But a true name resists passing fashion:
Il demeure immobile au milieu du néant.	It stands motionless amidst oblivion.

Roussel had the integrity, and something of the severity, of those who come from northern France. Without the influence of Debussy and Ravel, and the enlightening experience of world travel, he might have tended to the lugubrious seriousness which sometimes benighted his teacher d'Indy, and the Schola Cantorum in general. As it was, he had the best intellectual qualities of that institution's adherents; but his stature as a song composer—incomparably greater than, say, Ropartz—is thanks to a streak of real sensuality, a great feeling for poetry, an openness to the music of others, at the same time as an individual style—too acerbic and dry for some tastes, like brut champagne, but nevertheless his own.

We should remind ourselves that Roussel was a late starter, and that he was in his thirties when he wrote his first songs. The first group of these shows an array of somewhat undigested musical influences but, from a literary point of view, the composer proclaims a surprisingly mature allegiance to a great collaborator, Henri de Régnier. His first nine songs (including the orchestrally accompanied *La menace*) are settings of this poet. These texts are a mixed blessing as far as Roussel is concerned; the poetry is never less than interesting, but it leads the composer into long and extended settings when his real talent is for concision and epigram. Of the QUATRE POÈMES Op. 3 (1903), *Départ* and *Vœu* are rambling creations with the incessant pianistic triplets which are the hallmark of the Schola Cantorum. There are moments of beauty here, particularly at the apposite modulations at the end of paragraphs, but this is not yet the real Roussel. *Madrigal lyrique* has more direction, but it seems too much like d'Indy. On the other hand **Le jardin mouillé**, the third of the set, is a masterpiece. Admittedly this song shows the influence of Ravel's *Jeux d'eau*, and Debussy's *Jardins sous la pluie*, but this seems to be an agreeably healthy model for a composer still wet behind the ears; after all, Ravel's piano piece was inspired by Régnier, so there may have been a deliberate spirit of homage here to both Ravel and Régnier who were, in any case, firm friends. The accompaniment is eerily evocative of the gentle falling of rain on a leafy garden, and, for the first time in Roussel's mélodies, we find a perfect balance between form and content.

The QUATRE POÈMES Op. 8 (1907) show a great advance; all four songs are very fine indeed. *Adieux* is the longest—a heartfelt tribute to his wife from a man who, as a sailor, knows the agonies of parting, and who faces the threat of the final parting of death itself. This is almost a cantata in terms of its length and complexity, but it is held together by the depth of its feeling. This song was orchestrated by the composer. *Nuit d'automne* begins with an almost rhetorical grandeur, rare in Roussel, and it ends on an erotic note ('Et l'automne est si tiède encor | Que tu pourras t'endormir nue') that we will find again at the end of *Sarabande*. *Invocation* is perhaps the most successful of the group—another of Régnier's garden nocturnes for which the composer finds a mystery and transparency worthy of late Fauré. This was after all the epoch of that composer's LA CHANSON D'ÈVE. *Odelette* is an exercise in gradated diminuendo; it is a song which begins trumpetingly, in the grand manner, and becomes progressively more inward looking, and spare in texture, as the poet seeks to clothe his love in the humblest of garments. The feeling is of music gradually evaporating under the fingers.

Although the composer orchestrated seven of his mélodies, there is only one Roussel work in this field which was conceived for voice and orchestra in the first place. This is *La menace* (Op. 9, 1908) to a text by Henri de Régnier and written for medium voice. It is somewhat operatic in character, and with its theme of betrayed love is more melodramatic than any of the piano-accompanied songs. It is certainly for this reason that Roussel chose to work on a larger canvas than normal. It would be difficult to find a place on a concert programme for this work which is neither cycle nor miniature, and makes a curiously negative emotional impression. *Flammes* (Jean-Aubry, 1908) also stands alone as Op. 10, but it is more successful—a magnificent song written in a style which, by now, is recognizably Rousselian. The piano accompaniment admirably surges and flickers like flames themselves, a new idea in his always resourceful piano writing, but the theme of the music is the old one of partings and memories. How many times must the composer, in his earlier years, have bidden a tearful farewell to his wife as he parted for the Orient? This travel to the Far East produced some remarkable music—chiefly the opera-ballet *Padmâvatî*, of Indian inspiration, but also three sets (of two songs each) to Chinese texts which had been translated into English by Herbert Giles, and then into French by Henri-Pierre Roché. The first of these, DEUX POÈMES CHINOIS (Op. 12 1907–8), comprises the ode **À un jeune gentilhomme**, which was also set a few years earlier by Cyril Scott (in Giles's original translation) as *Don't come in sir, please!* Roussel's song is an oriental evocation worthy of Debussy's *Pagodes*, both tremulous and flirtatious. The much more dramatic **Amoureux** *séparés* contains a fantasy ride on horseback through the heavens to the beloved's side. The crest-fallen coda brings us back to reality. We begin to notice a pattern emerging where the composer delights in emotional transformation in his songs: they often end differently from how they began. The hallmark of a great Roussel mélodie is often to be found in the postlude (the best example is perhaps at the end of *Réponse d'une épouse sage*, with its poignantly poetic final page.

Roussel wrote no more songs until after the First World War was over. He had other tasks (now he was increasingly well-known), and there was no question in his mind but that it was his duty to fight for his country. *DEUX MÉLODIES* (Op. 19, 1918) contains the beautiful **Light** (Jean-Aubry), restless and sadly tormented until the final magical phrase which is pellucid in a way worthy of the song's title, and *A farewell* (E. Oliphant), a dark and bitter song which arrives once again at the theme of unhappiness in love—something of a Rousselian trade mark. Although both songs have English titles, only *A farewell* is an English poem, and not an easy one to grasp for one unversed in Anglo-Saxon irony. On the face of it these words are angry, but there is a note of black humour here too which Roussel fails to realise, it seems. The words 'sound my knell' inspire most ingenious bell-music. The two songs of Op. 20, *DEUX MÉLODIES* (René Chalupt, 1919), are, on the other hand, sheer perfection. **Le bachelier de Salamanque** is an immortal figure in song, and a triumph of mock-Spanish scene-painting. Typical of Roussel is the way that almost the whole mélodie depicts the serenader as devil-may-care. But on the last page, with a change of tempo, we hear that he has a heart after all: he is smitten—love-sick for the daughter of the Almirante, and we suddenly hear the vulnerability of the not-at-all heartless young man from the land of Don Juan. Right at the end the object of his adoration provides the last surprise—the pianist's murmured glissando across the whole keyboard does service for a derisory laugh, a flick of the fan, less of a slap on the face than a tickle. As a courtly outdoor evocation of romantic assignation in the gardens of a fairy-tale château, **Sarabande** is almost the equal of Fauré's *Clair de lune*. The formality of the dance, and its ever-repeated and modified motif, is magically balanced with the sensuality of the words. The music bristles with wrong-note accidentals, but is nevertheless sensual in its slightly spiky, crystalline way, and, to a marked degree, somehow evocative of a former century. For once, in a composer given to texts of renunciation and unhappiness, this scenario promises a measure of happiness and fulfilment. The poet's lady-love wears nothing under her cloak, and the composer is also left naked, unmasked at the costume ball as the only possible begetter of this harmonic world of his own creation. This music looks forward to the neo-classicism of the celebrated *Suite in F* for orchestra. Roussel orchestrated both these Op. 20 songs.

The *DEUX POÈMES DE RONSARD* (Op. 26, 1924) were Roussel's contribution to the celebrations of Ronsard's 400th anniversary. **Rossignol mon mignon,** in particular, is a fine addition to the repertoire for flute and voice. These songs (the other is *Ciel, aer et vens*) stand next to *Écoute*, Caplet's Tagore setting for flute and voice, also written in 1924, as the best examples of this genre-within-a-genre, a seemingly exclusively French preoccupation. It appears that the experience of setting Ronsard sharpened Roussel's taste for music which evoked the pleasures of former times. Like many French composers before him (admittedly of an earlier generation) he turned to Leconte de Lisle, this time not as a poet in his own right, but as a translator of the odes of Anacreon, the ancient Greek bard and bon viveur who had tempted many composers into song, including Schubert in German translation. There are six *ODES ANACRÉONTIQUES*, written for baritone in 1926 and comprising two opus numbers—31 and 32. These are fine songs, although at first hearing they may seem rather brusque and hermetic. Roussel seems to be aiming at some sort of Attic economy and leanness of texture. *Ode XIX: qu'il faut boire* is a lugubriously funny portrait of the poet in his cups; this, and another drinking song, *Ode XXVI: sur lui-même*, are equal in piquancy to Don Quixote's *Chanson à boire* by Ravel. Indeed, the hiccups in the piano part of that song are found here, rather more violently, eleven years earlier. *Ode XXXIV: sur une jeune fille* is a touching page, unusually simple with its sad, sombre chords in minims. Anacreon woos a young girl, though he himself has white hair. It was in similar circumstances that the ageing Goethe wrote *Phänomen* (set by Wolf and Brahms) in order to reassure himself that he still had the right to love. Three of these songs exist in orchestral versions.

DEUX POÈMES CHINOIS (Roché after Giles, Op. 35, 1927) are great successes. An oriental scenario encourages Roussel's taste for the hieratic; he is at home with cultures where formality is a *sine qua non*, where tears are hidden, and feelings are masked. This is ideal for a musical style which glitters on the surface, but which has an undertone of poetic melancholy for those with the ears to hear. Nothing could illustrate this better than the sublime **Réponse d'une épouse sage**, a poem which might have been written by Chang-chi a thousand years earlier, with Roussel's art in mind. The song opens with music of yearning, although always suppressed, and controlled by ritual. The middle section gives the oh-so-correct wife the chance to climb on her high-horse as consort to the captain of the royal guard. This proud and jarring music of keeping up appearances is the perfect foil for the melting moments to come. She vows to send back two pearls which had been offered to her by a suitor. First, she chides him for having behaved in a thoroughly inappropriate way. But in one of his typically magical codas, Roussel allows us to glimpse the wife's grief that she had not met her admirer sooner. The two tears she sends back with the pearls seem to glisten within the music itself, suspended like dew-drops on the lines of the stave as the little finger of the pianist's right hand picks out, as plaintively as an oboe, a falling motif of two minims. The tiny postlude says it all: the wife's loneliness, the unhappiness of her social-climbing marriage, the bleak desert of an unfulfilled life stretching before her. The composer orchestrated this song. *Des fleurs font une broderie* (dedicated to Pierre Bernac who gave its first performance) is also beautiful, though not the expressive match for its companion. Nevertheless, it is masterful how Roussel, in a flurry of staccato, evokes the percussive, tinkling sound of Chinese music, and the tightly sprung enthusiasm of a young man who is impatient to turn his dreams of love into reality. The composer's chromatic harmonic palette seems ideally suited to the kaleidoscope of quasi-instrumental colour which beguiles the ear, particularly in fast pieces like this where the music seems to jangle with an exotic energy. This particular sound, dry and *pétillant*, slightly more acid than fruit, is typical of the harvest from Roussel's musical vineyard; Dutilleux thought well enough of this song to orchestrate it.

The remainder of the songs fail to strike anything like the same form, which is not to say that Roussel was not still capable of writing beautiful music. **Jazz dans la nuit** (Dommange, 1928) is often to be found on the concert platform, but is not one of Roussel's greatest successes. On paper, this evocation of the new jazz craze seems fun, but just as most concert singers, keen to demonstrate their crossover skills, should be advised against excursions into jazz, so should most serious composers. Younger men like Milhaud and Auric just about got away with it, but Roussel's song is not at home with the new form. (I am reminded of Sir Peter Pears who, after a visit to a London theatre in 1972, found himself with me in a Soho bar with psychedelic rock music and strobe-light-ing, and asked, with great pride in being *au courant*, 'Is this jive?') The song, with a long piano intro-duction, sprawls in a number of awkward and disconnected sections, and never really gets started; it always seems as if it is about to erupt into the real thing, but it fails to swing. Here Ravel was bet-ter (after all, he named his pet dog 'Jazz'). Roussel's gaze was more fruitfully directed eastwards; judging by this, travelling west to New Orleans was not his forte. (Jean Wiéner recalls him ostenta-tiously walking out of a Billy Arnold jazz concert in 1921, banging the door behind him.) Pierre Vellones later orchestrated this piece of misplaced levity. The *DEUX IDYLLES* (Theocritus and Moskhos translated by Leconte de Lisle, 1931) are deft and clean classical evocations in the spiky manner of the Anacreon odes, but this time suitable for soprano voice. *Le kérioklèpte* is a delightful little song about the naughtiness of Cupid who steals honey and gets his own medicine from a bee, and *Pan aimait Ekhô* outlines a sad case of unrequited love (A loves B who loves C, and so on), which could only be cured by Oberon and Puck on a midsummer night in an Athenian wood.

The 1930s are rather bleak in terms of song. Roussel's harmonic language seems to be evolving to new levels of inscrutability—no doubt a logical evolution according to his own scrupulously moni-tored musical development. His contribution to *The James Joyce book* (1931) is entitled *A flower given to my daughter*, and is not one of his most accessible songs. It is a useful curiosity as the second of his efforts in English, bearing in mind that a much earlier generation of French-speaking composers (Massenet, Liszt, Gounod) had contributed to a similar book in honour of Tennyson in 1880. In 1934 there is another set of *DEUX POÈMES CHINOIS* Op. 47. *Favorite abandonée* is a very bleak page, as the title of the poem suggests. *Vois, de belles filles* is pleasant enough, without attaining any of the magic of the previous Chinese songs. *DEUX MÉLODIES* (René Chalupt, Op. 50) date from 1933–4, and the second of these, at least, has remained in the repertoire to an extent: **Cœur en péril.** This is a less confident cousin of *Le bachelier de Salamanque*, but it makes a pleasantly entertaining part of a Roussel group, and once again the love-lorn coda, in a slower tempo, elevates a potentially ordinary Spanish evoca-tion into something memorable. The conclusion of the song in Bernac's recording provides a model moment of Rousselian tenderness. The other song which belongs to this group is *L'heure du retour*, which is rather beautiful and unusual. Roussel adopts the extremely old-fashioned practice (found nowhere else in his songs) of a vocal refrain in rondo form. This slightly faster section ('voyageur, voyageur, ne vois-tu qu'il est l'heure de rebrousser chemin et de rentrer chez toi?') occurs three times in all, and gives a slightly popular feel to the song. It is the last of the composer's mélodies exploring departures, farewells, and the return of the sailor home from the sea, and not the least attractive of them. The final songs, Op. 55, are from 1935. These are *DEUX MÉLODIES* of Georges Ville: *Vieilles cartes, vieilles mains* is a nostalgic reminiscence of childhood when cousins, no longer exactly children, not yet adults, played cards in the attic with unspoken erotic overtones; but *Si quelquefois tu pleures* is the song of a composer who has already said all that he has to say. The aura of sadness and withdrawal which has always marked Roussel's songs here seems to inspire something disappointingly tame and subdued. On the other hand, it should perhaps be no surprise that this composer should have found such a self-effacing way to take his leave of the world of mélodie. One can only compare this to the inscrutable last works of Fauré, and the sensitive listener is moved by the stringent economy achieved with the minimum of outward fuss, and the maximum of self-searching. The songs of Roussel are sel-dom less than rewarding; and at least five or six of them are as great as any in the mélodie repertoire.

Three items remain to be mentioned: two vocalises (1927–8) which contain some beautiful music (Hoérée arranged the second for chamber ensemble), and Roussel's only folksong arrangement. This is entitled *Ô bon vin, où as-tu crû?* and is an old melody from the Champagne district. This dates from 1929, and Roussel had already proved himself adapt with drinking songs in the *ODES ANACRÉON-TIQUES*. Crushed acciaccaturas, very much a feature of this composer's style throughout his song output (one of his means of creating a quasi-orchestral sound of string pizzicato), admirably depict the cheeky high spirits of the harvest. It is the nearest that this composer got, thank heavens, and only briefly, to the style of Orff's *Carmina burana*.

1 *Le jardin mouillé*

(Henri de Régnier)

La croisée est ouverte; il pleut
Comme minutieusement,
À petit bruit et peu à peu,
Sur le jardin frais et dormant,

Feuille à feuille, la pluie éveille
L'arbre poudreux qu'elle verdit;
Au mur, on dirait que la treille
S'étire d'un geste engourdi.

L'herbe frémit, le gravier tiède
Crépite et l'on croirait là-bas
Entendre sur le sable et l'herbe
Comme d'imperceptibles pas.

Le jardin chuchote et tressaille,
Furtif et confidentiel;
L'averse semble maille à maille
Tisser la terre avec le ciel.

Il pleut, et, les yeux clos, j'écoute,
De toute sa pluie à la fois,
Le jardin mouillé qui s'égoutte
Dans l'ombre que j'ai faite en moi.

The drenched garden

The casement is open; the rain falls
Minutely, as it were,
Noiselessly and gradually
On the fresh and sleeping garden.

Leaf by leaf the rain awakens
The dusty tree it is turning green,
The climbing vine against the wall
Seems to stretch lethargically.

The grass trembles, the warm gravel
Crunches, as though over there
You could hear on sand and grass
The sound of indistinguishable steps.

The garden whispers and quivers,
Furtive and confiding;
Stitch by stitch the downpour seems
To weave together earth and sky.

The rain falls, and I with closed eyes listen,
As with all its rain at once
The drenched garden drips
In the darkness I've made in my heart.

2 *Flammes*

(Georges Jean-Aubry)

Je suis près de la porte où tu m'as dit adieu:
La chambre est monotone et douce,
Et la flamme inquiète du feu
Est une source
De souvenirs clairs et joyeux.

Flames

I am near the door where you bade me farewell:
The room is mellow and subdued,
And the fire's anxious flame
Is a source
Of bright and joyful memories.

Je suis près de la table où tu posas ta main:
La lampe a la même âme confidentielle
Et le même regard serein
Pour l'ombre qui l'appelle...

Près de la cheminée où tu rêvais
Je suis, ce soir d'octobre, solitaire,
Et la chambre monotone et douce s'éclaire
De mystérieux reflets.
J'écoute les branches frémir
Sous la caresse des flammes,
Et je regarde des formes surgir,
Brèves comme des passages d'âmes.

Je sens dans mon âme et ma chair
Naître un inexprimable émoi
Et je suis monotone et doux, ce soir, et clair
De la flamme que ton passé reflète en moi.

I am near the table where you placed your hand:
The lamp has the same confiding soul
And gazes with the same content
On the darkness that summons it...

By the fireplace where you used to dream
I am, this October night, alone,
And the room, mellow and subdued, is lit
By mysterious reflections.
I listen to the branches rustle
Beneath caressing flames,
And look as shapes loom up,
As ephemeral as fleeting souls.

I sense in my soul and my flesh
An ineffable emotion form,
And I am mellow and subdued tonight, and lit
By the flame your past reflects in me.

DEUX POÈMES CHINOIS

TWO POEMS FROM THE CHINESE

3 i   *À un jeune gentilhomme*

To a young gentleman

(Anonymous Chinese ode, trans. H. P. Roché
from the English of Herbert Giles)

N'entrez pas, Monsieur, s'il vous plaît!
Ne brisez pas mes fougères!
Non pas que cela me fasse grand' peine;
Mais que diraient mon père et ma mère?
Et même si je vous aime,
Je n'ose penser à ce qui arriverait.

Ne passez pas mon mur, Monsieur, s'il vous plaît!
N'abîmez pas mes primevères!
Non pas que cela me fasse grand' peine;
Mais, mon Dieu! que diraient mes frères?
Et même si je vous aime,
Je n'ose penser à ce qui arriverait.

Restez dehors, Monsieur, s'il vous plaît!
Ne poussez pas mon paravent!
Non pas que cela me fasse grand' peine;
Mais, mon Dieu! qu'en diraient les gens?
Et même si je vous aime,
Je n'ose penser à ce qui arriverait.

Don't come in, sir, please!
Don't break my willow-trees!
Not that *that* would very much grieve me;
But alack-a-day! what would my parents say?
And love you as I may,
I cannot bear to think what that would be.

Don't cross my wall, sir, please!
Don't spoil my mulberry-trees!
Not that *that* would very much grieve me;
But alack-a-day! what would my brothers say?
And love you as I may,
I cannot bear to think what that would be.

Keep outside, sir, please!
Don't spoil my sandal-trees!
Not that *that* would very much grieve me;
But alack-a-day! what the world would say!
And love you as I may,
I cannot bear to think what that would be.

3 ii *Amoureux séparés*

(Fu Mi, trans. H. P. Roché from the
English of Herbert Giles)

Dans le royaume de Yen
        un jeune galant réside,
Dans le royaume de Chao
        une belle demoiselle habite.
À vrai dire, ces royaumes
        ne sont pas très distants,
Mais une chaîne de monts à pic
        le sépare bel et bien.
Vous, nuages, sur vos fortes poitrines,
        emportez-moi,
Vents, soyez mes chevaux
        et galopez!
Les nuages du ciel
        n'écoutent pas la voix;
La brise changeante
        s'élève et retombe.
Je reste dans l'amertume
        de mes pensées,
Songeant à la bien-aimée
        que je n'atteindrai pas.

Lovers parted

In the kingdom of Yen
        a young gallant resides,
In the kingdom of Chao
        a fair damsel abides;
No long leagues of wearisome
        road intervene,
But a chain of steep mountains
        is set in between.
Ye, clouds, on your broad bosoms
        bear me afar,
The winds for my horses
        made fast to my car!
And the clouds in the sky
        they come not at call;
And the fickle breeze rises,
        alas, but to fall.
And so I am left
        with my thoughts to repine,
And think of that loved one
        who ne'er can be mine.

4 *Light*

(Georges Jean-Aubry)

Des larmes ont coulé
D'un cœur secret et tendre
Qui se crut exilé.
Que n'ai-je su comprendre,
Quand je m'en suis allé,
Ce cœur secret et tendre.

Une bouche a parlé,
Triste douceur d'entendre
Aujourd'hui révélé
Ce cœur secret et tendre.

Des larmes ont coulé,
Que n'ai-je su comprendre...
Mais pouvais-je m'attendre
À ce ciel étoilé?

Light

Tears have flowed
From a secretive, tender heart
That believed itself banished.
Why did I not understand,
When I departed,
This secretive, tender heart?

Lips have spoken,
What sad sweetness to hear
Today revealed
This secretive, tender heart.

Tears have flowed,
Why did I not understand...
But could I have foreseen
This starlit sky?

DEUX MÉLODIES	***TWO MÉLODIES***
(René Chalupt)	

5 i *Le bachelier de Salamanque*

Où vas-tu, toi qui passes si tard
Dans les rues désertes de Salamanque,
Avec ta toque noire et ta guitare,
Que tu dissimules sous ta mante?

Le couvre-feu est déjà sonné
Et depuis longtemps dans leurs paisibles maisons
Les bourgeois dorment à poings fermés.

Ne sais-tu pas qu'un édit de l'alcade*
Ordonne de jeter en prison
Tous les donneurs de sérénade,
Que les malandrins couperont ta chaîne d'or,
Et que la fille de l'Almirante,†
Pour qui vainement tu te tourmentes,
Se moque de toi, derrière son mirador.‡

The Salamanca student

Passer-by, where are you bound so late
In Salamanca's deserted streets,
With black cap and guitar
Concealed beneath your cloak?

The curfew has already sounded,
And for hours now in their peaceful homes
The burghers have been fast asleep.

Are you not aware—the Alcade has decreed
That all shall be cast into jail
Who sing their serenades,
That brigands will cut your golden chain,
And that the Almirante's daughter,
For whom you vainly languish,
Mocks you from her mirador?

5 ii *Sarabande*

Les jets d'eau dansent des sarabandes
Sur l'herbe parfumée des boulingrins;
Il y a des rumeurs de soie dans le jardin
Et de mystérieuses présences.
Sur le marbre rose d'une margelle,
Trois tourterelles
Se sont posées
Comme sur tes lèvres trois baisers;
Leurs plumes s'effeuillent dans le bassin.
Les fleurs fraîches des marronniers
Neigent lentement sur tes seins
Et font frissonner ta chair nue
Car tu es nue
Sous ton manteau.
Et c'est pour toi que les jets d'eau
Dansent de sveltes sarabandes,
Que le parc est plein de présences
Et que les tourterelles blanches,
Comme de vivantes guirlandes,
Viennent fleurir au bord de l'eau.

Saraband

The fountains are dancing sarabands
On the fragrant grass of the lawns;
Rustling silk is heard in the garden,
And mysterious presences too.
On a fountain's pink marble rim
Three turtle-doves
Have settled
Like three kisses on your lips;
Their feathers fall like leaves into the pool.
The fresh flowers of the chestnut trees
Shed their snowflakes slowly on your breast
And make your naked flesh shiver,
For you are naked
Beneath your cloak.
And it is for you that the fountains
Dance their slender sarabands,
That the park is full of presences,
And that the white turtle-doves,
Like living garlands,
Come to flower at the water's edge.

* Sheriff.
† Admiral, commander of a fleet.
‡ A turret or belevedere on the top of a Spanish house.

6 Rossignol mon mignon

(Pierre de Ronsard)

Rossignol mon mignon, qui dans cette saulaie
Vas seul de branche en branche à ton gré voletant,
Et chantes à l'envi de moi qui vais chantant
Celle qu'il faut toujours que dans la bouche j'aie.
   Nous soupirons tous deux; ta douce voix s'essaie
De sonner l'amitié d'une qui t'aime tant,
Et moi triste je vais la beauté regrettant
Qui m'a fait dans le cœur une si aigre plaie.
   Toutefois, Rossignol, nous différons d'un point,
C'est que tu es aimé, et je ne le suis point,
Bien que tous deux ayons les musiques pareilles:
   Car tu fléchis t'amie au doux bruit de tes sons,

Mais la mienne qui prend à dépit mes chansons
Pour ne les écouter se bouche les oreilles.

Nightingale, my sweet

Nightingale, my sweet, who flit as you please
From branch to branch through these willows alone,
And vie with me, as I walk and sing
Of her I must always have on my tongue.
   We sigh alike; your sweet voice seeks
To sing the affection of one who loves you so,
And I sadly lament the beauty
Who has dealt my heart so bitter a wound.
   And yet, nightingale, we differ in one regard,
It is that you are loved and I am not,
Even though our music be the same:
   For you move your love to mercy with your
      sounds,
While mine, who takes offence at my songs,
In order not to hear them stops her ears.

7 Réponse d'une épouse sage

(Chang Chi, trans. by H. P. Roché from the
English of Herbert Giles)

Connaissant, seigneur, mon état d'épouse,
Tu m'as envoyé deux perles précieuses.
Et moi, comprenant ton amour,
Je les posai froidement sur la soie de ma robe.

Car ma maison est de haute lignage,
Mon époux capitaine de la garde du Roi;
Et un homme comme toi devrait dire:
'Les liens de l'épouse ne se défont pas.'

Avec les deux perles, je te renvoie deux larmes:
Deux larmes—pour ne pas t'avoir connu plus tôt!

The chaste wife's reply

Knowing, fair sir, my matrimonial thrall,
Two pearls thou sentest me, costly withal.
And I, seeing that Love thy heart possessed,
I wrapped them coldly in my silken vest.

For mine is a household of high degree,
My husband captain in the King's army;
And one with wit like thine should say,
'The troth of wives is for ever and ay.'

With thy two pearls I send thee back two tears:
Tears—that we did not meet in earlier years!

8 Jazz dans la nuit

(René Dommange)

Le bal, sur le parc incendié,
Jette ses feux multicolores,
Les arbres flambent, irradiés,
Et les rugissements sonores
Des nègres nostalgiques, fous,
Tangos nerveux, cuivres acerbes,
Étouffent le frôlement doux du satin
Qui piétine l'herbe.

Jazz in the night

The ball, in the brightly lit park,
Casts its multicoloured beacons.
The trees are flaming, incandescent,
And the loud wailing
Of crazed, nostalgic negroes,
Sinewy tangos and biting brass
Muffle the soft drumming
Of satin on grass.

Que de sourires épuisés
À l'ombre des taillis complices,
Sous la surprise des baisers
Consentent et s'évanouissent...
Un saxophone, en sanglotant
De longues et très tendres plaintes,
Berce à son rythme haletant
L'émoi des furtives étreintes.

Passant, ramasse ce mouchoir,
Tombé d'un sein tiède, ce soir,
Et qui se cache sous le lierre;
Deux lèvres rouges le signèrent,
Dans le fard de leur dessin frais.
Il te livrera, pour secrets,
Le parfum d'une gorge nue
Et la bouche d'une inconnue.

So many wearied smiles,
In the shade of colluding bushes,
Surprised by kisses,
Consent and disappear...
A saxophone, sobbing
Its long and most tender lament,
Lulls with its panting rhythm
The excitement of furtive embraces.

Passer-by, pick up that handkerchief,
Fallen this evening from a warm breast
And lying hidden beneath the ivy;
Two red lips have marked it
With their outline of fresh rouge;
The secrets it will yield you
Are the scent of a naked bosom
And the lips of an unknown beauty.

9 *Cœur en péril*

(René Chalupt)

Que m'importe que l'Infante de Portugal
Ait le visage rond ou bien ovale,
Et une cicatrice sous le sein droit,
Qu'elle ait l'air d'une fille de roi
Ou d'une gardeuse d'oies,
Que m'importe?

Peu me chaut que la Princesse de Trébizonde
Soit rousse, châtaine ou blonde,
Qu'elle ait l'humeur prompte et le verbe haut,
Peu me chaut.

Point n'ai souci que la marquise de Carabas
Soit veuve et veuille reprendre mari,
Pour faire ici-bas son paradis!
Point n'ai souci!

Mais il suffit, jeune étourdie,
Du seul clin d'un de vos yeux moqueurs
Aux reflets irisés,
Pour que mon pauvre cœur
Batte à se briser.

Heart in peril

What do I care if the Infanta of Portugal
Has a round face or an oval one
And a scar beneath her right breast,
If she looks like a king's daughter
Or a gooseherd,
What do I care?

It matters little to me if the Princess of Trebizond
Be red-haired, brown-haired, or blonde,
Be quick-tempered or loud-mouthed,
It matters little to me.

I don't care a rap if the Marchioness of Carabas
Is a widow and wishes to marry again
To create her paradise here on earth!
I don't care a rap!

But it only takes, thoughtless girl,
A single flash of your mocking eyes
With their iridescent light,
To make my poor heart
Beat hard enough to break.

SAINT-SAËNS, Camille (1835–1921)

There is something inscrutable about the composer's gaze in the celebrated photograph by Nadar. Here he is at the greatest moment of fame, little dreaming that all too soon he was destined to become a footnote in French music, rather than the major chapter which he clearly thought his due. And somewhere in this expression of a grandee we can detect the heartbreak and sadness of a particularly lonely life. There is also a glint in the eye which suggests the touchy (and potentially vituperative) *maître*. His many secrets are his own, and to this day no one knows the real Camille Saint-Saëns. Perhaps as a result of this mask, fewer people today know his music. Obsessive privacy has a way of translating into anonymity, a quality which seeps into the compositions, and can render them all too easy to neglect. One finds in the songs neither the depth of Fauré (although the fact that Fauré achieved great things is partly thanks to Saint-Saëns, his teacher), nor the endless vistas of nebulous beauty of the languid Reynaldo Hahn. Instead there are other qualities: clarity, energy, humour (something rather lacking in the songs of the two composers mentioned above); a luxurious appreciation of foreign parts (for in his company we travel in both time and space, back into the seventeenth century and on to Persia); interesting and demanding piano writing (we would expect no less from a celebrated virtuoso); and an astonishing ability to write long-breathed melody that can rival the best of Gounod. If Fauré is the 'Master of Charms' as Debussy called him, Saint-Saëns is the 'Master of Disguises', and it is this which may perplex us when the innocent ear encounters these songs on the radio. 'Who is this composer?' we ask ourselves, enjoying the music the while, and wondering at its ease and urbane confidence. Saint-Saëns responds so readily to his texts, and fits his music out with such appropriate and clever local colour, that we sometimes forget where, and who, its creator is.

When Debussy was near death, Saint-Saëns, who outlived the younger composer by three years, was still judged by most foreigners to be unquestionably the greater French musician. Little by little, and then with the speed of the Wall Street Crash, his reputation declined. Composers of Poulenc's generation dismissed him as a ranting old reactionary, and this is more or less what he had become by as early as 1913, his *ex cathedra* pronouncements embittered by loneliness and spleen. Nadia Boulanger once remarked that 'Saint-Saëns knew his business admirably well. He only lacked what no one could give him.' This is a fair reflection of the plummeting of his posthumous reputation which has still not recovered. Perhaps there will one day be a major reassessment of someone who was after all one of the most interesting musical personalities of the time. Who else could claim to have performed for the Citizen King, Louis Philippe, at the Tuileries, and yet lived long enough to compose a chorus (*Aux conquérants de l'air*) in honour of 'those magnificent men in their flying machines', the brave airmen of the First World War and the Roaring Twenties?

After a glittering childhood, Saint-Saëns paid the heavy price, both emotional and musical, for his hothouse upbringing; his father had died when he was a baby, and he was brought up by a dominating and demanding mother. Even so, and despite the fact that he failed to win the Prix de Rome, the early period is full of good things. Saint-Saëns was a pioneer in the setting of Victor Hugo, and it might be argued that he is happier in finding music for Hugo's lyrics than any of his successors, certainly than Fauré. From this period date a number of significant settings of that poet's work, including *Rêverie* (later set by Hahn [HAHN 3]) and **Le pas d'armes du Roi Jean**, a ballad on a historical theme. This is one of the first well-known songs in the French repertoire which uses deliberate archaisms (now familiar as clichés of film music) and suggestions of modal harmony to evoke a world gone by of troubadours and brave knights. Saint-Saëns's devices and treatment of the various episodes are simple throughout and highly telling: at mention of the fair Yseult, cascading arpeggios as if painting the flow of her tresses; the fanfares of the joust and the excited stamping of the horses as they thunder in the lists; the outrageously sanctimonious appearance of monks and virgins to quasi-modal chords. All these things seem natural and unforced, and we realize that the composer himself was young enough to take this stirring evocation at face value. There is another Victor Hugo ballad setting, *La fiancée du timbalier*, which is even more ambitious in its depictions of knights, soldiers, and thwarted love in days of yore.

The first major work of Saint-Saëns to appear in print was the E flat major Symphony, published in 1855 as Op. 2. In this year he also composed **L'attente** (Hugo) which, alongside *Le pas d'armes du Roi Jean*, ranks as the composer's best-known work in the field of the mélodie, and which is anthologized in American song albums at the expense of many other delights. It gives the satisfying impression of a perfectly planned scherzo movement from a piece of chamber music. This suggests that Saint-Saëns might have known the music of Mendelssohn (the Octet for instance) or even some of the lieder like *Hexenlied* or *Neue Liebe*. Another big success of this period was **La cloche** (published 1856), yet another Hugo setting. The songs of the 1860s include a sprightly little setting of *La coccinelle*, the Hugo poem which Bizet set so imaginatively [BIZET 1], and one of Saint-Saëns's most noble and spacious mélodies, *Soirée en mer*, to words by the same poet.

In 1861 Saint-Saëns began his career as a teacher at the École Niedermeyer, where he met the young Gabriel Fauré. A special bond of friendship was formed between the 16-year-old pupil and the professor who, after all, was only ten years older. It was from Saint-Saëns that Fauré first heard the works of Schumann, Liszt, and Wagner—not prescribed composers for students at a school which concentrated on church music. Fauré was to remain a lifelong friend, and his family was adopted by the older composer as his own in his later, lonely years. Both composers are at one in their distrust of the self-consciously profound or sublime; they did not allow themselves to be dominated by the aesthetic of the Franck circle, and they understand the German lied without entertaining it as a blood relation. Once of the most attractive qualities of the Saint-Saëns songs to the modern listener is that they are almost all free of sentimentality and manipulative lack of taste. They are very seldom boring, and they have a spare quality and an economy of means which is as clean as a whistle. If we find Saint-Saëns's mélodies wanting in comparison to those of his pupil Fauré and his grand-pupil Ravel, we have to remind ourselves that his aesthetic influenced those younger masters to a large degree.

The Franco-Prussian War temporarily dashed several of the composer's hopes to expand further his ever-burgeoning European career as both composer and pianist. The songs of this period include the MÉLODIES PERSANES (Armand Renaud). The last of that set is **Tournoiement**, without doubt one of Saint-Saëns's finest songs. Whether or not he ever experienced the joys, or otherwise, of opium on his many travels we shall probably never know, but the composer provides us with a dizzy ride through the firmament of drug-enhanced perception. The difficulty of this, sheerly as a piano piece, is as good an indication as is to be found in the songs of the composer's own keyboard virtuosity—fleet, agile, and able to paint minute detail in the delicacy and evenness of his touch. Only Ravel might have written a mélodie like this, so abandoned and exotic in subject matter, and yet so classically restrained in its execution. *Dans ton cœur* (Henri Cazalis, later known under his pseudonym Jean Lahor, 1872) uses the same text that Duparc set as *Chanson triste* [DUPARC 1] and treats it quite differently. From 1870 and in quite another vein is *Si vous n'avez rien à me dire*, which is a lazily hypnotic salon song prophetic of the style of Reynaldo Hahn. The song **Danse macabre** (also Cazalis/Lahor, 1873) was to inspire the celebrated tone poem of 1874. The words 'Zig et zig et zag' and the conspiratorial 'Mais psit!' signal the composer letting his hair down in a manner which we can only describe as outrageously camp. From the very first strident tri-tones (the *intervalus diabolus*) twanging in the piano we are in for a Disneyland ride through the Haunted House (apart, that is, from the unacceptable-to-Disney descriptions of copulation, where the class barrier is forgotten between cartwright and marchioness—*Lady Chatterley's lover* encapsulated in a few bars of song).

For over thirty years Saint-Saëns had an atrocious time with the Parisian critics. *Samson et Dalila* failed to reach the French stage, despite a huge success in Weimar, and personal problems (a disastrous marriage, and the death of two young sons within six weeks of each other) added to the composer's burdens. He continued to compose indefatigably, and the output of songs was steady. He was by now a feared critic who tended to revel in polemical articles which seethed with anger, and which recalled the acerbic literary style of Berlioz. He was also a respected scholar and editor, undertaking the preparation of a complete edition of Gluck's works, and later Rameau's. The next great emotional setback was the death of his mother in 1888. He had been passionately devoted to her, although there is no doubt that their relationship was far from healthy, and it left Saint-Saëns emotionally stunted in certain respects. He found that he could no longer bear to live in Paris. Between 1890 and 1904, as he travelled the world, he had no fixed address, astonishing even for a busy professional pianist, but almost unthinkable for a composer. Nevertheless he continued to write and to work unabated, indeed with ever increasing productivity. Without a home of his own, he continued to be nomadic, living out of suitcases and composing in railway carriages, and in ship cabins. Algeria and Egypt were favourite ports of call and this exotic travel is reflected often in the music. Saint-Saëns's fondness for these sunny destinations (also Spain, Portugal, Italy, Greece, Uruguay) was partly to do with his health. His weak chest made it necessary for him to seek out comfortable climates. But there was no doubt another agenda for his visits to North Africa, and one calls to mind many French visitors to those parts of the world (Pierre Louÿs, Flaubert, Gide, among countless others) who were drawn there by the beauty of the inhabitants, and the air of sexual freedom so different from Europe. It was thus far away from Paris that Saint-Saëns made whatever arrangements were necessary to give him passing moments of happiness, illusions of intimacy, the coming to terms with love that had eluded him in the normal channels of life.

Songs of every kind poured from his pen throughout his long life. Despite the fact that the Hugo settings of the earlier years perhaps remain the best, there are many interesting mélodies for every kind of singer and mood. The composer had a penchant for writing for coloratura sopranos. Most notable of these are the valse chantée *La libellule* (written for Sybil Sanderson), the 'Bergerie Watteau' *Pourquoi rester seulette?*, the extraordinary *Thème varié* where the voice is truly treated as an instrument, and Saint-Saëns's riposte to Chausson's song of almost exactly the same name, the fleet and delicate *Papillons*. In terms of the duet repertoire, *Pastorale*, *El desdichado*, and *Viens!* are indispensable items. The last of these songs is from 1855, a setting of Hugo's *Une flûte invisible* [CAPLET 4]. Thirty years later the composer set the poem again, this time with a delightful flute obbligato, and using the same title as Caplet. There are also two other songs with violin, the enchanting **Le bonheur est chose légère** (where the addition of an instrument is optional) and the highly impressive *Violons dans le soir* (Anna de Noailles) which could not be bettered as a partnership between violin and voice, one complementing the other, both parts written with an idiomatic command that is Saint-Saëns at his best.

Another song to be recommended is the composer's setting of his own poem **Guitares et mandolines.** The repeated notes in the right hand of the accompaniment, an effect which suggests the plectrum at work, are the mark of a piano virtuoso who knows the tricks of the trade (the fingers have to change quickly on these repetitions). These mandolins are supported by guitar-like strummed chords in the left hand, and despite the fact that two instrumental evocations are at work simultaneously, the overall texture is as clear and bright as Spanish sunlight. On the whole, however, the songs of the final years have a chaste and moonlit classical quality, a sign of someone trying hard to shake off the velvet trappings of an old worn-out century. It is as if he is not impervious to the pathways trodden by Fauré, and though he disagrees with this former pupil's expeditions after 1900, he cannot remain uninfluenced by them.

Those interested in twin settings of famous poems will be somewhat astonished by what is to be found in Saint-Saëns's later output. From 1912 there is a song entitled *Le vent dans la plaine* which is this composer's only setting of Paul Verlaine—a truncated version of the immortal *C'est l'extase langoureuse* [DEBUSSY 6 i, FAURÉ 29 v]. The style of this music recalls the Fauré of *Nell*, and even the later cycles such as LE JARDIN CLOS. The trouble is that Verlaine and this composer are a strangely awkward mix. Even when he bowed to modernity and tried to write a song cycle in a manner fit for the new age—more introverted, less local colour—his choice of poetry let him down. LA CENDRE ROUGE (Georges Docquois), a large cycle of nine songs from 1914, finds the composer a fish out of water. Out of tune with the new literary sensibility, he selected grandiloquent, pretentious texts which no amount of musical skill could bring to life. And in this final phase, it was not always safe to stick with the classics. The last cycle of all is the strange VIEILLES CHANSONS (1921), with texts by Belleau, Charles d'Orléans, and Vacqueline de La Fresnaye. The central panel of this work is a setting of *Le temps a laissié son manteau* (entitled *Temps nouveau*) which was also set by Debussy in 1904 [DEBUSSY 12 i]. On either side of this, and rather less bizarre, are *Avril* and *Villanelle*. Saint-Saëns seems to have lost confidence in his old skills as a time-traveller, and failed to find an itinerary for a new journey. Much more enjoyable is *Grasselette et Maigrelette* (Ronsard), also from 1921. Only a French singer could cope with this dazzling patter song, where the virtues of two very different women are apostrophized. The music, in the manner of a *chanson-scie* at a *café-concert*, links hands with the modern generation of Les Six in a way that Saint-Saëns is unlikely to have suspected. There seems little to choose between this admirable song, and items from the CHANSONS GAILLARDES (e.g. *La belle jeunesse*) which Poulenc was to compose a few years later. It is as if the old boy has come full circle. He was alive and already composing when this type of ditty was all the rage in the cancan age of the Second Empire, and now he had lived long enough to encounter the phenomenon of frivolity enshrined as modernity, simplicity and economy praised as an antidote to 'boring old Duparc', artful banality praised to the skies as profundity under another guise. What a pity that he could not have lived his time all over again. Without the burdensome baggage of his long and unhappy past he might have been reborn as a deft and glittering composer of a less sentimental century.

1 *Le pas d'armes du Roi Jean*
   (Victor Hugo)

The tournament of King John

Par saint-Gille,
Viens-nous-en,
Mon agile
Alezan;
Viens, écoute,
Par la route,
Voir la joute
Du roi Jean.

By Saint Giles,
Let us set out,
My nimble
Chestnut steed;
Come, hear me:
We're off
To see King John's
Jousting contest.

Qu'un gros carme
Chartrier
Ait pour arme
L'encrier;
Qu'une fille,
Sous la grille,
S'égosille
À prier;

Let a portly Carmelite
Custodian of charters
Be armed
With an ink-well;
Let the maiden
In her convent parlour
Pray
Till she's hoarse;

Nous qui sommes,
De par Dieu,
Gentilshommes
De haut lieu,
Il faut faire
Bruit sur terre,
Et la guerre
N'est qu'un jeu.

We who are,
By the grace of God,
Noblemen
Of high rank
Must cause
a stir on earth,
And war
Is but a game.

Cette ville,
Aux longs cris,
Qui profile
Son front gris,
Des toits frêles,
Cent tourelles,
Clochers grêles,
C'est Paris!

This town,
Ringing with cries,
With its grey
Silhouette
Of delicate roofs,
Of a hundred turrets,
Of slender steeples,
Is Paris!

Los aux dames!
Au roi los!
Vois les flammes
Des champs clos,

Hooray for the ladies!
Hooray for the King!
See the banners
In the ring,

Où la foule,
Qui s'écroule,
Hurle et roule
À grands flots!

Sans attendre,
Çà, piquons!
L'œil bien tendre,
Attaquons
De nos selles
Les donzelles,
Roses, belles,
Aux balcons.

Là-haut brille,
Sur ce mur,
Yseult, fille
Au front pur;
Là-bas, seules,
Force aïeules
Portant gueules
Sur azur.

On commence!
Le beffroi!
Coups de lance,
Cris d'effroi!
On se forge,
On s'égorge,
Par saint-George!
Par le roi!

Dans l'orage,
Lys courbé,
Un beau page
Est tombé.
Il se pâme,
Il rend l'âme;
Il réclame
Un abbé.

Moines, vierges,
Porteront
De grands cierges
Sur son front;
Et, dans l'ombre
Du lieu sombre,
Deux yeux d'ombre
Pleureront.

Where the seething
Crowd
Roars and surges
Like breakers!

Without delay
Let's gallop off!
With amorous gaze,
Let us assail
From our saddles
The damsels,
Rosy-cheeked and lovely
On their balconies.

Gleaming up there
On that wall
Is the maiden Isolde
With her virginal brow;
Down there, on their own,
Throngs of old ladies
Are dressed in red
And blue.

Battle begins!
The alarm-bell rings!
Crash of lances,
Cries of fear!
Horses over-reach,
Throats are slit,
In the name of Saint George!
In the name of the King!

In the battle,
Like a wilted lily,
A handsome page
Has fallen.
He faints,
He breathes his last;
He begs for
A priest.

Monks, virgins
Will hold
Tall candles
Over his head;
And in the shadow
Of that dismal place,
Two dark eyes
Will weep.

Car madame
Isabeau
Suit son âme
Au tombeau.

Ça, mon frère,
Viens, rentrons
Dans notre aire
De barons.
Va plus vite,
Car au gîte
Qui t'invite,
Trouverons,

Toi, l'avoine
Du matin,
Moi, le moine
Augustin,
Ce saint homme
Suivant Rome,
Qui m'assomme
De latin,

Et rédige
En romain
Tout prodige
De ma main,
Qu'à ma charge
Il émarge
Sur un large
Parchemin.

Le vrai sire
Châtelain
Laisse écrire
Le vilain;
Sa main digne,
Quand il signe,
Égratigne
Le vélin.

For Lady
Isabeau
Follows his soul
To the grave.

Well, my brother,
Come, let's return
To our baronial
Hall.
Make haste,
For at home
Where we're awaited,
We shall find

Oats
For your breakfast,
And Friar Augustin
Waiting for me,
This holy man,
A follower of Rome,
Who bores me
With Latin,

And records
In Roman script
All my deeds
Of valour,
Which at my request
He lists
On a large
Parchment.

A true Lord
Of the manor
Lets a servant
Write for him;
His own noble hand,
When signing his name,
Scratches
The vellum.

2 L'attente

(Victor Hugo)

Monte, écureuil, monte au grand chêne,
Sur la branche des cieux prochaine,
Qui plie et tremble comme un jonc.
Cigogne, aux vieilles tours fidèle,
Oh! vole et monte à tire-d'aile
De l'église à la citadelle,
Du haut clocher au grand donjon.

Vieux aigle, monte de ton aire
À la montagne centenaire
Que blanchit l'hiver éternel.
Et toi qu'en ta couche inquiète
Jamais l'aube ne vit muette,
Monte, monte, vive alouette,
Vive alouette, monte au ciel!

Et maintenant, du haut de l'arbre,
Des flèches de la tour de marbre,
Du grand mont, du ciel enflammé,
À l'horizon, parmi la brume,
Voyez-vous flotter une plume
Et courir un cheval qui fume,
Et revenir mon bien-aimé?

Anticipation

Squirrel, ascend the towering oak,
To the branch right next to the sky
Bending and trembling like a reed.
Stork, faithful to the ancient towers,
Swiftly ascend and wing your way
From the church to the citadel,
From the lofty steeple to the mighty keep.

Old eagle, ascend from your eyrie
To the age-old mountain peak,
Whitened by eternal winter.
And you, whom in your unquiet nest,
Dawn never once saw silent—
Joyous lark, ascend, ascend,
Ascend into the sky!

And now, from the high tree-top,
From the spires of the marble tower,
From the great mountain, from the flaming sky,
On the sky-line, in the mist,
Can you see a bobbing plume,
A hurtling, steaming horse,
And my sweet love returning home?

3 La cloche

(Victor Hugo)

Seule en ta sombre tour, aux faîtes dentelés,
D'où ton souffle descend sur les toits ébranlés,
Ô cloche suspendue au milieu des nuées
Par ton vaste roulis si souvent remuées,
Tu dors en ce moment dans l'ombre, et rien ne luit
Sous ta voûte profonde où sommeille le bruit.
Oh! tandis qu'un esprit qui jusqu'à toi s'élance,
Silencieux aussi, contemple ton silence,
Sens-tu, par cet instinct vague et plein de douceur
Qui révèle toujours une sœur à la sœur,
Qu'à cette heure où s'endort la soirée expirante,

Une âme est près de toi, non moins que toi vibrante,
Qui bien souvent aussi jette un bruit solennel,
Et se plaint dans l'amour comme toi dans le ciel!

The bell

Alone in your dark and crenellated tower,
From where your breath drifts onto shaken roofs,
O bell suspended amid clouds
So often disturbed by your mighty swinging,
You sleep now in the shadows, no light gleams
Beneath your deep vault where sound is slumbering.
Ah! while a spirit, leaping towards you
And silent too, contemplates your silence,
Do you sense through that vague, sweet instinct
Which always discloses kindred spirits,
That at this hour when the dying evening falls
        asleep,
A soul, no less vibrant than your own, is near you,
Who also utters frequent solemn sounds,
And mourns in love as you do in the sky!

4 *Tournoiement: songe d'opium*

(Armand Renaud), from *MÉLODIES PERSANES*

Delirium: an opium-induced dream

Sans que nulle part je séjourne,
Sur la pointe du gros orteil,
Je tourne, je tourne, je tourne,
À la feuille morte pareil.
Comme à l'instant où l'on trépasse,
La terre, l'océan, l'espace,
Devant mes yeux troublés tout passe,
Jetant une même lueur.
Et ce mouvement circulaire,
Toujours, toujours je l'accélère,
Sans plaisir comme sans colère,
Frissonnant malgré ma sueur.

Dans les antres où l'eau s'enfourne,
Sur les inaccessibles rocs,
Je tourne, je tourne, je tourne,
Sans le moindre souci des chocs.
Dans les forêts, sur les rivages;
À travers les bêtes sauvages
Et leurs émules en ravages,
Les soldats qui vont sabre au poing,
Au milieu des marchés d'esclaves,
Au bord des volcans pleins de laves,
Chez les Mogols et chez les Slaves,
De tourner je ne cesse point.

Soumis aux lois que rien n'ajourne,
Aux lois que suit l'astre en son vol,
Je tourne, je tourne, je tourne,
Mes pieds ne touchent plus le sol.
Je monte au firmament nocturne,
Devant la lune taciturne,
Devant Jupiter et Saturne
Je passe avec un sifflement,
Et je franchis le Capricorne,
Et je m'abîme au gouffre morne
De la nuit complète et sans borne
Où je tourne éternellement.

Without so much as a pause,
I pirouette on my toe,
Spinning, spinning, spinning,
Like a withered leaf.
As at the moment of death,
The earth, the ocean and space
Pass before my clouded eyes,
Radiating the same light.
And as I rotate round and round,
I accelerate, accelerate,
Devoid of pleasure as of anger,
Shivering despite my sweat.

In caves aflood with foaming waves,
Standing on inaccessible rocks,
Spinning and spinning and spinning,
I've not the slightest fear of crashing.
In the forests and along the coasts,
Surrounded by savage beasts
And their havoc-wreaking rivals,
Soldiers brandishing their swords,
In the centre of slave-markets,
On volcano slopes awash with lava,
In the land of Slavs and Mogols,
I spin and spin unflaggingly.

Adhering to laws that none can defer,
The laws that the sun obeys in its course,
Spinning and spinning and spinning,
My feet no longer touch the ground.
I soar aloft to the starry sky,
I flit right past the silent moon,
Past Jupiter and Saturn,
Whirring on my way,
And I shoot past Capricorn,
And plunge into the dismal abyss
Of absolute and boundless night,
Where I spin and spin eternally.

5 *Danse macabre*
(Jean Lahor)

Zig et zig et zig, la mort en cadence
Frappant une tombe avec son talon,
La mort à minuit joue un air de danse,
Zig et zig et zag, sur son violon.

Le vent d'hiver souffle, et la nuit est sombre,
Des gémissements sortent des tilleuls;
Les squelettes blancs vont à travers l'ombre
Courant et sautant sous leurs grands linceuls.

Zig et zig et zig, chacun se trémousse,
On entend claquer des os des danseurs,
Un couple lascif s'asseoit sur la mousse
Comme pour goûter d'anciennes douceurs.

Zig et zig et zag, la mort continue
De racler sans fin son aigre instrument.
Un voile est tombé! La danseuse est nue!
Son danseur la serre amoureusement.

La dame est, dit-on, marquise ou baronne,
Et le vert galant un pauvre charron—
Horreur! Et voilà qu'elle s'abandonne
Comme si le rustre était un baron!

Zig et zig et zig, quelle sarabande!
Quels cercles de morts se donnant la main!
Zig et zig et zag, on voit dans la bande
Le roi gambader auprès du vilain!

Mais psit! tout à coup on quitte la ronde,
On se pousse, on fuit, le coq a chanté...
Oh! La belle nuit pour le pauvre monde!
Et vive la mort et l'égalité!

Dance of Death

Zig, zig, zig—Death, rhythmically,
Taps a tomb with his heel,
Death at midnight plays a gigue,
Zig, zig, zag, on his violin.

The winter wind blows, and the night is dark;
The lime-trees groan aloud;
White skeletons flit across the gloom,
Running and leaping beneath huge shrouds.

Zig, zig, zig, everyone's astir,
You hear the bones of the dancers knock;
A lustful couple sits down on the moss,
As if to savour past delights.

Zig, zig, zag, Death continues,
Endlessly scraping his shrill violin.
A veil has slipped! The dancer's naked!
Her partner clasps her amorously.

They say she's a baroness or marchioness,
And the callow gallant a poor cartwright.
Good God! And now she's giving herself,
As though the bumpkin were a baron!

Zig, zig, zig, what a saraband!
Circles of corpses all holding hands!
Zig, zig, zag, in the throng you can see
King and peasant dancing together!

But shh! Suddenly the dance is ended,
They jostle and take flight—the cock has crowed...
Ah! A splendid night for underlings!
And long live death and equality!

6 *Le bonheur est chose légère*
(Jules Barbier)

Le bonheur est chose légère,
Passagère,
On croit l'attendre, on le poursuit,
Il s'enfuit!
Hélas! Vous en voulez un autre

Happiness is a flighty thing

Happiness is a flighty,
Ephemeral thing;
You think it's imminent, you pursue it
It vanishes!
Alas, you covet something

Que le nôtre;	That's not ours;
Il faut à vos ardents désirs	Your fervent desires demand
Des plaisirs.	Fulfilment.
Dieu vous préserve des alarmes	May God shield you from alarms
Et des larmes	And tears
Qui peuvent assombrir le cours	Which might darken the course
Des beaux jours.	Of happy days.
Si jamais votre cœur regrette	If ever your heart misses
La retraite	The refuge
Qu'aujourd'hui vous abandonnez,	That today you forsake,
Revenez!	Return!
De tous les chagrins de votr'âme,	Of all your soul's sorrows
Je réclame	I crave
Pour notre fidèle amitié	For our friendship's sake
La moitié.	My half.

7 *Guitares et mandolines*   *Guitar and mandoline*

(Camille Saint-Saëns)

Guitares et mandolines	Guitar and mandoline
Ont des sons qui font aimer.	Cause you to fall in love.
Tout en croquant des pralines	While crunching pralines,
Pépa se laisse charmer	Pepa lets herself be charmed
Quand, jetant dièses, bécarres,	When, scattering sharps and flats,
Mandolines et guitares	Mandoline and guitar
Vibrent pour la désarmer.	Resound to disarm her.
Mandoline avec guitare	Mandoline and guitar
Accompagnent de leur bruit	Accompany with their sound
Les amants suivant le phare	Lovers who follow the beacon
De la beauté dans la nuit.	Of beauty in the night;
Et Juana montre, féline,	And feline Juana reveals
(Guitare avec mandoline)	(Guitar and mandoline)
Sa bouche et son œil qui luit.	Her mouth and gleaming eyes.

SATIE, Erik (1866–1925)

There is no one else like this in French music, and one is tempted to say the history of music as a whole. Is he a rogue or a saint, charlatan or genius, a disturbed crackpot or a man of fresh and inspired vision?—or is he just possibly a mixture of all these things? In any case, he is as much an enigma now as he was to his mystified contemporaries. How much was pose, and how much was unselfconscious eccentricity, how much was joking and how much was deadly serious? Reynaldo

Hahn was convinced that Satie was nothing more than a worthless *poseur*. At the Schola Cantorum, Albert Roussel, then a very young professor, was uncertain whether the 39-year-old Satie (he was what would today be called a 'mature student') really wanted to study composition. Just when Roussel had decided that Satie was laughing at him in the manner of a snide revolutionary who derides the outmoded and passé, the student, older than the teacher, revealed an astonishing humility in going back to school, and a real desire to master counterpoint. You never knew with Satie. He was the most childlike of adults, the most sophisticated of children. This in itself shaped a whole generation's responses to aesthetical questions, and freed French composers to be themselves and to trust their own hearts in a manner that had been impossible before. Picasso did the same for the painters, and Satie, had he a greater creative sweep, might have been called the Picasso of music. The shift in musical values which allowed Poulenc to present the six miniatures of *LE BESTIAIRE* (1919) as a serious song cycle, for example, had come about largely because of Érik Satie.

There is no other single person (César Franck and Nadia Boulanger included) whose influence, sometimes imperceptible, sometimes gigantic, stands behind the careers of so many composers in this book. Roland-Manuel calls him a 'weird Socrates' whose 'advice, devilment, artless audacity' inspired others to subvert the traditions of nineteenth-century music in favour of a new century. For thirty-five years Satie was 'the intimate advisor upon every type of bold and impudent experiment in French music'. Early in his career Satie met Debussy, and the influence was profound. It was thanks to this 'gentle medieval musician who strayed into this century' (as Debussy described Satie on a dedication flyleaf of the *CINQ POÈMES DE BAUDELAIRE* in 1892) that the younger composer was encouraged to make an opera out of a Maeterlinck text rather than use yet another botched libretto by Catulle Mendès. Satie's influence on Ravel was also profound, as it was on Koechlin too, and there was a corresponding depth of bitterness when he fell out with the former. But a younger generation beckoned and here Satie became an icon *sans pareil*. It goes without saying that Poulenc, Auric, and Milhaud were in his thrall, but the age-gap made the older composer extremely sensitive to slights, real or imagined. He had relationships of differing intimacy with all these young men, but he eventually quarrelled with Auric and Poulenc, for various reasons. Nevertheless, despite his personal prickliness, Satie was regarded as a shaman who could read the auguries for a new century. Even giants like Stravinsky were influenced by him: in contrast to *Les noces*, *Mavra* seems a Satie-inspired work.

At the first performance of *Socrate* at Adrienne Monnier's bookshop in the rue de l'Odéon, Gide, Claudel, Valéry, Fargue, Picasso, Braque, Derain, Stravinsky, and many others were in the audience. Satie was, in Roger Shattuck's words, 'part mascot, part primitive, part jester, part sage', a semi-official position in French musical life which, as he got older, he seemed uniquely able to fulfil. Even if one did not admire his music (Honegger described Satie as having 'an excessively precise mind, but bereft of all creative power') there could be no denying the influence he had on others. Later on there was a new school of composers and musicians who gathered around him, the so-called École d'Arcueil (named after the unfashionable area of Paris where Satie had his impoverished lodgings, a room full of umbrellas and an unplayable piano), and musicians like Desormière, Maxime Jacob, and Henri Sauguet now pledged their fealty. And when he was in Paris in the 1950s, long after Satie's death, the American composer Ned Rorem wrote of being moved to tears by *Socrate*, a score which every young composer of the time had under his arm as a talisman and a sign of his artistic alignment. In another direction, moving away from vocal music, composers like Varèse and Cage acknowledged a debt of gratitude to Satie, and his music remains a living tradition in the works he inspired from English composers like Gavin Bryars and Christopher Hobbs.

Satie's most influential works were probably those written in his fifties—the ballets *Parade* and *Relâche*, a number of the piano pieces and the extraordinary symphonic drama *Socrate*. The mélodie and chanson output from an earlier period cannot compete with these in terms of significance. But throughout his career, including the period between 1898 and 1910 when he all but retired from creative life, and was making his living as a piano player in Montmartre, Satie composed songs. These are sometimes gently challenging and whimsical, sometimes frankly populist and commercial. If we were to know Satie by his songs alone, his achievements would seem slighter than they are. In recitals one almost always finds the same handful of songs which show his abilities as a composer for the *café-concert*; it is seldom one hears the songs which represent his innovations and dead-pan pranks. This is probably because the 'serious' songs show little real interest in the human voice; they are vehicles for ideas rather than singers. The singers who enjoy performing the essential Satie are those who do not require a bel canto vehicle in order to display the beauty of their instruments.

The first set of songs, the TROIS MÉLODIES of 1886, date from just after his escape from the Paris Conservatoire—a period of wasted time by all accounts. Nevertheless when one listens to these songs, and considers that Chabrier's opera *Le roi malgré lui* was premièred in the same year (it was a work which would influence Satie greatly), they are startlingly modern. On the page they appear naive and simple to the point of parody. No one else was writing music that *looked* like this, and it is the spare minimalist texture (the third song *Sylvie* has no bar-lines) which seems even more modern than the succession of unresolved seventh and ninth chords. This is strange music, innocuous and bland at the same time as being revolutionary. We already detect a raffish spirit at work, a Puck who is teasing us and playing games, yet who reserves the right to claim his utter sincerity (and mean it) at any moment. The poet is Satie's great friend J. P. Contamine de Latour who was Satie's drinking companion and fellow spirit in various amorous adventures with the young *midinettes* who sewed until midday, and then sought protectors and gallants. In his early mélodies we can detect an evolution of Satie's musical personality; in the gentle swing of *Chanson* (1887) the composer of the *Gymnopédies* of the following year; in *Chanson médiévale* (1906) the man who was fascinated by Gothic art, Gregorian chant, and medieval music. *Les fleurs* (1887) is a perfect little gem, strangely moving in its flowing 3/4, and its tender minimalism. Was Poulenc's remarkably similar *Fleurs* from FIANÇAILLES POUR RIRE a homage to this song?

The composer's interest in mystical religion had led him to become the official composer of a spurious Rosicrucian sect. From this period of the early 1890s comes one song *Hymne* ('pour le "Salut Drapeau" du "Prince de Byzance" du Sâr Péladan'). This is perhaps Satie's most difficult song to perform because of the peculiarity of the vocal intervals based on an ancient Greek chromatic mode. The succession of first inversion chords accompanying the vocal line adds to the sense of this being a piece of moon-music. This marks the end of Satie's first period of 'serious' song composition. For further vocal music along these lines we have to wait more than twenty years. The composer was increasingly being drawn into the bohemian life of Montmartre, particularly the night life and bars like Le Chat Noir and the Auberge du Clou where he accompanied the singers and improvised waltzes for the customers. It was at the Auberge du Clou around 1891 that he met Debussy who was to become his closest friend and over whose development Satie watched like a guardian angel. Four years older than Satie, this composer was already counted a giant and Satie knew it. In a sense, Debussy's strivings (influenced by Satie to a certain degree) and his subsequent successes were a source of reproach to the lesser-known composer who felt himself musically ill-equipped in comparison, and was sometimes made to feel a 'poor relation'. It is little wonder that he declined to appear competitive, and that he never wanted to follow the same path. In fact the friendship with Debussy, far from inspiring Satie to greater creative activity, had the opposite effect. Montmartre and its cafés had become a way of life and the only way of earning his living. He withdrew into the popular world. There young Ravel heard him play at this time, and later acknowledged his influence, but at this point Satie seemed an oddity, his career as a composer (such as it was) already behind him.

There was now mostly light music. The first of his *caf' conc'* songs to be written was *Je te veux* (1897, Pacory), a waltz which has found an honoured place in almost every soprano's repertoire (although we are used to a modification of the original, more racy, text—the song was conceived at first for a male singer). There is a trace of the real Satie here, enough for the song to charm not only with its agreeable melody, but with a certain quirkiness. It evokes its time with Proustian precision. At first Satie lived up on the *butte* itself, but in 1898 he moved to the south of Paris—the suburb of Arcueil-Cachan. He walked the considerable distance back and forth from work each night. These were miserable years which the composer found 'a great lowering'. The turn of the century was the nadir of his life, just as it was the high point of Debussy's. Two stage works from this period (later rescued), *Jack-in-the-box* and *Geneviève de Brabant*, were conveniently lost for years behind the piano in Arcueil. And yet from this period come all the jolly songs. Less well known than *Je te veux* is *Tendrement*, another waltz written to the words of the popular chansonnier Vincent Hyspa. The recently published *NEUF CHANSONS DE CABARET ET DE CAF' CONC'* (Salabert, edited by Steven Moore Whiting) includes previously unknown cabaret material, and throws new light of this relationship. Occasionally these two would get a gig at a society function, and Satie would have to borrow clothes from his brother. From 1905 there are other fruits of the collaboration with Hyspa—*Chez le docteur* and *L'omnibus automobile*. In the right hands these songs can come off, but they need an artist skilled in the use of strophic song; and non-French singers, normally all-too-eager to sing anything by a famous composer with a hint of crossover, usually steer clear of this repertoire. In 1904 Satie wrote the song that most often appears on recital programmes, for better or worse. This is the celebrated Paulette Darty number *La Diva de l'Empire* (Bonnaud and Blès) which appeared in a revue entitled *Dévidons la bobine*, and was originally published as a 'marche chantée' although it shows a feeling for the syncopations of ragtime. English singers find this piece irresistible with its weird word stresses on words like 'gentlemen' and 'Piccadilly'. (In fact, with his penchant for velvet suits, Satie's nickname at this time was the 'Velvet gentleman'.) For a moment we glimpse the fact that London was almost as glamorous in Parisian eyes as Paris was in the fantasies of the sophisticated Londoner. Of course the 'Empire' was the Empire Theatre of Varieties, Leicester Square, where the promenade was a notorious meeting place for the 'ladies of the town' and their customers. The 'Diva' was very probably the beautiful Lilly Elsie (1886–1962), the young star who was to have her greatest success (particularly with her hats) in Lehár's *The Merry Widow* in 1907. There is one more well-known popular song by

Satie, truly irresistible in the hands of a great singing comedian like Gabriel Bacquier—this is *Allons-y chochotte* (Durante, 1906)—but foreigners beware!

And now Satie decided to go back to school, and study counterpoint, fugue, and orchestration at the Schola Cantorum. He did this for seven years (1905–12) and strove to integrate his new discoveries into his work. Whether we can hear this or not in his later songs is another matter—the main thing is that it seems to have given the composer the confidence to believe in himself once more after years in the wilderness. One of the extraordinary things about his life was this second youth when he re-emerged onto the musical scene and began a new, more serious, career as something of a reinvented personality. From this period date the extraordinary TROIS MÉLODIES SANS PAROLES (1907). These have fanciful titles (*Rambouillet, Les oiseaux,* and *Marienbad*) but no surviving words—which hardly encourages performance. In 1911 Satie was 'rediscovered' when both Ravel and Debussy arranged performances of his earlier work to illustrate that he had been a precursor of their own music. Debussy was astounded that the *Gymnopédies* (orchestrated by him) were such a success, and this sign of low esteem from an old friend wounded Satie deeply. From now on he would be an increasingly wild card, refusing to be merely a strangely influential name from the past, and insisting on his own individuality. The first fruits of this from the singer's point of view are TROIS POÈMES D'AMOUR (1914). These are tiny fragments to his own texts, and make a droll and strangely tender effect in performance. Only in 1916 would Satie write a set of songs which seems unafraid to stand up and be counted as songs written for real singers. Indeed two of the TROIS MÉLODIES (1916) were dedicated to the husband and wife singing-team Jane Bathori and Émile Engel whose names appear on the pages of Ravel's HISTOIRES NATURELLES. All of a sudden Satie enters the real world of the mélodie for the first time, seemingly given new strength by the efforts of Auric and Milhaud. He had been disinclined to publish songs when Debussy was the mélodiste of the moment, but these young men were more comfortable colleagues. In fact, Satie's time had come. Each of these three songs is understated and witty: after lugubrious music appropriate to a metal frog, the last page of *La statue de bronze* (Fargue, a writer we will hear of again in conjunction with Satie) contains night music of a certain elusive poetry that we will find again in *Socrate*. *Daphénéo* (the text by the mysterious 'God.'—in actual fact Satie's friend Mimi Godebska) is a perfect evocation of a child's world; when listening to this music we fancy we are hearing the workings of a young mind as tiny wheels and cogs grapple with a new concept. The final 'Ah!' never fails to elicit a murmur of delight from an audience. *Le chapelier* (dedicated to Stravinsky) is an affectionate parody of music from Gounod's *Mireille*, the poem by Chalupt inspired by *Alice in Wonderland*. The whole mock-solemn and zany mood of the mad hatter's tea-party is evoked in these two pages. The only problem is that this little set is too short in performance. One would like to ask for more, but Alice in Satieland has better manners than Oliver Twist.

From the last months of 1920 comes a perfect little cycle, QUATRE PETITES MÉLODIES, where each song is only a page long. But what is exceptional is the garland of poetry woven by the composer. The first, *Élégie*, sets only four lines of a long poem by Lamartine of all people—how strange it is to see this name together with Satie's! But it had been chosen as a touching tribute to Debussy, the old quarrel resolved by his death. At the top of the music Satie writes, 'En souvenir d'une admirative et douce amitié de trente ans.' The second song, *Danseuse*, is a Cocteau setting. (Honegger set the same poem at about the same time with the title *Une danseuse*, and not altogether dissimilarly.)

Chanson is a setting of an anonymous eighteenth-century poem and just as naughty as anything Poulenc composed in CHANSONS GAILLARDES. *Adieu* is a setting of a poem by Cocteau's lover Raymond Radiguet, then still only 17 and soon to lose his own life. Such knowledge makes the eloquence of this farewell even more touching; in musical terms Satie seems to be brushing away the 'mouches du passé', including the composers of an older generation, and looks to his new young colleagues for inspiration, as they to him. Satie's last vocal work with piano is a delightful little cycle called LUDIONS (Fargue, 1923). In *Song*, Carol Kimball explains this strange title: 'a *ludion* is a little figure suspended in a hollow ball, which descends or rises in a vase with water when one presses down on the elastic membrane covering the mouth of the vase.' Once again the set is very short and almost cryptic, though very varied and full of surprises. Its characters from the animal kingdom (rat, frog, and cat—not to mention poet) seem to be manipulated toy-like in any direction taking the fancy of poet or composer; it is difficult not to imagine this as a riposte to Poulenc's LE BESTIAIRE. It would perhaps be an interesting idea to place these two cycles next to each other on a programme. There is a confidence in this music, a swagger perhaps, which betokens a composer who knows that at last he is something of a celebrity.

There only remains one more work with piano, and certainly the most important. Perhaps *Socrate* (Plato translated by Victor Cousin, 1918) is not a work to discuss in a book about songs. It is sub-titled 'drame symphonique' and although it exists in a piano version, one senses that Satie preferred it with chamber orchestra. But who else would perform this work than an expert singer of mélodies—like Hugues Cuenod, for example, whose interpretation, with piano of course, is legendary? There is no better illustration than this piece of what Roger Shattuck meant when he said that Satie's songs 'resemble musical self-denial before a text'. The work was dedicated to, and commissioned by, the Princesse de Polignac. This was a sign of Satie's unique status at the end of the First World War—he was the Montmartre piano player who had come back from the dead to be a great composer, reborn as the spiritual familiar and mascot of the avant-garde. The work is divided into three long movements—*Portrait de Socrate*, *Bords de l'Ilissus*, and *Mort de Socrate*. The first two pieces are dialogues with never a suggestion that more than one singer should take part. The work has a curious effect in performance. It has a certain whiteness and blandness which makes the ear tire—it all seems so inconsequential. But listening beyond this, the culminative effect is not dissimilar to the experience of giving oneself up to certain music from the East: the very sameness engenders a sort of cosmic tranquillity, an elevation of the senses that goes to the heart of something about classical Greece that even the BILITIS evocations of Debussy, for example, cannot approach, much less the ÉTUDES LATINES of Hahn. There is a purity and a selflessness here, and a sort of unstrained goodness. We fancy that we are hearing the voice of the composer himself, simple and honest, as unspoiled by success as he had been unbowed by penury and obscurity. All this is incomprehensible to most people; for many, *Socrate* is no more than the Emperor's new clothes in music. But the ancient Greek philosopher and teacher of Plato was also incomprehensible to his contemporaries and only understood by a select group of younger men. Satie, one of the chief harbingers of the twentieth century in music, has acquired some of that sage's dignity and reputation for inscrutable wisdom. And yes, it is likely that somewhere in this mixture of sincerity and simplicity, the composer is laughing at us too.

TROIS MÉLODIES DE 1886

(J. P. Contamine de Latour)

I i *Les anges*

Vêtus de blanc, dans l'azur clair,
Laissant déployer leurs longs voiles,
Les anges planent dans l'éther,
Lys flottants parmi les étoiles.

Les luths frissonnent sous leurs doigts,
Luths à la divine harmonie.
Comme un encens montent leurs voix,
Calmes, sous la voûte infinie.

En bas, gronde le flot amer;
La nuit partout étend ses voiles,
Les anges planent dans l'éther,
Lys flottants parmi les étoiles.

I ii *Élégie*

J'ai vu décliner comme un songe,
Cruel mensonge,
Tout mon bonheur.
Au lieu de la douce espérance,
J'ai la souffrance
Et la douleur.

Autrefois ma folle jeunesse
Chantait sans cesse
L'hymne d'amour.
Mais la chimère caressée
S'est effacée
En un seul jour.

J'ai dû souffrir mon long martyre,
Sans le maudire,
Sans soupirer.
Le seul remède sur la terre
À ma misère
Est de pleurer.

THREE MÉLODIES OF 1886

The angels

Clothed in white in the bright blue sky,
Unfurling their long veils,
Angels hover in the clear heavens:
Lilies floating among the stars.

Lutes quiver beneath their fingers,
Lutes with a heavenly harmony.
Like incense their voices rise
Calmly up to the boundless vault.

Below—the thunder of briny waves,
Night on all sides spreads its veils,
Angels hover in the clear heavens:
Lilies floating among the stars.

Elegy

Like a dream I saw—
O cruel lie!—
All my fortune wane.
Sweet hope has given way
To suffering
And pain.

Long ago, my wild youth
Sang love's praises
Without cease.
But the cherished dream
Vanished
In a single day.

I have had to endure my long torment
Without demur,
Without sighs.
The sole earthly remedy
For my misery
Is to weep.

I iii *Sylvie*

Elle est si belle, ma Sylvie,
Que les anges en sont jaloux.
L'amour sur sa lèvre ravie
Laissa son baiser le plus doux.

Ses yeux sont de grandes étoiles,
Sa bouche est faite de rubis,
Son âme est un zénith sans voiles,
Et son cœur est mon paradis.

Ses cheveux sont noirs comme l'ombre,
Sa voix plus douce que le miel,
Sa tristesse est une pénombre
Et son sourire un arc-en-ciel.

Elle est si belle, ma Sylvie,
Que les anges en sont jaloux.
L'amour sur sa lèvre ravie
Laissa son baiser le plus doux.

Sylvie

My Sylvie is so fair
That angels are jealous of her;
Love on her enraptured lips
Left behind the sweetest kiss.

Her eyes are huge stars,
Her mouth is made of rubies,
Her soul is a sky without haze
And her heart is my paradise.

Her hair is black like the darkness,
Her voice more sweet than honey,
Her sadness is an eclipse
And a rainbow her smile.

My Sylvie is so fair
That angels are jealous of her;
Love on her enraptured lips
Left behind the sweetest kiss.

2 *Je te veux*
(Henry Pacory)

J'ai compris ta détresse,
Cher amoureux,
Et je cède à tes vœux:
Fais de moi ta maîtresse.
Loin de nous la sagesse,
Plus de détresse,
J'aspire à l'instant précieux
Où nous serons heureux:
Je te veux.

Je n'ai pas de regrets,
Et je n'ai qu'une envie:
Près de toi, là, tout près,
Vivre toute ma vie.
Que mon cœur soit le tien
Et ta lèvre la mienne,
Que ton corps soit le mien,
Et que toute ma chair soit tienne.

J'ai compris ta détresse,
Cher amoureux,
Et je cède à tes vœux:
Fais de moi ta maîtresse.

I want you

I've understood your distress,
Dear lover,
And yield to your desires:
Make of me your mistress.
Let's throw discretion
And sadness to the winds.
I long for the precious moment
When we shall be happy:
I want you.

I've no regrets
And only one desire:
Close, very close by you
To live my whole life long.
Let my heart be yours
And your lips mine,
Let your body be mine
And all my flesh yours.

I've understood your distress,
Dear lover,
And yield to your desires:
Make of me your mistress.

Loin de nous la sagesse,
Plus de détresse,
J'aspire à l'instant précieux
Où nous serons heureux:
Je te veux.

Oui, je vois dans tes yeux
La divine promesse
Que ton cœur amoureux
Vient chercher ma caresse.
Enlacés pour toujours,
Brûlés des mêmes flammes,
Dans des rêves d'amours,
Nous échangerons nos deux âmes.

Let's throw discretion
And sadness to the winds.
I long for the precious moment
When we shall be happy:
I want you.

Yes, I see in your eyes
The exquisite promise
That your loving heart
Is seeking my caress.
Entwined forever,
Consumed by the same desire,
In dreams of love
We'll exchange our souls.

3 *La Diva de l'Empire**   *The starlet of the Empire*

(Dominique Bonnaud and Numa Blès)

Sous le grand chapeau Greenaway,†
Mettant l'éclat d'un sourire,
D'un rire charmant et frais
De baby étonné qui soupire,
Little girl aux yeux veloutés,
C'est la Diva de l'Empire.
C'est la rein' dont s'éprennent
Les gentlemen
Et tous les dandys
De Piccadilly.

Beneath her large Greenaway hat,
Putting on her dazzling smile,
The fresh and charming laugh
Of a wide-eyed sighing babe,
A little girl with velvet eyes—
She's the Diva of the Empire,
She's the queen they're smitten with,
The gentlemen
And all the dandies
Of Piccadilly.

Dans un seul 'yes' elle met tant de douceur
Que tous les snobs en gilet à cœur,
L'accueillant de hourras frénétiques,
Sur la scène lancent des gerbes de fleurs,
Sans remarquer le rire narquois
De son joli minois.

She invests a single 'Yes' with such sweetness,
That all the fancy-waistcoated snobs
Welcoming her with frenzied cheers,
Hurl bouquets on the stage,
Without observing the wily smile
On her pretty face.

Elle danse presque automatiquement
Et soulève, oh très pudiquement,
Ses jolis dessous de fanfreluches,
De ses jambes montrant le frétillement.
C'est à la fois très très innocent
Et très très excitant.

She dances almost mechanically
And lifts—oh! so modestly—
Her pretty petticoat edged with flounces,
To reveal her wriggling legs.
It is very, very innocent
And very, very exciting too.

---

* The Empire Theatre of Varieties, Leicester Square.
† Kate Greenaway (1846–1901), English artist and illustrator of books, whose drawings of children, dressed in the style of the early 19th century, made her famous.

TROIS MÉLODIES DE 1916

4 i *La statue de bronze*
(Léon-Paul Fargue)

La grenouille
Du jeu de tonneau*
S'ennuie, le soir, sous la tonnelle...
Elle en a assez!
D'être la statue
Qui va prononcer un grand mot: Le Mot!

Elle aimerait mieux être avec les autres
Qui font des bulles de musique
Avec le savon de la lune
Au bord du lavoir mordoré
Qu'on voit, là-bas, luire entre les branches...

On lui lance à cœur de journée
Une pâture de pistoles
Qui la traversent sans lui profiter

Et s'en vont sonner
Dans les cabinets
De son piédestal numéroté!

Et le soir, les insectes couchent
Dans sa bouche...

4 ii *Daphénéo*
(Mimi Godebska)

Dis-moi, Daphénéo, quel est donc cet arbre
Dont les fruits sont des oiseaux qui pleurent?

Cet arbre, Chrysaline, est un oisetier.†

Ah! Je croyais que les noisetiers‡
Donnaient des noisettes, Daphénéo.

Oui, Chrysaline, les noisetiers donnent des noisettes,
Mais les oisetiers donnent des oiseaux qui pleurent.

Ah!...

THREE MÉLODIES OF 1916

The statue of bronze

The frog
Of the barrel-game
Gets bored at evening under the arbour...
She's had enough of it!
Being the statue
About to utter a weighty word: the Word!

She'd sooner be with the others
Blowing music-bubbles
With moon-soap,
By the reddish-brown washhouse
Shining down there through the branches...

All day they keep on throwing
Fodder of metal discs
That pass through her to no avail

And clatter
Into the compartments
Of her numbered pedestal!

And, at night, insects sleep
In her mouth...

Daphénéo

Tell me, Daphénéo, the name of that tree
Which sprouts weeping birds as fruit?

That tree, Chrysaline, is a bird-tree.

Ah! I thought nut-trees
Produced nuts, Daphénéo.

Yes, Chrysaline, nut-trees do produce nuts,
But bird-trees produce weeping birds.

Ah!...

* A garden game popular at the end of the 19th century; the aim was to throw metal discs through the frog's mouth.
† Un oisetier=a bird-tree; ‡ Un noisetier=a hazel tree.

4 iii *Le chapelier*
(René Chalupt)

Le chapelier s'étonne de constater
Que sa montre retarde de trois jours,
Bien qu'il ait eu soin de la graisser
Toujours avec du beurre de première qualité.
Mais il a laissé tomber des miettes
De pain dans les rouages,
Et il a beau plonger sa montre dans le thé,
Ça ne la fera pas avancer davantage.

The hatter

The hatter is astonished to find
That his watch is three days slow,
Despite always greasing it diligently
With butter of best quality.
But he has dropped
Breadcrumbs into the works,
And though he dip his watch in tea,
That will not make it go faster.

QUATRE PETITES MÉLODIES

FOUR LITTLE MÉLODIES

5 i *Élégie**
(Alphonse de Lamartine)

Que me font ces vallons, ces palais, ces chaumières?
Vains objets dont pour moi le charme est envolé;
Fleuves, rochers, forêts, solitudes si chères,
Un seul être vous manque, et tout est dépeuplé.

Elegy

What are these valleys, palaces, cottages to me?
Vain objects that for me have lost their charm;
Rivers, rocks, forests, solitudes so cherished—
A single being is absent from you, and all is void.

5 ii *Danseuse*
(Jean Cocteau)

Le crabe sort sur ses pointes
Avec ses bras en corbeille;
Il sourit jusqu'aux oreilles.

La danseuse d'Opéra,
Au crabe toute pareille,
Sort de la coulisse peinte,
En arrondissant les bras.

* In memory of Debussy.

Dancer

The crab walks out on its toes
With circular arms;
It smiles from ear to ear.

A ballerina,
Just like the crab,
Walks out from the painted wings,
Describing a circle with her arms.

5 iii *Chanson*

    (Anonymous, eighteenth century)

C'est mon trésor, c'est mon bijou,
Le joli trou par où
Ma vigueur se réveille...
Oui, je suis fou, fou, fou
Du trou de ma bouteille.

Song

What a treasure, what a jewel,
The pretty hole through which
My vigour is aroused...
Yes, I dote, dote, dote
On my bottle's orifice.

5 iv *Adieu*

    (Raymond Radiguet)

Amiral, ne crois pas déchoir
En agitant ton vieux mouchoir.
C'est la coutume de chasser
Ainsi les mouches du passé.

Farewell

Admiral, do not think you fall from grace
In waving your old handkerchief.
That is how we brush aside
The flies of yesteryear.

LUDIONS*

(Léon-Paul Fargue)

BOTTLE-IMPS

6 i *Air du rat*

Abi Abirounère
Qui que tu n'étais don?
Une blanche monère
Un jo
Un joli goulifon
Un œil
Un œil à son pépère
Un jo
Un joli goulifon.

The rat's air

Abi Abirounère
Who are you then?
A primitive white creature
A pret
A pretty glutton
An apple
An apple of the old boy's eye
A pret
A pretty glutton.

6 ii *Spleen*

Dans un vieux square où l'océan
Du mauvais temps met son séant
Sur un banc triste aux yeux de pluie
C'est d'une blonde
Rosse et gironde
Que je m'ennuie
Dans ce cabaret du Néant
Qu'est notre vie.

Spleen

In an old square where the ocean
Of bad weather deposits its derrière
On a sad bench with eyes of rain
Sits a blonde
Bitchy and buxom
How bored I feel
In this cabaret of nothingness
That is our life.

* These are nonsense poems that defy translation.

6 iii *La grenouille américaine*

La gouénouille améouicaine
Me regarde par-dessus
Ses bésicles de futaine.
Ses yeux sont des grogs massus
Dépourvus de jolitaine.
Je pense à Casadesus
Qui n'a pas fait de musique
Sur cette scène d'amour
Dont le parfum nostalgique
Sort d'une boîte d'Armour.

Argus de table tu gardes
L'âme du crapaud Vanglor
Ô bouillon qui me regardes
Avec tes lunettes d'or.

The American frog

The American frog
Peers at me over
His fustian spectacles.
His eyeballs are highballs
Stripped of pretty silvering.
I think of Casadesus
Who has not made music
For this scene of love
Whose nostalgic perfume
Rises from a tin of Armour.

Argus of the table you retain
The soul of Vanglor the toad
O bouillon watching me
With your golden spectacles.

6 iv *Air du poète*

Au pays de Papouasie
J'ai caressé la Pouasie...
La grâce que je vous souhaite
C'est de n'être pas Papouète.

The poet's air

In the land of Papua
I embraced Papoetry...
I do not desiderate
That you become a Papuoet.

6 v *Chanson du chat*

Il est une bebête
Ti Li petit nenfant
Tirelan
C'est une byronette
La beste à sa moman
Tirelan
Le peu Tinan faon
C'est un ti blanc-blanc
Un petit potasson?
C'est mon goret
C'est mon pourçon
Mon petit potasson.*

Il saut' sur la fenêtre
Et groume du museau
Pasqu'il voit sur la crête
S'découper les oiseaux
Tirelo

Song of the cat

'Tis a baby creature
Ti Li little enfant
Tirelan
A byronette
Mummy's best
Tirelan
The little en fawn
Is a ti blanc-blanc
A little potasson?
'Tis my piglet
My porker
My little potasson.

He jumps on the window sill
And grooms his snout
'Cos he sees on the roof
The clear outline of birds
Tirelo

* The name of Fargue's fat cat.

Le petit n'en faut	The little n'en faut
C'est un ti bloblo	'Tis a ti blo-blo
Un petit Potaçao	A little Potaçao
C'est mon goret	'Tis my piglet
C'est mon pourceau	My porker
Mon petit potasseau.	My little potasseau.

SAUGUET, Henri (1901–1989)

Born in Bordeaux, and only two years younger than Poulenc, Sauguet was just too young to be part of Les Six. However, he read Cocteau's manifesto *Le coq et l'arlequin*, and founded Les Trois in Bordeaux, with the composer Lizotte and the poet Louis Emié. He told me, during a memorable meeting towards the end of his life, that as a young man of 17 he hesitated for a long time as to whether he should write to Debussy, and eventually plucked up the courage to send him a letter. The next morning he heard that the great composer had died. In similar fashion, Sauguet seems to have missed the boat throughout his long career which, although filled with activity, seems at one remove from the centre of the musical scene. Certainly his works remain very much on the fringe of public awareness, particularly outside France. Milhaud encouraged him to move to Paris where he met Koechlin (who was to be his composition teacher) and Satie. His first work for the stage was *Le plumet du colonel* (1924), a one-act opera for which he wrote his own libretto. This contains an exquisite *Berceuse créole* which is sometimes performed in recital, and which is every bit as beautiful as Montsalvatge's ubiquitous *Canción de cuna para dormir a un negrito*. Sauguet was a member of the so-called École d'Arcueil (with Désormière, Cliquet-Pleyel, and Maxime Jacob), and Satie introduced him to Diaghilev, for whom he wrote the ballet *La chatte*. Other ballets followed, written for other companies, the most famous of which was *Les forains*. His most successful opera was *La chartreuse de Parme* (1927–36).

From this it is clear that Sauguet was a composer of much greater range and ambition than, say, Jacques Leguerney, who concentrated on writing songs which are as neglected today as Sauguet's. But whereas it is difficult to fault Leguerney's mélodies, where every note in his circumscribed world seems to have been weighed and considered, the prolific nature of Sauguet's output places him in the same tricky class as his mentor Milhaud. In the cycles (some thirty of them) there is a great deal of material of unequal quality; one feels that it was sometimes more important for him to put something down on paper at all costs than to refrain from writing anything inferior. Reading through Sauguet's music provides something of the same experience as playing Massenet's many songs one after the other: note-spinning is mixed with genuine inspiration, the dross threatens to overwhelm, and conceal, the threads of gold. In everything he does there is a sense of a man of wonderful manners (Sauguet was loved and respected by all who knew him in his long life, his relationship with the painter Jacques Dupont a rare model of sustained loyalty and fruitful collaboration), but at its least interesting, the music fails to reflect the charm of the man—it lacks contour and individuality. Sauguet could not rely on a ready melodic gift, and although his settings are never less than considerate to the poet, they all too often fail to impinge memorably on the listener's ear. The best of

Sauguet is a result of this exquisite literary sensibility where he was able to enter into the poet's world, and create an undeniable atmosphere appropriate to the texts, finding music which carries forward, rather than obscures, the literary ideas.

A good example of this is the very first cycle, *LES ANIMAUX ET LEURS HOMMES* (1921). This is an obvious riposte to Poulenc's *LE BESTIAIRE* of two years earlier. Instead of choosing Apollinaire's verses, however, Sauguet turns to Éluard, who was to become Poulenc's other great poet, and sets him to music a full fourteen years before the older composer. This type of literary coup was typical of Sauguet's culture; in this respect he was a benevolent, and less waspish, version of Auric. In all these farmyard songs the nature of the animal is conveyed in the piano (the spring of the horse, the flightiness of the bird, the lugubrious devotion of the dog, the pecking of the hen, and so on). The set has charm and the advantage of concision. I first encountered it in a taped BBC performance of Peter Pears and Viola Tunnard. From the same year comes the trippingly elegant note-spinning of the Cocteau setting *Îles* (an evocation of Palma de Majorca) and *Chanson de marins* by the same poet. Another cycle of miniatures is *CIRQUE* (Copperie, 1925), which owes something to Poulenc's *COCARDES*. The final song *Cloune étoilé* has a genuine and touching lyricism. The *SIX SONNETS DE LOUISE LABÉ* (1927) are more or less contemporary with Poulenc's excursions into ribald seventeenth-century texts. But Sauguet's style is much less abrasive; indeed these songs have much in common with the gentle style of Lennox Berkeley, who was also attracted to Labé's verse. With *QUATRE MÉLODIES SUR DES POÈMES DE SCHILLER* (1928) Sauguet displays an even greater catholicity of literary taste. As a memorial to a friend, he sets *Le souvenir*, a free translation of Schiller's *Amalia* (also set by the young Schubert) which emerges here with strong homoerotic overtones. The composer's own voice is to be heard plainly here, for the music is almost embarrassingly heartfelt. The next song in the cycle, *Le pèlerin*, is a setting, in French translation, of another famous Schiller poem—*Der Pilgrim*, once again also set by Schubert. The separate song *Amour et sommeil* (Swinburne, 1929), as well as the *DEUX POÈMES DE SHAKESPEARE* (Shakespeare, 1929), *POLYMÈTRES* (Jean-Paul, 1931), and the *CINQ POÈMES DE HÖLDERLIN* (1933), belong to this phase where the composer interested himself in foreign literature. The first of the Shakespeare poems—*Je te vois en rêve*—is a translation of Sonnet 43, 'When most I wink, then do mine eyes best see'. (Britten ends his *NOCTURNE FOR TENOR AND SEVEN OBBLIGATO INSTRUMENTS* with the same poem.) The second song, *Chanson*, is a translation of the much-set lyric (Quilter, Warlock, Rubbra among other English composers) 'Take, o take those lips away'. Chausson composed it, in a different translation, as *Chanson de clown*. The Hölderlin set contains an ardent love song, *Pardon* (beginning 'Divine créature! Oh! J'ai troublé le vermeil repos doré des dieux en toi'). It was at this period of his life, when he was still searching for a partner, that Sauguet's love songs are at their most ardent.

By 1938 Sauguet's songwriting had developed into more complex harmonic regions than that of his earlier work. One of his most interesting and successful *recueils* (dedicated to Jacques Dupont, who was to be the composer's lifelong friend) dates from that year—*SIX MÉLODIES SUR DES POÈMES SYMBOLISTES*. There are two interesting settings of Mallarmé—*Renouveau* and *Tristesse d'été*—two settings of Jules Laforgue (a poet not often encountered in mélodies) the first of which, *Crépuscule de mi juillet, huit heures*, is a hypnotic little nocturne, and two settings of Baudelaire. These cat pieces (**Le chat I** and *II*) are a splendid addition to the long-standing tradition of animal songs in the mélodie repertoire. Also from this period are three duets for soprano and tenor (*Lune inconstante,*

Crépuscule, and *L'instant*) to words by the Comtesse Murat. There are few duets in French song written after the time of Fauré, and these are attractive and useful additions to the modern repertoire. The tenor cycle NEIGES (Antoinette d'Harcourt, 1942) contains six short songs where the balance between music and poetry is admirable; particularly beautiful is the last song—*Les gens distraits qui rient*.

Occasionally the composer's choice of poetry is much more ambitious, and the two Max Jacob cycles come into this category. The first of these is LES PÉNITENTS EN MAILLOTS ROSES (1944). For the student of Jacob's poetry, and his extraordinary inner world where licentiousness mixed unselfconsciously with childlike purity and religious fervour, this work is as indispensable as Poulenc's *Le bal masqué*. One cannot pretend that the music is as beguiling, but it presents a portrait of the poet which is vivid and true. The final lines of the last song, *Ports de l'enfer*, are 'Seigneur! Seigneur! Secourez-moi! Secourez-moi, mon Dieu!' This *cri de cœur* is especially moving. As a Jew, Jacob had been arrested and taken to the concentration camp of Drancy where his death in 1944 spared him the otherwise inevitable transportation to Auschwitz. The horror of this Dante-like journey toward the underworld of the human spirit is aptly prophesied in **Voyage**, the opening song of VISIONS INFERNALES (1948), the second of the Max Jacob cycles. **Le petit paysan**, the tale of the little peasant boy whom the poet recognizes as himself, provides a real frisson as innocence and the horror of experience stand side by side, in the manner of a doppelgänger. This is perhaps Sauguet's most intense and harrowing set of songs; a well-sung performance can be a deeply moving experience. The work was composed for bass-baritone, thus very useful when so much in the French repertoire has been written for the high baritone (the so-called *bariton martin*). Poulenc was usually charming and supportive to Sauguet, but there is no doubt he was genuinely moved by this work which is as much a memorial to their mutual friend, the poet, as Sauguet's song *Cinq-mars* from 1953. Also dating from the war period is the Éluard cycle FORCE ET FAIBLESSE, a collection of seven miniatures, as well as the overtly political 'chant dissident' *Bêtes et méchants* (also Éluard, 1944). A setting of a poem by Seghers, *Chant funèbre pour de nouveaux héros*, which begins as a funeral march and works up into an epic requiem for the fallen youth of France, is as impassioned a song as Sauguet ever wrote.

Sauguet continued composing songs until the end of his life. For example, the most extensive setting of Marcel Proust in French song, the evocative COMME À LA LUMIÈRE DE LA LUNE, dates from 1967. Another late song cycle is JE SAIS QU'IL EXISTE (1973), twelve songs with texts by the Belgian Maurice Carême. In this way Sauguet follows in the footsteps of his old friend Poulenc ten years earlier with LA COURTE PAILLE, but this was far from his leave-taking. The impressively bulky *recueil* of songs published by Salbert in 1992 includes a cycle SEPT CHANSONS DE L'ALCHIMISTE (Raphaël Cluzel) which was written in 1978, and closes with *Dans la maison de paix*, composed in 1987 to words by the same poet. Perhaps it was easier to write songs after Poulenc's death for, like many composers of his generation, Sauguet worked in his old friend's shadow. This was a fact of life for a number of gifted men (Leguerney was another), but few were as significant a personality in the world of music as Sauguet. There are songs in this large output, if one has the patience to search them out, which deserve to be heard, in their own light, on the concert platform of today. During the best of Sauguet's songs, one somehow feels in the company of a man who embodies the great French virtues. If he is not often able to sing with the memorable lyricism of greater composers, his conversation is never less than civilized.

1 *Berceuse créole*

(Henri Sauguet)

Oiseau des îles, canari,
Tannanarive, île jolie,
Tous les paquebots se sont ligués
Pour nous amener.
A...

Petit oiseau chéri,
Endors-toi sur mes genoux,
En faisant tout doucement,
Petit oiseau chéri,
Endors-toi sur mes genoux.

Oiseau des îles, canari,
Tannanarive, île jolie,
Tous les paquebots se sont ligués
Pour nous amener.

Creole lullaby

Canary, bird of the isles,
Antananarivo, pretty isle,
All the steamers have joined together
To take us there.
A...

Beloved little bird,
Fall asleep on my knees,
Gently, take your time,
Beloved little bird
Fall asleep on my knees.

Canary, bird of the isles,
Antananarivo, pretty isle,
All the steamers have joined together
To take us there.

LES ANIMAUX ET LEURS HOMMES

(Paul Éluard)

ANIMALS AND THEIR MASTERS

2 i *Cheval*

Cheval seul, cheval perdu,
Malade de la pluie, vibrant d'insectes,
Cheval seul, vieux cheval.

Aux fêtes du galop,
Son élan serait vers la terre,
Il se tuerait.

Et, fidèle aux cailloux,
Cheval seul attend la nuit
Pour n'être pas obligé
De voir clair et de se sauver.

Horse

Lone horse, lost horse,
Sick with rain, seething with insects
Lone horse, old horse.

At riding fairs,
He would have hurtled to earth,
And killed himself.

And faithful to the stones,
Lone horse waits for night
To avoid being forced
To see clearly and escape.

2 ii *Vache*

On ne mène pas la vache
À la verdure rase et sèche,
À la verdure sans caresses.

Cow

You don't lead a cow
To verdure that's cropped and dry,
To verdure without caresses.

L'herbe qui la reçoit
Doit être douce comme un fil de soie,
Un fil de soie doux comme un fil de lait.

Mère ignorée,
Pour les enfants, ce n'est pas le déjeuner,
Mais le lait sur l'herbe

L'herbe devant la vache,
L'enfant devant le lait.

The grass that greets her
Must be sweet as a silken thread,
A silken thread sweet as a thread of milk.

Unknown mother,
For children, it is not lunch,
But milk on the grass

The grass in front of the cow
The child in front of the milk.

2 iii *Oiseau*   *Bird*

Charmée... Oh! pauvre fille!
Les oiseaux mettent en désordre
Le soleil aveuglant du toit,
Les oiseaux jouent à remplacer
Le soleil plus léger que l'huile
Qui coule entre nous.

Bewitched... Ah! poor girl!
The birds throw into confusion
The blinding sun of the roof,
The birds play at replacing
The sun that's lighter than the oil
Which flows between us.

2 iv *Chien*   *Dog*

Chien chaud,
Tout entier dans la voix, dans les gestes
De ton maître,
Prends la vie comme le vent,
Avec ton nez.

Reste tranquille.

Dog on heat,
Absorbed in the voice and gestures
Of your master,
Take life as you take the wind,
With your nose.

Stay calm.

2 v *Chat*   *Cat*

Pour ne poser qu'un doigt dessus
Le chat est bien trop grosse bête.
Sa queue rejoint sa tête,
Il tourne dans ce cercle
Et se répond à la caresse.

Mais, la nuit, l'homme voit ses yeux
Dont la pâleur est le seul don.
Ils sont trop gros pour qu'il les cache
Et trop lourds pour le vent perdu du rêve.

Not to put too fine a point on it
The cat is really too fat an animal.
Its tail meets up with its head,
It turns in this circle
And responds to its own caresses.

At night, however, man sees its eyes,
Whose pallor is its only gift.
They are too large to be hidden
And too heavy for dreams to take flight on.

Quand le chat danse
C'est pour isoler sa prison
Et quand il pense
C'est jusqu'aux murs de ses yeux.

When the cat dances
It is to isolate its prison
And when it thinks
It is right up to the walls of its eyes.

2 vi *Poule*

Hen

Hélas! ma sœur, bête bête,
Ce n'est pas à cause de ton chant,
De ton chant pour l'œuf
Que l'homme te croit bonne.

Alas! my sister, dumb creature,
It is not for your singing,
Your singing for the egg,
That man delights in you.

2 vii *Porc*

Pig

Du soleil sur le dos, du soleil sur le ventre,
La tête grosse et immobile
Comme un canon,
Le porc travaille.

Sun on his back, sun on his belly,
His head heavy and motionless
Like a canon
The pig toils.

3 *Le chat I*

(Charles Baudelaire)

The cat I

Dans ma cervelle se promène,
Ainsi qu'en son appartement,
Un beau chat, fort, doux et charmant.
Quand il miaule, on l'entend à peine,

Along my brain there walks,
As though in his own home,
A handsome cat, strong, gentle, full of charm.
When he meows, one scarcely hears,

Tant son timbre est tendre et discret;
Mais que sa voix s'apaise ou gronde,
Elle est toujours riche et profonde.
C'est là son charme et son secret.

So tender and discreet his tone;
Purring or complaining, his voice
Is always rich and deep.
That is the secret of his charm.

Cette voix, qui perle et qui filtre
Dans mon fonds le plus ténébreux,
Me remplit comme un vers nombreux
Et me réjouit comme un philtre.

This voice, which purls and filters down
Into the darkest depths of my being,
Fulfils me like a harmonious verse
And delights me as a potion would.

Elle endort les plus cruels maux
Et contient toutes les extases;
Pour dire les plus longues phrases,
Elle n'a pas besoin de mots.

It lulls to sleep the cruellest ills,
Contains all kinds of ecstasies:
To utter the longest phrases
It has no need of words.

Non, il n'est pas d'archet qui morde
Sur mon cœur, parfait instrument,
Et fasse plus royalement
Chanter sa plus vibrante corde,

Que ta voix, chat mystérieux,
Chat séraphique, chat étrange,
En qui tout est, comme en un ange,
Aussi subtil qu'harmonieux!

No, there is no bow, that biting
Across my heart—perfect instrument—
More regally draws a melody
From its most vibrant string,

Than your voice, mysterious cat,
Seraphic cat, exotic cat,
In whom all, as in an angel,
Is as subtle as harmonious!

4 *Voyage*

(Max Jacob), from VISIONS INFERNALES

Chemin de nuit, nuit du chemin! la lune est sur le lac, le lac est dans tes yeux. La voiture emportait notre voyage nocturne. Tes yeux sont les yeux des voyages, voyages des convalescents. Quand le postillon ne chantera plus je te dirai ma pensée, c'est une question de géologie architecturale au sujet de l'infini des montagnes, de la forme des montagnes. Il y avait sur la couverture à griffes un bol de porcelaine où la lune mettait un point. Dans le demi-sommeil de la voiture—le postillon chante, chante postillon—je croyais que la lune était le bol, que la couverture à griffes c'était les montagnes et que nous n'étions plus sur terre. Plus de lune! Ô nuit des chemins! Ô chemin des nuits: tes yeux sont les yeux de la mer et je ne te connais pas. C'est ainsi que nous avançons avec tout notre laisser-aller vers ce pays qui n'est pas loin que je ne souhaitais pas de connaître et où une certaine angoisse m'indique que le postillon me conduit en chantant. Maintenant c'est la peur!

Journey

Road of the night, night of the road! The moon is over the lake, the lake is in your eyes. The carriage bore us on our nocturnal journey. Your eyes are the eyes of journeys, journeys convalescents make. When the postilion sings no more, I shall tell you my thoughts. They concern architectural geology with reference to the infinity of mountains, the form of mountains. There was on the tarpaulin a porcelain bowl, marked by the shining moon. In the half-sleep of the carriage—the postilion sings, sings the postilion—I believed that the moon was the bowl, that the tarpaulin was the mountains and that we were no longer on earth. No more moon! O night of the roads! O road of the nights: your eyes are the eyes of the sea and I do not know you. That is how we progress with all our *laissez-faire* towards this country which is not far and which I did not wish to know and where a certain anguish shows me that the postilion is taking me as he sings. Now I'm afraid!

5 *Le petit paysan*

(Max Jacob), from VISIONS INFERNALES

Sous les ormeaux plus vieux que mon père et que mon grand'père, sous les ormeaux du Mont Frugy d'Odet. Sous les marronniers des bords d'Odet où je suis né, j'ai vu passer le petit paysan malade. Oh! ne me regarde pas comme si j'allais mourir car tu es moi-même et je te connais. L'enfant! l'enfant vient-il du ciel ou de l'enfer? Souris, je te connaîtrai par ton sourire.

The little peasant boy

Beneath the elms older than my father and my grandfather, beneath the elms of Mount Frugy d'Odet. Beneath the chestnut-trees on the shores of Odet where I was born, I saw the sick little peasant boy pass by. Oh! do not look at me as if I was going to die, for you are me and I know you. The child! Does the child come from heaven or hell? Smile, I shall know you by your smile.

SCHMITT, Florent (1870–1958)

The very name suggests a Germanic heaviness, and it is true that this composer, winner of the Prix de Rome on his fifth attempt in 1900, was much drawn to German romanticism and 'meaningful music'. In 1912 he composed a set entitled *QUATRE LIEDS*—grandiose settings of Richepin and, more successfully, of Maeterlinck in the final song *Ils ont tué trois petites filles*. His surest claims to fame are the monumental Piano Quintet, and *La tragédie de Salomé*, both works from his thirties which laid down the essential features of his style with some authority. He wrote a large amount of piano music, much of which seems to exceed the limitations of the instrument; the accompanist to the songs is also taxed by the feeling that he is playing from, and struggling with, an orchestral reduction. On the printed page, the look of this music has something in common with that of Caplet, and the two composers share a post-Debussian luxuriance in their pianistic writing, although Caplet is astringent in the typically French manner, Schmitt more touched by Franckian romanticism.

Of Schmitt's earlier songs, the *TROIS MÉLODIES* (Mauclair, Verlaine, Gavinet, 1894) are the most accessible. The first of these, *Lied* ('Les roses de l'autre année sont mortes') was admired by Koechlin, and *Il pleure dans mon coeur* (DEBUSSY 6 ii) shows a pianistic pudeur not evident in *Les barques* (Robert de Montesquiou, 1897) and *Musique sur l'eau* (Samain, 1898). The water imagery in these poems gives Schmitt ample chance to use the piano in extravagantly rippling fashion, and an ambitious pianist will relish the long and demanding introductions and postludes—although he might have to struggle to achieve an equable balance with the voice. A further Verlaine setting is *Ô triste était mon âme* (1892–1911). This last song seems to demand an orchestra; in actual fact it is one of the few mélodies which was not orchestrated by the composer himself.

Schmitt's vocal output is large and varied. He wrote all manner of music in various moods and for various combinations—duets and trios, as well as much choral music. (It is in the latter field where the composer seems to have enjoyed setting more humorous texts.) Not a great deal of this has survived in the concert hall. *QUATRE POÈMES DE RONSARD* (1942) is a much later work. Schmitt's empathy with the literature of this period is not to be compared to the inspired link with Ronsard enjoyed by Leguerney or even Milhaud, but one or two of these songs would find a worthy enough place in a song anthology devoted to the poet. The titles are *Si…*, *Privilèges*, *Ses deux yeux*, and *Le soir qu'amour*. The third of these is more obviously an evocation of the musical style of the Renaissance than the others, and the last, certainly the most beautiful song in the set, has a typical Schmitt trade mark, a difficult and impressive accompaniment with an extended piano prelude.

SÉVÉRAC, Déodat de (1872–1921)

It is not often in the history of the mélodie that we find a composer who turns his back on Paris in favour of the provinces. Sévérac, born in the south of France, was remarkably faithful to his roots, and after his long studentship only travelled to Paris when necessary. He was discovered in Toulouse by Bordes, and was encouraged to study at the Schola Cantorum, where he worked with d'Indy and

Magnard between 1896 and 1907. He completed Albéniz's *Navarra* for piano after that composer's death; his understanding of Spanish music is hardly surprising as he chose, as his final home, Céret, in the shadow of the Pyrenees, not far from Perpignan. This town was known as the 'Mecca of Cubism' and many of the painters whom Sévérac numbered among his friends, including Pablo Picasso, moved there to live. Much of this composer's piano music (works like *Le chant de la terre* and *En Languedoc*) bears testimony to his passion for the south of France.

Sévérac's music is a very individual amalgam of styles: Debussy was an obvious influence, but then so was Mussorgsky, a composer who had helped shape the musical language of Debussy himself. In his earlier songs we can detect his allegiance to Bizet, and he shared with Ravel a love of the music of the Basque region. He was more inclined to impressionistic effects than many a graduate of the Schola, but he was not ashamed to blossom into romanticism. All in all, he was a very independent southerner, a *petit maître* perhaps, but one with his own voice. There is a touch of that other southerner, Chabrier, about him—in his humour, his integrity, and his gift for melody.

The songs fall into two categories. Because he was interested in folksong and popular chanson he made two books of arrangements (recently republished by Salabert as a part of a *recueil* devoted to Sévérac) for the great diseuse and chansonnière Yvette Guilbert (1865–1944). These are CHANSONS DU XVIIIÈME SIÈCLE and LES VIEILLES CHANSONS DE FRANCE. Much of Guilbert's repertoire has been published, but she never had a more distinguished composer than Sévérac to write her accompaniments, which seems a perfect excuse for the right singer to revive this repertoire in recital. Of course, to bring off these songs it takes someone with a gift for comedy as well as tragedy, and absolutely at home in colloquial French. But Sévérac's delicate (and always simple) little arrangements for these strophic ditties add a touch of 'class' to a genre of performance that belongs to another epoch, and is all but forgotten. The eighteenth-century set includes such items as *Ba, be, bi, bo bu* (a prophecy of Poulenc's Carême setting of the same name), *Le vieil époux, Le berger indiscret, Ne dérangez pas le monde, L'homme est jamais content*, and so on. The other volume contains songs of the same type (*Le boudoir d'Aspasie* especially delicious with its refrain of 'Sur son sopha, dans son boudoir'). Sévérac's arrangements are more modern here as they are no longer obliged to provide a pastiche background in the old style. Indeed the arrangement *Le roi a fait battre tambour* is so witty and pithy, and uses the piano in such an adventurous yet economical manner, that it could be passed off as one of Benjamin Britten's French folksong settings.

The serious mélodies are of a remarkably high quality. The Salabert selection contains twelve of the best of these, though outside this volume *Soleils couchants* (Verlaine, 1901) and *L'infidèle* (Maeterlinck, 1900) are worth tracking down. The latter song is a delicate and mysterious little dialogue, all the more remarkable for pre-dating the performance of Debussy's *Pelléas et Mélisande*, and the inevitable interest in Maeterlinck's poetry which that work brought about. Salabert's *recueil* opens with *Le ciel est par-dessus le toit* (1898) which is in seven flats, one more than Fauré's E flat minor setting [FAURÉ 31]; but it is only in this respect that Sévérac attempts to outdo the old master. There is hardly a note of bitterness here, just a soft melancholy, aptly caught in the remarkably fluid piano writing for the tolling of bells (to illustrate 'La cloche, dans le ciel qu'on voit, | Doucement tinte'). Roussel must have remembered this effect when he came to write *Le jardin mouillé*, for the openings of both songs weave similar pianistic spells high on the stave in a murmuring moto perpetuo between the hands. The bird song at 'Un oiseau, sur l'arbre qu'on voit, |

Chante sa plainte' is charmingly illustrated by acciaccaturas in the piano. This is Sévérac in his Debussian mode: other settings reflecting his debt to this composer are *Un rêve*, a rare setting of Poe in Mallarmé's translation (1902), dedicated to the painter Odilon Redon (a real selection of celebrities on the title page, this), and *Temps de neige* (Gauthier-Villars, 1904). Side by side with these poetic evocations, Sévérac was also interested in writing a simpler, sturdier music. *Temps de neige* is a Parisian scene, but *À l'aube dans la montagne* to the composer's own words (1903) vibrates with an earthy rhythmical energy which shows us the folksong collector and enthusiast from the Pyrenees. We also remember Sévérac's links with d'Indy, and in *Chanson de la nuit durable* (Espinasse-Mongenet, 1910) we get the best of a number of worlds: Debussian sensuality in the harmony, Franckian seriousness woven into the texture of the incessant triplets, and the melodic freshness of Sévérac himself. Different from this are other songs which seem melodically similar to the material which the composer arranged for Yvette Guilbert: *Chansons de Jacques* (Magre), which is subtitled 'dans le style populaire' and is an extract from the composer's only opera *Le cœur du moulin*; *Chant de Noël* (a translation by Gravollet from the language of Languedoc which Sévérac set on a number of other occasions); the charming *Philis*, and *Aubade* (Marguerite de Navarre—a contemporary poet from the Languedoc, not the Queen Margot of Bourdet's play), both of which are pastiches of music of the eighteenth and sixteenth centuries respectively.

This leaves four of the very best Sévérac songs for consideration. The earliest of these is a setting of Baudelaire, **Les hiboux** (1898), which cleverly depicts the hollow sound of the owls' 'to-witto-woo' with crushed notes and open fourths in the piano. This song is mournful in a way that recalls Mussorgsky. Because it does not attempt too much, it seems worthy of a poet who is notoriously difficult to set—only Duparc knew the secret unerringly. This gentle song stands next to Sauguet's cat mélodies as a fine and rare contribution to the Baudelairian menagerie, less famous than Apollinaire's bestiary, but no less fascinating. *Chanson pour le petit cheval* (Prosper Estieu) is a masterful song which has something of Roussel's quality of briskness-concealing-melancholy, and a final page which plunges into tragedy. The canter of the little horse is perfectly caught as a motif which binds the various tempi together, and is skilfully modified according to the mood of the poem. We have already mentioned *À l'aube dans la montagne.* Here we see several of Sévérac's best qualities: his ability as a man of literature (the poem is his own); his mastery of piano colour (this is his greatest and most complex study of bell sonorities); his complete absorption of the lessons Debussy had to teach about French prosody, and the way speech rhythm can enliven music and provide a vocal line with a searing eloquence independent of melody as such. In this remarkable mélodie the excitement is generated by the slow yet inevitable progress of the dawn and its attendant sounds. This is one of the few songs in the French song repertoire (Caplet's *Fôret* is another) which succeeds in building tension over a long span in a manner reminiscent of *Pelléas et Mélisande.* Sévérac must have had in his mind the love music of Act IV scene iv which is also about the contest between light and dark, and the recklessness of self-abandon and final surrender. And finally there is **Ma poupée chérie** (1914) to the composer's own text which remains the work by Sévérac that everybody remembers. Is it sentimental? Certainly! But somehow the real love of a father for his only child, his daughter Magali, has been lavished on this music, and the tune is a heavenly inspiration. Once again Mussorgsky comes to mind, whose own set of ground-breaking nursery songs avoids the twee with similar mastery. It is the naturalness of the melody, childlike but not childish, which rescues this song from the squirm of embarrassment which is the usual reaction for kiddy music from times gone by. It is an apt reminder that, had Sévérac's career been longer, he might have left us many more songs of this very special quality—fresh, unaffected, written far away from the centre of French musical life, and all the more interesting for gaining strength and nourishment from different roots.

1 *Les hiboux*

(Charles Baudelaire)

Sous les ifs noirs qui les abritent,
Les hiboux se tiennent rangés,
Ainsi que des dieux étrangers,
Dardant leur œil rouge. Ils méditent.

Sans remuer ils se tiendront
Jusqu'à l'heure mélancolique
Où, poussant le soleil oblique,
Les ténèbres s'établiront.

Leur attitude au sage enseigne
Qu'il faut en ce monde qu'il craigne
Le tumulte et le mouvement;

L'homme ivre d'une ombre qui passe
Porte toujours le châtiment
D'avoir voulu changer de place.

Owls

Beneath the shelter of black yews,
The owls perch in a row,
Like alien gods, whose
Red eyes flash. They meditate.

Motionless they will perch
Till the melancholy hour
When, pushing aside the slanting sun,
The shadows will settle into place.

From their pose the wise man learns
That in this world he ought to fear
All movement and commotion;

The man drunk on fleeting shadows
Will always pay the penalty
For having wished to roam.

2 *À l'aube dans la montagne*

(Déodat de Sévérac)

Le long du ciel grenat, d'un grenat d'iris, et roux, d'un roux à peine émeraudé, les cimes s'éveillent une à une nimbées de gaze brodée d'opales et de poussières d'or.

Quelques nuages ténus oubliés par la brise se sont attardés aux caresses grisantes des bruyères, les vallées dans des voiles de lys poudrés de lilas semblent errer autour des peupliers qui fusent à l'infini vers le regard narquois de la lune.

At dawn in the mountains

Along the skies of garnet-red, of a rainbow's garnet-red, of russet, emerald-tinged, the summits awaken one by one, haloed in a veil embroidered with opals and gold-dust.

A few frail clouds, forgotten by the breeze, have lingered by the heather's intoxicating caresses; the valleys, veiled in lilies sprinkled with lilac, seem to hover around the poplars that melt to infinity towards the quizzical gaze of the moon.

Peu à peu l'horizon s'affirme en des gestes de flamme qui planent un instant et s'essorent vers les plaines baignées de sommeil; et des sommets ensanglantés un ruissellement de rubis se précipite le long des roches.

Les grives stridulent, dans les taillis, vers les échos rieurs. Et les voiles errants se déchirent et se fondent, poussières d'iris, dans l'orfèvrerie des haies.

Lors, une rumeur de joie s'élève des hameaux et des villes, et soudain triomphant, l'astre Dieu paraît!

Gradually the horizon focuses in a flash of flame that soars for an instant and takes flight towards the plains, steeped in slumber; and from the crimson heights, a shimmer of rubies dashes down the rocks.

Thrushes chirr in the thickets towards laughing echoes. And the wandering mists are torn apart and dissolve, rainbow dust in the bejewelled hedges.

Then, a sound of joy is heard in the hamlets and towns, and triumphant of a sudden, the sun god appears!

3 Ma poupée chérie

(Déodat de Séverac)

Ma poupée chérie ne veut pas dormir!
Petit ange mien, tu me fais souffrir!
Ferme tes doux yeux, tes yeux de saphir,
Dors, poupée, dors, dors, ou je vais mourir.

Il faudrait, je crois, pour te rendre sage,
Un manteau de soie de riches corsages!
Tu voudrais des roses à ton clair béguin,
Des bijoux d'or fin et mille autres choses!

Ma poupée chérie ne veut pas dormir!
Petit ange mien, tu me fais souffrir!
Ferme tes doux yeux, tes yeux de saphir,
Dors, poupée, dors, dors, ou je vais mourir.

Quand parrain viendra, sur son âne gris,
Il t'apportera de son grand Paris,
Un petit mari qui dira: 'papa',
Et qui dormira quand on le voudra.

Ma poupée chérie vient de s'endormir!
Bercez-la bien doux, ruisseaux et zéphirs!
Et vous chérubins, gardez-la-moi bien!
Sa maman jolie l'aime à la folie!

My dearest dolly

My dearest dolly will not go to sleep!
Little angel, you cause me such grief!
Close your eyes, your sweet sapphire eyes,
Sleep, dolly, sleep, or I shall die.

I suppose you'll want, to make you behave,
A cloak of silk with a gorgeous bodice!
And roses to put on your plain bonnet,
Jewels of pure gold and thousands of things!

My dearest dolly will not go to sleep!
Little angel, you cause me such grief!
Close your eyes, your sweet sapphire eyes,
Sleep, dolly, sleep, or I shall die.

When your godfather comes on his grey donkey,
He'll bring you from Paris, that big city,
A little husband, who will say 'papa'
And go to sleep when ordered to.

My dearest dolly has just gone to sleep!
Rock her gently, streams and breezes!
And you, angels, guard her well,
Her pretty mummy loves her so!

SORABJI, Kaikhosru (1892–1988)

This extraordinarily eccentric composer (his real name was Leon Dudley) was the son of a Spanish-Sicilian mother and a Parsi father. He spent most of his life in England, where he was a critic and railed in alarming hyperbole against his many enemies, real and imagined. His taste was for the monumental and sublime—his *Opus clavicembalisticum* for piano lasts nearly three hours, and the 'Jami' Symphony is a thousand pages long. It seems surprising, then, that he has a relatively large song output (only some of it published) which is almost exclusively in French. (The biggest exception is a set of Michelangelo sonnets for baritone and orchestra.) There is an early setting (1915) of Mallarmé's *Apparition* [DEBUSSY 5] but after this he concentrates on the two greatest of French song-poets. Of Baudelaire there is *Correspondances* (1918), *L'irrémédiable* (1927), and *Les chats* (1941). Of Verlaine, *L'heure exquise* [HAHN 1 v], which dates from 1916, *Crépuscule du soir mystique*, and *Pantomime* (both 1918). *Le faune* [DEBUSSY 13 ii] and *Dernière fête galante* were both composed in 1941. The *TROIS FÊTES GALANTES* is a set which dates from 1924. This comprises *L'allée*, *À la promenade*, and *Dans la grotte*. The appearance of this music without time or key signature on the page is rather like that of Bernard van Dieren, dazzling black patterns on a page which defy every practicality of performance—both in terms of the pianist's ability to play the notes, and the almost mystical rapport that he would have to enjoy with the singer in order to get anything like the required ensemble—not to mention balance. There is no doubt that Sorabji had a fine ear, and heard a wonderful performance of these pieces in his head, but of singers he knew nothing. In any case, he would have thought that his was music for the elite, not the common herd, and might have preferred it to remain unperformed. (Such was this composer's gift for vituperative rebuttal, that the present writer is grateful that this evaluation did not have to be written in Sorabji's lifetime.) These songs could well be taken as an illustration of how English-speakers can employ the mystique of French language and aesthetics as a weapon of cultural one-upmanship.

STRAVINSKY, Igor (1882–1971)

French was Stravinsky's second language, and he left Russia to live in France, so it is hardly surprising that many of the titles of his published works are in French. The only songs to original French texts, however, are two settings of Verlaine which were composed in Brittany in 1910. These are *Sagesse*, Stravinsky's version of *Un grand sommeil noir* [RAVEL 2], and *La bonne chanson*, which is none other than the famous 'La lune blanche' [FAURÉ 30 iii]. Both songs take their titles, of course, from the collections of Verlaine's poetry in which they appear. The first song is nearer to the sombre mood of Ravel's rather bizarre setting (and that of Varèse) than anything by the established masters—Fauré, Debussy, Hahn—who set this poet regularly. Indeed, Stravinsky throws away the words 'C'est l'heure exquise' in a decidedly casual manner at the end of his second song; this is light years away from the musical world of Reynaldo Hahn where the phrase is delicately cherished in a sensual setting which has withstood the test of time in the concert-hall. Music of Stravinsky's type, full of precisely imagined sonorities, and of an undeniable nocturnal atmosphere, seems strangely insensitive to old-fashioned things like prosody. Indeed the time was not far away when the composer would enrage his collaborator André Gide with the deliberate metrical distortions of *Perséphone*. The Verlaine songs display vividly how Stravinsky heard everything in terms of shape and instrumental colour, and that the piano as an accompanying instrument is merely a makeweight. At the end of *La bonne chanson* when the piano writing goes into three staves it is completely unplayable, even by a Horowitz. Stravinsky returned to these two songs to orchestrate them in 1951–2.

It should be mentioned that many of the Stravinsky songs were first heard in French translation. The composer's Pushkin suite for mezzo-soprano and piano, Op. 2, was published as *Le faune et la bergère*; the TROIS HISTOIRES POUR ENFANTS were Russian songs with a French translation by Ramuz (Stravinsky's Swiss collaborator on *L'histoire du soldat*). No less a musical personality than Maurice Delage made the French translation of THREE JAPANESE LYRICS. M.-D. Calvocoressi translated the TWO POEMS OF BALMONT into French, and he also provided both English and French singing translations of the two Gorodetsky songs, Op. 6. Nowadays, however, one seldom encounters this music in anything but the original Russian.

As a footnote one should mention that the composer's son Soulima Stravinsky (born 1910) was rather a more enthusiastic composer for voice and piano than his father. He published CHANTEFABLES, a cycle of ten children's songs to words by André Truffert. These are rather charming little fragments—and, in their economy and clarity, a classic example of a musical style tutored by Nadia Boulanger.

SZULC, Jósef (1875–1956)

Szulc was born into a famous family of Polish musicians—his father Henryk was a celebrated violinist who celebrated his jubilee in Warsaw by playing Beethoven's Septet with six of his sons, and a Beethoven trio with his son and grandson. Szulc studied under Moszkowski and moved to Paris where he composed a large number of successful operettas—including the famous *Flup* which had over five thousand performances. Like his compatriot Poldowski, Szulc is remembered today on the concert platform (if at all), as a composer of the lyrics of Paul Verlaine. His DIX MÉLODIES SUR DES POÉSIES DE VERLAINE (Op. 83) are divided between high and low voice—six for soprano or tenor, and four for baritone. The most famous of these (probably because Maggie Teyte recorded it with Gerald Moore) is *Clair de lune* [FAURÉ 25], which is an exceptionally well-made song. It may not match Fauré or Debussy, but it easily stands up to competition from anyone else. The same may be said for a beguiling *En sourdine* [FAURÉ 29 ii] and an incredibly fleet *Mandoline* [FAURÉ 29 i] which should be better known, as it is an ideal vehicle for a singer with an easy top register. There are also settings of poems less well known, and which are not to be found elsewhere: *J'ai peur d'un baiser* is charmingly hesitant in a 5/4 metre, and *Les coquillages* is also a decent and ingenious attempt at setting a difficult poem. This music is part of that time-honoured tradition of Polish musicians living in Paris and adopting France and French culture as their own. Szulc wrote songs in his own language too.

A setting of Adam Mickiewicz such as *Gdygym sie zmienil* was published as *Mon triste cœur* with a singing translation of the original Polish poem by Jean Bénédict.

TAILLEFERRE, Germaine (1892–1983)

Satie named her his 'musical daughter', and Cocteau described her as 'une Marie Laurencin pour l'oreille', comparing her musical style to that of the painter—light-hearted, feminine, yet highly individual and instantly recognizable—who provided the decor for Poulenc's *Les biches*. Of all Les Six, it was probably Tailleferre who preserved, more or less throughout her career, the neo-classical ethic of the group when it was under the influence of Cocteau. Her early work (such as the ballet *Le marchand d'oiseaux* and the Piano Concerto) show her affinity with the *clavecinistes*, and unlike her male contemporaries she kept in touch with Fauré and Ravel, both of whom she admired. It is sad that for a combination of reasons, often encountered by women composers attempting to make their way in a male-dominated world, Tailleferre's most successful period was during her earlier career when she was part of a group. She nevertheless remained a prolific composer, numbering no less than twelve operas in her catalogue, four ballets, a huge amount of works for film and televi- sion, orchestral, choral, and chamber music, and many pieces for piano. Her style is fluent, charm- ing, often piquant, in the best tradition of her contemporaries, music-making which aims to divert and please. She flirted with serialism and other fashions, but she remained essentially level-headed, and practical.

The best -known of her songs are the SIX CHANSONS FRANÇAISES (1929), where she chooses texts from the fifteenth, seventeenth, and eighteenth centuries—some anonymous—in line with her interest in a neo-classical style. At first glance these may seem to be Tailleferre's equivalent of Poulenc's CHAN- SONS GAILLARDES, but they show a gentler, less confrontational musical personality, and a strain of wistful thoughtfulness; indeed the music of Jacques Leguerney (and later, Jean Françaix) comes to mind rather than the rumbustious high-living Poulenc of the 1920s whose GAILLARDES songs are dis- tinctly male chauvinist, not to say phallocentric. Tailleferre has made a cycle which seems specifically suited for female performance—she cleverly chooses texts which score points off men, as in the third song *Mon mari m'a diffamée*. The end of the fifth song *On a dit mal de mon ami* defiantly says it all—'je coucherais avec-que lui'. Even the opening song of the set, *Non, la fidélité* (Laitaignant), has a feminine tone to it despite the fact that the text was written by a man. Neither are these songs merely pastiche in the time-honoured manner of much music of the time. The Voltaire setting **Souvent un air de vérité**, *Vrai Dieu, qui m'y confortera* (anon., fifteenth century), and *Les trois présents* (Sarasin) seem especially beautiful and individual—they are neither Poulenc nor Auric, less sump- tuous than Ravel, more lyrical than Jean Françaix—simply Tailleferre! This is a cycle that should re- enter the repertoire and deserves to be championed. Tailleferre went on to write many other songs: *La chasse à l'enfant* (Prévert, 1934); the cycle PARIS SENTIMENTAL (Laclochle, 1949); CHANSONS DU FOLK- LORE DE FRANCE (1952–5); UNE ROUILLE À L'ARSENIC (Centore, 1955); *L'adieu du cavalier* (Apollinaire, 1963), and so on. There is no doubt that Tailleferre suffered from the inability to push herself or her work, but she was always a superb professional. In 1963 she composed *L'adieu du cavalier*

(Apollinaire), a short song in memory of Poulenc. The time has come to reassess a composer who really benefited from the camaraderie of Les Six, and whose career never fully recovered, in the eyes of the public at least, from the collapse of that group's communal *esprit*.

1 *Souvent un air de vérité*
  (Voltaire)

The crudest lie

Souvent un air de vérité	The crudest lie will often contain
Se mêle au plus grossier mensonge:	An element of truth:
Une nuit, dans l'erreur d'un songe,	One night, deluded by a dream,
Au rang des rois j'étais monté.	I rose to the rank of kings.
Je vous aimais alors et j'osais vous le dire!	I loved you and dared to confess my love!
Les dieux à mon réveil ne m'ont pas tout ôté;	The gods, when I awoke, did not deprive me of all;
Je n'ai perdu que mon empire.	Self-control was all I lost.

TOSTI, Sir Paolo (1846–1916)

This most popular of Victorian composers is now undergoing a thorough reassessment thanks to the gradual appearance of a complete edition of his works published by Ricordi. He was born in Italy, and had a limited success there before he moved to England in 1880. He became singing teacher to the British royal family, and was knighted in 1908, returning to Italy in 1912. He was a friend of d'Annunzio, of whose poetry he made many settings, and he was also taken up by the Italian royal family. The new edition features no less than six volumes of Tosti's Italian songs, two of English, and two of French. Although he was a superb businessman with an eye for the popular market (his *Goodbye* was so celebrated that Liza Lehmann made a parody of it), Tosti was very selective in terms of texts, and his French songs reflect a certain literary taste. *Rêve* dates from 1893; it is a setting of Verlaine's *Green* [FAURÉ 29 iii] and is more or less contemporary with the most famous settings of this poem. From the same year is *Suzon* on the Musset poem which Bizet had set as *Adieux à Suzon*.

   The most substantial work in Tosti's French song collections is a Victor Hugo cycle entitled LA FILLE D'O-TAÏTI. This divides a single Hugo poem (which is very much in the manner of the same poet's celebrated *Les adieux de l'hôtesse arabe*) into six sections, and the effect is of a narrative cycle like Gounod's BIONDINA, only for mezzo-soprano rather than tenor. The cycle is a little catalogue of styles of other composers, a sign that Tosti was aware of the work of famous mélodistes of the past, as well that of his more serious (and less seriously rich) contemporaries. Thus *Dis-moi, tu veux fuir?* suggests the Schubert of *Mein*; *Te souvient-il du jour*, Saint-Saëns in his *La brise* from MÉLODIES PERSANES; *Tu rempliras mes jours*, Massenet; and *Loin des mes vieux parents*, Gounod and Bizet in their oriental vein. The cycle is framed, in the cyclical manner of César Franck, by a matching *Petit prélude* and final song made up of the same musical material.

TOURNEMIRE, Charles (1870–1939)

He is one of the greatest of church musicians (he was organist at Sainte-Clotilde from 1898), and like others of his fraternity—Franck, Widor, Pierné, Vierne, Dupré—Tournemire did not scorn the song repertoire. In his twenties he wrote mélodies to Victor Hugo texts, and then a sequence of songs to the poetry of Le Braz. Albert Samain (best known in connection with Fauré) was another favourite poet (POÈME, 1908, TRYPTIQUE, 1910, and TROIS LIEDER, 1912). The main work, however, by which Tournemire will be remembered by recitalists (if at all) is the large and imposing Verlaine cycle SAGESSE from 1908, a work contemporary with Maurice Emmanuel's deeply religious IN MEMORIAM MATRIS. Both sets were conceived for the tenor Rodolphe Plamondon, and both aim to transcend the normal limits of recital music. SAGESSE is also a precursor (and probably the inspiration) of Vierne's SPLEENS ET DÉTRESSES of 1916, another Verlaine cycle of immense seriousness.

The greatest settings of Verlaine, those by Fauré and Debussy, take words from the collections entitled *Romances sans paroles* and *Fêtes galantes*. Fewer lyrics were taken from the collection entitled *Sagesse*, mainly because musicians were seldom interested in Verlaine in religious mood; the radiance of *La bonne chanson* is easier to handle, and the Watteau-inspired character pieces of *Fêtes galantes* are the epitome of the throwaway charm and gentle ennui which characterized the salon. The musical garb of this poet is usually dictated by his voluptuary adventures during his vagabond years (as in Debussy's ARIETTES OUBLIÉES). Vierne, in particular, explored another side of Verlaine where desperate and dark lyrics, written in a mood of profound religious introspection and repentance, were threaded into his *Sagesse*. Here the poet focuses not on his romantic adventures, but on his tortured search for spiritual peace. The same is true in Tournemire's work (he too was a deeply religious man), but there is still a Wagnerian sensuality and grandiloquence to the music which marks it out as a *fin-de-siècle* work, in style if not chronology. It is a setting of ten sonnets, divided into three large sections separated by piano interludes. Tournemire subtitles it a 'Poème', and is unashamedly influenced by Franckian ideals of motival unity; cleverly worked out, it is a touch lugubrious, as if composed to resound in a large acoustic. Thus the mood and grandeur of the music suggests church performance, but the accompaniment indicates the concert hall. The exalted and somewhat over-heated tone seems dated; it is probably for that reason that the work is all but unknown. But it does throw a fascinatingly different light on Verlaine for the enthusiasts of the poet; and it could be affecting in the right circumstances, and given the right performers.

TRENET, Charles (b. 1913–2001)

Trenet is part of the tradition that goes back to Aristide Bruant (1851–1925), where the chansonnier, capable of captivating a wide public with his singing, was also both a poet and composer. There can be few people of the older generation who do not remember his great hits *Boum* (1936) and *La mer* (1945). Trenet composed over 500 songs, and many of them have become classics—part of the fabric of French everyday life. His inclusion in this book (which cannot claim in any way to be a survey of French popular music) is on the same grounds that Josef Kosma merits an entry: both men showed an appreciation of, and sensitivity to, literature which is the hallmark of the composer of mélodies. Trenet was a serious poet, much influenced by Max Jacob, one of Poulenc's favourite writers. Most of his chansons were composed to his own texts, but there are also a number to poems by such poets as Louis Codet (*La chanson du joli feu de bois*, 1943), Rimbaud (*Les corbeaux*, 1956), La Fontaine (*La cigale et la fourmi*, 1955) [CAPLET 3 ii], and Pierre Dupont-Rossini (*Les bœufs*, 1956). Trenet's piano parts, like those of many of Kosma's songs, are somewhat rudimentary and suggest that as a composer he needed the help of musical collaborators. His strengths were his melodic lines, his lyrics (which entered the consciousness of the French nation), and, of course, his inimitable singing voice.

VARÈSE, Edgard (1883–1965)

He was born in France, and spent his adolescence in Italy. Varèse returned to Paris to study with Roussel, Bordes, and d'Indy, and went on to work with Widor. He then moved to Berlin and fell under the influence of Busoni, Strauss, and Schoenberg. All this pre-dates Varèse's move to the United States in 1915 where he began a new career, and where he became one of the fathers of avant-garde music. Not a great deal of this composer's music survives; some of the early music was lost in a fire, and the composer himself destroyed other works. The very first piece in his work catalogue is a sombre E flat minor setting of Verlaine's *Un grand sommeil noir* (1906) [RAVEL 2]. Like Ravel's setting of 1895 it is in a ponderous four beats in a bar, suggesting a funeral march. Perhaps Stravinsky decided to set this poem in his own quirky way as a result of getting to know Varèse's song. There is another vocal work for soprano and small orchestra—*OFFRANDES* (1921), which consists of two songs: *Chanson de là-haut* (V. Huidobro) and *La croix du sud* (J. J. Tablada).

VELLONES, Pierre (1889–1939)

Vellones was a gifted composer of songs and it is a pity that his name and his work have disappeared so entirely from view. There was something about him of the dilettante, and he could never quite make up his mind whether to become a musician or a painter—he was also a gifted visual artist. (In this respect he was similar to Déodat de Séverac and Georges Migot.) He had originally decided to follow his father's path as a doctor, but the horrors of the First World War convinced him to follow his heart and become a composer. He was interested in ethnomusicology and exploring new instruments—his favourite saxophone and the Ondes Martenot among others—and he was an accomplished composer for theatre and cinema. His greatest public success was with the Tibetan-inspired ballet *Le paradis d'Amitabha*, for which he wrote the book as well as the music, and also designed the costumes and scenery. But it is as a composer of songs that Vellones deserves to be remembered.

His *CINQ POÈMES DE MALLARMÉ* (1929) are a fascinating adjunct to Ravel's set (the cycle includes a

Sainte [RAVEL 3]), particularly if heard in the version accompanied by four harps, two saxophones, and contrabass. His CINQ ÉPITAPHES (various eighteenth-century texts, 1935) are delicious miniatures, as pithy and amusing as Poulenc's LE BESTIAIRE. It is perhaps these which inspired the American composer Theodore Chanler to write his EIGHT EPITAPHS (1937), a standard work in American song literature. The work has been delicately orchestrated. *À mon fils* (1934) is a moving prayer to a text of the sixteenth-century poet Charles Fontaine, which Bernac and Poulenc thought enough of to record. This was also the composer's favourite song. The DEUX POÈMES DE PAUL FORT (1949), duets for mezzo and baritone, explore well-known literature with some distinction; but Vellones wrote a great deal to poems by lesser-known writers. A surprising choice of texts by a twentieth-century composer was the work of the eighteenth-century poet J. P. Claris de Florian: FABLES DE FLORIAN (1930) is a large work for voice and orchestra, equally influenced by jazz and by the sound-world of *Pelléas*. The piano reduction is actually very playable; certain songs in the set, *Le poisson volant* and *Le charlatan* for example, are worthy of revival.

Another work for voice and orchestra has the astonishing title *John Shag 35*, a single song to the prose of Gilbert Voisin about the narrator's relationship with twelve women—music-hall dancers in Indo-China. This seedy colonial evocation is less suitable for piano performance. The composer's other excursion into the oriental vein familiar in the mélodie is CHANSONS D'AMOUR DE LA VIEILLE CHINE (1931), which uses Chinese poems from the fifth century BC (*Le collet bleu* is the best of the four). Three individual songs also seem vivid enough to single out: *Chanson* (a beautiful butterfly song with a text by Louis de la Salle, 1931); and *Soir d'Idumée* (Gabriel Boissy) and *Pluies* (Théophile Briant)—both of which were published posthumously in 1947.

VIARDOT, Pauline (1821–1910)

The name of the Spanish-born Pauline Viardot belongs in the annals of French song with such figures as Meyerbeer, Offenbach, Rossini, Liszt, and other distinguished visitors who made Paris their home. This was an epoch when international and polyglot artists seemed inhabitants of a *Europe sans frontières* which would be the dream of any Euro-enthusiast today. For jet-setters of the time, diversity of background was taken for granted. In the Europe following the fall of Napoleon, and before the re-emergence of nationalism as a respectable artistic credo, everyone seems to have spoken as many languages as was necessary, and lived where they wished. It was the temporary collapse of these barriers which helped smuggle the lied into France, and hastened the advance of the mélodie.

Viardot, mezzo-soprano sister of the soprano of Callas-like fame and temperament, Maria Malibran, was a famous and charismatic artist, and years after she stopped singing, she remained an influential force in both French and German music (Schumann admired her, and Brahms wrote his *Alto Rhapsody* for her; Clara Schumann is said to have remarked that of all the women she had ever met, Viardot was the most gifted). Her two daughters were also singers, and Fauré as a young man fell in love with one of them, Marianne, and was even engaged to her. The young Reynaldo Hahn met Viardot as an old lady, and left an enthusiastic report of her charm and gaiety. Viardot's lover and companion was the great novelist Turgenev, and it is hardly surprising that there is a strong Russian dimension to her songwriting—two volumes of songs were published in St Petersburg to texts by Pushkin, Fet, Lermontov, and Turgenev himself (albeit often translated into French and German for wider European consumption). Of these, Turgenev's CHANSONS DE LA PLUIE and *Berceuse cosaque* achieved some celebrity as French songs in their own right.

Of course there were also lieder, including a setting of Mörike's *Die Soldatenbraut*, but the majority of Viardot's published songs are in French. An album of ten mélodies was published in 1850, but a number of songs appeared separately. Some of the best of these are a simple, heartfelt little Ronsard setting *Bonjour mon cœur*, a delicate *Rossignol, rossignolet* (Joseph Boulmier) with bird-like flutterings in the accompaniment, and a merry bolero setting of Musset's *Madrid*. *Le chêne et le roseau* to an anonymous poem has virtuoso piano writing which teeters on the borders of the comical; it was first accompanied by Chopin, no less, and the composer no doubt thought she had better give him something to show off his prowess. We also find the French language employed in some of Viardot's rather notorious adaptations of famous instrumental pieces which are turned into songs. Here she was following the example of the German composer Silcher who had arranged the Beethoven symphonies in this way, sometimes to unintentionally hilarious effect. Viardot's arrangements include waltzes by Schubert, *Les cavaliers*, a duet based on one of Brahms's *Hungarian Dances*, various arrangements of movements from Haydn string quartets for voice and piano, and twelve adaptations of selected Chopin *Mazurkas* for voice and piano which have been republished in the USA. At one time these concoctions might have struck the listener as highly tasteful, but they now seem more suitable for one of the 'camp' evenings of the late Cathy Berberian who made her audiences howl with laughter at adaptations with such titles, open to send-up, as *Seize ans!* One might imagine Mme Viardot herself, deep in middle age, artfully essaying such a piece, and pretending to be sixteen, going on seventeen. This was the crossover of the time, a source of fun and relaxation for serious artists, and it was a vogue which lasted until the 1940s and beyond. (An artist as distinguished as Ninon Vallin unashamedly recorded a deeply sentimental song entitled *Intimité*, based on Chopin's Third Étude.) In Viardot's time, before the radio and gramophone disseminated great music, such arrangements played their part in spreading knowledge about the repertoire. In this respect, as in others, Pauline Viardot was a tireless propagandist on behalf of the music she loved and admired and, in this respect, she takes a rather more modest place next to her piano teacher, Franz Liszt. She was above all a powerfully influential musical figure thoughout the Europe of her time, and her work as a composer makes us regret that the great divas of today do not write some of their own material, even as a means of sharpening their sense of living in the real world, rather than a musical museum. To rediscover this spark of creative genius in a singer-composer in twentieth-century terms we should probably have to look to the late Cathy Berberian, singer and composer; such jazz giants as Billie Holiday were also descendants of Viardot in that they composed their own material, and improvised during live performances with a flair that amounted to genius.

VIERNE, Louis (1870–1937)

This composer belongs to an honourable tradition of French organists who composed songs for voice and piano—Franck is the most obvious example of course, but there was also Widor, Vierne's predecessor at Saint-Sulpice, and, later, Charles Tournemire and Marcel Dupré. His fame rests on the music for his own instrument, in particular the six organ symphonies, four of which were composed before the First World War. The main set of songs from this earlier period of his career was *STANCES D'AMOUR ET DE RÊVE* (Sully Prudhomme, 1910), which was also orchestrated. During the upheaval of war, ill health made him take refuge in Switzerland (Vierne was born almost totally blind). Tournemire had composed his Verlaine cycle *SAGESSE* Op. 34 in 1908, and now another great organist was drawn to the poet. *SPLEENS ET DÉTRESSES* (1916) is a major cycle of ten rather gloomy songs, far away in mood from the delicacies of the Fauré and Debussy settings of this poet. The work reflects the anguish of those years of exile when Vierne was cut off from his work at Notre-Dame, his teaching, and his recitals. The set has a Franckian amplitude, with many of the chosen poems not otherwise set. There are however some celebrated texts: an unsurprisingly bleak *Un grand sommeil noir* [RAVEL 2]; *Spleen* [DEBUSSY 6 vi], where the hammered double octaves seem prophetic of Messiaen's *Quatuor pour la fin du temps*; and a *Le son du cor* [DEBUSSY 9 ii] which recalls the harmonic world of this text's most famous composer. The cycle was orchestrated in 1924.

Vierne returned to Paris only in 1920. By then he seemed to be a musical relic of another age, but with great determination, and the help of the wife of the poet Jean Richepin, he re-established himself, undertaking many concert tours, and publishing his music. This included two collections of songs which both date from 1924: *CINQ POÈMES DE BAUDELAIRE* (some thirty-five years after Debussy's collection of the same name) and, the most substantial *recueil* of all, *POÈMES DE L'AMOUR* by Richepin, a writer who was out of favour by this time, but a hardly surprising choice considering the composer's connection with the poet's spouse. The work consists of fifteen songs, and is divided into four movements which take their titles from the Revolutionary calendar—*Floréal*, *Thermidor*, *Brumaire*, and *Nivôse*. *Psyché* (1926) is an extended setting for voice and orchestra to a text by Hugo, although it can also be performed with piano. *QUATRE POÈMES GRECS* Op. 60 is a much later cycle published only in 1946. It is skilfully written for voice and harp, and the poems are by the comtesse de Noailles. This is a useful addition to the comparatively sparse repertoire of harp-accompanied songs.

VIEU, Jane (1871–1955)

Vieu was a composer of operas, chamber music, and piano works, as well as the author of technical works on *solfège*, but she is utterly forgotten today. The publishing house of Vieu (established together with her husband Maurice) was situated in the rue de Rome, and published many of her compositions as well as other unfashionable titles. She was also published by such houses as Enoch and Ricordi, however. Unlike composers such as Duchambge and Puget, Vieu composed in relatively modern times, but like them she seems to have been a determined guardian of old, fast-vanishing traditions. History was not on her side, for her songs are accomplished in the tradition of the salon, as opposed to the new world of Debussy and the late Fauré. The anachronistic flavour of the works is sometimes charming as in the valse chantée *La belle au bois dormant* (Métivet, 1902); indeed this work is reminiscent of Satie's *Je te veux*. Like many of her contemporaries Vieu was interested in pastiche, a good example of which is the *Chanson fleurie* (Louis Alotte) subtitled *Chanson Louis XV*. The accompaniment here suggests the delicacy of harpsichord writing. Perhaps the most original of the songs (and certainly the most free in terms of rhythm and harmony) are the TROIS MÉLODIES SUR DES TANKAS JAPONAIS (Serge Rello), which unexpectedly bring to mind the early songs of Charles Koechlin, such as *Le thé*. The optional flute part strengthens this exotic impression. The music of Vieu (she composed at least forty-five songs) seems worthy of some re-evaluation.

WAGNER, Richard (1813–1883)

Wagner's handful of French songs all date from his Parisian period (1839–42) when he attempted to play Meyerbeer at his own game as a German-speaking operatic cosmopolitan. This included the ability to write lieder (Wagner's first German songs date from as early as 1831) as well as being adaptable enough to write French songs. Somewhat down on his luck at the time (he even spent a short time in a debtor's prison), he was also forced, among other things, to make vocal scores of operas by Donizetti and Halévy, and a four-handed arrangement of a work by Herz. The writing of songs for the salon seems to have come into this category of music written for the Parisian market. It is no surprise that some of the music seems very reminiscent of Meyerbeer, in particular the extended scène *Adieux de Marie Stuart* (Béranger, 1840) in which, despite the vocally extravagant writing, we can detect very little trace of the great dramatist-in-music of the future. The song *Tout n'est qu'images fugitives* (Reboul), which is sometimes known as *Soupir*, generates a certain excitement with its agitato tempo, but it is rather commonplace as a piece of music, and there are mistakes in the prosody which betray someone not quite at home in French. Less operatic by far is a set of TROIS MÉLODIES composed in 1839, where the composer seems to have made some attempt to marry the thriving lied tradition from his own country with the prevailing French taste for the romance. In this set, two Hugo settings, *Dors, mon enfant* and *L'attente* (later to be set by Saint-Saëns [SAINT-SAËNS 2] in similarly agitated fashion), stand on either side of *Mignonne*, an interestingly early choice of Ronsard for a song text, and perhaps Wagner's best song in French. Here the composer seems to enter the spirit of the mélodie, and his work bears a certain resemblance to some of the songs of Berlioz and Bizet, for example. At the same time, Wagner also started work on setting two other Hugo texts, *Extase* and *La tombe dit à la rose*. The first of these runs to seventeen bars of completed music, and the second exists only as a sketch with a vocal line and a few indications of the harmonies the composer had in mind.

By far Wagner's most famous French song is **Les deux grenadiers** (1840), a setting of Heine's *Die beiden Grenadiere* in a French translation by François-Adolphe Loeve-Veimar. There was some justification for making a translation of this poem: Heine himself was resident in Paris at the time, a famous expatriate, highly critical of Germany; and the poem is, after all, the conversation of two loyal members of Napoleon's straggling army returning from the horrors of the Russian campaign. This was still a recent memory for many people. The song has a certain stirring effectiveness, although, as a piece of music, it is no match for Schumann's setting (dating from exactly the same time), which benefits from the poetic concision of the original German text. It has often been remarked what a coincidence it was that Schumann and Wagner, without knowing each other's song, should both have quoted *La Marseillaise* as a crowning *coup de théâtre* for their settings—Schumann in the vocal line, Wagner in the piano. Apart from a *pièce d'occasion* written in 1844, this was to be Wagner's last song with piano until the WESENDONCK LIEDER of seventeen years later.

1 *Les deux grenadiers*

(Heinrich Heine, trans. F. A. Loeve-Veimar)

Longtemps captifs chez le Russe lointain,
Deux grenadiers retournaient vers la France;
Déjà leurs pieds touchent le sol germain,
Mais on leur dit: pour vous plus d'espérance.
L'Europe a triomphé, vos braves ont vécu,
C'en est fait de la France, et de la Grande Armée,
Et rendant son épée,
L'empereur, l'empereur est captif et vaincu!

Ils ont frémi; chacun d'eux sent tomber
Des pleurs brûlants sur sa mâle figure;
Je suis bien mal, dit l'un, je vois couler
Des flots de sang de ma vieille blessure...
Tout est fini, dit l'autre, ô je voudrais mourir!
Mais au pays mes fils m'attendent, et leur mère,
Qui mourrait de misère;
J'entends leur voix plaintive; il faut vivre et souffrir!

Femmes, enfants, que m'importe! Mon cœur
Par un seul vœu tient encore à la terre.
Ils mendieront, s'ils ont faim. L'empereur,
Il est captif, mon empereur! Ô frère,
Écoute-moi, je meurs! Aux rives que j'aimais
Rends du moins mon cadavre, et du fer de ta lance
Au soldat de la France
Creuse un funèbre lit, sous le soleil français!

Fixe à mon sein, glacé par le trépas,
La croix d'honneur que mon sang a gagnée;
Dans le cercueil couche-moi, l'arme au bras,
Mets sous ma main la garde d'une épée.
De là je prêterai l'oreille au moindre bruit,
Jusqu'au jour où tonnant sur la terre ébranlée,
L'écho de la mêlée
M'appellera du fond de l'éternelle nuit!

The two grenadiers

For long held prisoner in far-off Russia,
Two grenadiers were returning to France;
Even now their feet touch German soil,
But they are told: all hope is lost!
Europe has triumphed, your warriors are dead,
It's all over with France and the Grande Armée,
And surrendering his sword,
The emperor, the emperor is captured and
    conquered!

They shuddered; each felt a burning tear
Fall down his manly cheek;
I'm badly hurt, said one, I see
Blood welling from my old wound.
All is finished, said the other, oh I would die,
But my sons and their mother await me at home,
And would die of hunger;
I hear their plaintive voices; I must live and suffer!

What do I care for wife and child! My heart
Here on earth is bound by a single vow.
If they be hungry, let them beg. The emperor
Is captured, my emperor! O brother,
Listen to my dying wish! To the shores that I loved,
Bring at least my body, and with your iron blade,
For a soldier of France
Dig a dismal grave beneath the French sun!

Fasten to my breast, chilled by death,
The cross of honour, won with my blood;
Lay me in my coffin, rifle at the ready,
Place the hilt of a sword in my hand.
From there I'll listen for the slightest noise,
Until, thundering over the trembling earth,
The sounds of battle
Shall summon me from the depths of eternal night!

Peut-être bien qu'en ce choc meurtrier	Perhaps in the midst of that murderous clash,
Et sous la mitraille et les feux de la bombe,	Beneath the hail of grape-shot and bomb,
Mon empereur poussera son coursier	My emperor will spur his steed
Vers le gazon qui couvrira ma tombe.	Towards the turf that covers my grave.
Alors je sortirai du cerceuil tout armé,	Then bristling with arms I'll arise from my coffin
Et sous les plis sacrés du drapeau tricolore,	And beneath the tricolore's sacred folds
J'irai défendre encore	I shall march to defend once more
La France et l'empereur, l'empereur bien aimé!	France and the emperor that I so love!

WHITE, Maude Valérie (1855–1937)

Lovers of English music are only now beginning to rediscover the significance of this highly gifted composer whose settings of such poets as Byron and Shelley show the, perhaps unexpectedly, aristocratic side of late nineteenth-century English song. The decline in the fashion for Victorian and Edwardian ballads swept into undeserved obscurity much vocal music of real worth and imagination, White's along with it. She was born in Dieppe, spent some time in South America, and studied in Vienna, so it is hardly surprising that she was a talented linguist, and that her song output contains songs in French, Spanish, and German, as well as English. Her music is characterized by a real melodic gift, an accomplished use of the piano, and a choice of poetry which shows uncommon literary sensibility. Two of her most attractive songs are the Victor Hugo settings *À une jeune fille inspirée* (a real *trouvaille* this, for a Hugo programme) and *Ici-bas*, and there is also a set of *TROIS CHANSONS TZIGANES* (1913) which are French translations of Russian poems.

WIDOR, Charles-Marie (1844–1937)

Who would have thought that this famous organist, composer of a ubiquitous Toccata, should also be an accomplished composer of mélodies? He composed his best songs between 1870 and 1880 and these constitute a veritable treasure-trove of Victor Hugo settings in particular. Widor, like Massenet, had a real melodic gift. His piano writing, on the other hand, has a higher profile and is more demanding; in this respect he may be said to take after Saint-Saëns. In his music it is easy to perceive a man of great education and urbanity, with a fine feel for significant poetry. He was a great raconteur and was proud to have numbered among his acquaintances composers ranging from Rossini to Milhaud. He had no need to make his living in the salon or opera house (although he wrote at least one successful opera and his ballet *Le korrigane* was famous at one time). His devotion to the music of the church and above all his knowledge of Bach gives his music an undertone of seriousness, though it is not at all lacking in humour.

The opening of the first set of songs (Op. 14) is *Nuit d'étoiles* (Banville) [DEBUSSY 1]. It announces the marks of Widor's style: graciousness, fluidity, and a surprising sensitivity to the voice. It is the next set, however, which contains the first of his Hugo settings, all of them interesting, and some of them very fine. These are: *Sois heureuse* (a long cantilena in the manner of Fauré's *Après un rêve*); *L'aurore*, a virtuoso setting, in the manner of Gounod's *Chanson de printemps*, of a poem which Fauré also composed and never published (*Le matin* by Saint-Saëns is also the same text); a sprightly *Aubade*; the most demanding and the most exciting song of the set, *À toi*. The composer's gift for melody, however, is perhaps best shown in *Invocation*. The Op. 43 set (1878) contains a setting of *Le vase brisé* (Sully Prudhomme) which was also set by César Franck, as well as probably Widor's best Hugo setting of all, a slow and ravishing *Contemplation*. (This was set as *Souvenir* by Lalo [LALO 4].) Continuing on the Hugo trail, Op. 47 (1879) contains a deceptively simple setting of *La captive* [BERLIOZ 6], worthy of revival. Another effective Hugo orientalism is *Albajdé*.

A later song is a setting of Sully Prudhomme, *Ne jamais la voir, ni l'entendre* (also set by Duparc [DUPARC 2] as *Soupir*), where the style is beginning to show signs of a certain inflation of style and manner. In later works like the cycle SOIRS D'ÉTÉ (Bourget, 1883) Widor's music takes on a rather more self-consciously exalted note with recitations between the songs in the manner of Massenet's POÈME D'AVRIL. The earlier Hugo settings remain his freshest and most valuable contribution to the repertoire, all the more welcome for being so unexpected from this source. Widor's duets for soprano and mezzo also feature Hugo. There are three opus numbers of these ensemble pieces, collected together as SIX DUOS. The best of these are Hugo's *Qu'un songe au ciel m'enlève*, the energetic *L'hiver* by the same poet, and *Guitare*, this time not the all-too-familiar Hugo text, but one by D. Marval.

1 *Sois heureuse*

(Victor Hugo)

Sois heureuse, ô ma douce amie,
Salue en paix la vie et jouis des beaux jours;
Sur le fleuve du temps mollement endormie,
    Laisse les flots suivre leur cours!

Bientôt tu peux m'être ravie:
Peut-être, loin de toi, demain j'irai languir.
Quoi, déjà tout est sombre et fatal dans ma vie!
    J'ai dû t'aimer, je dois te fuir!

Be happy

Be happy, O my sweet beloved,
Greet life in peace and enjoy days of happiness;
Recline drowsily on the river of time,
    And allow the streams to flow where they must!

Soon you may be torn from my side:
I may languish far from you tomorrow.
What! Already my life is destined for darkness!
    I had to love you, I have to abandon you!

2 *L'aurore*

(Victor Hugo)

L'aurore s'allume,
L'ombre épaisse fuit;
Le rêve et la brume
Vont où va la nuit;
Paupières et roses
S'ouvrent demi-closes;
Du réveil des choses
On entend le bruit.

Tout chante et murmure,
Tout parle à la fois,
Fumée et verdure,
Les nids et les toits;
Le vent parle aux chênes,
L'eau parle aux fontaines;
Toutes les haleines
Deviennent des voix!

Ô terre! ô merveilles
Dont l'éclat joyeux
Emplit nos oreilles,
Éblouit nos yeux!
Bords où meurt la vague,
Bois qu'un souffle élague,
De l'horizon vague
Plis mystérieux!

Saint livre où la voile
Qui flotte en tous lieux,
Saint livre où l'étoile
Qui rayonne aux yeux,
Ne trace, ô mystère!
Qu'un nom solitaire,
Qu'un nom sur la terre,
Qu'un nom dans les cieux!

Dawn

Dawn catches alight,
Thick darkness flees;
Dreams and mists recede
Where night recedes;
Eyelids and roses
Open half-closed;
You hear the sound
Of things awakening.

All things sing and murmur,
All things babble at once,
Smoke and verdure,
Nests and roofs;
The wind babbles to the oaks,
The water to the fountains;
Everything that has breath
Becomes a voice!

O Earth! O wonders,
Whose joyful brilliance
Fills our ears,
Dazzles our eyes!
Shores where waves ebb,
Woods that a wind denudes,
Mysterious folds
Of the hazy horizon!

Hallowed book where the sail
That ripples everywhere,
Hallowed book where the star
Shining before our eyes
Inscribes, O mystery,
But a single name,
But a single name on earth,
But a single name in heaven!

WIENER, Jean (1896–1982)

Wiener was an important figure in the Paris of the 1920s. He was a fringe member of Les Six, never quite belonging to their number, but friendly with all the same people. Because he played the piano at the famous bar and nightclub Le Bœuf sur le Toit, he was perhaps regarded as more of a jazz musician than a serious composer by the Cocteau set, although he played classical piano music with ease. His two-piano duo with Clément Doucet was renowned. Wiener was also something of an entrepreneur (Milhaud called him a 'mécène artiste'), and his concerts promoted the music of such composers as Falla and Stravinsky, as well as members of the unknown second Viennese school— Schoenberg, Berg, and Webern. Milhaud conducted *Pierrot lunaire* (a first performance in France) at a concert organized by Wiener.

As a song composer, very little of the *avant-gardiste* is detectable, but a great deal of the crossover artist. He has the knack of writing enchanting songs absolutely within the scope of his talent, and now seems an unjustly neglected figure awaiting rediscovery. The DEUX POÈMES DE JEAN COCTEAU (1921) are as good as any settings of this poet at the time; the first song *Aéronautes* has a madcap gaiety and, above all, a sweeping sense of continuity that we do not find in Poulenc's COCARDES; and the second, *Souvenirs d'enfance*, covers some of the same ground as the Poulenc cycle, if not with the same tenderness, at least with a similar wit. The TROIS BLUES CHANTÉS (1923) are wordless vocalises, the voice required to sound like a saxophone and, on one occasion, 'comme un trombone'. This is the music of someone who really knows something about American jazz—a stark contrast to Roussel's song *Jazz dans la nuit*, composed a few years later. The dedications of these blues (to Vera Janacopolous, Bernac's singing teacher, and Jane Bathori) show how well connected Wiener was at the time with the most influential people in French musical life—singers of new music.

SEPT PETITES HISTOIRES take their texts from *L'alphabet instantané* by René des Alyscamps. Each song is in a different musical form ('Marche', 'Valse', 'Rag-Time', 'Fuga', and so on) and each takes a letter of the alphabet—as in the second song which begins 'Hermine, Hilare, Harcelle, Hardiment, le Homard pour le Happer habilement dans le haveneau'. It is true that Auric had more or less the same idea (at more or less the same time) with his Radiguet cycle ALPHABET, but the Wiener cycle yields nothing to the work of his more famous contemporary. Certainly the later songs of Auric have nothing to rival the two cycles that Wiener composed in the 1950s, to the splendid poetry of Robert Desnos. In these works we can sense Wiener's experience as a composer of film music, so perfectly timed seems each vignette. The first of these faux-naïf works is TRENTE CHANTE-FABLES POUR LES ENFANTS SAGES (1955), and consists of a bestiary, or rather a large menagerie, of animal poems, no less than thirty in number. Henri Barraud also set a number of these poems, but the larger scope of Wiener's achievement in this substantial work is extraordinary. There are a number of animal songs in the mélodie repertoire (by such composers as Chabrier, Ravel, Durey, Sauguet— and Poulenc of course) and this set deserves to be known among their number. The cabaret style of the music is charming, but in order for interest to be sustained in a work as long as this, everything depends on a singer who can bring out the piquant humour of the text. It would be wise to make a selection from the songs for performance. In any case, this is the cream of crossover music by a composer profoundly at home in jazz and light music, but who also knows the musical developments of the twentieth century from within. The follow-up cycle, LES CHANTEFLEURS (also Robert Desnos, 1959), is no less engaging, this time a veritable florilegium of fifty flower songs, each one as exquisite a miniature as the bloom it describes. These two books of Desnos settings range from the wistful and gently rocking berceuse of **Le gardénia,** to the racy and jazzy **L'alligator.** That these works outdo Milhaud's CATALOGUE DE FLEURS in charm and wit is without question, although they cannot pretend to that work's pithy brevity. Perhaps Witold Lutoslawski, some thirty years later, was encouraged to make his own selection from these two Desnos collections after hearing this witty, unpretentious music.

The beauties of CHANTEFLEURS bring to mind the work of an Austrian, Franz Salmhofer's charming HEITERES HERBARIUM, which seems to have learned much from French music in terms of its understated wit and elegant economy of means. As we end this book, it seems appropriate to mention an example of twentieth-century lieder, because it was nineteenth-century German song, and the music of Schubert and Schumann in particular, which was the greatest influence on French song in its infancy. In the Salmhofer work, the mélodie and the lied (distant cousins with shared relatives going back to the 1840s) have come full circle and once more link hands, both of them threatened with extinction by passing fashion, and the indifference of composers and audiences. And the same applies to song in our own language of course. We hope that these precious blooms will survive well into the twenty-first century and beyond, continuing to re-flower with each generation's interpreters. It is up to all of us to play our part in keeping the art of song alive. It has proved itself amazingly resilient thus far, but there are forces in our brash commercial world which would crush the flower underfoot without even noticing (as in Mozart's *Das Veilchen*), unless those who love this music continue to listen, learn, and nurture.

1 *Le gardénia*

Dans un jardin en Angleterre
      Il était un gardénia.
Pour en fleurir sa boutonnière,
Un vieux lord se l'appropria.
    Depuis, au jardin, il n'y a,
      N'y a plus de gardénia.

The gardenia

In an English garden there
    Once grew a gardenia.
      An old lord stole
      It for his buttonhole.
Now in the garden there
      Isn't a gardenia.

2 *L'alligator*

    Sur les bords du Mississipi
      Un alligator se tapit.
    Il vit passer un négrillon
Et lui dit: 'Bonjour, mon garçon.'
Mais le nègre lui dit: 'Bonsoir,
La nuit tombe, il va faire noir,
    Je suis petit et j'aurais tort
    De parler à l'alligator.'
    Sur les bords du Mississipi
    L'alligator a du dépit,
Car il voulait au réveillon
Manger le tendre négrillon.

The alligator

    On the Mississipi shore
      An alligator lay,
    Saw a black boy passing by
And called to him: 'Good day.'
But the boy replied: 'Goodbye,
Night draws in and there'll be no light,
    I am small and it wouldn't be right
      To address an alligator.'
      On the Mississipi shore
      The alligator's full of ire,
For at the midnight feast he had a ploy
    To eat the tender negro boy.

AFTERWORD

with a list of eighty suggestions for further reading

(Key numbers to the bibliography are given in square brackets)

The process of getting to know the song repertoire is immeasurably enriched by understanding the context in which the works were written—and this applies to both poems and music. Having discovered the world of the mélodie, the interested listener will begin to explore aspects of this vast realm in more detail. It may not be long before this general appreciation is honed into dedicated enthusiasm. At this point, the *mélomane* (as the French would say) will look in different directions to deepen his or her knowledge. In throwing a well-aimed stone of curiosity into the bottomless lake of background information, the rings of resonance (in the form of words, sights, and sounds) ripple outwards in all directions from the original source of impact—as in *Reflets dans l'eau* from *MIRAGES* [FAURÉ 44 ii]: 'Si je glisse, les eaux feront | Un rond fluide... un autre rond... | Un autre à peine.'

When writing their songs, composers often feel entitled to indulge themselves personally: they allow themselves to be susceptible to emotions which are more subject to biographical circumstances in the span of a day's work than during the hatching of any mightier opus. In composing in this miniature form, many a composer may be glimpsed in the confessional, or at least caught 'off duty' from his more public tasks. This personal touch is mirrored by the song form itself, and its practitioners. Singers have a reputation—among string players for example—for being performer-personalities (thus more temperamental, vulnerable, mercurial, and unreliable) rather than musicians *pur sang*. To work in the world of vocal music as a composer (or accompanist, come to that) is to encounter a series of strong, though not necessarily intellectual, personalities; to navigate a sea of vivid and immediate emotions. It was ever thus, and all real song composers have been attracted to a milieu which liberates music from the rarefied and cerebral: working with singers has brought many an esoteric musician into touch with the practicalities of life in the theatre. The song scholar must follow suit with interdisciplinary interests similar, though not identical, to those required in opera studies.

Let us take, as a random example of this, Poulenc's song cycle to the words of Paul Éluard, *TEL JOUR TELLE NUIT* [POULENC 5 i–ix]. Affection for this work's undoubted musical beauties might make the listener curious about Poulenc's other music, and where and how the cycle fits into his overall output. He might be curious about the crucial year of its composition: 1936 when the composer reconverted to Catholicism because of a mystical experience at the shrine of the Black Virgin in Rocamadour; established his musical partnership with Pierre Bernac; and mourned the violent death of his fellow composer Pierre Octave Ferroud. This might lead to a reading of a Poulenc biography [66, 78], some of his letters [50, 51], as well as his *Journal de mes mélodies* [48]. The crucial part played by Bernac in the work's evolution and first performance leads to the singer's own writing about French song, and this cycle in particular [1, 30], as well as the duo's classic HMV recording of the cycle. (Bernac is the dedicatee of the eighth song, *Figure de force brûlante et farouche*—whose words perhaps have some special significance. Here speculation is aided by knowledge of the background to their friendship.) Then the listener might wish to find out more about Paul Éluard, not only because of the major role he played in Poulenc's song output, but because he is one of the great French poets of the twentieth century. (Song has led many English-speaking musicians to an appreciation of foreign writers who would otherwise have remained unknown to them.) Fascination with Éluard may lead to a more general study of the surrealist movement, and along the way an appreciation of the poet's extraordinary relationship with his wife Nusch, who is a central figure in the cycle's literary *raison d'être*, as well as the dedicatee of the third song. There is a fine, recently published book which addresses these issues [31], so far the only one in the series entitled 'Music, art and literature' devoted entirely to a French composer. Other figures who feature in the dedicatory pages of *TEL JOUR TELLE NUIT* are: Pablo Picasso, whose name stands at the head of the opening mélodie, a musical canvas bathed in sunlight (this opens up the whole colourful vista of Poulenc and the painters, leading to his later cycle *LE TRAVAIL DU PEINTRE* [POULENC 21 i–vii]); the mysterious 'Freddy' who, a decade later, was to become the mother of Poulenc's daughter Marie-Ange; the society hostess Valentine Hugo, whose name conjures up *le tout Paris* of the 1930s, just as her salon typified it, and who illustrated some of Éluard's collections; the soprano Marie Blanche de Polignac, daughter of the queen of *haute couture*, Jeanne Lanvin, talented and rich, whose song *Une herbe pauvre* is as beautiful and unaffected as its dedicatee; Yvonne Gouverné, whose achievements as a choral conductor are central to Poulenc's achievements in church and choral music—another separate study which, like the other divergent trails flowing from this work, is an important aspect of the cycle's overall meaning and significance.

The musicologists who favour pure musical analysis in order to unlock a song's secrets will also have much to occupy them in a study of Poulenc's mélodies, but when pure music is 'adulterated' by the alien presence of words by a collaborator-poet whose literary ideas set the composer thinking in terms of words-to-music relationships, and newly minted tonal analogues for poetic imagery, the normal apparatus of analysis seems cold and inadequate. And words themselves have sometimes to bow to the power of visual images. There is a wonderful photograph taken at a picnic which catches Paul Éluard and Nusch (stretched like a cat, defiantly bare-breasted in the sunshine of the south of France) kissing each other in a moment of spontaneous passion. The great photographer Man Ray is also in the picture, as well as Ronald Penrose, two men in the life of the invisible person behind the camera whom we know to have been the stunningly beautiful Lee Miller. These people all take their place, at one remove, in Poulenc's world. In my experience, the hedonism and *camaraderie*, the defying of convention and the unashamed emotion which come across in this voluptuous photographic image have done more to help singers and pianists instinctively understand the last song of *TEL JOUR TELLE NUIT* than any amount of harmonic or formal analysis.

There are countless works mentioned in this book which inspire similar trails of further reading and interdisciplinary investigation. And if I were to even attempt to list the books, articles, poems, pictures, films which one might peruse to follow up a study of this field (even if I knew them all), the result would be a huge list of countless tomes and tracts, an *omnium gatherum* of French cultural life for the past 300 years. Such a list would be neither possible nor desirable, for it is surely part of the fun behind any enthusiasm that one should find things out without a guide-list, slowly and lovingly acquiring knowledge through the exercise of ear, eye, brain, and sensibility. This all comes under the general imperative of 'cherchez la mélodie!' In the process the enthusiast may peruse, even purchase, a range of books, scores, films, and pictures (if finances allow) which are a testimony to the artistic loves of one's life, each field of study nourishing the other and, as the years go by, building into a single grand tapestry of many interwoven threads—a tapestry, moreover, which is one's own unique creation. Life itself is illuminated, and made more bearable, by music which, in turn, is the product of a composer's multi-faceted experiences as a human being. Whilst we cannot hope to experience these for ourselves, it is amazing how we may at least capture something of times long past, and otherwise out of reach, by following composers down the path of their own interests. By putting ourselves in *their* place (an accompanist does just this when he plays a song—standing in for the composer himself) we are able to see the world through *their* eyes. When a performer achieves this empathy, the result is music-making of vision and insight. But a 'mere' listener can also experience song at a deeper level where patiently acquired knowledge is not the enemy of sensual pleasure; indeed, it clears all avenues leading to the heart by exciting the senses and nourishing the mind.

In the meantime, before we are able to grasp the totality of the picture (a life's work, surely) there are a select number of books—directly related to the French mélodie and the song output of its composers—which will repay study. The list is, of necessity, highly personal, and even rather arbitrary.

Twenty books on French song in general

The first guide to the mélodie that came my way as a student remains a classic in its field—Bernac's study of *The interpretation of French song* [1], which is divided into chapters about the best known of the composers, and includes practical and useful, if necessarily pithy, hints on performance—encapsulations of years of teaching experience. The translations by Winifred Radford are supplemented by Bernac's suggestions for liaisons, or breaks, between words. Bernac, and his way of singing, are regarded as precious and passé by some French singers of the younger generation, although memories of his teaching are still very much alive, particularly in Britain and America. To the charge, sometimes made, that Bernac pontificates, one must allow that his teaching belongs to the magisterial style of an earlier epoch where pupils were reassured by firm opinions. His art, at once patrician and poignant, has given me more pleasure on disc than any other singer of the mélodie. (How invidious are comparisons! This enthusiasm cannot detract from admiration and gratitude for the lifework of the Fischer-Dieskau and Gerald Moore of French song, Bernac's pupil Gérard Souzay and his pianist Dalton Baldwin; Hugues Cuenod has a way with song that is life-enhancing and unique; Dame Maggie Teyte provided the passport to the sybaritic French repertoire for countless English speakers; and I learned the accompanist's art in tandem with that latter-day mistress of the mélodie, Dame Felicity Lott.)

And then there was the marvellous soprano Claire Croiza, a reissue of whose records on an LP in the 1970s was a revelation to many of us—many of the tracks featuring famous composers as her accompanist. The book which bears testimony to her work as a teacher (she was, incidentally one of Bernac's mentors) consists of scrupulous notes taken verbatim from Croiza's masterclasses in the 1930s. The original enthralled auditor was Hélène Abraham, but the editor and translator of this book in the English edition is Betty Bannerman, herself a Croiza pupil [2]. Croiza's observations, though less practical and down-to-earth than Bernac's, are often perceptive and poetic. She was an important figure, both historically and artistically, and the book is a fascinating resource. There is a chapter devoted to the songs of Gounod, Bizet, and Chabrier, and then separate sections on Fauré, Duparc, Chausson, Debussy, Ravel, Caplet, and Milhaud. Another book by a famous French singer seems to me, on the whole, to have fewer insights; nevertheless *50 mélodies françaises* by Charles Panzéra [3]—performance hints for fifty French songs by nineteen composers (in a bilingual edition)—covers a surprising range of composers, and is a testimonial to the dedicated sincerity and artistry of the last interpreter to work with Fauré himself. Panzéra's manuals of singing technique are perhaps better known.

There is a chapter on French diction and pronunciation at the beginning of Bernac's book, but perhaps the definitive work on the subject is by Thomas Grubb, who teaches at the Juilliard school in New York. This book [4] is required reading for singers and coaches, but also fascinating for those members of the public who are interested in the exigencies of French diction. It also contains a useful list of French repertoire (including French opera arias) classified into voice types. Another book of the highest accomplishment is *The art of accompanying and coaching* by Kurt Adler [5] (no relation to the conductor and opera Intendant). This contains a fascinating section devoted to French musical style (in particular, extracts from the heated correspondence between Romain Rolland and Richard Strauss on the subject of Debussy's prosody) and a detailed introduction to French diction (alongside chapters on singing in German, Italian, and Spanish). This compendium of a life's expertise is as interesting for singers as for pianists. The British coach Joan Thompson has also circulated a privately printed booklet with concisely presented information on French diction [6]. There is a shorter, and more general, introduction to singing in French as an introduction to Roger Nichols's anthology of French song in two volumes [7]. These gather together a representative selection of the mélodies, and are a good introduction for enthusiasts anxious to make the acquaintance of this field through the printed music, yet who are daunted by the expense of building up a library of individual composers' works.

The classic of the history of the mélodie (although it only deals with the song repertoire composed between Berlioz and Duparc) is by Frits Noske [8]; it was originally published in French, but has achieved wider circulation in its American edition. This scholarly work seems rather old-fashioned in its opinions at times, but it remains a very useful, and thorough, survey of the earlier history of the form. It is invaluable for its exhaustive work-lists—although there are new thoughts about some of the datings of songs by more recent scholars. Interestingly enough, there are remarkably few specific studies of the mélodie as such which have emanated from France (while the German lied has inspired its countrymen to countless expositions and treatises, not all of them interesting). There is a useful (and refreshingly informal) survey of the mélodie until 1924 which was written by Koechlin as a chapter in a much larger enterprise, the handsome pair of books entitled *Cinquante ans de musique française* [9]. This work, sumptuously produced and illustrated, is still occasionally to be found (at high prices) in French second-hand bookshops. Much more recently there have been published an impressive set of three large volumes entitled *Dictionnaire des œuvres de l'art vocal* [10], where individual mélodies (rather than composers) find their place, alphabetically, and by title, beside classical vocal music from all European countries. It is a bold and new means of presenting information which emphasizes the fact that each song and vocal work has a character (and thus an entry) of its own; as in any compilation of this sort, some of the articles are more revealing than others. Highly impressive in range and detail is *Guide de la mélodie et du lied* in the series *Les indispensables de la Musique* [11]. An astonishing amount of information about song of all nationalities (including a few surprisingly well-informed entries about rather obscure English composers) is packed into a compact alphabetical format. This volume is useful as an easily portable source-book of works and dates, containing brief musical descriptions of the repertoire concerned. It is, however, rather impersonal in its thoroughness—it refrains from both enthusiastic and unfavourable judgements on the composers' outputs, and one is left with little sense of their comparative standing.

Of books by English writers on French song, the chapters on individual mélodies of Debussy, Duparc, Fauré, Hahn, Ravel in Gerald Moore's *Singer and accompanist* [12] remain a treasury of practical advice; indeed, it is in getting through to the ordinary man in the street, or the ambitious amateur performer, that Moore displays his invaluable common touch. An excellent bird's-eye view of French song by David Cox is to be found in *A history of song*, edited by Denis Stevens [13]. Another introduction to the history of the mélodie, with different emphases, is to be found in Charles Osborne's *The concert song companion* [14], a book dedicated to Lotte Lehmann in friendship. That great singer's own pronouncements on the French repertoire are more remarkable for the sweep of their imaginative fantasy than their scholastic accuracy. It is surprising enough that a great German singer of her generation should have become interested in the mélodie; it was no doubt the experience of teaching in Santa Barbara for many years that brought her in touch with an American enthusiasm for these songs. The present author's account of concerts in London given by *The songmakers' almanac* [15] is an anthology which includes reprints of various essays on the mélodie, as well as examples of programme-building in recitals of this kind.

America has long been a source of enthusiasm for the mélodie. French song forms a central panel to James Husst Hall's *The art song* [16]. The book, simply written, packs a great deal of information (admittedly about a limited number of composers, and all seen from a perspective of the early 1950s) into a small space with an attractive ease and charm. A fairly recent publication is Carol Kimball's *Song* [17], which is a very practical volume, honed to the needs of the younger, and perhaps less experienced, student. It essays a survey of world song, country by country, and the section on France contains a decently comprehensive account of composers from Berlioz to Leguerney. Kimball's down-to-earth approach is well suited to those still unfamiliar with the repertory; this is a book which will, for example, encourage aspiring opera singers to embark on a study of song, and arm them with enough information to begin the journey without feeling at sea. Kimball gives scrupulously informative bibliographies and suggestions for further study. More esoteric is the book by Barbara Meister, *Nineteenth-century French song* [18], which concentrates on the song outputs of Fauré, Chausson, Duparc, and Debussy. Whilst taking the reader through the songs in some detail, and printing the complete poems in French, the English translations are awkwardly split between sections of the commentaries; they also contain numerous inaccuracies. Less ambitious, but probably more useful, is Sergius Kagen's *Music for the voice* [19], which has a substantial French section.

This remarkable teacher and coach is severely practical. Introductions to the composers (some strange choices) are short and to the point, and the songs themselves are simply listed with notes concerning their compass, tessitura, voice type, and a terse description of musical characteristics. Here is a man who understands the mentality of those singers who, in searching for songs to suit their own voices, will not wish to read anything about the composers which has no strict relevance to their immediate needs.

One more fruit of the American enthusiasm for French song may be mentioned here, all the more remarkable because there have been so few books published anywhere that offer good translations of the song repertoire. Philip Miller's *The ring of words* [20] was among the first of its kind, and the best. Because it is devoted to the song literatures of the world, Miller offers less than sixty French song translations. These are fastidiously arranged under the poets, not by composer (a sign of the author's literary sympathies), and there are short biographies of the poets as well. Miller addresses such issues as variants in the texts between the composers' versions and the original poems, and notes different settings of the same poem. What a contrast this approach is to Kagen's book, which fails to mention the poets of his recommended songs, unless they form part of the work's title.

[1] Pierre Bernac, *The interpretation of French song* (London, 1970; 2nd edn. 1976).

[2] Betty Bannerman (ed. and trans.), *The singer as interpreter: Claire Croiza's masterclasses* (London, 1989).

[3] Charles Panzéra, *50 mélodies françaises* (Brussels, 1964).

[4] Thomas Grubb, *Singing in French: a manual of French diction and French vocal repertoire*, foreword by Pierre Bernac (New York, 1979).

[5] Kurt Adler, *The art of accompanying and coaching* (Minneapolis, 1965; 2nd edn. New York, 1971).

[6] Joan Thompson, *French pronunciation for English-speaking singers* (privately printed, n.d.).

[7] Roger Nichols, *The art of French song*, 2 vols. (London, 1999).

[8] Frits Noske, *La mélodie française de Berlioz à Duparc* (Paris, 1954); English translation, *French song from Berlioz to Duparc* (New York, 1970).

[9] Charles Koechlin, *La mélodie*, in vol. ii of *Cinquante ans de musique française 1874–1925* (Paris, 1925).

[10] Marc Honegger and Paul Prévost, *Dictionnaire des œuvres de l'art vocal*, 2 vols. (Paris, 1991).

[11] Brigitte François-Sappey and Gilles Cantagrel, *Guide de la mélodie et du lied* (Paris, 1994).

[12] Gerald Moore, *Singer and accompanist: The performance of fifty songs* (London, 1953; 2nd edn. 1982).

[13] David Cox, 'France', in *A history of song*, ed. Denis Stevens (London, 1960; 2nd edn. 1971).

[14] Charles Osborne, *The concert song companion* (London, 1974).

[15] Graham Johnson, *The Songmakers' Almanac: twenty years of song recitals in London* (London, 1996).

[16] James Husst Hall, *The art song* (Norman, Okla., 1953).

[17] Carol Kimball, *Song* (Seattle, 1996).

[18] Barbara Meister, *Nineteenth-century French song* (Bloomington, Ind., 1980).

[19] Sergius Kagen, *Music for the voice: a descriptive list of concert and teaching material* (Bloomington, Ind., 1968).

[20] Philip Miller, *The ring of words: an anthology of song texts* (New York, 1963; 2nd edn. 1973).

Monographs on single composers and their mélodies

And now we move from the general to the specific. A book such as *A French song companion* could never attempt to take the place either of a comprehensive music encyclopaedia like *The New Grove*, or of specialist books devoted to each of the composers. Of these, there are only a handful of books which are given over specifically to studies of mélodies by separate composers. The monograph on Debussy's songs [23] and Bernac's extended study on the Poulenc mélodies [30] have the stamp of historical accuracy because of the writers' first-hand connections with the composers. Bathori was one of the most influential and ubiquitous of singers in the history of the mélodie, and the Bernac study is indispensable to the performance of Poulenc's songs. The book on the Fauré mélodies by Vladimir Jankélévitch [27] is simply one of the most poetic works about the song repertoire ever written. Part of its power lies in the author's mastery of perfumed and highly-charged description in the manner of French criticism of the time, but there is a profound understanding of the composer at the book's core. The study of Debussy and his poets by Margaret Cobb [24] is clearly presented, and delicately edited to match the subtlety of the music. (Margaret Cobb is also the compiler of a Debussy discography—1902–1950—which was published by Minkoff in 1975.)

The programme notes by the present author, accompanying various volumes of CDs in the Hyperion French Song Edition, discuss selected mélodies of Bizet, Gounod, Hahn, Saint-Saëns, and Séverac in rather more detail than may be found elsewhere. Further volumes issued in this ongoing series (Chausson, Chabrier, and Durey to be released in 2001) will be similarly annotated.

Listed alphabetically under composer:

[21] Graham Johnson, notes for *Songs by Bizet* with Ann Murray (Hyperion Records, 1998) CDA 66976.

[22] Isabelle Bretaudeau, *Les mélodies de Chausson* (Arles, 1999)

[23] Jane Bathori, *Sur l'interprétation des mélodies de Claude Debussy* (Paris, 1953). English translation of original edition by Linda Laurent.

[24] Margaret G. Cobb, *The poetic Debussy: a collection of his song texts and selected letters* (Boston, 1982).

[25] Sydney Northcote, *The songs of Henri Duparc* (New York, 1950).

[26] Rémy Stricker, *Les mélodies de Duparc* (Paris, 1996).

[27] Vladimir Jankélévitch, *Gabriel Fauré: ses mélodies, son esthétique* (Paris, 1938).

[28] Graham Johnson, notes for *Songs by Charles Gounod* with Felicity Lott, Ann Murray, Anthony Rolfe Johnson (Hyperion Records, 1993) CDA 66801/2.

[29] Graham Johnson, notes for *Songs by Reynaldo Hahn* with Felicity Lott, Sue Bickley, Stephen Varcoe (Hyperion Records, 1996) CDA 67141/2.

[30] Pierre Bernac, *Francis Poulenc: the man and his songs* (London, 1977).

[31] Sydney Buckland and Myriam Chimènes (eds)., *Francis Poulenc*, in the series Music, art and literature (London, 1999).

[32] Graham Johnson, notes for *Songs by Saint-Saëns* with François Le Roux (Hyperion Records, 1997) CDA 66856.

[33] Graham Johnson, notes for *Songs by Déodat de Séverac* with François Le Roux (Hyperion Records, 1998) CDA 66983.

The composer's voice

Of all the composers of the mélodie, only Francis Poulenc was moved to write at some length about his own songs. This unique document, *Journal de mes mélodies* [48] is an indispensable aid to discovering the composer's tone of voice and sense of style. It is less helpful for the student, in practical terms, than the Bernac book; casual and highly cultivated at the same time, throwaway yet deeply serious, it contains, however, the essence of the songs. Also by Poulenc is an unusual and allusive biography of Emmanuel Chabrier [49] which affectionately discusses that master's mélodies, but which is chiefly valuable for communicating Poulenc's enthusiasm for a composer whose music was so influential in the shaping of his own style. Milhaud preferred to write about someone he actually knew, Érik Satie [47]. The Fauré and Debussy biographies by Charles Koechlin [44, 45] are organized in a more scholarly way, and have illuminating chapters on the vocal music of each composer. (Ravel also wrote an article on Fauré's songs for the *Revue musicale*, but I have resisted the temptation to expand this bibliography to include the vast number of contributions to various journals on the mélodie, not only by distinguished critics of the past but by modern authorities on song such as Susan Youens.) Although they tackle topics outside the song repertoire, the essays of Reynaldo Hahn [40, 41, 42] are always highly revealing, as are the letters written to the composer by Marcel Proust [52]—the composer's words at one remove, as it were, but nevertheless fascinating for a student of the period. Apart from his song journal and volumes of conversations [51], Poulenc never attempted an autobiographical study. But three of his colleagues from Les Six—Auric, Honegger, and Milhaud—wrote books which placed their lives in the context of their music [32, 43, 46]. Apart from these, we have the memoirs and correspondence of a number of other composers, including Berlioz, Chabrier, Poulenc, and Ravel [35, 37, 50, 53], which also offer first-hand information about their life and times, and sometimes also about their mélodies. The diaries and writings of the American composer and mélodie enthusiast Ned Rorem [54] offer a unique perspective on life in the Parisian musical circle of the 1950s and 1960s, and his articles on the songs of his colleagues and friends are written from the standpoint of a fellow song composer. *Settling the score*, for example, has interesting reflections on the songs of Ravel and Poulenc, as does *An absolute gift*.

Listed alphabetically under composer:

[34] Georges Auric, *Quand j'étais là* (Paris 1979).

[35] Hector Berlioz, *Mémoires* (Paris, 1870); English translation by David Cairns (London, 1969).

[36] Hector Berlioz, *À travers chants* (Paris, 1862; 2nd edn. 1971); English translation (London, 1913–18).

[37] Emmanuel Chabrier, *Lettres à Nanine* (Paris, 1909); also Joseph Desaymard, *Chabrier d'après ses lettres* (1934).

[38] Claude Debussy, *Monsieur Croche et autres écrits*, ed. F. Lesure (Paris, 1971); English translation (London, 1976).

[39] Gabriel Fauré, *Correspondance*, ed. Jean-Michel Nectoux (Paris, 1980); English translation by J. A. Underwood, *Gabriel Fauré: his life through letters* (London, 1984).

[40] Reynaldo Hahn, *Du chant* (Paris, 1957); English translation by Léopold Simoneau, *On singers and singing* (Portland, Ore., 1990).

[41] Reynaldo Hahn, *Thèmes variés* (Paris, 1946).

[42] Reynaldo Hahn, *L'oreille au guet* (Paris, 1956).

[43] Arthur Honegger, *Je suis compositeur* (Paris, 1951); English translation, *I am a composer* (London, 1966).

[44] Charles Koechlin, *Gabriel Fauré* (Paris, 1927); English translation (London, 1946).

[45] Charles Koechlin, *Claude Debussy* (Paris, 1927).

[46] Darius Milhaud, *Notes sans musique* (Paris, 1949; 2nd edn. 1974, under the title *Ma vie heureuse*); English translation *Notes with music* (London, 1952).

[47] Darius Milhaud, *Notes sur Érik Satie* (New York, 1946).

[48] Francis Poulenc, *Journal de mes mélodies*, foreword by Henri Sauguet (Paris, 1964; 2nd edn. 1993, unexpurgated edition with commentary); English translation of original edition by Winifred Radford, *Diary of my songs*, introd. by Graham Johnson (London, 1985).

[49] Francis Poulenc, *Emmanuel Chabrier* (Paris, 1961); English translation by Denise Jolly (London, n.d.).

[50] Francis Poulenc, *Echo and source: selected correspondence (1915–1963)*, trans. Sidney Buckland (London, 1991).

Francis Poulenc, *Correspondance 1910–1963*, ed. Myriam Chimènes (Paris, 1994). (Both these books supersede the collection of correspondence by H. de Wendel, 1963.)

[51] Francis Poulenc, *Entretiens avec Claude Rostand* (Paris, 1954)—transcriptions of radio interviews with the composer. Francis Poulenc, *Moi et mes amis*—conversations with Stéphane Audel (Paris, 1963); English translation by James Harding, *My friends and myself* (London, 1978).

[52] Marcel Proust, *Lettres à Reynaldo Hahn* (Paris, 1956).

[53] Maurice Ravel, *Ravel au miroir de ses lettres*, ed. Marcelle Gerar and René Chalupt (Paris, 1956).

[54] Ned Rorem, *The Paris diary of Ned Rorem* (New York, 1966). Much of the composer's Parisian period is covered in more depth in *Knowing when to stop* (New York, 1994). Of his remaining publications two of the more recent are: *Setting the tone: essays and a diary* (New York, 1983); *Settling the score* (New York, 1988).

[55] Ornella Volta (ed.), *Satie seen through his letters*, with introd. by John Cage (London, 1989).

[56] Nigel Wilkins (ed. and trans.), *The writings of Érik Satie* (London, 1980).

[57] Pierre Guillot (ed.), *Déodat de Sévérac: écrits sur la musique* (Liège, 1993).

Biographies and reminiscences

In *A French song companion* there is, of necessity, only limited biographical information about the composers—no more than a skeleton framework on which to present the songs in a more palatable way than the publication of simple lists of works (which are, in any case, generally available in reference books). It goes without saying that there was much more to say about the composers' achievements in other musical fields, all of which is important in placing the song œuvre into context. For this information the reader must consult biographies of composers, and these are too numerous to list here in any comprehensive way (such bibliographies are to be found under each of the composers in *Grove 6*).

I confine myself here to a handful of biographies or collections of reminiscences which seem particularly useful to the student of the mélodie, or which are especially successful in evoking the atmosphere of the composer's life and times. In the first category is Jean-Michel Nectoux's magisterial study of the music of Fauré [68] which contains useful and fascinating chapters on the songs—particularly the Verlaine settings and the later cycles—as well as a study of Fauré's highly creative way of altering poets' texts to suit his musical purposes. In the second, more information-related, category it would be difficult to better the astonishing breadth and depth of Marcel Marnat's biography of Ravel [67].

[58] Jean-Pierre Barricelli and Leo Weinstein, *Ernest Chausson: the composer's life and works* (Norman, Okla., 1955).

[59] Winton Dean, *Bizet* (in the Master musician series) (London, 1975).

[60] Bernard Gavoty, *Reynaldo Hahn: le musicien de la belle époque* (Paris, 1976).

[61] James Harding, *Gounod* (London, 1973).

[62] Christopher Headington, *The songs* in *Liszt: the man and his music*, ed. Alan Walker (London, 1970).

[63] Henri Hell, *Francis Poulenc: musicien français* (Paris, 1978).

[64] Demar Irvine, *Massenet: a chronicle of his life and times* (Portland, Ore., 1994).

[65] Hélène Jourdan-Morhange, *Ravel et nous*, foreword by Colette (Paris, 1945).

[66] Edward Lockspeiser, *Debussy: his life and mind*, 2 vols. (London, 1962; 2nd edn. 1978).

[67] Marcel Marnat, *Maurice Ravel* (Paris, 1986).

[68] Jean-Michel Nectoux, *Gabriel Fauré: les voix du clair-obscur* (Paris, 1990); English translation by Roger Nichols, *Gabriel Fauré: a musical life* (London, 1991).

[69] Roger Nichols, *Debussy remembered* (London, 1992).

[70] Roger Nichols, *Ravel remembered* (London, 1987).

[71] Roger Nichols, *Messiaen* (London, 1975).

[72] Robert Orledge, *Gabriel Fauré* (London, 1975).

[73] Robert Orledge, *Satie remembered* (London, 1995).

[74] Brian Rees, *Camille Saint-Saëns—A Life* (London, 1999).

[75] Ornella Volta, *La banlieue d'Erik Satie* (Paris, 1999).

Iconographical volumes

There are occasional volumes which are especially valuable because of their iconography. The sumptuous volumes in the Editions Minkoff & Lattès series are in this category [76, 77] and the Poulenc biography, though small and concise, is delightfully illustrated with a number of rare photographs. The volume on Satie by Nigel Wilkins [56] listed above is also splendidly illustrated.

[76] Roger Delage, *Chabrier* (Paris, 1982).

[77] François Lesure, *Debussy* (Paris, 1980).

[78] Renaud Machart, *Poulenc* (Paris, 1995). (Apart from its iconographical excellence, this is a very useful and up-to-date account of the composer's life and work.)

[79] The Garland series of French song

Although it is not the purpose of this bibliography to list musical publications, the series issued by Garland publishing and edited by David Tunley (*Romantic French song 1830–70*) is in a class of its own for those interested in the early history of the mélodie. These handsome (and expensive) volumes contain facsimiles of songs by obscure but interesting composers. There are also commentaries on the composers and songs which contain much information not available elsewhere.

Volume i: *Early romances by Bérat, Berlioz, Duchambge, Grisar, Meyerbeer, Monpou, Morel, Panseron and Romagnesi: selected settings of Louis Niedermeyer and Ernest Reyer* (1994).
Volume ii: *Songs by Félicien David* (1995).
Volume iii: *Songs by Henri Reber and Édouard Lalo* (1995).
Volume iv: *Songs by Victor Massé and Georges Bizet* (1995).
Volume vi: *Songs by Jules Massenet, Louis Lacombe and Auguste Vaucorbeil* (1995).

[80] In a similar spirit to the Garland series is a publication of songs by French women composers, edited and introduced by Judy Tsou and Susan C. Cook. This *Anthology of songs* (New York, 1988) contains facsimiles of works published by Pauline Duchambge, Loïsa Puget, Pauline Viardot, and Jane Vieu. These are taken from the Women's Music Collection at the University of Michigan Music Library.

The following is an index of this bibliography. The only books that are not cross-referenced here are the alphabetically arranged dictionaries (10 and 11) which have a very comprehensive coverage of French song, with articles covering the majority of composers in *A French song companion*. Of the composers listed below, for example, only Duchambge, Dutilleux Massé, Monpou, Puget, Reber, Reyer, Rorem, and Vieu do not have separate articles in *Guide de la mélodie et du lied*, and a number of the earlier composers are mentioned in the alphabetical article 'Romance' in that book.

INDEX I. SELECTED POETS

INDEX 2. COMPOSERS IN TRANSLATION